WORLD HISTORICAL FICTION GUIDE

An Annotated, Chronological, Geographical and
Topical List of Selected Historical Novels

Second Edition

by

Daniel D. McGarry

and

Sarah Harriman White

The Scarecrow Press, Inc.
Metuchen, N. J.   1973

Library of Congress Cataloging in Publication Data

McGarry, Daniel D
  World historical fiction guide.

  Edition for 1963 published under title: Historical
fiction guide: annotated chronological, geographical,
and topical list of five thousand selected historical
novels.
    1. Historical fiction--Bibliography. I. White,
Sarah Harriman, joint author. II. Title.
Z5917.H6M3 1973   016.80883'81   73-4367
ISBN 0-8108-0616-9

FOREWORD

Historical fiction enjoys justifiable and ever-growing popularity among the reading public. Joining in the admiration for this genre, the compilers of the present Guide--one a professional historian, the other a homemaker and specialist in English--have considered it a labor of love and a service to readers to prepare an up-to-date World Historical Fiction Guide. This work is designed especially for use by adults and by students in senior high schools, colleges, and universities; but books suitable for junior high school students as well as adult readers are also included and are marked "YA" (Young Adult).

Both authors have long read historical fiction for recreational purposes, and the historian has long required such reading in his introductory survey courses. Thus the authors have become acutely aware of the need for an up-to-date guide. With the increasing demand for historical fiction, the preparation of a current, convenient guide has become ever more imperative. As a stop-gap, some librarians have attempted to accumulate special file cards for historical fiction, to prepare their own typed or mimeographed lists, to assemble historical novels in a separate section of the library, or to mark books of historical fiction with some distinguishing color. Helpful as such measures may be, they do not satisfy the need for a concise, general guide, which may, incidentally, be marked to show the holdings of a particular library, as well as to plan future acquisitions.

Much earlier in the century, general guides to historical fiction were compiled by Jonathan Nield,[1] Ernest Baker,[2] and James R. Kaye,[3] but these, unfortunately, have long been out of date, as well as out of print, although they are still often used for lack of something more recent. A good guide intended mainly for younger persons was prepared by Hannah Logasa in 1927.[4] This has gone

iii

through several subsequent editions and revisions,[5] but has continued to be especially useful for juvenile readers. Miss Logasa unfortunately died in 1967.

In recent times, some more specialized introductions to historical fiction in United States history have been appearing. An early instance was a volume by Otis W. Coan and Richard G. Lillard,[6] arranged thematically rather than historically.[7] Another example is Ernest E. Leisy's work on American historical fiction,[8] which incorporates extensive summaries of historical novels in its running text. Still another is that of Robert A. Lively,[9] which lists some five hundred novels on the Civil War, most without annotations. A convenient guide to American historical novels by A. T. Dickinson, Jr. was published by Scarecrow Press in 1958.[10] The Dickinson work can profitably be used along with this volume, whose references to historical fiction concerning the United States are necessarily limited because of its broader scope. More specialized is Jack W. Vanderhoof's bibliography of novels related to American frontier and colonial history.[11] Although valuable for their own purposes, these limited treatises do not satisfy the need for a general guide.

In preparing this Guide, the compilers have followed the view that fiction is historical if it includes reference to customs, conditions, identifiable persons, or events in the past. Thus, a novel concerning the everyday way of life, outlook, mores, and living conditions in fourteenth century France is historical fiction just as much as one which features Charles VII, Edward III, or the Battle of Crécy. Since many biographies, in which the author uses considerable imagination along with established facts, may be classified as historical fiction as well as biography, several such are included.

This Guide is also selective, and endeavors to include only better works of historical fiction. Among factors considered are literary excellence, readability, and historical value. Much weight has been attached to opinions of competent reviewers as well as to those of other bibliographers. However, in some categories there is a dearth of historical fiction, and it has been necessary to include less distinguished works. In the final analysis, the entries in this Guide are representative rather than all-inclusive. The book is meant to be a serviceable reference for persons desiring to find generally approved fiction concerning particular periods and fields of history. Poetry and drama have been generally excluded as better suited to oral and visual presentation than to silent reading.

For practical purposes the authors have made the year 1900 their terminal date. This is partly because fiction concerning our own twentieth century is so much more abundant and more readily available, and partly because this period is more contemporary than historical.

Only works available in English have been included, but these are often translations from books written in other languages. Thus many notable works originally written in foreign tongues are listed. Each translated book has been so marked.

Our historical subdivisions as to time and place are those commonly accepted in the historical profession. While to some extent arbitrary, they are generally similar to those followed by the Guide to Historical Literature.

In making particular entries, the compilers have usually observed the authoritative, accepted practices of the Library of Congress. Where a writer uses a pseudonym, the work is usually listed under the author's real name, with reference and cross-reference to the pseudonym. The exceptions have been where general usage prescribes otherwise, as in the cases of "George Eliot" and "Maurice Druon, " and where several authors have collaborated under one pseudonym (for example: Janet, Lillian, pseud. for Janet Cicchetti and Lillian Ressler Groom). Where the name under which a book was published differs from the name under which it is listed here, the name that appears on the title page is given after the title (for example: Stephens, Eve. Anne Boleyn, by Evelyn Anthony, pseud. ; Turnbull, Francese Hubbard. The Golden Book of Venice, by Mrs. Lawrence Turnbull). Where a woman has written under both her maiden and her married names, her latest or most consistently used name is listed for the main entry, with reference and cross-reference to the other (for example: Lenanton, Carola Oman. Crouchback, by Carola Oman). The Index, as well as the text, provides as complete a listing as possible of these multiple names.

Sometimes a work has appeared under various titles, as is the case where a book has one title in England and another in the United States. In such cases the American or more common title is preferred. When a book is re-issued with a new title, the later title is used. In known circumstances involving more than one name or title, explanation has been made in the text and cross references are provided in the Index.

Where there have been a great many editions of a work, as often happens in the case of classics, reference has usually been made to an earlier edition as more indicative of the author's milieu, style, and tendence. In the case of more contemporary novels, where information has come to hand of later editions, these are usually listed with reference to first or earlier publication dates. This is on the theories that later editions are more readily available and that a re-issue is an indication of the popularity and value of a particular book. Chance has had its part in these matters, so that the editions cited are sometimes, perhaps, not the earliest or the most recent. Where there have been several publishers, the one listed is likewise fortuitous, since no attempt has been made to choose between them, except that American publishers are usually given preference, since this Guide is initially published in the United States. The Library of Congress Catalogue has been the main reference here, as being the best yardstick of books available in this country. Publishers are American or English unless otherwise noted.

A common fault of many annotated bibliographies of historical fiction is that they are inclined either to be so diffuse that they tell the story in advance, or so concise as to be satisfied with unadorned entries that give practically no information. An attempt has been made here to tread the middle path. Ordinarily, information as to the general time and locale is already given by the chronological and geographical classification. It goes without saying that most of the works included involve exciting action, an element of adventure, and romantic suspense.

Long descriptive sub-titles, so popular in many older novels, have seldom been included unless they provide additional information. In some instances a sub-title has been used for the annotation, in which case it is enclosed in quotation marks.

The authors wish to express their profound gratitude to the various libraries which have so generously helped them in their work, including the Saint Louis University and Webster College-Eden Seminary Libraries, and the St. Louis (Central and Carpenter Branch), Cincinnati, and Los Angeles County Public Libraries, especially the last mentioned. Gratitude is also due to the authors' families, whose help and cooperation were both essential and supportive.

Although the authors have worked several years and expended much time and money in the preparation of this modest volume, they realize its inevitable limitations. For these they cannot apologize, since they have done their best, and, to quote Martial: "Otherwise, dear Avitus, there would be no book." At the same time they ask any users of the work who have criticisms, suggestions, or constructive comments to advise them. They will regard this as a special favor. Suggestions as to additions, subtractions, or other alterations will, as far as possible, be gratefully incorporated into subsequent editions.

And now we bid farewell to the patient reader: "Happy journeys along the picturesque paths of historical fiction! If this Guide be of any service in lighting your way, it will have fulfilled its purpose."

Notes

1. Jonathan Nield, A Guide to the Best Historical Novels and Tales (London and New York, 1902), which went through five successive, revised editions, the last in 1929.

2. Ernest A. Baker, History in Fiction . . . (London and New York, 1907). This reappeared in revised form as A Guide to Historical Fiction in 1914 and in 1969.

3. James R. Kaye, Historical Fiction, Chronologically and Historically Related (Chicago, 1920).

4. Hannah Logasa, Historical Fiction Suitable for Junior and Senior High Schools (Philadelphia, 1927). The ninth edition of this work, revised, appeared at Brooklawn, N. J., in 1968.

5. Generally these have been entitled, Historical Fiction and Other Reading References for Classes in Junior and Senior High Schools.

6. Otis W. Coan and Richard G. Lillard, America in Fiction . . . (Stanford University, 1941; revised in 1945).

7. "Farm and Village Life," "Industrial America," "Politics . . . ," "Religion," etc.

8. Ernest F. Leisy, The American Historical Novel (Norman, Okla., 1950).

9. Robert A. Lively, Fiction Fights the Civil War (Chapel Hill, N. C., 1957).

10. A. T. Dickinson, Jr., American Historical Fiction (New York, 1958). A revised edition appeared in 1971.

11. Jack W. Vanderhoof, A Bibliography of Novels Related to American Frontier and Colonial History (Troy, N. Y., 1971).

CONTENTS

xiii

xiv

INTRODUCTION

Attempts to reconstruct the past by using the imagination
to amplify traditions and other historical evidences are
among the oldest and dearest activities of man. Since
the earliest times of which we have record, man has
taken pleasure in picturing the past in folktales, song,
epic poems, and dramatic compositions. Although the
skeleton of these works is usually historical, their flesh
is decidedly fictional.

The great epic poems which have so often constituted the
fundamental literature and history of ancient peoples were essential-
ly historical: partly true, partly imaginative. It is accepted as a
fact that traditions concerning past events were incorporated into the
great epic poems of antiquity, such as Homer's Iliad and Odyssey,
Vergil's Aeneid, the early German Nibelungenlied (Song of the
Nibelungs), the French Chansons de geste such as the Song of
Roland, the Spanish Cid Campeador, the Byzantine Digenes Akrites,
and many Scandinavian Sagas and Eddas.

The like may be said of many outstanding dramas of earlier
times. Many of the greatest dramatists have composed works on
historical themes, for example: Aeschylus, Calderón, Corneille,
Racine, and especially Shakespeare. Dramatic presentations of historical subjects still have their attraction, as is evidenced by
several recent motion pictures and television presentations.

Thus writers of historical fiction stand in a distinguished
company and a great tradition. The main difference is that whereas epic poetry was composed primarily to be recited, and drama
to be presented both orally and visually, novels are written simply
to be read.

In comparatively recent times, as a result of the increased
diffusion of the printed word and public literacy, fiction has become the principal form of literature, and the historical novel the
prevailing form of historically oriented belles lettres. Both the

art and the popularity of historical fiction were ably promoted in the first half of the nineteenth century by Sir Walter Scott, as well as by other writers such as Alexandre Dumas, the Brontë sisters, James Fenimore Cooper, Nathaniel Hawthorne, Charles Kingsley, and Leo Tolstoy, to mention only a few examples. In our own day we see such figures as Thomas B. Costain, Louis de Wohl, Dmitri Merezhkovsky, Rafael Sabatini, Frank G. Slaughter, Shirley Seifert, and Janice Holt Giles among authors of historical fiction.

The same thing draws such writers and their readers to historical fiction as attracted great ancient writers to epic poetry and semi-historical drama. Historical fiction is a powerful medium which includes, at one and the same time, the attractions of fiction and those of history, and it appeals to a broad audience.

One of the charms of fiction is that it seeks "verisimilitude" and clothes itself in the semblance of truth. Historical fiction adds the realistic details and trappings of actuality that belong to a past, often remote time. The task of the author of historical fiction is thus the more difficult and the more exacting, since he must familiarize himself with the facts and features of life in the past as well as the present.

In addition to sharing the values of fiction in general, historical fiction has values all its own. Among shared attributes are the powers to inform and instruct, awaken sympathies and appreciations, communicate experiences and emotions, inspire and uplift, as well as the ability to entertain, amuse, and relax. But over and beyond these things, historical fiction is also an introduction to history: a threshold and a gateway leading into formal history. After reading historical fiction, as after seeing a film version of the story of Samson and Delilah, or Caesar and Cleopatra, for example, one is drawn to consult authentic historical accounts and sources to see how far the presentation has followed the facts.

The famous nineteenth century German historian Leopold von Ranke is said to have been turned to the study of history by reading the novels of Sir Walter Scott. As Robert A. Lively remarks: "The devotee of historical novels moves toward formal history rather than away from it; he rises from excitement at

fictions to seek the truth of the matter. "[1]   And, as the versatile
English author, historian, and statesman, Sir John Morley, has
forcibly put it: "The great Duke of Marlborough said that he had
learnt all the history he ever knew out of Shakespeare's historical
plays. "[2]

Good historical fiction, besides being an introduction and
enticement to history, is itself a form of history.   It not only contains many historical elements, but is also a legitimate approach
to history.   Hervey Allen has observed: "Neither historian nor
novelist can reproduce the real past, " but by use of his particular
art, the novelist may give "the reader a more vivid, adequate, and
significant apprehension of past epochs than does the historian. "[3]

The conscientious historian has this limitation: he is unable
to re-create a full historical picture "in the round" or "in the
concrete. " Although he may be informed as to the various historical elements which could go to make up a full picture of any
past event, he never knows for sure just which of these elements
were actually in conjunction at any given time.   The hero and
heroine might well have been attired thus and so according to the
styles of the day, but what did they actually wear on this occasion?
What did they actually say? What were the trivial details as well
as the more important elements that are essential to construct the
living yet accurate picture of any past event? Who can say? Cer-
tainly not the historian. By virtue of his profession he is disbarred
from simply imagining or improvising; he must stick to ascertained
facts.   It is here that he must call in his colleague--and we use
the term advisedly--the historical novelist.

The author of historical fiction is at liberty to reconstruct,
with his broader leeway, a detailed, colorful picture of the past as
it must have been.   He is able to provide "the selective litter of
unique detail that . . . warms fiction with the breath of reality. "[4]
As Lively further remarks, "While the historian labors to authenti-
cate each tile he laboriously assembles, the novelist, with broad
brush and vivid colors, may capture with a few broad strokes an
impression of the age recalled. "[5]

In earlier times there was not the distinction that we have

today between the historian and the historical novelist. Accordingly, in order to infuse life into his story and create a more striking picture of the past, the historian often acted as an historical novelist, and filled in the details from his imagination or from questionable traditions. In modern times, however, this distinction has been drawn, so that we can now trust the historian to retain his objective accuracy with greater integrity, and, at the same time, enjoy and appreciate the freer picture painted by the historical novelist.

Thomas Carlyle noted that Scott's publication of his absorbing tales known as the Waverley Novels "taught all men this truth . . . . that the bygone ages of the world were actually filled by living men, not by protocols, state papers, controversies, and abstractions of men. "[6]

In a way, it might even be argued that historical fiction is more truthful than history itself. History supposedly presents all that it records as factual, yet everyone knows that much of what it says is insufficiently proven, doubtful, or even, in many instances, in error, by virtue of the inadequacy of human knowledge. But historical fiction, on the other hand, merely suggests that much of its content is true to life and much fictional, leaving to the discriminating reader the determination of just what is objective and what is imaginative. In a broad sense most history is partly fictional, and most fiction is partly true. But whereas history makes claim to thorough-going objectivity, historical fiction displays no such presumption. The famous English novelist Thackeray declared, with some exaggeration, over a century ago, that "fiction contains a greater amount of truth in solution than the volume that purports to be all true. "[7]

The reading of historical fiction is recreational, and both relaxes and gratifies. But it is also profitable. It leaves us with something to show for our time. While being entertained, we are also instructed. This is to some extent true of all good fiction; but it is doubly true of good historical fiction. The latter adds more dimension to ordinary fiction. As one lady somewhat untactfully, but also with some truth, remarked: "Historical fiction

sugar-coats the historical pill. " It is a godsend for the tired
businessman, the fatigued mother, the weary working girl, laborer,
and student, who wish for and need a certain degree of relaxation,
but still do not want it to be entirely without profit. They are perhaps not up to digesting a more serious tome of formal history.
At the same time, they may not be content with a steady, monoto-
nous diet of television, newspapers, and magazines. For them
historical fiction, which can carry them back to the past on a
magic carpet, is "just what the doctor ordered. " For them the
historical novelist may fulfill in modern days the function that used
to be performed by epic poets, troubadors, and dramatic authors.

Notes

1. Robert A. Lively, Fiction Fights the Civil War (Chapel Hill,
   N. C. , 1957) p. 190.

2. The quotation is from John Morley, The Great Commonplaces
   of Reading, quoted in Jonathan Nield, A Guide to the Best
   Historical Novels and Tales (London, 1929) p. xvi.

3. Hervey Allen, "History in the Novel, " in Atlantic Monthly,
   CLXXIII, No. 2 (1944) 119-120.

4. Lively, op. cit. , p. 72.

5. Ibid. , p. 7.

6. Thomas Carlyle, Critical and Miscellaneous Essays (Century
   Edition), IV, 77.

7. Quoted in Nield, op. cit. , p. xvi.

PART I

ANTIQUITY (TO ABOUT 400 A.D.)

A. THE NEAR EAST, EUROPE AND THE MEDITERRANEAN AREA

1. ANCIENT NEAR EAST (to about 336 B.C.)

a) Ancient Egypt

Bell, Archie. King Tut-Ankh-Amen. St. Botolph Soc., 1923. Of
the love of the Prince of Hermonthis for a priestess--and its
outcome.   1

Ebers, Georg. An Egyptian Princess. (tr.) Macmillan, 1887.
Romance of Egypt and Persia in the sixth century B.C. with
good historical background.   2

_____. Uarda. (tr.) Caldwell, 1877. Life under the power-
ful Rameses II--social, military, religious, political--revolving
on a plot of mistaken identity.   3

Eckenstein, Lina. Tutankh-aten. Cape, 1924. Events during
monotheistic Aken-aten's reign in fourteenth century B.C.
Thebes.   4

Gautier, Théophile. The Romance of a Mummy. (tr.) Lippincott,
1886. About the plagues in ancient Egypt and the Exodus, with
details of life based on archeological findings.   5

Glowacki, Aleksander. The Pharaoh and the Priest. (tr.)
Little, 1902. Conflict between religious and political forces
in the reign of Rameses XIII.   6

Grant, Joan. Lord of the Horizon. British Bks., 1948. A
vivid story of the Middle Kingdom in Egypt under Amenem-
het I.   7

_____. Winged Pharaoh. Harper, 1938. An Egyptian princess
of about 4000 B.C., with ancient culture and ideals as background.   8

Haggard, H. Rider. The Ancient Allan. Longmans, 1920. A

1

flash-back transports us to fifth century B. C. Egypt.   9

_____. Morning Star. Longmans, 1910. A story of romance
and the supernatural in the face of danger with the Pharaoh's
daughter as a figure.   10

_____. Queen of the Dawn. Doubleday, 1925. Romance during
King Apepi's rule in the eighteenth century B. C.   11

Hall, Arthur Dana. Golden Balance. Crown, 1955. Son of a
farmer becomes a member of the Pharaoh's court.   12

Hardy, William George. All the Trumpets Sounded. Coward,
1942. The story of Moses as adopted Prince of Egypt and as
leader of the Hebrews.   13

Hawkes, Jacquetta. King of the Two Lands. Chatto, 1966.
Elevated monotheism and reform-efforts of the idealistic
Pharaoh Akhenaton and his lovely wife Nefertiti.   14

Kelly, William P. The Stonecutter of Memphis. Dutton, 1904.
During the period of animal worship the hero is sentenced to
be sold into slavery for killing a sacred cat.   15

McGraw, Eloise Jarvis. The Golden Goblet. Coward, 1961. YA.*
About life in ancient Egypt, a precious goblet stolen from a
Pharaoh's tomb, and a boy who aspires to be a goldsmith.   16

_____. Mara, Daughter of the Nile. Coward, 1953. YA. A
picture of the daily life, both in the marketplace and in court
circles, emerges in this tale of a slave's romance.   17

_____. Pharaoh. Coward, 1958. Queen Hatshepsut, acting as
regent, proclaims herself Pharaoh and rules Egypt.   18

Mann, Thomas. Joseph in Egypt. (tr.) Knopf, 1938. Joseph's
rise from slavery to a position of trust. (followed by Joseph
the Provider)   19

_____. Joseph the Provider. (tr.) Knopf, 1944. The height of
Joseph's power in Egypt and his reunion with his family.   20

Merezhkovsky, Dmitri. Akhnaton, King of Egypt. (tr.) Dutton,
1924. Association of the Cretan maiden-priestess Dio with
the monotheistic Pharaoh Akhnaton (Akenaten).   21

· Morrison, Lucile. The Lost Queen of Egypt. Lippincott, 1937.
YA. Princess Ankhsenamon marries King Tutankhamon and
becomes Queen of Egypt at twelve years of age.   22

_____

*YA. Young Adult. Suitable for junior high and high school stu-
dents as well as adults. See p. iii.

Norton, Alice Mary. Shadow Hawk. by Andre Norton, pseud.
Harcourt, 1960. YA. Conflict between the Pharaoh Kamose and
the Hyksos invaders of Egypt in the sixteenth century B. C.   23

Patterson, Emma L. Sun Queen: Nefertiti. McKay, 1967. The
marriage and reign of Akhenaton and Nefertiti and his attempt
to convert the people of Egypt to the worship of Aton, the
peaceful, gentle Sun-God.   24

Pier, Garrett Chatfield. Hanit, the Enchantress. Dutton, 1921.
An archeologist goes back thirty centuries to experience life
in Amenhotep's court.   25

Rawlins, Eustace. The Hidden Treasures of Egypt. by R. Eustace,
pseud. Stratford, 1926. About the Prophet Moses and his
people.   26

Stacton, David. On a Balcony. Faber & Faber, 1958. The
monotheistic Pharaoh Amenhotep IV, who took the name
Ikhnaton (Akhenaton), his shrewd wife, Nefertiti, and his
forthright general, Horemheb.   27

Vidal, Nicole. Goddess Queen. (tr.) McKay, 1965. About
Queen Nefertiti and her husband Amenhotep IV (Akhenaton)
and their influence on Egyptian religion.   28

Walloth, Wilhelm. The King's Treasure House. Gottsberger,
1886. Egypt before the Exodus.   29

Waltari, Mika. The Egyptian. (tr.) Putnam, 1949. Life in
Egypt a thousand years before the coming of Christ.   30

Whisper, A., pseud. King and Captive. Blackwood, 1910.
Romance of a monarch and a dancing girl in ancient
Thebes.   31

Whyte-Melville, George John. Sarchedon. Longmans, 1871.
Romance of a soldier and a maiden in the time of Semiramis
in Egypt and Assyria.   32

Williamson, W. H. The Panther Skin. Holden, 1924. Set in
Egypt during Amenhotep IV's (Akhnaton's) eventful reign.   33

Willis, Anthony Armstrong. The Love of Prince Rameses. by
Anthony Armstrong, pseud. Paul, 1921. Royal romance in
Egypt in the twelfth century B. C.   34

_____. When Nile Was Young. by Anthony Armstrong,
pseud. Hutchinson, 1923. Religious conflict in Egypt in the
fourteenth century B. C.   35

Wilson, Dorothy Clarke. A Prince of Egypt. Westminster, 1949.
Based on the life of Moses to the time of the Exodus.   36

b) Ancient Mesopotamia and Persia

Beddoes, Willoughby. A Son of Ashur. Sonnenschein, 1905.
The glory of Babylon in the days of King Nebuchadnezzar.   37

Crawford, M. Marion. Zoroaster. Macmillan, 1885. A
Persian romance of the time of Daniel--the fall of Babylon
and the feast of Belshazzar.   38

Davis, William Stearns. Belshazzar. Doubleday, 1902. "A tale
of the fall of Babylon. "   39

De Camp, Lyon. The Dragon of the Ishtar Gate. Doubleday,
1961. Adventures of an intelligent Greek and a brawny Persian in quest of the elixir of youth for Xerxes the Great.   40

Gardiner, G. S. Rustem, Son of Zal. Greening, 1911. Legendary
Iranian fighter whose tragedy was unknowingly to kill his son
in battle.   41

Jenkins, R. Wade. "O King, Live for Ever!" Watts, 1911. A
novel of the fall of Babylon.   42

Lofts, Norah. Esther. Macmillan, 1950. A warm, human story
of Esther, Queen of Persia.   43

Morgan, Barbara E. Hand of the King. Random House, 1963,
c. 1962. YA. Revolt against a hated Assyrian king in the
valley of the Euphrates in 1750 B. C.   44

Peple, Edward. Semiramis. Moffat, 1907. Based on the life
of the legendary Assyrian queen, Semiramis.   45

Potter, Margaret Horton. Istar of Babylon: A Phantasy. Harper,
1902. A fantasy about the moon god's daughter, who takes
human form as a beautiful woman.   46

Walker, Agnese Laurie. Hadassah, Queen of Persia. Scott,
1912. Includes a picture of the Persian court and of Esther,
whose earlier Jewish name was Hadassah.   47

Weinreb, Nathaniel Norsen. The Babylonians. Doubleday, 1953.
Swift-moving tale of a spy in the household of
Nebuchadnezzar.   48

_____. Esther. Doubleday, 1955. Based on the Biblical
story of the Jewish heroine who became Queen of Persia.   49

Williams, Earl Willoughby. Court of Belshazzar. Bobbs, 1918.
Liberation of the Jews from Babylon.   50

c) The Hebrews and Other Peoples

Asch, Sholem. Moses. (tr.) Putnam, 1951. An impressive retelling of the Biblical tale of Moses and the Exodus.   51

_____ . The Prophet. (tr.) Putnam, 1955. Isaiah the Prophet
at the end of the Babylonian captivity.   52

Ashton, Mark. Jezebel's Husband. Page, 1904. A story which
includes the Biblical characters Obadiah, Ahab, Jezebel, and
Elijah.   53

Baker, Amy J. Tyrian Purple. Long, 1919. Tyre and Samaria
provide the background for this novel of Ahab and Jehu.   54

Bauer, Florence Anne. Abram, Son of Terah. Bobbs, 1948.
Abraham's search for and fidelity to the one true God.   55

Blaker, Richard. Thou Art the Man. McBride, 1937. Vivid
study of three men of the Bible--Samuel, Saul, and David.   56

Bolt, David Langstone. Adam. Day, 1961, c.1960. Imaginative account of the creation, temptation, fall, and punishment
of Adam and Eve, based on the Bible.   57

Brady, Cyrus Townsend. When the Sun Stood Still. Revell,
1917. A story of the Israelites under the leadership of
Joshua.   58

Buchanan, Thompson. Judith Triumphant. Harper, 1905. The
siege of Bethulia, based on the Biblical story of Judith.   59

Cabries, Jean. Jacob. Dutton, 1958. Humanizes the Biblical
figures of Jacob, Esau, Rachel, Leah, and Joseph.   60

Cahun, Léon. The Adventures of Captain Mago. Scribner, 1876.
Imaginative account of a Phoenician expedition about 1000 B.C.
                                                               61
Chinn, Laurene. The Unanointed. Crown, 1959. The heroic fi-
delity of Joab, David's military commander.   62

_____ . Voice of the Lord. Crown, 1961. The life of the
gentle but fearless Jeremias and his prophecy concerning the destruction of Jerusalem.   63

Clark, Alfred. Lemuel of the Left Hand. Low, 1909. The war
between Jerusalem and Syria at the time of Ahab and Obadiah.
                                                               64
Davenport, Arnold. By the Ramparts of Jezreel. Longmans,
1903. The invasion of the Syrians into the land of the Jews in
the time of Elisha and Ahab.   65

Davis, Christopher. Ishmael. Harper, 1969, c.1967. Ishmael,

the son of Abraham by a slave girl, Hagar, is banished to the
desert, where he reflects on reality.   66

De Wohl, Louis. David of Jerusalem. Lippincott, 1963. A story
of David: his boyhood, his rise to Kingship, his reign, and
his eventual old age.   67

Feuchtwanger, Lion. Jephta and His Daughter. (tr.) Putnam,
1958. Jephta's determination to fulfill his rash vow to sacrifice
his beloved daughter.   68

Fineman, Irving. Jacob. Random, 1941. Novel presenting the
story of Isaac, Jacob, Esau, Rachel, and Joseph, purportedly
in the words of Jacob himself.   69

_____. Ruth. Harper, 1949. Fictionalized version of the life
of Ruth.   70

Fisher, Vardis. The Valley of Vision. Abelard, 1951. A novel
based on the life of King Solomon and showing him as an impressive, realistic person.   71

Grant, Joan. So Moses Was Born. Methuen, 1952. A story
of the birth of Moses and intrigue in the royal Egyptian court
of the time.   72

Haggard, H. Rider. Moon of Israel. Longmans, 1918. The
Hebrews in Egypt and their exodus through the Red Sea.   73

_____, and Andrew Lang. The World's Desire. Longmans,
1891. The flight of the Israelites from Egypt.   74

Hesky, Olga. The Painted Queen. Obolensky, 1962, c.1961.
A defense of Queen Jezebel, wife of King Ahab of Israel and
target of the Prophet Elijah.   75

Ibn-Sahav, Ari. David and Bathsheba. (tr.) Crown, 1951. The
romance of King David and the lovely Bathsheba, supposedly
told by the King on his deathbed.   76

Ilton, Paul and MacLennan Roberts. Moses and the Ten Commandments. Dell, 1956. Over three thousand years ago
Moses received the Commandments on Mount Sinai and led his
people to a rendezvous with God.   77

Ingram, Tolbert R. Maid of Israel. Broadman, 1955. Portrays
slavery and life in the ancient Near East.   78

Israel, Charles Edward. Rizpah. S. & S., 1961. A beautiful
young Hebrew girl, who had been captured and enslaved by the
Philistines, is rescued and develops a deep and lasting love
for King Saul.   79

Jacobson, Dan.   The Rape of Tamar.   Macmillan, 1970.   The
   rape of King David's only daughter by her brother Amnon and
   its violent sequel, told in modern idiom.   80

Jenkins, Gwyn.   King David.   Doubleday, 1961.   A tale of the
   shepherd-turned-king, set in Old Testament days.   81

Kellner, Esther.   The Promise.   Westminster, 1956.   The marriage of Sarah and Abraham and their journey to the Promised
   Land.   82

Kelly, William P.   The Assyrian Bride.   Dutton, 1905.   Conflict
   between opposing religions and nationalities in the forbidden
   marriage of a Jew to a heathen.   83

Kossak-Szczucka, Zofja.   The Covenant.   (tr.)   Roy, 1951.
   Abraham as a prophet and a leader in the Euphrates Valley,
   in the desert, and in Egypt.   84

Ley-Piscator, Maria.   Lot's Wife.   Bobbs, 1954.   The wanderings of Abraham, his nephew Lot, and the latter's wife.   85

Linklater, Eric.   Husband of Delilah.   Harcourt, 1963, c.1962.
   Sympathetic reconstruction of the story of Samson with details
   of his personal life.   86

McLaws, Lafayette, i.e. Emily Lafayette McLaws.   Jezebel.
   Lothrop, 1902.   A story of Israel when Ahab was king.   87

Malvern, Gladys.   The Foreigner.   McKay, 1954.   YA.   The
   story of Ruth, who left her own people and went to live in a
   foreign land.   88

Mann, Thomas.   Joseph and His Brothers.   (tr.)   Knopf, 1934.
   The story of Jacob, Leah, and Rachel and of their sons.
   (followed by Young Joseph)   89

_____.   Young Joseph.   (tr.)   Knopf, 1935.   Joseph's life
   from his seventeenth year until he was sold into slavery.
   (followed by Joseph in Egypt)   90

Michener, James A.   The Source.   Random House, 1965.   Successive civilizations are portrayed as different levels are revealed in an archeological dig in Israel, giving rise to dramatic stories of man's past.   91

Miller, Elizabeth.   The Yoke.   Bobbs, 1904.   "A romance of
   the days when the Lord redeemed the children of Israel from
   the bondage of Egypt."   92

More, E. Anson.   A Captain of Men.   Page, 1905.   About
   Hiram, King of Tyre, in whose reign Phoenician commerce ·
   flourished.   93

Murphy, Edward F. Song of the Cave. Bruce, 1950. A Biblical novel of the Jewish Naomi and her Moabite daughter-in-
law, Ruth.   94

Noller, Ella M. Ahira, Prince of Naphtali. Eerdmans, 1947.
Fictional account of the journey of the Hebrews to the land of
Canaan.   95

Ormonde, Czenzi. Solomon and the Queen of Sheba. Farrar,
1954. Based on the visit of the Queen of Sheba to Solomon. 96

Parker, Gilbert. The Promised Land. Stokes, 1928. King
David and Hebrew life.   97

Penfield, Wilder. No Other Gods. Little, 1954. A search for
the one true God, to the time Abraham sets out for the land
of Canaan.   98

Pitzer, Robert C. Daughter of Jerusalem. Liveright, 1956.
Trials of the Jews in the days of the Prophet Jeremias.   99

Rees, Jean A. Jacob Have I Loved. Eerdmans, 1963, c.1962.
The story of Isaac's son, Jacob, who eventually brought his
troubled people into Egypt.   100

Rijen, Adolf Josef Hubert Frans van. Cain. (tr.) by Rogier
van Aerde, pseud. Regnery, 1954. Imaginative expansion of
the Biblical account of Cain's rebellion.   101

Schmitt, Gladys. David the King. Dial, 1946. Vivid recrea-
tion of the story of David.   102

Shamir, Moshe. David's Stranger. (tr.) Abelard, 1965,
c.1964. The perplexity of the faithful Uriah the Hittite, husband of Bathsheba, sent by King David to the front to be
killed in battle.   103

Slaughter, Frank G. The Curse of Jezebel. Doubleday, 1961.
Portrays Queen Jezebel as an evil and faithless wife whose
wiles entrap Prince Michael.   104

_____. The Purple Quest. Doubleday, 1965. A seafaring
merchant's two great drives--one his love for Queen Dido,
the other the search for a rare purple dye.   105

_____. Scarlet Cord. Doubleday, 1956. Story of Rahab,
woman of Jericho, told against a well-detailed background
of the time.   106

_____. The Song of Ruth. Doubleday, 1954. A novel based
on the Biblical story of Ruth.   107

Tandrup, Harald. Reluctant Prophet. Knopf, 1939. The adventures of Jonah--told with a dash of humor.   108

Todres, Max. Man in the Ancient World. Meador, 1948.
Fictional account concerning the Patriarch Abraham.   109

Watkins, Shirley. The Prophet and the King. Doubleday,
1956. Story of the aging prophet Samuel and the young
king Saul.   110

Weinreb, Nathaniel Norsen. The Sorceress. Doubleday, 1954.
Action-filled story of the Hebrew prophetess Deborah.   111

Werfel, Franz. Hearken Unto the Voice. Viking, 1938. Life
of the Prophet Jeremias presented by way of flashback.   112

Wilchek, Stella. Judith. Harper, 1969. Based on the Biblical
story of Judith and her heroism in seducing and slaying the
Babylonian general, Holofernes.   113

Williams, Jay. Solomon and Sheba. Random, 1959. The
great love and the insurmountable political conflict between
King Solomon and Queen Sheba.   114

Williamson, Joanne S. Hittite Warrior. Knopf, 1960. YA.
Journeys and adventures of a Hittite youth after his province
had been destroyed.   115

Wilson, Dorothy Clarke. The Herdsman. Westminster, 1946.
Amos, the prophet, who perceived the love as well as the
justice of God.   116

_____. Jezebel. McGraw, 1955. Based on the biblical
story, this tells of Jezebel's powers against a background of
contemporary social life and customs.   117

Zador, Heinrich. Hear the Word. (tr.) McGraw, 1962.
Deals with the efforts of two Old Testament prophets, Elijah
and Elisha, to carry out God's plans for them.   118

2. GREECE AND THE AEGEAN (to about 336 B.C.)

Atherton, Gertrude. The Immortal Marriage. Boni & Liveright,
1927. Romance of Pericles and Aspasia in the Golden Age of
Athens.   119

_____. The Jealous Gods. [En. title: Vengeful Gods]

Liveright, 1928. Romance and marriage of Alcibiades.   120

Ayrton, Michael. The Maze Maker. Holt, 1967. Supposed
autobiography of Daedalus, Greek engineer and architect,
reflecting the Aegean mind and culture.   121

Baker, George E. Paris of Troy. [En. title: Fidus Achates]
Ziff-Davis, 1947. Fictionalized account of the siege and fall
of Troy with its Homeric heroes.   122

Bromby, Charles H. Alkibiades. Simpkin, 1905. A story
sympathetic to the Athenian demogogue Alcibiades and based
on his life.   123

Brun, Vincenz. Alcibiades. Putnam, 1935. Life and politics
in Athens in the second half of the fifth century B.C.   124

Buchan, John. The Lemnian. Blackwood, 1912. Graphic eye-
witness account of the tragic battle of Thermopylae.   125

Coolidge, Olivia. The King of Men. Houghton, 1966. YA. An
exciting tale of Agamemnon based on ancient legends, telling
of his struggle for power and romance.   126

Davis, William Stearns. A Victor of Salamis. Macmillan,
1907. Critical naval battle of Themistocles versus the Persians, with a description of the Isthmian games.   127

De Camp, Lyon. The Bronze God of Rhodes. Doubleday, 1960.
The life of the sculptor of one of the seven wonders of the
ancient world--the Colossus of Rhodes.   128

_____. An Elephant for Aristotle. Doubleday, 1958. A
story with a sense of humor--Alexander's bizarre gift of
an elephant to Aristotle.   129

Dodd, Anna Bowman. On the Knees of the Gods. Dodd, 1908.
The Peloponnesian War and the impulsive Athenian leader,
Alcibiades.   130

Eckstein, Ernst. Aphrodite. (tr.) Gottsberger, 1886. "A
romance of ancient Hellas."   131

Erskine, John. The Private Life of Helen of Troy. Bobbs,
1925. Set in Sparta after the return of Menelaus from Troy
with Helen.   132

Faulkner, Nancy. The Traitor Queen. Doubleday, 1963. YA.
Religious ritual, intrigue and romance combine in this novel
of ancient Crete.   133

Gaines, Charles Kelsey. Gorgo. Lothrop, 1903. Athens and
Sparta during the Peloponnesian War.   134

Gay, Geraldine M. The Astrologer's Daughter. Drane, 1906.
Set in Athens during its "Golden Age" in the fifth century
before Christ. 135

Gerson, Noel B. The Trojan. Doubleday, 1962. Recounts the
taking of Troy by the Greeks and its recovery by loyalists
with Hebrew and Arabian help. 136

Grazebrook, Owen Francis. Nicanor of Athens. Macmillan,
1947. Imaginary autobiography of a wealthy Athenian in the
fifth century B.C. 137

Green, Peter. Achilles His Armour. Doubleday, 1967. The
unpredictable but popular Athenian leader, Alcibiades, who
involved the Athenians in a ruinous expedition against Syracuse. 138

_____. The Laughter of Aphrodite. Doubleday, 1966, c.1965.
Tragic story of the Greek poetess of love, Sappho, based on
fragments of her writings. 139

Green, Roger Lancelyn. Mystery at Mycenae. Barnes, 1959.
The adventurous hearts of the men of Mycenae were fired
by the abduction of Helen from her husband by the Trojans. 140

Grosser, Karlheinz. Tamburas. (tr.) Holt, 1967. Forced
into exile by a hoax, a Greek boy rises to high position
among the Persians but loses his beloved. 141

Gudmundsson, Kristmann. Winged Citadel. (tr.) Holt, 1940.
A good picture of the religion and civilization of early
Crete. 142

Hamerling, Robert. Aspasia. (tr.) Gottsberger, 1882. The
activities of a beautiful, intelligent woman, friend of Pericles,
Socrates, and Anaxagoras. 143

Hansen, Eva Hemmer. Scandal in Troy. (tr.) Random House,
1956. A light-hearted version of the story of Helen of Troy.
144

Harris, Clare Winger. Persephone of Eleusis. Stratford,
1923. Romance of a soldier during the Persian invasion of
Greece. 145

Homer. The Iliad. (tr. by Ennis Rees and pub. as The Iliad
of Homer) Random House, 1963. The epic tale of Troy
translated into iambic pentameter blank verse. 146

_____. The Odyssey. (tr. by Robert Fitzgerald) Double-
day, 1961. A translation into modern English blank verse
of the classic epic of the wanderings of Odysseus. 147

Ingles, James Wesley. Test of Valor. Tempo Bks., 1965,

c. 1953.   The Olympic Games demanded the ultimate in
strength and skill, as Nicias found when he avenged his
crippled father by defeating the mighty Ajax.   148

Johnson, Dorothy.   Witch Princess.   Houghton, 1967.   YA.
The story of a princess possessed of magical powers who is
taken by Jason on his quest for the Golden Fleece.   149

Kelly, William P.   The Stranger from Ionia.   Dutton, 1911.
The conflict between democracy and aristocracy forbids the
marriage of an Athenian girl to a foreigner.   150

Landor, W. Savage.   Pericles and Aspasia.   Dent, 1836.   The
romance of Pericles and Aspasia in defiance of Athenian law,
which forbade citizens to marry foreigners.   151

Lawrence, Isabelle.   Niko.   Viking, 1956.   An apprentice to
the sculptor Phidias aids in making the figures on the Parthe-
non.   152

Lytton, Edward Bulwer, 1st. baron.   Pausanias, the Spartan.
Routledge, 1873.   An unfinished novel concerning Pausanias
who, by a tragic mistake, killed the woman he loved.   153

Marshall, Edison.   Earth Giant.   Doubleday, 1960.   The marvelous adventures and the twelve heroic labors of Hercules
explained in terms of human ability.   154

Mauthner, Fritz.   Mrs. Socrates.   International Pub., 1926.
A tale of the famous philosopher and his spirited wife,
Xanthippe.   155

Merezhkovsky, Dmitri.   The Birth of the Gods.   (tr.) Dutton,
1924.   The island of Crete about fourteen centuries before
Christ as seen by an Egyptian envoy and the Cretan maiden-
priestess, Dio.   (followed by Akhnaton, King of Egypt)   156

Mitchison, Naomi.   Cloud Cuckoo Land.   Harcourt, 1926.
Spartan superiority in the Peloponnesian War.   157

Penfield, Wilder.   The Torch.   Little, 1960.   The career of
Hippocrates and the practice of medicine in the fourth century B.C.   158

Pick, Robert.   The Escape of Socrates.   Knopf, 1954.   A delightful story of Socrates based on the writings of Plato.   159

Plowman, Stephanie.   The Road to Sardis.   Houghton, 1966,
c. 1965.   Ancient Athens during the Peloponnesian War:
features Lycius, his cousins Pericles and Alcibiades, and
his friends Euripides and Socrates.   160

Poole, Lynn and Gray.   The Magnificent Traitor.   Dodd, 1968.

A novel of Alcibiades in the Golden Age of Pericles, including such events as the Peloponnesian War and the Olympic Games.   161

Powell, Richard. Whom the Gods Would Destroy. Scribner,
1970. A Trojan youth, captured by the Achaeans, tells both
sides of the Trojan War, with life-like pictures of legendary
heroes.   162

Ray, Mary. The Voice of Apollo. Farrar, 1965, c.1964. YA.
Seeking to appease the wrath of Apollo, whose temple had
burned, a young Greek finds his true vocation.   163

Renault, Mary, pseud. The Bull from the Sea. Pantheon,
1962. A continuation of the legend of Theseus during his
adult years.   164

_____. The King Must Die. Pantheon, 1958. The legend-
ary Greek hero Theseus tells of his eventful youth. (followed
by The Bull from the Sea)   165

_____. The Last of the Wine. Pocket Bks., 1971, c.1956.
Athens in the days of Socrates and the Third Peloponnesian
War.   166

_____. The Mask of Apollo. Pantheon, 1966. A Greek
actor becomes involved in political intrigue in Athens and
Syracuse in a novel which also tells much of backstage life
in the theater of the time.   167

Sallaska, Georgia. Priam's Daughter. Doubleday, 1970. A
pro-Trojan version of the Achaean conquest of Troy, with
Priam's daughter Cassandra predicting disaster.   168

Schmitt, Gladys. Electra. Harcourt, 1965. Electra hated her
mother, Clytemnestra, for infidelity and the murder of Agamemnon, and spent years plotting revenge.   169

Schnabel, Ernst. Story for Icarus. (tr.) Harcourt, 1961.
Fictional life-story of the mythological Greek engineer and
artificer Daedalus, told as though he related it to his son,
Icarus.   170

_____. Voyage Home. (tr.) Harcourt, 1958. A novel
based, like the Odyssey, on the homeward journey of
Ulysses.   171

Snedeker, Caroline Dale. The Perilous Seat. Doubleday,
Page, 1923. A priestess in Greece at the time of the Persian invasion in 480 B.C.   172

Stacpoole, Henry de Vere. The Street of the Flute-Player.
Duffield, 1912. Athens in the days of Socrates and

Aristophanes.   173

Stewart, George Rippey. Years of the City. Houghton, 1955.
Chronicle of a Greek colonial city from its founding to its
fall.   174

Sutcliff, Rosemary. The Flowers of Adonis. Coward, 1970,
c.1969. Presents differing views of the Athenian General,
Alcibiades, who persuaded his countrymen to make a disastrous expedition against Syracuse.   175

Treece, Henry. The Eagle King. [En. title: Oedipus] Random House, 1965, c.1964. A re-creation of the Oedipus
legend with the confusion attendant on concealed identity and
the cryptic prophecy of the Delphic oracle.   176

_____. The Windswept City. Meredith Pr., 1968. YA.
The Trojan War told from the viewpoint of one of Helen's
slaves.   177

Warner, Rex. Pericles the Athenian. Little, 1963. Life of
the brilliant Athenian, Pericles, in the Golden Age of Athens
as told by his former teacher, the philosopher Anaxagoras. 178

Yerby, Frank. Goat Song. Dial, 1968, c.1967. A captured
Spartan youth eventually becomes a successful and powerful
man in Athens.   179

3.   THE HELLENISTIC (EASTERN MEDITERRANEAN) WORLD
     (c. 336-31 B.C.)

Aimery de Pierrebourg, Marguerite. The Life and Death of
Cleopatra. (tr.) ·by Claude Ferval, pseud. Doubleday,
Page, 1924. The story of Cleopatra from about her eigh-
teenth year.   180

Beck, Lily Adams. The Laughing Queen. by E. Barrington,
pseud. Dodd, 1929. A light romance about Cleopatra--
part deified queen, part bewitching woman.   181

Dickeson, Alfred. Tychiades. Unwin, 1903. The reign of
Ptolemy II in Alexandria.   182

Druon, Maurice, pseud. for Maurice Kessel. Alexander the
God. Scribner, 1960. Alexander's military victories and
his efforts to prove himself semi-divine.   183

Duggan, Alfred. Besieger of Cities. Pantheon, 1963. A biographical novel of Demetrius of Macedonia who sought to re-
vive the Empire of Alexander the Great.   184

Ebers, Georg. Arachne. (tr.) Appleton, 1898. Centers

around discussions of realism in Hellenistic art.   185

_____. Cleopatra. (tr.) Appleton, 1894. The final part
of Cleopatra's life.   186

_____. The Sisters. (tr.) Gottsberger, 1880. Egypt under
the Ptolemy dynasty in the mid-second century B.C.   187

Eiker, Karl V. Star of Macedon. Putnam, 1957. The genius
and cruelty of Alexander the Great, told by a slave.   188

Fast, Howard. My Glorious Brothers. Little, 1948. The liberation of Israel from Syrian-Greek overlords.   189

Fisher, Vardis. Island of the Innocent. Abelard, 1952. "A
novel of Greek and Jew in the time of the Maccabees."   190

Fuller, Robert H. The Golden Hope. Macmillan, 1905. The
victories and dreams of Alexander the Great in the East and
Egypt.   191

Gerson, Noel B. The Golden Lyre. Doubleday, 1963. The
love of Ptolemy, one of Alexander's leading lieutenants, and
the witty, beautiful courtesan Thais.   192

_____. That Egyptian Woman. Doubleday, 1956. Rather
frothy account of Julius Caesar and Cleopatra.   193

Haggard, H. Rider. Cleopatra. Longmans, 1889. About the
last of the Ptolemies, who charmed both Julius Caesar and
Mark Anthony.   194

Kirkman, Marshall Monroe. (1) The Romance of Alexander the
Prince. Simpkin, 1909. (2) The Romance of Alexander the
King (sequel). Simpkin, 1909. (3) The Romance of Alexander and Roxana (sequel). Simpkin, 1909. A series of novels tracing the life of Alexander.   195-7

Marshall, Edison. Conqueror. Doubleday, 1962. First person
story of Alexander the Great which records his thoughts and
feelings as he moves on to "world conquest."   198

Menen, Aubrey. A Conspiracy of Women. Random House,
1965. Alexander's plan to consolidate his empire by marry-
ing his officers to daughters of local, defeated leaders meets
the organized opposition of his army's campfollowers.   199

Mitchison, Naomi. The Corn King and the Spring Queen. Harcourt, 1931. Panoramic view of Greek civilization and religion in the third century B.C.   200

Mundy, Talbot. Purple Pirate. Appleton, 1935. Intrigue involving Cleopatra in the two years after Caesar's death.   201

Payne, Robert. Alexander the God. Wyn, 1954. Alexander
   the Great from his conquest of Thaissa to his death.   202

Phillpotts, Eden. The Treasures of Typhon. Richards, 1924.
   A romance of Athens including the philosopher Epicurus and
   the poet Menander.   203

Polland, Madeleine. To Tell My People. Holt, 1968. YA.
   A young Briton, enslaved by Julius Caesar's conquest of
   Britain, is taken to Rome.   204

Shamir, Moshe. The King of Flesh and Blood. (tr.) Vanguard, 1958. The destructive reign of Alexander Jannaeus,
   descendant of Simon Maccabeus.   205

Strauss, Frederick. Helon's Pilgrimage to Jerusalem. Mawman,
   1824. Pictures Judaism just prior to the advent of Christ. 206

4.   ROME AND THE WESTERN
     MEDITERRANEAN WORLD (to c. 31 B.C.)

Atherton, Gertrude. Dido, Queen of Hearts. Liveright, 1929.
   The beautiful Queen of Carthage, successful in all things except her love for Aeneas.   207

Baumann, Hans. I Marched with Hannibal. (tr.) Walck, 1962,
   c.1961. YA. The first-person account of a youth in the Second Punic War, with a detailed report of crossing the Alps
   with elephants.   208

Bentley, Phyllis. Freedom, Farewell! Macmillan, 1936.
   The career of Julius Caesar and a picture of Roman society
   and politics.   209

Blasco-Ibañez, Vicente. Sonnica. (tr.) Duffield, 1912. Hannibal's bloody, ruthless three-month siege of Saguntum, based
   on Livy's history.   210

Bryher, Winifred (Annie Winifred Macpherson). The Coin of
   Carthage. Harcourt, 1963. The paths of two traders cross
   and re-cross in Italy and North Africa during the Second
   Punic War.   211

_____. Gate to the Sea. by Bryher. Pantheon, 1958. The
   Greek inhabitants of Poseidonia (Paestam), oppressed by the
   Italic Lucanians, plot to found a city elsewhere in Italy. 212

Caldwell, Taylor, pseud. for Janet Taylor Caldwell Reback and
   Marcus Reback. A Pillar of Iron. Doubleday, 1965. A
   novel concerning Cicero--lawyer, orator, and statesman in
   the period of Rome's decay.   213

Davis, William Stearns. A Friend of Caesar. Macmillan, 1900. The "friend" is a young Roman nobleman during Caesar's conquests and the fall of the Republic.   214

De Camp, Lyon. The Golden Wind. Doubleday, 1969. About a Greek who sailed a direct trading route to the East and his experiences in Egypt.   215

Dixon, Pierson. Farewell, Catullus. British Bks., 1960. Portrays contemporary influences on one of Rome's most famous poets, Catullus.   216

Dolan, Mary. Hannibal of Carthage. Macmillan, 1955. Believable account of Hannibal from the Carthaginian point-of-view.   217

Donauer, Friedrich. Swords Against Carthage. (tr.) Longmans, 1932. Campaigns of Scipio Africanus in the Second Punic War.   218

Dored, Elisabeth. I Loved Tiberius. (tr.) Pantheon, 1963. The tragic Julia, daughter of Caesar Augustus, whose three marriages were matters of state and whose children were objects of jealous plotting.   219

Duggan, Alfred. Children of the Wolf. [En. title: Founding Fathers] Coward, 1959. The struggle for power in the new city of Rome.   220

_____. Three's Company. Coward, 1958. Concerns Lepidus, one of the triumvirate ruling Rome after Ceasar's death.   221

_____. Winter Quarters. Coward, 1956. Two young Gallic noblemen join the Roman army to flee the wrath of a goddess.   222

Eckstein, Ernst. Prusias. (tr.) Gottsberger, 1882. This story of Rome tells of Spartacus and the revolt of the slaves and gladiators.   223

Gérard, Francis. Scarlet Beast. Longmans, 1935. Swift-moving tale of the Second Punic War told with a definite prejudice against Carthage.   224

Ghnassia, Maurice. Arena. Viking, 1969. Account of the slave revolt of 73-71 B.C. led by the Thracian gladiator Spartacus.   225

Gilkes, A.H. Kallistratus. Frowde, 1897. An account of the Second Punic War in autobiographical form.   226

Green, Peter. The Sword of Pleasure. World Pub., 1958. The memoirs of the illustrious Lucius Cornelius Sulla, Dictator of Rome in Caesar's boyhood.   227

Hardy, William George. City of Libertines. Appleton, 1957.
Realistic account of Rome during Caesar's coming to glory. 228

_____. Turn Back the River. Dodd, 1938. Roman politics
and romance have startling likenesses to those of our own
day.   229

Jensen, Johannes Vilhelm. The Cimbrians. (tr.) Knopf, 1923.
The author carries the story of civilization through the Stone,
Bronze, and Iron Ages, ending with the Cimbrian migration
to Italy. (followed by Christopher Columbus)   230

Kent, Louise Andrews. He Went With Hannibal. Houghton,
1964. YA. The story of a young hostage who becomes a
messenger of Hannibal during the latter's campaigns.   231

King, Clive. The Twenty-Two Letters. Coward, 1967, c.1966.
YA. The travels of three adventurous Phoenicians and the
origin of the alphabet.   232

Koestler, Arthur. The Gladiators. Macmillan, 1939. The
revolt of the gladiators and slaves, led by Spartacus.   233

Lindsay, Jack. Rome for Sale. Harper, 1934. A fine narrative of the confusion in Rome which led up to Catiline's
rebellion.   234

Mabie, Mary Louise. Prepare Them for Caesar. Little, 1949.
Caesar's ambitions, conquests, and rise to dictatorial power.
                                                             235
Marston, William M. Venus With Us. Sears, 1932. The
human aspects of Julius Caesar against a backdrop of Roman
patrician life.   236

Merrell, Elizabeth Leigh. Prisoners of Hannibal. by Leigh
Merrell, pseud. Nelson, 1958. YA. When a proud Roman
senator refuses to ransom his captured son, the youth plots
a dangerous escape to regain his citizenship and claim his
betrothed.   237

Mitchison, Naomi. The Conquered. Harcourt, 1923. The conquest of Gaul by the Romans arouses a tardy sense of Gallic
nationalism.   238

Mundy, Talbot. Tros of Samothrace. Appleton, 1934. One of
the leading lieutenants of Julius Caesar and the first Roman
invasion of Britain.   239

Osborne, Duffield. The Lion's Brood. Doubleday, 1901. Hannibal's victory at Cannae and his winter camp at Capua.   240

Radin, Max. Epicurus My Master. U. of N.C. Press, 1949.
The atmosphere of Rome, re-created by Atticus, corre-

spondent of Cicero and follower of Epicurus.   241

Smith, E. M. Aneroestes the Gaul. Unwin, 1899. Hannibal's
campaigns in the Second Punic War, describing the crossing
of the Alps.   242

Taylor, Anna. The Gods Are Not Mocked. Morrow, 1968.
Conflict between a spirited Druid priestess and her high-
placed Roman lover during Caesar's invasion of Britain in
55 B.C.   243

Wagner, John and Esther. The Gift of Rome. Little, 1961.
Cicero defends, in his capacity as a lawyer, Cluentius Habitus
who is being tried for murder at the instigation of his own
mother in her desire for revenge.   244

Waltari, Mika. The Etruscan. (tr.) Putnam, 1956. The remarkable life of a "semi-divine" pagan woman some twenty-
five hundred years ago.   245

Warner, Rex. Imperial Caesar. Little, 1960. Julius Caesar's
recollection, shortly before his death, of the later years of
his life.   246

_____. The Young Caesar. Little, 1958. Caesar's review
of his childhood and rise to power. (followed by Imperial
Caesar)   247

Wilder, Thornton. The Ides of March. Harper, 1948. Events
leading up to Caesar's assassination told in purportedly ancient documents.   248

Williamson, Joanne S. The Eagles Have Flown. Knopf, 1957.
YA. The people and customs of ancient Rome are portrayed
in this novel of a boy in the time of Julius Caesar.   249

5. THE ROMAN EMPIRE AND CHRISTIANITY
    (c. 31 B.C. to 400 A.D.)

    a) The Roman Empire at Its Height and Early
        Christianity (c. 31 B.C. to 180 A.D.)

Abbott, Edwin A. Onesimus. Roberts, 1882. The book tells
of the ministry of St. Paul.   250

_____. Philochristus. Macmillan, 1878. "The memoirs
of a disciple of Christ."   251

_____. Silanus the Christian. Macmillan, 1906. The
changed belief of a Stoic philosopher who became a disciple
of Christ.   252

Asch, Sholem. The Apostle. (tr.) Putnam, 1943. A story
of the Jewish Roman citizen, Paul, and his preaching,
starting seven weeks after the Crucifixion.   253

_____. Mary. (tr.) Putnam, 1949. The love of the Virgin
Mary, Mother of Jesus Christ, for her Son.   254

_____. The Nazarene. (tr.) Putnam, 1939. The life of
Christ told from the viewpoints of a Pharisee's disciple,
Judas Iscariot, and a modern Polish Jew.   255

Atherton, Gertrude. Golden Peacock. Houghton, 1936. A
stirring and exciting account of a girl's part in discovering a
plot against Augustus Caesar.   256

Bacheller, Irving. The Trumpets of God. [same as: Dawn]
Macmillan, 1927. The spread of Christianity in various areas
--Jerusalem, Antioch, Jericho--between 30 and 70 A.D.   257

_____. Vergilius. Harper, 1904. A patrician in Rome
learns of the coming of Christ.   258

Baring-Gould, S. Domitia. Stokes, 1898. The unhappy life
of Domitian's wife and the deaths of Nero, Vitellius, and
Domitian.   259

Bauer, Florence Anne. Behold Your King. Bobbs, 1945.
Story of the nephew of Joseph of Arimathea in the last years
of Christ's life.   260

Becker, Wilhelm Adolf. Gallus. (tr.) Longmans, 1838.
This novel gives many details of the manners and customs
of Augustan Rome.   261

Bekessy, Emery with Andreas Hemberger. Barabbas. (tr.)
Prentice-Hall, 1946. Imaginative portrait of the violent
Barabbas and other characters of the time of Jesus.   262

Bell, Sallie. Until the Day Break. Zondervan, 1950. A novel
based on the daily life, customs, and intrigue at the court of
Herod.   263

Berstl, Julius. The Cross and the Eagle. (tr.) Muhlenberg,
1955. The experiences of St. Paul from the time of his conversion until his death.   264

_____. The Tentmaker. (tr.) Rinehart, 1952, c.1951.
About St. Paul, from the time he was sixteen until his conversion. (followed by The Cross and the Eagle)   265

Billings, Edith S. Cleomenes. by Maris Warrington Billings,
pseud. Lane, 1917. Account of Cleomenes, the sculptor of

the famous "Medici Venus."   266

Blythe, LeGette. Bold Galilean. U. of N.C. Press, 1948.
A compelling portrayal of Christ as He appeared to His
contemporaries.   267

_____. Brothers of Vengeance. Morrow, 1969. The bitter
mutual hatred of a pagan youth and a Jewish bandit comes
under the calming influence of the growing Christianity. 268

_____. The Crown Tree. Knox Pr., 1957. Concerns the
Roman centurion who believed that his spear-thrust killed
the crucified Christ.   269

_____. Hear Me, Pilate! Holt, 1961. A picture of Pontius
Pilate, the official who let the thief Barabbas go free while
condemning Christ to death at the hands of the mob.   270

_____. Man on Fire. Funk, 1964. The inspired life and
labors of the zealous missionary St. Paul, together with some
of his Christian and pagan contemporaries.   271

_____. A Tear for Judas. Bobbs, 1951. A novel of Judas
Iscariot, inquiring into his reasons for betraying Christ. 272

Brod, Max. The Master. (tr.) Philosophical Lib., 1951. An
account, purportedly by a disciple of Jesus, telling of Palestine during His ministry.   273

Byatt, H. The Testament of Judas. Long, 1909. The story
of the arch-traitor, Judas Iscariot.   274

Byrne, Donn. Brother Saul. Century, 1927. The spiritual
and intellectual growth of St. Paul from youth to death. 275

Caldwell, Taylor, pseud., for Janet Taylor Caldwell Reback
and Marcus Reback. Great Lion of God. Doubleday, 1970.
The inner conflicts of the intense Saul of Tarshish (St. Paul)
who is converted from a persecutor to a missionary of
Christianity.   276

Carling, John R. The Doomed City. Clode, 1910. A narrative of besieged Jerusalem culminating in destruction of the
temple.   277

Carrel, Frederic. Marcus and Faustina. Long, 1904. His
pleasure-seeking wife complicates the rule of Stoic Emperor
Marcus Aurelius.   278

Carter, Russell Kelso. Amor Victor. by Orr Kenyon, pseud.
Stokes, 1902. Gives a picture of the Christians' position
in Roman life about 100 A.D.   279

Chinn, Laurene. Marcus. Morrow, 1965. Conversion and
  labors of the apostle St. Mark, who eventually became
  Bishop of Alexandria.   280

Cooley, William Forbes. Emmanuel. Dodd, 1889. The ministry of Christ and the labors of His apostles and disciples.
                                                            281
Coolidge, Olivia. People in Palestine. Houghton, 1965. YA.
  Sketches of Jewish people in Palestine at the time of Christ
  reflect the atmosphere of the time.   282

Corelli, Marie. Barabbas. Lippincott, 1893. A story of the
  betrayal and Crucifixion of Christ, and of the criminal freed
  in His stead.   283

Cosgrove, John. Cedar of Lebanon. McMullen, 1952. The influence of Christ and His apostles upon a contemporary Roman
  and the complete faith of the early Christians, even in the
  face of torture.   284

Costain, Thomas B. The Silver Chalice. Doubleday, 1952.
  Gripping tale on the Holy Grail theme telling the adventures of
  Basil, an artist.   285

Couperus, Louis. The Comedians. Doran, 1926. Informative
  novel about the decadence of Rome under the despot Domitian.
                                                            286
_____. The Tour. Dodd, 1920. A young lord tours Egypt
  to consult oracles about his lost love--and finds a new and
  better one.   287

Cramp, Walter S. Psyche. Little, 1905. Emperor Tiberius
  appointed the corrupt Sejanus commander of the Praetorian
  Guards with unhappy consequences.   288

Crockett, Vivian. Messalina. Boni & Liveright, 1924. The
  corrupt wife of Emperor Claudius I, who was executed by
  him after a serious scandal.   289

Crozier, William Percival. The Fates Are Laughing. Harcourt,
  1945. Life on the senatorial level in the Rome of Tiberius
  and Caligula.   290

Daringer, Helen Fern. The Golden Thorn. Harcourt, 1956.
  YA. Two young Judeans are separated and later reunited
  in this romantic novel of the time of Christ.   291

Deamer, Dulcie. The Street of the Gazelle. Fisher Unwin,
  1922. A story of the Zealots in Jerusalem at the time of
  Christ.   292

De Ropp, Robert S. If I Forget Thee. St. Martins, 1956.
Romance in Judaea on the eve of revolt against the Romans. 293

De Wohl, Louis. Glorious Folly. Lippincott, 1957. A story
about early Christianity featuring St. Paul.   294

_____. The Spear. Lippincott, 1955. Cassius Longinus,
the Roman centurion who pierced Christ's side with his
spear.   295

Dobraczynski, Jan. The Letters of Nicodemus. (tr.) Newman,
1960, c.1958. A detailed picture of the public life of Christ,
told in supposed letters of Nicodemus, who was convinced
that Christ was sent by God.   296

Douglas, Lloyd C. The Big Fisherman. Houghton, 1948.
Account of Peter and his associates in the Christian ministry.   297

Dunscomb, Charles, pseud. Behold, We Live. Houghton, 1956.
Cedonius, a slave, comes to believe and follow the doctrines
of Christianity.   298

_____. The Bond and the Free. Houghton, 1955. Account
of the beginnings of Christianity told in correspondence.   299

Ebers, Georg. The Emperor. (tr.) Gottsberger, 1881. Concerns the Emperor Hadrian and events in Egypt.   300

Eckstein, Ernst. Nero. (tr.) Gottsberger, 1889. Nero as
a man and an emperor, with important people and events of
his reign.   301

_____. Quintus Claudius. (tr.) Gottsberger, 1882. De-
scriptive of social life, political thought, and religious persecution in Domitian's reign.   302

Farrar, Frederick W. Darkness and Dawn. Longmans, 1892.
The darkness of pagan immorality contrasted with the dawn
of Christian purity.   303

Fast, Howard. Agrippa's Daughter. Doubleday, 1964. About
the daughter of Herod the Great, Berenice--her struggle with
divisive Jewish factions and Roman conquerors, her tragic
marriage, and her brief romance with Emperor Titus.   304

_____. Spartacus. Citadel, 1952. Revolt of the slaves
against their overbearing Roman masters.   305

Feuchtwanger, Lion. (1) Josephus. (tr.) Viking, 1932.

(2) The Jew of Rome. (tr.) Viking, 1936. (3) Josephus
and the Emperor. (tr.) Viking, 1942. Based on the life of
Josephus, Jewish historian--his life in Rome, his search for
social justice, his relations with the Emperor Domitian.   306-8

Fisher, Aileen Lucia. Fisherman of Galilee. Nelson, 1959.
The personality and ministry of St. Peter from the time
Jesus called him to be a "fisher of men."   309

Fox, Paul H. Daughter of Jairus. Little, 1951. One of Christ's
miracles told against the background of Jewish life and customs.
                                                               310

France, Anatole (name originally Anatole Thibault). The Procurator of Judaea. (tr.) Lane, 1908. A sardonic picture
of Pilate, who was questioned years later about the death of
Christ.   311

_____. Thais. (tr.) Smith, 1891. Hermit from the desert
attempts to convert a libertine beauty, Thais.   312

Frieberger, Kurt. Fisher of Men. Appleton, 1954. A novel of
the apostle Peter.   313

Frost, Elizabeth H. Mary and the Spinners. Coward, 1946.
About Mary and several of her friends who spent some time
as spinners in the Temple.   314

Gann, Ernest K. The Antagonists. S. & S., 1970. The siege
of Masada in the year 73 A.D. by Roman General Flavius Silva
in which Eleazar ben Yair led nine hundred Jews in desperate
resistance.   315

Gibbs, Willa. A Fig in Winter. Morrow, 1963. The philosopher-
emperor Marcus Aurelius as seen by his admiring slave who is
a Christian convert.   316

Gibran, Kahlil. Jesus the Son of Man. Knopf, 1928. The story
of Jesus as told by people who met Him.   317

Gibson, John, pseud. Patrician Street. Vanguard, 1940. The
brutal persecution of the early Christians by Roman emperors.
                                                               318

Goldthorpe, John. The Same Scourge. Putnam, 1956. The events
leading up to the Crucifixion.   319

Graham, John W. Neaera. Macmillan, 1886. The lavish, dissolute life of the last part of Tiberius' reign.   320

Haggard, H. Rider. Pearl Maiden. Longmans, 1902. Vivid account of the destruction of Jerusalem in 70 A.D.   321

Hannah, Ian Campbell. Voadica. Longmans, 1928. Romance
of a Roman patrician and a barbaric princess in occupied

Britain.   322

Harington, Joy. Jesus of Nazareth. Doubleday, 1957. A well-
illustrated life of Christ based on a TV film produced in England in 1956.   323

Hartley, J. M. The Way. Crowell, 1944. Interest in Palestine
concerning the promised Messiah about the year 20 A. D.   324

Hastings, Peter. S. P. Q. R. Holden, 1926. A barbarian gladiator becomes a Praetorian Guard at the time of Domitian and
Nerva.   325

Haugaard, Erik Christian. The Rider and His Horse. Houghton,
1968. YA. A fifteen-year-old boy takes part in the Roman
siege of the Jewish fortress of Masada.   326

Hausrath, Adolf. Antinous. (tr.) by George Taylor, pseud.
Gottsberger, 1882. Contrasting principles of Christianity and
paganism appear in this story of a page deified by Hadrian. 327

Henkle, Henrietta. And Walk in Love. by Henrietta Buckmaster,
pseud. Random, 1956. A perceptive story of St. Paul.   328

Hobbs, Roe R. The Court of Pilate. Fenno, 1906. Shows the
hatred of the Jews for their Roman oppressors personified by
Pontius Pilate.   329

Hoppus, Mary A. M. Masters of the World. Bentley, 1888.
The power and glory of Rome in the reign of Domitian with
an account of his murder.   330

Horia, Vintila. God Was Born in Exile. (tr.) St. Martin's,
1961. Living in exile, the poet Ovid, disillusioned with the
Roman gods, hears of the new Christian religion from Judaea.
                                                               331

Hubler, Richard G. The Soldier and the Sage. Crown, 1966.
Conflicting ideals of a proud Roman tribune and his friend, a
brave young Jew.   332

Ingles, James Wesley. Woman of Samaria. Longmans, 1949.
The life and marriages of Photina, a woman Christ met in
Samaria.   333

Jacobs, Joseph. As Others Saw Him. Houghton, 1895. The
story of Jesus as told in a letter by one of the Jews who demanded His death.   334

Johnson, Gillard. Raphael of the Olive. Century, 1913. Jerusalem at the time of the Maccabees, showing their efforts to recover the city.   335

Kellner, Esther. Bride of Pilate. Appleton, 1959. The story

of Claudia, granddaughter of Augustus and wife of Pontius
Pilate.   336

_____. Mary of Nazareth. Appleton, 1958. A warm, sympa-
thetic story of Mary in a setting of Hebrew traditions and everyday life.   337

Kelly, William P. The Senator Licinius. Dutton, 1909. A desperately worried senator, his daughter's romance, and the ultimate justice of the capricious Caligula.   338

Kingsley, Florence M. Veronica. Appleton, 1913. A tale of
Pilate and his wife, ending at the time of the Crucifixion.   339

Koch, Werner. Pontius Pilate Reflects. (tr.) S. & S., 1962,
c.1961. Later reflections of the stolid, conscientious, re-
morseful Pontius Pilate.   340

Komroff, Manuel. In the Years of Our Lord. Harper, 1942.
A novel based on the life and times of Christ.   341

Kossoff, David. The Book of Witnesses. St. Martin's, 1971.
An account of the life of Christ, as though told by men and
women who knew Him at various times.   342

Lagerkvist, Pär. Barabbas. Random, 1951. A powerful study
of the bandit who was released to the mob instead of Christ.
                                                                           343
_____. Herod and Mariamne. (tr.) [Swedish & En. title:
Mariamne] Knopf, 1968. The self-centered Herod is almost
redeemed by his love for the lovely, unselfish Mariamne.   344

_____. The Sibyl. (tr.) Random House, 1958. The wander-
ing Jew, cursed by Christ, seeking a solution to his doubts,
hears the story of her life from an outlawed pagan priestess.
(followed by The Death of Ahasuerus)   345

Laut, Agnes C. Quenchless Light. Appleton, 1924. About early
Christianity in Ephesus, and a slave boy who became a bishop.
                                                                           346
Levin, Dan. Son of Judah. Appleton, 1961. A learned young
Alexandrian Jew roams throughout the Roman Empire search-
ing for truth, and is variously soldier, scribe, slave, actor,
and fighter.   347

Lloyd, Roger Bradshaigh. Letters from the Early Church. Macmillan, 1960. Lives of first century Christians as told in a
series of imaginary letters.   348

Lockhart, John Gibson. Valerius. Blackwood, 1821. Descriptive of social life and religious persecution in Rome under
Trajan.   349

Loewenstein, Hubertus. The Eagle and the Cross. Macmillan,
1947. An Irish prince takes the lance of the Centurion Longinus to Tiberius, Emperor of Rome.   350

Lytton, Edward Bulwer, 1st. baron. The Last Days of Pompeii.
Dutton, 1834. The luxurious life of Pompeii and the destructive eruption of Vesuvius.   351

McGerr, Patricia. Martha, Martha. Kenedy, 1960. An elabora-
tion of what the Gospels tell us of Mary, Martha, and Lazarus
and their relationship with Jesus.   352

Mack, Elsie. A Woman of Jerusalem. Doubleday, 1962. Inter-
action between conquered and ruler, conflict between social
classes, and the growing influence of Christ weave a vivid picture of life in Jerusalem.   353

Maier, Paul L. Pontius Pilate. Doubleday, 1968. About the
Roman Prefect who condemned Christ to death, with contrasting Jewish, Roman, and Christian viewpoints.   354

Malvern, Gladys. Rhoda of Cyprus. Macrae Smith, 1958. YA.
A girl returns to Jerusalem from a visit to find that her family has become Christian.   355

_____. Secret Sign. Abelard, 1961. YA. A young actor
attempts to rescue his beloved who has been arrested and
condemned to death during Nero's perseuction of Christians. 356

_____. Tamar. Longmans, 1952. YA. The central figure
in this story of Capernaum and Jerusalem is the daughter of
Jairus, Tamar, who was raised from the dead by Jesus.   357

Martin, James. The Empty Tomb. [En. title: Letters of Caiaphas to Annas] Harper, 1960. Supposed letters from Caiaphas
relate events from the crucifixion of Jesus to the conversion
of St. Paul.   358

Mason, Caroline A. The White Shield. Griffith & Rowland, 1904.
The persecution to which early Christians were subjected is described in this legend of St. Thekla.   359

Meisels, Andrew. Son of a Star. Putnam, 1969. About the daring Simon Bar Kockba and his leadership of the Jewish revolt
against the Romans in 132 A.D.   360

Miller, Elizabeth. The City of Delight. Bobbs, 1908. A romance
of the city of Jerusalem during its siege and destruction by
Titus.   361

_____. Saul of Tarsus. Bobbs, 1906. The Roman Empire
in the early days of Christianity, with Mary of Magdala as a
character.   362

Mitchison, Naomi. Blood of the Martyrs. McGraw, 1948.
Nero's persecution of the Christians, who came from all
levels of society.   363

Mosley, Jean Bell. The Crosses at Zarin. Broadman, 1967.
The brothers James and John, sons of Zebedee, and their association with Christ.   364

Murphy, Edward F. Scarlet Lily. Bruce, 1944. A sympathetic
portrait of St. Mary Magdalene--the scarlet lily.   365

Mygatt, Tracy D. and Frances Witherspoon. Armor of Light.
Holt, 1930. A thrilling story of the trials of the early Church
in the catacombs.   366

Newcomb, Robert T. Janissa. Destiny, 1943. Egypt and
Palestine during the early Christian era.   367

Nuñez Alonso, Alejandro. The Purple Sash. (tr.) McKay, 1969.
About a rich and powerful Jewish shipping magnate who is intent upon subverting the Roman Empire.   368

O'Hanlon, Richard. What if This Friend. by Richard Hanlon,
pseud. Kendall, 1935. Concerns Syria's deputy governor
Lucius Vitellius and his Christian wife.   369

Oxenham, John, pseud. for William Arthur Dunkerley. The
Splendor of the Dawn. Longmans, 1930. A young Roman's
search for knowledge of Christ.   370

Pater, Walter. Marius the Epicurean. Macmillan, 1885. Philosophical thought in Marcus Aurelius' time.   371

Perkins, Jacob Randolph. Antioch Actress. Bobbs, 1946.
Features pagan attacks on Christianity by means of satirical
theatrical presentations.   372

_____. Emperor's Physician. Bobbs, 1944. Two physicians
meet Jesus and are convinced of His healing powers.   373

Perri, Francesco. The Unknown Disciple. Macmillan, 1950.
Early Christianity in the unrest caused by politics and conflicts with paganism.   374

Petersen, Nis. The Street of the Sandalmakers. (tr.) Macmillan, 1933. The poorer people of Rome in the days of
Marcus Aurelius.   375

Powers, Anne. No King but Caesar. Doubleday, 1960. Marriage of two high-born Romans engenders a love which enables
them to escape the intrigue surrounding Tiberius Caesar's
death and to defy the tyrant Caligula.   376

Roberson, Harriette Gunn. Mary of Magdala. Greening, 1909.
Story of Mary Magdalene, supposedly told by St. John.   377

Ronalds, Mary Teresa. Nero. Doubleday, 1969. Nero tells
the story of his career from his start as a popular youth to
his fall from public favor and his fear of reprisals for his
many rash acts.   378

Rosegger, Peter. I. N. R. I. (tr.) Hodder, 1905. A prisoner
condemned to death tells the story of Christ's life.   379

Sackler, Harry. Festival at Meron. Covici, 1935. Simeon ben
Yohai leads a Jewish revolt against Roman persecution.   380

Saunders, W. J. The Nazarene. Murray & Evenden, 1915. A
first-person narrative by a young man in Pilate's service.   381

Scharlemann, Dorothy Hoyer. My Vineyard. Concordia, 1946.
Christians and Jews in Palestine at the time of Christ.   382

Schuré, Edouard. The Priestess of Isis. Rider, 1910. Sorcery
and religious rites in Pompeii in the year of Vesuvius' eruption.   383

Schuyler, William. Hope of Glory. Four Seas Co., 1916. Christianity in Nero's day as seen in supposed correspondence between a Stoic and a Christian.   384

_____. Under Pontius Pilate. Funk & Wagnalls, 1906.
Letters about Christ from a nephew of Pontius Pilate to a
Greek friend.   385

Scott, Barbara M. Magdalen. Hutchinson, 1953. Novel based
on the changes in Mary Magdalen's life after conversion to the
teachings of Christ.   386

Seton, Anya. The Mistletoe and Sword. Doubleday, 1955. Love
of a Roman soldier and a native girl during the uprising against
Roman rule in Britain at the time of Queen Boadicea.   387

Seward, Florence Augusta. Gold for the Caesars. Prentice-Hall,
1961. A young Roman, sold into slavery by an insolvent
father, seeks to find gold for Rome and gain his fortune and
restoration of his patrician rank.   388

Sheean, Vincent. Beware of Caesar. Random House, 1965.
Intrigues and plots of members of Nero's court with especial
emphasis on the relations between Nero and Seneca.   389

Shipway, George. The Imperial Governor. Doubleday, 1968.
Noble Roman governor rules Britain on behalf of his Emperor
and deals with the revolt of hostile natives.   390

Shore, Maxine. Captive Princess. Longmans, 1952. Concerns
the supposed first Christian Princess of Britain.   391

Siegel, Benjamin. Sword and the Promise. Harcourt, 1959.
A young Greek physician enslaved by the Romans participates
in a Jewish revolt.   392

Sienkiewicz, Henryk. Quo Vadis? (tr.) Little, 1896. A vivid
account of the conflict of Imperial Rome and early Christianity.
                                                                393
Simons, Katherine D. M. First the Blade. by Drayton Mayrant,
pseud. Appleton, 1950. A biographical novel of Claudia Pro-
cula, granddaughter of the Emperor Augustus and wife of Pontius Pilate.   394

Slaughter, Frank G. The Galileans. Doubleday, 1953. Based
on the life of Mary Magdalene.   395

_____. God's Warrior. Doubleday, 1967. The pious and
fanatical Jewish tentmaker, Saul, who became a zealous
apostle of Christ and labored tirelessly to spread Christianity.
                                                                396
_____. The Sins of Herod. Doubleday, 1968. The Apostles
Peter, John, and James preach Christianity against the dark
and corrupt background of Herod and Emperor Caligula.   397

_____. The Thorn of Arimathea. Doubleday, 1959. A Roman
centurion-physician who travels from Judaea to Britain with
Joseph of Arimathea and Veronica of the Holy Veil.   398

_____. Upon This Rock. Coward, 1963. The strength and
friendliness of St. Peter, the "rock" Christ used as cornerstone for His Church on earth.   399

Snedeker, Caroline Dale. The Forgotten Daughter. Doubleday,
1933, c.1929. YA. Chloe spent her childhood as a hard-
working, sometimes abused slave, until she was finally ac-
knowledged as the daughter of a Roman patrician.   400

_____. The White Isle. Doubleday, 1940. YA. A Roman
girl, exiled with her family to Britain, finds Christianity and
romance there.   401

Solon, Gregory. The Three Legions. Random, 1956. Picture
of the deterioration which led to the defeat of the Roman army
in Germany.   402

Southworth, John V. D. The Pirate from Rome. Crown, 1965.
Adventures of two Romans who are captured and held by
pirates in the Mediterranean in the time of Julius Caesar. 403

Speare, Elizabeth George. The Bronze Bow. Houghton, 1961.
YA. A young man's bitterness over the deaths of his parents

is softened when he learns the love taught by Christianity.   404

Spurrell, Herbert. <u>At Sunrise.</u> Greening, 1904. Traders and
sun-worshippers in Britain under the Romans.   405

Steinberg, Milton. <u>As a Driven Leaf.</u> Bobbs, 1940. A second
century Jewish rabbi's personal search for truth.   406

Stuart, Frank S. <u>Caravan for China.</u> Doubleday, 1941. Exciting experiences of a Roman trading expedition to China.   407

Sullivan, Richard. <u>The Three Kings.</u> Harcourt, 1956. The
journey of the three Magi who followed the star to find the
promised King.   408

Sutcliff, Rosemary. <u>The Eagle of the Ninth.</u> Walck, 1954. YA.
A young Roman centurion stationed in ancient Britain seeks a
lost standard.   409

_____. <u>The Mark of the Horse Lord.</u> Walck, 1965. YA.
A gifted slave who gains his freedom as a gladiator goes to
Roman Britain and becomes the leader of a warlike tribe.   410

Treece, Henry. <u>The Dark Island.</u> Random, 1952. The Roman
armies defeat the barbarian Celtic tribes in Britain.   411

_____. <u>Red Queen, White Queen.</u> Random, 1958. The re-
bellion led by Boadicea against the Romans in Britain.   412

Twells, Julia H. <u>Et Tu, Sejane!</u> Chatto, 1904. A romance
of the court of Tiberius on the island of Capri.   413

Van Santvoord, Seymour. <u>Octavia.</u> Dutton, 1923. The dark
period of Julio-Claudian Rome and the tragic story of Octavia.
                                                           414
Venter, François Alwyn. <u>Man from Cyrene.</u> (tr. ?) by Frans
Venter. Muhlenberg, 1962. Story of the strong and forthright Simon of Cyrene who, though not one of His followers,
helped Jesus carry His cross.   415

Wallace, Lew. <u>Ben Hur.</u> Airmont, 1965, c.1880. Hardships
of a noble Jew under Roman rule and his conversion to
Christianity.   416

Walloth, Wilhelm. <u>Empress Octavia.</u> Little, 1900. A story
of Rome in the reign of the infamous Nero.   417

Waltari, Mika. <u>The Roman.</u> (tr.) Putnam, 1966. (orig. pub.
in Finland in 1964) The rise to power in Nero's Rome of a
talented, ambitious man who was also passionate and ruthless.
                                                           418
_____. <u>The Secret of the Kingdom.</u> (tr.) Putnam, 1961.
About a Roman who joined the Jewish followers of Christ

after the Crucifixion.   419

Warmington, Gertrude R. King of Dreams. Doran, 1926. Based
  on the story of the rich young man of the New Testament and
  located in Palestine and Egypt.   420

Westbury, Hugh. Acté. Bentley, 1890. Illustrates the moral
  depravity of Nero's court.   421

White, Helen C. Four Rivers of Paradise. Macmillan, 1955.
  The decadence of Rome at the time of Alaric's invasion, seen
  by a Christian from Gaul.   422

White, Leslie Turner. Scorpus the Moor. Doubleday, 1962.
  The difficulties of an Arab accused of murder in Nero's
  Rome.   423

Whyte-Melville, George John. The Gladiators. Appleton, 1863.
  Roman persecution; the siege of Jerusalem; and a British
  slave's love for a Roman lady.   424

Wibberley, Leonard. The Centurion. Morrow, 1966. Interwoven
  lives of Christ and the Roman centurion whose servant He cured
  and who supervised His execution.   425

Williamson, Thames Ross. The Gladiator. Coward, 1948. A
  gladiator joins the forbidden Christian religion and barely escapes the burning of Rome.   426

Willis, Anthony Armstrong. The Heart of a Slave-Girl. by Anthony Armstrong, pseud. Paul, 1922. A tale of Rome when
  Nero was emperor.   427

Young, Patricia. The Prophecy. Bruce, 1965. Political maneuvering of people who lived simultaneously with Christ but
  who had no direct contact with Him.   428

Yourcenar, Marguerite. Memoirs of Hadrian. (tr.) Farrar,
  1954. Written as a letter from the Emperor Hadrian to his
  adopted grandson, Marcus Aurelius.   429

  b) The Later Roman Empire and Christianity (c. 180 to 400)

Albertini, Alberto. Two Years. (tr.) Viking, 1936. Philosophical study of a young Roman who, through prayer, receives a two-year reprieve from death.   430

Armstrong, Martin. Desert. Harper, 1926. An account of
  monastic life in Alexandria and the Egyptian desert in the
  late fourth century.   431

Baring-Gould, S. Perpetua. Dutton, 1897. A story of the

persecution of Christians at Nîmes in 213.   432

Baron, Alexander, name originally Alec Bernstein. Queen of the
East. Washburn, 1956. Conflict between Zenobia, Queen of
the East, and Aurelian, Emperor of Rome.   433

Baxter, J. Dowling. The Meeting of the Ways. Greening, 1908.
Fighting between Picts and Romans in early Britain, with descriptions of forts.   434

Bickerstaffe-Drew, Francis. Faustula. by John Ayscough,
pseud. Benziger, 1912. A girl from a pagan family who,
despite her belief in Christianity, was forced to become a
vestal virgin.   435

Bryher, Winifred (Annie Winifred Macpherson). Roman Wall.
Pantheon, 1954. A Helvetian outpost of the Roman Empire,
and its commander, Valerius.   436

Dahn, Felix. A Captive of the Roman Eagles. (tr.) McClurg,
1902. Story depicting relations between Romans and Germans
in the area around Lake Constance.   437

Deeping, Warwick. The Man Who Went Back. Knopf, 1940.
While recovering from an accident, a man seems to live in
the olden days of Roman Britain.   438

De Wohl, Louis. Imperial Renegade. Lippincott, 1950. The
career of Julian the Apostate, Emperor of Rome.   439

_____. Living Wood. Lippincott, 1947. Helena, mother of
Constantine, and her quest of the True Cross.   440

_____. The Restless Flame. Lippincott, 1951. St. Augus-
tine, from his riotous youth to his exemplary old age.   441

Du Bois, Theodora M. Captive of Rome. Crown, 1962. An
Irish princess is captured by the Goths and sold as a slave
into the Roman Emperor's household.   442

Duggan, Alfred. Family Favorites. Pantheon, 1961. The brief,
notorious reign of adolescent Heliogabalus, who became Emperor at the age of fourteen.   443

Dulin, Ralph. The Unconquered Sun. Macmillan, 1963. Political marriage of the Illyrian peasant who became Emperor
Aurelian, "Restorer of the Roman Empire."   444

Ebers, Georg. Homo Sum. (tr.) Gottsberger, 1880. A Christian anchorite accepts false accusation and unmerited exile. 445

_____. Per Aspera. (tr.) Low, 1893. Religious conflict
in Alexandria in the early third century.   446

_____. Serapis. (tr.) Paul, 1885. The conflict between
Christianity and paganism is described in this story of a
girl's conversion.   447

Eckstein, Ernst. The Chaldean Magician. (tr.) Gottsberger,
1886. "An adventure in Rome in the reign of Diocletian." 448

Fergusson, Adam. Roman Go Home! Putnam, 1969. Love between a noble Roman and a Celtic princess in the twilight of
Roman rule in Britain.   449

Fidelis, Sister Mary. In Holiest Troth. Burns & Oates, 1903.
"The story of St. Eucratida, one of the martyrs of Saragossa,
A.D. 304."   450

Harré, T. Everett. Behold the Woman! Lippincott, 1916.
About Mary of Egypt, converted from a life of sin in fourth
century Alexandria to a life of penance in the desert.   451

Jeske-Choinski, Teodor. The Last Romans. Duquesne U., 1936.
Pagan revolt against Christianity results in victory for Emperor
Theodosius I over Arbogast.   452

Jókai, Maurus. A Christian but a Roman. (tr.) Doubleday,
1900. The Christians in Rome and its vicinity under the Emperor Carinus.   453

Jordan, Mildred A. Miracle in Brittany. Knopf, 1950. A young
Breton priest tries to spread Christianity in a pagan society.
                                                              454

Maurice, C. Edmund. Telemachus. Independent Press, 1927.
An heroic monk amidst the conflicting religious and social
currents of the late Empire.   455

Merezhkovsky, Dmitri. The Death of the Gods. (tr.) Putnam,
1896. The struggle between Christianity and paganism at the
time of Emperor Julian. (followed by The Forerunner)   456

Newman, John Henry. Callista. Longmans, 1890. The savage
persecution of Christians by the Emperor Decius.   457

Perry, W.C. Sancta Paula. Sonnenschein, 1902. A romance
of the fourth century with Saints Jerome and Paula well portrayed.   458

Rydberg, Viktor. The Last Athenian. (tr.) Petersen, 1883.
The end of antiquity and the rise of Christianity in Greece. 459

Saylor, Carol. The Equinox. Lippincott, 1966, c.1965. A
young officer in the service of Emperor Commodus is converted to Christianity by the self-sacrifice of his beloved. 460

Schmitt, Gladys. Confessors of the Name. Dial, 1952. Emperor's nephew finds the meaning of life in Christianity.   461

Sherren, Wilkinson. Eelen of Bringard. Palmer, 1923. A
romance of Britain toward the end of the fourth century.   462

Sutcliff, Rosemary. The Silver Branch. Walck, 1959. YA.
The recovery of Britain by Rome in the late third century provided an opportunity for two legionaries to prove their loyalty.
463

Tollinton, Bartram. Pyrrho. Williams & Norgate, 1926. A
young man's search for religion in the early third century. 464

Vidal, Gore. Julian. Little, 1964. About Julian the Apostate
who tried to restore paganism and restrain Christianity when
he became Emperor of Rome in 361 A.D.   465

Ware, William. Aurelian. Burt, 1838. Emperor Aurelian's
persecution of Christians.   466

_____. Julian. Estes, 1841. Lavish spectacle of pagan civili-
zation at the time of Julian the Apostate.   467

_____. Zenobia. Burt, 1836. A Roman noble describes
Zenobia and her court and the destruction of Palmyra.   468

Waugh, Evelyn. Helena. Little, 1950. The life of Constantine's mother and her search for the True Cross.   469

Westcott, Arthur. The Sun God. Heath Cranton, 1914. Religious conflict in Rome at the time of Emperor Elagabalus
(Heliogabalus).   470

White, Edward Lucas. Andivius Hedulio. Dutton, 1921. A
young nobleman, suspected of treason, experiences every
facet of Roman life.   471

Wiseman, Nicholas P. Fabiola. Benziger, 1855. Classic tale
of Diocletian's perseuction of the Christians, who took refuge
in the catacombs.   472

6. EUROPEAN AND OTHER BARBARIANS
    (to about 400 A.D.)

Adkin, J.H. Knight. The Woman Stealers. Pitman, 1905. The
Celts in Britain in their daily struggles against other tribes
and prehistoric animals.   473

Barringer, Daniel Moreau. And the Waters Prevailed. Dutton,
1956. YA. A story of Stone Age life in which a thinking
man warns of the approach of a disastrous flood.   474

Begouen, Max. Bison of Clay. (tr.) Longmans, 1926.

Magdalenians of the Upper Paleolithic Stone Age in the
Pyrenees.   475

Carbery, Mary. Children of the Dawn. Heinemann, 1923. A
tale of Druidic Ireland based on ancient legends concerning
the coming of sun-worshippers from Hellas.   476

Du Chaillu, Paul Belloni. Ivar the Viking. Scribner, 1893.
Adventures of a Norse boy at the turn of the third to the
fourth century.   477

Farrar, Frederick W. Gathering Clouds. Longmans, 1896.
Antioch and Constantinople at the time of Alaric and his
Goths.   478

Faulkner, Nancy. The Sacred Jewel. Doubleday, 1961. YA.
Love and experiences of a druid's daughter and a young bard
training for the pagan priesthood in Celtic Britain about
30 A.D.   479

Fisher, Vardis. Darkness and the Deep. Vanguard, 1943.
Primitive man in the period before the development of lan-
guage.   480

Golding, William Gerald. The Inheritors. Harcourt, 1962,
c. 1955. The remnant of a prehistoric race struggles for ex-
istence against the primitive, but more advanced, homo
sapiens.   481

James, John. Votan. New American Lib., 1967, c.1966. The
tale of wanderer and teacher Photinus, who becomes deified
as Votan in a time of barbarous customs and pagan practices.
                                                                            482

Jensen, Johannes Vilhelm. Fire and Ice. (tr.) Knopf, 1923.
The first stages in the development of civilization, primitive
religion, and use of fire. (followed by The Cimbrians)   483

Kipling, Rudyard. (1) Puck of Pook's Hill. Doubleday, 1906.
(2) Rewards and Fairies (sequel). Doubleday, 1910. The
fairy Puck tells of England in ancient times.   484-5

London, Jack. Before Adam. Macmillan, 1907. Imaginative
tale of life in the Pleistocene or Glacial Age.   486

Marshall, Edison. Dian of the Lost Land. Chilton, 1966. YA.
A modern day observer lives with a Cro-Magnon type of man
whose rivals are of the earlier Neanderthal type.   487

Masters, John. The Rock. Putnam, 1970. A novel of Gibraltar
with stories of various inhabitants from its formation in the
Jurassic period of prehistory to the present and projected into
the future to 1985.   488

Paul, Louis. Dara, the Cypriot. S. & S., 1959. Supposed
autobiography of a Cypriot wanderer which tells much about
the ninth century B.C. Mediterranean world.   489

Roberts, Charles G. D. In the Morning of Time. Stokes, 1922.
Life and inventions in the early Stone Age.   490

Tapsell, R. F. The Year of the Horsetails. Knopf, 1967.
Primitive warfare between nomadic tribes and an attack on
a fortified town.   491

Treece, Henry. The Golden Strangers. Random House, 1957,
c. 1956. Metal-using Aegean strangers dispossess Neolithic
men of the New Stone Age in southern England.   492

_____. Men of the Hills. Criterion, 1958. YA. Two boys
build a friendship and a hope for the future after the nomadic
sun-worshippers have overpowered the hill people in Neolithic
England.   493

Wallis, Henry M. The Master Girl. by Ashton Hilliers, pseud.
Putnam, 1910. Prehistoric man's struggle against animals,
hostile tribes, and the elements.   494

Wibberley, Leonard. Attar of the Ice Valley. Farrar, 1968.
YA. A search for food leads Neanderthal people to a valley
from which the ice has just receded.   495

B.   ASIA, AFRICA, AND OCEANIA

Carus, Paul. Amitabha. Open Court, 1906. Includes a discussion of the philosophies of Buddhism and Brahminism in
first century India.   496

Caskie, Jaquelin Ambler. Figure in the Sand. Am. Library
Serv., 1924. Brief romance of North African nomads followed by condemnation to death in a Roman arena.   497

Croly, George. Salathiel, the Immortal. [pub. in 1901 as:
Tarry Thou Till I Come] Funk & Wagnalls, 1827. A tale
of the Wandering Jew, rich in Oriental background.   498

De Camp, Lyon. The Arrows of Hercules. Doubleday, 1965.
A young Greek engineer invents a dart-throwing catapult for
Dionysius of Syracuse and finds love and adventure in his
travels.   499

Efremov, Ivan A. The Land of Foam. (tr.) by Ivan Yefremov.
Houghton, 1959. YA. Three slaves from different lands band
together and brave revolt, captivity and hostile jungle in their
quest for liberty.   500

Elegant, Robert S. The Seeking. Funk, 1969. Pursuit of a
magnificent wild white stallion by a disinherited prince and
his companions in Central Asia is a sort of religious ordeal.
                                                                    501

Faludy, Gyorgy. City of Splintered Gods. (tr.) [En. title:
Karoton] by George Faludy. Morrow, 1966. A Christian
noble in fourth century Alexandria has to choose between com-
peting sects as well as between fair ladies.   502

France, Anatole (name originally Anatole Thibault). Balthazar.
(tr.) Lane, 1909. Based on the Bible story of the Three
Wise Men.   503

Gjellerup, Karl. The Pilgrim Kamanita. (tr.) Heinemann,
1911. The last years of Buddha's life, his death, and his
philosophy.   504

Jacobson, Sheldon A. Fleet Surgeon to Pharaoh. Oregon State
Univ. Pr., 1971. A vivid description of the first sea voyage
from Egypt around the coast of Africa featuring a Jewish
physician who studies medicine in Egypt.   505

Karney, Evelyn S. The Dust of Desire. Scott, 1912. The influence and limited appeal of Buddha's philosophy.   506

Lo, Kuan-chung, supposed author. Romance of the Three Kingdoms. (tr.) (2 v.) Tuttle, 1959. A novel of third century
ambition and intrigue, highly esteemed by the Chinese and
based on actual events.   507

Merwin, Samuel. Silk: A Legend. Houghton, 1923. Imaginary
journals concerning life in China about 100 A. D.   508

C. THE WESTERN HEMISPHERE

Harvey, James O. Beyond the Gorge of Shadows. Lothrop,
1965. YA. Three young men from an isolated tribe set out
to find if there are other tribes in prehistoric America.   509

Hyne, C. J. Cutcliffe. The Lost Continent. Hutchinson, 1900.
The supposed disappearance of the flourishing continent of
Atlantis.   510

Kidwell, Carl. The Angry Earth. Viking, 1964. YA. The
way of life in ancient Mexico shown in the life of a boy who
becomes a slave in a different tribe.   511

_____. Arrow in the Sun. Viking, 1961. YA. Battles for
power and supremacy in pre-Aztec Mexico.   512

PART II

THE MIDDLE AGES AND EARLY RENAISSANCE
(c. 400-1500)

A. EUROPE, THE NEAR EAST,
AND THE MEDITERRANEAN

1. THE EARLY MIDDLE AGES (c. 400-1000)

a) The British Isles (England, Wales,
Scotland, Ireland)

Babcock, William Henry. Cian of the Chariots. Lothrop, 1898.
A romance of the days of Arthur of Britain and his knights of
the Round Table.   513

_____. The Two Lost Centuries of Britain. Lippincott, 1890.
Britain in the turbulent period after the departure of the
Romans.   514

Baker, Amy J. The King's Passion. Long, 1920. Based on
the life of King Edmund, who died in the Danish invasion of
866-70.   515

Bishop, Farnham and Arthur Gilchrist Brodeur. The Altar of the
Legion. Little, 1926. Romantic novel of heroism and masquerade during the Saxon invasion of Britain.   516

Borowsky, Marvin. The Queen's Knight. Random House, 1955.
A story of King Arthur and the knights of the Round Table
which differs from the well-known version offered by Tennyson.   517

Borroff, Marie, tr. Sir Gawain and the Green Knight. Norton,
1967. A new verse translation of the classic tale.   518

Bowers, Gwendolyn. Brother to Galahad. Walck, 1963. YA.
This novel presents the chivalric activities at Camelot while
telling the story of Hugh of Alleyn, supposedly a relative of
Sir Galahad.   519

_____. The Lost Dragon of Wessex. Walck, 1957. YA.
A rousing tale of a thirteen-year-old follower of King Arthur
as he searches for treasure.   520

Breslin, Howard. The Gallowglass. Crowell, 1958. Irish
lords settle their differences and join together to drive the
Danes from Dublin.   521

Bryher, Winifred (Annie Winifred Macpherson). Ruan. by Bryher.
Pantheon, 1960. The adventures of Ruan, who prefers the excitement of sea travel to his inherited post as Druid priest.
                                                                       522
Castle, Frances. The Sisters' Tale. Little, 1968. YA. Two
motherless girls face many difficulties in the paganistic and
superstition-ridden Ireland of the sixth century.   523

Collingwood, W. G. The Likeness of King Elfwald. Titus Wilson,
1917. Tale of the Viking raids on Northumbria and West Scotland.   524

_____. Thorstein of the Mere. Arnold, 1895. A saga of
the Northmen in Lakeland.   525

Crosfield, Truda H. A Love in Ancient Days. Mathews, 1907.
Romance and warfare in southwestern Britain during the period
of the conquering Saxons.   526

Davis, Mrs. M. H. The Winter Serpent. McGraw, 1958. The
proud daughter of a Scots chieftain is sold to Vikings by a
jealous foster brother.   527

Deeping, Warwick. Love Among the Ruins. Cassell, 1904.
Picturesque romance of knightly exploits in Avalon.   528

_____. Uther and Igraine. Outlook, 1903. Purported ro-
mance of King Arthur's parents.   529

Donaldson, Mary E. M. The Isles of Flame. Gardiner, Paisley,
1912. A romance in the Hebrides with St. Columba as a
background figure.   530

Du Bois, Theodora M. Emerald Crown. Funk, 1955. Faith
and superstition, royalty and commoners mingle in this tale
of an Irish queen.   531

Duggan, Alfred. Conscience of the King. Coward, 1952. A
witty story of the reputed founder of the West Saxon Kingdom.   532

_____. The Little Emperors. Coward, 1953. About a Roman
official stationed in Britain to uphold Roman authority.   533

Erskine, John. Galahad. Bobbs, 1926. A clever adaptation of
one aspect of the Arthurian legends.   534

Farnol, Jeffery. The King Liveth. Doubleday, 1943. Action
galore as Alfred the Great fights the Danes.   535

Finkel, George. Watch Fires to the North. [En. title: Twilight Province] Viking, 1967. YA. Arthur and the knights
   of his court are characters in this story of the defense of
   northern Britain from Saxons and Celts.   536

Forrest, Thorpe. Builders of the Waste. Duckworth, 1899. A
   romance in Britain during a sixth century Saxon invasion.   537

Griffin, Gerald. The Invasion. Duffy (Dublin), 1832. Western
   Ireland in the last part of the eighth century.   538

Hodges, C. Walter. The Marsh King. Coward, 1967. YA.
   The battles that King Alfred of Wessex must win to bring
   peace and civilization to his kingdom.   539

_____. The Namesake. Coward, 1964. YA. A one-legged
   scribe tells of King Alfred's dual purpose in ruling--to repel
   the invading Danes and to encourage education as a tool of
   peace. (followed by The Marsh King)   540

Keith, Chester. Queen's Knight. Allen, 1920. An Arthurian
   romance about Britain in the sixth century.   541

Leighton, Margaret. Journey for a Princess. Farrar, 1960.
   YA. While Alfred the Great hesitates between two royal
   suitors for her hand, his daughter Elstrid is sent on a pilgrimage which has a surprising ending.   542

_____. Judith of France. Houghton, 1948. YA. Judith,
   princess and descendant of Charlemagne, endures two political marriages and finally, after much danger, marries for
   love.   543

Macnicol, Eona K. Colum of Derry. Sheed, 1954. Fictionalized account of the life of St. Columba of Ireland in the sixth
   century A.D.   544

Malory, Sir Thomas. Le Morte D'Arthur. (tr. by A.W. Pollard)
   University Bks., Inc., 1962, c.1961. A complete edition of
   Arthurian romances by Sir Thomas Malory, translated into
   modern English.   545

Marshall, Edison. The Pagan King. Doubleday, 1959. The
   successes in warfare and tribulations in private life of King
   Arthur during the barbarian invasions of Britain.   546

Nathan, Robert. The Fair. Knopf, 1964. Flight of a Celtic
   girl and her companions during the Anglo-Saxon conquest of
   Britain following King Arthur's defeat at Salisbury Plain. 547

Oliver, Jane, pseud., for Rees, Helen Christina Easson. Isle
   of Glory. Putnam, 1964. The energetic Irish monk and
   missionary St. Columba who eventually became Abbot of

Iona and Apostle of Scotland.   548

O'Meara, Walter. The Duke of War. Harcourt, 1966. Arthur
fought the Saxons for supremacy in Britain.   549

Powys, John Cowper. Porius. Macdonald, 1952. King Arthur
and his knights, with the help of the people, drive off invading Saxons and repel a rebelling Welsh tribe.   550

Reid, J. M. The Sons of Aethne. Blackwood, 1923. Celtic life
in west Scotland about the eighth century.   551

Roberts, Dorothy James. Kinsmen of the Grail. Little, 1963.
The search for the Holy Grail by Gawin of Rhos, nephew of
King Arthur, and Perceval, an impulsive youth, in Wales. 552

_____. Launcelot, My Brother. Appleton, 1954. The Ar-
thurian legend, told by Launcelot's brother, Bors de Ganis.
                                                         553
_____. Return of the Stranger. Appleton, 1958. A tale
based on the Irish legend of Etain, a homeless child raised
by foster parents to become the bride of the High King of
Ireland and mistress of the Seat of Kings of Tara.   554

Rooney, Theresa J. The Last Monarch of Tara. by Eblana,
pseud. Gill (Dublin), 1889. Tale of Ireland depicting Irish
civilization in the sixth century.   555

Senior, Dorothy. The Clutch of Circumstance. Macmillan,
1908. About King Arthur and his knights of the Round
Table.   556

Serrailier, Ian. The Challenge of the Green Knight. Walck,
1967. YA. A modern telling, in verse, of the story of Sir
Gawain and the Green Knight.   557

Sterling, Sara Hawks. A Lady of King Arthur's Court. Jacobs,
1907. Romance of a lady-in-waiting to Queen Guenevere. 558

Sterne, Emma and Barbara Lindsay. King Arthur and the Knights
of the Round Table. Golden, 1962. YA. The Arthurian
legends especially re-written for young people.   559

Stewart, Mary. The Crystal Cave. Fawcett, 1971, c. 1970.
Merlin's boyhood and his growing awareness of his magical
powers, with vivid pictures of the religion and superstition
of fifth century England.   560

Sutcliff, Rosemary. Dawn Wind. Walck, 1962, c. 1961. YA.
Loyalty and heroism of a young British farm boy who survives the battle of Aquae Sulis during the Saxon invasions. 561

_____. The Lantern Bearers. Walck, 1959. YA. A

Roman soldier stays with his Saxon family when the Roman
legions leave, and finds Britain a harsh and barbaric
country.   562

_____. Sword at Sunset. Coward, 1963. A telling, without
chivalric trappings, of King Arthur's leadership of the native
British resistance to invading Anglo-Saxons.   563

Taylor, C. Bryson. Nikanor, Teller of Tales. McClurg, 1906.
A story of Britain at the close of the Roman period.   564

Trease, Geoffrey. Escape to King Alfred. Vanguard, 1958.
YA. Two young people escape from a Viking camp and
seek refuge with King Alfred.   565

Treece, Henry. The Great Captains. Random, 1956. Rich
tale of Celtic Britain in the days of King Arthur.   566

Trevor, Meriol. The Last of Britain. St. Martins, 1956.
Noble Britons eat, drink, and make merry while the Saxons
prepare to invade.   567

Turton, Godfrey. The Emperor Arthur. Doubleday, 1967. A
member of the Round Table depicts King Arthur as a product
of Roman civilization.   568

Walsh, Gillian Paton. Hengest's Tale. St. Martin's, 1967.
YA. A first-person narrative of the fighting between Jutes,
Frisians, and Saxons in the fifth century.   569

White, Terence Hanbury. The Sword in the Stone. Putnam,
1939. Delightful fantasy based on the Arthurian legends.   570

Widgery, Jeanne Anne. The Adversary. by Jan Widgery.
Doubleday, 1966. Two brothers advocate different ways of
dealing with the Danish invasions of England in the ninth cen-
tury.   571

Williams, Patry. Alfred the King. Faber & Faber, 1951.
Story of Alfred the Great, who did so much to prepare England for future greatness.   572

  b) Western and Central Europe

  1) Fifth and Sixth Centuries: Ages of Barbarian Invasions and
       Early Germanic Kingdoms

Breem, Wallace. Eagle in the Snow. Putnam, 1970. Conflict of
the Twentieth Roman Legion and Germanic barbarians on the
Rhine in the early fifth century.   573

Costain, Thomas B. The Darkness and the Dawn. Doubleday,

1959.   Young lovers of a neutral tribe are caught up in the
struggle between Attila and Aetius.   574

Dahn, Felix.   Felicitas.   (tr.)   McClurg, 1883.   Germanic invasion of the Danubian regions.   575

De Wohl, Louis.   Throne of the World.   Lippincott, 1949.   The
invasion of the Roman Empire by the great Hunnic leader,
Attila.   576

Fuller, Roger.   Sign of the Pagan.   Dial, 1954.   Fifth century
Europe with Attila the Hun as a chief figure.   577

Gladd, Arthur Anthony.   The Saracen Steed.   Dodd, 1960.   A
youth from Aquitaine catches a runaway Saracen battle charger
and plays a significant part in the battle of Tours-Poitiers
(732).   578

Hausrath, Adolf.   Jetta.   (tr.) by George Taylor, pseud.   Paul,
1886.   Heidelberg under the Romans of the Later Empire.   579

James, G. P. R.   Attila.   Dutton, 1837.   The experiences of a
young Roman exile in the camp of Attila the Hun.   580

Pruette, Lorine.   Saint in Ivory.   Appleton, 1927.   Touching
story of St. Genevieve of Paris and Nanterre in Roman-
ruled France.   581

Simon, Edith.   Twelve Pictures.   Putnam, 1955.   Colorful fifth
century tapestry--part Christian, part pagan.   582

Treece, Henry.   The Green Man.   Putnam, 1966.   A sixth century Danish prince, Amleth, seeks revenge against his unscrupulous uncle in Scandinavia (based on the original "Hamlet" story).   583

Webb, Christopher.   Eusebius, the Phoenician.   Funk, 1969.
YA.   Eusebius, by his skill and wisdom, brings back safely
the ship of the stricken Viking, Harald the Hammer, and
continues his search for the Holy Grail.   584

2)   Seventh and Eighth Centuries:
     Age of Frankish Ascendance

Almedingen, Martha Edith von.   A Candle at Dusk.   by E. M.
Almedingen.   Farrar, 1969.   YA.   While his country is in
danger of Saracen invasion, a young Frankish boy achieves
his dream--to learn to read and write at an abbey near his
home.   585

Bennet, Robert Ames.   For the White Christ.   McClurg, 1905.
The mighty deeds of Charlemagne against the Moors, Arabs,

and Saxons.   586

Finkel, George. The Long Pilgrimage. Viking, 1969, c.1967.
A Norseman, exiled from Northumberland in 778, fights under Charlemagne, later travels throughout the known western
world.   587

Hardy, Arthur S. Passe Rose. Houghton, 1889. A romance
of the semi-barbarian Franks and savage Saxons of Charlemagne's time.   588

Pyle, Katharine. Charlemagne and His Knights. Lippincott,
1932. A novel based on stories and legends of Charlemagne.   589

Treece, Henry. The Road to Miklagard. Criterion, 1957. YA.
Saga of Viking wanderings from Norway to Ireland, Moorish
Spain, Byzantium, and Russia. (followed by Viking's Sunset)
                                                                590

_____. Viking's Dawn. Phillips, 1956. YA. An early
Viking voyage made by daring explorers before anyone had
a clear idea of geography. (followed by The Road to Miklagard)   591

_____. Viking's Sunset. Criterion, 1960. YA. Harald
Sigurdson's pursuit of an enemy leads him to a perilous
voyage across uncharted seas to Iceland, Greenland, and
finally North America. (completes trilogy)   592

   3) Ninth and Tenth Centuries:
      Early Feudal Era

Almedingen, Martha Edith von. The Golden Sequence. Westminster, 1949. Peasant and monastic life in and about a
French abbey.   593

Bengtsson, Frans Gunnar. The Long Ships. (tr.) Knopf,
1954. Exploits of Red Orm, a Dane, on land and sea.   594

_____. Red Orm. Scribner, 1943. Red Orm, once a Spanish
galley slave, lives in Denmark, later invades and settles in
England.   595

Burgess, J. Haldane. The Viking Path. Blackwood, 1894. The
wild, violent life of the Vikings.   596

Dasent, George Webbe. The Vikings of the Baltic. Chapman & Hall,
1875. The land and sea adventures of the Vikings of Jomsburg.
                                                                597

Eddison, Eric Rucker. Styrbiorn the Strong. A & C Boni, 1926.
Saga-based account of the attempts of an heir to the Swedish
throne to gain his heritage.   598

Gross, Myra Geraldine. The Star of Valhalla. Stokes, 1907. A
  romance of early Christianity in Norway and the people's initial
  resistance to it.   599

Gunnarsson, Gunnar. The Sworn Brothers. (tr.) Knopf, 1921.
  A rousing story of Vikings in the reign of Harold Fairhair of
  Norway.   600

Haggard, H. Rider. Eric Brighteyes. Longmans, 1891. A tale
  of the Norsemen in Iceland.   601

Hewlett, Maurice. Gudrid the Fair. Dodd, 1918. About a
  Norse girl who fulfills a prophecy.   602

_____. A Lover's Tale. Scribner, 1915. A novel based on
  sagas of ninth and tenth century Iceland, Norway, and Greenland.   603

_____. Thorgils of Treadholt. Scribner, 1917. A tale of
  adventure in the Scandinavian area in the early Middle Ages.
                                                                  604
Hough, Clara Sharpe. Leif the Lucky. Century, 1926. "A
  romantic saga of the sons of Erik the Red."   605

Kamban, Gudmundur. I See a Wondrous Land. Putnam, 1938.
  Saga-based novel of Leif Ericsson and his expeditions to Iceland, Greenland, and Labrador.   606

Linklater, Eric. The Men of Ness. Farrar, 1933. A saga
  of the Vikings of the Orkney Islands.   607

Marshall, Edison. The Viking. Farrar, 1951. Story of a
  Northman based on the Saga of Ogier the Dane, who loved a
  Welsh princess and sailed toward unknown lands.   608

Myers, Henry. The Utmost Island. Crown, 1951. Full of the
  daring of the Vikings and the clashes of Christianity with
  pagan mythology.   609

Myers, John. The Harp and the Blade. Dutton, 1941. An
  Irish minstrel's strange curse--a compulsion to help everyone.   610

Polland, Madeleine. Beorn the Proud. Holt, 1961. YA. About
  a Viking raider who took an Irish Christian girl as a slave. 611

Ritchie, Rita. Ice Falcon. Norton, 1963. YA. A young German boy captures and trains a white gyrfalcon, and thereby
  secures his father's release from Viking captors.   612

Roberts, Dorothy James. Fire in the Ice. Little, 1961. Saga-
  based story of a woman's desire for wealth and luxury which
  leads to tragedy among the early Norsemen.   613

Roth, Richard. King Otto's Crown. (tr.) Concordia, 1917.
   Fictional account of Emperor Otto I of Germany and Italy.   614

Scheffel, Joseph Viktor von. Ekkehard. (tr.) Dutton, 1927.
   A tale about the Magyar raids of the mid-tenth century.   615

Seton, Anya. Avalon. Fawcett, 1969, c.1965. French prince
   becomes enamoured of a peasant girl and pursues her even
   to America when she is captured by Viking raiders.   616

Sprague, Rosemary. Heroes of the White Shield. Oxford Univ.
   Pr., 1955. YA. A novel of tenth century Norway telling,
   in part, of King Olav's attempts to establish Christianity.   617

Treece, Henry. Splintered Sword. Duell, 1966, c.1965. YA.
   Disillusionment of a young Scandinavian who joins a band of
   Viking raiders.   618

Undset, Sigrid. Gunnar's Daughter. (tr.) Knopf, 1936. Saga-
   like story of a Norwegian girl and an Icelandic youth in the
   late tenth century.   619

Walton, Evangeline. The Cross and the Sword. Bouregy &
   Curl, 1956. The Northmen and their incursions into tenth
   century England.   620

Young, Charles. Harald, First of the Vikings. Crowell, 1911.
   About Harald Fairhair, King of Norway.   621

   c) Southern Europe (Iberian Peninsula, Italy,
       Adjacent Islands)

Collins, Wilkie. Antonina. Harper, 1850. The Gothic invasion of Italy and Alaric's first blockade of Rome.   622

Cresswell, Clarice M. Making and Breaking of Almansur. Dodd,
   1916. The career of an ambitious Moslem in the glorious
   period of Cordova under the Caliphate.   623

Dahn, Felix. A Struggle for Rome. (tr.) Bentley, 1878. The
   Gothic Kingdom and its collapse after Theodoric's death; the
   Roman Empire restored by Junstinian the Great.   624

De Camp, Lyon. Lest Darkness Fall. Holt, 1941. Fantasy of
   a present-day archeologist sent back into sixth-century Italy by
   a bolt of lightning.   625

De Wohl, Louis. Citadel of God. Lippincott, 1959. This novel
   traces St. Benedict's religious development and the growth of
   his order.   626

Gallizier, Nathan. The Sorceress of Rome. Page, 1907. The

love-story of King Otto III of the Germans and the wife of a
Roman senator.   627

Gay, Laverne. The Unspeakables. Scribner, 1945. A beautiful
Catholic queen of the hated Lombards works for their civilization and conversion.   628

Gissing, George. Veranilda. Dutton, 1905. Military tactics,
heresy, and love during the siege of Rome in the Byzantine
War to take Italy.   629

Mann, Thomas. The Holy Sinner. (tr.) Knopf, 1951. Story of
Pope Gregory I based on an old legend.   630

Park, Mrs. Kendall. Riquilda. Murray, 1912. Christian Bar-
celona and Catalonia during the tenth century Moorish offen-
sive.   631

Pei, Mario Andrew. Swords of Anjou. Day, 1953. The Moors
in Spain--with the Song of Roland as the basis of the story. 632

Raynolds, Robert. The Sinner of St. Ambrose. Bobbs, 1952.
This picture of the decay of the Roman Empire includes
Alaric the Goth and Sts. Ambrose and Augustine.   633

Schmirger, Gertrud. Gregory the Great. (tr.) by Gerhart Ellert,
pseud. Harcourt, 1963. The many-faceted life of Pope Gregory the Great, supposedly told by his secretary.   634

Treviño, Elizabeth Borton de. Casilda of the Rising Moon.
Farrar, 1967. YA. Knighthood, royalty, romance, and
mysticism abound in this tale of medieval Spain.   635

Vaughan, Agnes Carr. Bury Me in Ravenna. Doubleday, 1962.
Action-packed life of the remarkable, twice-widowed Galla
Placidia, who became regent for Emperor Valentinian III.   636

Williamson, Joanne S. The Iron Charm. Knopf, 1964. YA.
A young boy who is captured and sold into slavery has many
adventures in Constantinople and England before he finally
escapes.   637

  d) Eastern Europe (including the Byzantine Empire, the
      Balkans, and Russia), the Near East, and North Africa

Butcher, C.H. Armenosa of Egypt. Blackwood, 1897. The Arab
conquest of Egypt in the seventh century.   638

Coray, Henry W. Son of Tears. Putnam, 1957. Augustine of
Hippo, after some years of luxurious, worldly life, undergoes
a deep spiritual change and becomes a bishop and a saint.   639

Dahn, Felix. The Scarlet Banner. (tr.) McClurg, 1903. The
war between the Byzantine General Belisarius and the Vandal
King Gelimer.   640

Daringer, Helen Fern. Yesterday's Daughter. Harcourt, 1964.
YA. A fifth-century Greek girl faces the thought of a marriage arranged by her father.   641

Davis, William Stearns. The Beauty of the Purple. Macmillan,
1924. A romance about Leo III, the Isaurian peasant who became Emperor of Christian Constantinople.   642

Dumke, Glenn S. Tyrant of Bagdad. by Glenn Pierce, pseud.
Little, 1955. Charlemagne's European court and the opulent
splendor of the Moslem East.   643

Ebers, Georg. The Bride of the Nile. (tr.) Gottsberger, 1887.
A romance of divided Egypt during the period of Moslem conquest.   644

Gallizier, Nathan. The Lotus Woman. Page, 1922. The court
of Constantinople under the semi-barbaric Emperor Nicephorus
Phocas.   645

Gerson, Noel B. Theodora. by Samuel Edwards, pseud.,
Prentice-Hall, 1969. Concerns the sparkling, indomitable
wife of Justinian I, the Great.   646

Gordon, Samuel. The Lost Kingdom. Shapiro, Vallentine, 1926.
A story of the Kingdom of Khazaria, in the Crimean region.
                                                                   647

Haggard, H. Rider. The Wanderer's Necklace. Longmans,
1914. Tells of the Empress Irene, widow of the Emperor
Leo IV.   648

Harrison, Frederic. Theophano. Harper, 1904. The Byzantine Empire during its great struggle with the Saracens.   649

Hoyt, Edwin. The Voice of Allah. Day, 1970. A lucid, sympathetic version of the life of the Prophet Mohammed, including
his career as a businessman, his marriage, and the vision
that started his preaching.   650

Kingsley, Charles. Hypatia. Macmillan, 1853. Clash between
the comparatively new Christianity and deep-rooted paganism
in fifth century Egypt.   651

Lamb, Harold. Theodora and the Emperor; the Drama of
Justinian. Doubleday, 1952. A detailed picture of life in
Constantinople in the sixth century.   652

Masefield, John. Basilissa. Macmillan, 1940. The amazing
Theodora, who became the wife of Justinian I, Emperor of

the East.   653

_____. Conquer. Macmillan, 1941. Dramatic story of a
Byzantine uprising at the time of Justinian and Theodora.   654

O'Connor, Richard. The Vandal. Doubleday, 1960. An officer
in General Belisarius' army sees the schemings of the Empress and the General's wife.   655

Pottinger, Henry. Blue and Green. Chapman, 1879. The bloody
Nika insurrection of 532 against Justinian proves the courage
of his wife, Theodora.   656

Treece, Henry. The Amber Princess. [En. title: Electra]
Random House, 1963. The tragic story of participants in the
Trojan War-- Agamemnon, Clytemnestra, Orestes, Helen,
and others--as told by Electra in her old age.   657

_____. Jason. Random House, 1961. Quest of Jason and
his companions for the Golden Fleece together with their
seizure of power in Corinth and its aftermath.   658

Warner, Rex. The Converts. Little, 1967. Fictional life of
the great western Church Father, St. Augustine of Hippo, as
told by his friend, Alypius.   659

Wellman, Paul I. The Female. Doubleday, 1953. Empress
Theodora and sixth century Constantinople are vividly pic-
tured.   660

2.   THE HIGH MIDDLE AGES (c. 1000-1300)

    a)   The British Isles (England, Wales, Scotland, Ireland)

Adams, Doris Sutcliffe. Power of Darkness. Walker, 1968,
c.1967. A youth defends a girl accused of witchcraft and murder, and thereby places himself in great danger.   661

Andrew, Prudence. Ordeal by Silence. Putnam, 1961. Story
of a twelfth century deaf-mute who lived an extraordinary,
highly influential life, becoming both a favorite of Henry II
and a candidate for canonization.   662

Baring-Gould, S. Pabo, the Priest. Stokes, 1899. Henry I's
attempt to subdue the Welsh people by weakening their Church.
                                                                               663

Barnes, Margaret Campbell. The Passionate Brood. Macrae
Smith, 1945. A story of Richard Plantagenet and the minstrel
Blondel.   664

Barringer, Leslie. Kay, the Left-Handed. Doubleday, 1935.
England under John during the absence of Crusader-King

Richard Lion-Heart.   665

Bowker, Alfred. Armadin. Causton & Sons, 1908. Civil war
in the reign of Stephen against the forces of Matilda and
Henry of Anjou.   666

Bryher, Winifred (Annie Winifred Macpherson). The Fourteenth
of October. Pantheon, 1952. Vivid account of the Norman
invasion of 1066.   667

_____. This January Tale. by Bryher. Harcourt, 1966.
The plight of the ordinary people whose lives, culture, and
homes fell victim to the Norman Conquest.   668

Burroughs, Edgar Rice. The Outlaw of Torn. McClurg, 1927,
c.1914. A son of Henry III, kidnapped as a small child, is
brought up as an expert swordsman and a feared outlaw.   669

Carlos, Louisa Cooke Don-. A Bottle in the Smoke. Fenno,
1908. Benedictine monastic life at the time of Henry II and
Richard I.   670

Chidsey, Donald Barr. This Bright Sword. Crown, 1957. YA.
Society and warfare in thirteenth century England during the
conflict between Richard Lion-Heart and his brother John.   671

Costain, Thomas B. Below the Salt. Doubleday, 1957. Panoramic view of England and the Magna Carta in a modern
American frame.   672

_____. The Black Rose. Pocket Bks., 1970, c.1945.
Travels, adventures and romance of an Englishman in the
Orient.   673

Cunningham, Allan. Sir Michael Scott. Colburn, 1828. Based
on the career of the famous British scholar and magician at
the court of Frederick II.   674

Dane, Joan. Prince Madog, Discoverer of America. Stock,
1909. Based on the legend that a Welsh prince discovered
America in the twelfth century.   675

Davidson, Mary M. Edward the Exile. Hodder, 1901. Based
on the life of Edward the Atheling, son of Margaret of Scotland.   676

Davies, Naunton. The King's Guide. Simpkin, 1901. Concerns
a period in the life of Prince Llewelyn ap Gruffydd, leader of
the thirteenth century Welsh fight for independence.   677

Deeping, Warwick. The Red Saint. McBride, 1940. The
Barons' Wars in Kent and Sussex, including the Battle of
Lewes.   678

Douglas, Donald. The Black Douglas. Doran, 1927. Powerful
tale of the daring Black Douglas and of the girl who loved
him.   679

Du Bois, Theodora M. Love of Fingin O'Lea. Appleton, 1957.
The adventures and studies of a young doctor who becomes a
famous physician.   680

Duggan, Alfred. The Cunning of the Dove. Pantheon, 1960. A
plausible picture of Edward the Confessor, England's last king
before the Norman Conquest.   681

_____. Devil's Brood. Coward, 1957. Vigorous account of
the unpleasant family of Henry II and Eleanor of Acquitaine.
                                                                  682

_____. Leopards and Lilies. Coward, 1954. The conflict-
ing loyalties and ambitions of a selfish English noblewoman.
                                                                  683

Edmondston, C. M. and M. L. F. Hyde. King's Man. Longmans, 1948. Penniless squire who rose to important posi-
tions with Henry II, Richard I, and John.   684

Farnol, Jeffery. Beltane the Smith. Little, 1915. Romance
of an outlaw and rebel in medieval England.   685

Gellis, Roberta. Bond of Blood. Doubleday, 1965. A club-
footed Welsh knight who marries the Earl of Pembroke's
daughter finds that his father-in-law is plotting against him
at court.   686

_____. Knight's Honor. Doubleday, 1964. A young Earl,
who is pro-Angevin, strives to dethrone King Stephen as well
as to subdue his own wilful wife.   687

Gerson, Noel B. The Conqueror's Wife. Doubleday, 1957.
The busy lives of two strong-willed people--William the Conqueror and his consort, Matilda.   688

Gibney, Somerville. John o' London. Ward & Downey, 1887.
Some of the researches and experiments of Roger Bacon's
early life.   689

Gibson, G. B. Dearforgil, the Princess of Breffny. Hope, 1857.
About the little-known abduction of the Princess by Diarmuid
MacMurrough.   690

Greenberg, Joanne. The King's Persons. Holt, 1963. The life
and trials of a Jewish money-lender, his son, and a Christian
servant girl in twelfth century England, displaying the prejudices of the day.   691

Greenleaf, Margery. Banner Over Me. Follett, 1968. YA.
Events leading up to the Norman Conquest, in which two

brothers find themselves fighting on opposite sides.   692

Griffiths, D. Ryles. Elgiva, Daughter of the Thegn. Unwin,
  1901. The Welsh border in the time of Edward the Confessor and Harold.   693

Grindrod, Charles F. The Shadow of the Raggedstone. Mathews,
  1908. About a twelfth century monk; the shadow of the Raggedstone is a sign of death.   694

Gull, C. Ranger. The Serf. Greening, 1902. The oppression
  and injustice involved in the feudal system are illustrated. 695

Hall, Hubert. Court Life Under the Plantagenets. Dutton,
  1890. A story of twelfth century England based on documents of the period.   696

Harris, Edwin. William D'Albini. Harris, 1901. The second
  siege of Rochester castle, an incident in John's dispute with
  refractory landholders.   697

Hay, Agnes Grant. Malcolm Canmore's Pearl. Hurst & Blackett, 1907. A romance about Malcolm III and his beautiful
  wife--St. Margaret of Scotland.   698

Haycraft, Molly Costain. The King's Daughters. Lippincott,
  1971. About the political and subsequent marriages of two
  of the daughters of Edward I.   699

Hewlett, Maurice. The Forest Lovers. Macmillan, 1898.
  Romance of a knight and a peasant girl, with good descriptions of medieval customs and ideas.   700

_____. The Life and Death of Richard Yea-and-Nay. Mac-
  millan, 1900. The pageantry and panoply of the chivalric
  age.   701

Heyer, Georgette. The Conqueror. Bantam Bks., 1968,
  c.1931. Colorful account of the forceful William the Bastard
  of Normandy who became the Conqueror and King of England.
                                                             702

Holland, Cecelia. The Earl. Knopf, 1971. Fulk of Stafford
  supports Henry of Anjou against King Stephen and seeks to
  secure his inheritance against his unscrupulous uncle.   703

_____. The Kings in Winter. Pocket Bks., 1969, c.1967.
  A tale of heroic leaders and of bloody battles between Irish,
  Vikings, and Danes, culminating in the Battle of Clontarf in
  1014.   704

Horne, Roland. The Lion of De Montfort. Dent, 1909. "A
  romance of the Barons' Wars."   705

James, G. P. R.   Forest Days.   Dutton, 1843.   England in the
    period of the Barons' Wars against King John.   706

Kingsley, Charles.   Hereward the Wake.   Macmillan, 1874.
    A saga-like account of the unruly Hereward, who refused
    to accept the Norman Conquest.   707

Knowles, Mabel Winifred.   Let Erin Remember.   by May Wynne,
    pseud.   Greening, 1908.   The Norman victory over the unity-
    lacking Irish in the 1170s.   708

Lenanton, Carola Oman.   The Empress.   by Carola Oman.
    Holt, 1932.   The Empress Matilda and her life in England
    and France.   709

Lewis, Hilda Winifred.   Harold Was My King.   McKay, 1970,
    c.1968.   In 1064 the fate of England was in question as
    Edward the Confessor died leaving three claimants to the
    throne--his son, Edgar the Atheling; Harold, Earl of Wes-
    sex; and William, Duke of Normandy, later known as the
    Conqueror.   710

_____.   Wife to the Bastard.   McKay, 1967, c.1966.   About
    Matilda, daughter of the Duke of Flanders, who became the
    wife of William the Conqueror and the mother of two more
    rulers, William Rufus of England and Robert of Normandy.   711

Lofts, Norah.   Eleanor the Queen.   Doubleday, 1955.   YA.   The
    life of one of the most interesting women of the Middle Ages,
    Eleanor of Aquitaine, consort of Henry II.   712

_____.   Madselin.   Bantam Bks., 1970, c.1968.   The life of
    a tiny English community under the rule of a hated enemy im-
    mediately following the Norman Conquest.   713

Lytton, Edward Bulwer, 1st. baron.   Harold, the Last of the
    Saxon Kings.   Longmans, 1848.   The Norman invasion, the
    Battle of Hastings, and the fall of the last Saxon king.   714

Maberley, Kate Charlotte.   The Lady and the Priest.   Clarke,
    1851.   The story is about Henry II, Rosamund, and Thomas
    à Becket.   715

MacFarlane, Charles.   The Camp of Refuge.   Longmans, 1846.
    Hereward the Wake's famous stand against William the Con-
    queror.   716

_____.   A Legend of Reading Abbey.   Dutton, 1904.   Con-
    flict between Matilda and the usurper Stephen.   717

Mackay, Charles.   Longbeard.   Routledge, 1841.   William
    FitzOsbert, Longbeard, led the Londoners against the
    Norman oppressors.   718

Maiden, Cecil. Harp Into Battle. Crowell, 1959. The eventful
life of Llewelyn the Great of Wales.   719

Marsh, John B. The Life and Adventures of Robin Hood. Dutton, 1875. Based on the career of the legendary outlaw-
hero.   720

Marshall, Bernard G. Walter of Tiverton. Appleton, 1923.
Heroic exploits in the chivalric days of Richard Lion-
Heart.   721

Miller, Thomas. Fair Rosamond. Darton, 1839. Romance of
Henry II and his contest with Becket.   722

_____. Royston Gower. Colburn, 1838. The background of
this Robin Hood tale is King John's quarrel with Pope Innocent III.   723

Muddock, J.E. Preston. Maid Marian and Robin Hood. Lippincott, 1892. Opposition to the treacherous John, who seized
his crusading brother's throne.   724

Muntz, Hope. The Golden Warrior. Scribner, 1949. Powerful
account of the Norman Conquest as vivid as a medieval tapestry.   725

Mydans, Shelley Smith. Thomas. Doubleday, 1965. Action-
filled life and career of the brilliant Thomas à Becket, cleric,
royal companion, chancellor, archbishop, and saint.   726

Napier, Charles. William the Conqueror. Routledge, 1858.
William's preparations for the invasion of England and the
Battle of Hastings.   727

O'Byrne, Miss M. L. The Court of Rath Croghan. Simpkin,
1887. Disunity among the Irish princes during the Norman
Conquest.   728

O'Grady, Standish. The Departure of Dermot. Talbot Press
(Ireland), 1917. King Dermot of Leinster and his departure
for Bristol in 1166.   729

O'Hannrachain, Michael. When the Norman Came. Maunsel
(Dublin), 1918. King Dermot of Leinster and his Norman
ally Strongbow.   730

Oliver, Jane, pseud. for Rees, Helen Christina Easson. Alexander, the Glorious. Putnam, 1965. Political successes
and personal sorrows of the great thirteenth century Scottish
king, Alexander III.   731

_____. Sing Morning Star. Putnam, 1956. Inspiring ro-
mance of Malcolm III, King of Scotland, and his saintly wife,

Margaret.   732

Pargeter, Edith. The Heaven Tree. Doubleday, 1960. This
medieval tapestry includes the construction of a Gothic
cathedral.   733

Peacock, Thomas Love. Maid Marian. Dutton, 1905. Account
of the Robin Hood legend, with some satire.   734

Peart, Hendry. Red Falcons of Tremoine. Knopf, 1956. YA.
The kidnapping of a young knight-to-be sparks fighting between
two noble houses in twelfth century England.   735

Picard, Barbara Leonie. Lost John. Criterion, 1963, c.1962.
YA. Young man leaves his home to avenge his father's death,
but joins a band of forest outlaws instead.   736

Potter, Margaret Horton. Uncanonized. McClurg, 1900.
Monastic life in England under King John.   737

Reznikoff, Charles. Lionhearted. Jewish Pub., 1944. The
persecution of the Jews in medieval England.   738

Scott, Sir Walter. The Betrothed. Lovell, 1885. Warfare on
the Welsh border in the reign of Henry II.   739

_____. Ivanhoe. Constable, 1821. Scott's most popular book
displays the pageantry and romance of the chivalric tradition.
                                                                 740
Sheppard, Alfred Tresidder. Here Comes an Old Sailor.
Doubleday, 1928. Chronicle of a Kentish family in the reign
of King John.   741

Shipway, George. The Knight. Doubleday, 1970, c.1969. (pub.
in 1969 as Knight in Anarchy) The story of a not-so-gentle
knight whose first battle sets the tenor of his life.   742

Sutcliff, Rosemary. Knight's Fee. Walck, 1960. YA. A young
man's arduous life which raises him from lowly dogboy to his
ultimate chance at knighthood, told against a background rich
in detail.   743

_____. Shield Ring. Oxford Univ. Pr., 1956. YA. A girl,
orphaned when the Normans invade her home, takes refuge
with the Vikings.   744

Swan, Edgar. The Sword and the Cowl. Digby & Long, 1909.
Pictures the Battle of Hastings and domestic life at the time.
                                                                 745
Talbot, L.A. Jehanne of the Forest. Melrose, 1914. Vigor-
ous England in the early part of Henry II's reign.   746

Treece, Henry. Man With a Sword. Pantheon, 1964, c.1962.

YA. A young fighting man travels from one country and one
master to another, spending some time with both Harold
Hardrada and William the Conqueror.   747

Turnbull, Clara. The Damsel Dark. Melrose, 1912. Romance
of the reigns of Stephen and Henry II.   748

Walworth, Alice. Shield of Honor. Doubleday, 1957. One of
Simon de Montfort's knights in the struggle for the rights of
Englishmen.   749

_____. The Vows of the Peacock. Doubleday, 1955. Isabel
of France, Elizabeth, daughter of Warwick, and intrigue surrounding the throne.   750

Ward, Bryan W. The Forest Prince. Digby & Long, 1903.
About the Barons' Wars of the mid-thirteenth century.   751

Weenolsen, Hebe. The Last Englishman. Doubleday, 1951. Eventful narrative of Hereward's resistance to William the Conqueror.
                                                            752
_____. To Keep This Oath. Doubleday, 1958. Pictures mining,
medicine, and the conflict between Henry Plantagenet and King
Stephen.   753

b) Western and Central Europe

1) France

Addison, Julia de Wolf. Florestane the Troubadour. Estes,
1903. Southern France and Italy near the end of the thirteenth century, with the artist Cimabue.   754

Aveling, Francis. Arnoul the Englishman. Herder, 1908.
Based on the Paris University debates over such philosophers
as Plato and Aristotle.   755

Bailey, H.C. The Fool. Dutton, 1927. The Civil War between
Stephen and Matilda in England and the exploits of Henry of Enjou,
who became Henry II, in France.   756

Barrington, Michael. The Lady of Tripoli. Chatto, 1910. A
romance of Odierna, widow of Raymond I of Tripoli, at the
time of the Crusades.   757

Blissett, Nellie K. The Most Famous Loba. Appleton, 1901.
The persecution of the Albigenses by Simon de Montfort.   758

Closs, Hannah. Deep Are the Valleys. Vanguard, 1960. An
idealistic knight seeking to avenge a friend during the Albigensian Wars is tempted to join the Cathari. (followed by

The Silent Tarn)   759

_____. High Are the Mountains. Vanguard, 1959. Richly
detailed descriptions of medieval scenes and life during the
crusade against the Albigenses. (followed by Deep Are the
Valleys)   760

_____. The Silent Tarn. Vanguard, 1963. Wolf, bastard
son of the Count of Foix, is involved in political and religious controversies in the time of the Albigensian heresy
and the Inquisition. (completes trilogy)   761

Davis, William Stearns. Falaise of the Blessed Voice. [later
   pub. as: The White Queen] Macmillan, 1904. A romance
   based on the lives of King Louis IX, the Saint, and his
   Queen, Marguerite of Provence.   762

Hewlett, Maurice. The Heart's Key. Harper, 1905. Romance
   and revenge under the feudal system in France.   763

James, G. P. R. Philip Augustus. Dutton, 1831. Philip II's
   quarrel with Innocent III and the case of Arthur Plantagenet.
                                                                 764
Jeffries, Graham Montague. Courts of Love. [En. title:
   Court of Love] by Peter Bourne, pseud. Putnam, 1958.
   Bound by a chivalric oath to his cousin's service, a young
   knight is sent to kidnap a beautiful heiress.   765

Lindsey, William. The Severed Mantle. Houghton, 1910.
   A tale of the troubadours in twelfth century Provence.   766

Maturin, Charles Robert. The Albigenses. Hurst & Blackett,
   1824. The Civil War in Languedoc which followed Montfort's
   crusade against the Albigenses.   767

Oldenbourg, Zoe. Cities of the Flesh. (tr.) Pantheon, 1963.
   The story of a knight whose religious beliefs caused him to
   have trouble with the Inquisition during the days of the Albigensian heresy.   768

_____. Destiny of Fire. (tr.) Pantheon, 1961. Reactions
   of members of a devout Albigensian family of the lesser nobility who are persecuted as heretics for their beliefs.   769

Pouillon, Fernand. The Stones of the Abbey. (tr.) Harcourt,
   1970. The final nine months of an anonymous Cistercian
   monk who was the architect of Le Thoronet Abbey in Provence.   770

Prescott, Hilda Frances Margaret. The Lost Fight. Dodd,
   1956. (orig. pub. in 1928) Left by a crusader friend to
   safeguard the friend's wife, Adam Morteigne proves himself
   unworthy of the trust.   771

_____. Son of Dust. Macmillan, 1956. A rich tapestry of
life in medieval Normandy.   772

_____. Unhurrying Chase. Dodd, 1925. The quest for re-
venge of a young Frenchman who has lost his estates to
Richard Lion-Heart.   773

Rawson, Maud Stepney. Morlac of Gascony. Hutchinson, 1915.
French plots concerning the Cinque Ports, keys of English
maritime defense.   774

Rossiter, Leonard. Bernadin, My Love. [En. title: The Tale
of Magali] Doubleday, 1962, c.1961. A tragic love story in
chivalric twelfth century Provence.   775

Stephens, Eve. The Cardinal and the Queen. by Evelyn Anthony, pseud. Coward, 1968. The difficulties of the wife
of Louis XIII, beset by her husband's dislike, her mother-
in-law's hatred, and the supposed passion of Cardinal Richelieu.   776

Stevens, Clifford J. Flame Out of Dorset. Doubleday, 1964.
The story of Stephen Harding, founder of the austere Cistercian religious order, related by a contemporary.   777

Symons, Beryl. Prince and Priest. Paul, 1912. Story based
on the Albigensian heresy.   778

Treece, Henry. Perilous Pilgrimage. Criterion, 1959. YA.
A brother and sister run away from home to join the ill-
fated Children's Crusade led by Stephen of Cloyes.   779

Waddell, Helen Jane. Peter Abelard. Holt, 1933. The famous
romance of Abelard and Heloise.   780

Webb, Henry B. Dew in April. by John Clayton, pseud. Kendall & Sharp, 1935. Convent life and daring romance in thirteenth Provence. (followed by Gold of Toulouse)   781

_____. Gold of Toulouse. by John Clayton, pseud. Heine-
mann, 1932. Brotherly devotion, romance, and sadistic torture in thirteenth century Toulouse.   782

    2) The Empire and Central Europe (including the Germanies,
    Netherlands, Switzerland, Poland, and Hungary)

Barr, Robert. The Countess Tekla. Stokes, 1898. Love
affair of the countess with an emperor in disguise in the
Rhine area.   783

Conscience, Hendrik. The Lion of Flanders. (tr.) Kelly,
1838. Uprising in Flanders against the French occupa-

tion; the Massacre of Bruges and the Battle of Courtrai.   784

Davis, William Stearns. The Saint of Dragon's Dale. Macmillan, 1903. Fantastic tale of the suppression of robber
knights in Thuringia by Rudolf I.   785

Ebers, Georg. In the Time of the Forge. (tr.) Low, 1895.
Novel of thirteenth century Nuremberg, reflecting life both
in and outside of the cloister.   786

Haughton, Rosemary. Elizabeth's Greeting. Lippincott, 1968.
The spiritual and physical beauty of St. Elizabeth of Hungary
and her boundless love for her husband and for God's poor. 787

Holland, Cecelia. Antichrist. Atheneum, 1970. The unconventional, learned, ambitious Holy Roman Emperor Frederick II
who made himself King of Jerusalem in 1229.   788

_____. The Firedrake. Atheneum, 1966. A wandering Irish
knight who serves in Thuringia and Flanders eventually becomes a follower of William the Conqueror.   789

James, G. P. R. The Castle of Ehrenstein. Dutton, 1847.
The atmosphere of Germany in the early thirteenth century. 790

Josika, Miklos. 'Neath the Hoof of the Tartar. (tr.) Jarrold
and Sons, 1905. The Mongol invasion of Hungary in the
1240's.   791

Prior, Loveday. A Law Unto Themselves. Little, 1934.
Robber barons in the Austrian Tyrol in the thirteenth century.   792

Robertson, Frances F. The Wanton. by Frances Harrod,
pseud. Greening, 1909. A romance of the Empire at the
time of the conflict between Frederick II and the Papacy.   793

Schmitt, Gladys. The Godforgotten. Harcourt, 1972. A village and a monastery, cut off from the world a hundred years,
develop strange religious ideals and social customs in their
isolation.   794

3) Scandinavia and the Baltic

Best, Herbert. The Sea Warriors. Macmillan, 1959. YA.
The way of life of eleventh century Norsemen is well pictured in this tale of Viking adventure in Ireland and Greenland.   795

Drummond, Hamilton. A Man's Fear. Ward & Lock, 1903.
A story of Norway when Christian teachings were replacing
pagan superstitions.   796

Hewlett, Maurice. Frey and His Wife. McBride, 1916. A
saga of Norway telling of the introduction of Christianity.   797

_____. The Light Heart. Holt, 1920. Saga of Thormod of
the light heart whose loyalty never falters at danger.   798

_____. Outlaw. Dodd, 1920. A strong, tense saga of a
craftsman turned outlaw and a sword which carried a curse.
                                                          799

Ingemann, Bernard S. Waldemar. Bentley, 1864. A novel
of adventure in thirteenth century Denmark.   800

Kennedy, C. Rann. The Winterfeast. Harper, 1908. A Viking,
after twenty years in America, discovers his father had in-
terfered with his romance.   801

Treece, Henry. The Burning of Njal. Criterion, 1964. YA.
Tales based on the saga of Njal and his sons in eleventh
century Iceland.   802

_____. The Last Viking. [En. title: The Last of the Vi-
kings] Pantheon, 1966. YA. The exciting career of the
adventurous Norwegian King Harald Hardrada as Vikings,
Anglo-Saxons, and Normans fought for ascendancy.   803

Undset, Sigrid. Master of Hestviken. (tr.) Knopf, 1934.
[Contains: The Axe. Knopf, 1928; The Snake Pit. Knopf,
1929; In the Wilderness. Knopf, 1929; The Son Avenger.
Knopf, 1930] Exquisite, powerful tetralogy portraying life,
love, and violence in Norway.   804

c) Southern Europe (Iberian Peninsula, Italy, Adjacent
    Islands)

Alexander, Eleanor. The Lady of the Well. Longmans, 1906.
The adventures and experiences of a troubadour.   805

Bailly, Auguste. The Divine Minstrels. (tr.) Scribner, 1909.
Based on the lives of St. Francis of Assisi and his companions.   806

Barton, Hester. The Baron of Ill-Fame. Paul, 1911. Corso
Donati, whose actions won him the unusual nickname of
Baron of Ill-Fame.   807

Bickerstaffe-Drew, Francis. San Celestino. by John Ayscough,
pseud. Putnam, 1909. Story of the hermit who became
Pope Celestine II for a period of five months.   808

Deiss, Joseph Jay. The Great Infidel. Random House, 1963.
Fictional biography of the brilliant and skeptical Emperor
Frederico II and his struggles with the North Italians and

the Papacy.   809

De Wohl, Louis. The Joyful Beggar. Lippincott, 1958. About
a young soldier who became a joyful beggar and founder of
a religious order--St. Francis of Assisi.   810

_____. The Quiet Light. Lippincott, 1950. Novel based on
the life and philosophy of Thomas Aquinas.   811

Drummond, Hamilton. The Betrayers. Dutton, 1919. Stirring
account of the struggle for power between Emperor Frederick
II and Pope Innocent IV.   812

_____. Greater Than the Greatest. Dutton, 1917. Fred-
erick II's conflict with Pope Gregory IX.   813

Feuchtwanger, Lion. Raquel: The Jewess of Toledo. (tr.)
Messner, 1955. Alfonso VIII, King of Castile, his Jewish
finance minister, and the latter's daughter, Raquel.   814

Gallizier, Nathan. Castel del Monte. Page, 1905. Romantic
and political developments attending the coronation of Manfred as King of Sicily.   815

_____. The Hill of Venus. Page, 1913. A young man
forced by his father to become a monk.   816

Gifford, Evelyn H. Provenzano the Proud. Smith & Elder,
1904. Siena during the bitter strife between Guelfs and
Ghibellines.   817

Goldston, Robert. The Legend of the Cid. Bobbs, 1963. YA.
Based on the legendary adventures of the knight, Rodrigo de
Vivar, who won the title of "El Cid Campeador."   818

Hewlett, Maurice. Buondelmonte's Saga. Harper, 1905. A
tragic romance of Florence.   819

Lee-Hamilton, Eugene. The Lord of the Dark Red Star. Scott,
1903. "Supernatural influences in the life of an Italian despot of the thirteenth century."   820

Le Fort, Gertrud von. The Pope From the Ghetto. (tr.) Sheed,
1934. Dramatic story of a Jew who became a Catholic and
ruled for a time as anti-Pope Anacletus II.   821

Lewis, Arthur. The Pilgrim. Blackwood, 1910. A Welsh
pilgrim visits Rome during the conflict between Pope Gregory VII (Hildebrand) and Emperor Henry IV.   822

Llewellyn, Richard. Warden of the Smoke and Bells. Doubleday, 1956. Marco Polo returns from Cathay through thirteenth century Assisi.   823

McCarthy, Justin Huntly. The God of Love. Harper, 1909.
A story of the romance between Dante and Beatrice.   824

Osgood, Claude Jack. Eagle of the Gredos. Reynal, 1942. A
Spanish noble fights against Moslem invaders.   825

Schachner, Nathan. The Wanderer. Appleton, 1944. Dante's
undying love for Beatrice.   826

Scollard, Clinton. The Vicar of the Marches. Sherman &
French, 1911. Padua in the days of Conrad III.   827

Stewart, Newton V. The Cardinal. Paul, 1911. Ottaviano
Ubaldini is the Cardinal in this novel of thirteenth century
Italy.   828

_____. A Son of the Emperor. Methuen, 1909. Emperor
Frederick II's son Enzio and the contention of Guelphs and
Ghibellines.   829

Trease, Geoffrey. The Red Towers of Granada. Vanguard,
1967. YA. Adventures of a boy wrongly suspected as a
leper in England and Europe.   830

Underdown, Emily. Cristina. Sonnenschein, 1903. The struggle
in Italy between Ghibelline (Imperial) and Guelph (Papal) parties.   831

White, Helen C. Bird of Fire. Macmillan, 1958. The development of Francis of Assisi from a young cloth merchant to
the founder of a religious order.   832

_____. Not Built With Hands. Macmillan, 1935. About
Matilda, Countess of Tuscany, who attempted to settle the
differences between Henry IV and Pope Gregory VII (Hildebrand).   833

_____. A Watch in the Night. Macmillan, 1933. A worldly
lawyer becomes a devoted Franciscan.   834

d) Eastern Europe (including the Byzantine Empire, the
    Balkans, and Russia), the Near East, and North Africa

Dole, Nathan Haskell. Omar the Tentmaker. Page, 1899.
Imaginary romance of the Persian savant, Omar Khayyam,
author of the Rubáiyát.   835

Duggan, Alfred. The Lady for Ransom. Coward, 1953. Informative story of mercenary soldiers in the service of
Byzantine emperors.   836

Harrison, Edith. Princess Sayrane. McClurg, 1910. Mistaken identity and romance in an Egyptian setting.   837

Holland, Cecelia. Until the Sun Falls. Atheneum, 1969,
c.1968. The Mongol invasion of Russia and East Central
Europe in the thirteenth century as seen from the viewpoints of a veteran general and his arrogant son, also a
general.   838

Lagerkvist, Pär. The Death of Ahasuerus. (tr.) Random
House, 1962. After centuries of roaming and searching, the
Wandering Jew finds peace on a pilgrimage.   839

MacFall, Haldane. The Three Students. Knopf, 1926. Based
on the life of Omar Khayyam from his student days.   840

Phillpotts, Eden. Eudocia. Macmillan, 1921. Intrigues surrounding a Byzantine imperial widow and her reluctant promise
not to remarry.   841

Pickthall, Marmaduke. Knights of Araby. Collins, 1917. Tale
of adventure in eleventh century Arabia.   842

Treece, Henry. The Golden One. Criterion, 1962, c.1961.
Adventures of young Constantine and his sister, Theodora, who
flee a Constantinople torn by the chaos of the Crusades.   843

_____. Swords From the North. Pantheon, 1967. YA.
Battles, marches, and court intrigue facing Harold Hardrada
when he was Captain of the Greek Emperor's Guard in Constantinople.   844

Weigall, Arthur. The Garden of Paradise. Fisher Unwin, 1923.
A romance set in the exotic Persia of Omar Khayyam.   845

  e) Overseas Exploration, Enterprise, and Expansion
      (including the Crusades)

Adams, Doris Sutcliffe. No Man's Son. Walker, 1969, c.1961.
During the time of the Third Crusade a young man and his
friends try to claim his rightful inheritance.   846

Baerlein, Henry. On the Forgotten Road. Murray, 1909.
Twenty-three years of captivity in Egypt told in a fictional
autobiography.   847

Barr, Gladys. Cross, Sword, and Arrow. Abingdon, 1955.
A member of the Children's Crusade is captured by the
Saracens.   848

Begbie, Harold. The Distant Lamp. Hodder, 1912. Events of
the Children's Crusade in France, Egypt, and the Holy Land.
                                                           849

Boucher, Alan. The Sword of the Raven. Scribner, 1969. YA.
The wanderings of Halli Thordarson around Iceland, Greenland, and Ireland, based on Icelandic sagas.   850

Brady, Charles Andrew. This Land Fulfilled. Dutton, 1958.
Supposed narrative of a priest who, as a youth, accompanied Leif Ericsson on his voyage to Vinland.   851

Brooke, Teresa. Under the Winter Moon. Doubleday, 1958.
A tapestry of the Middle Ages including romance and crusading.   852

Butcher, C. H. The Oriflamme in Egypt. Dent, 1905. The
First Crusade of Louis IX of France with initial scenes of
English rural life and later of the Coptic Church.   853

Byrne, Donn. Crusade. Little, 1928. The capture, escape,
and romance of a crusading Irishman.   854

Charques, Dorothy. Men Like Shadows. Coward, 1953. A
narrative of the Third Crusade to the Holy Land.   855

Crawford, F. Marion. Via Crucis. Macmillan, 1899. The
Second Crusade, introducing Bernard of Clairvaux and other
religious and political figures.   856

Cronyn, George W. The Fool of Venus. Covici, 1934. Stirring
tale of the Fourth Crusade with Pierre Vidal, troubadour of
Provence, as the central character.   857

Davis, Christopher. Belmarch. Viking, 1964. Recounts the
actions and spiritual distress of a Crusader who took part in
the massacre of the Jews of Mainz.   858

Davis, William Stearns. God Wills It. Macmillan, 1902. A
tale of the First Crusade--the exploits and romance of a
young Norman.   859

Duggan, Alfred. Count Bohemond. Pantheon, 1965, c.1964. A
favorable portrait of the ambitious, controversial Crusader who
became the Prince of Antioch.   860

_____. Knight With Armour. Coward, 1951. A picture
of the feudal way of life including battle scenes.   861

Duncan, David. Trumpet of God. Doubleday, 1956. Perceptive story of the human aspect of the Children's Crusade. 862

Faust, Frederick. The Golden Knight. by George Challis,
pseud. Greystone, 1937. A tale of Richard I of England
as a captive in Austria.   863

Gallizier, Nathan. The Crimson Gondola. Page, 1915. Con-

flict between Venice and Constantinople during the Fourth
Crusade.   864

Gartner, Chloe. The Infidels. Doubleday, 1960. A young
knight of mixed origins is torn between conflicting feelings
on the First Crusade.   865

Gay, Laverne. Wine of Satan. Scribner, 1949. Vivid account
of the First Crusade centering on Bohemond, Prince of Anti-
och.   866

Haggard, H. Rider. The Brethren. McClure, 1904. Life of
Englishmen in Syria preceding the Third Crusade.   867

Haycraft, Molly Costain. My Lord Brother the Lion Heart.
Lippincott, 1968. Joan, the widowed daughter of Henry II,
accompanies her brother King Richard on the Third Crusade.
                                                                              868

Jeffries, Graham Montague. When God Slept. by Peter Bourne,
pseud. Putnam, 1956. Picaresque adventures of two Englishmen captured by the Arabs.   869

Johnston, Mary. The Fortunes of Garin. Houghton, 1915. A
young knight, true to the chivalric tradition, sings of a princess but loves a shepherdess.   870

Kossak-Szczucka, Zofja. Angels in the Dust. (tr.) Roy Pub.,
1947. Three Polish brothers, driven from their lands, answer Urban II's call to crusade.   871

_____. Blessed Are the Meek. (tr.) Roy Pub., 1944. A
story concerning the Children's Crusade with St. Francis of
Assisi as a character.   872

_____. The Leper King. (tr.) Roy Pub., 1945. The wise
reign of Baldwin IV of Jerusalem who played a valiant role
despite his leprosy.   873

Lamb, Harold. Durandal. Doubleday, 1931. A crusader falls
into the hands first of the Saracens and then of the Mongol-
ian horde.   874

Lofts, Norah. The Lute Player. Fawcett, 1971, c.1951.
Richard Lion-Heart and the musician who rescued him from
a dungeon.   875

Ludlow, James M. Sir Raoul. Revell, 1905. Diversion of the
Fourth Crusade to Constantinople for the benefit of Venice. 876

Mason, Van Wyck. Silver Leopard. Doubleday, 1955. Melo-
drama of twin brother and sister during the First Crusade. 877

Meakin, Nevill Myers. The Assassins. Holt, 1902. An Arab

is the hero of this novel of the Third Crusade, featuring
Richard Lion-Heart, Philip Augustus, and Saladin.   878

Myers, Henry. Our Lives Have Just Begun. Stokes, 1939.
The French contingent of the tragic Children's Crusade.   879

Oldenbourg, Zoe. The Cornerstone. (tr.) Pantheon, 1955.
Rich panorama of the era of faith and chivalry.   880

_____. The Heirs of the Kingdom. (tr.) Pantheon, 1971.
The hardships of humble weavers from Arras who join the
First Crusade.   881

_____. The World Is Not Enough. (tr.) Pantheon, 1948.
A petty knight's home life and crusading.   882

O'Meara, Walter. The Devil's Cross. Knopf, 1957. Excitement, romance, and tragedy during the ill-fated Children's
Crusade.   883

Scarfoglio, Carlo. The True Cross. Pantheon, 1956. Forceful account of the problems of a young Knight Templar.   884

Schoonover, Lawrence. Golden Exile. Macmillan, 1951. A
crusader's attempt to reclaim his lands and end his exile. 885

Scott, Sir Walter. Count Robert of Paris. Bazin & Ellsworth,
1833. Concerns romance and dissension among members of
the First Crusade.   886

_____. The Talisman. Harper, 1879. About the Third Cru-
sade, with Saladin, Richard Lion-Heart, and Kenneth of Scotland, loyal follower of the King.   887

Shelby, Graham. The Kings of Vain Intent. Weybright & Talley,
1971, c. 1970. Daring King Richard Lion-Heart and his fellows
during the Third Crusade.   888

_____. The Knights of Dark Renown. Weybright & Talley,
1969. The downfall of the Crusader Kingdom of Jerusalem is
precipitated by the villainy of the irresponsible Reynald of Chatil-
lon. (followed by The Kings of Vain Intent)   889

Shellabarger, Samuel. The Token. Little, 1955. A silver
girdle, symbol of nobility and strength, is the focus of the
story.   890

Simpson, Evan John. Ride Home Tomorrow. By Evan John,
pseud. Putnam, 1951. The atmosphere of the crusades
is captured in this narrative.   891

Smith, Arthur D. Howden. Spears of Destiny. Doran, 1919. Tells
of the Fourth Crusade and the capture of Constantinople.   892

Tapsell, R. F. The Unholy Pilgrim. Knopf, 1968. Adventures
  of a Norman knight on a pilgrimage to the Holy Land in the
  thirteenth century.   893

Vidal, Gore. Search for the King. Dutton, 1950. Blondel's
  search through Europe for the imprisoned Crusader, Richard
  Lion-Heart.   894

Wiles, John. The March of the Innocents. Chatto, 1964. A
  story based on the adventures and tragedies of the Children's
  Crusade of 1212.   895

Williams, Jay. The Siege. Little, 1955. Stirring descriptions
  of battles and of ideal and corrupt aspects of chivalry.   896

_____. Tomorrow's Fire. Atheneum, 1964. Adventures of
  a wandering troubadour who joins Richard Lion-Heart on the
  Third Crusade.   897

Yerby, Frank. The Saracen Blade. Dial, 1952. An Italian
  armorer's son, on a crusade, finds love with a slave girl
  in Egypt.   898

Zimmermann, Samuel. Sir Pagan. by Henry John Colyton,
  pseud. Creative Age, 1947. A swift-paced adventure story
  of the crusades.   899

3. THE LATER MIDDLE AGES AND EARLY RENAISSANCE
    (c. 1300-1500)

  a) The British Isles

  1) England and Wales

Andrew, Prudence. The Constant Star. Putnam, 1946, c.1963.
  Conflict between loyalty and ambition in an English village
  during the Peasants' Revolt of 1381.   900

_____. The Hooded Falcon. New Authors Guild, 1960. A
  border baron is torn between loyalty to England or to Wales.
                                                                 901

_____. A Question of Choice. Putnam, 1962. The monks
  of Woodchester Abbey are subject to unusual pressures in
  electing a new abbot when national politics enters the picture.   902

_____. A Sparkle From the Coal. Hutchinson, 1964. A
  student leaves Oxford to live a hermit's life in his search
  for God's truth.   903

Bailey, H.C. The Merchant Prince. Dutton, 1929. Concerns

the growth of English commerce in the second half of the
fifteenth century.   904

Barber, Margaret Fairless. The Gathering of Brother Hilarius.
by Michael Fairless, pseud. Murray, 1903. A religious is
sent from the monastery to learn the ways of the world during the Black Plague.   905

Barnes, Margaret Campbell. Isabel the Fair. Macrae Smith,
1957. The problems facing the French Princess Isabel who
became the wife of Edward II of England.   906

_____. The King's Bed. Macrae Smith, 1962, c.1961.
Love of Richard III's bastard son for an innkeeper's daughter
and intrigue surrounding the time of the Battle of Bosworth
Field.   907

_____. Tudor Rose. Macrae Smith, 1953. Elizabeth, con-
sort of Henry VII and mother of Henry VIII.   908

_____. Within the Hollow Crown. Macrae Smith, 1947.
Based on the life of Richard II from his fifteenth year.   909

Bauer, Florence Anne. Lady Besieged. Bobbs, 1960. The
young wife of an older lord manages to reorganize his estate
and become involved in religious affairs while he is cam-
paigning in Spain.   910

Begbie, Harold. Rising Dawn. Doran, 1913. A romance of
1377-78 introducing Chaucer, Wycliff, John of Gaunt, and
John Ball.   911

Benson, Robert Hugh. Richard Raynal, Solitary. Pitman, 1906.
Fifteenth century Quietism in the England of Henry VI and
Cardinal Beaufort.   912

Breton, Frederic. God Save England. De la More Press, 1899.
England in the latter part of Edward III's reign and at the
accession of Richard II.   913

Carleton, Patrick. Under the Hog. Dutton, 1938. Richard
III's unscrupulous seizure of the throne and its sequel.   914

Chesson, Nora. Father Felix's Chronicles. Wessels, 1907.
A monk's account of the poor living conditions of the people
in fifteenth century England.   915

Church, Richard. The Bells of Rye. Day, 1961, c.1960. YA.
Coastal war between English, French, and Spanish in the four-
teenth century after the disturbance caused by the Black
Death.   916

Converse, Florence. Long Will. Houghton, 1903. Story of

William Langland, author of Piers Plowman, and other
people notable in the Peasants' Revolt.   917

Cooke, J. H.   Ida.   Mackie, 1912.   English monastic life in the
reigns of Edward I, II, and III.   918

Cripps, Arthur S.   Magic Casements.   Duckworth, 1905.   Daily
life in restless England during the troubled reigns of Henry
VI and Edward IV.   919

Deeping, Warwick.   The King Behind the King.   McBride, Nast,
1914.   In southern England at the time of the Peasants' Revolt.   920

_____.   The Shield of Love.   McBride, 1940.   Exciting ad-
ventures in England during Richard II's reign.   921

Duros, Edwin.   Otterbourne.   Bentley, 1832.   The Scottish invasion of England and Douglas' deafeat of Hotspur at the
Battle of Otterbourne.   922

Eckerson, Olive.   The Golden Yoke.   Coward, 1961.   A tale of
the kaleidoscopic convolutions of the Wars of the Roses focus-
ing on the controversial Richard III, his accession and marriage.   923

Edmondston, C. M. and M. L. F. Hyde.   The Ragged Staff.   Longmans, 1932.   Romance and adventure during the Wars of the
Roses.   924

Ellis, Beth.   A King of Vagabonds.   Blackwood, 1911.   Deals
with Perkin Warbeck's contention that he was of royal blood
and had a claim to the throne of England.   925

Ellis, Kenneth M.   Guns Forever Echo.   Messner, 1941.   Yar-
mouth during the Hundred Years War.   926

Estrange, H. O. M.   Mid Rival Roses.   Selwyn & Blount, 1922.
The swift march of events during the Wars of the Roses.   927

Eyre, Katherine W.   Song of a Thrush.   Oxford Univ. Pr., 1952.
YA.   Margaret and Edward Plantagenet and their uncle who
usurped the throne, Richard III.   928

Faulkner, Nancy.   The Yellow Hat.   Doubleday, 1958.   YA.
The Peasants' Revolt brings a serf to London, where he
falls in love with a maid servant of Chaucer.   929

Ford, Ford Madox (name originally Ford Madox Hueffer).
Ladies Whose Bright Eyes.   Lippincott, 1935.   Due to an accident, a twentieth century businessman returns to fourteenth
century England.   930

Forster, R. H. In Steel and Leather. Long, 1904. The Wars
of the Roses, with Henry VI and Queen Margaret's escape to
Scotland.   931

_____. The Mistress of Aydon. Long, 1907. Border
clashes in fourteenth century Northumberland.   932

Fullerton, Georgiana. A Stormy Life. Bentley, 1867. Written
as the journal of Henry VI's queen, Margaret of Anjou.   933

Greener, William. The Men of Harlech. Ward & Downey, 1896.
The scene is laid in Wales during the struggle of Henry VI
and Edward IV for the throne.   934

Haggard, H. Rider. Red Eve. Doubleday, Page, 1911. Tells
of the disastrous Black Death in England and the decisive
Battle of Crécy.   935

Hamilton, Bernard. Coronation. Ward & Lock, 1902. Events
during the reign of Henry V, ending with the decisive Battle
of Agincourt.   936

Harding, T. Walter. The Abbot of Kirkstall. Heffer, 1926.
Features such leaders as John of Gaunt, the Black Prince,
and Wycliff.   937

Hardy, Blanche. Dynasty. Philip Allan, 1925. Romance in
England in the time of Henry VII.   938

_____. Sanctuary. Philip Allan, 1925. Concerns the reign
of Richard III and his murder of the little Princes in the
Tower.   939

Harnett, Cynthia. Caxton's Challenge. [En. title: The Load
of Unicorn] World, 1960, c.1959. YA. The opposition of
scriveners, whose business is handwritten books, to William
Caxton and his new art of printing.   940

Harwood, Alice. Merchant of the Ruby. Bobbs, 1950. Romance of a cousin of the Scottish king, and Perkin Warbeck,
Pretender to the English throne.   941,

Hawtrey, Valentina. In a Desert Land. Duffield, 1915. Traces
a family from the early fourteenth century to modern times
and includes the Peasants' Revolt and Wycliff's Preachers. 942

Haycraft, Molly Costain. The Lady Royal. Lippincott, 1964.
Princess Isabella, daughter of Edward III, finds a husband
during the Hundred Years' War in France.   943

Hesse, Hermann. Narcissus and Goldmund. (tr.) Farrar,
1968. (orig. pub. in German in 1930; in En. as Death and
the Lover in 1932 and as Goldmund in 1959) The quest of

two men for happiness--one as a scholarly monk, the other
as a travelling wood-carver.   944

Heyer, Georgette. Simon the Coldheart. Small, Maynard,
  1925. Life during the thrilling times of Henry IV and
  Henry V.   945

Hibbert, Eleanor. The King's Mistress. by Jean Plaidy, pseud.
  Pyramid, 1971. (orig. pub. in 1950 as The Goldsmith's
  Wife) The scandalous love affairs of a woman in Edward
  IV's court who was greatly loved for her beauty and good-
  ness and greatly hated for her sins and her power.   946

Hudson, H. Wild Humphrey Kynaston, the Robber Troglodyte.
  Paul, 1899. About Kynaston who, outlawed by Henry VII,
  led a Robin Hood-type life.   947

Hughes, Beatrix. Joan of St. Albans. Heath Cranton, ·1926.
  Includes the Yorkist King Edward IV, the printer Caxton,
  and the second Battle of St. Albans.   948

Israel, Charles Edward. Who Was Then the Gentleman? S. &
  S., 1963. The Peasants' Revolt of 1381, in which Wat Tyler and John Ball led an early social upheaval, provides the
  focus for this story.   949

Jackson, Dorothy V.S. Walk With Peril. Putnam, 1959. A
  country boy's advance in the service of Henry V at Agincourt.   950

James G.P.R. Agincourt. Harper, 1844. Concerns Henry V
  and his victory at Agincourt.   951

_____. The Woodman. Newby, 1849. The scene is Eng-
  land under Richard III, ending with the Battle of Bosworth
  Field.   952

Jarman, Rosemary H. We Speak No Treason. Little, 1971.
  A maiden, a jester, and an archer tell about King Richard
  III as their lives touched his.   953

Jefferis, Barbara. Beloved Lady. Sloane, 1955. Norfolk
  manor house life and romance during England's Wars of
  the Roses.   954

Kelly, Regina Zimmerman. Young Geoffrey Chaucer. Lothrop,
  1952. YA. The story of Chaucer as a boy, telling of his
  training as a student at Oxford and a page at court.   955

Knowles, Mabel Winifred. The Red Rose of Lancaster. by
  May Wynne, pseud. Holden & Hardingham, 1922. Romance
  of Brittany in which the future Henry VII of England appears.
                                                             956

Lawrence, George Alfred. Brakespeare. Routledge, 1868.
Battles in England and France in the days of Edward III and
the Black Prince.   957

Leary, Francis W. Fire and Morning. Putnam, 1957. The
turbulent times of Richard III and the Wars of the Roses.   958

_____. The Swan and the Rose. Wyn, 1953. The Wars of
the Roses as seen by a young Lancastrian soldier.   959

Lenanton, Carola Oman. Crouchback. by Carola Oman. Holt,
1929. Presents a favorable picture of the controversial character of Richard III.   960

Lewis, Hilda Winifred. The Gentle Falcon. Phillips, 1957. YA.
Story of the French princess Isabella who married Edward
II of England.   961

_____. Harlot Queen. McKay, 1970. Conflicting drives
and tragic ending of the ill-mated Edward II of England and
Isabella of France.   962

_____. Here Comes Harry. Criterion, 1960. YA. The
boy King, Henry VI, leads a lonely life due to the struggle
of men to control England during his minority.   963

_____. Wife to Henry V. Putnam, 1957. Emphasis on the
private life of Catherine of Valois.   964

Lindsay, Philip. London Bridge Is Falling. Little, 1934.
London citizens defend the city from Jack Cade's rebellion.   965

Lofts, Norah. The Town House. Doubleday, 1959. A serf attains freedom by living, undetected, in a walled town for a
year and a day. (followed by The House at Old Vine)   966

Lytton, Edward Bulwer, 1st. baron. The Last of the Barons.
Dutton, 1843. Edward IV and Warwick the King-maker are
prominent characters.   967

McChesney, Dora Greenwell. The Confession of Richard
Plantagenet. Smith & Elder, 1913. Absorbing defense of
the controversial Richard III.   968

Mackintosh, Elizabeth. Daughter of Time. by Josephine Tey,
pseud. Macmillan, 1952, c.1951. A contemporary English
detective does extensive research to determine whether Richard III was really responsible for the deaths of his royal
nephews in the Tower.   969

Mann, F.O. The Golden Quill. Blackwell, 1924. Novel of
southern England and London in Chaucer's period.   970

Matthew, Anne Irwin. Warm Wind, West Wind. Crown,
   1956. Social life in London and adventures of ships which
   dare to sail far seas.   971

Maude, Sophie. The Hermit and the King. Washbourne, 1916.
   England during the Wars of the Roses seen from a Catholic
   viewpoint.   972

Maughan, A. Margery. Harry of Monmouth. Sloane, 1956.
   Fictionalized account of Henry V and English campaigns in
   France.   973

Meyer, Annie N. Robert Annys, Poor Priest. Macmillan,
   1901. The powerful emotions engendered by the Peasants'
   Revolt.   974

Minto, William. The Mediation of Ralph Hardelot. Harper,
   1888. An account of the Peasants' Revolt of 1381.   975

Morris, William. The Dream of John Ball. Longmans, 1888.
   The awakening of social consciousness in the insurrection
   that had Jack Ball, Jack Straw, and Wat Tyler as leaders. 976

Muddock, J. E. Preston. Jane Shore. Long, 1905. A romance
   of the charming and notorious Jane Shore.   977

Newbolt, Henry. The New June. Dutton, 1909. The reigns
   of Richard II and Henry IV, ending with the Battle of
   Shrewsbury.   978

Oakeshott, Ronald. The Merchant at Arms. Longmans, 1920.
   Career of an English merchant in the late fifteenth century. 979

Palmer, Marian. The White Boar. Doubleday, 1968. Sympathetic account of Richard III and his loyal followers during the
   Wars of the Roses and the actions he took to secure the
   throne. (followed by The Wrong Plantagenet)   980

_____. The Wrong Plantagenet. Doubleday, 1972. Was
   this pretender to the English throne one of the young princes
   supposedly murdered in the Tower by their uncle, Richard
   III, or was he the low-born Perkin Warbeck?   981

Phelps, Charles Edward. The Accolade. Lippincott, 1905.
   Chaucer's travels on the Continent as an English diplomat. 982

Powers, Anne. Ride East! Ride West! Bobbs, 1947. England and Ireland during the Hundred Years War.   983

_____. Ride With Danger. Bobbs, 1958. YA. This is
   the author's book Ride East, Ride West (listed above) about
   Irish spy Thomas Gilman, rewritten for young readers.   984

Powys, John Cowper. Owen Glendower. S. & S., 1940.
About the famous leader of the Welsh bid for independence. 985

Pyle, Howard. Men of Iron. Harper, 1919. YA. A young
man attains knighthood and avenges his father, who was
wrongly accused of treason.   986

Raine, Allen, pseud. Hearts of Wales. Hutchinson, 1905.
Events in the period of Owen Glendower and the Welsh rebellion against Henry IV.   987

Rhys, Ernest. The Whistling Maid. Hutchinson, 1900. Pictures South Wales, Lord Mortimer, and Queen Isabella at
the time of Edward II.   988

Richings, Emily. In Chaucer's Maytime. Unwin, 1902. About
Chaucer, his wife, and his sister-in-law, Katherine, wife of
John of Gaunt.   989

_____. White Roseleaves. Drane, 1912. Court life center-
ing on the queen of Edward IV of York.   990

Ridge, Antonia. The Royal Pawn. [En. title: The Thirteenth
Child] Appleton, 1963, c.1962. A story of Catherine of Valois, consort and widow of Henry V of England.   991

Schuster, Rose. The Triple Crown. Chapman, 1912. Henry
VI, his unpopular marriage to Margaret of Anjou, and his
insanity.   992

Scott, John Reed. Beatrix of Clare. Lippincott, 1907. Shows
Richard III as a strong king in an unsettled era.   993

Seibert, Elizabeth. White Rose and Ragged Staff. Bobbs, 1968.
YA. A young girl in London is drawn into the struggle for
the English crown during the Wars of the Roses.   994

Seton, Anya. Katherine. Houghton, 1954. The romance of
John of Gaunt and Katherine Swynford, Chaucer's sister-in-
law.   995

Shelley, Mary. The Fortunes of Perkin Warbeck. Routledge,
1830. About Perkin Warbeck, who claimed to be the lost
Duke of York with a right to the English crown.   996

Simon, Edith. The Golden Hand. Putnam, 1952. Chronicle of the Widowson family in feudal England.   997

Stevenson, Robert Louis. The Black Arrow. Dutton, 1958.
YA. (orig. pub. 18--) A tale of knighthood and chivalric
romance during the Wars of the Roses.   998

Trease, Geoffrey. Snared Nightingale. Vanguard, 1958.

Youth raised in Italy goes to England to claim an earldom
on the Welsh border.   999

Treece, Henry. Ride Into Danger. Criterion, 1959. YA. A
young soldier learns, in the battle of Crécy, how to protect
his home and family from marauding Welsh and a scheming
neighbor.   1000

Tyler-Whittle, Michael Sidney. Richard III: The Last Plantagenet. by Tyler Whittle. Chilton, 1970. [pub. in 1968 as
The Last Plantagenet] This novel gives a picture of Richard
III as a loyal brother, a brave warrior, and a popular king--
not at all the same as Shakespeare's portrayal.   1001

Vance, Marguerite. Song for a Lute. Dutton, 1958. YA. The
tragic marriage of Richard III and Anne Neville, political intrigue, and the controversial character of Richard are the
theme of this novel.   1002

Warner, Sylvia Townsend. The Corner That Held Them.
Viking, 1948. A tapestry of convent life from the Black
Death to the Peasants' Revolt.   1003

Wheeler, Thomas Gerald. All Men Tall. Phillips, 1969. YA.
A young man works with Hugh the Armourer to develop new
weapons--for the Battle of Crécy.   1004

Widgery, Jeanne Anne. Trumpet at the Gates. by Jan Widgery.
Doubleday, 1970. A young man searches for the real meaning of honor and loyalty in the political upheaval resulting
from contention for the throne between Richard II and Henry
IV.   1005

Willard, Barbara. The Lark and the Laurel. Harcourt, 1970.
YA. When her father must flee an accusation of treachery,
a girl learns a new way of life and solves a life-long mystery.   1006

Woods, William Howard. Riot at Gravesend. Duell, 1952.
Swift, eventful story of Wat Tyler's Rebellion.   1007

2) Scotland and Ireland

Buchan, John. The Riding of Ninemileburn. Blackwood,
1912. Involvement of innocent farmers in a Scottish border
quarrel.   1008

Crockett, Samuel R. The Black Douglas. Doubleday, 1899.
Beheading of William, Earl of Douglas, and his brother in
the reign of the Scotch boy-king, James II. (followed by
Maid Margaret of Galloway)   1009

_____. **Maid Margaret of Galloway.** Dodd, 1905. The
family tragedy of the "Fair Maid of Galloway," wife of the
murdered eighth Earl of Douglas.   1010

Douglas, William A. **Long John Murray.** Coward, 1936. Story
of the descendants of Long John Murray, a Scotch Presbyter-
ian who settled in Ulster in the time of James I of Scotland.
                                                              1011
Ferguson, Dugald. **The King's Friend.** Gardner, 1907. The
war for Scottish Independence at the time of the early
Edwards.   1012

Fremantle, Anne. **James and Joan.** Holt, 1948. James I of
Scotland spent his youth as a prisoner in England, where he
married Joan Beaufort.   1013

Galt, John. **The Spaewife.** Oliver & Boyd (Scotland), 1823.
Tale of the early fifteenth century based on Scottish chronicles.   1014

Hamilton, Ernest. **The Mawkin of the Flow.** Unwin, 1898.
Romance of a peasant girl in fifteenth century Scotland.   1015

Hibbert, Eleanor. **The Thistle and the Rose.** by Jean Plaidy,
pseud. Hale, 1963. The marriage-of-state of twelve-year-
old Margaret Tudor and James IV of Scotland.   1016

Hill, Pamela. **Marjorie of Scotland.** Putnam, 1956. Concerns
a little-known princess, the daughter of Robert the Bruce. 1017

Knowles, Mabel Winifred. **A King's Tragedy.** by May Wynne,
pseud. Long, 1905. The conspiracy of Graham and the
assassination of James I of Scotland.   1018

Lenanton, Carola Oman. **King Heart.** by Carola Oman. Fisher
Unwin, 1926. Set in Scotland at the time of James IV.   1019

Muddock, J. E. Preston. **Kate Cameron of Brux.** Digby &
Long, 1900. A deadly feud between rival Scottish clans.   1020

O'Byrne, Miss M. L. **Art MacMurrough Kavanagh, Prince of
Leinster.** Simpkin, 1885. Reaction of an independent Irish
chieftain to Richard II's offer of knighthood.   1021

Oliver, Jane, pseud. for Rees, Helen Christina Easson. **The
Lion Is Come.** Putnam, 1957. Pictures the life and times
of Robert the Bruce, king of Scotland.   1022

Powers, Anne. **The Gallant Years.** Bobbs, 1946. Life in Ireland in the fourteenth century.   1023

Scott, Sir Walter. **Castle Dangerous.** Munro, 1885. As a
condition of marriage, a youth is bidden to defend Douglas

Castle, which has changed hands repeatedly.   1024

_____. The Fair Maid of Perth. Munro, 1885. The turbu-
lent Scotland of Robert III, torn by strife of nobles and feuds
of clans.   1025

Simpson, Evan John. Crippled Splendour. by Evan John, pseud.
Dutton, 1938. James I of Scotland from his imprisonment in
England to his assassination in 1437.   1026

Willard, Rachel. Catherine Douglas. Jarrold & Sons, 1905.
Instability in Scotland during the reign of the well-intentioned
James I.   1027

b) Western and Central Europe

1) France

Angellotti, Marion Polk. The Burgundian. Century, 1912.
Concerns international tensions caused by the insanity of King
Charles VI.   1028

Atkinson, Henry H. The King's Favourite. Allen, 1912. Tale
of the French court during the early reign of Louis XI.   1029

Bailey, H.C. Knight at Arms. Dutton, 1925. Events after
the youthful Charles VIII assumed the throne of France.   1030

Baring-Gould, S. Noémi. Appleton, 1894. Domestic conditions
and struggles between England and France in the time of
Charles VII.   1031

Bataille, Michel. Fire From Heaven. (tr.) Crown, 1967. Life
of a fifteenth century Bluebeard, Gilles de Rais, as seen by
a modern screenwriter.   1032

Beevers, John. Saint Joan of Arc. Hanover, 1959. YA. Joan
of Arc's mission in the service of France, her subsequent
imprisonment, trial, and execution.   1033

Bowen, Marjorie, pseud. for Gabrielle Campbell Long. The
Leopard and the Lily. Doubleday, Page, 1909. An account
of Civil War in Brittany, full of romance and passion.   1034

Bray, Anna Eliza. The White Hoods. Chapman & Hall, 1884.
Philip van Artevelde's revolt of 1381-2 against the Count of
Flanders.   1035

Butler, Mildred Allen. Twice Queen of France. Funk, 1967.
YA. Anne of Brittany, to protect the independence of her
province, had happy marriages with two successive kings of
France.   1036

Carton, Jacques. La Belle Sorel. (tr.) Washburn, 1956. A biographical novel of Agnes Sorel, who was the mistress of Charles VII. 1037

Catherwood, Mary H. The Days of Jeanne d'Arc. Century, 1897. About Jeanne d'Arc with emphasis on the important years, 1429-31. 1038

Comstock, Seth Cook. Marcelle the Mad. Appleton, 1906. A feminine counterpart of Robin Hood in the forests of France. 1039

Costain, Thomas B. The Moneyman. Doubleday, 1951. Influence of a wealthy merchant, Jacques Coeur, on trade and politics in the reign of Charles VII. 1040

Deeping, Warwick. Bertrand of Brittany. Harper, 1908. Incidents in the life of the clever Bertrand du Guesclin, military leader for Charles V. 1041

Deutsch, Babette. Rogue's Legacy. Coward, 1942. François Villon, the gay thief who brought sensitive poetry out of sordid surroundings. 1042

Doyle, Sir Arthur Conan. Sir Nigel. McClure, 1906. The adventures of an Englishman abroad at the time of the Black Death; the Battle of Poitiers. (followed by The White Company) 1043

_____. The White Company. Caldwell, 1890. A company of English bowmen fighting in France and Castile. 1044

Drummond, Hamilton. Chattels. Paul, 1922. The hard lot of French peasants in the reigns of Charles VII-Louis XI. 1045

_____. A King's Scapegoat. Ward & Lock, 1905. Attempt of the power-greedy Louis XI to seize the heir to Foix and his possessions. 1046

_____. A Lord of the Soil. Ward & Lock, 1902. The feudal period, depicting monastic life and conditions among the peasants. 1047

_____. The Seven Houses. Stokes, 1901. Astrology figures prominently in this story of a girl's life. 1048

Druon, Maurice, pseud. for Maurice Kessel. The Iron King. (tr.) Scribner, 1956. Romantic, political, religious, and financial conflicts at the court of Philip the Fair. (The Accursed Kings--v. 1) 1049

_____. The Lily and the Lion. (tr.) Scribner, 1962, c.1961. Struggles for power both in France and England concerning Philippe of Valois, Edward III, Robert of Artois,

Mahaut, and Roger Mortimer. (The Accursed Kings--v. 6
& last, containing a bibliography for the whole series)   1050

_____. The Poisoned Crown. (tr.) Scribner, 1957. The
ill-fated marriage of Louis X and his consort Clémence.
(The Accursed Kings--v. 3)   1051

_____. The Royal Succession. (tr.) Scribner, 1958.
Maneuvering for succession among sons of Philip the Fair
and Louis X. (The Accursed Kings--v. 4)   1052

_____. The She-Wolf of France. (tr.) Scribner, 1961. The
fortunes of Isabella of France, consort of Edward II of England. (The Accursed Kings--v. 5)   1053

_____. The Strangled Queen. (tr.) Scribner, 1957. Con-
cerns part of the brief reign of the weak Louis X, "the Self-
Willed." (The Accursed Kings--v. 2)   1054

Gamo, Jean. The Golden Chain. (tr.) McKay, 1958, Purported manuscript by the squire of a doughty knight, telling
of valorous deeds and romantic intrigue.   1055

Hawtrey, Valentina. Peronelle. Lane, 1904. Compelling story
of the common people of Paris in the fifteenth century.   1056

_____. Suzanne. Holt, 1906. A story of France and
Flanders including an account of Philip van Artevelde's revolt of 1381.   1057

Hewlett, Maurice. The Countess of Picpus. Scribner, 1911.
The adventures of Captain Brazenhead, who pretends to be
a count.   1058

Hugo, Victor. The Hunchback of Notre Dame. (tr.) [same as
Notre Dame de Paris] Bentley, 1833. The classic, tragic
story of Quasimodo, the bellringer of the Cathedral, who
loves Esmeralda, a beautiful gypsy girl.   1059

James, G. P. R. The Jacquerie. Dutton, 1841. The Peasants'
Insurrection in France in 1358.   1060

James, Grace. Joan of Arc. Dutton, 1910. Gives an account
of the period and trends which influenced Joan.   1061

Jefferies, Ian. A Kingdom for a Song. by Ira J. Morris,
pseud. Dutton, 1963. The adventures, romantic and military, of Charles, Duke of Burgundy and master of the Low
Countries.   1062

Kaye, Michael W. The Duke's Vengeance. Greening, 1910.
The scheming of Louis XI against the Dukes of Burgundy and
Guienne.   1063

Knowles, Mabel Winifred. A Maid of Brittany. by May Wynne,
pseud. Greening, 1906. The hatred between Bretons and
French is typified in the conflict between the Dutchess Anne
and Charles VIII.   1064

_____. The Tailor of Vitre. by May Wynne, pseud. Gay
& Hancock, 1908. A narrative disclosing "the power behind
the throne" in Brittany.   1065

Koningsberger, Hans. A Walk With Love and Death. S. & S.,
1961. Romance of two doomed young lovers during peasant
uprisings in the fourteenth century in France.   1066

Lang, Andrew. A Monk of Fife. Longmans, 1895. The tale of
a Scotsman in France during the period of the valorous Jeanne
d'Arc.   1067

Leslie, Doris. Vagabond's Way. Doubleday, 1962. Intimate
details concerning the dissolute and unconventional life of the
gifted poet François Villon.   1068

McCarthy, Justin Huntly. The Flower of France. Harper, 1906.
Concerns Jeanne d'Arc and her services to France.   1069

_____. (1) If I Were King. Harper, 1902. (2) Needles
and Pins (sequel). Harper, 1907. Two light romances
loosely based on the career of François Villon, beggar-
poet.   1070-1

McComas, Ina Violet. The Mark of Vraye. by H.B. Somerville, pseud. Hutchinson, 1917. Revolt of the nobles against
Pierre Landais in Brittany.   1072

Merliss, Reuben. The Year of the Death. Doubleday, 1965.
A young physician who seeks to determine the cause of the
Black Death experiences the heavy hand of the Inquisition.   1073

Morley, Iris. The Proud Paladin. Morrow, 1936. The powerful, lovely Duchess of Montpellier and an English military
captain.   1074

Neumann, Alfred. The Devil. (tr.) Knopf, 1928. The influence of his barber on superstitious King Louis XI.   1075

Potter, Margaret Horton. The Castle of Twilight. McClurg,
1903. The feudal period in Brittany, showing the status of
women.   1076

Rickert, Edith. Golden Hawk. Baker & Taylor, 1907. Provence and Avignon during the Avignon residence of the Papacy.   1077

Ridding, Laura. By Weeping Cross. Hodder, 1899. Rural

life in southern France during the fifteenth century.   1078

Schoonover, Lawrence. The Burnished Blade. Macmillan, 1948.
Adventure-packed life of a young Frenchman who witnessed
the death of Jeanne d'Arc.   1079

_____. The Spider King. Macmillan, 1954. Pictures Louis
XI, the "spider" who reached out for lands on all sides.   1080

Scott, Sir Walter. Anne of Geierstein. Harper, 1829.
Swiss involvement in the conflict of Louis XI and Charles
the Bold.   1081

_____. Quentin Durward. Constable, 1823. A Scottish
archer in the service of Louis XI.   1082

Stuart, Dorothy M. Martin the Mummer. Constable, 1910.
The court of Burgundy is the scene of a masquerade in the
time of Philip the Good.   1083

_____. St. Lo. Holden, 1912. Life of a noble at the time
of Louis XI, Pope Sixtus IV, and Emperor Maximilian.   1084

Symons, Beryl. A Lady of France. Paul, 1910. A romance
showing life during the reign of Philip the Fair.   1085

Vansittart, Peter. The Lost Lands. Walker, 1964. The
struggles of a feudal lord to hold and defend his land in the
time of Philip the Fair.   1086

_____. The Tournament. Walker, 1961, c.1959. Colorful
pageantry and chivalrous customs contrast with poverty and
plague in fifteenth century France.   1087

2) The Empire and Central Europe (including the Germanies,
    Netherlands, Switzerland, Poland, and Hungary)

Baker, James. The Cardinal's Page. Chapman & Hall, 1898.
Henry Beaufort is the Cardinal in this story of the Hussites
in Bohemia. (companion volume to The Gleaming Dawn)   1088

_____. The Gleaming Dawn. Chapman & Hall, 1896. Based
on the Wycliffite Movement in England and especially the Huss-
ite Wars in Bohemia. (companion volume to The Cardinal's
Page)   1089

Barr, Robert. The Sword Maker. by Luke Sharp, pseud.
Stokes, 1910. Germany at the time of Rudolf of Hapsburg's
death, showing the power of Prince Roland and the Robber

Barons of the Rhine.   1090

Bertram, Paul. The Fifth Trumpet. Lane, 1912. The background is the great ecumenical Council of Constance.   1091

Crockett, Samuel R. Joan of the Sword-Hand. Dodd, 1900.
Exploits of a north German princess in the fifteenth century.
                                                             1092
Feuchtwanger, Lion. The Ugly Duchess. (tr.) Viking, 1928.
A striking picture of central European life and events, with
Margarete of Tyrol as heroine.   1093

Fisher, F. Hope. Written in the Stars. Harper, 1951. A
novel of Albrecht Dürer in the city of Nuremberg.   1094

Grattan, Thomas C. Jacqueline of Holland. Colburn & Bentley,
1831. A tale of Jacoba, Countess of Hainault and Holland. 1095

Häring, Wilhelm. The Burgomaster of Berlin. (tr.) by Wilibald Alexis, pseud. Saunders & Otley, 1843. Frederick's
attempts to smooth strained relations between nobles and
townspeople.   1096

James, G. P. R. Mary of Burgundy. Dutton, 1833. The daughter of Charles the Bold and her marriage to Maximilian of
Austria.   1097

Kelly, Eric P. From Star to Star. Lippincott, 1944. Students
at the University of Cracow--one of whom was Copernicus. 1098

Kingsley, Henry. Old Margaret. Longmans, 1871. Portrays
the growth of art and trade in the Netherlands under Philip
the Good of Burgundy.   1099

Laughlin, Clara Elizabeth. Heart of Her Highness. Putnam,
1917. The struggle of Mary of Burgundy for a happy marriage.   1100

Lennep, Jacob van. The Rose of Dekama. (tr.) Bruce & Wyld,
1847. Set in Holland in the turbulent times of William IV. 1101

Maass, Edgar. Magnificent Enemies. Scribner, 1955. Flaring action as the Hanseatic League's power is challenged by
merchant seamen.   1102

Major, Charles. Yolanda, Maid of Burgundy. Macmillan, 1905.
Tells of Mary, daughter of Charles the Bold, and Maximilian,
son of Emperor Frederick.   1103

Mellor, Dora. Bewitched. Drane, 1922. The German Empire
in the troubled days of the Hussites.   1104

Mills, Lois. So Young a Queen. Lothrop, 1961. YA. The
    lavish splendor of the court of King Louis of Hungary, father
    of Jadwiga, is the background for her romance, marriage,
    and accession as Queen.   1105

Reade, Charles. The Cloister and the Hearth. Dodd, 1861.
    A travelogue of western Europe in the fifteenth century with
    the father of Erasmus as hero.   1106

Rosegger, Peter. The Godseeker. (tr.) Putnam, 1902. Ac-
    count of a religious crime with descriptions of pagan cere-
    monies.   1107

Ross, Ronald. The Revels of Orsera. Murray, 1920. Romantic
    novel depicting Switzerland in 1495.   1108

Sienkiewicz, Henryk. The Knights of the Cross. (tr.) Little,
    1897. Struggles of Poland and Lithuania against aggressive
    Teutonic Knights.   1109

3) Scandinavia and the Baltic

Rydberg, Viktor. Singoalla. (tr.) Scott, 1904. Sweden at
    the time of the Black Death, showing survivals of heathen-
    ism and superstition.   1110

Undset, Sigrid. Kristin Lavransdatter. (tr.) Knopf, 1929.
    [Contains: The Bridal Wreath. Knopf, 1923. The Mistress
    of Husaby. Knopf, 1925. The Cross. Knopf, 1927] The
    dramatic account of a woman's life in fourteenth century
    Norway.   1111

c) Southern Europe

1) Iberian Peninsula

Ardagh, W. M. The Knightly Years. Lane, 1912. Spain and
    the Canary Islands at the time of Ferdinand and Isabella. 1112

_____. The Magada. Lane, 1910. A romance of the Span-
    ish conquest of the Canary Islands.   1113

Aronin, Ben. The Moor's Gold. Argus, 1935. A novel of the
    Spanish Inquisition and its persecution of the Jews.   1114

Drummond, Hamilton. The Grain of Mustard. Paul, 1916.
    A young lady's experiences during the Spanish conquest of
    Granada.   1115

Dumas, Alexandre. Agénor de Mauléon. (tr.) Little, 1897.
    The international conflict over the rule of Pedro the Cruel

of Castile.   1116

Eça de Queiroz, José María de. <u>Our Lady of the Pillar.</u> (tr.)
Constable, 1906. Mystery, romance, and passion combine
to make a thrilling story.   1117

Fast, Howard. <u>Torquemada.</u> Doubleday. 1966. The Prior of
Segovia is appointed Grand Inquisitor of Spain and given the
duty of removing heretics, even when his friends are accused.
                                                                           1118

Gerson, Noel B. <u>Master of Castile.</u> by Samuel Edwards, <u>pseud.</u>
Morrow, 1962. About Alvaro de Luna, a Spanish nobleman's
natural son, who acted as regent for the King of Castile, Juan
II.   1119

Haggard, H. Rider. <u>Fair Margaret.</u> Longmans, 1907. Experiences of a young Jewess with the Inquisition in Spain.   1120

Hamilton, Bernard. <u>His Queen.</u> Hutchinson, 1927. Imaginative
account of the friendship between Queen Isabella and Columbus.
                                                                           1121
Hibbert, Eleanor. <u>Castile for Isabella.</u> by Jean Plaidy, <u>pseud.</u>
Hale, 1960. Life of Isabella of Spain to her accession to the
throne of Castile.   1122

_____. <u>Isabella and Ferdinand.</u> by Jean Plaidy, <u>pseud.</u>
Hale, 1970. An omnibus volume containing three previously
published novels: <u>Castile for Isabella;</u> <u>Spain for the Sover-</u>
<u>eigns</u> (both listed separately); and <u>Daughters of Spain.</u>   1123

_____. <u>Spain for the Sovereigns.</u> by Jean Plaidy, <u>pseud.</u>
Hale, 1960. The story of Queen Isabella from the time of
her accession to the return of Columbus in triumph.   1124

Humphreys, Jeanne. <u>The Count Without Castles.</u> Duell, 1956.
The love of Pedro the Cruel, King of Castile, for María and
her reaction.   1125

Kesten, Hermann. <u>Ferdinand and Isabella.</u> Wyn, 1946. Story
of the "Catholic Monarchs" who ruled Spain with such success.
                                                                           1126
Lee, Albert. <u>The Black Disc.</u> Digby & Long, 1897. Moorish
power in Spain is contested by the armies of Ferdinand and
Isabella.   1127

Lytton, Edward Bulwer, 1st. baron. <u>Leila.</u> Dutton, 1838. The
Spanish Christian invasion of Moorish Granada.   1128

Miller, Elizabeth. <u>Daybreak.</u> Scribner, 1915. Romance of a
niece of Ferdinand and Isabella with a youth in a voyage led
by Columbus.   1129

Paterson, Isabel. The Singing Season. Boni & Liveright, 1924.
Spain in the period of Pedro the Cruel of Castile.   1130

Richings, Emily. Broken at the Fountain. Heath Cranton, 1916.
Royal romance and violence in fourteenth century Portugal. 1131

Sabatini, Rafael. Columbus, a Romance. Houghton, 1942. A
story of Columbus which emphasizes his personality and romance with Beatriz Enriquez.   1132

Schoonover, Lawrence. Key of Gold. Little, 1968. Jewish doctors in three different generations in Spain, Holland, and America in the fifteenth, seventeenth, and eighteenth centuries. 1133

_____. The Queen's Cross. Sloane, 1955. Isabella of Spain
as a woman and as a queen.   1134

Slaughter, Frank G. The Mapmaker. Doubleday, 1957. About
an actual Venetian mapmaker and the days of Prince Henry
the Navigator.   1135

Snaith, John Collis. Fortune. Moffatt, 1910. Adventures of
an English knight in Spain and France.   1136

2) Italy and Adjacent Islands

Anderson, Arthur J. His Magnificence. Paul, 1913. Story of
Lorenzo de Medici from 1478 to his death in 1492, supposedly told by a contemporary.   1137

_____. The Romance of Fra Filippo Lippi. Paul, 1909.
The romance of the gifted painter and a nun.   1138

_____. The Romance of Sandro Botticelli. Paul, 1912.
Based on the life of artist Botticelli with some reference to
the influence of reformer Savonarola.   1139

Andrewes, A.G. In the Days of Lorenzo the Magnificent. Foulis,
1924. Political activities of the powerful Lorenzo de Medici.   1140

Andrews, Marian. Felicita. by Christopher Hare, pseud.
Stokes, 1909. A romance of Siena during the time of the
Black Death, illustrated with photographs.   1141

Bailey, H.C. Springtime. [same as: Under Castle Walls]
Appleton, 1906. A romance of Lombardy at the time of
Boccaccio--a time of passion and superstition.   1142

Borden, Lucille Papin. White Hawthorn. Macmillan, 1935.
Romance in the days of Petrarch and Boccaccio.   1143

Bowen, Marjorie, pseud. for Gabrielle Campbell Long. The
Carnival of Florence. Dutton, 1915. Based on the rise
and fall of Savonarola.   1144

_____. The Sword Decides. McClure, 1908. Story of Joanna
of Naples and her unfortunate husband, Andrea of Hungary.   1145

_____. The Viper of Milan. Penguin, 1963, c.1906. Wars
between the Count of Milan and the free towns of northern
Italy.   1146

Capes, Bernard. Bembo; A Tale of Italy. [same as: A Jay of
Italy] Dutton, 1906. About a zealous youth who preaches in
the court of the cruel Galeazzo Sforza, Duke of Milan.   1147

_____. The Love Story of St. Bel. Methuen, 1909. A story
of Siena in 1374 with St. Catherine as the central figure. 1148

Carter, Barbara Barclay. Ship Without Sails. Dutton, 1934.
Based on the life of Dante during his composition of the
Divine Comedy.   1149

Crawford, F. Marion. Marietta: A Maid of Venice. Macmillan, 1901. Romance of a glass blower's daughter with
one of his workmen.   1150

Cronquist, Mabel. Bianca. Putnam, 1956. Political events during the heyday of the Medici family.   1151

De Wohl, Louis. Lay Siege to Heaven. Lippincott, 1961. Story
of St. Catherine of Siena, one of the fourteenth century's outstanding personages.   1152

Drummond, Hamilton. Maker of Saints. Dutton, 1920. A tale
of the peasant-artist Fieravanti, sculptor of saints, at the
time of Dante.   1153

_____. Sir Galahad of the Army. Paul, 1913. Adventures
of a soldier in the army of the French King Charles VIII during his Italian campaign.   1154

Eliot, George, pseud. for Mary Ann Evans. Romola. Unwin,
1863. Contrast between good and evil sides of Florentine
life during the Renaissance.   1155

Faust, Frederick. Firebrand. by George Challis, pseud.
Harper, 1950. Excitement and adventure in Renaissance
Italy.   1156

Formont, Maxime. The She-Wolf. Paul, 1913. Features exploits of the capable, ruthless Cesare Borgia.   1157

Gallizier, Nathan. The Leopard Prince. Page, 1920. A novel

filled with political and romantic intrigues.   1158

Gaunt, Richard. Blood for a Borgia. Roy, 1968. A picture of
politics and warfare in fifteenth century Rome and Italy, including members of the notorious Borgia family.   1159

George, Arthur. The House of Eyes. Gay & Hancock, 1913.
Intrigues focus on the Lady Valentine Visconti, daughter of
the Duke of Milan.   1160

Goodwin, Ernest. Duchess of Siona. Houghton, 1919. A tale
of suitors for the hand of the lovely young Duchess of an
Italian principality.   1161

Green, Anne. Lady in the Mask. Harper, 1942. A bright panorama of Renaissance Italy with a charming rogue as hero.   1162

Grossi, Tommaso. Marco Visconti. (tr.) Macmillan, 1881.
Feuds between Guelfs and Ghibellines in Italy in the period
of discord between Emperor Frederick II and the Pope.   1163

Hewes, Agnes D. Swords on the Sea. Knopf, 1928. Venetian
romance, trade, and warfare in the fourteenth century.   1164

Hewlett, Maurice. Brazenhead the Great. Smith & Elder, 1911.
About a professional killer in the service of the Duke of Milan.   1165

_____. The Love Chase. Harper, 1905. Three men seek
the hand of a lady-in-waiting to the Duchess of Milan.   1166

Hibbert, Eleanor. Light on Lucrezia. by Jean Plaidy, pseud.
Hale, 1958. Matrimonial ventures of Lucrezia Borgia, who
was esteemed for her beauty and goodness once she escaped
her family's influence.   1167

James, G.P.R. Leonora d'Orco. Dutton, 1857. Has as background the French King Charles VIII's invasion of Italy and
his marriage to Anne of Brittany.   1168

James, Katherine. A City of Contrasts. Chapman & Hall,
1913. A study of Renaissance Florence where art and culture flourished.   1169

Kenny, Louise M. Stacpoole. At the Court of Il Moro. Long,
1912. Pictures Milanese society under Ludovico Sforza (Il
Moro) and includes Leonardo da Vinci.   1170

Knowles, Mabel Winifred. The Master Wit. by May Wynne,
pseud. Greening, 1911. The creative mind of Boccaccio
is at work in a friend's behalf in this romance of Florence. 1171

Knowles-Foster, Frances G. Jehanne of the Golden Lips.

Lane, 1910. The magnificent court of Joanna, Queen of
Naples and Sicily, where Boccaccio was a visitor.   1172

Ladd, Anna Coleman. Hieronymus Rides. Macmillan, 1912.
Episodes in the life of a knight and jester at the court of
his half-brother, Maximilian.   1173

Lance, Rupert. The Crowning Hour. Blackwood, 1910. Romance and adventure in medieval Italy.   1174

Livingston, Margaret Vere Farrington. Fra Lippo Lippi.
by Margaret Vere Farrington. Putnam, 1890. Based on the
life of this famous fifteenth century artist.   1175

Long, William. Sword of Il Grande. by Will Creed, pseud.
Little, 1948. Politics and swordplay in fifteenth century
Florence.   1176

Lytton, Edward Bulwer, 1st. baron. Rienzi, the Last of the
Tribunes. Macmillan, 1835. The political situation in fourteenth century Italy which did not favor Rienzi's dream of a
united Italy.   1177

Maugham, H. Neville. Richard Hawkwood. Blackwood, 1906.
Features Lorenzo de Medici and the notorious Pazzi Conspiracy (1477).   1178

Muddock, J.E. Preston. The Scarlet Seal. Long, n.d. A
complicated tale of the notorious Borgia family.   1179

Osborne, Duffield. The Angels of Messer Ercole. Stokes, 1907.
Italy in the later fifteenth century at the time of the Umbrian
painter Perugino.   1180

Rolfe, Frederick W. Don Tarquinio. Chatto, 1905. Customs,
manners, and events in Rome at the time of the Borgias.   1181

Sabatini, Rafael. Bellarion. Houghton, 1926. Fast-paced story
of a young man's career in and about Milan.   1182

_____. Chivalry. Houghton, 1935. Interplay of sword and
poison in fifteenth century Italy.   1183

Samuel, Maurice. Web of Lucifer. Knopf, 1947. Tapestry of
Renaissance Italy with Cesare Borgia as villain.   1184

Scollard, Clinton. The Cloistering of Ursula. Page, 1902.
Imaginary memoirs of the Marquis of Ucelli in central Italy. 1185

_____. A Man-at-Arms. Page, 1898. Gian Galeazzo Vis-
conti, Duke of Milan, and his wars with free Italian cities. 1186

Scudder, Vida O. The Disciple of a Saint. Dutton, 1907. This

purported biography of her secretary tells of St. Catherine
of Siena.   1187

Shellabarger, Samuel. Prince of Foxes. Little, 1947. How
Cesare Borgia's power affected the lives of many people.   1188

Shelley, Mary. Valperga. Whittaker, 1823. Romances of Cas-
truccio Castracani, Duke of Lucca.   1189

Stowe, Harriet Beecher. Agnes of Sorrento. Houghton, 1862.
Romance of a pious girl and an irreligious man during the
time of Savonarola's preaching.   1190

Turnbull, Francese Hubbard. The Royal Pawn of Venice. by
Mrs. Lawrence Turnbull. Lippincott, 1911. The marriage
of Caterina Cornaro of Venice and King James II of Cyprus. 1191

Unruh, Fritz von. The Saint. (tr.) Random House, 1950. A
biographical novel of the fourteenth century Italian mystic, St.
Catherine of Siena.   1192

Warde, Evelyn B. Elena. Simpkin, 1910. Cesare Borgia and
his sister Lucrezia figure in this tale of the time of Charles
VIII's invasion.   1193

Westcott, Jan. Condottiere. Random House, 1962. The strong
mercenary captain Bartolomeo Colleoni who laid siege to the
heart of aristocratic Tisbe de Martinengo after their marriage
at her father's orders.   1194

_____. The White Rose. Putnam, 1969. The rise, reign,
and troubles of Edward IV, telling of his unpopular, stormy
love affair with Elizabeth Woodville.   1195

Williams, Egerton R., Jr. Ridolfo. McClurg, 1906. Based
on the history of the notorious Baglioni family of Perugia. 1196

d)   Eastern Europe (including the Byzantine Empire, the
     Balkans, and Russia), the Near East, and North Africa

Crawford, F. Marion. Arethusa. Macmillan, 1907. Account
of life in Constantinople in the late fourteenth century.   1197

McCarthy, Justin Huntly. The Dryad. Harper, 1905. A fantasy of the romance of a Dryad whose love made her mortal.
                                                             1198
Morrison, Lester M. and Richard G. Hubler. Trial & Triumph.
Crown, 1965. Eventful life of Maimonides, the famous Jewish philosopher, theologian, and medical doctor who eventually became Saladin's physician.   1199

Motta, Luigi. Flames on the Bosphorus. (tr.) Odhams Press,

1920. Struggle between Turks and Christians culminating in
the Ottoman capture of Constantinople.   1200

Neale, John Mason. Theodora Phranza. S. P. C. K., 1857.
Romance and war during the siege of Constantinople by the
Turks.   1201

O'Neal, Cothburn. Master of the World. Crown, 1952. The
military and romantic conquests of Timur the Great (Tamer-
lane), ruler of Samarkand in the fourteenth century.   1202

Schoonover, Lawrence. The Gentle Infidel. Macmillan, 1950.
The richness of medieval Turkey and the siege of Constantinople.   1203

Waltari, Mika. The Dark Angel. (tr.) Putnam, 1953. The
fall of Constantinople with a vivid account of the siege.   1204

e) Overseas Exploration, Enterprise,
   and Expansion

Baumann, Hans. The Barque of the Brothers. (tr.) Walck,
1958. YA. Two boys from a fishing village join an expedition planned by Prince Henry the Navigator down the coast
of Africa.   1205

_____. Son of Columbus. (tr.) Oxford Univ. Pr., 1957.
YA. An account of Columbus' fourth voyage to the New
World as seen by his fourteen-year-old son.   1206

Belfrage, Cedric. My Master, Columbus. Doubleday, 1961.
An Indian woman who is a servant of Columbus gives a satirical anti-Christian account of the coming of the Spanish.   1207

Blasco-Ibañez, Vicente. Unknown Lands. (tr.) Dutton, 1929.
Features details of shipboard life during Columbus' first
voyage to America.   1208

Coatsworth, Elizabeth. Door to the North. Holt, 1950. YA.
An expedition of Norsemen to Greenland in the fourteenth
century.   1209

Cooper, James Fenimore. Mercedes of Castile. Lea & Blanchard, 1840. The loves of a companion of Columbus for a
Spanish maiden and an Indian princess.   1210

Engle, Eloise. Sea Challenge. C. S. Hammond, 1962. YA.
Two young men join Magellen's expedition and circumnavi-
gate the world.   1211

Forester, C. S. To the Indies. Little, 1940. The third voyage
made by Columbus to America and his career as viceroy of

the Indies.   1212

Jensen, Johannes Vilhelm. Christopher Columbus. (tr.)
     Knopf, 1924. Vivid re-creation of the famous voyage is the
     culmination of Mr. Jensen's trilogy of the wanderings of
     mankind.   1213

Johnston, Mary. 1492. [En. title: Admiral of the Ocean Sea]
     Little, 1922. Christopher Columbus from his first voyage
     until his death, as seen by one of his sailors.   1214

Kent, Louise Andrews. He Went With Christopher Columbus.
     Houghton, 1940. YA. The English deckboy on the Santa
     Maria sees Columbus as a loyal, dedicated, and religious
     man.   1215

_____ . He Went With Vasco da Gama. Houghton, 1938.
     YA. Two boys sail on the first voyage around Africa to
     India and encounter perverse weather, unfriendly natives,
     and mutinous sailors.   1216

Lytle, Andrew Nelson. At the Moon's Inn. Bobbs, 1941. Based
     on the life and adventures of Hernando de Soto.   1217

Street, James Howell. The Velvet Doublet. Doubleday, 1953.
     From the perils of the Inquisition to the glory of discovery
     with Columbus.   1218

Tourgée, Albion W. Out of the Sunset Sea. Merrill & Baker,
     1893. Supposed story of an English sailor on Columbus'
     expedition of 1492.   1219

              B.   ASIA, AFRICA, AND OCEANIA
              IN THE MIDDLE AGES (c. 400-1500)

1.   ASIA

     a) India

Anatanarayanan, Madavayya. The Silver Pilgrimage. (tr. ?)
     Criterion, 1961. A melancholy young prince and his com-
     panion are joined on a pilgrimage by assorted characters
     who travel with them, a la Canterbury Tales.   1220

Clifford, Hugh. The Downfall of the Gods. Dutton, 1911.
     Passionate romance combined with religious and political
     upheaval in the thirteenth century.   1221

Leighton, Margaret. Voyage to Coromandel. Farrar, 1965.
     YA. Two young Vikings travel from Alfred the Great's
     court to Rome and from there on a pilgrimage to Coro-
     mandel.   1222

Potter, Margaret Horton. The Flame-Gatherers. Macmillan,
   1904. A story of India before and during the Mohammedan
   Conquest of 1250.   1223

Steel, Flora Annie. King Errant. Stokes, 1912. Based on the
   life of Baber, founder of the Mogul Empire in India.   1224

b) China

Akutagawa, Ryunosuke. Tu Tze-Chun. (tr.) Kodansha Intl.,
   1965. A tale, based on a ninth century Chinese story, of
   a youth who spent his fortune in the quest of magical power.
                                                                     1225
Bauer, Wolfgang and Herbert Franke, ed. The Golden Casket.
   (tr.) Harcourt, 1964. Forty-six tales of Chinese ceremonial
   life and elegant society, written from the third century B.C.
   through the eighteenth century.   1226

Byrne, Donn. Messer Marco Polo. Century, 1921. The
   travels and exploits of Marco Polo in the Far and Near East,
   and his love for the daughter of Kublai Khan.   1227

Eaton, Evelyn. Go Ask the River. Harcourt, 1969. Rise
   of the lovely poetess Hung Tu from the position of a concubine
   in the "Blue House" to that of poet laureate of the province
   of Shu.   1228

Gulik, Robert Hans Van. The Chinese Bell Murders. Harper,
   1959, c.1958. Judge Dee, seventh century Chinese magistrate, uses deceptive suavity and shrewd deduction to solve
   murder mysteries.   1229

_____. The Chinese Lake Murders. Harper, 1960. The
   clever, exciting detective work of Judge Dee, confronted by
   puzzling murders.   1230

_____. The Chinese Gold Murders. Harper, 1961, c.1959.
   Judge Dee, magistrate of Pen-lai, continues his suspenseful
   detective work in the authentic atmosphere of seventh century China.   1231

_____. The Chinese Nail Murders. Harper, 1961. A story
   about three cases of master-detective Judge Dee, based on ancient Chinese plots.   1232

_____. The Emperor's Pearl. Scribner, 1964, c.1963.
   The murders of Lady Amber, a crew member of a dragon
   racing boat, and his associate are solved by Judge Dee.   1233

_____. The Haunted Monastery. Scribner, 1969, c.1961. Judge
   Dee discovers three crimes committed in a ghostly Chinese monastery, when he takes shelter there from a storm.   1234

_____. The Lacquer Screen. Scribner, 1970, c. 1962.
Judge Dee lives incognito in the underworld to find the answer to a complicated murder problem.   1235

_____. The Monkey and the Tiger. Scribner, 1966, c. 1965.
Two stories of seventh century China in which Judge Dee
solves murders by exposing robbery and smuggling: "The
Morning of the Monkey" and "The Night of the Tiger."   1236

_____. Murder in Canton. Scribner, 1967, c. 1966. An ar-
ray of fascinating characters figures in a detective story concerning the murder of an imperial official in Canton.   1237

_____. Necklace and Calabash. Heinemann, 1967. Detec-
tive Judge Dee is helped by a crippled Taoist sage in his
effort to recover the stolen necklace of the Third Princess. 1238

_____. The Phantom of the Temple. Scribner, 1966. Mur-
der, mystery, and hidden treasure in a Buddhist temple show
the different clothing and customs of seventh century China
but the same human emotions of all times.   1239

_____. Poets and Murder. Scribner, 1968. Seething pas-
sion erupts into murder in the seemingly calm surroundings
of the literary world and Judge Dee has another mystery to
solve.   1240

_____. The Red Pavilion. Scribner, 1968. Judge Dee fer-
rets out the reasons for a suicide and two murders at the
holiday resort, Paradise Island.   1241

_____. The Willow Pattern. Scribner, 1965. Three seem-
ingly unrelated murders of a merchant, a philanthropist, and
a serving girl are solved by Judge Dee.   1242

Kent, Louise Andrews. He Went With Marco Polo. Houghton,
1935. YA. A Venetian gondolier accompanied Marco Polo
on his journey to the court of Kublai Khan.   1243

Ko lien hua ying. Flower Shadows Behind the Curtain. (tr.)
Pantheon, 1959. Version of a classic Chinese novel concerning life in turbulent fourteenth century.   1244

Lane, Kenneth Westmacott. Winter Cherry. by Keith West,
pseud. Macmillan, 1944. Witty romance of the Emperor's
court in China in the eighth century.   1245

Lin, Yutang. Lady Wu. Putnam, 1965. Rise from obscurity
of a young woman who was determined to become Empress
of China in the seventh century.   1246

Marshall, Edison. Caravan to Xanadu. Farrar, 1953. Marco
Polo's travels to the exotic land of Kublai Khan.   1247

Wingate, Lititia Beryl. A Servant of the Mightiest. by Mrs.
Alfred Wingate. Lockwood, 1927. A stirring account of
Genghis Khan's conquests in China.   1248

c) Japan and Korea

Jennings, William Dale. The Ronin. Tuttle, 1968. A daring
twelfth century samurai mends his evil ways to become a
beloved hero.   1249

Stacton, David. Segaki. Pantheon, 1959. Depicts Buddhist
monasticism in fourteenth century Japan.   1250

Yoshikawa, Eiji. Heiké Story. (tr.) Knopf, 1956. A warrior
clan, the Heiké, in twelfth century Japan.   1251

d) Other Asiatic Peoples

Baumann, Hans. Sons of the Steppe. (tr.) Oxford Univ. Pr.,
1958, c.1957. YA. Two grandsons of Genghis Khan, trained
in his army, find they have different desires for war or
peace.   1252

Caldwell, Taylor (full name: Janet Taylor Caldwell). The
Earth is the Lord's. Scribner, 1941. The childhood and
early career of Genghis Kahn, portraying his skill in unit-
ing the Mongols.   1253

Clou, John. Caravan to Camul. Bobbs, 1954. The story of a
soldier and philosopher in the service of Jenghiz Khan.   1254

Collis, Maurice. She Was a Queen. Criterion, 1962. (orig.
pub. in En. in 1937) A village girl becomes Queen and
struggles to survive successive regimes in thirteenth century
Burma (founded on written Burmese history).   1255

Kneen, Eleanor. Lordless. Putnam, 1936. The life of Tamer-
lane's youngest wife after his death.   1256

Ritchie, Rita. The Golden Hawks of Genghis Khan. Dutton,
1958. YA. A youth finds answers to old problems and a
new purpose to life in the court of Genghis Khan.   1257

_____. The Year of the Horse. Dutton, 1957. YA. A
swiftly-moving tale of a boy and a horse told with a background of Mongol customs and warfare.   1258

2. AFRICA

[No entries in this section.   See sections II-A-1-d and II-A-2-d
for novels pertaining to North Africa during this period.]

3. OCEANIA

Michener, James A. Hawaii. Random, 1959. A panoramic
  novel of Hawaii and its successive inhabitants from eleven
  centuries ago to the present.   1259

C.   THE WESTERN HEMISPHERE
IN THE MIDDLE AGES (400-1500)

Allen, Dexter. Jaguar and the Golden Stag. Coward, 1954.
  Young Aztec prince of Mexico vies with his uncle to claim
  his throne.   (followed by Coil of the Serpent)   1260

Bo'ld, Paul. The Temple of Dreams. Ham Smith, 1912. The
  civilization of old Peru--its society, religion, mores, and
  valor.   1261

Haggard, H. Rider. The Virgin of the Sun. Cassel, 1922.
  An Englishman's adventures in Peru in the late fourteenth
  century.   1262

PART III

THE MODERN WORLD (c. 1500-1900)

A. EUROPE, THE NEAR EAST,
AND THE MEDITERRANEAN

-1. SIXTEENTH CENTURY: AGE OF THE
REFORMATION AND LATER RENAISSANCE

a) The British Isles

1) England, Wales, and Scotland

Ainsworth, W. Harrison. Cardinal Pole. Routledge, 1863. The
political, religious, and national controversy over Mary Tudor's
marriage.   1263

_____. The Constable of the Tower. Dutton, 1861. The story
of Somerset, the Protector.   1264

_____. The Tower of London. Dutton, 1840. The conflicting
elements in the struggle for the crown from Henry VIII's death
until Lady Jane Grey's execution.   1265

_____. Windsor Castle. Dutton, 1843. Much is told about
the castle itself, chiefly during the time of Henry VIII's marriage to Anne Boleyn.   1266

Albert, Edward. Kirk o' Field. Hodder, 1924. A novel of
Scotland and some of the tragic events surrounding Mary
Queen of Scots.   1267

Anderson, Robert Gordon. The Tavern Rogue. Farrar & Rinehart, 1934. Adventures in London of an outlaw whose life
depended on his writing a play Elizabeth liked.   1268

Bailey, H.C. Bonaventure. Methuen, 1927. Relations between
England and Spain in the years just before the attack of the
Armada.   1269

_____. The Lonely Queen. Methuen, 1911. The people and
influences which molded Elizabeth's character in her formative
years.   1270

_____. The Master of Gray. Longmans, 1903. Episodes
during the captivity of Mary Queen of Scots, with a deserter
of her cause as "hero."   1271

Balin, Beverly. King in Hell. Coward, 1971. The rugged,
courageous border lord, James Hepburn, Lord Bothwell,
allowed nothing to stand in the way of his love for Mary. 1272

Baring-Gould, S. Guavas, the Tinner. Methuen, 1897. Events
centering around a tin mine in Dartmoor and a Cornish
"foreigner."   1273

Barker, Shirley. Liza Bowe. Random, 1956. Story of a young
country maid in London in the days of "Good Queen Bess."
                                                           1274

Barnes, Margaret Campbell. Brief Gaudy Hour. Macrae Smith,
1949. Life-like picture of Anne Boleyn from the age of eighteen to her trial for her life.   1275

_____. King's Fool. Macrae Smith, 1959. The shrewd ob-
servations of Henry VIII's jester present a behind-the-scenes
view of the court.   1276

_____. My Lady of Cleves. Macrae Smith, 1946. Shows
the character of Anne of Cleves, fourth wife of Henry VIII. 1277

Barrington, Michael. David Arnot. Crosby Lockwood, 1927.
A medical student becomes involved with superstitious beliefs
currently popular in Scotland.   1278

Beahn, John E. A Man Born Again. Bruce, 1954. Fictional
autobiography of St. Thomas More.   1279

Beck, Lily Adams. Anne Boleyn. by E. Barrington, pseud.
Doubleday, 1932. Includes some of Henry's letters to the
clever woman who, for a time, fascinated him.   1280

_____. Duel of the Queens. by E. Barrington, pseud.
Doubleday, 1930. Competition between Mary Queen of Scots
and Elizabeth of England.   1281

Beebe, Elswyth Thane. The Tudor Wench. by Elswyth Thane.
Harcourt, 1932. A richly colored picture of Elizabeth to
the time of her coronation.   1282

Benson, Robert Hugh. By What Authority? Pitman, 1904.
Conflict between conscience and loyalty to the crown over
religious issues; hardships of English Catholics.   1283

_____. Come Rack! Come Rope! Hutchinson, 1912. Dar-
ing exploits of hunted priests who defied a hostile government
to bring religion to Elizabethan England.   1284

_____ . The King's Achievement. Pitman, 1905. Conflict between brothers over opposing loyalties to Church and Crown under Henry VIII.   1285

_____ . The Queen's Tragedy. Pitman, 1906. Reports and attempts to explain the harsh methods Mary employed to bring religious unity to England.   1286

Beresford-Howe, Constance. My Lady Greensleeves. Ballantine, 1955. Trials of an aristocratic lady married to a man of the middle class.   1287

Borden, Lucille Papin. Starforth. Macmillan, 1937. The Starforth family in Tudor England.   1288

Bowers, Gwendolyn. At the Sign of the Globe. Walck, 1966. YA. A former tanner's apprentice finds odd jobs at Shakespeare's Globe Theatre in London.   1289

Boyce, John. The Spae-Wife. by Paul Peppergrass, esq., pseud. Murphy, 1853. Unusual story of a remarkable Scots lady endowed with second sight and involved in royal circles.   1290

Brady, Charles Andrew. Stage of Fools. Dutton, 1953. About Sir Thomas More, called a fool for placing devotion to God before loyalty to Henry VIII.   1291

Brookfield, Frances Mary. A Friar Observant. Herder, 1909. A friar observes the closing of the English monasteries and meets Luther.   1292

_____ . My Lord of Essex. Pitman, 1907. The expedition of the Earl of Essex to Cadiz against the Spanish fleet. 1293

Brophy, John. Gentleman of Stratford. Harper, 1940. A story of Shakespeare with emphasis on the man rather than on his plays.   1294

Buchan, John. The Blanket of the Dark. Houghton, 1931. An attempt to displace Henry VIII from the throne of England. 1295

Byrd, Elizabeth. Immortal Queen. Ballantine, 1956. Mary Stuart's childhood in France, reign in Scotland, and eventual imprisonment in England.   1296

Calhoun, Mary. White Witch of Kynance. Harper, 1971, c.1960. YA. A girl learns the art of herbs and healing from the wise woman of Kynance.   .1297

Capes, Bernard. Where England Sets Her Feet. Collins, 1918. Land and sea adventures of a young Englishman of mysterious birth.   1298

Catherine, Sister Mary. Storm Out of Cornwall. by S.M.C.,
pseud. Kenedy, 1959. A tale of the Prayerbook Rebellion,
when Cornishmen fought for freedom of religion.   1299

Champion de Crespigny, Rose. The Mischief of a Glove. by
Mrs. Philip Champion de Crespigny. Unwin, 1903. A romance in England in mid-century.   1300

Charques, Dorothy. The Nunnery. Coward, 1960, c.1959.
Doubts about the status of religious houses and vocations in
the upheaval of Henry VIII's reign combine with romance in
this tale of 1535.   1301

Chidsey, Donald Barr. Captain Bashful. Crown, 1955. Efforts
of the hero to win his lady love and recover his lands.   1302

_____. Reluctant Cavalier. Crown, 1960. A man of good
birth becomes an unwilling courier in secret diplomatic negotiations; voyages of Sir Francis Drake.   1303

Chute, Marchette. The Wonderful Winter. Dutton, 1954. YA.
A boy leaves his country home and becomes an actor with
Shakespeare's company.   1304

Coker, Elizabeth Boatwright. Lady Rich. Dutton, 1963. The
heart of Penelope Devereaux, the elusive "Stella" of Sir
Philip Sidney's sonnets, is bared in this purported diary. 1305

Comstock, Harriet T. The Queen's Hostage. Little, 1906.
Elizabeth's court with emphasis on the theater of the day--
Shakespeare, Jonson, the Globe Theater.   1306

Cronyn, George W. Mermaid Tavern. Knight, 1937. Life and
adventures of Christopher Marlowe in England during Mary
Stuart's time.   1307

Cullen, W.R. The Unwedded Bride. Long, 1910. Religious
dissent in Scotland under Mary Queen of Scots.   1308

Curtis, Felicia. Under the Rose. Sands, 1912. Romance of
Elizabethan England features Richard Topcliffe, persecutor of
Roman Catholics.   1309

Dakers, Elaine. Parcel of Rogues. by Jane Lane, pseud.
Rinehart, 1948. A tale of those who opposed Mary Stuart in
her reign as Queen of Scots.   1310

Davidson, Diane. Feversham. Crown, 1969. Efforts of Sir
Thomas Cheyney to save Alice Arden and her lover who are
accused of murdering her husband along with four others. 1311

Delves-Broughton, Josephine. The Heart of a Queen. [En.
title: Crown Imperial] McGraw, 1949. The loves of Eliza-

beth--the foremost being her love for England.   1312

Dunnett, Dorothy. The Game of Kings. Putnam, 1961. Story
of an aristocratic young Scotsman who is accused of being a
renegade and a traitor. (followed by Queen's Play)   1313

Eckerson, Olive. My Lord Essex. Holt, 1955. Excellent
character portrayal in this romance of Elizabeth and Essex.
                                                            1314

Ellis, Amanda Mae. Elizabeth, the Woman. Dutton, 1951.
Portrait of Elizabeth against the pageantry, extravagance,
and cruelty of Tudor England.   1315

Elsna, Hebe, pseud., for Ansle, Dorothy Phoebe. The Queen's
Ward. Beagle Bks., 1971, c.1967. A homeless girl, befriended by Amy Robsart, becomes the ward of Queen Elizabeth after the sudden death of her benefactress.   1316

_____. The Wise Virgin. Beagle Bks., 1971, c.1967. A
pretty girl, by a desperate ruse, avoids becoming the fifth
wife of Henry VIII and remains free to marry the man of her
choice.   1317

Farnol, Jeffery. A Jade of Destiny. Little, 1931. Sentimental
romance of England during Elizabeth's reign.   1318

Fecher, Constance. Heir to Pendarrow. Farrar, 1969. YA.
A wicked uncle has his nephew's father imprisoned in an effort to secure the estate for himself.   1319

Filon, Augustin. Renégat. Armand Colin (France), 1894.
England's growth in sea power with her defeat of the Spanish
Armada.   1320

Fisher, Edward. The Best House in Stratford. Abelard, 1965.
Shakespeare's life as a family man, playwright, and actor,
his friendship with Ben Jonson, and his purchase of an old
house in Stratford. (completes The Silver Falcon trilogy) 1321

_____. Shakespeare & Son. Abelard, 1962. Young William
Shakespeare and his attraction to the theatre despite his
father's plans for him. (The Silver Falcon--v. 1)   1322

_____. Love's Labour's Won. Abelard, 1963. William
Shakespeare's "lost years," 1583-93 before he was estab-
lished as a playwright, ending with his partnership with
Dick Burbage. (The Silver Falcon--v. 2)   1323

Foote, Dorothy Norris. The Constant Star. Scribner, 1959.
The story of Frances Walsingham and her marriages, first
to Sir Philip Sidney, then to the Earl of Essex.   1324

Ford, Ford Madox (name originally Ford Madox Hueffer). The

Fifth Queen. Vanguard, 1963. A trilogy containing: The
Fifth Queen; Privy Seal; and The Fifth Queen Crowned
(listed separately).   1325

_____. The Fifth Queen and How She Came to Court. Rivers,
1906. Henry VIII's reception of Catherine Howard after
his disappointing marriage to Anne of Cleves. (followed by
Privy Seal)   1326

_____. The Fifth Queen Crowned. Nash, 1908. Catherine
Howard's reign as queen of Henry VIII.   1327

_____. Privy Seal. Rivers, 1907. The downfall of Crom-
well after he had displeased Henry VIII. (followed by The
Fifth Queen Crowned)   1328

Forster, R. H. The Arrow of the North. Long, 1906. The
Battle of Flodden Field is the high point of this story of war
between England and Scotland.   1329

_____. The Last Foray. Long, 1903. Adventures of one of
Cardinal Wolsey's men.   1330

_____. Midsummer Morn. Long, 1911. Romance and
cattle stealing along the border.   1331

Fulton, D. Kerr. The Witch's Sword. Arnold, 1908. The
Battle of Flodden Field and the period following, with a man
mistaken for King James IV.   1332

Garnier, Russell M. The White Queen. Harper, 1899. The
quest for happiness of Mary Tudor, Henry VIII's sister, who
contracted a state marriage.   1333

Gibbon, Charles. The Braes of Yarrow. Harper, 1881. The
Regent of Scotland, Queen Margaret Tudor, and the youthful
King, James V, after the Battle of Flodden Field.   1334

Goudge, Elizabeth. Towers in the Mist. Coward, 1938. A
story of Oxford University with a visit from Queen Elizabeth
as a high point.   1335

Graham, Winston. The Grove of Eagles. Doubleday, 1964,
c. 1963. The son of the governor of a castle in Wales serves
under Sir Walter Raleigh, is captured by the Spanish, and
returns to England having had many exciting adventures.   1336

Grant, James. Bothwell. Dutton, 1851. The political career
of Bothwell and his disastrous romance with Mary Queen of
Scots.   1337

Gregory, Charles. His Sovereign Lady. Melrose, 1919.
Drake's search for fame and fortune on the high seas.   1338

Gull, C. Ranger. House of Torment. Greening, 1910. Persecutions in England and Spain in the time of Mary Tudor and Philip II.   1339

Hackett, Francis. Queen Anne Boleyn. Doubleday, 1939. The beautiful, scheming woman who became Henry VIII's second queen.   1340

Haggard, H. Rider. The Lady of Blossholme. Hodder, 1909. Time of the closing of the monasteries and the Pilgrimage of Grace in Henry VIII's reign.   1341

Hale, John. Mary, Queen of Scots. New American Lib., 1972. Mary, who was betrayed by her own romantic nature, lost her kingdom and her life because she was more woman than Queen (novel from movie script).   1342

Hamilton, Ernest. Mary Hamilton. Methuen, 1901. A romance of Mary Hamilton, lady-in-waiting to Mary Queen of Scots.   1343

_____. The Outlaws of the Marches. Dodd, 1897. Adventures of Liddesdale and the country along the border.   1344

Hancock, Sardius. Tonford Manor. Unwin, 1903. A chivalric story of England early in Henry VIII's reign before his break with Rome.   1345

Harwood, Alice. The Lily and the Leopards. [En. title: She Had to Be Queen] Bobbs, 1949. The sweet and innocent Lady Jane Grey was sacrificed for her family's ambition for power.   1346

_____. No Smoke without Fire. Bobbs, 1964. Mary Stuart's loving illegitimate brother, James, the Earl of Moray, and his devotion to Scotland.   1347

_____. Seats of the Mighty. Bobbs, 1956. The loyalty of James Stuart, illegitimate half-brother of Mary Queen of Scots.   1348

_____. So Merciful a Queen, So Cruel a Woman. Bobbs, 1958. Queen Elizabeth kept a watchful eye on the younger sisters of Lady Jane Grey, for they stood close in the line of succession.   1349

Haycraft, Molly Costain. The Reluctant Queen. Lippincott, 1962. Steadfast love of Mary, sister of Henry VIII, for a commoner, despite her political marriage to Louis XII of France.   1350

_____. Too Near the Throne. Lippincott, 1959. About the Lady Arbella Stuart, who had a near enough claim to the throne to be a problem and a threat to both Elizabeth and later James I.   1351

Henham, Ernest George. The Custom of the Manor. by John
Trevena, pseud. Mills & Boon, 1924. England's reaction
to Thomas Cromwell's dissolution of the monasteries.   1352

Hewlett, Maurice. The Queen's Quair. Macmillan, 1904.
A fine romance about the tense period in Mary Queen of Scot's
life ending with Darnley's death.   1353

Hibbert, Eleanor. The Captive Queen of Scots. by Jean Plaidy,
pseud. Putnam, 1970, c.1963. The stormy life of Mary
Stuart who, after Darnley's death, exchanged one prison and
one plot for another, time after time.   1354

_____. Gay Lord Robert. by Jean Plaidy, pseud. Putnam,
1971, c.1955. The romance of Robert Dudley and Queen
Elizabeth and the mysterious death of his wife, Amy Robsart.   1355

_____. The King's Pleasure. by Jean Plaidy, pseud. Apple-
ton, 1949. Anne Boleyn's swift rise to power and her sudden
downfall.   1356

_____. The King's Secret Matter. by Jean Plaidy, pseud.
Hale, 1962. Catherine of Aragon strives to preserve her
rightful position and that of her daughter Mary as Henry
VIII seeks a divorce.   1357

_____. Royal Road to Fotheringay. by Jean Plaidy, pseud.
Putnam, 1970, c.1956. The tragic story of Mary Queen of
Scots, who lived out her life as a prisoner because she was
an inept ruler and a threat to Queen Elizabeth.   1358

_____. St. Thomas's Eve. by Jean Plaidy, pseud. Putnam,
1970, c.1954. Tells of the happy home life of Sir Thomas
More, which he gave up, along with the King's pleasure, to
follow his duty to God.   1359

_____. The Sixth Wife. by Jean Plaidy, pseud. Fawcett,
1970, c.1953. The tragic story of Katharine Parr, who
walked a. precarious line as the sixth wife of Henry VIII. 1360

Hill, Pamela. King's Vixen. Putnam, 1954. Romance and
adventure in the Scotland of James IV.   1361

Innes, J.W. Brodie. For the Soul of a Witch. Rebman, 1910.
Witchcraft and superstition, based on contemporary documents.   1362

Ireland, James. Master Secretary. Hodder & Stoughton, 1826.
The chief character is the politically crafty secretary Sir
William Cecil.   1363

Irwin, Margaret. Elizabeth and the Prince of Spain. Har-
     court, 1953. Elizabeth during the precarious period of the
     marriage of Mary Tudor and Philip II, with her own safety
     subject to Mary's whims. (completes trilogy)   1364

_____. Elizabeth, Captive Princess. Harcourt, 1948. The
     tense, fateful time from Edward VI's death to the marriage
     of Queen Mary and Philip II of Spain. (followed by Elizabeth
     and the Prince of Spain)   1365

_____. The Gay Galliard. Harcourt, 1942. Romance of
     Mary Queen of Scots and James Hepburn, Earl of Both-
     well.   1366

_____. Young Bess. Harcourt, 1944. Elizabeth Tudor in
     the uncertain days from her twelfth year to the death of her
     brother, Edward VI. (followed by Elizabeth, Captive Prin-
     cess)   1367

James, G. P. R. Darnley. Dutton, 1830. Interesting account of
     the relations between England and France in 1520.   1368

James, Miss W. M. Court Cards. by Austin Clare, pseud.
     Unwin, 1904. A story of sheep stealing which involves the
     court circles of England and Scotland.   1369

Johnston, Mary. Silver Cross. Little, 1922. The rivalry for
     worldly glory between two abbeys.   1370

Johnston, Sue (Sister Mary Francis Johnston). Star Inn. Ave
     Maria Pr., 1953. A loyal subject of Queen Elizabeth is
     sent to track down recalcitrant priests defying the royal
     edict.   1371

Jones, E. Brandram. (1) In Burleigh's Days. Long, 1916.
     (2) The Second Cecil. Long, 1917. Two historical novels
     of the Elizabethan period with such literary and political
     figures as Shakespeare, Bacon, Essex, and Jonson.   1372-3

Jones, Gwyn. Garland of Bays. Macmillan, 1938. A novel
     about Robert Greene, poet and playwright, with a realistic
     Elizabethan background.   1374

Kaye-Smith, Sheila. Superstition Corner. Harper, 1934.
     Elizabeth's persecution of Catholics is intensified by the
     threat of the Armada.   1375

Kenyon, Frank Wilson. Mary of Scotland. Crowell, 1957.
     The exciting times of Mary Queen of Scots.   1376

_____. Shadow in the Sun. Crowell, 1958. Queen Eliza-
     beth loved three men but could not marry any of them.   1377

Knight, Charles Brunton. My Lord Cardinal. Long, 1924.
Cardinal Wolsey in the period of his waning political
power.   1378

Knipe, John. The Hour Before the Dawn. Lane, 1921. The
tense atmosphere in Scotland about the time of James V's
death.   1379

_____. The Watch-Dog of the Crown. Lane, 1920. A ro-
mance of the Tower of London about Sir Henry Talbot and
the lovely prisoner Frances Grey in the reign of Edward VI.
                                                            1380

Knowles, Mabel Winifred. A King's Masquerade. by May Wynne,
pseud. Greening, 1910. Scotland's James V as a young man
in the disguise which almost resulted in his death.   1381

Lee, Albert. The Gentleman Pensioner. Appleton, 1900.
Conspiracy to free Mary Queen of Scots from imprisonment
and place her on the throne of England.   1382

Lenanton, Carola Oman. The Road Royal. by Carola Oman.
Fisher Unwin, 1924. Mary Queen of Scots' childhood marriage to the French Dauphin and subsequent events in Scotland.   1383

Lethbridge, Olive and John de Stourton. The King's Master.
Paul, 1912. The chief characters are Thomas Cromwell
and Queen Anne Boleyn.   1384

Letton, Jennette and Francis. Robsart Affair. Harper, 1956.
Tale of the early love of Queen Elizabeth and Robert Dudley
--and of Amy Dudley's mysterious death.   1385

Lewis, Hilda Winifred. I Am Mary Tudor. McKay, 1971. An
account, told in the first person, of Mary Tudor's life, her
reactions to her father's marriages, her brother's reign, and
her own accession to the throne.   1386

Lindsay, Philip. Here Comes the King. Little, 1933. The
marriage of Henry VIII and Catherine Howard, his fifth
wife.   1387

Lofts, Norah. Here Was a Man. Knopf, 1936. Romantic
novel based on the career of Sir Walter Raleigh.   1388

_____. The House at Old Vine. Doubleday, 1961. An epi-
sodic tale of successive inhabitants of an English residence
from the fall of Richard III in 1485 to the reign of James II
in 1679. (followed by The House at Sunset)   1389

Lusk, Lewis. Sussex Iron. Ouseley, 1913. Life in a Sussex
village and the defeat of the Spanish Armada.   1390

McCarthy, Justin Huntly. Henry Elizabeth. Lane, 1920.
Elizabethan romance concerning a country boy turned
courtier; Dr. Dee is mentioned.   1391

McChesney, Dora Greenwell. The Wounds of a Friend. Smith
& Elder, 1908. A romance of Raleigh's part in colonizing
the New World.   1392

MacFarlane, James. The Red Fox. Lang, 1912. "A story of
the Clan Macfarlan."   1393

McIlwraith, Maureen Mollie Hunter. The Spanish Letters. by
Mollie Hunter, pseud. Funk, 1967, c.1964. YA. Intrigue
involves English, Scottish, and Spanish people in plotting for
the kidnapping of King James and a Spanish invasion.   1394

MacInnes, Colin. Three Years to Play. Farrar, 1970. A
story of a rustic's adventures in London and the country and
his meeting with Shakespeare, who used his adventures as
the basis for As You Like It.   1395

Macleod, Alison. The Heretic. [En. title: The Heretics]
Houghton, 1966, c.1965. Concerns Anne Askew, who was
burned at the stake as a heretic during the reign of Henry
VIII.   1396

_____. The Hireling. Houghton, 1968. Courtier Thomas
Vaughan, involved in intrigue at the court of Henry VIII,
finds that he must make many hard decisions concerning
family, country, and religion. (followed by City of Light)
                                                   1397

McMahon, Norbert. St. John of God. McMullen Bks., 1953?
About St. John of God, patron of the sick and dying, of nurses
and hospitals.   1398

Major, Charles. Dorothy Vernon of Haddon Hall. Macmillan,
1902. Based on the legendary romance of Dorothy Vernon.
                                                   1399

_____. When Knighthood Was in Flower. by Edwin Casko-
den, pseud. Bowen-Merrill, 1898. Romance of Mary Tudor,
Henry VIII's sister, and Charles Brandon, Duke of Suffolk. 1400

Manning, Anne. The Household of Sir Thomas More. Dutton,
1851. Written as the diary of More's daughter Margaret,
this pictures the saint as a family man.   1401

Mason, A.E.W. Fire Over England. Doubleday, 1936. England in the uncertain days of the Spanish Armada threat.   1402

Mason, Van Wyck. Golden Admiral. Doubleday, 1953. Sir
Francis Drake and the Spanish Armada.   1403

Mathew, Frank. Defender of the Faith. Lane, 1899. Offers

fine characterizations of many people prominent in Henry
VIII's reign, including several of his wives.   1404

_____. One Queen Triumphant. Lane, 1899. The Babing-
ton Plot and the execution of Mary Queen of Scots to end her
threat to Elizabeth's throne.   1405

_____. The Royal Sisters. Long, 1901. The wary, uneasy
relationship between Mary and Elizabeth Tudor.   1406

Meadows, Denis. Tudor Underground. Devin-Adair, 1950.
Jesuit efforts to keep Catholicism alive although outlawed by
the Oath of Supremacy.   1407

Michelson, Miriam. Petticoat King. McBride, 1929. Romance
in Queen Elizabeth's court.   1408

Moubray, Douglas. Fair Helen of Kirkconnell Lea. Hayes,
1920. A romance of Scotland in 1565.   1409

Muddock, J.E. Preston. Fair Rosalind. Long, 1902. London
in the stormy reign of Henry VIII.   1410

_____. In the King's Favour. Digby & Long, 1899. A ro-
mance of Flodden Field and the weak Scottish King James
IV.   1411

Mundt, Klara. Henry VIII and His Court. (tr.) by Louisa
Mühlbach, pseud. Appleton, 1867. The conspiracies and
corruption of the English court; Catherine Parr, queen-
consort.   1412

Nicolls, William Jasper. The Daughters of Suffolk. Lippincott, 1910. Lady Jane and Lady Catherine Grey are figures
in the battle for royal succession.   1413

Oliphant, Margaret O. Magdalen Hepburn. Munro, 1885.
Scotland during Mary Stuart's reign, with John Knox as a
character.   1414

Oliver, Jane, pseud., for Rees, Helen Christina Easson.
Flame of Fire. Putnam, 1961. The work and dedication of
the scholar Tyndale, who defied laws and tradition by trans-
lating the Bible into English.   1415

_____. The Lion and the Rose. Putnam, 1959. Sympathetic
telling of the romance of Mary Queen of Scots and Lord Darnley.   1416

_____. Mine Is the Kingdom. Lippincott, 1937. The life
of James I of England (James VI of Scotland), son of Mary
Stuart.   1417

_____. Sunset at Noon. Putnam, 1963. James IV of Scot-
land was a popular and successful king until he invaded Henry
VIII's England and was killed at Flodden Field in 1513.   1418

Parry, Edward Abbott. England's Elizabeth. Smith & Elder,
1904. The dangerous course Elizabeth followed to become
and remain Queen.   1419

Paterson, Isabel. The Fourth Queen. Boni & Liveright, 1926.
The love of a waiting maid and Fighting Jack Montagu in
Elizabeth's court.   1420

Pemberton, Max. I Crown Thee King. Methuen, 1902. Rebellious elements in England's troubled Tudor period.   1421

Potter, Jeremy. A Trail of Blood. McCall, 1971, c.1970. An
examination of Richard III's involvement in the deaths of the
princes in the Tower made by a sixteenth century monk who
wishes to discredit Henry VIII and replace him with a Plantagenet.   1422

Power, Edith Mary. A Knight of God. Sands, 1909. The
plight of persecuted Catholics in Elizabethan England.   1423

Powers, Anne. No Wall So High. Bobbs, 1949. Treachery,
duels, and the attack of the Spanish Armada.   1424

Preedy, George, pseud. for Gabrielle Campbell Long. Queen's
Caprice. King, 1934. A picture of Mary Queen of Scots at
the time of her first meeting with Darnley.   1425

Prescott, Hilda Frances Margaret. The Man on a Donkey.
Macmillan, 1952. Comprehensive account of English life including the Pilgrimage of Grace during Henry VIII's eventful
reign.   1426

Richings, Emily. Sir Walter's Wife. Drane, 1900. Sir Walter
Raleigh's romance in the face of royal disapproval.   1427

Robertson, William. The Dule Tree of Cassillis. Menzies
(Scotland), 1904. Fighting over property during the unrest
in mid-sixteenth century Scotland.   1428

_____. The Lords of Cuninghame. Gardner, 1891. Family
feuds in Scotland as related in original documents.   1429

Robinson, Emma. Westminster Abbey. Routledge, 1854. An
account of London during the religious and moral upheavals
of Henry VIII's reign.   1430

Salmon, Geraldine Gordon. The Lost Duchess. by J.C. Sarasin,
pseud. Doran, 1927. Romance based on the story of Lady
Arabella Stuart, wife of William Seymour.   1431

Saunders, John. A Noble Wife. Jarrold & Sons, 1895. Story
of the wife of Archbishop Cranmer.   1432

Scott, Sir Walter. The Abbot. Bazin & Ellsworth, 1831.
Good picture of Mary Queen of Scots and her flight into England.   1433

_____. Kenilworth. Bazin & Ellsworth, 1831. Robert Dud-
ley's lavish entertainment for Queen Elizabeth at his home,
Kenilworth.   1434

_____. The Monastery. Bazin & Ellsworth, 1830. Set in
the border country during the Reformation. (followed by
The Abbot)   1435

Sheppard, Alfred Tresidder. Brave Earth. Doran, 1925. Confusion caused by the Reformation is reflected in this romance
of Henry VIII's reign.   1436

Siegel, Benjamin. A Kind of Justice. Harcourt, 1960. A
Spanish Jew encounters religious persecution in Elizabethan
England.   1437

Snaith, John Collis. Anne Feversham. [En. title: The Great
Age] Appleton, 1914. Romance of Elizabethan England with
Shakespeare appearing prominently.   1438

Stephens, Eve. All the Queen's Men. [En. title: Elizabeth]
by Evelyn Anthony, pseud. Crowell, 1960. The story involves Queen Elizabeth, Robert Dudley, and Mary Queen of
Scots.   1439

_____. Anne Boleyn. by Evelyn Anthony, pseud. Crowell,
1957. Convincing portrait of the clever woman who held
Henry VIII for ten years.   1440

Stephens, Robert Neilson. Captain Ravenshaw. Page, 1901.
A romance of London under Elizabeth.   1441

_____. A Gentleman Player. Page, 1899. A comedian in
the Lord Chamberlain's company at the time of Shakespeare.
                                                            1442
Strode-Jackson, Myrtle B.S. Tansy Taniard. Scribner, 1945.
Romance of Tansy Taniard, whose beautiful red hair made
a wig for Queen Elizabeth.   1443

Sutcliff, Rosemary. Lady in Waiting. Coward, 1957. About
Sir Walter Raleigh's wife, who spent many years as a lady-
in-waiting.   1444

Sutcliffe, Halliwell. The Crimson Field. Ward & Lock, 1916.
Relations between England and Scotland ending with the Battle
of Flodden Field.   1445

_____. Pam the Fiddler. Laurie, 1910. An adventure-
romance during the period of Mary Queen of Scots' imprisonment.   1446

Swallow, Henry J. Love While Ye May. Jarrold & Sons, 1907.
Based mainly on the Rising of the North in 1569.   1447

Taylor, Mary Imlay. The House of the Wizard. McClurg,
1899. The first two marriages of Henry VIII.   1448

Travers, Hettie. A Stormy Passage. Digby & Long, 1913.
Queen Catherine Howard in the two years before Henry VIII
caused her execution.   1449

Turton, Godfrey. My Lord of Canterbury. Doubleday, 1967.
Fictional autobiography of Thomas Cranmer, Archbishop of
Canterbury, who further Protestantized the early Anglican
Church.   1450

Uttley, Alison. A Traveler in Time. Viking, 1964. A girl
visiting the ancestral home goes back in time three hundred
years to become involved in the Babington attempt to rescue
Mary Queen of Scots.   1451

Vaughan, Owen. The Shrouded Face. by Owen Rhoscomyl,
pseud. Pearson, 1898. The tribal system in effect in turbulent Wales.   1452

Vining, Elizabeth Gray. I Will Adventure. by Elizabeth J. Gray.
Viking, 1962. YA. A country boy comes to London and finds
life there surprisingly different from what he had experienced
at home.   1453

Walford, Lucy Bethia. The Black Familiars. Longmans, 1903.
Religious intrigue during the early part of Elizabeth's reign.
                                                            1454
Walpole, Hugh. The Bright Pavilions. Doubleday, 1940. A
romance of the Herries family in Elizabethan England.   1455

Ward, Josephine. Tudor Sunset. Longmans, 1932. Persecution of Catholics toward the close of Elizabeth's reign; the
Queen's maid, secretly a Catholic.   1456

Westcott, Jan. The Border Lord. Crown, 1946. Thrilling,
romantic tale of Francis Hepburn, Lord Bothwell, whose
popularity and power were feared and envied by King James
VI of Scotland.   1457

_____. The Hepburn. Crown, 1950. Border war and in-
trigue in Scotland during the reign of James IV.   1458

_____. The Queen's Grace. Crown, 1959. Sweet, sensible
Catherine Parr, who had four marriages, including one with

Henry VIII.   1459

_____. Walsingham Woman. Crown, 1953. Frances
Walsingham, whose second husband was Queen Elizabeth's
favorite, the Earl of Essex.   1460

Wheelwright, Jere Hungerford. The Strong Room. Scribner,
1948. Adventures of a young noble twice committed to the
Tower of London.   1461

White, Beatrice. Royal Nonesuch. Macmillan, 1933. A tapestry of the Tudor court--Henry VIII, his sister Mary, and her
husband.   1462

White, Leslie Turner. Magnus the Magnificent. Crown, 1950.
Quest of a pirate for love, fame, and riches.   1463

White, Olive B. The King's Good Servant. Macmillan, 1936.
The last years of Sir Thomas More, who defied his king,
Henry VIII, rather than deny his God.   1464

_____. Late Harvest. Macmillan, 1940. The Catholic side
of the many changes in Elizabeth's time.   1465

Whyte-Melville, George John. The Queen's Maries. Longmans,
1864. The romances of four ladies-in-waiting to Mary Queen
of Scots.   1466

Wilby, Noel Macdonald. Merry Eternity. Benziger, 1934. Fictional account of the household of Sir Thomas More.   1467

Williams, Jay. The Witches. Random, 1957. Spy investigates
a rumored conspiracy of witches against James VI.   1468

Wilson, John Anthony Burgess. Nothing Like the Sun. by Anthony Burgess, pseud. Norton, 1964. A picture of Shakespeare which shows him as a man who lived and enjoyed life
to the fullest in a London of many extremes.   1469

Wilson, Mary J. The Knight of the Needle Rock and His Days.
Stock, 1905. Written as a family journal of English life.   1470

    2) Ireland

Craig, R. Manifold. The Weird of "The Silken Thomas."
Moran (Aberdeen), 1900. The customs and traditions of
Ireland in the 1530s and the revolt of Lord Thomas Fitz-
gerald.   1471

Knowles, Mabel Winifred. For Church and Chieftain. by May
Wynne, pseud. Mills & Boon, 1909. Thrilling romance
of the Geraldine rebellion in Ireland.   1472

Lawless, Emily. Maelcho. Appleton, 1894. A sober account of the hard conditions of the Irish under English
oppression.   1473

_____. With Essex in Ireland. Lovell, 1890. The expe-
dition led by Essex to put down the Irish Rebellion and win
prestige.   1474

Linington, Elizabeth. The Proud Man. Viking, 1955. Shane
O'Neill, prince of Ulster, attempts to oust the English.   1475

Machray, Robert. Grace O'Malley, Princess and Pirate.
Stokes, 1898. About a woman whose courage inspired rebellion against English cruelty and oppression.   1476

O'Brien, William. A Queen of Men. Unwin, 1898. The daring
Grace O'Malley, who led her fierce clan in rebellion against
English oppression.   1477

O'Byrne, Miss M. L. The Pale and the Septs. Gill (Dublin),
1876. A story of rebellious Ireland under English domina-
tion in mid-century.   1478

O'Grady, Standish. The Flight of the Eagle. Sealy & Bryers
(Dublin), 1889. Oppression in Ireland in Elizabeth's reign.
                                                        1479

Rhys, Grace. The Charming of Estercel. Dutton, 1913.
Northern Ireland during the Irish Rebellion and the English
attempt, led by Essex, to quell it.   1480

Sadlier, Mary Anne. MacCarthy More! by Mrs. James Sadlier.
Kenedy, 1868. Struggle of an Irish family to retain its religion and possessions during persecution.   1481

Taunton, M. The Last of the Catholic O'Malleys. Kenedy,
1870. Exploits of courageous Grace O'Malley and her resistance to the English.   1482

Walsh, Maurice. Blackcock's Feather. Stokes, 1932. A Scotch-
Irish romance during the struggle against Queen Elizabeth.
                                                        1483

b) Western and Central Europe

1) France

Ainsworth, W. Harrison. Crichton [same as: The Admirable Crichton] Routledge, 1873. The adventurer James
Crichton, son of the Scottish Lord Advocate, at Paris.   1484

Balzac, Honoré de. About Catherine de Medici. (tr.) Macmillan, 1897. Centers chiefly on Catherine and her relations with other court personages.   1485

Bedford-Jones, Henry. King's Pardon. Covici, 1933. A
swift-moving adventure story full of swordplay and bloodshed.   1486

Bloundelle-Burton, John. The King's Mignon. Everett, 1909.
Features the assassination of the Duke of Guise and following
events.   1487

_____. Under the Salamander. Everett, 1911. Intrigue and
romance during France's struggle with Spain.   1488

Bolton, Muriel Roy. The Golden Porcupine. Doubleday, 1947.
Story of the Duc d'Orleans, who became Louis XII of France.
                                                       1489
Champion de Crespigny, Rose. The Grey Domino. by Mrs.
Philip Champion de Crespigny. Nash, 1906. Romance of
southern France with scenes at the court of Henry IV. 1490

Clark, Janet M. The Bourgeois Queen of Paris. Greening,
1910. Life in Paris during the reign of Henry II is marked
by dissension between Catholics and Protestants.   1491

Conyers, Dorothea. For Henri and Navarre. Hutchinson,
1911. A romance beginning with the Massacre of St. Bartholomew's Day and featuring Henry of Navarre.   1492

Crockett, Samuel R. The White Plumes of Navarre. [same as:
The White Plume] Dodd, 1906. Henry of Navarre is a cen-
tral figure in this tale of the French Religious Wars and the
Spanish Inquisition.   1493

Curties, Henry. Renée. Richards, 1908. A broken state-
marriage contract between Austria and France, the battle of
Marignano, and the meeting on the Field of the Cloth of
Gold.   1494

De La Fayette, Madame. The Princess of Cleves. (tr.) Routledge, 1925. Psychological novel dealing with the French
court.   1495

Drummond, Hamilton. The Cuckoo. White, 1906. A gentle
mother and a rough peasant father vie for the control of
their son.   1496

_____. (1) For the Religion. Smith & Elder, 1898. (2)
A Man of His Age (sequel). Harper, 1900. Novels of the
French Wars of Religion, Coligny's plan to colonize Florida,
and the conflicts between Catholics and Huguenots.   1497-8

_____. A King's Pawn. Doubleday, Page, 1901. Adventures
of a follower of Henry of Navarre in France and Spain. 1499

_____. Little Madame Claude. Paul, 1914. The daughter

of Anne of Brittany, the Queen of Louis XII.   1500

Dumas, Alexandre. Ascanio. (tr.) Munro, 1878. Visit
of Benvenuto Cellini to the court of Francis I, mecca of
artists and authors.   1501

_____. The Page of the Duke of Savoy. (tr.) Munro,
1878. Portrays a large number of historic people and events
including Emmanuel Philibert, Henry II, Catherine de Medici,
and the conflicts at St. Quentin and Calais.   1502

_____. The Two Dianas. (tr.) Munro, 1879. Wars of
France during the reigns of Francis I, Henry II, and Francis
II; romances of Diana of Poitiers and her daughter, Diana.
(followed by The Page of the Duke of Savoy)   1503

_____. The Valois Cycle: (1) Marguerite de Valois. (tr.)
Routledge, 1857. (2) Chicot, the Jester (sequel). (tr.)
[same as: La Dame de Monsoreau] Munro, 1880. (3) The
Forty-Five (sequel). (tr.) [same as: The Forty-Five Guards-
men] Little, 1889. A series of novels about the French
court including Marguerite de Valois, Charles IX, Henry III,
Catherine de Medici, Henry of Navarre, the jester Chicot,
and Henry III's bodyguard, the Forty-Five.   1504-6

Dunnett, Dorothy. Pawn in Frankincense. Putnam, 1969. Perilous
journey of a Scotsman in quest of his illegitimate son during
the confrontation between the Ottoman and Holy Roman Empires.   1507

_____. Queen's Play. Putnam, 1964. Exertion of a
versatile agent to protect the young Mary Stuart against
plots on her life at the court of Henry II of France.   1508

Gobineau, Joseph Arthur, comte de. The Lucky Prisoner.
(tr.) Doubleday, Page, 1926. A romance having the antag-
onism between Catholics and Huguenots as background.   1509

Gosse, Edmund. The Secret of Narcisse. Tait, 1892. Manners,
superstitions, and entertainments in court circles.   1510

Hartley, Percy J. The Hand of Diane. Unwin, 1911. A romance of the court of Henry II and of his mistress and her
younger sister.   1511

Hibbert, Eleanor. Madame Serpent. by Jean Plaidy, pseud.
Appleton, 1951. Court life of the merchant's daughter,
Catherine de Medici, consort of Henry II.   1512

_____. Queen Jezebel. · by Jean Plaidy, pseud. Appleton,
1953. Catherine de Medici, widow of Henry II, during the
Religious Wars in France.   1513

Hope, Jessie. A Cardinal and His Conscience. by Graham
   Hope, pseud. Smith & Elder, 1901. Rivalry between Catholics and Huguenots, with the Cardinal of Lorraine as central figure.   1514

_____. The Gage of Red and White. by Graham Hope,
   pseud. Smith & Elder, 1904. The marriage of Jeanne
   d'Albret and Antoine de Bourbon, parents of Henry of Navarre.   1515

Houston, June Dimmitt. The Faith and the Flame. Sloane,
   1958. Romance of a Catholic lady-in-waiting to Catherine de
   Medici with a Huguenot captain.   1516

Isham, Frederic S. Under the Rose. Bobbs, 1904. An adventure-romance during the reign of Francis I.   1517

James, G. P. R. The Brigand. Dutton, 1841. About an adventurer, with Diane de Poitiers and Henry II of France prominent.   1518

_____. Henry of Guise. Dutton, 1839. The War of the
   Three Henrys, depicting Henry of Navarre, King Henry III,
   and Henry Duke of Guise.   1519

_____. The Man-At-Arms. Dutton, 1840. Religious Wars
   and the Massacre of St. Bartholomew's Day.   1520

_____. One in a Thousand. Harper, 1835. A vivid account
   of Henry IV's victory in the Battle of Ivry in 1590.   1521

_____. Rose d'Albret. Dutton, 1844. Intrigue and romance
   in France at the time of the Battle of Ivry.   1522

Johns, Cecil Starr. With Gold and Steel. Lane, 1917. Royal-
   sponsored treasure hunt for a wrecked Spanish galleon.   1523

Johnson, William Henry. (1) The King's Henchman. Little,
   1898. (2) Under the Spell of the Fleur-de-Lis (sequel).
   Little, 1899. These stories of France during the Religious
   Wars depict Henry IV as a romantic hero.   1524-5

Knowles, Mabel Winifred. Henry of Navarre. by May Wynne,
   pseud. Putnam, 1904. A romance of August, 1572, during
   the Wars of Religion.   1526

_____. The Silent Captain. by May Wynne, pseud. Paul,
   1914. Struggle between Catholics and Huguenots, culminating in the Conspiracy of Amboise.   1527

_____. A Trap for Navarre. by May Wynne, pseud. Holden,
   1922. Intrigue in Henry of Navarre's court.   1528

Levett-Yeats, Sidney. The Chevalier d'Auriac. Longmans,
1897. The court of Henry of Navarre--romance, intrigue,
and petty jealousies.   1529

_____. Orrain. Longmans, 1904. The rivalry between
Catherine de Medici, queen of Henry II, and Diane de Poitiers,
his mistress.   1530

_____. The Traitor's Way. Stokes, 1901. The Conspiracy
of Amboise--a scheme aimed at King Francis II.   1531

Lewis, Ada Cook. The Longest Night. Rinehart, 1958. A
spirited account of the bloody Massacre of St. Bartholomew's
Day.   1532

Lewis, Janet. The Wife of Martin Guerre. Colt, 1941. Romance set in sixteenth century Languedoc.   1533

McComas, Ina Violet. Ashes of Vengeance. by H. B. Somerville, pseud. Hutchinson, 1913. An adventure story of the
closing quarter of the century.   1534

_____. Raoul the Hunchback. by H. B. Somerville, pseud.
Hutchinson, 1921. Love, intrigue, and adventure in sixteenth
century Provence.   1535

Macquoid, Katherine S. A Ward of the King. Buckles, 1898.
A conspiracy against Francis I, his capture, and his beautiful mistress, the Countess of Chauteaubriand.   1536

Mann, Heinrich. Henry, King of France. (tr.) Knopf, 1939.
Politics and intrigues during the reign of Henry IV.   1537

_____. Young Henry of Navarre. (tr.) [En. title: King
Wren] Knopf, 1937. The childhood and youth of Henry IV.
(followed by Henry, King of France)   1538

Mérimée, Prosper. A Chronicle of the Reign of Charles IX.
(tr.) Nimmo, 1889. Depicts a Huguenot's experiences in the
St. Bartholomew's Day Massacre and pictures Charles IX,
Coligny, Catherine de Medici, and Henry of Navarre.   1539

Montgomery, K. L., pseud. for Kathleen and Letitia Montgomery.
The Ark of the Curse. Hurst, 1906. A romance of the time
of Henry III with an appearance by Don Juan of Austria.   1540

Orczy, Baroness Emmuska. Flower o' the Lily. Doran, 1919.
Sufferings during the siege of Cambrai led by the Duke of Parma in 1581.   1541

Pater, Walter. Gaston de Latour. Macmillan, 1896. An unfinished though distinguished romance of France's Wars of
Religion.   1542

Peterson, Margaret. The Love of Navarre. Melrose, 1915.
Henry of Navarre from the War of the League to his Coronation as Henry IV.   1543

Radcliffe, Ann. The Mysteries of Udolpho. Dutton, 1931. A
romance of Henry III's reign.   1544

Runkle, Bertha. The Helmet of Navarre. Century, 1901. A
young follower of Henry IV at the latter's entry into Paris
in 1594.   1545

Sabatini, Rafael. The Romantic Prince. Houghton, 1929. A
French prince chooses between his heritage and a commoner's
daughter.   1546

Salmon, Geraldine Gordon. Quest of Youth. by J. G. Sarasin,
pseud. Hutchinson, 1923. A romance of the 1570s with the
Duc de Guise prominent.   1547

Schoonover, Lawrence. The Chancellor. Little, 1961. The be-
hind-the-throne machinations of Antoine Duprat who allowed no
personal or moral considerations to interfere in his dedication
to France's glory.   1548

Shellabarger, Samuel. The King's Cavalier. Little, 1950.
Swordplay and intrigue in a conspiracy against Francis I. 1549

Stephens, Robert Neilson. An Enemy to the King. Page, 1898.
Struggle for power among Henry III, Henry of Navarre, and
Henry of Guise.   1550

Stevenson, Philip L. A Gallant of Gascony. Hurst, 1907.
Unhappy marriage of Marguerite de Valois and Henry of
Navarre.   1551

_____. Love in Armour. Paul, 1912. Romance of court
personages near the end of Charles IX's reign.   1552

_____. The Rose of Dauphiny. Paul, 1910. Events incident
to conspiracies in the Religious Wars concerning the Sieur de
Roquelaure, later a trusted aide of Henry IV.   1553

Stilson, Charles B. A Cavalier of Navarre. Watt, 1925.
The romance of a young couple coincides with Henry of Navarre's rise to the throne.   1554

Walder, Francis. The Negotiators. (tr.) McDowell, Obolensky, 1959. The wrangle between Admiral de Coligny
and Catherine de Medici over the religion of four towns.   1555

Weyman, Stanley J. The Abbess of Vlaye. Burt, 1904.
Peasant unrest in the early part of Henry of Navarre's
reign.   1556

_____. Count Hannibal. Longmans, 1901. Scenes during Charles IX's reign including the St. Bartholomew's Day Massacre. 1557

_____. A Gentleman of France. Longmans, 1893. A pleasing mixture of warlike exploits and court romance. 1558

_____. The House of the Wolf. Longmans, 1890. Vivid picture of the St. Bartholomew's Day Massacre. 1559

Wheelwright, Jere Hungerford. Wolfshead. Scribner, 1949. Adventures of John Aumarie, outlaw and pirate. 1560

2) Central Europe (including Germany, the Netherlands, Switzerland, Austria, Hungary, Czechoslovakia, and Poland)

Antal-Opzoomer, Adèle Sophia Cornelia von. In Troubled Times. (tr.) by A. S. C. Wallis, pseud. Sonnenschein, 1883. Account of growing unrest in the Netherlands, chiefly during the regency of Margaret of Parma. 1561

Bailey, H. C. My Lady of Orange. Longmans, 1901. An Englishman joins William of Orange in opposing the Duke of Alva. 1562

_____. Raoul: Gentleman of Fortune. Hutchinson, 1907. Romance amid such historic events as the sieges of Leyden and Antwerp. 1563

Beahn, John E. A Man of Good Zeal. Newman, 1958. The life of St. Francis de Sales provides the basis for this novel. 1564

Bertram, Paul. The Shadow of Power. Lane, 1912. The absolute rule of Jaime de Jorquera, representative of Philip II, over the Netherlands, then chafing under Spanish oppression. 1565

Bowen, Marjorie, pseud. for Gabrielle Campbell Long. (1) Prince and Heretic. Dutton, 1915. (2) "William, by the Grace of God." Dutton, 1917. William the Silent, Prince of Orange, and the rebellion of the Netherlands against the Spanish. 1566-7

Breton, Frederic. True Heart. Dent, 1898. Reflects the religious, political, and intellectual turmoil of the early sixteenth century. 1568

Coleridge, Gilbert and Marion. Jan van Elselo. Macmillan, 1902. Reports, adventures, and schemes of a diplomat in Holland, England, Spain, and France. 1569

Comstock, Seth Cook. Monsieur le Capitaine Douay. Long,

1904.   The cruel Spanish sack of prosperous Antwerp.   1570

_____. The Rebel Prince. Long, 1905. Adventure in the
Netherlands during the time of William of Orange and Don
Juan of Austria.   1571

Conscience, Hendrik. Ludovic and Gertrude. (tr.) Murphy,
1895. Resentment of the people of Antwerp to Spanish rule
in the person of Alva.   1572

Cornford, L. Cope. The Master Beggars. Lippincott, 1897.
The Netherlands following the success of the Beggars' Rebellion.   1573

Davis, William Stearns. The Friar of Wittenberg. Macmillan,
1912. A story of Martin Luther from his posting of the
Ninety-five Theses.   1574

Dekker, Maurits. Beggars' Revolt. Doubleday, 1938. This
novel of rebellion in the Netherlands against Spanish rule
encompasses all levels of society.   1575

Ebers, Georg. Barbara Blomberg. (tr.) Appleton, 1897.
The German court of Charles V and the passionate, ambitious mother of Don Juan of Austria.   1576

_____. The Burgomaster's Wife. (tr.) Macmillan, 1882.
The siege of Leyden, the cutting of the dikes, and activities
of the revolutionary Dutch "Beggars."   1577

_____. In the Blue Pike. (tr.) Appleton, 1896. Travellers
at the Blue Pike Inn reflect the contemporary ecclesiastical
abuses which aroused Luther.   1578

Gerson, Noel B. The Gentle Fury. by Paul Lewis, pseud.
Holt, 1961. A story of Margaret of Austria, who served
very capably as regent of the Netherlands.   1579

Grattan, Thomas C. Agnes de Mansfelt. Saunders & Otley,
1835. The Wars of Independence in the Netherlands from
mid-sixteenth to mid-seventeenth century.   1580

Haggard, H. Rider. Lysbeth. Longmans, 1901. Sieges of
Haarlem and Leyden in the revolt of the Netherlands against
Philip II.   1581

Hauff, Wilhelm. Lichtenstein. (tr.) [En. title: Marie of
Lichtenstein] Bruce & Wyld, 1846. A romance of Swabia
describing customs and living standards.   1582

Hausrath, Adolf. Klytia. (tr.) by George Taylor, pseud.
Munro, 1885. The theological atmosphere of Heidelberg
during the dissension between Catholics, Lutherans, and

Calvinists.   1583

Hill, Pamela. Here Lies Margot. Putnam, 1958. Margaret
of Burgundy, her three state marriages, and her regency
for her nephew, Emperor Charles V.   1584

Hocking, Joseph. The Sword of the Lord. Dutton, 1900.
An Englishman in Germany during the Reformation.   1585

Holland, Cecelia. Rakóssy. Atheneum, 1967. A courageous
Hungarian nobleman endeavors to defend his land and people
against Turkish invaders.   1586

Kleinhans, Theodore J. Printer's Devil from Wittenberg. Augsburg, 1962. YA. A young man, confined in Wittenberg by
an injury, learns of Martin Luther's teachings.   1587

Klingenstein, L. Great Infanta. Putnam, 1911. Isabel of
Spain, eldest daughter of Philip II, and her role as sovereign
of the Netherlands.   1588

Lee, Albert. The Key of the Holy House. Pearson, 1898.
The escape of prisoners from the dungeons of the Inquisition and popular opposition to Spanish rule in the Netherlands.   1589

Liefde, Jacob B. de. The Beggars. Scribner, 1868. Fighters
for freedom in the Netherlands unite to protest the Inquisition.   1590

Maas, Mabel. The Two Flames. (tr.) Cape, 1922. Conditions in Leyden and Bruges early in the century.   1591

Macleod, Alison. City of Light. Houghton, 1969. Amorous
and religious adventures of Thomas Vaughan in Geneva after
his exile from England.   1592

Mally, Emma Louise. The Tides of Dawn. Sloane, 1949.
Sixteenth century Netherlands with a picture of contemporary
religious dissension.   1593

Malo, Henri. The Romantic Passion of Don Luis. (tr.)
Harrap, 1925. Life in the Low Countries in the days of
the Duke of Parma.   1594

Mason, Caroline A. A Lily of France. Griffith, 1901. The
career of William of Orange, Dutch revolutionary, and
Charlotte de Bourbon, his third wife.   1595

Nietschmann, Hermann Otto. Prince Albrecht of Brandenburg.
German Literary Board, 1907. Features Tetzel, who
aroused Luther's opposition by his misuse of indulgences. 1596

Orczy, Baroness Emmuska. Leatherface. Doran, 1916.
    Story of the "Beggars" following the arrival of the Duke of
    Alva in the Netherlands.   1597

Ritchie, Rita. The Enemy at the Gate. Dutton, 1959. YA.
    A young gunsmith has a part in breaking the 1529 siege of
    Vienna.   1598

Rothberg, Abraham. The Sword of the Golem. McCall, 1970.
    A story of the Golem, a man-made human being of Jewish
    folklore, in the historical setting of sixteenth century Prague.
                                                                1599
Sargent, H. Garton. A Woman and a Creed. Blackwood, 1902.
    Religious persecution in Antwerp.   1600

Sinclair, Kathleen. The Valiant Lady. by Brigid Knight, pseud.
    Doubleday, 1948. Wars between Holland and Spain and emer-
    gence of the Dutch Republic.   1601

Stevenson, John P. Captain General. Doubleday, 1956. Ac-
    tion against backdrop of Netherlands' resistance to Spain's
    Philip II.   1602

Vansittart, Peter. The Siege. Walker, 1962. Account of the
    Anabaptist dream of "a kingdom of God on earth" during
    their temporary control of Münster, Germany.   1603

Walker, Frances M. Cotton. Cloister to Court. Longmans,
    1909. Princess Charlotte leaves a convent to contract mar-
    riage with William of Orange.   1604

Weyman, Stanley J. The Story of Francis Cludde. Longmans,
    1898. A young man embarks on a life of adventure in the
    Netherlands to escape persecution.   1605

Williams, Jay. The Rogue from Padua. Little, 1952. A
    wandering rascal's adventures in Germany during the
    Peasants' War.   1606

Zara, Louis. Against This Rock. Creative Age, 1943. The
    life of the powerful Emperor Charles V.   1607

    3) Scandinavia and the Baltic

Antal-Opzoomer, Adèle Sophia Cornelia von. Royal Favour.
    (tr.) by A.S.C. Wallis, pseud. Sonnenschein, 1884. Story
    of Goran Person, who becomes Chancellor to the weak and
    cruel King Eric XIV of Sweden.   1608

Jensen, Johannes Vilhelm. The Fall of the King. (tr.) Holt,
    1933. Adventures of a student who becomes a messenger
    and friend of Denmark's Christian II.   1609

Jensen, Wilhelm. Karine. (tr.) McClurg, 1896. A romance
of the reign of Gustavus Vasa of Sweden.   1610

Waltari, Mika. The Adventurer. (tr.) Putnam, 1950. A
Finn wanders about Europe early in the century, meeting
leading characters of the day. (followed by The Wanderer)
                                                            1611

c) Southern Europe

1) Iberian Peninsula

Blake, Gladys. Doña Isabella's Adventures. Appleton, 1928.
Gay story of a lady-in-waiting to the Queen and a young
soldier, Miguel Cervantes, who later wrote Don Quixote
[listed in this section under Cervantes].   1612

Bloundelle-Burton, John. The Sea Devils. White, 1912. Adventures of a sailor in the Spanish Armada and his later imprisonment and suffering in the Inquisition.   1613

Borton, Elizabeth. The Greek of Toledo. Crowell, 1959.
The life of El Greco both as a man and a great artist.   1614

Bowen, Marjorie, pseud. for Gabrielle Campbell Long. A
Knight of Spain. Methuen, 1913. Successes of Don Juan
of Austria at Lepanto and in the Netherlands, which displeased
his half-brother, Philip II.   1615

Braider, Donald. Color From a Light Within. Putnam, 1967.
Based on the life of El Greco, whose ambition and talent
combined to produce marvelous expressions of faith in his
religious paintings.   1616

Cervantes Saavedra, Miguel de. Don Quixote de la Mancha.
(tr.) Dodd, 1885. An excellent picture of the times is given
in this satire on chivalric romances with the hero a would-be
knight tilting at windmills.   1617

Crawford, F. Marion. In the Palace of the King. Macmillan,
1900. Suspense-filled story about a romance of Don Juan
of Austria which conflicted with the plans of King Philip II.
                                                            1618
De Wohl, Louis. The Golden Thread. Lippincott, 1952. Story
of St. Ignatius Loyola, interwoven with a tale of young
lovers.   1619

_____. Last Crusader. Lippincott, 1956. Don Juan of
Austria and the Battle of Lepanto.   1620

Frank, Bruno. A Man Called Cervantes. Viking, 1935. Life-
like picture of the creator of Don Quixote [listed in this section under Cervantes], with a vivid account of the Battle of

Lepanto.   1621

Hibbert, Eleanor. The Scarlet Cloak. by Jean Plaidy, pseud.
    Hale, 1969. (prev. pub. under the pseud. of Ellalice Tate
    in London in 1957) A tale of religious persecution in Spain,
    France, and England.   1622

_____. The Spanish Bridegroom. by Jean Plaidy, pseud.
    Putnam, 1971, c. 1956. Fictionalized effort to penetrate the
    true character of the enigmatic Philip II.   1623

Hocking, Joseph. A Flame of Fire. Revell, 1903. The hero,
    during a stay in Spain, obtains information which helps in
    England's defeat of the Armada.   1624

Kaye, Michael W. For Braganza. Greening, 1911. A romance
    of Portugal under Spanish rule.   1625

Larreta, Enrique. The Glory of Don Ramiro. Dutton, 1924.
    Don Ramiro's involvement in a plot for a Moorish uprising.
                                                             1626
Moore, H.C. A Devonshire Lass. Scott, 1908. Adventure in
    Spain during the Inquisition.   1627

O'Brien, Kate. For One Sweet Grape. [En. title: That Lady]
    Doubleday, 1946. Romance in the court of Philip II involving
    both the King and his minister.   1628

Sabatini, Rafael. The Hounds of God. Houghton, 1928. The
    Inquisition, Philip of Spain, and Elizabeth of England figure
    in this romance of a Spanish gentleman and an English
    lady.   1629

Schoonover, Lawrence. The Prisoner of Tordesillas. Little,
    1959. About Juana the Mad of Castile, imprisoned almost
    fifty years for insanity.   1630

Slaughter, Frank G. Divine Mistress. Pocket Bks., 1969,
    c. 1949. Romance during the Spanish Inquisition with art,
    medicine, and torture as ingredients.   1631

        2) Italy and Adjacent Islands

Ainsworth, W. Harrison. The Constable de Bourbon. Dutton,
    1866. This novel depicts the struggle for Milan between
    Francis I and Charles V; the bloody sack of Rome.   1632

Astor, William Waldorf. Sforza, A Story of Milan. Scribner,
    1886. Events in Milan in the sixteenth century with Ludo-
    vico Sforza, Duke of Milan, prominent.   1633

_____. Valentino. Scribner, 1885. Intrigues and exploits

of the notorious Cesare Borgia.   1634

Barton, Florence. Olympia. Fortress Pr., 1965. Since
Olympia Morata was not of noble blood and did not conform
to the popular religion, her artistic and literary gifts were
only partially realized.   1635

Cleveland, Treadwell, Jr. A Night With Alessandro. Holt,
1904. Episode in Florence under the last Medici.   1636

Drummond, Hamilton. The Half-Priest. Paul, 1916. Life in
Italy under the powerful and unscrupulous Borgia family.   1637

Dunnett, Dorothy. The Disorderly Knights. Putnam, 1966.
The defense of Malta against the Turks by the Knights of the
Order of St. John; and the role of knights in political affairs
at home in Scotland.   1638

Durbin, Charles. The Mercenary. Houghton, 1963. The fortunes
of Gianpaolo Baglioni, a mercenary captain in Renaissance
Italy who came into contact with most of the era's important
persons.   1639

Faust, Frederick. Bait and the Trap. by George Challis,
pseud. Harper, 1951. Narrative of a man in the service
of Duke Cesare Borgia.   1640

Gallizier, Nathan. The Court of Lucifer. Page, 1910. The
complicated entanglements of the Borgias in Rome and the
innocence of Lucrezia from involvement.   1641

_____. The Red Confessor. Page, 1926. Sensational story
of political and moral corruption in Rome in mid-century. 1642

Gardner, Edmund G. Desiderio. Dent, 1902. A novel of the
political dealings of Pope Julius II and King Louis XII.   1643

Gladd, Arthur Anthony. Galleys East! Dodd, 1961. YA. Adventure story of a youthful sponge diver who recovers sunken
jewels, is captured and used as a galley slave, escapes and
fights in the Battle of Lepanto.   1644

Godwin, William. St. Leon. Colburn & Bentley, 1831. Story
of a man who gains wealth but finds it does not bring happiness.   1645

Guerrazzi, Francesco D. Beatrice Cenci. (tr.) Ward & Lock,
1858. The tragic story of Beatrice Cenci, whose father's
cruelties drove her to desperate measures.   1646

Hausrath, Adolf. Father Maternus. (tr.) [same as: Pater
Maternus] by George Taylor, pseud. Dent, 1911. The
visit of two Augustinians from Germany discloses conditions

of religious life in Rome in 1511.   1647

Hicks Beach, Susan. A Cardinal of the Medici. Macmillan,
   1937. Ippolito de Medici, contemporary of Leo X, Clement
   VII, and Cardinal Bembo.   1648

Kaye, Michael W. The Honour of Bayard. Greening, 1912.
   Attempt to undermine Bayard's defense of a town.   1649

Kelland, Clarence Budington. Merchant of Valor. Harper,
   1947. Italy in the sixteenth century during the period of
   Medici ascendance.   1650

Kenyon, Frank Wilson. The Naked Sword. Dodd, 1968. Lucrezia Borgia, attractive daughter of Pope Alexander VI, and
   her unscrupulous brother, Cesare Borgia.   1651

Levett-Yeats, Sidney. The Honour of Savelli. Appleton, 1895.
   An adventure story telling of many famous persons--Machia-
   velli, the Borgia family, Cardinal d'Amboise.   .   1652

McCarthy, Justin Huntly. The Gorgeous Borgia. Harper,
   1908. A thrilling tale of the Borgia family.   1653

Marshall, Rosamond. The Rib of the Hawk. Appleton, 1958.
   Romance and conquest in Renaissance Rome.   1654

Merezhkovsky, Dmitri. The Forerunner. (tr.) [also titled:
   The Resurrection of the Gods; Leonardo da Vinci; and The
   Romance of Leonardo da Vinci] Constable, 1902. The blend-
   ing of pagan and Christian elements during the Renaissance;
   a vivid picture of Leonardo da Vinci. (followed by Peter and
   Alexis)   1655

Montgomery, K. L. , pseud. for Kathleen and Letitia Montgomery.
   The Cardinal's Pawn. McClurg, 1904. A colorful picture of
   the scheming Medici family of the High Renaissance.   1656

Mujica-Laiñez, Manuel. Bomarzo. (tr.) S. & S. , 1969.
   Life of the hunchbacked Duke of Bomarzo who fought in the
   Battle of Lepanto, told as an autobiography.   1657

Payne, Robert. Caravaggio. Little, 1968. Fictional autobiography of a great Italian painter who became famous for his
   dramatic use of light against a dark background.   1658

Prokosch, Frederic. A Tale for Midnight. Little, 1955. The
   murder of Francesco Cenci and his family's trial for the
   crime.   1659

Pugh, John J. Captain of the Medici. Little, 1953. The
   perilous adventures of the blacksmith captain of the notorious
   "Black Band."   1660

_____. High Carnival. Little, 1959. Pre-Lenten
carnival in prosperous Venice.   1661

Ritson, Arthur. My Lady Lucia. Mills & Boon, 1925. Italy
at the outset of the century, with a picture of Cesare
Borgia.   1662

Robinson, Emma. Caesar Borgia. Routledge, 1846. Rome in
the days when the Borgias wielded so much power.   1663

Sabatini, Rafael. Love at Arms. Hutchinson, 1907. Italy during the period of Borgia power early in the century.   1664

_____. The Shame of Motley. Hutchinson, 1908. The
Borgia family figures in this novel of the early sixteenth
century.   1665

_____. The Sword of Islam. Houghton, 1939. Genoese naval
action, romance, and captivity mark this typical Sabatini
tale.   1666

Sand, George, pseud. for Mme. Dudevant. The Master Mosaic-
Workers. (tr.) Little, 1895. Concerns craftsmen who
made the beautiful mosaics of St. Mark's Church.   1667

Scollard, Clinton. Count Falcon of the Eyrie. Page, 1903.
Venice and Milan are the setting for this romance.   1668

Spinatelli, Carl J. Baton Sinister. Little, 1959. Picaresque
tale of the natural son of a murdered nobleman.   1669

_____. The Florentine. Prentice-Hall, 1953. A biographi-
cal novel of Benvenuto Cellini and his life in Renaissance
Florence and Rome.   1670

Stacton, David. A Dancer in Darkness. Pantheon, 1962,
c. 1960. The opposition of her brothers to her love for
Antonio, her steward, leads the Duchess of Amalfi to ultimate tragedy (based on a 1613 play by John Webster).   1671

Stone, Irving. The Agony and the Ecstasy. Doubleday, 1961.
Michelangelo's personal life and career in Florence and
Rome.   1672

Tapparelli-D'Azeglio, Massimo. The Challenge of Barletta.
(tr.) Allen, 1880. Dissension between French and Spanish
after they jointly invaded Naples.   1673

_____. The Maid of Florence. (tr.) Bentley, 1853. De-
fense of Florence against the army of Emperor Charles V.
                                                           1674
Toye, Nina. The Death Rider. Cassell, 1916. Rome during
the time of Pope Julius II.   1675

Turnbull, Francese Hubbard. The Golden Book of Venice. by
  Mrs. Lawrence Turnbull. Century, 1900. Pictures Venice
  in the period of its dispute with Pope Paul V.   1676

Whiting, Mary B. The Plough of Shame. Dent, 1906. In the
  background are the accession and conquests of Charles V. 1677

  d) Eastern Europe (including Russia and the Balkans),
      the Near East, and North Africa

Bartos-Höppner, B. The Cossacks. (tr.) Walck, 1963,
  c.1962. YA. Cossack conquests in the Oryol region of Siberia, including the crossing of the Ural Mountains.   1678

_____. Save the Khan. (tr.) Walck, 1964. YA. The last
  part of the sixteenth century is the setting for this adventure
  story of the Tartars' struggle against the Russian invaders.
                                                            1679
Gogol, Nikolai V. Taras Bulba. (tr.) Crowell, 1886. The
  fierce fighting of the Cossacks against the Poles who invaded their territory.   1680

Lindsay, Philip. The Knights at Bay. Loring & Mussey, 1935.
  The Knights Hospitallers and their fighting against the Turks.
                                                            1681
Waltari, Mika. The Wanderer. (tr.) Putnam, 1951. A
  Finnish adventurer in North Africa and the Ottoman Em-
  pire.   1682

Whishaw, Frederick J. A Boyar of the Terrible. Longmans,
  1896. The ruthless Ivan IV, the Terrible, and his diplomatic relations with other countries.   1683

_____. The Tiger of Muscovy. Longmans, 1904. A lively
  English girl in Russia at the court of Ivan the Terrible. 1684

White, Leslie Turner. Sir Rogue. Crown, 1954. Swashbuckling tale of Russia and Ivan the Terrible.   1685

  e) Overseas Exploration, Enterprise and Expansion

Balfour, Andrew. By Stroke of Sword. Lane, 1897. Adventures in Scotland, England, and on the sea during the
  troubled times following Mary of Scotland's imprisonment. 1686

Cornford, L. Cope. Sons of Adversity. Page, 1898. A sea
  story of England and Holland.   1687

De Wohl, Louis. Set All Afire. Lippincott, 1953. Compelling
  account of the dedication and missionary labors of St. Francis
  Xavier.   1688

Griffith, George. John Brown, Buccaneer. White, 1908.
Success of English sea power as Spain's national power
diminishes.   1689

Haggard, H. Rider. Montezuma's Daughter. Longmans, 1893.
An Englishman seeks his mother's murderer in Spain and
Mexico.   1690

Hodgson, W. H. The Boats of the Glen-Carrig. Chapman, 1907.
Old mariner's tale of adventures in the South Seas.   1691

Jennings, John. The Golden Eagle. Putnam, 1958. A romance of the conquistador De Soto is related along with an
account of his explorations.   1692

Johnston, Mary. Sir Mortimer. Houghton, 1904. The Spanish
Main in the time of Drake, when Queen Elizabeth was offi-
cially unaware of pirating.   1693

Kent, Louise Andrews. He Went With Magellan. Houghton, 1943.
YA. A young sailor accompanies Magellan on his circum-
navigation of the globe.   1694

Kingsley, Charles. Westward Ho! Macmillan, 1855. Adventures of English seamen who defeated the Spanish Armada
and established English naval supremacy.   1695

Knight, Frank. Remember Vera Cruz! Dial, 1966. YA.
Slave trading, sea battles, and daring escapes hasten the
growing up process of a young sailor.   1696

Koningsberger, Hans. The Golden Keys. Rand, 1956. YA.
A tale of a courageous Dutch boy who sailed with the explorer Barents to find a northeast passage to the Indies.   1697

Lomask, Milton. Ship's Boy with Magellan. Doubleday, 1960.
YA. A boy, running away from a scheming uncle, joins
Magellan's fleet for a three-year voyage around the world. 1698

Raynolds, Robert. The Quality of Quiros. Bobbs, 1955. A
tale of Spanish and Portuguese exploration in the Pacific. 1699

Sabatini, Rafael. The Sea-Hawk. Houghton, 1915. Adventures
of the lusty sea-rover Sir Oliver Tressilian.   1700

Schmeltzer, Kurt. Long Arctic Night. (tr.) Watts, 1952.
YA. The Barents Expedition left Amsterdam in 1594 in a
tragic attempt to find a passage through the Arctic to the
Orient.   1701

Smith, Ralph. The Dragon in New Albion. by S.H. Paxton,
pseud. Little, 1953. Sir Francis Drake, called the
"Dragon" by the Spaniards, claimed California for the Eng-

lish under the name of "New Albion."   1702

Wibberley, Leonard. King's Beard. Farrar, 1952. YA. Sir
Francis Drake's expedition "to singe the King of Spain's
beard" included two adventurous Devon boys.   1703

2. SEVENTEENTH CENTURY: AGE OF ABSOLUTISM

   a) The British Isles

   1) England, Wales, and Scotland

Ainsworth, W. Harrison. Boscobel; or, The Royal Oak.
Dutton, 1872. The escape of Charles II after the Battle of
Worcester.   1704

_____. Guy Fawkes. Dutton, 1841. Causes and failure
of the Gunpowder Plot which involved Catholics suffering
under harsh penal laws.   1705

_____. James the Second. Carey. & Hart, 1848. Includes
accounts of the Seven Bishops' Trial and the revolution of
1688.   1706

_____. The Lancashire Witches. Dutton, 1848. A story
of the persecution of supposed witches in Lancashire. 1707

_____. The Leaguer of Lathom. Routledge, 1880. Color-
ful tale of Lancashire during the Civil War, with the siege
of Lathom House and the execution of the Earl of Derby. 1708

_____. Old St. Paul's. Dutton, 1841. A grocer's family
in London during the plague and great fire of mid-century. 1709

_____. Ovingdean Grange. Dutton, 1860. Charles II's
escape to France after his defeat at Worcester.   1710

_____. The Star Chamber. Dutton, 1854. Activities of
the Court of the Star Chamber and general customs of the
period of James I.   1711

Anderson, H. M. Kelston of Kells. Blackwood, 1927. Rivalry
in Scotland between Episcopalians and Presbyterians.   1712

Arthur, Mary Lucy. The Baton Sinister. by George David
Gilbert, pseud. Long, 1903. A sympathetic account of
the personal life of the Duke of Monmouth.   1713

Bailey, H. C. Beaujeu. Murray, 1905. A story of the last
days of the Stuart dynasty recounting the downfall of James
II.   1714

_____. Colonel Greatheart. [En. title: Colonel Stow]
Bobbs, 1908. A Civil War story which includes the
Battle of Newbury and presents both sides of the conflict.   1715

_____. The Plot. Methuen, 1922. Written around the
Popish Plot of 1678.   1716

Baker, H. Barton. For the Honour of His House. Digby &
Long, 1906. Court life from Monmouth's defeat until
James II's downfall.   1717

Bamfylde, Walter. The Road to Arcady. Low, 1917. Love
surmounts differences of nationality, religion, and political
belief.   1718

Baring-Gould, S. Urith. Methuen, 1891. The rough, rugged
moor people of Dartmoor during the controversy over Monmouth's movement.   1719

Barnes, Margaret Campbell. Mary of Carisbrooke. Macrae
Smith, 1956. Royalist intrigue involves a sergeant's daughter in the life of Charles I.   1720

_____. With All My Heart. Macrae Smith, 1951. A novel
of Catherine of Braganza, consort of Charles II.   1721

_____, and Hebe Elsna, pseud. for D. P. Ansle. Lady
on the Coin. Macrae Smith, 1963. The duties and
pleasures of a Maid of Honor to Charles II's Queen.   1722

Barnes-Austin, Edgar. Mark Eminence. by E. Wynton
Locke, pseud. McBride, 1947. English life and customs
during the rule of Charles II.   1723

Barney, Helen Corse. Light in the Rigging. Crown, 1955.
A rousing tale of an officer in the English Navy.   1724

Barr, Amelia E. Friend Olivia. Dodd, 1898. England in
the days of Cromwell with events involving Puritans and
members of the new Quaker sect.   1725

Barr, Robert. Over the Border. Stokes, 1903. Adventures
of a messenger to the king during the mid-century Civil
War.   1726

Barrett, Frank. The Obliging Husband. Chatto, 1907. Tale
of a spirited girl whose forced marriage turns out to be
successful.   1727

_____. A Set of Rogues. Innes, 1896. A company of
poverty-stricken actors tours in the country while the
plague rages in London.   1728

Barrington, Michael. The Knight of the Golden Sword. Chatto,
1909. Plots and events during Restoration times with an un-
sympathetic account of Covenanter activities.   1729

Bates, Arthur. Cromwell. Popular Lib., 1970. The role of
Cromwell in an England threatened by rival factions for power
--King, people, Parliament, the Army.   1730

Bayly, Ada. In Spite of All. by Edna Lyall, pseud. Longmans, 1901. Vicissitudes of Puritans in England at the time
of Charles I.   1731

_____. To Right the Wrong. by Edna Lyall, pseud. Harper,
1893. Romance of Civil War England with John Hampden as
a chief character.   1732

Beatty, John and Patricia. Campion Towers. Macmillan, 1965.
YA. A Puritan girl from Massachusetts faces problems
while visiting her relatives in England in Cromwellian times.
                                                          1733
_____. Witch Dog. Morrow, 1968. YA. Story of the Eng-
lish Civil War centers on a dog believed to have supernatural
powers.   1734

Beck, Lily Adams. The Great Romantic. by E. Barrington,
pseud. Doubleday, 1933. Based on the public and the tumultuous private lives of Samuel Pepys and his lovely French
wife, Elizabeth.   1735

Beebe, Elswyth Thane. Queen's Folly. by Elswyth Thane.
Harcourt, 1937. Four-generation story of a family living
in a house presented to an ancestor who had performed a
service for Queen Elizabeth.   1736

Benson, Claude E. Miles Ritson. Low, 1925. An adventure
tale of the late 1880s with Claverhouse appearing.   1737

Benson, Robert Hugh. Oddsfish! Hutchinson, 1914. Clever,
compelling novel of political and religious intrigue in Restoration England.   1738

Bentley, Phyllis. The Power and the Glory. Macmillan, 1940.
Inter-relationships between two families--one Royalist and
one Puritan.   1739

Berridge, Jesse. The Stronghold. Melrose, 1926. Stresses
the religious aspect of the English Civil War at the time of
Cromwell.   1740

Besant, Walter. For Faith and Freedom. Harper, 1888.
The plight of the Puritans during the reign of James II. 1741

Binns, Ottwell. The Sword of Fortune. by Ben Bolt, pseud.

Ward & Lock, 1927.   Adventures in England during Monmouth's Rebellion against James II.   1742

Blackmore, R. D. Lorna Doone. Harper, 1874. Romance of Lorna and her captor, the robber Doone.   1743

Blayney, Owen. The MacMahon. Constable, 1898. Novel centering on the Battle of the Boyne.   1744

Blissett, Nellie K. The Silver Key. Smart Set, 1905. The royal families of the English and French courts.   1745

Blyth, James. The King's Guerdon. Digby & Long, 1906. Recounts the naval battle off Lowestaft and the great plague and fire of the 1660s in London.   1746

Bowen, Marjorie, pseud. for Gabrielle Campbell Long. The Glen o' Weeping. Beagle Bks., 1971, c.1953, 1907. The Glencoe Pass Massacre of 1692 and the clan feud between Macdonalds and Campbells.   1747

_____. The Governor of England. Dutton, 1914. Well-written account of Cromwell's rise to power.   1748

_____. (1) I Will Maintain. Methuen, 1910. (2) Defender of the Faith. Methuen, 1911. (3) God and the King. Methuen, 1911. Political undercurrents during the Revolution and the reign of William III and Mary, with significant people and events.   1749-51

Braddon, Mary E. In High Places. Hutchinson, 1898. The assassination of the Duke of Buckingham, the English Civil War, and contemporary France.   1752 ⅴ

_____. London Pride. Simpkin, 1896. The execution of Charles I and the later restoration of Charles II.   1753

Bray, Claude. A Cuirassier of Arran's. Sands, 1900. Action during the so-called "Glorious Revolution"--the landing of William and the flight of James II.   1754

Brebner, Percy J. The Brown Mask. Cassell, 1910. Adventure story of Monmouth's Rebellion and the Bloody Assize with infamous Judge Jeffreys.   1755

Bryher, Winifred (Annie Winifred Macpherson). The Player's Boy. Pantheon, 1953. A vivid picture of decline in England after Elizabeth's reign.   1756

Buchan, John. John Burnet of Barns. Lane, 1898. University life in Scotland and the Netherlands during persecution of the Covenanters.   1757

_____. Witch Wood. Houghton, 1927. The hero's opposi-
tion to the persecution of witches incurs abuse and condemnation.   1758

Bunbury, Selina. Coombe Abbey. Willoughby, 1843. "An historical tale of the reign of James the First."   1759

Burchell, Sidney Herbert. Daniel Herrick. Gay & Hancock,
1900. Romance of a news-writer in London during the plague
of 1665.   1760

_____. The Duke's Servants. Little, 1899. A troupe of
players in rural England in the period of the Duke of Buckingham's assassination.   1761

_____. The Prisoner of Carisbrooke. Gay & Hancock, 1904.
The flight of Charles I to the Isle of Wight.   1762

Burnett, Frances Hodgson. (1) A Lady of Quality. Scribner,
1896. (2) His Grace of Osmonde (sequel). Scribner, 1897.
The adventurous life of an apparent lady who achieves position and honor.   1763-4

Caine, Hall. The Shadow of a Crime. Caldwell, 1885. Exciting murder mystery set in Quaker England.   1765

Carr, John Dickson. The Devil in Velvet. Harper, 1951.
History professor finds a way to return to Restoration England in this historical fantasy.   1766

_____. Murder of Sir Edmund Godfrey. Harper, 1936.
An historical murder-mystery concerning a real crime committed in 1678.   1767

Caute, David. Comrade Jacob. Pantheon, 1963, c.1961. The
utopian dreams of a small, semi-religious community of
Diggers in Cromwellian times.   1768

Chalmers, Stephen. When Love Calls Men to Arms. Richards,
1912. Feuds and fighting under James VI of Scotland based
on a seventeenth century manuscript.   1769

Chapman, Hester W. Lucy. Reynal, 1966, c.1965. A serving
maid is changed into a successful actress by Richard Nash, a
leading actor and stage manager, but his unkindness to her
dog causes complications.   1770

Charques, Dorothy. Dark Stranger. Coward, 1957. Combina-
tion of romance, religion, politics, and witchcraft in Cromwell's time.   1771

Church, Samuel Harden. Penruddock of the White Lambs.
Stokes, 1902. The daring revolt of Royalists under Colonel

Penruddock against Cromwell's forces.   1772

Clark, Justis Kent. The King's Agent. Scribner, 1958. Sir
Ralph Barnard decides his exiled master, James II, has no
chance to regain the throne of England.   1773

Clarke, Mary Stetson. Piper to the Clan. Viking, 1970. YA.
The inspiring story of Scotsmen who were taken prisoner by
Cromwell's army and sent to Massachusetts to work for
seven years.   1774

Cobban, J. MacLaren. The Angel of the Covenant. Fenno,
1898. Montrose and the struggle with the Presbyterians in
Scotland.   1775

Cooke, W. Bourne. Her Faithful Knight. Cassell, 1908. The
English Civil War as seen by a Roundhead soldier.   1776

Cowen, Laurence. Bible and Sword. Hodder & Stoughton, 1919.
The Cromwells, Charles I, John Milton, and his wife Mary
Powell all figure in this story.   1777

Crockett, Samuel R. The Cherry Ribband. Barnes, 1905.
Romance between a Covenanter boy and a girl of a different
belief.   1778

_____. The Gray Man. Harper, 1896. Exciting story of
feuds and discord in Scotland during the early seventeenth
century.   1779

_____. Lochinvar. Harper, 1897. Rousing military action
and romances of a soldier under both William of Orange and
Claverhouse.   1780

_____. The Men of the Moss-Hags. Macmillan, 1895.
The sufferings of the persecuted Covenanters.   1781

_____. The Standard Bearer. Appleton, 1898. Persecu-
tion and oppression of the Covenanters in Scotland.   1782

Dakers, Elaine. The Sealed Knot. by Jane Lane, pseud.
Beagle Bks., 1971. "The Sealed Knot" was a secret or-
ganization pledged to work for the restoration of the King
during the time of the Protectorate.   1783

_____. Thunder on St. Paul's Day. by Jane Lane, pseud.
Newman, 1954. A novel of the Popish Plot in England in
1678.   1784

Deeping, Warwick. Lantern Lane. Cassell, 1921. A story
of romance and adventure climaxing in a duel.   1785

_____. Mad Barbara. Cassell, 1908. A murder story

set in England at the time of the plague.   1786

_____. Orchards. Cassell, 1922. Life in Royalist England
in the seventeenth century.   1787

Defoe, Daniel. Memoirs of a Cavalier. Macmillan, 1720. A
military journal of wars in Germany (under Gustavus Adolphus)
and in England (under Charles I).   1788

De Morgan, William. An Affair of Dishonour. Holt, 1910.
Naval warfare between the English-French fleets and the
Dutch navy in 1672.   1789

Dexter, Charles. Street of Kings. Holt, 1957. Murder and
intrigue in the court of James I.   1790

Dilnot, Frank. Mad Sir Peter. Macmillan, 1932. An action-
filled tale of England in the time of William and Mary.   1791

Dix, Beulah M. The Fair Maid of Graystones. Macmillan,
1905. A young Cavalier prisoner of a Puritan family--his
adventures and marriage.   1792

_____. The Fighting Blade. Holt, 1912. Romantic adven-
tures of a German in the service of Cromwell.   1793

_____. The Life, Treason, and Death of James Blount of
Breckenhow. Macmillan, 1903. A subaltern assumes the
blame for another's act of cowardice.   1794

Dodge, Constance. Graham of Claverhouse. Covici, 1937.
Religious struggles resulting from Charles II's attempt to
establish Episcopacy in Scotland.   1795

_____. The Pointless Knife. Covici, 1937. A tale of the
MacGregor clan, forbidden to carry any weapons except a
pointless knife.   1796

Douglas, Alan. For the King. Macrae Smith, 1926. Masquerade of a Roundhead as his Cavalier brother leads to danger.
                                                             1797
Doyle, Sir Arthur Conan. Micah Clarke. Longmans, 1888. Adventure-
packed account of the fighting in Monmouth's Rebellion.   1798

Du Maurier, Daphne. Frenchman's Creek. Doubleday, 1942.
The love of a noble lady for a pirate in the reign of
Charles II.   1799

_____. The King's General. Doubleday, 1946. Cloak and
dagger tale of Cornwall during England's Civil Wars.   1800

Eccott, W. J. Fortune's Castaway. Blackwood, 1905. Sympathetic
account of the Rye House Plot and Monmouth's Rebellion.   1801

Ellis, Beth. <u>Barbara Winslow, Rebel.</u> Blackwood, 1903. A
girl's rebellious activities point up the prejudice and injustice
of the latter part of the century.   1802

_____. <u>The King's Spy.</u> Dodd, 1910. A romance of Marl-
borough's plot to put Anne on the throne of England.   1803

Eyre-Todd, George. <u>Anne of Argyle.</u> [later pub. as: <u>Cavalier
and Covenant</u>] Stokes, 1895. Charles II's exile after the
execution of his father; Cromwell's invasion of Scotland.   1804

Fairbairn, Roger. <u>Devil Kinsmere.</u> Harper, 1934. A dashing
young provincial joins the "secret service" of Charles II.   1805

Farnol, Jeffery. <u>Martin Conisby's Vengeance.</u> Little, 1921.
Highly colored adventure story of pirates in seventeenth century England and of the Spanish Inquisition.   1806

Fea, Allan. <u>My Lady Wentworth.</u> Mills & Boon, 1909. Story
of Monmouth and the rebellion he led.   1807

Felton, Ronald Oliver. <u>For the King.</u> by Ronald Welch, pseud.
Criterion, 1962, c.1961. YA. The younger son of a Welsh
nobleman who fought for Charles I.   1808

Finkel, George. <u>The Loyal Virginian.</u> Viking, 1968. YA. A
Virginian, in England to market American tobacco, is drawn
into plots to rescue King Charles.   1809

Finnemore, John. <u>The Red Men of the Dusk.</u> Lippincott, 1899.
Adventures of a fugitive Cavalier and a band of outlaws.   1810

Fox, Marion. <u>The Hand of the North.</u> Lane, 1911. A story
of border warfare which gives a good picture of Essex's
plot against the aging Elizabeth.   1811

Galt, John. <u>Ringan Gilhaize.</u> Greening, 1899. Stirring account of the Battle of Killiecrankie in the Scottish uprising
of 1688.   1812

Garnett, Henry. <u>Gamble for a Throne.</u> Barnes, 1959, c.1958.
A Royalist uprising against the Roundheads in England in the
mid-seventeenth century.   1813

Garnier, Russell M. <u>His Counterpart.</u> Harper, 1898. "An
historical romance of the early days of John Churchill,
first Duke of Marlborough."   1814

Garrett, George. <u>Death of the Fox.</u> Doubleday, 1971. Sir
Walter Raleigh rose into high favor with Queen Elizabeth,
but so displeased King James I that he lost his head on the
executioner's block.   1815

Gerson, Noel B. The White Plume. by Samuel Edwards, pseud. Morrow, 1961. Events in the life of the versatile Rupert of the Rhine,
who distinguished himself in the service of the Stuarts--his uncle,
Charles I, and his cousin, Charles II.   1816

Gissingham, James. For Prince or Pope. Greening, 1910.
Country life in England shortly before the coming of William
of Orange.   1817

Gore, Catherine Grace. The Courtier. Weldon, 1877. A story
of the court of Charles II.   1818

Goudge, Elizabeth. The Child From the Sea. Pyramid, 1971,
c. 1970. The fascinating life story of Lucy Walter, child of
the turbulent Welsh coast, who became the secret wife of
exiled Charles II.   1819

_____. The White Witch. Coward, 1957. A "white witch,"
part gypsy, who used her influence for good in Puritan England.   1820

Grierson, Edward. Dark Torrent of Glencoe. Doubleday,
1960. The feud between the Campbell and Macdonald clans
leading to the Massacre of Glencoe in 1632.   1821

Griffin, E. Aceituna. A Servant of the King. Blackwood, 1906.
Background is the story of Thomas Wentworth's service to
Charles I, his trial, and execution.   1822

Griffin, Gerald. The Duke of Monmouth. Duffy (Dublin) 1857.
The scene is Somerset; the action is Monmouth's Rebellion
from his landing to his execution.   1823

Grogan, Walter E. The King's Cause. Milne, 1909. Prince
Rupert's capture of Bristol.   1824

Hales, A. G. Maid Molly. Treherne, 1907. A romance of
fighting in Yorkshire--the Battle of Naseby.   1825

Hamilton, John A. Captain John Lister. Hutchinson, 1906.
Effects of the Civil War on English and Dutch commoners.
                                                                1826
_____. The Ms. in a Red Box. Lane, 1903. The first
successful drainage of the Fens of Lincolnshire by Cornelius
Vermuyden.   1827

Hartley, J. Wesley. In the Iron Time. Jennings & Graham,
1908. Adventures of a youthful soldier in Cromwell's
service.   1828

Hartley, Percy J. My Lady of Cleeve. Dodd, 1908. Continued plotting of the Jacobites after William's victory.   1829

Hatton, Joseph. The Dagger and the Cross. Fenno, 1897.
Conditions resulting from the plague of 1665.   1830

Hawkins, Anthony Hope. Simon Dale. by Anthony Hope, pseud.
Stokes, 1897. A romance of Charles II's court with Nell
Gwyn as the object of affection.   1831

Henkle, Henrietta. All the Living. by Henrietta Buckmaster,
pseud. Random House, 1962. An exciting year (1600) in
the life of William Shakespeare when he was deeply involved
with the Dark Lady of his sonnets.   1832

Heyer, Georgette. The Great Roxhythe. Small, 1923. The
Marquis of Roxhythe was Charles II's close political friend;
his only desire was to serve his king.   1833

_____. Royal Escape. Dutton, 1967, c.1938. The escape of
Charles II from Worcester to France.   1834

Hibbert, Eleanor. A Health Unto His Majesty. by Jean Plaidy,
pseud. Hale, 1956. A story of Charles II, his wife, and
his mistress.   1835

_____. Here Lies Our Sovereign Lord. by Jean Plaidy,
pseud. Hale, 1957. Spotlights actress Nell Gwyn, the extraordinary mistress of King Charles II.   1836

_____. Murder in the Tower. by Jean Plaidy, pseud. Hale,
1964. Ambition and scheming run afoul of murder in England during the reign of James I.   1837

_____. The Wandering Prince. by Jean Plaidy, pseud.
Putnam, 1971. (pub. in En. in 1956) Charles II as a wandering prince in exile prior to the Restoration.   1838

Hill, Frank Ernest. King's Company. Dodd, 1950. YA.
About the people who worked at the Globe Theatre in London
and presented Shakepeare's plays.   1839

Hill, William K. Under Three Kings. Routledge, 1907. Reflects the political scene in the time of Charles II, James
II, and William III.   1840

Hillary, Max. The Blue Flag. Ward & Lock, 1898. Somer-
setshire during the unrest incident to Monmouth's Rebellion.
                                                          1841

Hocking, Joseph. The Chariots of the Lord. Eaton & Mains,
1909. Plots and counter-plots involving James II, Judge
Jeffreys, and Monmouth before the landing of William of
Orange.   1842

_____. The Coming of the King. Ward & Lock, 1904.
The early years of Charles II's reign and enforcement of

the Act of Uniformity.   1843

Hooper, I. His Grace o' the Gunne. Black, 1898. Life and
adventures of a vagabond thief.   1844

Hope, Elizabeth. My Lady's Bargain. Century, 1923. A story
with a surprise ending set in England during the Protectorate.   1845

Hope, Jessie. The Lady of Lyte. by Graham Hope, pseud.
Methuen, 1905. Conflict within the court at the time of the
Popish Plot of 1678.   1846

_____. My Lord Winchenden. by Graham Hope, pseud.
Elder, 1902. Village life--social and political--during the
Restoration period.   1847

Hunt, J.H. Leigh. Sir Ralph Esher. Colburn, 1832. About
the ravages of the Great Plague and sea fights with the
Dutch.   1848

Hunt, Mabel Leigh. Beggar's Daughter. Lippincott, 1963. YA.
About a girl whose penniless mother sold her as an infant to
a Quaker family who suffered religious persecution in England.   1849

Hunter, P. Hay. Bible and Sword. Hodder, 1905. A story of
the Covenanters' fight for freedom from persecution.   1850

Irwin, Margaret. The Bride. Harcourt, 1939. The Stuart cause
during the months between the executions of Charles I and the
Marquis of Montrose.   1851

_____. The Proud Servant. Harcourt, 1934. James Graham,
first Marquis of Montrose, and his efforts to win Scotland for
Charles I.   1852

_____. Stranger Prince. Harcourt, 1937. Prince Rupert,
son of Elizabeth of Bohemia, and his part in the English
Civil War.   1853

Jahoda, Gloria. Annie. Houghton, 1960. The love of a manor
house maid and the crippled son of the house's owner.   1854

James, G. P. R. Arabella Stuart. Dutton, 1844. Romance of
William Seymour and Arabella Stuart.   1855

_____. Arrah Neil. Dutton, 1845. A romance of the early
part of the English Civil War.   1856

_____. The Fate. Newby, 1851. Social life in the Lincoln-
shire-Nottinghamshire area of England during Monmouth's Rebellion.   1857

_____. Gowrie. Dutton, 1851. Based on the Gowrie Con-
spiracy of 1600.   1858

_____. Henry Masterton. Colburn & Bentley, 1832. Ad-
ventures of a young Cavalier at the Royalist downfall. (followed by Life and Adventures of John Marston Hall)   1859

_____. The King's Highway. Dutton, 1840. Jacobite con-
spiracy against William III.   1860

James, Miss W. M. The Carved Cartoon. by Austin Clare,
pseud. S. P. C. K., 1874. London just after mid-century
during the disastrous fire and plague.   1861

Jeffries, Graham Montague. Soldiers of Fortune. by Peter
Bourne, pseud. Putnam, 1963, c. 1962. Emigrants waiting
for favorable sailing weather explain why they are leaving
the England of James I for the Virginia colony.   1862

Jenkins, Burris Atkins. The Bracegirdle. Lippincott, 1922.
The wooing of Anne Bracegirdle, star of the London theater.   1863

Johnston, Mary. The Witch. Houghton, 1914. Life in England under James I, featuring trials of accused witches.   1864

Jones, Dora M. A Soldier of the King. Cassell, 1901.
Centers on the Royalist defeat at Maidstone.   1865

Jordan, Helen Rosaline. The Swan of Usk. Macmillan, 1940.
Concerning the life of the poet Henry Vaughan.   1866

Judah, Charles Burnet. Christopher Humble. Morrow, 1956.
Adventure on two continents as the hero, involved in the
Titus Oates Plot, finally returns to Virginia.   1867

Kamm, Josephine. Return to Freedom. Abelard, 1962. YA.
A story of the persecution suffered by the Jews in England
and of its abatement.   1868

Kaye-Smith, Sheila. Gallybird. Harper, 1934. Strange marriage of a widower and a young gypsy.   1869

Keddie, Henrietta. The Witch-Wife. by Sarah Tytler, pseud.
Chatto, 1897. A grim story of the witch burnings in Scotland.   1870

Kenyon, Frank Wilson. The Glory and the Dream. Dodd, 1963.
The pomp and glamour of the reigns of James II, William
and Mary, and Queen Anne, reflected in the lives of John
and Sarah Churchill, the first Duke and Duchess of Marlborough.   1871

_____. Mistress Nell. [En. title: Mrs. Nelly] Appleton,
1961. Life and adventures of Eleanor Gwyn, actress and
favourite of King Charles II.   1872

Keynes, Helen Mary. Honour the King. Chatto & Windus,
1914. The scene is Charles I's England, including the
Siege of Bristol.   1873

_____. The Spanish Marriage. Chatto & Windus, 1913.
Trip of Prince Charles, son of James I, to Madrid in 1623
for a secret discussion of a possible state marriage.   1874

Knowles, Mabel Winifred. Hey for Cavaliers. by May Wynne,
pseud. Greening, 1912. The siege of Pontefract Castle. 1875

Lambert, Frederick Arthur. The Accuser. by Frederick
Arthur, pseud. Nash & Grayson, 1927. Titus Oates and
the Popish Plot from an anti-Puritan viewpoint.   1876

Lance, Rupert. The Golden Pippin. Allen & Unwin, 1917.
Plots against Charles II after the Restoration.   1877

Lane, Elinor Macartney. All for the Love of a Lady. Appleton, 1906. Romance of a French duke and a Scots lady. 1878

LeGallienne, Richard. There Was a Ship. Doubleday, Doran,
1930. A light, lyrical novel of romance and search for
hidden treasure.   1879

Lewis, Hilda Winifred. Call Lady Purbeck. St. Martin's,
1962. Frances Coke, forced to marry the half-insane Vi-
count Purbeck at age fifteen, fell in love with her handsome
cousin and suffered the revenge of her husband's family. 1880

_____. Catherine. Putnam, 1966, c.1965. Portuguese
Princess Catherine of Braganza, wife of Charles II of England, is compelled to compete with a succession of mis-
tresses.   1881

_____. Wife to Great Buckingham. Putnam, 1960. The
Duke of Buckingham's life as recounted by his wife, Catherine.   1882

Linington, Elizabeth. The Kingbreaker. Doubleday, 1958.
Spying in Oliver Cromwell's household during the English
Civil War.   1883

Lobdell, Helen. The King's Snare. Houghton, 1955. YA.
A boy's view of Sir Walter Raleigh's expedition to the Orin-
oco and his fall from political favor which cost him his
life.   1884

Lorraine, Rupert. The Woman and the Sword. McClurg, 1908.

Troubles in England and Germany at the time of the Star
Chamber and the Thirty Years War.   1885

Mabie, Mary Louise. The Pale Survivor. Bobbs, 1934. A
disillusioned English lady sails for America and is captured by pirate Henry Morgan.   1886

Macaulay, Rose. The Shadow Flies. Harper, 1932. This
novel, written in contemporary language, treats of Herrick,
Milton, and other poets of the day.   1887

McCarthy, Justin Huntly. In Spacious Times. Hurst & Blackett,
1916. Romantic tale of Elizabethan England in the last years
of the Queen's life.   1888

_____. The Lady of Loyalty House. Harper, 1904. A
light romance of the Civil War period.   1889

_____. The O'Flynn. Harper, 1910. Tale of a follower
of the deposed James in his search for Irish support in opposition to William III.   1890

McChesney, Dora Greenwell. Cornet Strong of Ireton's Horse.
Lane, 1903. Puritan-slanted story of the battles and sieges
of the Civil War.   1891

_____. Miriam Cromwell, Royalist. Blackwood, 1897.
English society at the time of Oliver Cromwell reflected
in the lives of his niece, Miriam, and Royalist Prince
Rupert.   1892

_____. Rupert, by the Grace of God. Macmillan, 1899.
The siege of Bristol and an unauthorized plot to make
Prince Rupert king are spotlighted.   1893

_____. Yesterday's To-Morrow. Dent, 1905. Life in
Restoration England with an undercurrent of religious unrest.   1894

Macdonald, George. St. George and St. Michael. Munro,
1875. Romance between a Roundhead and a Royalist and
the exploits of Somerset in the Civil War.   1895

MacDonald, Ronald. The Sword of the King. Century, 1900.
England and Holland under James II and William of Orange.
                                                              1896
McKemy, Kay. Samuel Pepys of the Navy. Warne, 1970.
YA. An account of the Restoration of Charles II supposedly
told by the famous diarist, Pepys, together with events of
the latter's own life.   1897

Mackenna, Robert William. Flower o' the Heather. Murray,
1922. A romance which shows the sufferings and the zeal

of the Covenanters.   1898

_____. Through Flood and Fire. Murray, 1925. Romance
and adventure in Covenanter times, with a good picture of
Claverhouse.   1899

Macmillan, Malcolm. Dagonet the Jester. Macmillan, 1886.
The story of a jester in Puritan England.   1900

Macrae, J. A. For Kirk and King. Blackwood, 1911. Scottish lowland life at mid-century.   1901

Magnay, William. The Amazing Duke. Unwin, 1906. A romance whose central character is the Duke of Buckingham.
                                                               1902

Maitland, Alfred L. I Lived as I Listed. Wells Gardner,
1899. An adventure-romance of the road in Restoration England.   1903

Major, Charles. The Touchstone of Fortune. Macmillan,
1912. The memoirs of Baron Clyde, who thrived and fell
in the reign of Charles II.   1904

Marryat, Mrs. F. T. Romance of the Lady Arbell. White,
1899. Story of Arabella Stuart, whose proximity to England's
throne endangered her life.   1905

Marryat, Frederick. Snarleyyow. Carey & Hart, 1837. The
"dog fiend" has a leading role in this tale of smuggler
hunters.   1906

Marsh, John B. For Liberty's Sake. Strahan, 1873. A character study of Robert Ferguson, involved in a Jacobite
plot.   1907

Martin, A. D. Una Breakspear. Clarke, 1926. Reflects religious and political problems of the Commonwealth and
Restoration periods.   1908

Mason, A. E. W. The Courtship of Morrice Buckler. Macmillan, 1896. Romance-adventure of an Englishman in
Monmouth's Rebellion and in Europe in the 1680s.   1909

Mason, Caroline A. The Binding of the Strong. Revell, 1908.
Turbulent course of the marriage of John Milton and Mary
Powell.   1910

Mills, J. M. A. The Way Triumphant. Hutchinson, 1926.
Royalist romance of Scotland with the ill-fated Montrose
as hero.   1911

Montgomery, K. L., pseud. for Kathleen and Letitia Montgomery. Major Weir. Unwin, 1904. About Thomas Weir,

tried, convicted, and executed as a wizard in Scotland.   1912

Moore, F. Frankfort. Nell Gwyn--Comedian. Brentano's,
1901. A romance of the court of Charles II.   1913

Morley, Iris. We Stood for Freedom. Morrow, 1942. Monmouth's Rebellion and the fight for the cause of the common
people.   1914

Morrow, Honoré. Yonder Sails the "Mayflower." Morrow, 1934.
A story of the Puritans before they sailed for America.   1915

Munro, Neil. John Splendid. Dodd, 1898. War in the highlands with the Royalists under Montrose.   1916

Murdoch, Gladys. Mistress Charity Godolphin. Murray,
1914. Includes the trial and execution of Lady Alice Lisle,
implicated in Monmouth's Rebellion.   1917

Musters, Mrs. Chaworth. A Cavalier Stronghold. Simpkin,
1890. A romance of the Vale of Belvoir--Nottinghamshire.
                                                         1918

Mylechreest, Winifred Brookes. The Fairest of the Stuarts.
Low, 1912. Tells the story of Elizabeth and Henry, two
children of James I, and current superstition.   1919

Neill, Robert. Elegant Witch. Doubleday, 1952. Puritan
girl comes in contact with witchcraft in Lancashire, England.   1920

_____. Rebel Heiress. Doubleday, 1954. Adventure and
romance amid Restoration politics.   1921

_____. Traitor's Moon. Doubleday, 1952. Internal strife
in England around 1679.   1922

Nepean, Evelyn Maud. (1) Lanterns of Horn. Lane, 1923.
(2) Ivory and Apes. Bale, Sons & Danielson, 1921.
(3) My Two Kings. Dutton, 1918. all by Mrs. Evan
Nepean. A Stuart trilogy of Charles II's reign in which
each novel stands as a separate romance although many
of the same characters appear in all three.   1923-5

Orczy, Baroness Emmuska. Fire in Stubble. Methuen, 1912.
An English nobleman and a French tailor's daughter at the
time of the Popish Plot.   1926

_____. His Majesty's Well-Beloved. Doran, 1920. A
picturesque romance of the days of Charles II centered on
the actor, Thomas Betterton.   1927

_____. The Honourable Jim. Doran, 1924. Martial dis-
cord occasioned by political differences between Round-

heads and Cavaliers.   1928

Parker, Katherine. My Ladie Dundie. Gardner, 1926. About
the wife of the Scottish Jacobite chieftain, John Graham of
Claverhouse.   1929

Paterson, Arthur. Cromwell's Own. Harper, 1899. Cromwell's army in the English Civil War ending with the Battle
of Marston Moor.   1930

_____. The King's Agent. Appleton, 1902. Marlborough's
plotting in favor of Anne against William III.   1931

Payne, Robert. Roaring Boys. Doubleday, 1955. Shakespeare
and his players in rowdy Elizabethan England.   1932

Pease, Howard. (1) Magnus Sinclair. Constable, 1904.
(2) Of Mistress Eve (sequel). Constable, 1906. Scotland
and northern England during the Commonwealth and under
Charles II. (followed by The Burning Cresset)   1933-4

Pilgrim, David, pseud. for John Leslie Palmer and Hilary
Aiden St. George Saunders. The Grand Design. Harper,
1943. Charles II's natural son travels in Europe on missions for his father.   1935

_____. No Common Glory. Harper, 1941. Adventure story
of England centering on a natural son of Charles II. (followed by The Grand Design)   1936

Plant, C. P. The King's Pistols. Sonnenschein, 1902. A
story about the Court of Common Pleas.   1937

Porter, T. H. A Maid of the Malverns. Lynwood, 1911. A
romance of the Blackfriars Theater in Elizabethan London. 1938

Poynter, H. May. A Merry Heart. S. P. C. K., 1893.
Exile of Lady Grizel Baillie from James II's England and
her triumphant return with William.   1939

Quiller-Couch, Arthur T. The Splendid Spur. by Q., pseud.
Scribner, 1889. A messenger of Charles I finds adventure
in the performance of his duties.   1940

Raymond, Walter. In the Smoke of War. Macmillan, 1895.
Interesting account of Somerset in 1645 and the suffering
brought on by the Civil War.   1941

Reid, Hilda S. Two Soldiers and a Lady. Dutton, 1932. Attempts to obtain an incriminating document in Puritan-ruled
England.   1942

Reynolds, George W. M. The Rye House Plot. Dicks, 1884.

Based on the Rye House conspiracy of 1683.   1943

Richards, H. Grahame. Richard Somers. Blackwood, 1911.
England during the Civil War and Restoration.   1944

Roberton, Margaret H. A Gallant Quaker. Methuen, 1901.
Trials of the Quakers under the Stuarts, presenting William
Penn and George Fox.   1945

Robertson, William. The Kings of Carrick. Hamilton, 1890.
Historical romance of the feud among the Kennedys of Ayr-
shire.   1946

Robinson, Emma. Whitefriars. Dutton, 1844. A panoramic
view of people and events in the days of Charles II.   1947

_____. Whitehall. Mortimer, 1845. Recounts the capture,
trial, and execution of Charles I.   1948

Rodenberg, Julius. King by the Grace of God. (tr.) Bentley,
1871. Characters include Cromwell and other politicians at
the time of the King's capture.   1949

Sabatini, Rafael. Fortune's Fool. Houghton, 1923. A soldier
of Cromwell's army in exile after the Restoration, and his
return to England.   1950

_____. The King's Minion. Houghton, 1930. The Earl of
Somerset and the Countess of Essex become implicated in a
murder.   1951

_____. The Stalking Horse. Houghton, 1933. Romance and
adventure amid Jacobite plotting in England.   1952

_____. The Tavern Knight. De la More Press, 1904. A
wild, unruly Cavalier condemned to death for his part in
Charles II's escape.   1953

Salmon, Geraldine Gordon. The Black Glove. by J.G. Sarasin, pseud. Doran, 1925. London and Hampton Court with
scenes illustrating the Plague and the fire of 1666.   1954

_____. Chronicles of a Cavalier. by J.G. Sarasin, pseud.
Hutchinson, 1924. Secret missions and spying at the time
of the Restoration.   1955

Scott, Thomas. Morcar. Greening, 1903. A story of hidden
treasure and claim to fortune early in the century.   1956

Scott, Virgil. I, John Mordaunt. Harcourt, 1964. Story of a
Royalist who risked his life to plot the overthrow of Protector Cromwell and the return of King Charles II.   1957

Scott, Sir Walter. The Bride of Lammermoor. Tauchnitz,
1858. Scottish romance of a couple whose families are
enemies of long standing.   1958

_____. The Fortunes of Nigel. Dean & Munday, 1822.
Good picture of James I of England and the young noblemen
who followed him from Scotland.   1959

_____. The Legend of Montrose. Lovell, 1885. Story of
the Royalists under Montrose in the Scottish Highlands.   1960

_____. Old Mortality. Tauchnitz, 1846. About an old man
who wandered about Scotland caring for the graves of the
Covenanters slain by.Claverhouse.   1961

_____. Peveril of the Peak. Dean & Munday, 1823. Com-
plicated plot of romance and revenge during the hostility between Roundheads and Cavaliers.   1962

_____. Woodstock. Constable, 1826. A Roundhead's kind
treatment of the fugitive Prince Charles.   1963

Seawell, Molly Elliot. The House of Egremont. Scribner, 1900.
Jacobite life during and after the Glorious Revolution.   1964

Shorthouse, Joseph Henry. John Inglesant. Macmillan, 1881.
Romance of the English Civil War with some account of diplomatic and religious affairs.   1965

Simpson, Violet A. The Parson's Wood. Nash, 1905. Religious confusion and controversy in an English village during the 1680s.   1966

Sinnott, Patrick J. Simon the Fox. Comet, 1956. Early life
of Simon Fraser, Scottish lord and Jacobite intriguer.   1967

Smith, Mrs. Fowler. Journal of the Lady Beatrix Graham.
Bell, 1875. Concerned with Montrose and the Covenanters
in Scotland.   1968

Smith, Horace. Brambletye House. Weldon, 1826. Romance
of Cavaliers and Roundheads in Commonwealth and Restoration England.   1969

Smith, Vian. The Wind Blows Free. Doubleday, 1968. An independent Dartmouth farmer fights to retain his land and freedom despite the Enclosure Act before becoming an emigrant.
                                                                 1970
Snaith, John Collis. Mistress Dorothy Marvin. Appleton, 1895.
A novel with the overthrow of James II as background.   1971

_____. Patricia at the Inn. Dodge, 1906. Events at a
coastal inn during the Civil War between Roundheads and

Cavaliers.   1972

Speas, Jan Cox.   Bride of the MacHugh.   Bobbs, 1954.   Resistance of a Highland clan which refused to give up its
sovereignty to James VI.   1973

_____.   My Lord Monleigh.   Bobbs, 1956.   The companion
to a Cromwellian must conceal her love for a political
enemy.   1974

Stephens, Eve.   Charles the King.   by Evelyn Anthony, pseud.
Doubleday, 1961.   Two sides of Charles I--the happy family
man and the sovereign whose belief in "the divine right of
kings" had fallen prey to a changing world.   1975

Steuart, John A.   The Red Reaper.   Hodder & Stoughton, 1905.
The last fifteen years of Montrose's career.   1976

Stewart, Charlotte.   The Safety of the Honours.   by Allan Mc-
Aulay, pseud.   Blackwood, 1906.   Desperate efforts to hide
the Scottish emblems of royalty during the siege of Dunnottar
Castle.   1977

Stucken, Eduard.   Dissolute Years.   (tr.)   Farrar, 1935.
Love and politics at the court of James I in Stuart Eng-
land.   1978

Sutcliff, Rosemary.   Rider on a White Horse.   Coward, 1959.
A Baroness and her little daughter accompany her husband
as he rides to fight with Cromwell.   1979

_____.   Simon.   Oxford, 1953.   Vivid description of battles
during the English Civil War.   1980

Sutcliffe, Halliwell.   The White Horses.   Ward & Lock, 1915.
Sieges and fighting during the English Civil War.   1981

Syrett, Netta.   Lady Jem.   Hutchinson, 1923.   The atmosphere
of plague-stricken London pervades this romance.   1982

Tanqueray, Mrs. Bertram.   The Royal Quaker.   Methuen, 1904.
Religious conflict of a natural daughter of the Duke of York,
later James II.   1983

Taunton, Winefrede Trafford-.   The Romance of a State Secret.
Simpkin, 1910.   Intrigue in London after the restoration of
Charles II.   1984

Taylor, Mary Imlay.   My Lady Clancarty.   Little, 1905.   Describes many prominent people and their activities in the
closing years of the century.   1985

Teague, John J.   The Broken Sword.   by Morice Gerard,

pseud. Hodder, 1906. The revolution against Catholic James II.
                                                                      1986

_____. Check to the King. by Morice Gerard, pseud. Hodder,
1906. Set during the revolution of the English people against
James II.   1987

_____. The King's Signet. by Morice Gerard, pseud.
Hodder, 1909. The Restoration of Charles II and the part
played by George Monk.   1988

_____. Purple Love. (Formerly titled: Love in the Purple)
by Morice Gerard, pseud. Hodder, 1908. Courtship of
William of Orange and the Stuart Princess Mary.   1989

Thomas, H. Elwyn. The Forerunner. Lynwood, 1910. The
calling and romance of a young Welsh evangelist.   1990

Thynne, Arthur Christopher. Sir Bevill. Lane, 1904. Account of life in Cornwall, particularly among the lower
classes.   1991

Tremlett, C. H. Civil Dudgeon. Blackwood, 1914. Historical
allusions abound in this novel of the Popish Plot and Rye
House Plot period.   1992

Vallings, Harold. By Dulvercombe Water. Macmillan, 1902.
Shows the discontent that prompted rebellion in James II's
reign.   1993

_____. The Lady Mary of Tavistock. Milne, 1908. Life
of the people showing the advent of a plague and the punishment of criminals.   1994

Vance, Wilson. Big John Baldwin. Holt, 1909. A Roundhead
fights in Ireland and settles in America.   1995

Varble, Rachel M. Three Against London. Doubleday, 1962.
YA. Lives of two young fishermen, one of whom is implicated in the Great Fire of London, imprisoned, and rescued
with the aid of a customer, diarist Samuel Pepys.   1996

Vaughan, Owen. Battlement and Tower. by Owen Rhoscomyl,
pseud. Longmans, 1896. Events in north Wales during the
English Civil War recounting the siege of Conway.   1997

_____. Sweet Rogues. by Owen Rhoscomyl, pseud. Duck-
worth, 1907. Disappearance of an important message after
the Battle of Naseby.   1998

Vining, Elizabeth Gray. Take Heed of Loving Me. Lippincott, 1964, c.1963. Intrigue, adventure, romance, and
political ambition all figure in the life of the great writer,
John Donne, whose marriage for love damaged rather than

advanced his career.   1999

Walpole, Hugh. Katherine Christian. Doubleday, 1943.
The Herries family from Queen Elizabeth's death (1603)
to the outbreak of the Civil War at mid-century.   2000

Walsh, Maurice. The Dark Rose. Chambers, 1938. Rescues
of two women during the revolt in Scotland against the Covenanters (1644-45).   2001

Watson, H.B. Marriott. Captain Fortune. Methuen, 1904.
Adventure and romance during the Civil War.   2002

_____. (1) Galloping Dick. Lane, 1895. (2) The High
Toby (sequel). Methuen, 1906. (3) The King's Highway
(sequel). Mills & Boon, 1910. The entertaining adventures of a likeable rogue--Dick Ryder.   2003-5

_____. The Rebel. Harper, 1900. The corrupt, brittle
way of life of Charles II's court.   2006

Watson, John. Graham of Claverhouse. by Ian Maclaren,
pseud. Cupples, 1908. The Jacobite Claverhouse, his wife
Lady Jean Cochrane, and William of Orange are prominent
figures.   2007

Watson, Sally. Lark. Holt, 1964. YA. A girl runs away
from her Puritan uncle to live with Scottish relatives during the fighting between Roundheads and Royalists.   2008

Weyman, Stanley J. Shrewsbury. Smith & Elder, 1898.
Deals with the Jacobite conspiracy led by Fenwick and
Robert Ferguson.   2009

White, Leslie Turner. Highland Hawk. Crown, 1952. Resistance to Cromwell results in Scottish guerrilla warfare. 2010

Whyte-Melville, George John. Holmby House. Longmans,
1860. Describes the battles of Newbury and Naseby and
the trial of Charles I.   2011

Williamson, Hugh Ross. James, by the Grace of God. Regnery, 1956. The intermingling of religious intolerance and
political intrigues in the Glorious Revolution.   2012

Wood, Lydia C. For a Free Conscience. Revell, 1905.
Trials of Quakers in England, resulting in the colonization of Pennsylvania.   2013

Woodruffe-Peacock, Dennis Max Cornelius. The King's Rogue.
[En. title: Colonel Blood] by Max Peacock, pseud. Macrae

Smith, 1947. A dispossessed Irish landowner attempts to
steal the English crown jewels.   2014

Yeoman, William Joseph. A Woman's Courier. Chatto, 1896.
Based on the plot of Jacobites Fenwick and Charnock.   2015

Young, Margaret. The Wreathed Dagger. Cassell, 1909.
Features Cromwell's siege of Thirlsby House in 1648.   2016

2) Ireland

Banim, John. The Boyne Water. Duffy (Dublin), 1826. A
vivid account of the Jacobite Rebellion and the siege of
Limerick.   2017

_____. The Denounced. Harper, 1830. Protestant perse-
cution of Irish Catholics after the Williamite Wars.   2018

Blake-Forster, Charles F. The Irish Chieftains. Whittaker,
1874. Accurate, comprehensive account of Ireland during
and following the Williamite Wars.   2019

Burchell, Sidney Herbert. My Lady of the Bass. Gay & Hancock, 1903. The seizure and holding of the Bass Rock by
four dauntless Jacobites.   2020

Butt, Isaac. The Gap of Barnesmore. Smith & Elder, 1848.
"A tale of the Irish highlands and the Revolution of 1688." 2021

Canning, Albert S. Baldearg O'Donnell. Marcus Ward, 1881.
Story of an Irish leader who joined the English enemy.   2022

Carleton, William. Redmond, Count O'Hanlon, the Irish
Rapparee. Duffy (Dublin), 1862. Exploits of an Irish outlaw whose fortune was ruined by the English Revolution.   2023

Church, Samuel Harden. John Marmaduke. Putnam, 1889.
Describes Cromwell's taking of Drogheda in 1649.   2024

Field, Louise. Ethne. by Mrs. E. M. Field. Wells Gardner,
1888. Diary of an Irish girl caught in the upheavals caused
by Cromwell's invasion.   2025

Finlay, T. A. The Chances of War. Gill (Dublin), 1877. The
Catholic Confederation of Kilkenny and the wars in Ireland,
1648-49.   2026

Fitzpatrick, Thomas. The King of Claddagh. Sands, 1899.
A story of the Cromwellian occupation of Galway and its
attending cruelties.   2027

Hinkson, Henry A. Silk and Steel. Chatto & Windus, 1902.

Fighting, politics, and secret orders in the wars of
Charles I.   2028

Le Fanu, J. Sheridan.   The Fortunes of Colonel Torlogh
O'Brien.   Routledge, 1847.   Shows the bitter feuds and rivalries current during the Wars of King James.   2029

Leigh, Michael.   Rogue Errant.   Crowell, 1951.   An Irishman,
accused of a crime he did not commit, flees unjust impris-
onment.   2030

McChesney, Dora Greenwell.   Kathleen Clare.   Blackwood,
1895.   Story of Thomas Wentworth, Lord-Deputy of Ireland
under Charles I.   2031

McDonnell, Randal.   My Sword for Patrick Sarsfield.   Gill
(Dublin), 1907.   Exploits of a cavalry colonel in the Jaco-
bite War in Ireland.   2032

_____. When Cromwell Came to Drogheda.   Gill (Dublin),
1906.   Military account of Cromwell's subjugation of Ire-
land.   2033

Macken, Walter.   Seek the Fair Land.   Macmillan, 1959.   One
man's quest for freedom after Cromwell's ruthless subjec-
tion of Ireland.   2034

MacManus, Francis.   Stand and Give Challenge.   Loring &
Mussey, 1935.   The oppression of Irish peasants by absentee
landlords.   2035

McManus, Miss L.   Nessa.   Sealy & Bryers (Dublin), 1904.
The Cromwellian Settlement causes the quartering of Puritan soldiers in resentful County Mayo.   2036

_____. The Wager, or, In Sarsfield's Days.   Buckles,
1906.   The siege of Limerick in 1690 and the midnight
cavalry action led by Sarsfield.   2037

Mathew, Frank.   Love of Comrades.   Lane, 1900.   A romantic
tale of adventure during Wentworth's service in Ireland.   2038

Moore, F. Frankfort.   (1) Castle Omeragh.   Appleton, 1903.
(2) Captain Latymer (sequel).   Cassell, 1907.   Conditions
in the west of Ireland during and after Cromwell's taking
of Drogheda.   2039-40

O'Byrne, Miss M. L.   Leixlip Castle.   Gill (Dublin), 1883.
Religious friction and the flight of James II, with various
battles and sieges.   2041

_____. Lord Roche's Daughters of Fermoy.   Sealy &
Bryers (Dublin), 1892.   Account of the wars following the

Catholic Confederation of Kilkenny.   2042

O'Grady, Standish. <u>In the Wake of King James.</u> Dent, 1896.
Jacobite activities in the years after James II was driven
from Ireland.   2043

_____. <u>Ulrick the Ready.</u> Dodd, 1896. Feuds among the
clans, the siege of Dunboy, and general unrest.   2044

Sadlier, Mary Anne. <u>The Confederate Chieftains.</u> by Mrs.
James Sadlier. Gill (Dublin), 1860. Owen Roe O'Neill and
his part in the Irish Rebellion of 1641.   2045

_____. <u>The Daughter of Tyrconnell.</u> by <u>Mrs.</u> James Sad-
lier. Kenedy, 1863. The story of Mary Stuart O'Donnell,
who fled Ireland to avoid marriage outside her religion.   2046

b) <u>Western and Central Europe</u>

1) France

Achard, Amédée. <u>Belle-Rose.</u> (tr.) Street & Smith, 1895.
A Dumas-type novel of romance, fighting, and adventure.   2047

_____. <u>The Golden Fleece.</u> (tr.) Page, 1900. Romance
and adventure set amid the Turkish Wars of Louis XIV's
early reign.   2048

Andrews, Marian. <u>In the Straits of Time.</u> by Christopher
Hare, <u>pseud.</u> Cassell, 1904. Depicts the conditions under
which the Huguenots pursued their religion in southern
France.   2049

Arnott, Peter. <u>Ballet of Comedians.</u> Macmillan, 1971. A
dramatic story of the playwright, Molière, who rose from a
bourgeois family fo the glittering, superficial life of the theater
and royal court.   2050

Barr, Robert. <u>Cardillac.</u> Stokes, 1909. Blois is the locale
of this romance of Louis XIII's early reign, showing influences of his mother, Richelieu, and Luynes.   2051

Beattie, William B. <u>The Werewolf.</u> Paul, 1910. A lord's
cruel treatment of his peasants in the time of Mazarin and
Anne of Austria.   2052

Bedford-Jones, Henry. <u>D'Artagnan; the Sequel to The Three
Musketeers.</u> Covici, 1928. The author completes an unfinished manuscript by Dumas.   2053

Bloundelle-Burton, John. <u>The Clash of Arms.</u> Methuen, 1897.
General Turenne's brilliant work in Louis XIV's wars for

more territory.   2054

_____. Fate of Henry of Navarre. Lane, 1911. A story
leading up to and including the tragic death of King Henry
of Navarre.   2055

_____. In the Day of Adversity. Appleton, 1895. The
dueling, imprisonment, and military service of a youth
whose inheritance is threatened.   2056

_____. Knighthood's Flower. Hurst & Blackett, 1906.
The fifteen-month siege of La Rochelle over the issue of
religious freedom.   2057

_____. Traitor and True. Long, 1906. Based on a plot
to bring about a Dutch invasion and remove Louis XIV from
power in France.   2058

_____. Within Four Walls.· Milne, 1909. An assassination
attempt against Henry of Navarre is revealed to his wife by
a maid-of-honor.   2059

Brebner, Percy J. Gallant Lady. Duffield, 1919. The treachery and intrigues of Louis XIV and his courtiers.   2060

Bungener, Louis F. The Preacher and the King. (tr.)
Lothrop, 1853. A story of the reign of Louis XIV, dealing with religion, written by a Protestant.   2061

Caldwell, Taylor (full name: Janet Taylor Caldwell). The Arm
and the Darkness. Scribner, 1943. Politics, intrigue, and
religious strife in Richelieu's time.   2062

Chatfield-Taylor, H.C. Fame's Pathway. Chatto, 1910. Has
Molière as hero and Corneille as a prominent character. 2063

Colin, Gerty. Say No to Love. (tr.) Coward, 1958. A romance concerning Louis XIV as a young man.   2064

Coryn, Marjorie. Sorrow by Day. Appleton, 1950. Royal
romance featuring La Grande Mademoiselle, Louise de
Bourbon.   2065

Courtney, Etta. Checkmate. Arnold, 1904. Diplomatic
scheming under Louis XIV at Versailles.   2066

Doyle, Sir Arthur Conan. The Refugees. Harper, 1891.
Rivalry at court between Madame de Maintenon and the
Marquise de Montespan, and the flight of oppressed Hugue-
nots to Canada.   2067

Drummond, Hamilton. The Great Game. Paul, 1918. The
carefully planned schemes of French War Minister Louvois

provide the background.   2068

Dumas, Alexandre. The D'Artagnan Romances, the many dar-
ing adventures of three guardsmen, Porthos, Athos, and
Aramis, and their Gascon companion, D'Artagnan. (1) The
Three Musketeers. (tr.) Little, 1888. The feud between
Richelieu and Queen Anne. (2) Twenty Years After (sequel).
(tr.) Munro, 1878. In the service of Mazarin; the Fronde;
the execution of Charles I in England. (3) The Vicomte de
Bragelonne (sequel). (tr.) [same as: Ten Years Later]
Routledge, 1857. The time of Louis XIV's increasing power,
with the son of Athos as hero; contains the story of the "Man
in the Iron Mask."   2069-71

_____. The War of Women. (tr.) Little, 1895. The end
of the second Fronde and Mazarin's defeat of Condé, stressing the part played by the latter's wife.   2072

Eccott, W.J. A Demoiselle of France. Blackwood, 1910.
Dashing adventure in this novel featuring an Abbé and relating the downfall of Finance Minister Fouquet.   2073

_____. His Indolence of Arras. Blackwood, 1905. A ro-
mantic tale of Louise de la Valliere and the Marquise de
Montespan, court favorites of Louis XIV.   2074

_____. The Red Neighbour. Blackie, 1908. A romance
which has Louvois, Minister of War under Louis XIV, as
the leading character.   2075

Fifield, William. The Devil's Marchioness. Dial, 1957. The
determined Marquise de Brinvilliers resorted to the use of
poison to rid herself of unwanted people.   2076

Frischauer, Paul. Shepherd's Crook. Scribner, 1951. The
daughter of a Huguenot martyr flees court to join fellow re-
ligionists in hiding in the mountains.   2077

Fuller, Iola. All the Golden Gifts. Putnam, 1966. The mistress and ex-mistress of Louis XIV seek to rid themselves
of a young newcomer from the country, sent to court by her
uncles in hopes she will gain the King's favor.   2078

Gallet, Louis. Captain Satan. [same as Adventures of Cyrano
de Bergerac] Fenno, 1900. A story of the swaggering Cyrano
de Bergerac.   2079

Gautier, Théophile. Captain Fracasse. (tr.) Page, 1897.
Daring exploits in a romance which pictures travelling
actors and the homes of nobles.   2080

Gay, Madame Sophie. Marie de Mancini. (tr.) Lawrence
& Bullen, 1898. A story of mid-century court life reflect-

ing military and political developments.   2081

Gerson, Noel B. The Anthem. Fawcett, 1968, c.1967. Sweep-
ing story of the de Montauban family from the reign of Henry
IV to the twentieth century illustrating changes in religious
freedom.   2082

Golon, Sergeanne, pseud. for Anne and Serge Golon. Angèlique.
(tr.) Bantam Bks., 1971, c.1958. Historical romance of a
dazzling, appealing girl at the spectacular court of Louis
XIV.   2083

_____. Angèlique and the King. (tr.) Bantam Bks., 1971,
c.1960. The heroine becomes a favorite of the "Sun King,"
Louis XIV.   2084

_____. Angèlique in Revolt. (tr.) Bantam Bks., 1971,
c.1961. Angèlique returns to France after escaping from
Morocco to find herself pitted against the King in a bloody,
brutal religious war as she leads a Huguenot rebellion.   2085

Grant, James. Arthur Blane. Dutton, 1858. The Scottish
Guard in France in the third decade of the century.   2086

Hill, Pamela. The Crown and the Shadow. Putnam, 1955.
Social life at the time of Louis XIV centered on Madame
de Maintenon.   2087

Hooper, I. The Singer of Marly. Methuen, 1897. The slave
market is featured in this story which embraces events in
France, Ireland, and Martinique.   2088

Irwin, Margaret. Royal Flush. Harcourt, 1932. A moving
story of the royal houses of France and England in the age
of Louis XIV.   2089

James, G.P.R. The Huguenot. Dutton, 1838. The persecutions that resulted when the Edict of Nantes was revoked. 2090

_____. Life and Adventures of John Marston Hall. Dutton,
1834. The exploits of an adventurous Scotsman in France
during the first Fronde outbreak.   2091

_____. Richelieu. Dutton, 1829. Based on the career of
Richelieu, with emphasis on the Cinq-Mars Conspiracy.   2092

Jordan, Humfrey. My Lady of Intrigue. Blackwood, 1910.
Court intrigues involve Louis XIII, Richelieu, Marie de
Rohan, and Anne of Austria.   2093

Kaye, Michael W. The Cardinal's Past. Greening, 1910.
Tells of plotting against France's great politician, Cardinal
Richelieu.   2094

Kenny, Louise M. Stacpoole. Love Is Life. Greening, 1910.
The exiled soldier, Sarsfield, in the employ of Louis XIV. 2095

Lee, Albert. The Frown of Majesty. Hutchinson, 1902.
French court and village life when Madame de Maintenon
was most influential.   2096

Lewis, Janet. Ghost of Monsieur Scarron. Doubleday, 1959.
Louis XIV punishes a bookbinder for possessing a pamphlet
attacking the king's scandalous behavior.   2097

Maass, Edgar. A Lady at Bay. (tr.) Scribner, 1953. The
Marquise de Brinvilliers, notorious poisoner, at the court
of Louis XIV.   2098

McCarthy, Justin Huntly. The Duke's Motto. Harper, 1908.
Adventure story of the time of Louis XIII and Richelieu. 2099

MacDougall, Sylvia B. A Duchess of France. by Paul Waine-
man, pseud. Hurst & Blackett, 1915. Court of Louis XIV
at Versailles up to the time of the revoking of the Edict of
Nantes.   2100

MacGrath, Harold. The Grey Cloak. Bobbs, 1904. France
during the period of Cardinal Mazarin, successor to Richelieu.   2101

Macquoid, Katharine S. His Heart's Desire. Hodder, 1903.
A story based on the career of Cardinal Richelieu, with
Louis XIII portrayed.   2102

Mallet-Joris, Françoise. The Witches. (tr.) Farrar, 1969.
A novel about three French women who became separately
involved in witchcraft and how this involvement affected
their lives.   2103

Mann, Millicent E. Margot, the Court Shoemaker's Child.
McClurg, 1901. A romance of the time of Louis XIV.   2104

Manning, Anne. Jacques Bonneval. Dodd, 1869. The days
of the Dragonnades under Louis XIV.   2105

Meeker, Arthur. Ivory Mischief. Houghton, 1942. Two
sisters are the heroines of this French romance.   2106

_____. The Silver Plume. Knopf, 1952. The Duc de
Rohan's fight to prove his right to his title.   2107

Melbury, John. Monsieur Desperado. Murray, 1924. Includes the submission of Huguenot La Rochelle to Richelieu.   2108

Mundt, Klara. Prince Eugene and His Times. (tr.) by

Louisa Mühlbach, pseud. Appleton, 1869. European poli-
tics and warfare during the years from about 1680 to 1718.
                                                              2109
O'Shaughnessy, Michael. Monsieur Molière. Crowell, 1959.
French theater and theatrical society in Molière's time.   2110

Pemjean, Lucien. Captain D'Artagnan. (tr.) Doubleday,
1933. Adventures of D'Artagnan from the death of his
beloved Irene to his trip to England.   2111

_____. When D'Artagnan Was Young. (tr.) Doubleday,
1932. Based on the life in Paris of the historical figure,
D'Artagnan. (followed by Captain D'Artagnan)

Sabatini, Rafael. St. Martin's Summer. Hutchinson, 1909.
Domestic life in a feudal chateau early in the century.   2113

Sanders, Joan. Baneful Sorceries. Houghton, 1969. A beautiful heiress, married to an impoverished Count, is threatened
by the witchcraft of jealous women, even as her husband is
threatened by that of envious men.   2114

Smith, Albert. The Marchioness of Brinvilliers. Bentley,
1846. A novel based on the activities of an infamous
poisoner.   2115

Stilson, Charles B. The Ace of Blades. Watt, 1924. The
extraordinary swordsmanship of an untitled lad is his key
to success.   2116

Taylor, Mary Imlay. The Cardinal's Musqueteer. McClurg,
1900. Contest for power between Marie de Medici and
Cardinal Richelieu.   2117

Tessin, Brigitte von. The Bastard. (tr.) McKay, 1959. Relations between a man and his three sons against a background of religious warfare.   2118

Thompson, E. Perronet. A Dragoon's Wife. Greening, 1907.
Features Louis XIV's Dragonnades and an escaped Huguenot.   2119

Trouncer, Margaret Lahey. The Nun. Sheed, 1955. Imaginative account of the life and trials of a seventeenth century
religious who was a mystic, St. Marguerite Marie Ala-
coque.   2120

Vigny, Alfred Victor, comte de. Cinq-Mars. (tr.) Low, 1847.
Attempt to assassinate the despotic Richelieu.   2121

Weyman, Stanley J. The Man in Black. Longmans, 1894.
Adventure-romance during the time of Louis XIII and Richelieu.   2122

_____. Under the Red Robe. Longmans, 1894. A spy
in the service of Cardinal Richelieu struggles with his
conscience.   2123

2) Central Europe (including Germany, the Netherlands,
    Switzerland, Austria, Hungary, Czechoslovakia, and Poland)

Auerbach, Berthold. Spinoza. Holt, 1882. The development
of Spinoza's philosophy, his romance, interest in Christianity,
and break with Judaism.   2124

Bailey, H.C. Karl of Erbach. Longmans, 1903. Adventures
during the Thirty Years War reflecting Richelieu's masterly
diplomacy.   2125

Braider, Donald. An Epic Joy. Putnam, 1971. The story of
the Flemish Pieter Paul Rubens who, besides his great artistic talent, served his country as a diplomatic envoy to Spain,
France, and England.   2126

Brebner, Percy J. The Turbulent Duchess. Little, 1915.
Romance involving the Duchess of Podina.   2127

Brod, Max. Redemption of Tycho Brahe. (tr.) Knopf, 1928.
Recounts clash between famous old Danish astronomer, Tycho
Brahe, living in a Bohemian castle, and his brilliant young
German disciple, Johann Kepler, over the heliocentric theory
of the solar system.   2128

Crockett, Samuel R. The Red Axe. Harper, 1898. Lawlessness and violence in seventeenth century Germany.   2129

DeQuincy, Thomas. Klosterheim. Black, 1896. A mysterious
apparition unsettles a superstitious man who holds power in
the palace unjustly.   2130

Dumas, Alexandre. The Black Tulip. (tr.) Munro, 1877.
Struggles of the rising Dutch Republic; William of Orange
and the De Witt brothers; the tulip industry craze.   2131

Dunlop, Agnes Mary Robertson. Princess of Orange. by Elisabeth Kyle, pseud. Holt, 1966, c.1965. YA. The reign of
William and Mary, which grew from a marriage of state to
a real love match, as they ruled Holland and eventually England.   2132

Durych, Jaroslav. Descent of the Idol. (tr.) Dutton, 1936.
Romance and adventure during the Thirty Years War.   2133

Eccott, W.J. The Mercenary. Blackwood, 1913. A Scotsman in the Thirty Years War in Germany and Austria.   2134

Gerson, Noel B. The Queen's Husband. by Samuel Edwards, pseud. McGraw, 1960. The course of the political marriage of Holland's William of Orange and England's Mary II. 2135

_____. Rock of Freedom. Messner, 1964. YA. The wanderings of the Plymouth Colony from England to Holland and eventually to the New World. 2136

Grimmelshausen, Hans J. Von. The Runagate Courage. (tr.) Univ. of Nebr. Pr., 1965. High-spirited girl of illegitimate birth becomes successively a camp-follower, an officer's wife, a nobleman's betrothed, and a gypsy-queen. 2137

_____. Simplicius Simplicissimus. (tr.) Bobbs, 1965. The son of a nobleman, reared by a peasant in utmost simplicity, has numerous experiences in various parts of Europe during the Thirty Years' War. 2138

Habeck, Fritz. Days of Danger. (tr.) Harcourt, 1963. YA. Exciting action involves a youthful art student during the siege of Vienna by the Turks and Tartars. 2139

Hamilton, Cosmo. His Majesty the King. Doubleday, Page, 1926. Charles II during the final period of his exile in the Low Countries. 2140

Harsányi, Zsolt. Lover of Life. (tr.) Putnam, 1942. The compelling personality and great work of artist Peter Paul Rubens. 2141

Hay, Marie. The Winter Queen. Houghton, 1910. Concerns the daughter of James I of England who, as wife of Frederick V, the Elector Palatine, was briefly Queen of Bohemia. 2142

Innes, Norman. My Lady's Kiss. Rand McNally, 1908. Hardships, destruction, and tensions during the Thirty Years War. 2143

James, G. P. R. Heidelberg. Smith & Elder, 1846. The beautiful district of Heidelberg, the court of Frederick I, King of Bohemia and Elector Palatine. 2144

Jókai, Maurus. (1) 'Midst the Wild Carpathians. (tr.) Page, 1894. (2) The Slaves of the Padishah. (tr.) Jarrold & Sons, 1902. The feudal, semi-barbaric society of Transylvania at the time of warfare between Turks and Hungarians. 2145-6

_____. Pretty Michal. (tr.) Doubleday, 1892. The state of affairs in Hungary under Turkish rule. 2147

Koerner, Herman T. Beleaguered. Putnam, 1898. "A story of the uplands of Baden." 2148

Kossak-Szczucka, Zofja. The Meek Shall Inherit. (tr.) Roy
Pub., 1948. An aristocrat lives among the poor in seventeenth century Poland-Lithuania.   2149

Lawrence, Isabelle. Night Watch. Rand McNally, 1952. YA.
A story of the artist Rembrandt and his household in Amsterdam.   2150

Lons, Hermann. Harmwulf. (tr.) Minton, Balch, 1931. The
much-oppressed peasants fight back against both sides in the
Thirty Years War.   2151

McCarthy, Justin Huntly. A Health Unto His Majesty. Doran,
1912. The life of Charles II during his exile in Holland. 2152

Mason, A.E.W. Königsmark. Doubleday, Doran, 1939. Picturesque novel of the small German state of Celle.   2153

Meinhold, Wilhelm. Mary Schweidler, the Amber Witch. (tr.)
Scribner, 1844. An interesting account of a witchcraft trial
assertedly based on a manuscript by the accused's father. 2154

_____. Sidonia the Sorceress. (tr.) Reeves & Turner,
1894. Vivid account of the woman who supposedly destroyed
the reigning ducal house of Pomerania by black magic.   2155

Molander, Harald. The Fortune-Hunter. (tr.) Heinemann,
1905. Experiences during the Thirty Years War including
the siege of Magdeburg.   2156

Orczy, Baroness Emmuska. (1) The Laughing Cavalier.
Doran, 1914. (2) The First Sir Percy (sequel). Doran,
1921. The Netherlands in the early years of their hard-
won independence.   2157-8

Pauli, Hertha. The Two Trumpeters of Vienna. Doubleday,
1961. YA. Two teenagers serve as trumpeters when Vienna
is besieged by the Turks in 1683.   2159

Pick, John B. Last Valley. [En. title: Fat Valley] Little,
1960. A wandering philosopher's influence on mercenary
soldiers in the Thirty Years War.   2160

Purtscher, Nora. Woman Astride. Appleton, 1934. International adventures of a German noblewoman who fought in the
Thirty Years War.   2161

Schmitt, Gladys. Rembrandt. Random House, 1961. A vivid
account of the great painter of tremendous vitality who lived
every moment to the fullest.   2162

Sienkiewicz, Henryk. The Deluge. (tr.) Little, 1891. The
Swedish invasion of Poland in the third quarter of the cen-

tury. (followed by Pan Michael)   2163

_____. On the Field of Glory. (tr.) [same as: The
Field of Glory] Little, 1906. Unfinished romance of Poland
at the time of King John Sobieski and the Turkish invasions.
                                                     2164
_____. Pan Michael. (tr.) Little, 1893. Domestic life in
Warsaw and the invasion of 1672-73.   2165

_____. With Fire and Sword. (tr.) Little, 1890. An up-
rising of the Cossacks on the Dnieper. (followed by The
Deluge)   2166

Singer, Isaac. Satan in Goray. (tr.) Noonday, 1955. Religious hysteria among Polish Jews in mid-seventeenth century.   2167

Stevenson, Philip L. The Black Cuirassier. Hurst & Blackett,
1906. Adventures of an Irish hero in the Thirty Years War,
featuring Wallenstein.   2168

Vansittart, Robert. John Stuart. Murray, 1912. Adventures
of John Stuart, who claimed to be a son of Charles II.   2169

Wassermann, Jacob. The Triumph of Youth. (tr.) Boni &
Liveright, 1927. Experiences of a youth in Germany confronted by superstition and fanaticism.   2170

Weyman, Stanley J. The Long Night. McClure, 1903. Chiefly
concerns the attack of the Savoyards on Geneva, 1602.   2171

_____. My Lady Rotha. Longmans, 1899. Shows the
Thirty Years War with the countryside overrun by soldiers
and bandits.   2172

Zangwill, Israel. The Maker of Lenses. Harper, 1898. A
novel based on the career of Spinoza.   2173

3) Scandinavia and the Baltic

Elwood, Muriel. Dorothea. Bobbs, 1962. The romance of
Swedish princess Sophia Dorothea and Count Philip of Konigs-
mark.   2174

Jacobsen, ·Jens Peter. Marie Grubbe. (tr.) Knopf, 1925. A
Danish tragic novel of romance, warfare, and high politics.
                                                     2175
Lewis, Janet. Trial of Soren Quist. Doubleday, 1947. Tragic
drama rooted in an old folk tale of seventeenth century Denmark.   2176

Stacton, David. People of the Book. Putnam, 1965. Parallel

lives of a Swedish chancellor and two orphans during the
Thirty Years' War.   2177

Stephan, Ruth. The Flight. Knopf, 1956. Purported autobiography of Queen Christina of Sweden, who was converted to
Catholicism. (followed by My Crown, My Love)   2178

c) Southern Europe

1) Iberian Peninsula

Ainsworth, W. Harrison. The Spanish Match. Routledge, 1865.
Charles Stuart and Buckingham go to Madrid in quest of a
royal Spanish bride.   2179

Burr, Amelia Josephine. A Dealer in Empire. Harper, 1915.
Statesmanship and diplomacy in Spain under the youthful
Philip IV.   2180

Drummond, Hamilton. Loyalty. Nash, 1921. Maneuverings
at the Madrid court of Philip IV.   2181

Hunt, Frederick. Royal Twilight. by John Fitzgay, pseud.
Roy Pub., 1946. International intrigue centered on Maria
Luisa, consort of the idiot Carlos II.   2182

Keyes, Frances Parkinson. I, the King. McGraw, 1966.
Spain's Philip IV and the women who were involved, in various ways, in his life.   2183

Thomas, Gwyn. A Wolf at Dusk. [En. title: The Love Man]
Macmillan, 1959, c.1958. A witty, readable novel of the
decline of the legendary Spanish gentleman, Don Juan Ten-
orio.   2184

Treviño, Elizabeth Borton de. I, Juan de Pareja. Farrar,
1965. YA. A young negro slave who serves the great
artist Velasquez secretly teaches himself to paint.   2185

2) Italy and Adjacent Islands

Candler, Pat. Testore. Dutton, 1916. Story of a fiddle-
maker of Milan.   2186

Cotton, Albert Louis. The Company of Death. Blackwood,
1905. Neapolitan revolt against strict Spanish rule.   2187

Crawford, F. Marion. Stradella. Macmillan, 1909. Elopement and flight of musician Alessandro Stradella.   2188

Harsányi, Zsolt. The Star-Gazer. (tr.) Putnam, 1939.

Galileo's teachings, inventions, discoveries, and trouble
with the Inquisition. 2189

Manzoni, Alessandro. The Betrothed. (tr.) Macmillan, 1875.
Obstacles to a peasant marriage are met and overcome in a
story descriptive of Milan. 2190

Montgomery, K. L., pseud. for Kathleen and Letitia Montgomery.
'Ware Venice. Hutchinson, 1927. Exciting adventure based
on the Spanish Conspiracy of 1618. 2191

Stephan, Ruth. My Crown, My Love. Knopf, 1960. Christina
of Sweden in the period after she relinquished her crown and
joined the Catholic faith. 2192

d) Eastern Europe (including Russia and the Balkans),
   the Near East, and North Africa

Donchev, Anton. Time of Parting. (tr.) Morrow, 1968,
c. 1967. Parallel narratives of seventeenth century Bulgaria
under the yoke of Islam told by an enslaved French nobleman and a local priest. 2193

Groseclose, Elgin Earl. The Carmelite. Macmillan, 1955.
Contrast of the simplicity and austerity of Fray Juan to the
Persian pageantry which surrounded him. 2194

Knowles, Mabel Winifred. A Prince of Intrigue. by May Wynne,
pseud. Jarrolds Ltd., 1920. Mazeppa and his relations with
Russia's Peter the Great and Sweden's Charles XII. 2195

Lamb, Harold. The Curved Saber. Doubleday, 1964. A collection of short stories concerning the adventures of the shrewd,
scar-faced Cossack, Khlit of the Curved Saber. 2196

Taylor, Mary Imlay. On the Red Staircase. McClurg, 1896.
Confusion and intrigue in Russia following Czar Feodor'a death.
2197
_____. The Rebellion of the Princess. McClure, 1903.
The heroine is Sophia, sister of Peter the Great and regent
of Russia. 2198

Tolstoi, Alexei N. Peter the Great. (tr.) Covici, 1932.
Account of Peter I from boyhood to young manhood. 2199

Whishaw, Frederick J. Mazeppa. Chatto, 1902. A story of
Mazeppa and the Cossacks. 2200

_____. Nathalia. Digby & Long, 1913. Depicts Moscow
court life, the romance of Peter the Great's parents, and
his questioned birth. 2201

_____. A Splendid Impostor. Chatto, 1903. An impostor
claims to be the murdered son of Ivan the Terrible.   2202

e) Overseas Exploration, Enterprise, and Expansion

Bailey, H.C. The Gentleman Adventurer. Doran, 1915. The
hero, a sort of gentleman pirate, has many thrilling experiences in the West Indies.   2203

Bullen, Frank T. Sea Puritans. Hodder, 1904. The navy of
the Puritan Commonwealth and the career of Admiral Blake.
                                                              2204
Chidsey, Donald Barr. The Legion of the Lost. Crown,
1967. Experiences of an indentured seaman who is sent to
sea with the notorious pirate, Captain Kidd, on a voyage to
Madagascar.   2205

Costain, Thomas B. For My Great Folly. Putnam, 1942.
English piracy in the Mediterranean under the dashing John
Ward.   2206

Davies, John Evan Weston. The Road and the Star. by Berkely
Mather, pseud. Scribner, 1965. An English lord, fleeing
from Cromwell, observes colonialism in action in South Africa
and India.   2207

Farnol, Jeffery. Black Bartlemy's Treasure. Little, 1920.
Adventures of an English nobleman on the high seas in quest
of vengeance and treasure. (followed by Martin Conisby's
Vengeance)   2208

Forbes, George. Adventures in Southern Seas. Dodd, 1920.
Voyages in search of treasure, based on the journeys of
the Dutch navigator, Hartog.   2209

Ford, Ford Madox (name originally Ford Madox Hueffer). The
Half Moon. Doubleday, Page, 1909. Harsh conditions under
James I led to such expeditions as Henry Hudson's voyage to
the New World.   2210

Godtsenhoven, Oscar van. The Sable Lion. (tr.) by Jan Van
Dorp, pseud. Putnam, 1954. An adventure story of Flemish
corsairs who preyed on shipping in the English channel.   2211

Golon, Sergeanne, pseud. for Serge and Anne Golon. Angélique
in Love. (tr.) Bantam Bks., 1968, c.1961. On board ship
bound for Canada, Countess Angélique discovers that the
swashbuckling captain is her first love.   2212

Heyer, Georgette. Beauvallet. Bantam Bks., 1969, c.1929.
Pirating on the Spanish Main and the capture of an explosive
Spanish girl.   2213

Hyne, C.J. Cutcliffe. Prince Rupert the Buccaneer. Stokes,
1900. Prince Rupert's voyage to the West Indies and his
adventures with Caribbean buccaneers.   2214

Judah, Charles Burnet. Tom Bone. Morrow, 1944. Slave
trading, a romantic triangle, and plenty of action.   2215

Marshall, Edison. Great Smith. Farrar, 1943. Fictionalized
account of the remarkable travels and adventures of Captain
John Smith.   2216

Masefield, John. Captain Margaret. Lippincott, 1908. Combines romance and adventure on the Spanish Main.   2217

_____. Lost Endeavour. Nelson, 1910. Buccaneering
on the Spanish Main at the end of the seventeenth century. 2218

Niven, Frederick. The Island Providence. Lane, 1910. Experiences of an Englishman on the Spanish Main and as a
prisoner at Cartagena.   2219

Orcutt, William Dana. Robert Cavalier. McClurg, 1904. La-
Salle's experiences in Old World and New, crowned by his
exploration of the Mississippi.   2220

Parrish, Randall. Wolves of the Sea. McClure, 1918. A sea
story about a man who had been condemned to slavery in
Virginia.   2221

Quiller-Couch, Arthur T. The Blue Pavilions. by Q., pseud.
Scribner, 1891. Tale of a youthful orphan and two old sea
captains who were once his mother's suitors.   2222

Reach, Angus B. Leonard Lindsay. Routledge, 1850. Exploits of English and Scottish buccaneers in the West Indies
near the end of the century.   2223

Sabatini, Rafael. Captain Blood. Houghton, 1922. A tale of
buccaneering with an Irishman who was doctor, slave, pirate,
and politician.   2224

Van Zile, Edward Sims. With Sword and Crucifix. Harper,
1900. Exploration of the Mississippi Valley by La Salle and
Jesuit missionaries.   2225

Vaughan, Owen. The Jewel of Ynys Galon. by Owen Rhoscomyl, pseud. Longmans, 1895. The infamous pirate,
Sir Henry Morgan, is the leading character.   2226

Westerman, Percy F. The Quest of "The Golden Hope." Blackie,
1911. The sea adventures of a fugitive from Monmouth's Rebellion.   2227

Williams, R. Memoirs of a Buccaneer. Mills & Boon, 1909.
A tale of pirating and naval warfare between English and
Spanish.   2228

Wilson, R.A. A Rose of Normandy. Little, 1903. Explorations of La Salle and De Tonty in the Mississippi Valley. 2229

3. EIGHTEENTH CENTURY: AGE OF
ENLIGHTENMENT AND REVOLUTION

a) The British Isles

1) England, Wales, and Scotland

Ainsworth, W. Harrison. Beau Nash. Dutton, 1880. Social
life in the resort town of Bath.   2230

_____. The Miser's Daughter. Wilson, 1842. A tale of
London society in 1744.   2231

_____. Preston Fight. Dutton, 1877. Romance at the time
of the Jacobite Rebellion of 1715.   2232

_____. Rookwood. Dutton, 1931. The notorious highwayman,
Dick Turpin, is the inspiration here.   2233

_____. The South Sea Bubble. Routledge, 1868. The wild
speculation of investors in the South Sea Company and the
eventual results.   2234

Allardyce, Alexander. Balmoral. Blackwood, 1893. Elopement of a young couple in Scotland at the beginning of the
Jacobite Rebellion.   2235

Andrew, Prudence. A New Creature. Putnam, 1968. Contrasting effects of John Wesley's preaching on a slave trader
and a mine owner.   2236

Andrews, Robert. Burning Gold. Doubleday, 1945. Surgeon's
adventures as ship's doctor with a crew of pirates.   2237

Arblay, Frances Burney. Evelina. by Fanny Burney. Lowndes,
1791. A series of letters discloses the gay social whirl of
late eighteenth century London.   2238

Arthur, Mary Lucy. To My King Ever Faithful. by George
David Gilbert, pseud. Nash, 1909. The love story of
Maria Fitzherbert, whose marriage to the Prince of Wales
(George IV) was declared illegal when he married Caroline
of Brunswick.   2239

Ashton, Blair. Deeds of Darkness. Little, 1957. A fashion-

able London gentleman is, secretly, a dashing highwayman.   2240

Bailey, H.C. The Golden Fleece. Methuen, 1925. Jacobite
plans and romances in mid-century.   2241

_____. The Highwayman. Dutton, 1918. A tale of the
open road in the reign of Queen Anne, told with a backdrop
of Jacobite scheming.   2242

Baker, Emily. Peggy Gainsborough, the Great Painter's
Daughter. Griffiths, 1909. Social life of artistic and literary families, the Gainsboroughs and Sheridans, in London
and Bath.   2243

Balfour, Andrew. To Arms! Page, 1898. Experiences of a
Scottish medical student who views the prisons of Paris and
is involved in the Scottish rebellion of 1715.   2244

Balfour, Melville. The Blackbird. Hodder & Stoughton, 1925.
A story of the Old Pretender and intrigues and schemes
surrounding the throne.   2245

Banks, G. Linnaeus. Forbidden to Wed. Heywood, 1883. A
story of Manchester in the late 1700s showing the social and
economic status of the tradespeople.   2246

_____. God's Providence House. Paul, 1865. Growing
sentiment to free the slaves results in the Emancipation Act
of 1833.   2247

Baring-Gould, S. Bladys of the Stewponey. Methuen, 1897.
About such diverse characters as a highwayman, a hangman,
an innkeeper's daughter, and a woman condemned to death
by fire.   2248

_____. The Broom-Squire. Stokes, 1895. A story of
murder and violence in Hindhead in 1786.   2249

Barke, James. Crest of the Broken Wave. Macmillan, 1953.
Burns' attempts to farm Ellisland, and his marriage to Jean
Armour. (His Immortal Memory--v. 4)   2250

_____. The Song in the Green Thorn Tree. Macmillan,
1948. Robert Burns' two years on the Mossgiel farm, ending
with the death of Highland Mary. (His Immortal Memory--
v. 2)   2251

_____. The Well of the Silent Harp. Macmillan, 1954.
The final volume in the series telling of poet Robert Burns,
his family, and his friends. (His Immortal Memory--
v. 5)   2252

_____. The Wind that Shakes the Barley. Macmillan, 1947,
c. 1946. A story of poet Robert Burns, beginning with his
father and continuing into Robert's early twenties. (His Immortal Memory--v. 1)   2253

_____. The Wonder of all the Gay World. Macmillan,
1950. The life of Robert Burns in Edinburgh, Scotland.
(His Immortal Memory--v. 3)   2254

Barker, Shirley. Swear by Apollo. Random, 1958. A doctor
from the American colonies goes to Edinburgh to learn new
medical techniques.   2255

Barr, Amelia E. Bernicia. Dodd, 1895. Social and political
life following the Jacobite Rebellion of 1745, showing influence
of the Methodist Revival.   2256

Barrington, Michael. The Reminiscences of Sir Barrington
Beaumont, Bart. Richards, 1902. This supposed autobiog-
raphy affords glimpses of cultured and corrupt society in
England and France during the French Revolution.   2257

Beatty, John and Patricia. At the Seven Stars. Macmillan,
1963. YA. A young colonial from Pennsylvania becomes
involved in a plot to overthrow George II.   2258

_____. The Royal Dirk. Morrow, 1966. YA. The adven-
tures of a youth who led Bonnie Prince Charlie through the
hills to escape the English armies.   2259

Beck, Lily Adams. The Chaste Diana. by E. Barrington,
pseud. Dodd, 1923. About the actress Lavinia Fenton,
star of The Beggar's Opera.   2260

_____. The Divine Lady. by E. Barrington, pseud. Dodd,
1924. The historic romance of Lord Nelson and Lady Hamilton, with her life before she met him.   2261

_____. The Exquisite Perdita. by E. Barrington, pseud.
Dodd, 1926. Theatrical and private life of Mary Robinson,
an actress who worked with Sheridan and Garrick.   2262

_____. The Irish Beauties. by E. Barrington, pseud.
Doubleday, 1931. The Irish Gunning sisters take a brilliant
place in the social whirl of London.   2263

Bennett, Alice Horlock. The Prince's Love Affair. Longmans,
1926. The romance and illegal marriage of the Prince of
Wales (later George IV) and Marie Fitzherbert.   2264

Bentley, Phillis. Manhold. Macmillan, 1941. Features a
cloth manufacturer in the Yorkshire district of eighteenth
century England.   2265

Besant, Walter. Dorothy Forster. Chatto, 1884. A view of
Northumberland noble society during the tumultuous first
part of the century.   2266

_____. A Fountain Sealed. Stokes, 1897. George II and
George the Prince of Wales in the closing months of the
king's reign.   2267

_____. The Lady of Lynn. Dodd, 1901. Romance of an
English beauty in the late 1740s.   2268

_____. No Other Way. Dodd, 1902. The desperate actions
of a debt-ridden lady reflect conditions of the lowest levels of
London society.   2269

_____. The Orange Girl. Dodd, 1899. Theatrical life in
London in the 1760s with glimpses of taverns, mansions,
and prisons.   2270

_____. St. Katherine's by the Tower. Harper, 1891. The
activities of the Jacobin Clubs just before the close of the
century.   2271

_____ and James Rice. The Chaplain of the Fleet. Chatto,
1881. Manners and customs of London and Epsom in the
middle of the century.   2272

Blackmore, R. D. The Maid of Sker. Burt, 1872. Thrilling
events in the life of a well-born girl raised as a foundling.
                                                         2273
_____. Mary Anerley. Burt, 1880. Characters are people
along the Yorkshire coast; events include smuggling and naval
serivce.   2274

Blake, Bass. A Lady's Honour. Appleton, 1902. Chiefly a
character study of John Churchill, first Duke of Marlborough.
                                                         2275
Bleackley, Horace. A Gentleman of the Road. Lane, 1911.
Adventure-romance of the road between Portsmouth and
London in the early part of George III's reign.   2276

Bloundelle-Burton, John. Denounced. Appleton, 1896. Followers of Stuart Prince Charlie in England and France after
his defeat.   2277

_____. Fortune's My Foe. Appleton, 1899. Adventure on
shipboard in action between British and French.   2278

_____. The Intriguers' Way. Religious Tract Soc., 1908.
Implication of an innocent man in a conspiracy to assassinate George I shortly before his coronation.   2279

Blundell, Mary E. Noblesse Oblige. by M. E. Francis, pseud.

Long, 1909.   The exile of French émigrés to London during
the early part of the French Revolution.   2280

Bodkin, M. McDonnell.   Lord Edward Fitzgerald.   Chapman &
Hall, 1896.   Career of an English soldier who served in the
American Revolution, in Ireland, and in Canada.   2281

Bone, Florence.   The Morning of To-Day.   Eaton & Mains,
1907.   Reaction of the people to Methodist preaching.   2282

Bowen, Marjorie, pseud. for Gabrielle Campbell Long.   The
Rake's Progress.   Rider, 1912.   A light romance of highly
fashionable society.   2283

Bowles, Emily.   Auriel Selwode.   Sands, 1908.   The story of an
Oxford scholar and his niece, Auriel, with scenes at Queen
Anne's court.   2284

Braddon, Mary E.   The Infidel.   Simpkin, 1900.   Reflects English thought and feeling during the Methodist Revival led by
the Wesley brothers.   2285

_____.   Mohawks.   Simpkin, 1886.   Life in London in the
early eighteenth century.   2286

Brady, Cyrus Townsend.   The Adventures of Lady Susan.
Moffat, 1908.   Experiences of a lady who crosses the Atlantic fleeing from her husband.   2287

_____.   The Two Captains.   Macmillan, 1905.   Conflict be-
tween Nelson and Bonaparte in the Mediterranean.   2288

Brandane, John.   My Lady of Aros.   Duffield, 1910.   Depicts
Jacobite plotting in Scotland as much as ten years after their
defeat at Culloden.   2289

Brandreth, Charles A.   The Honourable Roger.   Hutchinson,
1926.   A picture of Methodists, Jacobites, Whigs, and
Tories in Lincolnshire at mid-century.   2290

Bray, Anna Eliza.   Hartland Forest.   Chapman & Hall, 1871.
A domestic tragedy of western England in the rebellious
early eighteenth century.   2291

Briton, E. Vincent.   Some Account of Amyot Brough.   Seeley,
1884.   A romance of England which includes an account of
James Wolfe and the taking of Quebec in Canada.   2292

Broster, Dorothy K.   (1)   The Flight of the Heron.   Dodd,
1926.   (2)   The Gleam in the North.   Coward, 1931.   (3)
The Dark Mile.   Coward, 1934.   Series of three books
dealing with the unrest in Scotland during the Jacobite Rebellion and the fierce loyalty of the Highlanders to the

cause of Bonnie Prince Charlie.   2293-5

Buchan, John. A Lost Lady of Old Years. Lane, 1899. The
Jacobite period in Scotland with Lord Lovat and Murray of
Broughton pictured.   2296

_____. Midwinter. Doran, 1923. Dr. Johnson and General
Oglethorpe appear in this story of the Jacobite unrest.   2297

Burchell, Sidney Herbert. The Mistress of the Robes. Hurst,
1905. The court of Queen Anne.   2298

Byng, N.W. The Lawless Lover. Methuen, 1926. Story of
an English highwayman about the middle of the eighteenth
century.   2299

Calthorp, Dion Clayton. Little Flower of the Street. Hodder &
Stoughton, 1923. Romance of eighteenth century London. 2300

Campbell, Grace MacLennan. Torbeg. Duell, 1953. The daily
life of loyal Scots who aided Bonnie Prince Charlie.   2301

Capes, Bernard. Jemmy Abercraw. Brentano, 1910. A well-
born youth's career as a highwayman.   2302

_____. Our Lady of Darkness. Dodd, 1899. A novel using
the French Revolution as background.   2303

Carey, Wymond. (1) Monsieur Martin. Blackwood, 1902.
(2) For the White Rose (sequel). Blackwood, 1903.
Jacobite activities in England and on the Continent between
1700 and 1720.   2304-5

Carmichael, Miss E.M. The House of Delusion. Melrose,
1925. Pictures Lord Lovat and the Rebellion of '45 in
Scotland.   2306

Carr, John Dickson. The Demoniacs. Harper, 1962. Murder
mystery concerning a young couple in eighteenth century London.   2307

Castle, Agnes and Egerton. (1) The Bath Comedy. Stokes,
1900. (2) Incomparable Bellairs. Stokes, 1904. (3)
Love Gilds the Scene, and Women Guide the Plot. Smith
& Elder, 1912. Accounts of society life in these three romances of Bath are supposedly based on fact.   2308-10

_____. French Nan. Smith & Elder, 1905. A comedy of
manners in the London of George II.   2311

_____. Pamela Pounce. Appleton, 1921. Life at court
and in high society.   2312

Champion de Crespigny, Rose. The Rose Brocade. by Mrs.
Philip Champion de Crespigny. Nash, 1905. The court of
George I at Leicester House and a surprising marriage.   2313

Charles, Elizabeth. Diary of Mrs. Kitty Trevelyan. Nelson,
1864. The manners, customs, and thought of the time reflected in this tale of Cornish domestic life.   2314

Chidsey, Donald Barr. His Majesty's Highwayman. Crown,
1958. A youth mistakenly captured as a highwayman escapes and joins the bandits until he can clear his name.   2315

Cobbold, Richard. The History of Margaret Catchpole. Frowde,
1845. Experiences of a woman jailed for stealing a horse
and later transported to Australia.   2316

Compton, Herbert. The Inimitable Mrs. Massingham. Chatto,
1900. Story of an actress in London, with scenes on a convict ship and at the Botany Bay colony.   2317

Cooke, H. Robswood. Alturlie. Hodder & Stoughton, 1925.
A Jacobite tale of France and Scotland.   2318

_____. Outlawed. Hodder & Stoughton, 1924. Adventures
of a man who was outlawed following the Battle of Culloden.
                                                                      2319

Cooper, Henry St. John. The Gallant Lover. Low, 1926.
An adventure story in Queen Anne's reign.   2320

Creswick, Paul. The Ring of Pleasure. Lane, 1911. About
Lady Emma Hamilton before her romance with Lord Nelson.
                                                                      2321

Crockett, Samuel R. (1) The Raiders. Macmillan, 1893.
(2) The Dark o' the Moon (sequel). Macmillan, 1902.
Pathos, romance, and adventure in Scotland in the 1720s.
                                                                   2322-3

Dakers, Elaine. Ember in the Ashes. by Jane Lane, pseud.
F. Muller, 1960. The disastrous marriage of a willful girl
affects her whole family during the Gordon Riots.   2324

_____. Madame Geneva. by Jane Lane, pseud. Rinehart,
1946. Effect on Londoners of the bursting of the South Sea
Bubble and the importation of cheap, poisonous gin.   2325

Dampier, E. M. Smith. Ineffectual Fires. Melrose, 1913.
Artistic circles in London and Florence with Sir Joshua
Reynolds a figure.   2326

_____. Oil of Spikenard. Melrose, 1911. A picture of
manners and character in the reign of George II.   2327

Dawson, A. J. The Fortunes of Farthings. Harper, 1904.
Contrasts peaceful life in rural Dorset with hardships of

a Christian slave of the barbaric Moors.   2328

Deane, Mary. The Rose-Spinner. Murray, 1904. English
life during the unrest caused by Jacobite activity and South
Sea Bubble speculation.   2329

Dearmer, Mabel. The Orangery. Smith & Elder, 1904.
Portrays London society--its parties, clubs, and gambling
rooms.   2330

Deeping, Warwick. Bess of the Woods. Harper, 1906. English country life in the mid-eighteenth century.   2331

Dickens, Charles. Barnaby Rudge. Chapman & Hall, 1849.
Dramatic account of the Gordon Riots of 1780 against modi-
fying the penal laws against Catholics.   2332

Dill, Bessie. My Lady Nan. Hurst, 1907. A light novel of
society life in resort areas.   2333

_____. The Silver Glen. Digby & Long, 1909. Schemes
of the Jacobites and Hanoverians with a portrait of the Old
Pretender.   2334

Dudley, Ernest. Picaroon. Bobbs, 1953. An engaging Irish
pickpocket mixes theft and romance in London.   2335

Duke, Winifred. Heir to Kings. Stokes, 1926. The Young
Pretender's attempts to attain the English throne.   2336

_____. Scotland's Heir. Chambers, 1925. Prince Charlie
is the central figure in this novel.   2337

Dundas, Norman. Castle Adamant. Murray, 1927. The adventures, imprisonment, and escape of a Jacobite hero.   2338

Eccott, W.J. The Hearth of Hutton. Blackwood, 1906. A
squire uses his knowledge of his own region to serve the
Young Pretender.   2339

Ellis, Beth. The Moon of Bath. [same as: The Fair Moon
of Bath] Dodd, 1907. Romance and Jacobite conspiracy
in the resort town of Bath.   2340

Elvin, Harold. Story at Canons. Roy Pub., 1952. Spirited
story of the Dukes of Canons.   2341

Elwood, Muriel. The Bigamous Duchess. Bobbs, 1960. A romantic novel about the scandal involving Elizabeth Chudleigh,
the Duchess of Kingston.   2342

Everett, Mrs. H.D. White Webs. by Theo. Douglas, pseud.
Secker, 1912. An imaginative romance of Henry Stuart and

Margaret Hay.   2343

Falkner, J. Meade. Moonfleet. Arnold, 1898. A tale of
smuggling along the coast of England.   2344

Farnol, Jeffery. Our Admirable Betty. Little, 1918. A
London belle and her train of admirers.   2345

Field, Bradda. Bride of Glory. [En. title: Miledi] Greystone,
1942. The romances of Emy Lyon, the blacksmith's daughter
who became Lady Hamilton.   2346

Fielding, Henry. The History of Tom Jones, a Foundling.
Millar, 1749. A novel of manners concerning mid-century
life with pictures of all levels of society.   2347

Findlater, Jane Helen. A Daughter of Strife. Methuen, 1897.
Domestic life in Scotland early in the century.   2348

_____. The Green Graves of Balgowrie. Methuen, 1896.
A charming story of family life in Scotland.   2349

Findlay, J. T. A Deal With the King. Digby & Long, 1901.
"A tale of the period of the Jacobite Rebellion of 1715." 2350

Fleming, Guy. Over the Hills and Far Away. Longmans,
1917. Land and sea adventures in the area of England,
Ireland, and Scotland.   2351

Fletcher, Joseph S. I'd Venture All for Thee! Nash, 1913.
Adventures of a Jacobite on the Yorkshire coast in 1746.   2352

Ford, Ford Madox (name originally Ford Madox Hueffer). The
Portrait. Methuen, 1910. Social life of fashionable young
dandies and their club activities.   2353

Forster, R. H. The Little Maister. Long, 1913. A tale of
Northumberland which includes an account of Prince Charlie
in Carlisle.   2354

_____. Strained Allegiance. Long, 1905. Romance during
the Jacobite Rebellion of 1715.   2355

Foster, Elizabeth. Children of the Mist. Macmillan, 1961.
An actual romantic scandal, the parties to which all lived
in the same house.   2356

Fox, Marion. The Bountiful Hour. Lane, 1912. A pleasing
account of late eighteenth century life having light touches
of humor.   2357

Francillon, Robert E. Ropes of Sand. Munro, 1885. Life in
North Devon at the end of the century.   2358

Francis, Marian. Where Honour Leads. Hutchinson, 1902.
Domestic life in confused mid-eighteenth century England. 2359

Frye, Pearl. A Game for Empires. Little, 1950. Admiral
Lord Nelson and his rousing-naval victories.   2360

Galt, John. The Annals of the Parish. Dutton, 1820. The
manners and thought-patterns of Scottish village life.   2361

Garfield, Leon. Smith. Pantheon, 1967. YA. A twelve-
year-old pickpocket becomes involved in murder and mystery
and ends up in Newgate prison.   2362

Gaskell, Elizabeth C. Sylvia's Lovers. by Mrs. Gaskell.
Scribner, 1863. A romance of the closing years of the
century during the war with France.   2363

Gaskin, Catherine. Blake's Reach. Lippincott, 1958. A young
woman, attempting to rebuild the family manor, becomes involved in smuggling.   2364

Gerson, Noel B. The Charlatan. by Carter A. Vaughan, pseud.
Doubleday, 1959. A court-martialed English Colonel undertakes to rescue a boy from a French citadel to redeem himself.   2365

Gilchrist, R. Murray. The Gentle Thespians. Milne, 1908.
A troupe of travelling actors in the country areas of England.
                                                            2366
Godwin, William. Things as They Are. Robinson, 1794. An
expression of the author's protest against eighteenth century
English penal laws.   2367

Goldring, Maude. Dean's Hall. Murray, 1908. English
Quaker life from a sympathetic point-of-view.   2368

Goldsmith, Oliver. The Vicar of Wakefield. Newbery, 1766.
The life of a vicar and his family in a small rural community.   2369

Goodridge Roberts, Theodore. Captain Love. by Theodore
Roberts. Page, 1908. Thrilling incidents and romances in
the company of gamblers and highwaymen.   2370

Goodwin, Maud W. Veronica Playfair. Little, 1909. Based
on the literary, political, and social life of George I's time
with Beau Nash as a figure.   2371

Gough, George W. Yeoman Adventurer. Putnam, 1917. A
farmer turns soldier in the Jacobite cause.   2372

Graham, Winston. The Renegade. Doubleday, 1951. Defiance of conventions in the colorful Cornwall countryside,

1783-1787.   2373

Grant, James. Lucy Arden. Dutton, 1859. A romance of
persons involved in the Jacobite rising of 1715.   2374

Harrison, Herbert. Dick Munday. Low, 1923. An adventure
story of London and Kent.   2375

Hastings, Phyllis. The House on Malador Street. Putnam, 1970.
The eldest of four impoverished orphaned sisters strictly con-
trols the others and teaches them dressmaking for self-sup-
port.   2376

Hayes, Frederick W. (1) A Kent Squire. Hutchinson, 1900.
(2) Gwynett of Thornhaugh (sequel). Hutchinson, 1900.
(3) The Shadow of a Throne (sequel). Hutchinson, 1904.
A series of adventures in England and France during the
disturbed eighteenth century.   2377-9

Hector, Annie French. The Heritage of Langdale. by Mrs.
Alexander, pseud. Hutchinson, 1877. A story of southern
England during the Jacobite Rebellion.   2380

Heyer, Georgette. The Black Moth. Dutton, 1968, c.1921.
High society life in fashionable English places at mid-century.   2381

_____. Devil's Cub. Dutton, 1966, c.1932. A hot-headed
young English nobleman, forced to fight a duel, carries off
the wrong girl as he flees to France.   2382

_____. The Masqueraders. Dutton, 1967, c.1929. Story of
a young man and his sister who are forced to flee in disguise
after an unsuccessful Jacobite uprising in 1745.   2383

Hinkson, Henry A. The King's Deputy. McClurg, 1899. Ireland during the viceroyalty of the Duke of Rutland, featuring social customs and traditions.   2384

Hocking, Joseph. The Birthright. Dodd, 1897. Exciting adventures, including smuggling, in mid-century Cornwall.   2385

_____. Mistress Nancy Molesworth. Doubleday, 1898.
Daily life and Jacobite activities in Cornwall at mid-century.   2386.

Hocking, Silas K. The Strange Adventures of Israel Pendray.
Warne, 1899. A didactic novel of Cornwall in the time of
Wesley.   2387

Innes, Norman. Parson Croft. Nash, 1907. Social life early
in the century.   2388

Jacob, Naomi Ellington. They Left the Land. Macmillan, 1940. Yorkshire yeomen leave the land for London but their descendants return to the country. 2389

Jacob, Violet. Flemington. Murray, 1911. Adventures of a spy in the Jacobite Rebellion of '45. 2390

James, G. P. R. The Smuggler. Dutton, 1845. The contest between smugglers and customs men in Kent. 2391

Jeffery, Walter. The King's Yard. Everett, 1903. The attempt of an American to set fire to the Portsmouth Dockyard at the outbreak of the American Revolution. 2392

Johnston, Mary. Foes. Harper, 1918. Boyhood friends become enemies due to their love for the same girl. 2393

_____. The Laird of Glenfernie. Harper, 1919. Adventures of the hero in Scotland and abroad in Jacobite times. 2394

Kaye-Smith, Sheila. Starbrace. Dutton, 1926. Life in the English countryside. 2395

_____. The Tramping Methodist. Dutton, 1922. The mission of an itinerant preacher. 2396

Keddie, Henrietta. Favours from France. by Sarah Tytler, pseud. Long, 1905. A Scottish Jacobite family in exile after 1745. 2397

_____. Innocent Masqueraders. by Sarah Tytler, pseud. Long, 1907. Domestic life in English villages. 2398

_____. Lady Bell. by Sarah Tytler, pseud. Chatto, 1885. The entertainments of noble society in the reign of George III and Queen Charlotte. 2399

_____. Lady Jean's Son. by Sarah Tytler, pseud. Jarrold & Sons, 1897. A novel of manners set in Scottish society. 2400

_____. The MacDonald Lass. by Sarah Tytler, pseud. Chatto, 1895. Flora MacDonald's part in the rescue and escape of Bonnie Prince Charlie. 2401

_____. The Poet and His Guardian Angel. by Sarah Tytler, pseud. Chatto, 1904. The literary circle at Olney, with the poet Cowper as chief figure. 2402

Keeling, Elsa d'Esterre. The Queen's Serf. Unwin, 1898. A romance of England in Queen Anne's reign. 2403

Kenyon, Frank Wilson. The Duke's Mistress. Dodd, 1969. Low-born, but charming and ambitious, Mary Ann Clarke

becomes the mistress of Frederick Augustus, playboy son
of King Edward III.   2404

King-Hall, Magdalen. Lovely Lynchs. Rinehart, 1947. Drawing
room society in Ireland, England, and France as it appears
in the lives of two sisters.   2405

Kirk, James Prior. Fortuna Chance. by James Prior, pseud.
Constable, 1910. Rural life on the secluded western border
of Sherwood Forest, affected little by current events.   2406

Knowles, Mabel Winifred. The Gipsy Count. by May Wynne,
pseud. McBride, 1909. Based on the adventures of Bamfylde Moore Carew, known as "king of the gypsies."   2407

_____. Honour's Fetters. by May Wynne, pseud. Paul,
1911. The search of a young French girl for her brother,
a prisoner-of-war in England.   2408

_____. Mistress Cynthia. by May Wynne, pseud. Green-
ing, 1910. Romance involving Jacobite intrigues with Spain
and France.   2409

Laing, Jan. Priscilla. Putnam, 1951. Story of a girl left in
the London Foundling Hospital.   2410

Lambert, Frederick Arthur. The Great Attempt. by Frederick
Arthur, pseud. Murray, 1914. Jacobite activity in northern
England in the 1730s.   2411

Lane, Elinor Macartney. Nancy Stair. Appleton, 1905. Romance and murder figure in this story of Nancy Stair and
Robert Burns.   2412

Lee, Albert. The Baronet in Corduroy. Appleton, 1903. Pictures English life from noble homes to prisons.   2413

Legge, Clayton Mackenzie. Highland Mary. Clark, 1906.
The story of Robert Burns and his romances with Mary
Campbell and Jean Armour.   2414

Lenanton, Carola Oman. Princess Amelia. by Carola Oman.
Duffield, 1924. Tragic romance of Princess Amelia at the
court of her father, George III.   2415

Lever, Charles. Sir Jasper Carew, Knight. Hodgson, 1855.
The early days of the Irish Parliament in the unrest preceding the open rebellion of 1798.   2416

Linington, Elizabeth. Monsieur Janvier. Doubleday, 1957.
A cloak-and-sword story of revenge and romance.   2417

Lofts, Norah. Afternoon of an Autocrat. Doubleday, 1956.

Two separate romances are told in this enjoyable picture
of manor and village life.   2418

_____. Colin Lowrie. Knopf, 1939. The varied life and loves
of a Scotsman driven from his home by the Jacobite Rebellion.   2419

_____. The House at Sunset. Doubleday, 1962. The proud
old house, passing from family to family, is finally divided
into apartments and shops, each of which adds to its history.
(Completes trilogy)   2420

Lyell, W. D. The Justice-Clerk. Hodge, 1923. Social and political life in high legal circles in Edinburgh.   2421

Lytton, Edward Bulwer, 1st. baron. Devereux. Dutton, 1829.
Based on activities of Lord Bolingbroke with literary figures
introduced.   2422

_____. Eugene Aram. Harper, 1832. Study of a murderer,
giving the man credit for his good points.   2423

McCarthy, Justin Huntly. The King Over the Water. Harper,
1911. A romance of the Old Pretender, James Stuart, and
Princess Clementina Sobieski.   2424

McFadden, Gertrude Violet. His Grace of Grub Street. Lane,
1918. Dependence of Grub Street writers on their rich and
powerful patron.   2425

Machray, Robert. Sir Hector. Constable, 1901. Shows the
influence of the Rebellion of '45 on financial matters. 2426

McIlwraith, Jean. The Curious Career of Roderick Campbell.
Constable, 1901. Thrilling adventures of a man involved in
the Rebellion of '45.   2427

Mackenzie, Compton. The Passionate Elopement. Lane, 1911.
The gay life and light entertainments of a resort town at the
turn of the century.   2428

Mackenzie, William Cook. The Lady of Hirta. Gardner, 1905.
The kidnapping and imprisonment of Lady Grange, involved
in Jacobite plotting.   2429

Maclean, Norman. Hills of Home. Hodder, 1906. The search
for Jacobites in hiding after the Battle of Culloden. 2430

McLennan, William. Spanish John. Harper, 1898. A Spanish
lieutenant sent by the king of Spain to the Young Pretender
arrives after the Battle of Culloden.   2431

Macquoid, Katharine S. Captain Dallington. Arrowsmith,

1907. Adventures of highwaymen and campaigns of Marlborough.   2432

Malling, Matilda. The Immaculate Young Minister. (tr.)
Constable, 1913. Centers around the career of William Pitt
the Younger and reflects politics and court life.   2433

Markham, Virgil. The Scamp. Macmillan, 1926. The fortunes
of Francis Talbot and his friends during the reign of George
I.   2434

Marsh, Frances. A Romance of Old Folkestone. Fifield,
1906. Romance of an English admiral and a goddaughter
of Marie Antoinette.   2435

Marshall, Edison. The Upstart. Farrar, 1945. The streets
of London and the provincial theaters are the setting. 2436

Marshall, Rosamond. The General's Wench. Pyramid Bks.,
1963, c.1953. Sabrina, as a poor relation, was counted
lucky to marry a rich old man--until she fell violently in
love with a lusty young general.   2437

Mason, A.E.W. and Andrew Lang. Parson Kelly. Longmans,
1899. Based mainly on the Jacobite plot in which Bishop
Atterbury was involved.   2438

Middleton, Ellis. The Road of Destiny. Mills & Boon, 1923.
Gambling and Jacobite activities in eighteenth century England.   2439

Milne, James. The Black Colonel. Lane, 1921. Adventures
of a Jacobite after the Rebellion.   2440

Montgomery, K.L., pseud. for Kathleen and Letitia Montgomery.
Colonel Kate. Methuen, 1908. A Scots girl resolves, against
her husband's wishes, to arouse her clan to Prince Charlie's
cause.   2441

Moore, F. Frankfort. Fanny's First Novel. Doran, 1913. A
novel based on the acceptance of Fanny Burney's first novel,
Evelina [listed in this section under Frances Burney Arblay].
                                                       2442

_____. The Jessamy Bride. Hutchinson, 1897. Oliver
Goldsmith and Mary Horneck are the central figures in this
novel of cultured circles.   2443

_____. A Nest of Linnets. Appleton, 1901. The court-
ship and marriage of Elizabeth Linley and the playwright
Sheridan.   2444

_____. Sir Roger's Heir. Hodder, 1905. A novel of
manners with characters such as those in Addison and

Steele's Spectator Papers.   2445

Morrow, Honoré. Let the King Beware! Morrow, 1936. Depicts the English government during Franklin's negotiations
concerning the American Revolution.   2446

Muddock, J. E. Preston. For the White Cockade. Long, 1905.
A tale of the double-dealing Simon Fraser during the 1740s.
                                                                  2447

_____. The Lost Laird. Long, 1898. The search for
hiding rebels after the Battle of Culloden.   2448

Munro, Neil. Doom Castle. Dodd, 1901. The French hero
searches for a traitor in western Scotland after Culloden. 2449

_____. The New Road. Blackwood, 1914. Scotland in
1740s.   2450

_____. The Shoes of Fortune. Dodd, 1901. A romance
concerning the Young Pretender ten years after his defeat
at Culloden.   2451

Murray, David Leslie. Commander of the Mists. Knopf,
1938. Charles Edward, the Young Pretender, and the valiant Scots who tried to help him.   2452

Neill, Robert. Black William. Doubleday, 1955. Romance
and details of life in bleak, austere Northumberland.   2453

_____. Hangman's Cliff. Doubleday, 1956. Exciting tale
of smuggling and murder on the English Channel coast.   2454

_____. The Mills of Colne. [En. title: Song of Sunrise]
Doubleday, 1959. The troubled depressed times just before
the Industrial Revolution.   2455

Nicholls, Frederick Francis. The Free Traders. Scribner,
1968, c.1967. YA. The desire for riches conflicts with
the ideals of honesty as a profitable smuggling operation
is set up in coastal Sussex.   2456

Oliver, Jane, pseud., for Rees, Helen Christina Easson.
Candleshine No More. Putnam, 1967. Daring attempt of
the Young Pretender, Bonnie Prince Charlie, to recover the
English throne from Hanoverians.   2457

O'Riordan, Conal. Yet Do Not Grieve. Scribner, 1928. Conditions under George III are reflected in the life of a loyal
subject.   2458

Ormerod, Frank. The Two-Handed Sword. Simpkin, 1909.
Jacobite and Methodist influences on English thought and
action.   2459

Overton, John. Hazard: A Romance. Melrose, 1920. A
   love story with Jacobite elements in George II's time.   2460

Pearce, Charles E. Madam Flirt. Paul, 1922. A romantic
   novel about actress Lavinia Fenton.   2461

Pease, Howard. The Burning Cresset. Constable, 1908.
   Lord Derwentwater and his associates in the Rising of '15.
                                                             2462
Peck, Theodora. The Sword of Dundee. Duffield, 1908. Ad-
   ventures of a girl who assisted Bonnie Prince Charlie.   2463

Pemberton, Max. Sir Richard Escombe. Harper, 1908.
   High society circles in mid-century Warwickshire.   2464

Picard, Barbara Leonie. The Young Pretenders. Criterion,
   1966. YA. A brother and sister shelter a wounded fugitive
   on their estate during the Jacobite Rebellion.   2465

Pinkerton, Thomas A. Blue Bonnets Up. Long, 1901. The
   time when Jacobite hopes were centering on the claim of
   the Young Pretender--about 1730.   2466

Ponsonby, Doris. If My Arms Could Hold. Liveright, 1947.
   "A vivid and colorful romance of Bath in the time of Beau
   Nash."   2467

Quiller-Couch, Arthur T. Hetty Wesley. Dutton, 1931. Tragic
   life of Hetty, sister of the famous John and Charles Wesley.
                                                             2468
Raymond, Walter. Jacob and John. Hodder, 1905. Rural
   life in Somerset at the time of South Sea Bubble speculation.   2469

_____. No Soul Above Money. Longmans, 1899. A domes-
   tic tragedy of village life in which murder figures.   2470

Reade, Charles. Peg Woffington. Scribner, 1853. Based
   on the life of a Covent Garden actress, Margaret Woffington.   2471

_____. The Wandering Heir. Chatto, 1882. The journeys
   and romance of a young heir.   2472

Rhys, Ernest. The Man at Odds. Hurst, 1904. Smuggling
   and piracy in Lundy and Wales.   2473

Richardson, Samuel. The History of Clarissa Harlowe. Dutton, 1748. Sentimental portrait of a young lady at mid-
   century.   2474

_____. The History of Sir Charles Grandison. Dutton,
   1753. Realistic story of a gentleman at mid-century.   2475

Ritchie, Anne Thackeray. Miss Angel. by Anne Thackeray.
Harper, 1875. The cultural life of Venice and London with
the painter Angelica Kauffmann as the main figure. 2476

Robertson, Frances F. The Taming of the Brute. by Frances
Harrod, pseud. Methuen, 1905. A young lady's attempts to
instill the social graces in her uncouth cousin. 2477

Robertson, William. The Stone of Dunalter. Gardner, 1901.
Set in Scotland during the turbulence of 1745. 2478

Rogers, Garet, pseud. Lancet. Putnam, 1956. Practice
of medicine in London by two very different men in a swift-
moving drama. 2479

Sabatini, Rafael. The Gates of Doom. Paul, 1924. Adventures
of a Jacobite agent during the Atterbury Plot. 2480

_____. The Lion's Skin. Appleton, 1911. Domestic crisis
after the bursting of the South Sea Bubble. 2481

Salmon, Geraldine Gordon. The Red Curve. by J.G. Sarasin,
pseud. Hutchinson, 1927. A romance of many historic
events in Scotland at mid-century. 2482

Schumacher, Henry. The Fair Enchantress. Hutchinson,
1912. The life of Emma, Lord William Hamilton's wife before her marriage to him. (followed by Nelson's Last Love)
2483

Scott, Sir Walter. The Antiquary. Tauchnitz, 1845. Lives
of gentry and fisherfolk on the coast of Scotland at the end
of the century. 2484

_____. The Black Dwarf. Lovell, 1885. A dwarf is the
central character in this tale of Scotland before the Rebellion of 1715. 2485

_____. Guy Mannering. Bazin & Ellsworth, 1829. Law-
lessness, smuggling, and a gypsy's curse in Galloway. 2486

_____. The Heart of Midlothian. Tauchnitz, 1858. Jeanie
Deane walks from Edinburgh to London to petition Queen
Caroline to pardon her sister. 2487

_____. The Pirate. Parker, 1822. Concerns a pirate in
the Shetland and Orkney Islands and pictures the life and
customs of the time. 2488

_____. Redgauntlet. Constable, 1824. A Scottish romance
which tells of the Young Pretender's farewell. 2489

_____. Rob Roy. Bazin & Ellsworth, 1817. Robert Mac-
Gregor, Highland robber-outlaw, in the beautiful Loch Lo-

mond area.   2490

_____. Waverley. Tauchnitz, 1845. Scotland during the
Jacobite Rebellion of 1745.   2491

Seton, Anya. Devil Water. Avon Bks., 1970, c.1962. Charles
Radcliffe's part in two abortive attempts to restore the Stuarts and his daughter's efforts to save him.   2492

Sheldon, Gilbert. Bubble Fortune. Dutton, 1911. A story of
the development and fate of the South Sea Company.   2493

Shellbarger, Samuel. Lord Vanity. Little, 1953. Elegant
and artificial mid-century English society is pictured here. 2494

Shepard, Odell and Willard Odell Shepard. Jenkins' Ear.
Macmillan, 1951. Concerns the results of the War of Jenkins' Ear.   2495

Silberrad, Una L. Sampson Rideout, Quaker. Nelson, 1911.
Peaceful life of a Quaker merchant in rural England.   2496

Sladen, Douglas. The Admiral. Pearson, 1898. Romance of
Lord Nelson and Lady Hamilton.   2497

Smith, Arthur D. Howden. Claymore. Skeffington, 1918. A
young man with Prince Charlie at Derby and Culloden.   2498

Smith, Frederick R. The Coming of the Preachers. by John
Ackworth, pseud. Hodder, 1901. The Methodist Revival in
northern, rural England.   2499

Snaith, John Collis. The Wayfarers. Ward & Lock, 1902.
London social life in the time of novelist Henry Fielding.   2500

Stephens, Eve. Clandara. by Evelyn Anthony, pseud. Doubleday, 1963, c.1962. A crisis is precipitated by love between
members of feuding Scottish families during Stuart efforts to
recapture the English throne.   2501

Stephens, Robert Neilson. The Flight of Georgiana. Page,
1905. Northern England is the scene for these events following the Battle of Culloden.   2502

_____ and George Hembert Westley. Clementina's Highwayman. Page, 1907. A gentleman turned highwayman for a
lark rescues a damsel in distress.   2503

Steuart, Catherine. By Allan Water. Elliot (Edinburgh), 1901.
Recounts meetings held in a certain house in '15 and '45.   2504

_____. Richard Kennoway and His Friends. Methuen, 1908.
A preacher and his associates at the turn of the century.   2505

Stevenson, Robert Louis.   (1) Kidnapped.   Scribner, 1886.
(2) David Balfour (sequel).   [En. title: Catriona] Scribner,
1892.   The exciting travels of two young Scots and conditions
in Scotland after the Rebellion of 1745.   2506-7

_____. The Master of Ballantrae.   Scribner; 1889.   The
tragic story of a fighting Scots family involved in the Jacobite
troubles of mid-century.   2508

Stewart, Charlotte.   Poor Sons of a Day.   by Allan McAulay,
pseud.   Nisbet, 1902.   A tale showing the sufferings and
heartbreak incident to the Rebellion of '45.   2509

_____. The Rhymer.   by Allan McAulay, pseud.   Scribner,
1900.   A Scottish romance concerning an episode in Robert
Burns' life.   2510

Strain, Euphans H.   A Prophet's Reward.   Blackwood, 1908.
Political unrest in Scotland before and during the French
Revolution.   2511

Stubbs, Jean.   The Case of Kitty Ogilvie.   Walker, 1970.   Harrowing details of an eighteenth century trial about the murder
of a wealthy man.   2512

_____. My Grand Enemy.   Stein & Day, 1967.   Based on
the case of Mary Blandy, who was accused of murdering her
father out of love for her fiancé.   2513

Sutcliffe, Halliwell.   The Lone Adventure.   Doran, 1911.   Reflects the attitude of the squire and yeoman classes during
the disturbances of '45.   2514

_____. The Open Road.   Ward & Lock, 1913.   In a case
of mistaken identity the hero is taken for Prince Charlie.   2515

_____. Ricroft of Withens.   Appleton, 1898.   A violent
story of the country folk of Yorkshire around 1745.   2516

_____. Willowdene Will.   Pearson, 1901.   Exploits of a
highwayman in Cornwall during the '45 Rebellion.   2517

Tarbet, W. G.   A Loyal Maid.   Arrowsmith, 1908.   A picture
of Galloway during Prince Charlie's scheming.   2518

Tarkington, Booth.   Monsieur Beaucaire.   McClure, 1900.
Complications arise when a nobleman disguised as a barber
falls in love with an aristocratic lady.   2519

Taylor, Winchcombe.   Ram.   St. Martin's, 1960.   Tale of an
Englishman whose military adventures and unsavory romances
range from India to London to the Georgia Colony.   2520

Teague, John J. A Rose of Blenheim. by Morice Gerard,
pseud. Hodder, 1907. The successful campaign of Marlborough at Blenheim.   2521

Thackeray, William Makepeace. The History of Henry Esmond,
Esquire. Harper, 1879. Noted English literary figures ap-
pear in this story of the era of Queen Anne. (followed by
The Virginians)   2522

Thompson, China, pseud. Starrbelow. Scribner, 1958. The
question of a child's origins is at the center of this novel of
eighteenth century London society.   2523

Thorndike, Arthur Russell. Christopher Syn. by Russell Thorndike and William Buchanan, pseud. Abelard, 1960. The
vicar of a church in the Kentish marshes becomes an accom-
plice of smugglers evading high taxes.   2524

Tunstall, Beatrice. The Long Day Closes. Doubleday, 1934.
An ancestral estate in the Midlands during the time of Bonnie
Prince Charlie.   2525

Tynan, Katharine. Rose of the Garden. Constable, 1912. The
story of Lady Sarah Lennox, with whom George III had a
brief romance.   2526

Walpole, Hugh. Judith Paris. Doubleday, 1931. A dramatic
tale of the fun-loving daughter of Rogue Herries' old age. 2527

_____. Rogue Herries. Doubleday, 1930. The Herries
come to live in the family castle in Keswick.   2528

Ward, Mary Augusta. Fenwick's Career. by Mrs. Humphry
Ward. Harper, 1906. Romantic tragedy involving artists
George Romney and Benjamin Haydon.   2529

Ware, Mrs. Hibbert. The King of Bath. Skeet, 1879. A
novel of manners at the fashionable resort.   2530

Watson, H.B. Marriott. The House Divided. Harper, 1901.
English social life of the nobility with scenes at court and
in London.   2531

Watson, William L. Sir Sergeant. Blackwood, 1899. Adventures of a French sergeant who had served the Jacobites until their defeat.   2532

Watt, Lauchlan Maclean. Edragil, 1745. Hodder, 1907.
Western Scotland at the time of Bonnie Prince Charlie's
landing.   2533

Weiss, Arthur. O'Kelly's Eclipse. Doubleday, 1968. An exiled Irishman seeks both a perfect racehorse and an ideal

woman in London.   2534

Wentworth, Patricia. **Queen Anne Is Dead**. Melrose, 1915.
London at the time of Queen Anne's death.   2535

Weyman, Stanley J. **The Castle Inn**. Longmans, 1898. Adventures of travellers on mid-century English roads.   2536

White, Leslie Turner. **Lord Fancy**. Doubleday, 1960. Prize-
fighting was a sport which required great endurance in 1791,
when Darcy Scott fought political odds as well as Slasher
Rucker, his opponent in the ring.   2537

Whitelaw, David. **The Little Lady of Arrock**. Chapman & Hall,
1921. Domestic tragedy in Jacobite times in Scotland.   2538

Whyte-Melville, George John. **Katerfelto**. Longmans, 1875.
A sportsman's story with a vivid description of stag hunting.   2539

Wilkins, William Vaughan. **Crown Without Sceptre**. Macmillan,
1952. Romance in England and Italy during the 1770s.   2540

Williamson, Joanne S. **The Glorious Conspiracy**. Knopf, 1961.
YA. A poor orphan escapes London for America where he
becomes involved in Federalist politics.   2541

Wingfield, Lewis Strange. **Lady Grizel**. Bentley, 1877. Society life at Bath in mid-century.   2542

Winstanley, L. **The Face on the Stair**. Hutchinson, 1927.
Mystery and adventure in England's Lake District.   2543

Woods, Margaret L. **Esther Vanhomrigh**. Murray, 1891. Portrays Jonathan Swift and many of his associates.   2544

_____. **A Poet's Youth**. Chapman & Dodd, 1923. Words-
worth's school days in England, his tours of the Continent,
and his romance with Annette Vallon.   2545

Yerby, Frank. **Jarrett's Jade**. Dial, 1959. A dashing Scottish
highland Lord, driven from his home by poverty, seeks his
fortune in London, then emigrates to Georgia with Oglethorpe.
                                                                2546
Yoxall, James Henry. **Smalilou**. Hutchinson, 1904. Gypsy
life in English rural areas.   2547

2) Ireland

Alexander, Miriam. **The House of Lisronan**. Melrose, 1912.
Ireland under William III and in Anne's reign, showing the
harshness of the Penal Laws.   2548

_____. The Port of Dreams. Putnam, 1912. Romance of
Irish Jacobites.   2549

Arthur, Mary Lucy. The Island of Sorrow. by George David
    Gilbert, pseud. Long, 1903. Account of Ireland at the close
    of the century centers around the career of Robert Emmet.
                                                             2550
Banim, John and Michael. The Croppy. Duffy (Dublin), 1828.
    An Irishman's view of the excesses of the Rebellion of
    1798.   2551

Bennett, Louie. A Prisoner of His Word. Maunsel (Dublin),
    1908. An Englishman, motivated by love of an Irish girl,
    joins the Irish cause for which he has little sympathy.   2552

Bodkin, M. McDonnell. In the Days of Goldsmith. Long, 1903.
    Pictures members of mid-eighteenth century literary circles.
                                                             2553
_____. The Rebels. Ward & Lock, 1899. Politics, capture,
    and imprisonment in the Irish Rebellion of 1798.   2554

Bowen, Marjorie, pseud. for Gabrielle Campbell Long. Dark
    Rosaleen. Houghton, 1933. A tragic story of Ireland's un-
    rest and rebellion in the late eighteenth century.   2555

Buckley, William. Croppies Lie Down. Duckworth, 1903.
    A realistic account of the more severe aspects of the
    1798 Rebellion.   2556

Burnett, William Riley. Captain Lightfoot. Knopf, 1954. Ex-
    ploits of a youthful highwayman who wanders through Ireland
    and Scotland.   2557

Byrne, Donn. Blind Raftery and His Wife Hilaria. Century,
    1924. Marriage of an Irish poet and a Spanish lady in the
    Connaught hills.   2558

Carleton, William. Willie Reilly and His Dear Colleen Bawn.
    Dutton, 1855. Portrays the hunting and persecuting of
    priests in mid-century.   2559

Crosbie, W.J. David Maxwell. Jarrold & Sons, 1902. A
    Loyalist view of the Rebellion of 1798.   2560

Edgeworth, Maria. Castle Rackrent. Dutton, 1800. The
    reminiscences of an old family retainer depict Irish life
    and character.   2561

Elsna, Hebe, pseud. for Ansle, Dorothy Phoebe. The Brimming
    Cup. John Cushman Assoc., 1965. Two poverty-striken
    gentlewomen in Dublin manage to make apparently good matches
    --one for love and one for ambition.   2562

Faly, Patrick C. 'Ninety-Eight. Downey, 1897. Life in
Dublin during the 1798 Rebellion.   2563

Froude, James Anthony. The Two Chiefs of Dunboy. Longmans, 1889. Shows Ireland chafing under the yoke of English oppression.   2564

Gilbert, Rosa Mulholland. O'Loghlin of Clare. by Rosa Mulholland. Kenedy, 1916. Catholic suffering under the harsh
Penal Laws.   2565

Gogarty, Oliver St. John. Mad Grandeur. Lippincott, 1941.
How the decay of the aristocracy and the desperation of the
peasants led to revolt.   2566

Graber, George Alexander. The White Cockade. by Alexander
Cordell, pseud. Viking, 1970. YA. A seventeen-year-old
boy rides on a hazardous journey to deliver a message to
Dublin as Ireland seethes in unrest in 1798.   2567

Gwynn, Stephen. John Maxwell's Marriage. Macmillan, 1903.
Conflict between Protestants and Catholics involving forced
marriage and political schemes.   2568

Hannay, James Owen. The Northern Iron. by George A. Birmingham, pseud. Maunsel (Dublin), 1909. Pictures intense
political feelings at the end of the century.   2569

Hinkson, Henry A. The Point of Honour. McClurg, 1901.
The restless Irish at mid-century.   2570

_____. Up For the Green. Lawrence & Bullen, 1898.
Based on the experiences of a man captured by the United
Irishmen in their uprising of 1798.   2571

Kerr, Archibald W. M. By the Pool of Garmoyle. Northern
Whig (Ireland), 1925. Jacobite schemings in the early
1700s.   2572

Knowles, Mabel Winifred. For the Sake of Charles the Rover.
by May Wynne, pseud. Fenno, 1909. Adventures of a follower of Prince Charlie after the Rebellion of 1745.   2573

Lepper, John Heron. A Tory in Arms. Richards, 1916.
Wool smuggling and other activities in Ireland.   2574

Lever, Charles. Maurice Tiernay. Harper, 1852. The capture and death of Wolfe Tone during the Irish Rebellion of
1798, and French attempts on Ireland.   2575

_____. The O'Donoghue. Routledge, 1845. Conflict between
Irish and French at the end of the century.   2576

Lover, Samuel. Rory O'More. Dutton, 1837. A novel of the
    Rebellion of 1798 blaming a desperate few for the horrors
    committed.   2577

McDonnell, Randal. Ardnaree. Gill (Dublin), 1911. An Eng-
    lish girl in Connaught during the Rebellion of 1798.   2578

_____. Kathleen Mavourneen. Sealy & Bryers (Dublin),
    1898. The Irish Rebellion and attempted intervention of
    France in the 1790s.   2579

McKown, Robin. The Ordeal of Anne Devlin. Messner, 1963.
    YA. Role of courageous young Anne Devlin in the Irish strug-
    gle for freedom and the Rebellion of 1798.   2580

Mathew, Frank. The Wood of the Brambles. Lane, 1896.
    Events during the Rebellion of 1798.   2581

Maxwell, William H. O'Hara, 1798. Andrews, 1825. Dealings
    with the United Irishmen imperil a landowner.   2582

Murphy, James. The House in the Rath. Sealy & Bryers (Dub-
    lin), 1909. Negotiations with France shortly before the Irish
    Rebellion of 1798.   2583

_____. The Shan Van Vocht. Gill (Dublin), 1883. Diplo-
    matic and military relations between France and Ireland in
    1798.   2584

Newcomen, George. A Left-Handed Swordsman. Smithers,
    1900. Social life in Dublin in the unsettled years before
    the Rebellion of 1798.   2585

O'Hannrachain, Michael. A Swordsman of the Brigade. Sands,
    1914. An adventure-romance in Ireland and Flanders.   2586

O'Neill, Egan. The Anglophile. [En. title: Pretender]
    Messner, 1957. Handsome Irish rebel falls in love with his
    English wife--jeopardizing his cause and his life.   2587

Orpen, Mrs. Corrageen In '98. New Amsterdam Bk. Co.,
    1898. A description of atrocities committed during the
    1798 Rebellion.   2588

Parker, Gilbert. No Defence. Lippincott, 1920. A novel of
    Ireland, England, and Jamaica including the French attack
    on Ireland.   2589

Pender, Mrs. M. T. The Green Cockade. Downey, 1898.
    Northern Ireland during the Rebellion of '98.   2590

Sadlier, Mary Anne. The Fate of Father Sheehy. by Mrs.
    James Sadlier. Duffy (Dublin), 1845. A parish priest is

accused of involvement in a murder.   2591

Sheehy-Skeffington, Francis. In Dark and Evil Days. Duffy
(Dublin), 1919. The United Irishmen Movement in the Rebellion of 1798.   2592

Sillars, John. The McBrides. Blackwood, 1922. Smuggling
and adventure on the Isle of Arran.   2593

Skinner, June O'Grady. O'Houlihan's Jest. by Rohan O'Grady,
pseud. Macmillan, 1961. Confrontation between a British
officer and the scion of a proud Irish family in the days of
Ireland's oppression.   2594

Thackeray, William Makepeace. The Memoirs of Barry Lyndon,
Esq. Lippincott, 1871. Exploits of an Irish scoundrel who
travels about Europe.   2595

Tynan, Katharine. A King's Woman. Hurst, 1900. A Quaker
lady's view of the Irish Rebellion of 1798.   2596

b) Western and Central Europe

1) France

Ainsworth, W. Harrison. John Law, the Projector. Chapman
& Hall, 1864. About John Law and his disastrous speculation, the Mississippi Bubble.   2597

Atkinson, Eleanor. Mamzelle Fifine. Appleton, 1903. "A
romance of the girlhood of the Empress Josephine on the island of Martinique."   2598

Aubry, Octave. The Lost King. (tr.) Stokes, 1927. Report
of a retired secret agent relating his attempts to trace the
Lost Dauphin, Louis XVII.   2599

Austin, F. Britten. Forty Centuries Look Down. Stokes, 1937.
Napoleon's Egyptian campaign and his suspicions about Josephine's loyalty.   2600

_____. The Road to Glory. Stokes, 1935. Napoleon's view
of his first Italian campaign. (followed by Forty Centuries
Look Down)   2601

Bailey, H.C. Barry Leroy. Dutton, 1920. About a spy for
Napoleon who changes loyalties and serves the British.   2602

_____. The God of Clay. Brentano, 1908. Napoleon's
career from the time he was a Lieutenant until he became
First Counsul.   2603

_____. _Storm and Treasure._ Methuen, 1910. The Reign
of Terror in provincial France--the Vendean Rebellion and
Carrier's wholesale drownings at Nantes.   2604

Balzac, Honoré de. _The Chouans._ (tr.) Little, 1896. Royalist activities and Fouché's far-flung spy system.   2605

Baring-Gould, S. _In Exitu Israel._ Macmillan, 1870. Relations
between Church and State in 1788-89, when revolution was
imminent.   2606

Beck, Lily Adams. _The Empress of Hearts._ by E. Barrington, _pseud._ Dodd, 1928. Sympathetic portrayal of the young
queen, Marie Antoinette, and the trouble caused by a costly
diamond necklace.   2607

Bedford-Jones, Henry. _Rodomont._ Putnam, 1926. "A romance
of Mont St. Michel in the days of Louis XIV."   2608

_____. _Saint Michael's Gold._ Putnam, 1926. A young Am-
erican involved in the politics of the Revolution.   2609

Belloc, Hilaire. _The Girondin._ Nelson, 1911. The experiences
of an adventurer impressed into the army of the Republic. 2610

Bloundelle-Burton, John. _A Fair Martyr._ Everett, 1910.
Story of a child during the plague at Marseilles.   2611

_____. _The Fate of Valsec._ Methuen, 1902. Family dis-
sent in the Revolution--a judge's disowned son loves the
daughter of a woman condemned by the judge.   2612

_____. _The Right Hand._ Everett, 1911. The Battle of Det-
tingen is an important event in this tale of dispute over the
right to a title.   2613

_____. _The Scourge of God._ Appleton, 1898. Romance of
the daughter of Baville, who figured in the insurrection of
the Camisards for religious freedom.   2614

_____. _Servants of Sin._ Methuen, 1900. Marseilles during
the plague; the banishment of a girl as a criminal and her,
rescue.   2615

_____. _A Woman From the Sea._ Nash, 1907. An actress
in England serves as a spy of the revolutionary French government.   2616

_____. _The Year One._ Dodd, 1901. Adventures of a lady
whose husband has joined the Revolutionists; the massacre of
the Swiss Guards.   2617

Bois, Helma de. _The Incorruptible._ Crown, 1965. The final

years of the stern revolutionary leader, Robespierre.   2618

Bowen, Marjorie, pseud. for Gabrielle Campbell Long. The
Burning Glass. Dutton, 1920. Paris at the time of the
Encyclopaedists.   2619

_____. Mr. Misfortunate. Collins, 1919. Bonnie Prince
Charlie's life in Paris and elsewhere on the Continent.   2620

_____. The Quest of Glory. Methuen, 1911. Sophisti-
cated Parisian society life and the War of Austrian Succession.   2621

_____. The Third Estate. Dutton, 1918. The rise to
power of representatives of the French people.   2622

Brebner, Percy J. A Gentleman of Virginia. Macmillan,
1910. A story of French life, which continued as usual
in many places despite the Revolution.   2623

Brinton, Selwyn J. The Jacobin. Besant, 1936. Activities of
the leftist Jacobins during the early part of the French Revolution.   2624

Broster, Dorothy K. Sir Isumbras at the Ford. Murray,
1918. Includes the kidnapping of a small child during the
French Revolution.   2625

_____ and G.W. Taylor. Chantemerle. Murray, 1912.
Romance dealing with the suppression of religious orders in
revolutionary France at the start of the Terror.   2626

Capes, Bernard. Adventures of the Comte de la Muette During
the Terror. Dodd, 1898. This tale of revolutionary Paris
includes scenes of prison life.   2627

Carey, Wymond. "No. 101." Blackwood, 1906. A spy of Louis
XV's court during the War of Austrian Succession.   2628

Champion de Crespigny, Rose. From Behind the Arras. by
Mrs. Philip Champion de Crespigny. Unwin, 1902. Life
of a young lady of the upper class.   2629

Chapman, Hester W. Fear No More. Reynal, 1968. Tragic
story of the young son of Louis XVI and Marie Antoinette. 2630

Christian, Catherine. A Stranger Passed. Putnam, 1961,
c.1960. Intrigue in the royal court involves a group of
French and English nobles and prompts them to flee to
England before the Revolution.   2631

Cleugh, Sophia. Anne Marguerite. Houghton, 1932. Romantic
adventures of an aristocratic young lady during the early

French Revolution.   2632

Coryn, Marjorie. Alone Among Men. Appleton, 1947. Napoleon and Josephine in the month between his return from
Egypt and his becoming First Consul.   2633

_____. Good-Bye, My Son. Appleton, 1943. Napoleon's
mother, the engaging Letizia Bonaparte, and her amazing
children. (followed by The Marriage of Josephine)   2634

_____. Incorruptible. Appleton, 1943. Compelling story
of Robespierre in the last five months of his life.   2635

_____. The Marriage of Josephine. Appleton, 1945. Beauti-
ful Josephine de Beauharnais and her marriage to Napoleon.
(followed by Alone Among Men)   2636

Crockett, Samuel R. Flower O' the Corn. McClure, 1902.
The insurrection of the Camisards under Jean Cavalier, a
movement of people greatly stirred by religious fervor.   2637

Cuninghame, Lady Fairlie. The Little Saint of God. Hurst,
1901. A heroine of the Red Terror in Brittany during the
French Revolution.   2638

Dale, Mrs. Hylton. Crowned With the Immortals. Nichols,
1896. Romance based on the life of journalist-revolutionary
Camille Desmoulins.   2639

Davis, Harold Lenoir. Harp of a Thousand Strings. Morrow,
1947. Novel of the French Revolution and the period immedi-
ately following.   2640

Davis, William Stearns. The Whirlwind. Macmillan, 1929.
The passionate, widespread excesses in Paris and at Court
during the Revolution.   2641

Dehon, Theodora. Heroic Dust. Macmillan, 1940. The lovely
Normandy countryside is the locale for this tale of the Chouan
revolt of 1792.   2642

Delderfield, Ronald Frederick. Farewell the Tranquil. Dutton,
1950. Adventures of an English smuggler who takes part in
the French Revolution.   2643

Dickens, Charles. A Tale of Two Cities. Chapman & Hall,
1859. Classic tale of the French Revolution's Reign of
Terror.   2644

Dumas, Alexandre. Andree de Taverney. (tr.) Peterson,
1862. Centering on the executions of Louis XVI and his
queen, this novel introduces many noted revolutionary personages.   2645

_____. (1) The Chevalier D'Harmental. (tr.) [same as: The Conspirators] Little, 1891. (2) The Regent's Daughter (sequel). (tr.) Harper, 1845. The conspiracy to overthrow Louix XV and his regent is foiled by Dubois, French foreign minister.   2646-7

_____. The Marie Antoinette Romances, a chronicle of history and court life from 1770 to 1793. (1) Memoirs of a Physician. (tr.) Little, 1893. Supposed memoirs of the swindler, Cagliostro, showing the decline of Louis XV's disastrous reign. (2) The Queen's Necklace (sequel). (tr.) Munro, 1877. Louis XVI's early reign; the scandal of the diamond necklace. (3) Ange Pitou, or The Taking of the Bastille (sequel). (tr.) [same as: Six Years Later] Little, 1890. The attack on the Bastille, where state political prisoners were kept. (4) La Comtesse de Charny (sequel). (tr.) Little, 1890. The king and queen's flight; their capture at Varennes; the king's execution. (5) The Chevalier de Maison-Rouge (sequel). (tr.) Little, 1890. The queen's imprisonment; unsuccessful attempts to rescue her; her execution.   2648-52

_____. Monsieur de Chauvelin's Will. (tr.) Munro, 1900. This novel of the end of Louis XV's life depicts his decadent court and his death by smallpox.   2653

_____. Sylvandire. (tr.) Little, 1897. Versailles during the ascendancy of Madame de Maintenon toward the closing part of Louis XIV's reign.   2654

_____. (1) The Whites and the Blues. (tr.) Little, 1894. The period of the Directory and Napoleon's seizure of power. (2) The Companions of Jehu (companion volume). (tr.) Little, 1894. The Chouan conspiracy, a Royalist movement against Napoleon.   2655-6

_____. The Woman with the Velvet Collar. (tr.) Munro, 1900. A scene from the Reign of Terror including the execution of Madame du Barry.   2657

Du Maurier, Daphne. The Glass-Blowers. Doubleday, 1963. Supposed memoirs of the author's ancestor discloses the history of a family of artists caught up in the Revolution.   2658

Dunlap, Katharine. Glory and the Dream. Morrow, 1951. The romance of an actress and a soldier.   2659

Edwards, Matilda Betham. A Romance of Dijon. Macmillan, 1894. The feelings of the peasant class just before the outbreak of the Revolution.   2660

_____. A Storm-Rent Sky. Hurst & Blackett, 1898. Provincial life in eastern France with a picture of Danton's execution in Paris.   2661

Ellis, Beth. The King's Blue Ribband. Hodder, 1912. A
swift-paced novel of intrigue in Louis XIV's court at Versailles.   2662

Endore, Guy. Voltaire! Voltaire! S. & S., 1961. Fictional
biography of the fiery Voltaire, showing his purported influence on Rousseau and vice-versa.   2663

Erckmann-Chatrian, pseud. for Emile Erckmann and Alexandre
Chatrian. Madame Thérèsa. (tr.) Scribner, 1869. Daily
life in a Vosges village in 1793 and the effect of the political turmoil in France.   2664

_____. The Story of a Peasant. (tr.) Dutton, 1915. Illus-
trates the lot of peasants during the Revolution and their attempts to prosper at the expense of the monarchy.   2665

Everett, Mrs. H.D. A Golden Trust. by Theo. Douglas, pseud.
Smith & Elder, 1905. The storming of the Tuileries; massacre
in the prisons; and the brutal murder of a friend of the queen.
                                                                 2666

Eversleigh, E.G. The Rose of Béarn. Paul, 1925. Romance
in Paris at the start of the Revolution.   2667

Felton, Ronald Oliver. Escape from France. by Ronald Welch,
pseud. Criterion, 1961, c.1960. The self-confidence of an
arrogant young Englishman is shaken by his experiences during an attempt to rescue relatives in the French Revolution.
                                                                 2668

Feuchtwanger, Lion. Proud Destiny. (tr.) Viking, 1947.
Benjamin Franklin's stay in France seeking aid for the American Revolution.   2669

_____. 'Tis Folly to Be Wise. (tr.) Messner, 1953.
Revolutionary France between the death of Rousseau and his
re-burial in Paris.   2670

Fezandié, Hector. Knight of the Third Estate. Kyle, 1938.
Romance of a lovely aristocrat during the Revolution.   2671

Fitchett, William H. A Pawn in the Game. Eaton & Mains,
1908. A narrative about the attack on the Tuileries, the
Reign of Terror, and Napoleon's campaigns in Egypt and
Syria.   2672

Forbes, Eveline Louisa. Leroux. by Mrs. Walter R.D. Forbes.
Greening, 1908. Career of a soldier of the Republic who becomes a general.   2673

France, Anatole (name originally Anatole Thibault). At the
Sign of the Queen Pédauque. (tr.) Gibbings, 1912. The

Abbé Coignard figures in this satiric picture of a Paris
inn.   2674

_____. The Gods Are Athirst. (tr.) Lane, 1913. Adven-
tures of a patriotic Parisian artist at the time of the downfall of Marat and Robespierre.   2675

Garnett, Henry. The Red Bonnet. Doubleday, 1964. YA. A
lively adventure story of a youth who helps rescue priests in
Paris during the Terror.   2676

Gaulot, Paul. The Red Shirts. (tr.) Greening, 1894. A
novel based on the Batz Conspiracy of 1794.   2677

Gerson, Noel B. Mohawk Ladder. Doubleday, 1951. A group
of Americans fight against Louis XIV in the War of Spanish
Succession.   2678

Gibbs, Willa. Seed of Mischief. Farrar, 1953. A novel of
the Lost Dauphin, Louis XVII of France.   2679

_____. Tell Your Sons. Farrar, 1946. This story empha-
sizes Napoleon's personal magnetism for those around him. 2680

_____. Twelfth Physician. Farrar, .1954. The conflict of
a young doctor in the turbulent time of Napoleon.   2681

Gorman, Herbert Sherman. The Mountain and the Plain.
Farrar, 1936. An excellent picture of the French Revolution seen through the eyes of a young American.   2682

Gras, Felix. (1) The Reds of the Midi. (tr.) Appleton,
1899. (2) The Terror (sequel). (tr.) Appleton, 1898.
(3) The White Terror (sequel). (tr.) Appleton, 1899.
Three novels of the Revolution covering the introduction of
"The Marseillaise," Marat in power, Louis XVI's execution,
and Napoleon's battles at Marengo, Austerlitz, Moscow, and
Waterloo.   2683-5

Green, Anne. The Silent Duchess. Harper, 1939. The story
of a French duchess during the Revolution.   2686

Grierson, Edward. Hastening Wind. Knopf, 1953. Efforts to
restore the Bourbons to the throne during Napoleon's rule.
                                                        2687
Guinagh, Kevin. Search for Glory. Longmans, 1946. YA.
About Pilatre de Rozier, pharmacist, scientist, and inventor.   2688

Haggard, Andrew C. P. Thérèse of the Revolution. White,
1921. A countess uses her influence to save many from
execution during the Revolution.   2689

Hamilton, Bernard. The Giant. Hutchinson, 1926. An account of Danton as a boy and in the Revolution.   2690

Harding, Bertita. Farewell 'Toinette. Bobbs, 1938. Light-
hearted tale of Marie Antoinette's wedding journey from
Vienna to Versailles.   2691

Heard, Adrian. Rose in the Mouth. Ward & Lock, 1927.
Tells of many prominent figures in the Revolution, including
the Dauphin, Robespierre, and Marie Antoinette.   2692

Heyer, Georgette. These Old Shades. Small, Maynard, 1926.
Light romance of court life under Louis XV.   2693

Hibbert, Eleanor. The Queen's Confession. by Victoria Holt,
pseud. Doubleday, 1968. A purported memoir of Marie
Antoinette showing her change from a spoiled, pampered
princess to a woman who achieved maturity only in the final
disaster.   2694

Holland, Clive. The Lovers of Mademoiselle. Hurst & Blackett,
1913. The French Revolution provides the background for this
romance, which includes an attack on a chateau.   2695

Hood, Arthur. Dragon's Teeth. Cassell, 1925. Record of a
nobleman of France during the Revolution, compiled from diaries and papers.   2696

Hough, Emerson. The Mississippi Bubble. Bobbs, 1903. John
Law's scheme to colonize and exploit the Mississippi Valley
for the French.   2697

Hugo, Victor. Ninety-Three. (tr.) Little, 1900. A romantic
account of the Royalist struggle in Brittany.   2698

Isham, Frederic S. The Lady of the Mount. Bobbs, 1908.
The efforts of a young lord to regain his inheritance, taken
by an unprincipled governor.   2699

James, G. P. R. The Ancient Régime. Longmans, 1841. The
corrupt court of Louis XV with a picture of the French police
system.   2700

James, Henry. Gabrielle de Bergerac. Boni & Liveright, 1918.
Courageous French girl who dared marry "beneath" her is
caught up in the Reign of Terror.   2701

Jennings, Edward W. Under the Pompadour. Brentano's,
1907. Embraces English-French smuggling and the court
of Louis XV.   2702

Jessop, George H. Desmond O'Connor. Long, 1914. Love
story of Louis XIV's ward and a captain in the Irish Brigade. 2703

Johnson, Owen. In the Name of Liberty. [En. title: Nicole]
Macmillan, 1905. Some of the grimmer aspects of the
Reign of Terror.   2704

Jones, Dora M. Camilla of the Fair Towers. Melrose, 1920.
A story of revolutionary Paris and southern England with
Madame Roland and Tom Paine.   2705

Kaye, Michael W. The King's Indiscretion. Paul, 1920. A
romance of Louis XV, with a plan for France to invade England.   2706

_____. A Patriot of France. Paul, 1909. Fighting in the
Revolution and the attempted rescue of Louis XVI.   2707

_____. A Robin Hood of France. Paul, 1912. Having
earned the displeasure of the powerful Madame de Pompadour, the hero becomes another Robin Hood.   2708

Keddie, Henrietta. Citoyenne Jacqueline. by Sarah Tytler,
pseud. Routledge, 1865. "A woman's lot in the great
French Revolution."   2709

Kenyon, Frank Wilson. Marie Antoinette. Crowell, 1956. A
novel of the unfortunate queen.   2710

_____. Royal Merry-Go-Round. Crowell, 1954. The gay,
extravagant court of Louis XV.   2711

Kingsley, Henry. Mademoiselle Mathilde. Longmans, 1868.
Life in England and France during the perilous time of the
Revolution.   2712

Knowles, Mabel Winifred. A Blot on the 'Scutcheon. by May
Wynne, pseud. Mills & Boon, 1910. The spreading of revolutionary ideas in England and France.   2713

_____. King Mandrin's Challenge. by May Wynne, pseud.
Paul, 1927. A wild-living nobleman incurs Madame de
Pompadour's wrath, leaves the court, and turns outlaw. 2714

_____. The Red Fleur-de-Lys. by May Wynne, pseud.
Paul, 1911. A story of the White Terror, the opposition
of aristocrats to revolutionists in 1791.   2715

_____. The Regent's Gift. by May Wynne, pseud. Chap-
man & Hall, 1915. Brittany and Paris during Orleans'
regency for Louis XV.   2716

_____. The Spendthrift Duke. by May Wynne, pseud.
Holden & Hardingham, 1920. The French court with Louis
XV, Madame de Pompadour, and the Duc de Choiseul.   2717

Lambert, Frederick Arthur. The Mysterious Monsieur Dumont.
  by Frederick Arthur, pseud. Murray, 1912. A woman disguised as a man during and after the Revolution's Reign of
  Terror.   2718

Landau, Mark Aleksandrovich. The Ninth Thermidor. (tr.)
  by M. A. Aldanov, pseud. Knopf, 1926. Travels in Europe
  of a diplomatic messenger.   2719

Levy, Barbara. Adrienne. Holt, 1960. The celebrated actress,
  Adrienne Lecouvreur, is the central figure; Voltaire appears
  as a character.   2720

Lindop, Audrey E. The Way to the Lantern. Doubleday, 1961.
  Experiences of an itinerant English actor turned spy in Paris
  during the French Revolution.   2721

Luther, Mark Lee. The Favour of Princes. Macmillan,
  1899. Exciting adventure in Louis XV's France.   2722

Maass, Edgar. Imperial Venus. Bobbs, 1946. A story of one
  of Napoleon's sisters, Pauline.   2723

McCarthy, Justin Huntly. Seraphica. Harper, 1907. The
  French court during the regency of Orleans when John Law
  was much in favor.   2724

Mahner-Mons, Hans. Sword of Satan. by Hans Possendorf,
  pseud. McKay, 1952. About Charlot, hangman of Paris. 2725

Malvern, Gladys. Patriot's Daughter. Macrae Smith, 1960.
  YA. The story of Anastasia, daughter of the Marquis de
  Lafayette, to the time of her marriage in 1798.   2726

Martin, Sylvia. I, Madame Tussaud. Harper, 1957. Concerns
  Madame Tussaud's famous waxworks in France during the
  Revolution and afterwards in England.   2727

Mitchell, S. Weir. The Adventures of François. Century,
  1898. Adventures of the wily hero during the Revolution. 2728

Mundt, Klara. The Empress Josephine. (tr.) by Louisa
  Mühlbach, pseud. Appleton, 1867. A sympathetic portrait
  of Josephine including Napoleon, the royal family, and national events.   2729

_____. Marie Antoinette and Her Son. (tr.) by Louisa
  Mühlbach, pseud. Appleton, 1867. The fate of the queen
  and the supposed escape of the Dauphin.   2730

Openshaw, Mary. The Loser Pays. Laurie, 1908. The
  writer of the stirring "Marseillaise" of the revolutionists
  is the hero.   2731

Orczy, <u>Baroness</u> Emmuska. <u>Petticoat Rule.</u> [En. title:
  <u>Petticoat Government</u>] Doran, 1910. The influence of
  women, especially Madame de Pompadour and the finance
  minister's wife, on public affairs.   2732

_____. (1) <u>The Scarlet Pimpernel.</u> Putnam, 1920. (2)
  <u>I Will Repay.</u> Lippincott, 1906. (3) <u>The Elusive Pimpernel</u>
  Dodd, 1908. (4) <u>The League of the Scarlet Pimpernel.</u>
  Doran, 1919. (5) <u>The Triumph of the Scarlet Pimpernel.</u>
  Doran, 1922. (6) <u>Lord Tony's Wife.</u> Doran, 1917. (7)
  <u>Eldorado.</u> Doran, 1913. (8) <u>Sir Percy Hits Back.</u> Doran,
  1927. (9) <u>Adventures of the Scarlet Pimpernel.</u> Doubleday, 1929. (10) <u>Way of the Scarlet Pimpernel.</u> Putnam,
  1934. (11) <u>Child of the Revolution.</u> Doubleday, 1932. An
  Englishman, whose wife is French, heads a group engaged
  in the hazardous enterprise of rescuing innocent victims of
  the Revolution.   2733-43

Oxenham, John, <u>pseud.</u> for William Arthur Dunkerley. <u>Queen</u>
  <u>of the Guarded Mounts.</u> Lane, 1912. English involvement
  in the Vendean revolt provides background for romance and
  adventure.   2744

Parker, Gilbert. <u>The Battle of the Strong.</u> Harper, 1898.
  The French invasion of Jersey during the revolutionary
  period.   2745

Pemberton, Max. <u>My Sword for Lafayette.</u> Dodd, 1906.
  "Episodes in the wars waged for liberty in France and
  America."   2746

Pickering, Sidney. <u>Paths Perilous.</u> Chapman, 1909. This
  story of life in revolutionary France includes scenes in the
  prisons of Paris.   2747

Potter, Margaret Horton. <u>The House of De Mailly.</u> Harper,
  1901. This romance contrasts life in New England with life
  in Louis XV's court.   2748

Praed, Rosa Caroline. <u>The Romance of Mlle. Aissé.</u> by Mrs.
  Campbell Praed. Long, 1910. The court life of a Circassian
  chief's daughter who had been captured by Turks, later educated in France.   2749

Preedy, George, <u>pseud.</u> for Gabrielle Campbell Long. <u>General</u>
  <u>Crack.</u> Dodd, 1928. The varying successes of a bold adventurer in politics and love.   2750

Rowsell, Mary C. <u>The Friend of the People.</u> Marshall, 1894.
  Efforts of an illegitimate son to have his brother guillotined.
                                                       2751
_____. <u>Monsieur de Paris.</u> Chatto, 1907. A story of
  Madame du Barry and her fate.   2752

Sabatini, Rafael. The Gamester. Houghton, 1949. Dramatic account of John Law and his fantastic financial manipulations.   2753

_____. Master-At-Arms. Houghton, 1940. French fencing master returns from London to take part in the Revolution.
                                                                   2754
_____. The Nuptials of Corbal. Houghton, 1927. Exciting romance of Paris and provincial France.   2755

_____. Scaramouche. Houghton, 1921. Brilliant romance of the French Revolution with a dashing and eloquent hero. 2756

_____. The Trampling of the Lilies. Hutchinson, 1906. A picture of Picardy at the start of the Revolution.   2757

Sage, William. Robert Tournay. Houghton, 1900. Danton and Robespierre figure prominently in this novel of the Revolution.   2758

Sanders, Joan. The Marquis. Houghton, 1963. Mainly the story of the scheming wife of the Marquis de Montespan, who became the mistress of the "Sun King," Louis XIV.   2759

Savage, Charles Woodcock. A Lady in Waiting. Appleton, 1906. About one of Marie Antoinette's attendants, who lost her family to the guillotine.   2760

Seawell, Molly Elliot. Francezka. Bobbs, 1902. A novel introducing the philosopher Voltaire, the actress Adrienne, and Marshal Saxe.   2761

_____. The Last Duchess of Belgarde. Appleton, 1908. A duke and duchess at Louis XVI's court and during the Reign of Terror.   2762

Selinko, Annemarie. Désirée. Morrow, 1953. About Désirée, early love of Napoleon, later wife of Bernadotte, and her relations with the Bonaparte family.   2763

Shay, Edith and Katharine Smith. Private Adventure of Captain Shaw. Houghton, 1945. Experiences of a Cape Cod sea captain during the Reign of Terror.   2764

Sheean, Vincent. A Day of Battle. Doubleday, 1938. The battle between French and English at Fontenoy in 1745.   2765

Sheehan, Patrick A. The Queen's Fillet. Longmans, 1911. Concerns Marie Antoinette, Louis XVI, and the slaughtering of the Swiss Guard during the Revolution.   2766

Simpson, Evan John. Kings' Masque. by Evan John, pseud. Dutton, 1941. Marie Antoinette of France and Gustav III of Sweden are central characters.   2767

Sinclair, Edith. His Honour and His Love. Blackwood, 1911.
Pictures many prominent people of the nobility at the court
of Louis XV.   2768

Smythe, David Mynders. Golden Venus. Doubleday, 1960. A
fictionalized biography of Madam DuBarry, beautiful mistress
of Louis XV.   2769

Spender, Harold. At the Sign of the Guillotine. Merriam, 1895.
Robespierre and his activities in the Reign of Terror.   2770

Spillman, J. Valiant and True. Sands, 1905. "Adventures of
a young officer of the Swiss Guards at the time of the French
Revolution."   2771

Stacpoole, Henry de Vere. Monsieur de Rochefort. Hutchinson,
1914. The hero becomes involved in politics at Louis XV's
court.   2772

_____. The Order of Release. Hutchinson, 1912. Concerns
Versailles and attempts to free a man unfairly imprisoned
in the Bastille.   2773

Stair, Grace. A Lady of France. Stokes, 1930. About the lovely Louise de Lamballe, ill-fated attendant to Marie Antoinette.
                                                      2774
Stephens, Eve. The French Bride. by Evelyn Anthony, pseud.
Doubleday, 1964. Contest between a faithful wife and a scheming mistress for the affections of a charming Scottish rascal,
at the court of Louis XV.   2775

Stevenson, Burton E. At Odds With the Regent. Lippincott,
1900. A story of the Cellamare Conspiracy, which occurred
during the regency of the Duke of Orleans.   2776

Sue, Eugène. The Sword of Honor. N.Y. Labor News, 1910.
A tale of the Revolution including the fall of the Bastille. 2777

Theuriet, André. The Canoness. Nelson, 1893. Eastern
France during the Revolution with an account of the Battle
of Valmy.   2778

Trollope, Anthony. La Vendée. Chapman, 1850. The struggles
and success of the Vendean insurgents during the Revolution.
                                                      2779
Vansittart, Robert. Pity's Kin. Murray, 1924. Conflicting
feelings and ideas of the people in Nantes during the Revolution.   2780

Wagnalls, Mabel. The Palace of Danger. Funk & Wagnalls, 1908.
The great influence of the king's mistress, Madame de Pom-

padour.   2781

Ward, Mary Augusta. Lady Rose's Daughter. by Mrs. Humphry Ward. Harper, 1903. A novel of manners based on
actual events in Louis XV's France.   2782

Watson, Frederick. Shallows. Dutton, 1913. Jacobite intrigues in France, England, and Scotland, with Prince
Charles Edward and the philosopher Condillac.   2783

Wentworth, Patricia. A Marriage Under the Terror. Putnam,
1910. A marriage is performed to save the bride from the
guillotine.   2784

Weyman, Stanley J. The Red Cockade. Longmans, 1895.
Revolutionary activity recounted by an aristocrat sympathetic
with the commoners.   2785

Wheatley, Dennis. The Man Who Killed the King. Putnam,
1965. Daring attempt of a British agent to rescue the
French King and his family during the French Revolution. 2786

Wheelwright, Jere Hungerford. Draw Near to Battle. Scribner,
1953. The exploits of an American in Napoleon's army. 2787

White, Helen C. To the End of the World. Macmillan, 1939.
The work of a priest to support religion during the Reign of
Terror in the French Revolution.   2788

White, Leslie Turner. Monsieur Yankee. Morrow, 1957.
Youthful American doctor becomes enmeshed in espionage
during the French Revolution.   2789

Whyte-Melville, George John. Cerise. Appleton, 1866.
France during the last days of Louis XIV and the regency
for Louis XV.   2790

Wilkins, William Vaughan. A King Reluctant. Macmillan, 1953.
The story of the Lost Dauphin, Louis XVII.   2791

_____. Lady of Paris. St. Martin's, 1957. Madame
Tallien, later Princesse de Chimay, against a backdrop of
the French Revolution and the Reign of Terror.   2792

Williams, Hugh Noel. The Hand of Leonore. Harper, 1904.
Adventure-romance of a poor Englishman and a wealthy
lady, telling of the Battle of Rossbach.   2793

Williams, Valentine. The Red Mass. Houghton, 1925. An
English soldier goes as a spy to revolutionary France.   2794

Winwar, Frances. The Eagle and the Rock. Harper, 1953.
A fresh story of Napoleon and the people around him.   2795

Yerby, Frank. The Devil's Laughter. Dial, 1953. A bold,
brilliant lawyer in the French Revolution.   2796

2) Central Europe (including Germany, the Netherlands,
   Switzerland, Austria, Hungary, Czechoslovakia, and
   Poland)

Ammers-Küller, Jo van. The House of Tavelinck. (tr.) Farrar,
1938. Holland at the time of the French Revolution, including a Dutch boy's exploits in France.   2797

Auerbach, Berthold. Poet and Merchant. Holt, 1877. The
time in which Mendelssohn lived.   2798

Bailey, H.C. The Gamesters. Dutton, 1919. The exciting adventures of owners of European gambling houses--the haunts
of nobility.   2799

_____. His Serene Highness. Dutton, 1922. Two English-
men on a trip through the Continent.   2800

Bett, Henry. The Watch Night. Paul, 1912. Religious thought,
mainly in Germany, at mid-century, with John Wesley prominent.   2801

Bloundelle-Burton, John. Across the Salt Sea. Stone, 1898.
Marlborough's victory at Blenheim in the War of the Spanish
Succession.   2802

_____. The Sword of Gideon. Cassell, 1905. A story of
the Netherlands during the War of the Spanish Succession. 2803

Bryher, Winifred (Annie Winifred Macpherson). The Colors
of Vaud. by Bryher. Harcourt, 1969. A French émigré
girl and a Swiss youth during the liberation of the Swiss
Canton of Vaud in the French Revolution.   2804

Casserley, Gordon. The Red Marshal. Clode, 1923. The
liberation of a small Austrian state.   2805

Castle, Agnes and Egerton. The Pride of Jennico. Macmillan, 1898. Memoirs of an Englishman who inherited Moravian estates.   2806

Conscience, Hendrik. Veva. (tr.) Burns & Oates, 1853.
The French taking of Belgium and the uprising of the
peasants against their rule.   2807

Feuchtwanger, Lion. Power. (tr.) [same as Jew Suss and
Jud Suss] Viking, 1926. Political and religious forces at
work on mid-European history.   2808

Grant, James. Second to None. Dutton, 1864. Action-filled
story of military service in Hanover under the Duke of
Cumberland.   2809

Grun, Bernard. Golden Quill. Putnam, 1956. A story of
Mozart as seen through his sister's diary.   2810

Innes, Norman. The Governor's Daughter. Ward & Lock, 1911.
Adventures of an Austrian spy in the Seven Years War.   2811

_____. The Lonely Guard. Ward & Lock, 1908. A story
of the Austro-Bavarian border giving the Austrian attitude
toward Frederick the Great's ambitions.   2812

Jókai, Maurus. The Strange Story of Rab Raby. (tr.) Jarrold & Sons, 1909. Social reform in Hungary under Emperor
Joseph II.   2813

Knowles, Mabel Winifred. Foes of Freedom. by May Wynne,
pseud. Chapman & Hall, 1916. The revolt of the Belgian
provinces against Joseph II of Austria.   2814

_____. The King of a Day. by May Wynne, pseud. Jar-
rolds Ltd., 1918. Stanislaus I and the War of Polish Suc-
cession.   2815

Kraszewski, Jósef I. The Countess Cosel. (tr.) Downey,
1901. The court of Augustus the Strong, Elector of Saxony.
                                                                                       2816

Lowe, Charles. A Fallen Star. Downey, 1895. A story of
Scots who saw action with Frederick the Great in the Seven
Years War.   2817

McHugh, Arona. The Luck of the Van Meers. Doubleday, 1969.
Chronicle of a Jewish family of merchants, seafarers, and
travelers and their extraordinary talents.   2818

Major, Charles. A Gentle Knight of Old Brandenburg. Macmillan, 1909. The domestic life and diplomatic relations
of Frederick William I of Prussia.   2819

Mundt, Klara. Goethe and Schiller. (tr.) by Louisa Mühlbach,
pseud. Appleton, 1868. Romantic story based chiefly on the
life of Schiller.   2820

_____. (1) Old Fritz and the New Era. (tr.) Appleton,
1868. (2) Frederick the Great and His Court. (tr.) Appleton, 1866. (3) Berlin and Sans Souci; or, Frederick the
Great and His Friends (sequel). (tr.) Appleton, 1867. (4)
Frederick the Great and His Family (sequel). (tr.) Appleton,
1867. (5) The Merchant of Berlin. (tr.) Appleton, 1867.
all by Louisa Mühlbach, pseud. A series of novels concerning the court of Frederick the Great and contemporary social,

political, and economic activities.   2821-5

Porter, Anna Maria. The Hungarian Brothers. Lippincott,
1807. Hungary, Austria, and Italy during the wars against
the French in Italy. 1797 ff.   2826

Porter, Jane. Thaddeus of Warsaw. Routledge, 1803.
Poland's struggle for survival inspired by the heroism of Kosciusko. 2827

Ramuz, Charles F. When the Mountain Fell. (tr.) Pantheon,
1947. Tragic avalanche in the Swiss Alps.   2828.

Sabatini, Rafael. Birth of Mischief. Houghton, 1945. Rise of
Prussia during the reigns of Frederick William I and Frederick II, the Great.   2829

Sand, George, pseud. for Mme. Dudevant. (1) Consuelo. (tr.)
Ticknor, 1846. (2) The Countess of Rudolstadt (sequel).
(tr.) Ticknor, 1847. The career of a woman singer in
Europe.   2830-1

Schuster, Rose. The Road to Victory. Chapman & Hall, 1913.
The relationship between Frederick William I and his son
Frederick II, the Great.   2832

Sheppard, Alfred Tresidder. The Red Cravat. Macmillan,
1905. An Englishman's adventures at the eccentric court
of Frederick William I.   2833

Stevenson, Philip L. A Gendarme of the King. Hurst, 1905.
Frederick the Great's battles in the Seven Years War. 2834

Stewart, Charlotte. Beggars and Sorners. by Allan McAulay,
pseud. Lane, 1912. Scottish and Jacobite influences in Amsterdam.   2835

Weiss, David. Sacred and Profane. Morrow, 1968. About the
musically triumphant but financially impoverished life of the
famous composer, Wolfgang Amadeus Mozart.   2836

Yoxall, James Henry. The Courtier Stoops. Smith & Elder,
1911. Based on the life and romance of Goethe.   2837

Zschokke, Heinrich. The Rose of Disentis. (tr.) Sheldon,
1873. Romance in Switzerland during the war between
France and Austria.   2838

3) Scandinavia and the Baltic

Brogger, Mae. Lindeman's Daughters. by Synnove Christensen,
pseud. Doubleday, 1958. Norwegian country life, an unhappy marriage, and a forbidden love.   2839

Caine, Hall. The Bondman. Appleton, 1890. Iceland and
the Isle of Man at the outset of the Napoleonic Wars.   2840

Coleridge, Mary E. The King With Two Faces. Arnold,
1897. Relations between Sweden and France with Gustavus
III a central figure.   2841

Freuchen, Peter. White Man. Rinehart, 1946. Couple finds a
new life in Greenland in a Danish settlement peopled largely
by former convicts.   2842

Heidenstam, Verner von. The Charles Men. American-Scandi-
navian Foundation, 1897-98. A powerful novel with Charles
XII of Sweden as chief character.   2843

Hesekiel, J. G. L. Two Queens. (tr.) Sonnenschein, 1869.
Queen Caroline Matilda of Denmark and Queen Marie Antoinette of France.   2844

Hornborg, Harald. Passion and the Sword. Appleton, 1941.
Attempts of a pastor in Finland to win over the people of
his parish.   2845

Hunt, Frederick. Royal Physician. by John Fitzgay, pseud.
Roy Pub., 1947. Secret intrigue and tangled plots in the
Danish court of King Christian VII.   2846

Lofts, Norah. The Lost Queen. Doubleday, 1969. The tragic
life of Queen Caroline Mathilda as the consort of mad King
Christian VII of Denmark and her love for the court physician.   2847

Maass, Edgar. Queen's Physician. Scribner, 1948. The
court of Christian VII of Denmark, his lovely queen, and
the royal physician.   2848

Neumann, Robert. The Queen's Doctor. (tr.) Knopf, 1936.
Struensee, the doctor who had great influence, personally
and politically, with Christian VII and his wife, Mathilda.
                                                           2849
Nisser, Peter W. The Red Marten. (tr.) Knopf, 1957. (orig.
pub. in Sweden in 1954) A stirring tale of a Swedish clan of
ambitious peasants in Sweden during the Swedish-Russian
(Northern) War.   2850

Pontoppidan, Henrik. (1) Emmanuel, or, Children of the Soil.
Dent, 1892. (2) The Promised Land. Dent, 1896. A Danish pastor espouses the cause of the peasants by vocation
and by marriage.   2851-2

Sand, George, pseud. for Mme. Dudevant. The Snow Man.
(tr.) Little, 1871. A dispute over inheritance provides
the plot for this story of winter life in Sweden.   2853

Undset, Sigrid. Madame Dorthea. (tr.) Knopf, 1940. Vicissitudes of a Norwegian family left without a father.   2854

c) Southern Europe

1) Iberian Peninsula

Bloundelle-Burton, John. The Last of Her Race. Milne, 1908.
The contest among Austria, France, and England in the War
of the Spanish Succession.   2855

Capes, Bernard. A Castle in Spain. Hutchinson, 1903. An
adventurer attempts to take the French Lost Dauphin, Louis
XVII, from a Spanish convent where he is allegedly hiding. 2856

Feuchtwanger, Lion. This Is the Hour. (tr.) Viking, 1951.
A novel of the eventful life of Goya, famous Spanish
painter.   2857

Griffiths, Arthur. Thrice Captive. White, 1908. Adventures
of an Englishman in Spain during the campaigns of the capable,
restless general, Peterborough.   2858

Knowles, Mabel Winifred. A Gallant of Spain. by May Wynne,
pseud. Paul, 1920. Jacobites in Spain during Philip V's
reign.   2859

Mackay, Margaret. The Wine Princes. Day, 1958. Two
cousins, named Prince, go to Portugal to learn the wine
business.   2860

White, Charles William. In the Blazing Light. by Max White,
pseud. Duell, 1946. Novel concerning the life and love of
Francesco Goya.   2861

2) Italy and Adjacent Islands

Calvino, Italo. Baron in the Trees. (tr.) Random, 1959.
An Italian baron fulfills his youthful vow of never setting
foot on the ground.   2862

Capes, Bernard. The Pot of Basil. Constable, 1913. A romance centering on state marriage plans between Italy and
Austria.   2863

_____. A Rogue's Tragedy. Methuen, 1906. A rogue,
Cartouche, undertakes to destroy a secret political society.   2864

Dumas, Alexandre. (1) The Neapolitan Lovers. (tr.) Brentano's, 1917. (2) Love and Liberty. (tr.) Peterson, 1874.

Naples during the French Revolutionary period, featuring
Lord Nelson.   2865-6

Eaton, Evelyn. In What Torn Ship. Harper, 1944. The liberation of Corsica from the Genoese by Pasquale Paoli.   2867

Forbes, Helen E. His Eminence. Nash, 1904. A Cardinal in
an Italian town under threat of invasion by Napoleon.   2868

Hewlett, Maurice. The Fool Errant. Macmillan, 1905. Adventures of an English gentleman who gives up rank and
wealth to do "penance" in Italy.   2869

Lambton, Arthur. The Splendid Sinner. Nash, 1911. A conspiracy against Queen Caroline's prime minister, Sir John
Acton.   2870

McManus, Miss L. Lally of the Brigade. Page, 1899. The
French service of an Irish brigade in Italy during the War
of the Spanish Succession.   2871

Mason, A.E.W. Clementina, Stokes, 1901. Marriage in
Rome of the Old Pretender of England and Princess Clementina Sobieski of Poland.   2872

Nievo, Ippolito. The Castle of Fratta. Houghton, 1958. The
fading days of the aristocracy during the time of Napoleon.
                                                         2873
Pemberton, Max. Beatrice of Venice. Dodd, 1904. Account
of Napoleon's Italian campaign.   2874

_____. Paulina. Cassell, 1922. "A story of Napoleon and
the fall of Venice."   2875

Pickering, Edgar. King for a Summer. Hutchinson, 1896.
An exciting tale of rebellion in Corsica in 1735.   2876

Pickering, Sidney. The Key of Paradise. Macmillan, 1903.
Romance of an English soldier and a girl married to an
Italian prince.   2877

Quiller-Couch, Arthur T. Sir John Constantine. by Q., pseud.
Scribner, 1906. "Memoirs of his adventures at home and
abroad, and particularly in the island of Corsica."   2878

Radcliffe, Ann. The Italian; or, The Confessional of the
Black Penitents. Cadell & Davies, 1811. The Inquisition
in and about Naples.   2879

Rodocanachi, Emmanuel. Tolla the Courtesan. (tr.) Heinemann, 1905. Life and manners at Rome featuring Tolla
Boccadileone and Prince Constantine Sobieski.   2880

Salmon, Geraldine Gordon.   Corsican Justice.   by J. G.
Sarasin, pseud.   Doran, 1927.   Adventure in Italy, with
Napoleon's military activities as the background.   2881

Schumacher, Henry.   Nelson's Last Love.   Hutchinson, 1913.
Lady Hamilton's life in Naples, showing especially her friend-
ships with Queen Maria Caroline and Nelson.   2882

Sheean, Vincent.   Sanfelice.   Doubleday, 1936.   Colorful account of the unsuccessful Revolution of 1799 in Naples. 2883

Spalding, Albert.   A Fiddle, a Sword and a Lady.   Holt, 1953.
The life story of eighteenth century violinist Giuseppe Tar-
tini written by a contemporary violinist.   2884

Stewart, Charlotte.   The Eagle's Nest.   by Allan McAulay,
pseud.   Lane, 1907.   Napoleon as a young man in Corsica.
                                                         2885
Wharton, Edith.   The Valley of Decision.   Scribner, 1902.
Gives an insight into European thought prior to the French
Revolution.   2886

   d)   Eastern Europe (including Russia and the Balkans),
        the Near East, and North Africa

Alexander, grand duke of Russia.   Evil Empress.   Lippincott,
1934.   A novel based on the career of Catherine the Great.
                                                         2887
Almedingen, Martha Edith von.   Young Catherine.   by E. M.
Almedingen.   Stokes, 1938.   A novel of Russia's Catherine
the Great telling of her childhood and tragic marriage. 2888

_____.   Young Mark.   by E. M. Almedingen.   Farrar, 1968,
c. 1967.   YA.   A Russian boy with a great ambition to be a
singer journeys to St. Petersburg.   2889

Beddoe, David M.   The Lost Mameluke.   Dutton, 1913.   Fall
of the Mameluke influence in Egypt and events of Napoleon's
Egyptian campaign.   2890

Carnegie, Sacha.   Scarlet Banners of Love.   Dodd, 1968.   The
romance of Kasia, who suffered abduction to a sultan's
harem and many other adventures before meeting again the
man she loved in the court of Catherine the Great.   2891

Chevigny, Hector.   Lost Empire.   Macmillan, 1937.   Nikolai
Rezánov's dream of an empire in Siberia is stirringly told.
                                                         2892
Danilévski, Grigovii P.   The Princess Tarakanova.   (tr.)
Sonnenschein, 1891.   A threat to the throne of Catherine
the Great by a supposed daughter of the preceding Empress,
Elizabeth.   2893

Dickson, Harris. She That Hesitates. Bobbs, 1903. Chiefly
about the marriage of the unscrupulous Alexis of Russia
and Charlotte of Brunswick.   2894

Drummond, Hamilton. Shoes of Gold. Paul, 1909. A French
diplomat's assignment to win Russia's friendship by charming
Catherine the Great.   2895

Durand, Henry Mortimer. Nadir Shah. Dutton, 1908. A romance of the great conqueror, Nadir Shah, against a rich
background of Persian customs.   2896

Gerson, Noel B. The Scimitar. by Samuel Edwards, pseud.
Farrar, 1955. An Englishman's adventures in the Near
East, told in a light vein.   2897

Helps, Arthur. Ivan de Biron. Isbister, 1874. The place in
Russian government held by the German, Biron, a favorite
of Empress Anna Ivanovna.   2898

Hope, Jessie. The Triumph of Count Ostermann. by Graham
Hope, pseud. Holt, 1903. The blending of Eastern and
Western civilizations in Russia during Peter the Great's
reign.   2899

Jókai, Maurus. Halil the Pedlar. (tr.) Jarrold & Sons, 1901.
A poor peddler who led a rebellion in Turkey and eventually
became Prime Minister.   2900

Jones, Maurice Bethell. Peter, Called the Great. Stokes,
1936. The cruelty, ability, and madness of Peter I, Emperor of Russia.   2901

Merezhkovsky, Dmitri. Peter and Alexis. (tr.) Putnam,
1905. The unhappy relationship between Peter the Great
and his son Alexis.   2902

Price, Jeramie. Katrina. Farrar, 1955. Russian life during
the time of Peter I and his peasant wife, Catherine.   2903

Pushkin, Alexander S. The Captain's Daughter. (tr.) Müller,
1846. A story of the peasants' insurrection led by Pouga-
chev.   2904

River, Walter Leslie. The Torguts. Stokes, 1939. Mass
migration of a southeastern Russian tribe to China.   2905

Stephens, Eve. Rebel Princess. by Evelyn Anthony, pseud.
Crowell, 1953. Young Catherine II overthrows her half-wit
husband, Peter III, to become a great Empress.   2906

_____. Royal Intrigue. by Evelyn Anthony, pseud. Cro-
well, 1954. Cruelty and intrigue in the Russia of Catherine

the Great and her son, Paul.   2907

Swan, Edgar.   The Mark of the Cross.   Digby & Long, 1911.
Elizabeth, daughter of Peter the Great, came to the throne
through a series of plots.   2908

Taylor, Mary Imlay.   An Imperial Lover.   McClurg, 1897.
A French diplomat at the court of Peter the Great and his
secretary's romance with the future Catherine I.   2909

Underwood, Edna.   Whirlwind.   Small, Maynard, 1918.   Catherine the Great's inexorable climb to ultimate power in
Russia.   2910

Whishaw, Frederick J.   At the Court of Catherine the Great.
[En. title: Many Ways of Love] Stokes, 1899.   Court of
Catherine and Peter III telling of his accession and mur-
der.   2911

_____.   An Empress in Love.   Paul, 1910.   The reign of
Catherine the Great who was more successful as a ruler
than as a wife.   2912

_____.   A Forbidden Name.   Chatto, 1901.   A story of the
child Czar Ivan VI who was imprisoned by the Empress
Elizabeth and later executed.   2913

_____.   Her Highness.   Long, 1906.   The Empress Cath-
erine as a bride.   2914

_____.   Near the Tsar, Near Death.   Chatto, 1903.   Peter
the Great's disappointment in his son Alexis.   2915

e)   Overseas Exploration, Enterprise,
     and Expansion

Allen, Hervey.   Anthony Adverse.   Farrar, 1933.   Young
man travels all over the world in quest of adventure.   2916

Ballard, Martin.   The Monarch of Juan Fernandez.   Scribner,
1968, c.1967.   YA.   The adventures of Alexander Selkirk,
real-life counterpart of the fictional Robinson Crusoe.   2917

Besant, Walter.   The World Went Very Well Then.   Harper,
1886.   Naval adventures on the Thames River and the
South Seas.   2918

Brant, Irving.   Friendly Cove.   Bobbs, 1963.   A Spanish boy,
who is also a spy, serves on an English ship in search of
sea otter in the North Pacific.   2919

Chambers, Robert W.   The Man They Hanged.   Appleton,

1926. Sympathetic account of the notorious Captain Kidd. 2920

Chamier, Frederick. Tom Bowling. Dutton, 1839. A tale of
sea action in the English war with France.   2921

Chidsey, Donald Barr. Captain Adam. Crown, 1953. A former
indentured servant becomes a ship's captain and engages in
trade, smuggling, and fighting pirates in the days of Queen
Anne.   2922

Defoe, Daniel. Life, Adventures, and Piracies of Captain
Singleton. Macmillan, 1720. Exciting career of an eighteenth century pirate.   2923

De Witt, James. In Pursuit of the Spanish Galleon. Criterion,
1961. YA. A cabin boy's adventures during Commodore
George Anson's chase of the Spanish treasure ship, the
Manila Galleon.   2924

Garstin, Crosbie. (1) The Owl's House. Stokes, 1924. (2)
High Noon. Stokes, 1925. (3) The West Wind. Stokes,
1926. Far-flung adventures of smugglers, gypsies, and
privateers.   2925-7

Gerson, Noel B. The Yankee Brig. by Carter A. Vaughan,
pseud. Doubleday, 1960. A Yankee captain, seeking enough
naval prizes to buy part ownership in a ship for himself, is
impressed as a common seaman.   2928

Kent, Alexander. Enemy in Sight! Putnam, 1970. Daring
Captain Bolitho both participates in a blockade of the French
coast and travels to South America.   2929

_____. The Flag Captain. Putnam, 1971. Bolitho serves
as flag captain for a British admiral during an effort to pene-
trate the Mediterranean in the difficult year of 1797.   2930

_____. Form Line of Battle! Putnam, 1969. Able captain
Bolitho commands a ship-of-the-line in action off the coast
of France during the French Revolution in 1793.   2931

_____. To Glory We Steer. Putnam, 1968. Captain Boli-
tho's British frigate scores successes against the French
and Spanish in the Caribbean during the American Revolution.   2932

Kent, Louise Andrews. He Went With John Paul Jones. Houghton, 1958. YA. The journal of a young sailor tells exciting
tales of serving under Captains James Cook and John Paul
Jones.   2933

McIntyre, John Thomas. Stained Sails. Stokes, 1928. An
early romance of John Paul Jones, slave trader, later

American naval hero.   2934

MacOrlan, Pierre. The Anchor of Mercy. (tr.) Pantheon,
1967. YA. Novel about the attempt to capture a French
pirate before he joins the British.   2935

Marryat, Frederick. The King's Own. Dutton, 1834. Sea
adventures, fighting, and mutiny on shipboard.   2936

Mason, Van Wyck. Manila Galleon. Little, 1961. The cir-
cumnavigation of the world by Commodore George Anson
and his fleet, which took from 1740 to 1744 and won him
the title of "Father of the British Navy."   2937

Miers, Earl Schenck. Pirate Chase. Holt, 1965. YA. A
young man captured by Blackbeard escapes and later, in
Governor Spottswood's expedition, helps defeat the pirate. 2938

Pope, Dudley. Drumbeat. Pocket Bks., 1970, c.1968. (first
pub. as Ramage and the Drumbeat) Lieutenant Lord Ramage
sails his sloop Kathleen to both glory and destruction during
the Napoleonic conflict. (followed by The Triton Brig) 2939

_____. Ramage. Lippincott, 1965. Unconventional British
naval Lieutenant Ramage rescues an Italian Marchesa who
sympathizes with British resistance to Napoleon. (followed
by Drumbeat)   2940

_____. The Triton Brig. Doubleday, 1969. Lieutenant
Lord Ramage surmounts a mutiny to deliver an important
message and capture privateers in the West Indies. (completes trilogy)   2941

Stevenson, Robert Louis. Treasure Island. Lovell, 1886.
Classic tale of pirates and buried treasure.   2942

Styles, Showell. The Sea Officer. Macmillan, 1962, c.1961.
Story of the capable, bluff, and salty Edward Pellew who
rose from a thirteen-year-old ship's boy to Rear Admiral
and Member of Parliament.   2943

Walsh, Joseph Patrick. King's Arrow. by Joseph Patrick,
pseud. Lippincott, 1951. Smuggling from Scotland to the
American colonies by way of the West Indies was frequent
because of British taxation just before the American Revolution.   2944

Wibberley, Leonard. The Secret of the Hawk. Farrar, 1953.
YA. The evils of the slave trade are pointed up in the dis-
cussions of two enslaved youths--one English, one African.
                                                        2945
Wilson, Erle. Adams of the Bounty. Criterion, 1959, c.1958.
From the point-of-view of a seaman, this tells of the famous

mutiny from the cruelty of Captain Bligh to the disastrous
settlement on Pitcairn Island.   2946

4.   NINETEENTH CENTURY: AGE OF
     NATIONALISM AND LIBERALISM

     a)   The British Isles

     1)   England, Wales, and Scotland

Ainsworth, W. Harrison. Mervyn Clitheroe. Dutton, 1857.
     Manchester in the time of industrial upheaval after the war
     with the French.   2947

Alington, Argentine. Gentlemen--the Regiment! by Hugh Tal-
     bot, pseud. Harper, 1933. Story of two military families
     in England during the Crimean War.   2948

Ashton, Helen. Footman in Powder. Dodd, 1954. The time of
     King George IV as seen by the royal servants.   2949

Ashton, Winifred. He Brings Great News. by Clemence
     Dane, pseud. Random, 1945. A British naval lieutenant
     brings the news of Trafalgar and of Nelson's death back
     to England.   2950

Austen, Jane. (1) Emma. Murray, 1816. (2) Mansfield
     Park. Egerton, 1814. (3) Northanger Abbey. Carey &
     Lea, 1833. (4) Persuasion. Bentley, 1848. (5) Pride
     and Prejudice. Egerton, 1813. (6) Sense and Sensibility.
     Egerton, 1813. Six separate novels of quiet country life
     containing excellent character studies and pictures of the
     morals and customs of the times, and of the preoccupation
     of young ladies with appropriate marriages.   2951-6

_____. The Watsons. (a fragment continued and com-
     pleted by John Coates) Crowell, 1958. Typical Austen
     story of a family of girls concerned with achieving good
     marriages.   2957

Avery, Gillian. Call of the Valley. Holt, 1968. YA. The
     experiences and responsibilities of a young boy on his own
     in Wales during the 1880s.   2958

Banks, G. Linnaeus. Bond Slaves. Griffith & Farran, 1893.
     The riots of the Luddite Society, an organization of workers
     in Yorkshire.   2959

_____. Caleb Booth's Clerk. Simpkin, 1878. An escaped
     convict and his sister insinuate their way into a respectable
     Lancashire household.   2960

_____. The Manchester Man. Heywood, 1895. A detailed picture of the Manchester region in the first quarter of the century.   2961

Baring-Gould, S. Cheap Jack Zita. Methuen, 1893. Conspiracy, rioting, and fear in England during the period of the decisive Battle of Waterloo.   2962

_____. Eve. Appleton, 1888. A romance of the moors, rampant in superstition, with a convict's escape from Dartmoor Prison.   2963

_____. In Dewisland. Methuen, 1904. Country folks' rebellion against the unpopular increase in highway tolls.   2964

_____. Kitty Alone. Dodd, 1894. About Kitty and her uncle, a man who commits arson to collect insurance money.   2965

_____. Red Spider. Appleton, 1888. A realistic picture of life in the village areas of England.   2966

_____. Royal Georgie. Methuen, 1901. A story of the Prince Regent, later George IV, with a glimpse of Dartmoor.   2967

Barker, Shirley. Corner of the Moon. Crown, 1961. The presence of her bridegroom's first love and the fear of Napoleonic invasion combine to disrupt a girl's honeymoon.   2968

Barr, Amelia E. Between Two Loves. Harper, 1886. Rural life in England.   2969

_____. A Daughter of Fife. Dodd, 1886. Romantic novel of life in a Scottish fishing village.   2970

_____. I, Thou, and the Other One. Dodd, 1899. Domestic scene at the time of the controversial Reform Bill agitation.
                                                                       2971

_____. Jan Vedder's Wife. Dodd, 1885. Domestic life in the Shetland Islands.   2972

_____. A Knight of the Nets. Dodd, 1896. Marriage of a landed youth and a poor girl in a village in Fifeshire.   2973

_____. Master of His Fate. [same as In Spite of Himself] Dodd, 1888. A man who marries an heiress finds happiness when he works for a living.   2974

_____. The Paper Cap. Appleton, 1918. The introduction of the factory system into England.   2975

_____. Paul and Christina. Dodd, 1898. Life and hardships of the simple fisherfolk of the Orkneys.   2976

Barrett, Frank. Perfidious Lydia. Chatto, 1910. The runaway marriage of a rebellious girl.   2977

Bartram, George. Lads of the Fancy. Duckworth, 1906. Concerns English sports-fanciers and features thrilling accounts
of prize-fighting.   2978

_____. The Longshoremen. Arnold, 1903. A tale of smug-
gling told from the viewpoint of those who tried to prevent it.
                                                       2979

Beaconsfield, Benjamin Disraeli, 1st. earl of. Coningsby.
Colburn, 1844. Political and social life of England in the
1830s.   2980

Beck, Lily Adams. The Glorious Apollo. by E. Barrington,
pseud. Dodd, 1925. The political, social, and romantic
life of Lord Byron and three women who were prominent
in it.   2981

Bellasis, Margaret. Mrs. Betsey. by Francesca Marton,
pseud. Coward, 1955. Period piece of the Victorian era,
reminiscent of Jane Austen.   2982

Bennett, Arnold. The Old Wives' Tale. Doran, 1908. Life
in the English midlands during the Victorian period.   2983

Bentley, Phyllis. Inheritance. Macmillan, 1932. Long struggle
between capital and labor in the Yorkshire district of England.
                                                       2984
Berckman, Evelyn. The Heir of Starvelings. Doubleday, 1967.
The daughter of a rural minister is given the task of re-
educating the heir of a broken-down English manor.   2985

Berstl, Julius. Kean. (tr. ?) Orion, 1962. (pub. in En. in
1946 as The Sun's Bright Child) The imaginary memoirs of
an actor, Edmund Kean, whose life and career were a series
of contrasts.   2986

Besant, Walter. By Celia's Arbour. Chatto, 1878. A girl receives a mistaken report of her sweetheart's death in the
Crimean War.   2987

Beyer, Audrey White. The Sapphire Pendant. Knopf, 1961.
YA. An English orphan girl, rebelling against her guardian,
runs away from home and becomes embroiled in the Napoleonic Wars.   2988

Bickerstaffe-Drew, Francis. Hurdcott. by John Ayscough,
pseud. Herder, 1911. Country life in England from a
Catholic viewpoint, with glimpses of Hazlitt as well as
Charles and Mary Lamb.   2989

Blackmore, R. D. Alice Lorraine. Burt, 1875. A romance
in England and some events in Spain during the Peninsular
War.   2990

_____. Perlycross. Harper, 1894. Scenes of village
life in eastern Devon.   2991

_____. Springhaven. Harper, 1887. Southern England
under threat of invasion by Napoleon.   2992

Bleackley, Horace. A Hundred Years Ago. Nash, 1917. Reflects some of the problems resulting from an increasingly
mechanized industry.   2993

_____. The Monster. Doran, 1921. The "monster" is the
English factory system, which was so cruel and demanding
of employees.   2994

Blundell, Mary E. Lychgate Hall. by M. E. Francis, pseud.
Longmans, 1904. Life in a haunted country mansion.   2995

_____. Yeoman Fleetwood. by M. E. Francis, pseud.
Longmans, 1900. A yeoman falls in love with a girl of
higher social status, and becomes involved in a Regency
court romance.   2996

Blyth, James. A Hazardous Wooing. Ward & Lock, 1907.
Set amidst the exploits of daring highwaymen.   2997

_____. Napoleon Decrees. White, 1914. Adventures of a
French spy in England.   2998

Bolton, Guy. The Olympians. World, 1961. The personal
life of the poet Percy Bysshe Shelley, who left his wife and
family to elope to Europe with Mary Wollstonecraft.   2999

Bonnet, Theodore. The Mudlark. Doubleday, 1949. About
Queen Victoria's palace, Disraeli, the mudlark (a slum
urchin), and the Queen's unconventional bodyguard, Brown. 3000

Bragg, Melvyn. The Hired Man. Knopf, 1970, c. 1969. The
unhappy lot of a Cumberland farm worker and his family who
are forced by economic necessity to move to a coal-mining
community.   3001

Brebner, Percy J. A Royal Ward. Little, 1909. Time is
1813 when there was still some fear of French invasion.   3002

Brontë, Charlotte. Jane Eyre. Harper, 1848. The classic
story of a governess who falls in love with her employer
and discovers a tragic family secret.   3003

_____. Shirley. Derby, 1856. Centers on the curtailment

of trade caused by the Napoleonic Wars and shows the contemporary position of women.   3004

Brontë, Emily. Wuthering Heights. Harper, 1848. Story of
terror and hatred in the Yorkshire moors.   3005

Broster, Dorothy K. "Mr. Rowl." Doubleday, Page, 1924.
The imprisonment in England of a young Frenchman early
in the nineteenth century.   3006

_____. Ships in the Bay! Coward, 1931. An Englishman
in Wales, involved with French foes and Irish rebels, defends himself against a charge of treason.   3007

Buchan, John. The Free Fishers. Houghton, 1934. Rescue
operations of a group of Scottish fishermen organized to do
espionage during the Napoleonic Wars.   3008

Burton, Hester. Time of Trial. World, 1964, c.1963.
YA. A teen-aged girl finds herself alone when her father
is imprisoned for his published protest after a tenement
building collapses.   3009

Capes, Bernard. The Secret in the Hill. Smith & Elder,
1903. Adventure story of smuggling and treasure hunting. 3010

Carey, Alfred E. Sir Waterloo. Selwyn & Blount, 1920.
Life in the period of early railway development around
Sussex and London.   3011

Castle, Agnes and Egerton. Wroth. Macmillan, 1908. Dra-
matic romance in aristocratic Regency society.   3012

Castle, Egerton. The Light of Scarthey. Macmillan, 1895.
The tense Hundred Days are the time and a lighthouse the
place for this tale of smuggling and adventure.   3013

Cawley, Winifred. Down the Long Stairs. Holt, 1965, c.1964.
YA. The many perilous adventures of a Royalist who leaves
home to fight for his political beliefs.   3014

Chalmers, Stephen. A Prince of Romance. Small, Maynard,
1911. Unusual romance of Jacobite Scotland around 1812. 3015

_____. The Vanishing Smuggler. Clode, 1909. Attempts
of customs officials to apprehend smugglers countered by
the latters' efforts to elude capture.   3016

Chamier, Frederick. Ben Brace: The Last of Nelson's Aga-
memnons. Routledge, 1835. Naval story based on the ca-
reer of Lord Nelson's servant, Allen.   3017

Cleland, Robert. Inchbracken. Wilson & M'Cormack (Glas-

gow), 1883. The effect on a Highland parish of the seces-
sion of the Free Church from the Church of Scotland.   3018

Clevely, Hugh. Stranger in Two Worlds. Appleton, 1959.
The varied life of a young man who survives the Lucknow
siege in India, tangles with Fenians in Ireland, lives in
London's slums, and sees the Great Fire in Chicago.   3019

Cloete, Stuart. The Abductors. Trident Pr., 1966. Exposé of
the extensive white slave trade in London amidst the hypocrisy
and prudery of the Victorian Era.   3020

Cobban, J. MacLaren. The King of Andaman. Methuen, 1895.
Interesting story of Scottish life in young Victoria's time. 3021

Compton, Herbert. The Palace of Spies. Treherne, 1903. Intrigue in the court of Caroline of Brunswick and the Prince
Regent, later George IV.   3022

_____. The Queen Can Do No Wrong. Chatto, 1904. Ex-
citing romance of the court of Queen Caroline.   3023

Conrad, Joseph. The Nigger of the Narcissus. Heinemann,
1897. A sailing ship's stormy voyage from India to England.   3024

Cookson, Catherine. The Dwelling Place. Bobbs, 1971. The
orphaned daughter of a tenant-farmer struggles to support
her family and bring the local Lord's son to accept his re-
sponsibilities.   3025

_____. The Glass Virgin. Bantam Bks., 1970, c.1969.
When she discovers her illegitimacy, an heiress runs away
and makes a respectable, though hard, life for herself by
the work of her own hands.   3026

_____. Katie Mulholland. Bobbs, 1967. A novel of three
generations in which we see how class distinctions and the
Industrial Revolution affected the life of the heroine. 3027

Cooper, Lettice U. The Old Fox. Hodder & Stoughton, 1927.
Southern England when French smuggling and talk of French
invasion were rampant.   3028

Cornish, Francis Warre. Sunningwell. Dutton, 1899. Social
life of villagers active in the church in Victoria's reign. 3029

Costain, Thomas B. Ride With Me. Doubleday, 1944. Sir
Robert Wilson--a general in the Napoleonic Wars--and a
crusading newspaper publisher.   3030

_____. The Tontine. Doubleday, 1955. Narrative of two
families entangled in the annuity-lottery-insurance scheme. 3031

Cowper, Edith E. Lady Fabia. S. P. C. K., 1909. "A story
of adventure on the south coast" in the first decade of the
century.   3032

Craigie, Mrs. Pearl Mary. Robert Orange. by John Oliver
Hobbes, pseud. Stokes, 1900. About an Englishman who
becomes a Catholic and a Member of Parliament.   3033

Craik, Dinah Maria. John Halifax, Gentleman. Harper, 1856.
The rise of a poor man to a position of wealth through the
Industrial Revolution.   3034

Crichton Smith, Iain. The Alien Light. [En. title: Consider
The Lilies] Houghton, 1969, c.1968. A spirited old Scotswoman resists the clearance movement which would destroy
her crofter's home to make room for sheep grazing.   3035

Crockett, Samuel R. The Banner of Blue. McClure, 1903.
A romance of Galloway with religious disturbances in the
background.   3036

_____. The Moss Troopers. Hodder & Stoughton, 1912.
Romance and smuggling in the second decade of the century.   3037

_____. Strong Mac. Dodd, 1904. A story of conditions
in the rough lowlands of Scotland and the siege of San Sebastian.   3038

Crouch, Archer Philip. Nellie of the Eight Bells. Long,
1908. A story of naval life centering in a Portsmouth
tavern popular with English sailors.   3039

Dale, Celia. Act of Love. Walker, 1969. The theme of love
and hatred predominates in this novel about a tutor and the
parents of his pupils.   3040

Deeping, Warwick. The House of Spies. McBride, 1938. A
French spy in southern England during the threat of Napoleonic invasion.   3041

Delderfield, Ronald Frederick. God Is an Englishman. S. &
S., 1971, c.1970. A veteran of English (East) Indian service starts a successful moving van business and achieves a
happy marriage. (followed by Theirs Was the Kingdom)   3042

_____. Theirs Was the Kingdom. S. & S., 1971. Various
members of the Swann family as their business and fortune
expand during the Industrial Revolution.   3043

De Morgan, William. Joseph Vance. Holt, 1906. A romance
of Victorian life and manners.   3044

Dickens, Charles. A Christmas Carol. Watts, 1969, c. 18--.
The beloved story of Scrooge and Tiny Tim.   3045

_____. David Copperfield. Bradbury & Evans, 1850. The
famous cast of characters includes Aunt Betsy Trotwood,
Peggotty, Steerforth, Barkis, and Uriah Heep.   3046

_____. Hard Times. Harper, 1883. Pictures life in a man-
ufacturing town and reflects Carlyle's criticism of contemporary conditions.   3047

_____. Little Dorrit. Bradbury & Evans, 1857. Satirizes
the civil service and depicts prison life in mid-nineteenth
century England.   3048

_____. Nicholas Nickleby. Chapman & Hall, 1839. The
hero is first a teacher in a severe school, then an actor
in a provincial company.   3049

_____. Oliver Twist. Bentley, 1838. Corruption of a youth
in an environment of crime and poverty.   3050

Dixon, W. Wilmott. The Rogue of Rye. Chatto, 1909. The
escape of many English people caught in France by the Napoleonic Wars.   3051

Dodd, Catherine. Clad in Purple Mist. Jarrolds Ltd., 1926.
Middle class life on the Isle of Man, in Liverpool, and in
Australia.   3052

Dolbier, Maurice. The Mortal Gods. Dial, 1971. A prominent theatrical family in London in 1895 provides a story of
stage life and memorable characters.   3053

Doyle, Sir Arthur Conan. Rodney Stone. Appleton, 1896.
A novel which deals with social life and prize fighting.   3054

Dudeney, Alice. The Battle of the Weak. by Mrs. Henry
Dudeney. Dillingham, 1906. Village life on England's
southern coast at the beginning of the century.   3055

_____. The Story of Susan. by Mrs. Henry Dudeney.
Heinemann, 1903. A deep, true love underlies the frivolous
actions of a girl who delights in parties and gaiety.   3056

Duggan, Alfred. The Right Line of Cerdic. Pyramid, 1967,
c. 1961. Convincing portrait of Alfred the Great, who rose
from the obscure position of fourth son to be king of Wessex and defeater of the Viking invaders.   3057

Du Maurier, Daphne. Jamaica Inn. Doubleday, 1936. An orphaned girl goes to live at her uncle's inn on the Cornish
moors and finds it filled with strange and frightening ac-

tivities.   3058

_____. Mary Anne. Pocket Bks., 1972, c.1954. Story of
the author's ancestress, a clever woman reminiscent of
Thackeray's Becky Sharp [see Vanity Fair by William Makepeace Thackeray].   3059

Dunlop, Agnes Mary Robertson. Girl With a Pen, Charlotte
Brontë. by Elisabeth Kyle, pseud. Holt, 1964. YA. A
novel about Charlotte Brontë and her two sisters, who pursued writing careers in an age when women writers were
not accepted.   3060

_____. Great Ambitions. by Elisabeth Kyle, pseud. Holt,
1968, c.1966. YA. A story which recounts the early days
in the life of Charles Dickens.   3061

Eden, Dorothy. Darkwater. Coward, 1964, c.1963. Chilling
suspense, murder, and romance haunt the eerie ancestral
home where Fanny Davenport lives as the orphaned ward of
her Uncle Edgar.   3062

_____. Lady of Mallow. [En. title: Samantha] Coward,
1962, c.1960. Family seeks to unmask an adventurer who
claims to be the legitimate heir to an English estate.   3063

_____. Ravenscroft. Coward, 1965, c.1964. Two orphaned
sisters fall into unscrupulous hands and have terrifying experiences when they come to Victorian London.   3064

_____. Winterwood. Coward, 1967. A spoiled, crippled
daughter, a ruthless, beautiful mother, and a father with
whom she falls hopelessly in love people the home where
Lavinia comes as the child's companion.   3065

Eden, Emily. The Semi-Attached Couple. Mathews & Marrat,
1860. English manners and life in nineteenth century high
Whig circles.   3066

Edwards, Matilda Betham. The Lord of the Harvest. Hurst
& Blackett, 1899. Farm life in Suffolk.   3067

_____. Mock Beggars' Hall. Hurst & Blackett, 1902.
Suffolk farm life before the repeal of the Corn Laws.   3068

_____. A Suffolk Courtship. Hurst & Blackett, 1900.
Romance of the farm people of Suffolk.   3069

Eliot, George, pseud. for Mary Ann Evans. Adam Bede.
Harper, 1859. Detailed account of village and country
life with the romance of a carpenter and a dairymaid.   3070

_____. Daniel Deronda. Harper, 1876. Social life and

Jewish character at mid-century.   3071

_____. Felix Holt, the Radical. Harper, 1866. A working
man marries into a "higher class" during the social upheaval
of the 1832 Reform Bill.   3072

_____. Middlemarch. Harper, 1872-3. A panoramic pic-
ture of everyday village happenings in the lives of two families.   3073

_____. The Mill on the Floss. Blackwood, 1860. The re-
sults of emotional conflict between a brother and a sister. 3074

_____. Silas Marner. Dutton, 1861. Novel of village life
in which a miserly weaver is rehabilitated by love for a
child.   3075

Elsna, Hebe, pseud. for Ansle, Dorothy Phoebe. The Love
Match. Beagle Bks., 1971, c.1967. The relentless plotting
of a ruthless mother-in-law forces a sensitive girl into a
scandalous affair with Lord Byron and to the brink of insanity.   3076

Everett, Mrs. H.D. Cousin Hugh. by Theo. Douglas, pseud.
Methuen, 1910. A tale of traffic in the escape of French
prisoners and the importation of false coins.   3077

Farnol, Jeffery. The Amateur Gentleman. Low, 1913. An innkeeper's son inherits a fortune and enters English society. 3078

_____. The Broad Highway. Little, 1911. A youth
scorns an inheritance conditioned on a certain marriage.   3079

_____. Heritage Perilous. McBride, 1947. A brave sailor
endeavors to claim an inherited title and fortune.   3080

_____. The High Adventure. Little, 1926. Conspiracy,
adventure, and prize fighting in southeast England.   3081

_____. The Loring Mystery. Little, 1925. A tale dealing
with murder in Sussex.   3082

Felton, Ronald Oliver. Nicholas Carey. by Ronald Welch,
pseud. Criterion, 1963. YA. A wealthy young man buys
a commission in the Army and becomes involved in affairs
in Italy, France, and the Crimea.   3083

Ferrier, Susan. Destiny. Macmillan, 1831. A picture of
Scottish life and manners early in the century.   3084

Findlater, Jane Helen. The Story of a Mother. Nisbet, 1903.
The everyday life of a Scots family.   3085

Foreman, Stephen. The Fen Dogs. Long, 1912. Two soldiers
   from the Fens in the Battle of Waterloo and in their rugged
   life at home.   3086

Forrest, Charles E. All Fools Together. Collins, 1925.
   Poaching, politics, and other elements of English country
   life about 1820.   3087

Fothergill, Jessie. Probation. Fenno, 1880. The cotton short-
   age of 1863 caused by the American Civil War; the struggle
   for women's rights.   3088

Foulds, Elfrida Vipont. Weaver of Dreams. by Elfrida Vipont.
   Walck, 1966. YA. The childhood of Charlotte Brontë and her
   brother and sisters gave promise of their future literary
   achievements.   3089

Fowles, John. The French Lieutenant's Woman. Little, 1969.
   Love triangle between an aristocratic young man, an heiress,
   and a scandalous woman who had been deserted by a French
   naval officer.   3090

Frye, Pearl. Sleeping Sword. Little, 1952. Concerns Lord
   Nelson, Lady Hamilton, and Nelson's naval warfare.   3091

Galt, John. The Gathering of the West. Johns Hopkins, 1939.
   Features George IV's first visit to Edinburgh.   3092

Garnett, Martha. The Infamous John Friend. by Mrs. R. S.
   Garnett. Holt, 1909. A tale of London and Brighton in
   1805, with the hero a spy for Napoleon.   3093

Gaskell, Elizabeth C. Mary Barton. by Mrs. Gaskell. Dutton, 1848. Set in industrial Manchester during the early
   Victorian period.   3094

_____. North and South. by Mrs. Gaskell. Dutton, 1855.
   Contrasts the "manufacturing north" and the "rural south" of
   the Industrial Revolution.   3095

Gerson, Noel B. The Nelson Touch. by Paul Lewis, pseud.
   Holt, 1960. The sea battles which brought fame to Lord
   Nelson are described here, as are his unhappy married life
   and his infatuation for Lady Hamilton.   3096

Gibbs, Willa. The Dedicated. Morrow, 1960. [pub. in En.
   in 1959 as The Two Doctors] Two doctors, Dr. Jenner and
   Dr. Woodville, offer different methods for the prevention of
   smallpox.   3097

Goudge, Elizabeth. The Dean's Watch. Coward, 1960. An
   old clockmaker and a cathedral dean demonstrate the power
   of love and respect to change human lives.   3098

_____. Gentian Hill. Coward, 1949. Romance of a mid-
shipman and a girl rescued from the sea; lore and legend of
the Devonshire coast in England.   3099

Graber, George Alexander. The Rape of the Fair Country. by
Alexander Cordell, pseud. Doubleday, 1959. Wales in the
1830s when mine owners controlled economics and thus whole
families. (followed by The Robe of Honour)   3100

_____. The Robe of Honour. [En. title: Hosts of Rebecca]
by Alexander Cordell, pseud. Doubleday, 1960. The Rebecca Movement in Wales in the 1830s and 1840s. (followed
by Song of the Earth)   3101

_____. Song of the Earth. by Alexander Cordell, pseud. S.
& S., 1970, c.1969. Hardships of a Welsh coal-mining family exploited by British mine-owners in the last century.
(completes trilogy)   3102

Graham, Winston. The Wreck of the Grey Cat. Doubleday,
1958. A mystery set in the Cornish port of Falmouth in
1898.   3103

Grant, James. Under the Red Dragon. Dutton, 1872. A
vivid picture of life during the Crimean War.   3104

Grierson, Edward. The Massingham Affair. Doubleday, 1963,
c.1962. A young lawyer who seeks justice for two poachers
convicted of a crime becomes enmeshed in a wierd mystery.
                                                             3105
Griffiths, Arthur. A Royal Rascal. Unwin, 1905. The story
of a career soldier who saw action in many campaigns.   3106

_____. The Thin Red Line. Macqueen, 1900. A story of
the Crimean War.   3107

Gunn, Neil. Highland Night. Harcourt, 1935. Eviction of Scots
peasants from their homes to make way for lucrative sheep
raising.   3108

Hall, Evelyn Beatrice. Basset: A Village Chronicle. [En.
title: Early Victorian] by S.G. Tallentyre, pseud. Moffat,
1910. A peaceful scene of village life early in Victoria's
reign.   3109

_____. Matthew Hargraves. by S.G. Tallentyre, pseud.
Putnam, 1914. The early years of Queen Victoria's reign
and the changing social and industrial conditions.   3110

Hamley, William G. Traseaden Hall. Blackwood, 1882. Pictures both English country life and military life during the
Peninsular War.   3111

Hardy, Thomas.   The Mayor of Casterbridge.   Random
House, 1950.   (orig. pub. in 1886) The lives of a man,
his wife, and their daughter from the time he auctions
them off to the highest bidder.   3112

_____. Tess of the D'Urbervilles.   Bantam Bks., 1971.
(prev. pub. in 1891) The romantic dilemma of an attractive
servant girl and her reactions to her suitors.   3113

_____. The Trumpet-Major.   Harper, 1879.   A soldier in
the war with Bonaparte and his brother in the merchant
service.   3114

Harwood, Alice.   The Strangeling.   Bobbs, 1954.   The often
misunderstood adventures of a well-meaning but impractical
daughter of a missionary.   3115

Hewlett, Maurice.   Bendish: A Study in Prodigality.   Scribner,
1913.   The literary and political circles of the 1830s with
several historical figures introduced.   3116

_____. Mainwaring.   Dodd, 1920.   An Irish-born adventurer,
after much wandering, becomes a member of the English
Parliament.   3117

_____. The Stooping Lady.   Dodd, 1907.   Romance of high
society life with its heroine wooed by a worthy butcher.   3118

Heyer, Georgette.   April Lady.   Putnam, 1957.   A young wife,
in love with her older husband but somewhat afraid of him,
entangles herself in a web of "little white lies."   3119

_____. Arabella.   Heinemann, 1966.   (prev. pub. in 1949)
When the daughter of a country minister visits her London
godmother, she sets her cap for the most eligible--and most
confirmed--bachelor in town.   3120

_____. Bath Tangle.   Heinemann, 1967, c.1955.   A novel
of manners with Regency Bath as background.   3121

_____. Black Sheep.   Dutton, 1966.   Endeavoring to protect
her niece from a fortune hunter, a young aunt suffers a similar fate herself.   3122

_____. A Civil Contract.   Putnam, 1961.   The marriage of
an impoverished Viscount, who is a veteran of the Napoleonic
Wars, to an heiress to replenish his fortune.   3123

_____. The Corinthian.   Dutton, 1966.   (pub. in 1941 as
Beau Wyndham) Their common desire to escape from family-
arranged marriages involves a young man and woman in adventure and romance.   3124

_____. Cotillion. Heinemann, 1965, c.1953. Light-
hearted tale of romance in Regency England.   3125

_____. Cousin Kate. Bantam Bks., 1970, c.1968. Sud-
denly bereft of parents and fortune, a girl accepts her aunt's
hospitality, only to find she doesn't agree with the lady's
plans for her.   3126

_____. False Colours. Dutton, 1964, c.1963. Tense and
humorous situations arise when an identical twin substitutes
for his absent brother in British high society.   3127

_____. Faro's Daughter. Dutton, 1967, c.1942. Battle of
wits between a lady who works in her aunt's gambling house
and a Lord who is attempting to prevent her marriage to his
cousin.   3128

_____. The Foundling. Heineman, 1966, c.1948. During
the period of betrothal for an arranged marriage, a young
man brings a beautiful foundling to his fiancée for her pro-
tection.   3129

_____. Frederica. Dutton, 1965. This story of two sis-
ters and three brothers shows the society of the Regency
period and increasing industrialization.   3130

_____. Friday's Child. Heinemann, 1965, c.1946. Novel
of high society activities and entangled romance.   3131

_____. The Grand Sophy. Heinemann, 1965, c.1950. Forth-
right girl, educated on the Continent, comes to live with con-
servative London relatives.   3132

_____. The Nonesuch. Heinemann, 1967, c.1962. An en-
tangled maze of love interests is engendered when a fashionable Londoner comes to the Yorkshire manor he has inherited.   3133

_____. Pistols for Two, and Other Stories. Dutton, 1964,
c.1960. Eleven short stories about a diversity of characters in a Regency setting.   3134

_____. Powder and Patch. Bantam Bks., 1970, c.1923.
(orig. pub. in En. as The Transformation of Philip Jettan)
A country girl becomes confused in her romantic life when
plunged into Regency society in London.   3135

_____. Quiet Gentleman. Ace Bks., 1968. (prev. pub. in
1951) The seventh Earl of St. Erth returns from the Napoleonic Wars to claim his heritage, only to find menacing enemies in his own household.   3136

_____. Regency Buck. Dutton, 1966. (prev. pub. in 1935)

An orphaned brother and sister, wishing for the gay life of
London society, leave their country home for the questionable welcome of a reluctant guardian.   3137

_____. Reluctant Widow. Putnam, 1946. An impoverished
governess is married, through a mistake in identity, to a
wealthy, but dying, man.   3138

_____. Sprig Muslin. Putnam, 1956. A light and lively
tale of love in Regency England.   3139

_____. Sylvester. Putnam, 1958. The tangled love affair
of an improbable pair has a happy ending.   3140

_____. The Talisman Ring. Dutton, 1967, c.1964. The
mystery of a stolen ring and a charge of murder give extra
excitement to this lively romance.   3141

_____. The Toll-Gate. Heinemann, 1965, c.1954. A veter-
an of the Napoleonic Wars finds toll-gate keeping in England
anything but dull.   3142

_____. The Unknown Ajax. Putnam, 1960. A lively story
of young love with an incidental picture of the new textile industry.   3143

_____. Venetia. Heinemann, 1968, c.1959. A charming
and sensible woman circumvents a planned marriage.   3144

Hibbert, Eleanor. Kirkland Revels. by Victoria Holt, pseud.
Fawcett, 1968, c.1962. The ordeals of a young bride in an
eerie Yorkshire manor house.   3145

_____. The Legend of the Seventh Virgin. by Victoria
Holt, pseud. Fawcett, 1965, c.1964. An illiterate cottage
girl sells herself as a servant as the first step in her ambition to become mistress of the mansion.   3146

_____. Menfreya in the Morning. [En. title: Menfreya]
by Victoria Holt, pseud. Fawcett, 1967, c.1966. A young
heiress marries for love, but in the confines of her husband's terrifying castle begins to have doubts about his
motives.   3147

_____. Mistress of Mellyn. by Victoria Holt, pseud. Faw-
cett, 1970, c.1960. About the young governess to the child
of a widowed Cornish manor lord.   3148

_____. The Secret Woman. by Victoria Holt, pseud.
Doubleday, 1970. A secret childhood romance continues
after a lapse of many years, as Anna Brett becomes governess to the young son of the man she still loves.   3149

_____. The Shivering Sands. by Victoria Holt, pseud. Doubleday, 1969. A young musician coming to a great estate to solve her sister's mysterious disappearance becomes far too deeply involved.   3150

Hodge, Jane Aiken. Marry in Haste. Doubleday, 1970, c. 1969. A marriage of convenience develops heart-breaking problems when man and wife are afraid to admit their true feelings to each other.   3151

_____. Maulever Hall. Doubleday, 1964. A beautiful girl loses her memory in a coach accident and thus becomes involved in a suspenseful gothic romance.   3152

_____. Watch the Wall, My Darling. Doubleday, 1966. An American girl visits her English grandfather and finds herself in the midst of spying and smuggling during the Napoleonic Wars.   3153

Hodges, C. Walter. The Overland Launch. Coward, 1970, c. 1969. YA. A gripping tale of rescue at sea when the lifeboat had to be taken overland to a sheltered launching area before it could brave the storm and aid a foundering ship.   3154

Hope, Matilda. Because of the Angels. Longmans, 1883. The early story of the Irvingite Church in Scotland.   3155

Howatch, Susan. The Shrouded Walls. Stein and Day, 1971, c. 1968. A penniless girl who has been forced to marry a rich landowner confronts the question whether or not he had murdered his father.   3156

Hughes, Thomas. Tom Brown's Schooldays. Dutton, 1964. YA. (first pub. in 1857) The classic tale of escapades at a boys' school in England.   3157

Hunt, Dorothy Alice Bonavia. Pemberley Shades. Dutton, 1949. A sequel to Jane Austen's Pride and Prejudice [q. v.] giving an account of Elizabeth and Darcy's marriage after three years.   3158

Hutchinson, Horace G. Crowborough Beacon. Smith & Elder, 1903. A tale of quiet country life early in the century.   3159

_____. A Friend of Nelson. Longmans, 1902. An account of Nelson's Baltic campaign of 1801.   3160

Jacob, Naomi Ellington. Time Piece. Macmillan, 1937. A Yorkshire squire and his family in the second half of the century.   3161

Jacob, Violet. The History of Aythan Waring. Dutton, 1908.

Thrilling activities of an outlaw band.   3162

_____. The Interloper. Heinemann, 1904. The effects of
a young laird's learning that there is some question about
his birth.   3163

_____. The Sheep Stealers. Putnam, 1902. Events con-
nected with the Highway Acts and resultant Turnpike Riots
in Welsh border regions.   3164

Jameson, Storm. Lovely Ship. Knopf, 1927. The two marriages of the niece of a shipyard owner in a mid-century
shipbuilding town.   3165

Jesse, F. Tennyson. Secret Bread. Doran, 1917. A novel
of domestic affairs in the last half of the century showing
the influence of religious and political developments.   3166

Jones, Gwyn. The Walk Home. Norton, 1963, c.1962. A
young man in search of his father encounters contrasting
characters in the hills and vales of Wales.   3167

Jones, Margam. The Stars of the Revival. Long, 1910. Religious feeling in Wales in the first quarter of the century. 3168

Kaye, Michael W. Devil's Brew. Paul, 1912. Social unrest
caused by economic insecurity following Waterloo.   3169

Kaye-Smith, Sheila. The Challenge to Sirius. Dutton, 1918.
Life in Sussex during the Crimean War and the American
Civil War.   3170

_____. Sussex Gorse. Knopf, 1916. Depicts Sussex rural
life and makes many allusions to politics and public events.
                                                                 3171
Keddie, Henrietta. A Daughter of the Manse. by Sarah Tytler,
pseud. Long, 1905. The plight of pastors whose financial
security was affected by the break in the Church of Scotland.
                                                                 3172
_____. Logan's Loyalty. by Sarah Tytler, pseud. Long,
1900. A family rift is caused by a daughter's elopement
with a man of her low-born mother's class.   3173

_____. Sir David's Visitors. by Sarah Tytler, pseud.
Chatto, 1903. A novel of Kensington during the Regency. 3174

Kennedy, Margaret. A Night in Cold Harbor. Macmillan,
1960. A picture of English village life.   3175

_____. Troy Chimneys. Rinehart, 1952. A refreshing
method of story telling depicts a young man's dual personality.   3176

Kenyon, Frank Wilson. The Absorbing Fire. Dodd, 1966.
The personal life of Lord Byron with his many love-affairs
and seductions.   3177

_____. Emma. Crowell, 1955. The Emma of the title is
Lady Hamilton, well-known for her scandalous romance with
Lord Nelson.   3178

_____. Golden Years. Crowell, 1959. A romantic novel of
the life and loves of poet Percy Bysshe Shelley.   3179

King, Louise W. The Rochemer Hag. Doubleday, 1967. A
governess who accepts a position on a rural estate becomes
embroiled in a murder mystery.   3180

Kingsley, Henry. Ravenshoe. Longmans, 1802. Recounts University life, political discussions, and scenes from the Crimean War.   3181

Kirk, James Prior. Forest Folk. by James Prior, pseud.
Dodd, 1901. The character and life of farm people affected
by the spread of industrialization.   3182

Leslie, Doris. Full Flavour. Macmillan, 1934. A family
chronicle of the Victorian and Edwardian eras.   3183

_____. Prime Minister's Wife. [En. title: The Perfect
Wife] Doubleday, 1960. Fictional biography of Mary Anne
Evans, the milliner who married Benjamin Disraeli.   3184

_____. Royal William. Macmillan, 1941. Lively fiction-
alized biography of William IV, England's "Sailor King."   3185

Lincoln, Victoria. Charles. Little, 1962. Recounts the family
life and ambitions of the great novelist, Charles Dickens,
and depicts life in Victorian England.   3186

Linklater, Eric. The House of Gair. Harcourt, 1954. Suspense on the Scottish moors.   3187

Linton, Lynn. Lizzié Lorton of Greyrigg. Ward & Lock, 1866.
A dedicated young minister finds his new parish rough and
superstition-ridden.   3188

Llewellyn, Richard. How Green Was My Valley. Macmillan,
1940. Life of a coal-mining family in southern Wales.   3189

Lobdell, Helen. Thread of Victory. McKay, 1963. YA.
Child labor conditions in a Scottish cotton mill in the nineteenth century are examined here.   3190

Lofts, Norah. The Brittle Glass. Knopf, 1943. About an embittered woman who is left a business at her father's death.   3191

_____. The Golden Fleece. Knopf, 1944. Diverse
events in an English inn during a day and night of 1817.   3192

_____. Letty. Pyramid, 1968. (orig. pub. in 1949 as
A Calf for Venus) A shy young girl grows up in a coffee-
house which is a center for smuggling.   3193

_____. Lovers All Untrue. Fawcett, 1971, c.1970. A
father, obsessed with keeping his daughters at home and away
from contact with men, sees a tragic result of his domina-
tion.   3194

_____. To See a Fine Lady. Knopf, 1946. Rise of an am-
bitious dairy-maid on a farm in post-Napoleonic Essex.   3195

Lowe, Marjorie G. Sudden Lady. Putnam, 1961. The romance
and adventures of gypsy life in the English countryside.   3196

Lucas, Audrey. Old Motley. Macmillan, 1938. Centers on
a Quaker community in London in the 1830s.   3197

Lysaght, Sidney Royse. One of the Grenvilles. Macmillan,
1899. Adventures of an Englishman who is, for a time, a
prisoner of the Arabs.   3198

Lytton, Edward Bulwer, 1st. baron. The Caxtons. Dutton,
1849. True-to-life novel of society in Victorian England. 3199

_____. Kenelm Chillingly. Dutton, 1873. A country squire
lives as a worker and discovers the contrast between luxury
and poverty.   3200

McCarthy, Justin. The Waterdale Neighbours. Chatto, 1867.
How two men met the challenge of personal profit versus
political loyalty.   3201

McCrone, Guy. Red Plush. Farrar, 1947. Fictional chronicle of a Scots family, the Moorhouses, 1870-1881.   3202

McFadden, Gertrude Violet. The Honest Lawyer. Doran,
1916. A novel of Wareham and Dorchester in the first
half of the century.   3203

_____. Maumbery Rings. Doran, 1921. A rural horse-
stealing episode in the time of George IV.   3204

_____. Preventive Man. Lane, 1920. A government agent
comes to the Dorset coast in search of smugglers.   3205

_____. The Roman Way. Doran, 1925. The local color of
the Dorchester district in the late eighteenth and early nineteenth centuries.   3206

_____. Sheriff's Deputy. Lane, 1924. A romance dur-
ing the time of the Machinery Riots in the Dorchester district.   3207

_____. So Speed We. Doran, 1926. Social life in Dorset-
shire in the early nineteenth century.   3208

_____. The Turning Sword. Lane, 1923. Presents people
of the picturesque market town and seaport of Poole in
1833.   3209

Mackenzie, Agnes Mure. The Quiet Lady. Doubleday, Page,
1926. The Outer Hebrides in the early nineteenth century.
                                                              3210
McLean, Allan Campbell. A Sound of Trumpets. Harcourt,
1966. YA. The trials of a Scottish crofter on the island of
Skye in 1884.   3211

Main, Mary Foster. The Girl Who Was Never Queen. Doubleday, 1962. The difficult life of Princess Charlotte Augusta,
daughter of frivolous George IV and coarse Caroline of
Brunswick.   3212

Marriage, Caroline. The Luck of Barerakes. Heinemann,
1903. About the rugged people who inhabit the Yorkshire
moors.   3213

Marshall, Edison. The Infinite Woman. Farrar, 1950. An
Irish adventuress determines to become a countess.   3214

Meade, L. T., pseud. The Witch Maid. Nisbet, 1903. The
persecution of a young girl accused of witchcraft.   3215

Meredith, George. Beauchamp's Career. Scribner, 1876.
Mid-century politics in the period of Carlyle's influence.   3216

Montgomery, K. L., pseud. for Kathleen and Letitia Montgomery.
The Gate-Openers. Long, 1912. A tale of the Turnpike
Riots and of some unusual Welsh customs.   3217

Munro, Neil. Children of Tempest. Blackwood, 1903. Customs, life, and romance among rural Catholics.   3218

_____. Gilian the Dreamer. Dodd, 1899. Highland village
life just after Napoleon's defeat at Waterloo.   3219

Neill, Robert. The Shocking Miss Anstey. Doubleday, 1965.
An English naval captain seeks to win the love of a high-
class courtesan whom he pursues from London to Chelten-
ham.   3220

Newbolt, Henry. Taken From the Enemy. Chatto & Windus,
1892. A tale of London and the sea concerned with an at-

tempt to rescue Napoleon from St. Helena.   3221

O'Brian, Patrick. Master and Commander. Lippincott, 1969.
About the commander of an English brig fighting the French
and Spanish on the Mediterranean in the early 1800s.   3222

Oliver, Jane, pseud., for Rees, Helen Christina Easson.
The Blue Heaven Bends Over All. Putnam, 1971. Sir
Walter Scott, by his determination and cheerful disposi-
tion, overcame the handicap of lameness and led a full,
rich life.   3223

Ollivant, Alfred. Devil Dare. Doubleday, 1924. The story of
a traitor in the conflict between Nelson and Napoleon.   3224

_____. The Gentleman. Macmillan, 1908. Attempt of a
Napoleonic spy to capture Nelson shortly before the Battle
of Trafalgar.   3225

O'Neil, George. Special Hunger. Liveright, 1931. Depicts
the tragic life of the poet Keats.   3226

Oxenham, John, pseud. for William Arthur Dunkerley. Lauris-
tons. Methuen, 1910. A London banking house during the
suspense-laden Hundred Days and at the news of Waterloo. 3227

Parker, Gilbert. The Judgment House. Harper, 1922. England in the period towards the end of the Boer War in South
Africa.   3228

Pearce, Charles E. Corinthian Jack. Paul, 1920. A tale of
prize fighting in Bristol, Bath, and London about 1823. 3229

Peard, Frances M. Catherine. Harper, 1893. Romance in
a normally peaceful English countryside upset by the threat
of Napoleon's ambition.   3230

Phillpotts, Eden. The American Prisoner. Macmillan,
1904. Pictures a harsh English prison where many Americans were held during the War of 1812.   3231

_____. Faith Tresilion. Macmillan, 1916. Smuggling and
adventure in nineteenth century Cornwall.   3232

_____. Minions of the Moon. Macmillan, 1935. Dartmoor
prison and the problem of escaping from it.   3233

Pinkerton, Thomas A. The French Prisoner. Sonnenschein,
1894. Piracy and smuggling during the threatened invasion
by Napoleon.   3234

Poynter, H. May. Scarlet Town. S. P. C. K., 1894. The
tale of a young naval officer who escapes Napoleon's im-

prisonment.   3235

Quiller-Couch, Arthur T. The Adventures of Harry Revel.
Scribner, 1903. The youth of a foundling in England and
his adventures in the Peninsular Wars.   3236

_____. The Mayor of Troy. Scribner, 1905. Exploits of
the Troy Volunteer Artillery when English civilians were preparing for Napoleonic invasion.   3237

_____. Poison Island. Scribner, 1907. Shows influences
of the Napoleonic Wars and the War of 1812.   3238

_____. The Westcotes. Coates, 1902. Pathetic romance
of an English spinster who falls in love with a much younger
French prisoner.   3239

_____ and Daphne du Maurier. Castle Dor. Doubleday,
1962. A tragic romance in Cornwall is a modern counterpart of the Tristan and Iseult legend.   3240

Rawson, Maud Stepney. The Apprentice. Hutchinson, 1904.
Life in the shipbuilding town of Rye in the 1820s.   3241

_____. A Lady of the Regency. Harper, 1900. The un-
happy life of Queen Caroline is shown in this story of one
of her ladies.   3242

Raymond, Walter. Two Men O' Mendip. Doubleday, 1899.
Strained relations between farmers and lead miners in the
Cheddar area.   3243

Reade, Charles. Foul Play. Estes, 1869. A novel which
treats of social conditions in a realistic manner.   3244

_____. Hard Cash. Estes, 1863. A realistic account of
the status of the insane; financial panic in early railroad development.   3245

_____. It Is Never Too Late to Mend. Scribner, 1856.
An attack on the harsh and unreasonable prison system.   3246

_____. Put Yourself in His Place. Estes, 1870. A seri-
ous treatment of the Trade Union question.   3247

Rives, Hallie Erminie. The Castaway. Bobbs, 1904. A
sympathetic novel based on the life of the poet Byron.   3248

Roberts, Janet Louise. Ravenswood. Avon, 1971. Marriage
between an impoverished gentlewoman and an austere nobleman endures despite his diplomatic errands and her secret
spying in affairs concerning Napoleon.   3249

Roberts, Morley. A Son of Empire. Lippincott, 1899. Vigorous adventures of a soldier and explorer.   3250

Russell, W. Clark. An Ocean Free-Lance. Macmillan, 1881.
A tale of privateering in the War of 1812.   3251

_____. The Yarn of Old Harbour Town. Jacobs, 1905. Nel-
son's naval operations in the English Channel.   3252

Sagon, Amyot, pseud. When George III Was King. Sands,
1899. Mystery story involving smugglers in Cornwall and
London.   3253

Scott, Sir Walter. St. Ronan's Well. Bazin & Ellsworth, 1832.
Local customs and manners at a small watering place in
Scotland.   3254

Sheppard, Alfred Tresidder. Running Horse Inn. Lippincott,
1906. A soldier returns from war to find his brother marry-
ing his sweetheart.   3255

Simpson, Violet A. The Bonnet Conspirators. Smith & Elder,
1903. Smuggling on the Sussex coast during the Napoleonic
Wars.   3256

_____. The Sovereign Power. Smith & Elder, 1904. A
romance set during the threat of Napoleonic invasion.   3257

Smith, Vian. The First Thunder. Doubleday, 1965. A young
labor leader works with a schoolteacher to improve the lot
of tenant farmers.   3258

_____. Genesis Down. Doubleday, 1963, c.1962. A daring
young peasant couple comes to the English moor as homesteaders.   3259

Snowden, James K. The Plunder Pit. Methuen, 1898.
Thrilling story of Yorkshire early in Victoria's reign.   3260

Stacton, David. Sir William. Putnam, 1963. The love affair
of Admiral Horatio Nelson and Lady Hamilton, wife of the
British Ambassador to Naples.   3261

Stephens, Eve. Victoria and Albert. by Evelyn Anthony, pseud.
Crowell, 1958. The one-sided love of the famous royal
couple.   3262

Stevenson, Anne. Ralph Dacre. Walker, 1967, c.1966. A
country boy who is adopted and raised by a wealthy man
falls in love with and competes for the hand of his bene-
factor's daughter.   3263

Stevenson, Robert Louis. St. Ives. Dutton, 1934. Adven-

tures of a French gentleman held at Edinburgh during the
Napoleonic Wars.   3264

_____. Weir of Hermiston. Scribner, 1896. Unfinished
romance, based on fact, concerning the unhappy relations
between a father and his son.   3265

Stewart, Charlotte. Black Mary. By Allan McAulay, pseud.
Unwin, 1901. A half-caste girl plagued by the accident of
her birth.   3266

Styles, Showell. The Admiral's Fancy. Longmans, 1958.
The daring romance of Lord Nelson and Lady Hamilton told
from the viewpoint of Nelson's friend, Captain Ben Hallo-
well.   3267

_____. His Was the Fire. Vanguard, 1957, c.1956. The
story of General Sir John Moore, who fought against Napoleon,
told by people who came in contact with him.   3268

Sutcliffe, Halliwell. Mistress Barbara. [En. title: Mistress
Barbara Cunliffe] Crowell, 1901. Pictures wool and cotton
producers on the Yorkshire moors.   3269

_____. Shameless Wayne. Dodd, 1900. A bloody feud be-
tween two respected Yorkshire families.   3270

_____. Through Sorrow's Gates. Unwin, 1904. Folklore
and superstition on the Yorkshire moors.   3271

Sykes, J. A. C. Mark Alston. Nash, 1908. Based on the personal life of the writer Ruskin.   3272

Teague, John J. A Gentleman of London. by Morice Gerard,
pseud. Nash, 1908. About a man who becomes Lord Mayor
of London early in the century.   3273

Tearle, Christian. Holborn Hill. Clode, 1909. Pictures the
locality and the people of Holborn, Highgate, and Kent.   3274

Thackeray, William Makepeace. The History of Pendennis.
Harper, 1850. Portrait of a typical young man about mid-
century.   3275

_____. The Newcomes. Harper, 1855. Good picture of
English social life in the first half of the century.   3276

_____. Vanity Fair. Bradbury & Evans, 1848. Classic
novel of society with an account of the Battle of Waterloo
and society's attitude toward it.   3277

Thirkell, Angela. Coronation Summer. Oxford, 1937.
Panorama of ceremonies and celebrations during Victoria's

coronation.   3278

Thomas, R. M.   Trewern.   Unwin, 1901.   The uncertainty and
change of political thought at the time of the Reform Act of
1832.   3279

Tilsley, Frank.   Mutiny.   Reynal, 1959.   The discontentment of
mistreated sailors aboard the H. M. S. Regenerate.   3280

Torday, Ursula.   English Wife.   by Charity Blackstock, pseud.
Coward, 1964.   A happy marriage is threatened when a wife
discovers her husband is capable of criminal activities.   3281

Trollope, Anthony.   Chronicles of Barsetshire: (1)   The Warden.
Munro, 1885.   (2)   Barchester Towers.   Munro, 1881.   (3)
Doctor Thorne.   Munro, 1882.   (4)   Framley Parsonage.
Smith & Elder, 1861.   (5)   Small House at Alington.   Dodd,
1904.   (6)   Last Chronicle of Barset.   Smith & Elder, 1867.
Separate but related novels of quiet country life around the
cathedral town of Barchester, containing numerous fine char-
acter studies.   3282-7

_____.   (1) Phineas Finn.   Ward & Lock, 1869.   (2) Phineas
Redux.   Ward & Lock, 1874.   The social side of political
life in the 1860s.   3288-9

_____.   The Way We Live Now.   Chatto, 1875.   An account
of contemporary English society.   3290

Trollope, Frances.   Life and Adventures of Michael Armstrong.
Colburn, 1840.   Illustrates the conditions of child labor in
factories.   3291

Waite, Helen Elmira.   How Do I Love Thee?   Macrae Smith,
1953.   A story about Elizabeth Barrett and how her love for
Robert Browning overcame the obstacles of her ill health and
her father's opposition to their marriage.   3292

Wallis, Henry M.   Demi-Royal.   by Ashton Hilliers, pseud.
Methuen, 1915.   The social and religious life of the early
part of the century in England and on the Continent.   3293

Walpole, Hugh.   The Cathedral.   Doran, 1922.   Life in an English cathedral city at the end of the nineteenth century.   3294

_____.   The Fortress.   Doubleday, 1932.   A feud between
Judith Paris and Walter Herries, whose family had grown
rich in commerce after Waterloo.   3295

Ward, Mary Augusta.   The Marriage of William Ashe.   by Mrs.
Humphry Ward.   Harper, 1905.   Romance in cultured circles
in Regency England.   3296

_____. Robert Elsmere. by Mrs. Humphry Ward. Mac-
millan, 1888. Centers on English intellectual life and the
Oxford Movement.   3297

Warry, C. King. The Sentinel of Wessex. Unwin, 1904.
The gaiety and uncertainty in London during the Napoleonic
Wars.   3298

Watson, H. B. Marriott. Chloris of the Island. Harper, 1900.
Dilemma of a youth who loves an Irish girl but differs politically with her family.   3299

_____. The House in the Downs. Dent, 1914. Smuggling,
naval activities, and threat of invasion in the Napoleonic
era.   3300

_____. Twisted Eglantine. Appleton, 1905. Vivid society
romance of the Regency period.   3301

Watson, Helen H. Andrew Goodfellow. by Mrs. Herbert
Watson. Macmillan, 1906. Romance of a lieutenant in Nelson's service with an account of Trafalgar.   3302

Watson, Margaret. Driven. Unwin, 1905. Economic problems
before the repeal of the hated Corn Laws.   3303

Webb, Mary. Precious Bane. Cape, 1924. Welsh border life
and ways at the beginning of the nineteenth century.   3304

Weyman, Stanley J. The Great House. Longmans, 1919. Centered on the controversies caused by the Corn Laws and their
repeal.   3305

_____. Ovington's Bank. Longmans, 1922. The Welsh
border after the Napoleonic Wars and during the development of industry.   3306

_____. Starvecrow Farm. Longmans, 1905. A young girl's
romances amidst social injustices in England early in the century.   3307

White, Hilda. Wild Decembers. Dutton, 1957. The story of
the poor, but very talented, Brontë family.   3308

White, William Hale. The Revolution in Tanner's Lane. by
Mark Rutherford, pseud. Dodd, 1887. Unrest of the lower
middle classes in the first half of the century.   3309

Wilkins, William Vaughan. And So--Victoria. Macmillan, 1937.
Plots and intrigue about the throne in the years before Victoria's accession.   3310

_____. Consort for Victoria. [En. title: Husband for Vic-

toria] Doubleday, 1959. Plot to discredit Albert and force
Victoria to relinquish the throne.   3311

Williams, Lawrence. I, James McNeill Whistler. S. & S.,
1972. The purported autobiography of Whistler, who lived
and painted in England and Europe, with an account of the
lawsuit between himself and Ruskin.   3312

Wilson, Margaret. The Valiant Wife. Doubleday, 1934. A
young wife goes to England to be near her husband, a prisoner at Dartmoor in the War of 1812.   3313

Wilson, Theodora Wilson. Jack O' Peterloo. Labour Pub.,
1924. Shows social injustice and unrest in England at the
outset of the century.   3314

_____. Moll O' the Toll Bar. Hutchinson, 1911. The
rugged, sometimes illegal pursuits of the Cumberland country
folk.   3315

Wright, Constance. Silver Collar Boy. Dutton, 1935. Tells
the story of a little Negro page in the age of Queen Anne. 3316

Wright-Henderson, R.W. John Goodchild. Murray, 1909.
Life in England during Victoria's reign.   3317

   2) Ireland

Ashton, Helen. Hedge of Thorns. Dodd, 1958. The tragic
failure of the potato crop in Ireland in 1846.   3318

Banim, Michael. Crohoore of the Bill-Hook. Duffy (Dublin),
1825. Savage revolt of the down-trodden peasants against
their oppressors in the first quarter of the century.   3319

_____. Father Connell. Newby, 1840. An Irish priest and
his flock in Kilkenny.   3320

Bodkin, M. McDonnell. True Man and Traitor. Duffy (Dublin),
1910. Robert Emmet's college career, romance, and political involvement with Napoleon as well as with the Irish rebellion.   3321

Byrne, Donn. The Field of Honor. Century, 1929. The love
story of a young Irishman in the service of the English minister, Castlereagh.   3322

Carleton, William. The Black Prophet. Sadlier, 1847. The
suffering and endurance of the Irish people during the dread
famine.   3323

_____. Rody the Rover. Duffy (Dublin), 1845. Exploits

of a Ribbonite agent.   3324

_____. The Tithe-Proctor. Duffy (Dublin), 1849. Some-
what biased account of the tithe rebellion of the Irish
peasants.   3325

Cary, Joyce. Castle Corner. Harper, 1963. The heirs of a
Protestant landholding family in Ireland eventually decide to
invest in a risky trading venture in Nigeria.   3326

Colum, Padraic. Castle Conquer. Macmillan, 1923. Conditions centering around the Land Question of the 1870s and
1880s.   3327

Coogan, Beatrice. The Big Wind. Doubleday, 1969. Love
between an Irish girl of noble birth and a young peasant in
the evil days of the potato famine and English oppression.
                                                          3328
Darcy, Clare. Georgina. Walker, 1971. The forbidden romance of a young Englishwoman and an Irish landowner.   3329

Dowsley, William George. Travelling Men. Stokes, 1926.
Entertaining tale of two Irish students which shows the depressed conditions following the Battle of Waterloo.   3330

Du Maurier, Daphne. Hungry Hill. Avon Bks., 1971, c.1943.
The struggle of a proud and passionate Irish family to
achieve the successes they felt due them.   3331

Eden, Dorothy. Never Call It Loving. Coward, 1966. Romance of the Irish leader Charles Stewart Parnell with
Katherine O'Shea, the wife of his Parliamentary colleague.
                                                          3332
Edgeworth, Maria. The Absentee. Macmillan, 1812. Trials
of the tenant farmers left by absentee landlords to the mercy
of unscrupulous agents.   3333

_____. Belinda. Macmillan, 1801. Contrasts between the
rich and the poor in their daily lives.   3334

_____. Ormond. Macmillan, 1817. Tenant farmers aban-
doned to their own resources by absentee landlords who pur-
sue gay and frivolous lives.   3335

_____. Vivian. Dent, 1893. The luxury of the rich in con-
trast to the hardships of the poor.   3336

Gilbert, Rosa Mulholland. Onora. by Rosa Mulholland. De
la More Press, 1900. A girl's pathetic life during the
Land League evictions.   3337

Gwynn, Stephen. Robert Emmet. Macmillan, 1909. Events
leading up to and resulting from the rising in Ireland in

1803 led by Robert Emmet.   3338

Hackett, Francis. The Green Lion. Doubleday, 1936. The
childhood and schooling of Gerald Coyne, who became, at
seven, a follower of Parnell.   3339

Hall, Anna Marie. The Whiteboy. by Mrs. S.C. Hall. Routledge, 1845. An attempt to improve conditions of impoverished peasants.   3340

Hannay, James Owen. The Bad Times. by George A. Birmingham, pseud. Methuen, 1908. Political experiences of a
landlord who advocates home rule in the tense 1870s.   3341

Hartley, May. Ismay's Children. Macmillan, 1887. The conditions of the poverty-stricken peasants and the military activities of the Fenians.   3342

Johnson, Myrtle. The Rising. Appleton, 1938. Irish resistance
to the English culminates in the Fenian uprising of 1867.   3343

Keary, Annie Maria. Castle Daly. Macmillan, 1875. The
anti-English feelings of the starving Irish peasants.   3344

Kelly, Peter Burrowes. The Manor of Glenmore. Butt, 1839.
The actual conditions of the Irish peasants, sympathetically
told.   3345

Keyes, Frances Parkinson. The Heritage. McGraw, 1968.
A Bostonian who inherits his uncle's earldom in Ireland is
confronted by the young widow of his predecessor.   3346

Kickham, Charles J. Knocknagow. Benziger, 1879. A character novel illustrating the arbitrary power of eviction exer-
cised by landlords in mid-century.   3347

King, Richard Ashe. The Wearing of the Green. by Basil, pseud.
Harper, 1885. A romance with the revolutionary Fenian
Brotherhood in the background.   3348

Lawless, Emily. Hurrish. Methuen, 1886. A strong story of
the peasants' attitude toward the land reform issue.   3349

Leslie, Shane. Doomsland. Chatto & Windus, 1923. Life and
politics in the late nineteenth century.   3350

Lever, Charles. Jack Hinton. Little, 1841. A tale of early
century life abounding in humorous character sketches.   3351

_____. The Knight of Gwynne. Routledge, 1847. Irish
life, politics, and character in the first quarter of the century.   3352

_____. St. Patrick's Eve. Munro, 1877. The cholera
epidemic and the general discontent of the Irish tenant
farmers form the background.   3353

McCarthy, Justin. A Fair Saxon. Sheldon, 1873. A member
of Parliament finds his career threatened by involvement
with the Fenians.   3354

_____. Mononia. Chatto, 1901. Combines accounts of a
romance and the attempted insurrection of 1848.   3355

Macken, Walter. The Silent People. Macmillan, 1962. A
young Irishman contends with the threat of starvation and
grasping landlords during the potato famine of the nineteenth
century.   3356

MacManus, Seumas. A Lad of the O'Friels. Digby & Long,
1903. A rather more cheerful than usual picture of the
poor peasants' lot.   3357

Marshall, Muriel. Lovely Rebel. Rinehart, 1950. An Irish
girl, married to an English aristocrat, takes an active part
in the Fenian Rebellion.   3358

Merry, Andrew. The Hunger. Melrose, 1910. Realistic
story based on actual records of the severe famine of the
1840s.   3359

Moran, James J. The Dunferry Risin'. Digby & Long, 1894.
A sympathetic report of the Irish Republican Brotherhood,
the Fenians.   3360

Morgan, Sydney Owenson. The O'Briens and the O'Flahertys.
by Lady Morgan. Colburn, 1827. A young patriot flees Ireland to escape harsh political and religious laws.   3361

_____. O'Donnel. by Lady Morgan. Colburn, 1814. About
a poor, but proud, Irish aristocrat much oppressed by the
cruel penal laws.   3362

_____. The Wild Irish Girl. by Sydney Owenson. Rout-
ledge, 1805. Romance between two young people whose
families have been feuding for centuries.   3363

O'Brien, Kate. Without My Cloak. Doubleday, 1931. An Irish
family of the Victorian era sacrifices freedom for position.
                                                               3364
O'Brien, R.B. The D'Altons of Crag. Duffy (Dublin), 1882.
Shows the desperate situation of the people during the great
famine.   3365

O'Brien, William. When We Were Boys. Longmans, 1890.
Account of the Fennian-Nationalist conflict, written from a

jail cell.   3366

O'Flaherty, Liam. <u>Famine.</u> Random, 1937. The potato
famine in Ireland during the 1840s.   3367

Reade, Amos. <u>Norah Moriarty.</u> Blackwood, 1886. Glad-
stone's advocacy of Irish land reform and home rule.   3368

Rhys, Grace. <u>The Prince of Lisnover.</u> Methuen, 1904. A
romance of Ireland during the Fenian Movement.   3369

Russell, T. O'Neill. <u>Dick Massey.</u> Gill (Dublin), 1869. The
sufferings and evictions of farmers in the first quarter of the
century.   3370

Savage, Marmion W. <u>My Uncle the Curate.</u> Harper, 1849.
A novel of Irish politics in the 1830s.   3371

Sheehan, Patrick A. <u>The Graves at Kilmorna.</u> Longmans,
1915. Tells of the Fenians and their struggles, mentioning
events at Dartmoor prison.   3372

_____. <u>Glenanaar.</u> Longmans, 1905. Conditions in Ireland
in the 1830s, with a family bearing a burden of "inherited
shame."   3373

Thynne, Robert. <u>Ravensdale.</u> Tinsley, 1873. A Loyalist
family during the attempted rebellion led by Emmet.   3374

_____. <u>The Story of a Campaign Estate.</u> Long, 1899.
Sympathetic view of the Irish drive for Home Rule and independence.   3375

Trench, W. Stewart. <u>Ieme.</u> Longmans, 1871. Explains
many aspects of the land question in the latter part of the
century.   3376

Trollope, Anthony. <u>Castle Richmond.</u> Ward & Lock, 1860.
Emphasizes the desperation and horror of the famine of
1845-48.   3377

Walsh, Louis J. <u>The Next Time.</u> Gill (Dublin), 1919. Political unrest from the Catholic Emancipation Bill of '29 to the
Rebellion of '48.   3378

Wibberley, Leonard. <u>Kevin O'Connor and the Light Brigade.</u>
Farrar, 1957. YA. A poor boy of a good old Irish family
runs away to war and takes part in the Battle of Balaklava.
                                                                    3379

b) Western and Central Europe

1) France

Aragon, Louis. Holy Week. (tr.) Putnam, 1961. (orig. pub.
in Fr. in 1958) Migration of Louis XVIII and his court from
Paris during the time of Napoleon's escape from Elba.   3380

Aubry, Octave. The Empress-Might-Have-Been. (tr.)
Harper, 1927. The love of the Polish Marie Walewska
and Napoleon, as well as his romances with Josephine
and Marie Louise of Austria.   3381

Balfour, Andrew. Vengeance Is Mine. New Amsterdam Bk.
Co., 1899. Napoleon at Elba, the Hundred Days, and the
Battle of Waterloo.   3382

Barry, William Francis. The Dayspring. Dodd, 1904. Romance of an Irishman in Paris during the Second Empire. 3383

Beck, Lily Adams. The Thunderer. by E. Barrington, pseud.
Dodd, 1927. The personal life of Napoleon and Josephine
with an account of the Coronation.   3384

Beyle, Marie Henri. The Red and the Black. (tr.) by Stendhal, pseud. Richmond, 1898. Depicts France following the
fall of Napoleon.   3385

Bickerstaffe-Drew, Francis. Dromina. by John Ayscough,
pseud. Putnam, 1909. A romance concerning the supposed "Lost Dauphin" of France, Louis XVII.   3386

Bill, Alfred H. The Clutch of the Corsican. Atlantic Monthly,
1925. A picture of the plight of British hostages in France
toward the end of Napoleon's power.   3387

_____. Highroads of Peril. Little, 1926. The adventures
of an American secret agent of exiled Louis XVIII during
the First Consulate.   3388

Black, Ladbroke and Robert Lynd. The Mantle of the Emperor.
Griffiths, 1906. The early career of Napoleon III (Louis
Napoleon)--his joining the Carbonari, his unsuccessful mili-
tary attempts, and his escape from Ham.   3389

Blake, M.M. Grantley Fenton. Jarrold & Sons, 1902.
Novel based on Napoleon's sojourn at Elba.   3390

Blyth, James. A Bid for Loyalty. Ward & Lock, 1909.
An agent of the Empress Eugénie is entrusted with her
jewels in an attempt to save France in the Franco-Prussian War.   3391

Bourchier, M. H. The Adventures of a Goldsmith. Elkin
Mathews, 1898. The involvement of an English goldsmith
in a plot against Napoleon.   3392

Bowen, Marjorie, pseud. for Long, Gabrielle Campbell.
Forget-Me-Not. Harper, 1953. The passionate battle between two women for the love of a man, and the brutal murder that involved them all.   3393

Bower, Marian. Skipper Anne. Hodder & Stoughton, 1913.
Spying for Napoleon during the Chouan Conspiracy.   3394

Braddon, Mary E. Ishmael. Harper, 1884. Political developments of 1848 and 1851 and their results, with a good account of the coup of 1851.   3395

Broster, Dorothy K. The Wounded Name. Doubleday, Page,
1923. A young French Royalist's romance and adventures,
chiefly during the Hundred Days.   3396

_____. The Yellow Poppy. McBride, 1922. Efforts of
Royalists to rebuild power by finding a buried treasure during the Directorate.   3397

Buchanan, Robert. The Shadow of the Sword. Appleton, 1875.
This novel of Breton shows the effects of war on the common
people.   3398

Campbell, A. Godric. Fleur-de-Camp. Chatto, 1905. This
story of a French girl reflects many important events during the first fifteen years of the century.   3399

Castle, Agnes and Egerton. Wind's Will. Appleton, 1916.
Post-war romance of an English officer and a French flower
girl.   3400

_____. Wolf-Lure. Appleton, 1917. Vigor, action, and
suspense in a tale of castles and counterfeiters.   3401

Chambers, Robert W. (1) Lorraine. Harper, 1898. (2)
Ashes of Empire. Stokes, 1898. (3) The Red Republic.
Putnam, 1895. A trilogy telling of Franco-Prussian War
events--the Declaration of War, Sedan, the eventual surrender of Paris, and ensuing conditions.   3402-4

_____. The Maids of Paradise. Harper, 1902. Contains
excellent descriptions of cavalry charges during the Franco-
Prussian War.   3405

Chamson, André. The Mountain Tavern. (tr.) Holt, 1933.
Tragic story of a young French officer on his way home
after defeat at Waterloo.   3406

Chapman, Hester W. Eugénie. Little, 1961. The life of
the dazzling Empress Eugénie and her efforts to continue
living by outdated standards in a rapidly changing world.   3407

Claretie, Jules. Agnes. (tr.) Stock, 1909. A romance during the German siege of Paris (1870-1).   3408

Coleridge, Mary E. The Fiery Dawn. Longmans, 1901.
Based on the Duchess of Berri's Vendean rebellion--an attempt to gain the throne for her son.   3409

Costain, Thomas B. The Last Love. Doubleday, 1963. Napoleon's friendship for a high-spirited English teen-ager,
Betsy Balcombe, during his exile on St. Helena while he
was imprisoned in her father's house.   3410

Daudet, Alphonse. Kings in Exile. (tr.) Little, 1900. A
Novel of King Christian II of Illyria and his family in exile
in Paris.   3411

_____. The Nabob. (tr.) Heinemann, 1878. Satirical story
of society in Paris during the Second Empire.   3412

_____. Robert Helmont. (tr.) Macmillan, 1896. Horrors
and sufferings during the siege of Paris, written from the
viewpoint of a recluse.   3413

Delderfield, Ronald Frederick. Seven Men of Gascony. Bobbs,
1949. Chronicle of a band of men from Gascony serving
in the Napoleonic campaigns.   3414

_____. Too Few for Drums. S. & S., 1971, c.1964. A
youthful British soldier finds himself in charge of a motley
crew trapped behind French lines.   3415

Dempster, Charlotte L.H. Iseulte. Harper, 1875. Life of
the nobility in the provinces during the Franco-Prussian
War.   3416

Desmond, Alice Curtis. Marie Antoinette's Daughter. Dodd,
1967. About the fascinating, capable woman who suffered
imprisonment and exile before living triumphantly in the
courts of two uncle-kings--Louis XVIII and Charles X.   3417

Doyle, Sir Arthur Conan. (1) The Exploits of Brigadier Gerard. Appleton, 1896. (2) Adventures of Gerard (sequel).
McClure, 1903. Loosely connected episodes in the adventurous career of a blustering, bragging French officer.
3418-9

_____. The Great Shadow. Arrowsmith, 1893. Romance
under the shadow of Napoleon's driving ambition; a fine
description of the Battle of Waterloo.   3420

_____. Uncle Bernac. Appleton, 1897. Northern France
during Napoleon's plans for an invasion of England.   3421

Dumas, Alexandre. The Count of Monte Cristo. (tr.) Routledge, 1888. Imprisoned unjustly on a charge of aiding
the exiled Napoleon, Edmond Dantes plots to escape and
becomes wealthy and powerful.   3422

_____. The She-Wolves of Machecoul. (tr.) Little, 1894.
Depicts the Vendean rebellion of 1832, led by the Duchess
of Berri, who sought to make her son king.   3423

Elwood, Muriel. So Much as Beauty Does. Liveright, 1941.
Romance of Amy Brown and the Duc de Berri, and the way
it was affected by the Bourbon restoration.   3424

Endore, Guy. King of Paris. S. & S., 1956. Fictional biography of Alexandre Dumas--as exciting as any of his novels.
                                                          3425

Erckmann-Chatrian, pseud. for Emile Erckmann and Alexandre
Chatrian. The Plebiscite. (tr.) [same as The Story of the
Plebiscite] Scribner, 1871. Conditions of unpreparedness in
France before and during the Franco-Prussian War.   3426

Fleischmann, Harriet. The Great Enchantment. Chilton, 1967.
The daughter of an Irish mother and a Yankee sea captain
father becomes a piano student of Chopin in Paris.   3427

Fleischmann, Hector. The Emperor's Spy. (tr.) Nash,
1913. The story of a woman who acted as a spy for Napoleon during a conspiracy against his life.   3428

Ford, Ford Madox (name orginally Ford Madox Hueffer). A
Little Less Than Gods. Viking, 1928. The hectic Hundred
Days of Napoleon's attempt to regain power.   3429

Gavin, Catherine Irvine. Madeleine. Beagle Bks., 1972,
c.1957. Romance of a Suez Canal engineer and of a lady-
in-waiting to the Empress Eugénie, wife of Napoleon III. 3430

Gennari, Genevieve. The Riven Heart. (tr.) McKay, 1956.
Seething France during Napoleon's rule and the subsequent
Bourbon restoration.   3431

Gerson, Noel B. The Emperor's Ladies. Doubleday, 1959.
The marriage of Marie Louise of Austria to Napoleon.   3432

Giono, Jean. Horseman on the Roof. (tr.) Knopf, 1954.
Difficult journey through Provence in the midst of a disastrous cholera epidemic. (followed by The Straw Man)   3433

Gonnard, Philippe. Exile of St. Helena. (tr.) Lippincott,
1909. Portrays the Napoleonic legend in its last phase.   3434

Gorham, Charles. Gold of Their Bodies. Dial, 1954. A
novel based on the life of the artist Paul Gauguin.   3435

_____. Wine of Life. Dial, 1958. A long biographical
novel of Honoré de Balzac, whose life was filled with action
and vitality.   3436

Gorman, Herbert Sherman. Brave General. Farrar, 1942.
The career of Georges Boulanger, demagogic military and
political figure.   3437

Gosselin, Louis L. T. The House of the Combrays. (tr.) by
G. Lenôtre, pseud. Dodd, 1903. The historical background
is the Chouan Conspiracy against Napoleon, led by Georges
Cadoudal.   3438

Graves, Clotilde Inez Mary. Between Two Thieves. by Richard Dehan, pseud. Heinemann, 1912. The poor government
and military leadership and the curtailment of popular rights
in Napoleon III's time.   3439

Gribble, Francis. The Dream of Peace. Chatto, 1904. The
retreat into Switzerland of General Bourbaki during the
Franco-Prussian War.   3440

_____. A Romance of the Tuileries. Chapman, 1902. A
romance of the court of Louis Napoleon with an account of
the Revolution of 1848.   3441

Haines, Donald H. The Return of Pierre. Paul, 1912. The
feelings and experiences of a peasant-soldier in the Franco-
Prussian War.   3442

Hall, Moreton. General George. Unwin, 1903. The Chouan
Conspiracy to assassinate Napoleon and Napoleon's unjust
revenge.   3443

Harris, John. Vardy. Sloane, 1965, c.1964. An English girl
turns down a rich suitor in favor of an American soldier
of fortune in the service of France.   3444

Hayes, Frederick W. Captain Kirke Webbe. Hutchinson, 1907.
A delightful rascal manages to be at once a French and an
English privateer.   3445

Herbert, Alan Patrick. Why Waterloo? Doubleday, 1953. Napoleon's activities, from his arrival at Elba to his defeat
at Waterloo.   3446

Hibbert, Eleanor. The King of the Castle. by Victoria Holt,
pseud. Doubleday, 1967. A young English artist who comes
to a French chateau to restore old paintings finds herself
deeply involved in the rather complicated family history.   3447

Hodge, Jane Aiken. The Adventurers. Doubleday, 1965. A
young card player of questionable repute escorts two gentle-
women through France and Germany in the wake of Napoleon's
army.   3448

Jacob, Naomi Ellington. Founder of the House. Macmillan,
1936. A Jewish family of art dealers amidst the life of
nineteenth century Paris, Vienna, and London.   3449

Johnson, David. Proud Canaries. [En. title: Sabre General]
Sloane, 1959. A cavalryman tells of Napoleon's European
campaigns from 1806 to 1809.   3450

Kane, Harnett T. The Amazing Mrs. Bonaparte. Doubleday,
1963. Outcome of the romantic marriage of the Baltimore
beauty, Betsy Patterson, to Jerome Bonaparte, brother of
Napoleon.   3451

Kavanagh, Julia. Madeleine. Appleton, 1848. The heroine,
disappointed in love, founds and runs an orphanage.   3452

Kenyon, Frank Wilson. The Emperor's Lady. Crowell, 1953,
c.1952. A story of the Empress Josephine, consort of Napoleon I, Emperor of the French.   3453

_____. Imperial Courtesan. Dodd, 1967. The wealthy
English mistress of Louis Napoleon financed his political
rise because of her love and of his written promise of
marriage.   3454

_____. My Brother Napoleon. Dodd, 1971. The story of
Caroline Bonaparte, Napoleon's charming, scheming sister,
who manipulated men and events to attain her own ends.   3455

_____. That Spanish Woman. Dodd, 1963, c.1962. (first
pub. in 1962 as I, Eugénia) Brilliance and character of the
charming Empress Eugénie, wife of Louis Napoleon III.   3456

Knowles, Mabel Winifred. A Spy for Napoleon. by May
Wynne, pseud. Jarrolds Ltd., 1917. Shows conspiracy
against the revolutionary government and the spy system of
Fouché.   3457

Komroff, Manuel. Waterloo. Coward, 1936. Napoleon's escape from Elba and his smashing defeat at Waterloo.   3458

La Mure, Pierre. Clair de Lune. Random House, 1962.
Many love affairs of the unconventional music composer,
Claude Debussy.   3459

Landau, Mark Aleksandrovich. Saint Helena, Little Island.
(tr.) by M.A. Aldanov, pseud. Knopf, 1924. A story
of Napoleon's last illness and death.   3460

Lansworth, Lew X. Over the River Charlie. Doubleday,
1956. Paris during the Prussian siege of 1870-71.   3461

Leblanc, Maurice. The Frontier. (tr.) Mills & Boon, 1912.
A border incident during the Franco-Prussian War.   3462

Lee, Albert. The Emperor's Trumpeter. Shaw, 1907. Napoleon's rise and a description of deserted Moscow between its
abandonment by the Russians and its burning by the French.
                                                            3463

Lenanton, Carola Oman. Major Grant. by Carola Oman.
Holt, 1932. About one of Wellington's spies during the
Peninsular War.   3464

Le Poer, John. A Modern Legionary. Methuen, 1904. A
realistic account of French Foreign Legion service in Algeria.   3465

Levy, Barbara. Place of Judgment. Doubleday, 1965. Based
on the 1840 trial of a Parisian girl accused of poisoning her
dullard husband.   3466

Lodi, Maria. Charlotte Morel. (tr.) (v.1) Putnam, 1969,
c.1965. A romantic novel about a provincial girl who marries and goes to live in Paris during the dictatorship of Napoleon III. (followed by Charlotte Morel: the Dream)   3467

_____. Charlotte Morel: the Dream. (tr.) (v.2) Put-
nam, 1970, c.1965. A tale of romance in the time of Napoleon III's crumbling empire, involving Thomas Becque,
editor of the revolutionary paper Le Surin. (followed by:
Charlotte Morel: The Siege)   3468

Longstreet, Stephen and Ethel. Man of Montmartre. Funk,
1958. An exciting picture of the artistic life of Paris
emerges in this biographical novel of Maurice Utrillo.   3469

Lovelace, Maud Hart. Petticoat Court. Day, 1930. The
court of the Empress Eugénie in the days of Napoleon III. 3470

Lytton, Edward Bulwer, 1st. baron. The Parisians. Dutton,
1873. A picture of the various types of French society.   3471

McAllister, Alister. The Two of Diamonds. by Anthony
Wharton, pseud. Collins, 1926. Paris during the Second
Empire with Napoleon III, Zola, and Flaubert.   3472

Malling, Matilda. A Romance of the First Consul. (tr.)
Heinemann, 1898. About a La Vendée girl who falls in
love with Napoleon.   3473

Malm, Dorothea. On a Fated Night. Doubleday, 1965. A
bride is received with coldness and resentment at her in-

laws' estate, and a suspenseful murder mystery ensues.   3474

Manceron, Claude. So Brief a Spring. Putnam, 1958. The
"brief spring" is Napoleon's one-hundred-day bid to regain
his former power.   3475

Margueritte, Paul and Victor. The Disaster. (tr.) Greening,
1898. An account of the Franco-Prussian War in the vicinity
of Metz.   3476

_____. Strasbourg. (tr.) Dutton, 1916. The courage of two
Strasbourg families during the Franco-Prussian War.   3477

Margueritte, Victor. The Frontiers of the Heart. (tr.) Stokes,
1913. Pressures in the home of a French girl and her Prussian husband during the Franco-Prussian War.   3478

Marsh, Frances. The Iron Game. Fifield, 1909. A story of
the Franco-Prussian War of 1870-71.   3479

Morrison, Peggy. I, Rachel. by March Cost, pseud. Vanguard, 1957. The life and career of Elisa Felix, who became a great European actress under the name of Rachel. 3480

Murray, David Leslie. Tale of Three Cities. Knopf, 1940.
The three cities of the title are Paris, London, and Rome.
                                                          3481
Murray, E.C. Grenville. The Member for Paris. Smith &
Elder, 1871. "A tale of the Second Empire."   3482

Neumann, Alfred. Another Caesar. (tr.) [En. title: The
New Caesar] Knopf, 1934. A story of Louis Napoleon III,
who believed in his destiny as emperor of the French.   3483

_____. The Friends of the People. (tr.) Hutchinson,
1940. The political unrest of Paris during the reverses
of 1870 and 1871.   3484

_____. The Gaudy Empire. (tr.) [En. title: Man of De-
cember] Knopf, 1937. Portrait of Napoleon III and his fall
from power, 1856 to 1870.   3485

Ohnet, Georges. The Eagle's Talon. (tr.) Putnam, 1913.
Displays the people's discontent with the revolutionary government.   3486

Orcutt, William Dana. The Flower of Destiny. McClurg,
1905. Louis Napoleon's escape, marriage, and taking
of the Imperial title.   3487

Orczy, Baroness Emmuska. The Bronze Eagle. Doran, 1915.
Conflict between Royalists and Bonapartists during the Hundred Days.   3488

_____. Castles in the Air. Doran, 1922. Adventures of
a charming rogue in Paris after Napoleon's defeat.   3489

_____. Joyous Adventure. Doubleday, 1932. An English
gentleman sets out to find the heir to the French throne,
who is in hiding in Normandy.   3490

_____. Sheaf of Bluebells. Doran, 1917. A French noble-
woman plots to overthrow Napoleon.   3491

_____. A Spy of Napoleon. Putnam, 1934. Romance and
intrigue in the police-state of Napoleon III.   3492

Oxenham, John, pseud. for William Arthur Dunkerley. Broken
Shackles. Lane, 1915. Military tale of Bourbaki's attack on
the Prussians and subsequent retreat.   3493

_____. Great-Heart Gillian. Hodder, 1909. The French
army's fateful march to Sedan and the battle which ensued. 3494

_____. Our Lady of Deliverance. Hutchinson, 1901. A
novel of the Dreyfus case, in which a man falsely convicted
of treason was finally cleared.   3495

Pardo Bazán, Emilia. The Mystery of the Lost Dauphin. (tr.)
Funk & Wagnalls, 1906. What became of the son of Marie
Antoinette?   3496

Paretti, Sandra. The Rose and the Sword. (tr.) Coward, 1969,
c.1968. An aristocratic French girl defends her purity amidst
the license and excesses of Napoleonic France.   3497

Pemberton, Max. The Hundred Days. Appleton, 1905. The
period of Napoleon's bid to regain power.   3498

_____. The Virgin Fortress. Cassell, 1912. Siege, cap-
ture, and spying at Metz in the Franco-Prussian War.   3499

Pilgrim, David, pseud. for John Leslie Palmer and Hilary
Aiden St. George Saunders. So Great a Man. Macmillan,
1937. Napoleon's life during the ten months from March,
1808, to January, 1809.   3500

Poldermans, Joost. Vincent. Holt, 1962. The talented but un-
stable Dutch painter Van Gogh in the revolutionary art world
of the late nineteenth century.   3501

Powers, Anne. The Thousand Fires. Bobbs, 1957. The
battles and adventures of the final years of Napoleon's
power.   3502

Praviel, Armand. The Murder of Monsieur Fualdès. (tr.)
Seltzer, 1924. Deals with the murder of an ex-prosecutor

and its discovery.   3503

Ralli, Constantine S.   The Tyranny of Honour.   Chapman, 1911.
A court trial concerning a contested fortune with a background
of the Franco-Prussian War.   3504

_____.   The Wisdom of the Serpent.   Griffith, 1907.   The
battle of Vionville-Mars la Tour in the Franco-Prussian War
is described.   3505

Rawson, Maud Stepney.   Journeyman Love.   Hutchinson, 1902.
The development of culture and politics in rebellious mid-
century Paris.   3506

Rayner, Denys Arthur.   The Long Fight.   Holt, 1958.   A little-
known British-French sea battle in the Indian Ocean in 1808.
                                                                  3507

Reitzel, William.   The Pinnacle of Glory.   by Wilson Wright,
pseud.   Macmillan, 1935.   The activities of Napoleon during
his exile on St. Helena.   3508

Renard, Jules.   Poil de Carotte.   (tr.)   Walker, 1967.   (first
pub. in Fr. in 1894)   Portrays a sad childhood in a bourgeois
French family in which the selfish mother continually abuses
the little boy.   3509

Rijen, Adolf Josef Hubert Frans van.   The Tormented.   (tr.)
[En. title: The Poor Wedding Guest]   Doubleday, 1960.   A
biographical novel of Paul Verlaine, brilliant, dissolute
poet.   3510

Ritchie, Rita.   Night Coach to Paris.   Norton, 1970.   YA. An
American searches for his cousin in France during the Reign
of Terror.   3511

Roth, Joseph.   The Ballad of the Hundred Days.   Viking, 1936.
Napoleon's return from Elba told from the viewpoint of a
laundress infatuated with him.   3512

Rudigoz, Roger.   French Dragoon.   (tr.)   Coward, 1959.   Adventures of a cavalryman after the French defeat at Leipzig
in 1813.   3513

Sabatini, Rafael.   The Lost King.   Houghton, 1937.   The mystery of the Lost Dauphin of France, Louis XVII.   3514

Savidge, Eugene Coleman.   The American in Paris.   Lippincott, 1895.   The turmoil during the siege of Paris by the
Germans.   3515

Schonthan, Gaby von.   The Roses of Malmaison.   (tr.)   Meredith, 1968.   The resilient Marie Beauharnais (Napoleon's
Josephine) who, after other loves, marries Napoleon and is

crowned Empress of France.   3516

Scott, Hugh S. The Last Hope. by H. Seton Merriman, pseud.
Scribner, 1904. A story of the Lost Dauphin, Louis XVII,
and his supposed son.   3517

Seawell, Molly Elliot. The Fortunes of Fifi. Bobbs, 1903.
The story of a French actress.   3518

Shackelford, Henry. The Lost King. Brentano's, 1903. One
theory of the escape of Marie Antoinette's son.   3519

Stacpoole, Henry de Vere. The Drums of War. Duffield,
1910. Competition between Prussia and France at the time
of Napoleon III and Bismarck.   3520

Stephens, Eve. Valentina. by Evelyn Anthony, pseud. Doubleday, 1966. A Polish countess finds both bitterness and love
as she is forced to become a spy during the Napoleonic
Wars.   3521

Stone, Irving. Lust for Life. Longmans, 1934. Story of the
tortured genius now recognized as a great artist, Vincent Van
Gogh.   3522

Strachey, John St. Loe. The Madonna of the Barricades. Harcourt, 1925. A dedicated young couple fights for freedom in
the Revolution of 1848.   3523

Troyat, Henri. The Brotherhood of the Red Poppy. (tr.) S. &
S., 1961. At the close of the Napoleonic Era a Russian lieutenant marries and takes to Russia a charming young Parisi-
enne.   3524

Ullman, James Ramsey. The Day on Fire. World, 1958. A
novel suggested by the life of Arthur Rimbaud, French poet
and adventurer.   3525

Vidalie, Albert. The Moonlight Jewelers. (tr.) Farrar, 1958.
Bandits who robbed at night terrified most French provincials,
but one girl fell deeply in love with a brigand and fled to the
forest with him.   3526

Wagner, Geoffrey A. Nicchia. Day, 1959, c.1958. Story of
the captivating Countess of Castiglione, who was sent by
Cavour to seduce Emperor Napoleon III.   3527

_____. Sophie. Ward, 1957. A smuggler's daughter be-
comes wealthy and influential by improper means.   3528

Weiss, David. Naked Came I. Morrow, 1963. Fictionalized
story of the life of Auguste Rodin, showing the many years
of work and frustration before he achieved acclaim as a

sculptor.   3529

Werfel, Franz. Song of Bernadette. (tr.) Viking, 1942. Account of fourteen-year-old St. Bernadette and her "beautiful lady," Mary.   3530

Wilkins, William Vaughan. Being Met Together. Macmillan, 1944. A young American is an agent for Napoleon and tries to rescue him from St. Helena.   3531

2) Central Europe (including Germany, the Netherlands, Switzerland, Austria, Hungary, Czechoslovakia, and Poland)

Abrahams, William Miller. Imperial Waltz. Dial, 1954. Empress Elizabeth of Austria and her marriage to Franz Joseph of Hungary.   3532

Agnon, Samuel Joseph. The Bridal Canopy. (tr.) Schoecken Bks., 1967. (orig. pub. in 1937) A poor Polish Jew wanders through Galicia with a friend in quest of dowries for his daughters and tells stories during the journey.   3533

Andric, Ivo. Bosnian Story. (tr.) London House & Maxwell, 1959. The people and atmosphere of the seven years before Napoleon's fall.   3534

_____. The Bridge on the Drina. (tr.) Macmillan, 1959. (first pub. in 1945) The bridge over the Drina, separating Bosnia from Serbia, was built by orders of the Sultan's Grand Vizier Mehmed Pasha Sokolli. (followed by Bosnian Story)   3535

Arnold, Michael P. The Archduke. Doubleday, 1967. The tragic love of Crown Prince Rudolph of Hapsburg for the beautiful Baroness Maria Vetsera.   3536

Asch, Shalom. Salvation. (tr.) Putnam, 1934. Story based on the activities of a Jewish rabbi in a small Polish village.   3537

Bass, Eduard. Umberto's Circus. (tr.) Farrar, 1951. A Czech mason in need of work joins a travelling European circus, leading to circus careers for both himself and his son.   3538

Baum, Vicki. Headless Angel. Doubleday, 1948. A German countess who sought happiness in Mexico returns to a reconciliation with her husband.   3539

Berckman, Evelyn. A Finger to Her Lips. Doubleday, 1971. The Duchess of Volingen-Ilm bears a bastard son whom her husband seeks to destroy.   3540

Beyerlein, Franz Adam. "Jena" or "Sedan"? (tr.) Heinemann, 1904. The military life of soldiers from all walks
of society.   3541

Bloem, Walter. The Iron Year. (tr.) Lane, 1914. A novel
of people and events in the Franco-Prussian War.   3542

Blum, Eliezer. Revolt of the Apprentices and Other Stories.
(tr.) by Eliezer Blum-Alquit. T. Yoseloff, 1969. Several
stories concerning Jews in Poland and old New York, translated from the Yiddish.   3543

Born, Edith de. Felding Castle. [En. title: Schloss Felding]
Knopf, 1959. The upbringing of a young girl in a family of
Austrian nobility at the turn of the century.   3544

Brenner, Jacques. Nephew to the Emperor. (tr.) World,
1959. Beethoven's nephew, although he loved his famous
uncle, found it hard to live in the shadow of genius.   3545

Brontë, Charlotte. Villette. Tauchnitz, 1853. School life in
the nineteenth century in Brussels, Belgium.   3546

Carr, Mildred E. A Knight of Poland. Smith & Elder, 1910.
Revolt is provoked by the impressment of Poles into the·
Russian army.   3547

_____. Love and Honour. Putnam, 1901. Shows the career
of Jerome Bonaparte, Napoleon's younger brother, as ruler
of Westphalia.   3548

Castle, Agnes and Egerton. If Youth But Knew! Macmillan,
1906. A romance in Westphalia during the rule of the weak
Jerome Bonaparte.   3549

Chatfield-Taylor, H.C. The Crimson Wing. Stone, 1902. Adventures of the crown prince, later to become Frederick III,
in the Franco-Prussian War.   3550

Cramb, J.A. Schönbrunn. Putnam, 1918. Napoleon at the
height of his power in the period of the Treaty of Schönbrunn (1809).   3551

Doderer, Heimito von. The Waterfalls of Slunj. (tr.) Harcourt,
1966. A detailed picture of Viennese life as an English family
of manufacturers settles there.   3552

Dodge, Mary Mapes. Hans Brinker; or, The Silver Skates.
World, 1946, c. 1865. YA. The touching story of the little
Dutch boy who had so great a yearning for the silver skates
and so great a devotion to his family that he would give them
up.   3553

Franzos, Karl Emil. For the Right. Clarke, 1888. An un-
educated rural judge does his best to dispense impartial
justice.   3554

Frenssen, Gustav. Jörn Uhl. (tr.) Estes, 1905. German
provincial life--the hero is a peasant--in the period of the
Franco-Prussian War.   3555

_____. The Three Comrades. (tr.) Estes, 1907. Life in
Schleswig-Holstein during the Franco-Prussian War.   3556

Freytag, Gustav. Debit and Credit. Ward & Lock, 1856. The
changing economic conditions in Germany during the Industrial
Revolution.   3557

Frischauer, Paul. A Great Lord. Random, 1937. A story of
life in Poland during Napoleonic times.   3558

Gasiorowski, Waclaw. Napoleon's Love-Story. (tr.) Dutton,
1905. The part played in his treatment of Poland by the
romance of Napoleon and Madame Walewska.   3559

Gregg, Hilda Caroline. A Brother of Girls. by Sydney C.
Grier, pseud. Blackwood, 1925. The political activities
and romantic affairs of an English diplomat in Europe.   3560

_____. (1) The Strong Hand. Blackwood, 1920. (2) Out
of Prison (sequel). Blackwood, 1922. both by Sydney C.
Grier, pseud. Laid chiefly in Germany between 1806 and
1814, these novels depict Napoleon's growing influence.   3561-2

Grogger, Paula. The Door in the Grimming. Putnam, 1936.
The Catholic peasantry in Styria during the Napoleonic invasion of Austria.   3563

Hartley, M. A Sereshan. Mills & Boon, 1911. A tale of action including the Vienna revolution and the rebellion of the
Hungarians in 1848.   3564

Hatton, Joseph. By Order of the Czar. Munro, 1890. Torture and revenge during the persecution of the Jews in
Poland.   3565

Hauser, Marianne. Prince Ishmael. Stein and Day, 1963. At-
temps of an actual Nuremberg youth, forcibly confined until
the age of sixteen, to adapt to civilized society.   3566

Hector, Annie French. Maid, Wife, or Widow? by Mrs.
Alexander, pseud. Munro, 1884. A romance of the Franco-
Prussian War.   3567

Heyer, Georgette. An Infamous Army. Doubleday, Doran,
1938. The Battle of Waterloo seen from Brussels with

the Duke of Wellington as man of the hour.   3568

Jeans, Alice. The Stronger Wings. Stock, 1909. Shows how
higher education and the spread of new ideas led to the uprising in Vienna in 1848.   3569

Jókai, Maurus. The Baron's Sons. (tr.) Page, 1900. A
widow and her sons in the Revolution of 1848.   3570

_____. The Day of Wrath. (tr.) McClure, 1900. Crime,
disease, and poverty leading up to the Magyar Revolution of
1848.   3571

_____. Debts of Honour. (tr.) Doubleday, 1900. Tale
of the Hungarian insurrection of 1848 and of a family pursued by a curse.   3572

_____. An Hungarian Nabob. (tr.) Doubleday, 1898.
The rich, extravagant way of life of a wealthy Hungarian
landowner.   3573

_____. Manasseh. (tr.) Page, 1901. The simple life
and brutal fighting of the Transylvanians in 1848.   3574

_____. The Nameless Castle. (tr.) Doubleday, 1898.
Based on a report that Marie Antoinette had a daughter who
was hidden in a castle in Hungary.   3575

_____. The New Landlord. (tr.) Macmillan, 1868. An
elderly Hungarian landowner offers passive resistance to the
hated Austrians in 1848.   3576

Komroff, Manuel. Feast of the Jesters. Farrar, 1947. A
troupe of French actors who entertained during the Congress
of Vienna.   3577

Longard de Longgarde, Dorothea Gerard. A Glorious Lie. by
Dorothea Gerard. Long, 1912. Domestic tragedy in Austria
during the conflict with Prussia.   3578

Lundegård, Axel. The Storm Bird. (tr.) Hodder, 1895. A
novel of Vienna in 1848.   3579

Mann, Thomas. The Beloved Returns. (tr.) Knopf, 1940.
The Lotte of Goethe's Sorrows of Werther visits the author
after forty years.   3580

_____. Buddenbrooks. (tr.) (2 v.) Knopf, 1924. (orig.
pub. about 1904 in Germany) Rise and decline of a prosperous merchant family in Lubeck through four generations.   3581

Marlowe, Derek. A Single Summer With Lord B. [En. title:
A Single Summer With L. B.] Viking, 1970, c.1969. The

summer of 1816, spent by Lord Byron in the company of
Shelley and three others at Switzerland's Lake Geneva.   3582

Meding, Oskar. For Sceptre and Crown. by Gregor Samarow,
pseud. King, 1875. A novel based on events in the Austrian
War.   3583

Meredith, George. The Tragic Comedians. Scribner, 1880.
A romance based on the later life of Ferdinand Lassalle,
a Socialist who agitated for labor unions.   3584

Mundt, Klara. Andreas Hofer. (tr.) by Louisa Mühlbach,
pseud. Appleton, 1868. An account of the Tyrol during and
after the 1809 revolt led by Hofer.   3585

_____. (1) Louisa of Prussia and Her Times. (tr.) Apple-
ton, 1867. (2) Napoleon and the Queen of Prussia (sequel).
(tr.) Appleton, 1867. (3) Napoleon and Blücher (sequel).
(tr.) Appleton, 1867. all by Louisa Mühlbach, pseud. Include Napoleon's campaigns against Prussia and Russia and
his treaty with Alexander of Prussia which resulted in the
formation of Westphalia.   3586-8

Neumann, Robert. A Woman Screamed. Dial, 1938. The revolt of the Hungarians against Hapsburg rule.   3589

Nordling, John. The Moonlight Sonata. (tr.) Sturgis & Walton, 1912. Based on the career of Beethoven during his
growing deafness.   3590

Openshaw, Mary. The Cross of Honour. Laurie, 1910. Warsaw romance of Napoleon and Madame Walewska.   3591

Oxenham, John, pseud. for William Arthur Dunkerley. John of
Gerisau. Hurst, 1902. European wars in the 1860s--Prus-
sia, Austria, Germany, France.   3592

Pemberton, Max. The Garden of Swords. Dodd, 1899. Effect of the Franco-Prussian War on those who remained at
home.   3593

Pidoll, Carl von. Eroica. (tr.) Methuen, 1956. Purported
narration by a friend of Beethoven telling of the musician's
career.   3594

Reuter, Fritz. In the Year '13. (tr.) Tauchnitz, 1867. A
spirited story of rural life showing the German reaction to
Napoleon's invading army.   3595

_____. Seed Time and Harvest. (tr.) Low, 1878. Daily
life in rural Mecklenburg, and reactions to the Revolution
of 1848.   3596

Rosegger, Peter. The Forest Schoolmaster. (tr.) Putnam,
1901. Story of a schoolmaster of Napoleonic times in the
Alpine forests.   3597

Scott, Hugh S. Barlasch of the Guard. by H. Seton Merriman, pseud. McClure, Phillips, 1903. About a family in
Danzig during the Napoleonic invasion of Russia.   3598

_____. The Vultures. by H. Seton Merriman, pseud.
Harper, 1902. Foreign secret agents, Polish revolt, and
the assassination of Czar Alexander II in 1881.   3599

Seidel, Ina. The Wish Child. Farrar, 1935. Two young
cousins in Germany during the Napoleonic era.   3600

Simpson, Helen D. Saraband for Dead Lovers. Doubleday,
1935. The story of Sophia Dorothea, Electress of Hanover,
divorced and imprisoned for infidelity.   3601

Singer, Isaac. The Estate. (tr.) Farrar, 1969. (written between 1952-1955) Vivid picture of the life of Polish Jews in
the late nineteenth century and the flight of some to America.   3602

_____. Gimpel the Fool and Other Stories. (tr.) Noonday,
1957. Tales concerning the Jewish ghetto of nineteenth century Poland, filled with folklore.   3603

_____. The Magician of Lublin. (tr.) Noonday, 1960.
A talented circus performer in Poland.   3604

_____. The Manor. (tr.) Farrar, 1967. (written between
1953-55) The changing fortunes of a Jewish family whose
head has profitably leased a Polish estate confiscated by the
Russians. (followed by The Estate)   3605

Skelton, Gladys. Barricade. by John Presland, pseud. Philip
Allan, 1926. A romance based on the uprising in Vienna in
1848.   3606

Spielhagen, Friedrich. The Hohensteins. (tr.) Holt, 1870.
Follows three generations of the Hohenstein family from
1848.   3607

Stone, Irving. The Passions of the Mind. New American Lib.,
1972, c.1971. Biographical novel of Sigmund Freud, Austrian physician who developed the modern method of psychoanaly-
sis and the theory of the role of sexual desire.   3608

Strachey, Marjorie. The Nightingale. Longmans, 1925.
Novel based on the life of the great Polish musician,
Chopin.   3609

Sudermann, Hermann. Regina. (tr.) Lane, 1905. A story
of eastern Prussia in which the sins of a father affect the
life of his son.   3610

Tautphoebus, Baroness Jemima von. At Odds. Lippincott,
1863. Bavaria is the scene for this tale of a romantic tri-
angle.   3611

Thompson, Morton. The Cry and the Covenant. Doubleday,
1949. Fictional biography of a famous Hungarian obstetri-
cian and early foe of infection, Ignaz Semmelweis.   3612

Tickell, Jerrard. Hussar Honeymoon. Doubleday, 1963. The
rivalry of two officer candidates for both the colonel's daughter and a military post in Budapest in 1900.   3613

Weiss, David. The Assassination of Mozart. Morrow, 1971.
In the early nineteenth century a young American composer
attempts to solve the mystery surrounding the death of Mozart
in 1791 and the disappearance of his body.   3614

Westall, William. A Red Bridal. Chatto, 1898. Resistance
of the Tyroleans, led by Hofer, to the French and Bavar-
ians.   3615

_____. With the Red Eagle. Chatto, 1897. An English-
Irish soldier joins the Tyrolese revolt. (followed by A Red
Bridal)   3616

Weyman, Stanley J. The Traveller in the Fur Cloak. Longmans, 1924. Adventures and misadventures of an English
diplomat abroad.   3617

White, Hilda. Song Without End. Dutton, 1959. YA. The love
story of Clara Wieck and Robert Schumann, both of whom
were music students of Clara's father.   3618

Zilahy, Lajos. Century in Scarlet. McGraw, 1965. Aristocratic Hungarian twins represent opposing forces of liberalism and conservatism in their own country and abroad during a period of social and economic revolution.   3619

3) Scandinavia and the Baltic

Dixelius, Hildur. The Minister's Daughter. Dutton, 1926.
Colorful novel of people and events in Lapland at the start
of the century.   3620

Dunlop, Agnes Mary Robertson. The Swedish Nightingale. by
Elisabeth Kyle, pseud. Holt, 1965, c.1964. YA. Spark-
ling life and career of the internationally famous singer,
Jenny Lind.   3621

Geelmuyden, Hans. Oceans Free. (tr.) Harper, 1962.
Rise of an enterprising young Norwegian seaman to the
position of ship's captain and his romance with a Boston
girl.   3622

Gulbranssen, Trygve. Beyond Sing the Woods. (tr.) Putnam,
1936. Saga of Norwegian farmers on their family estate in
the hills. (followed by The Wind From the Mountains)   3623

_____. The Wind From the Mountains. (tr.) Putnam,
1937. The strength and beauty of rugged Norway shows
in this tale of family life.   3624

Gunnarsson, Gunnar. The Black Cliffs. (tr.) Univ. of Wisc.
Pr., 1967. Psychological novel based on the sensational
trial of a man and woman for murder in Iceland in the early
nineteenth century.   3625

Hamsun, Knut. Mysteries. (tr.) Farrar, 1971. (orig. pub.
in Norway in 1892) Psychological novel concerning an eccentric stranger who briefly soujourned in a small Norwegian
coastal community.   3626

_____. Victoria. (tr.) Farrar, 1969. (first pub. in 1898)
A miller's son and the daughter of a land-owner fall in love,
but the difference in their fortunes forbids marriage.   3627

Hubbard, Margaret Ann. Flight of the Swan. Bruce, 1946.
Based on the life of story teller Hans Christian Andersen. 3628

Lagerlöf, Selma. Gosta Berling's Saga. Amer. Scandinavian
Foundation, 1891. A Swedish novel depicting life about
1820.   3629

Laxness, Halldor. The Fish Can Sing. (tr.) Crowell, 1967.
The growing-up of a young man shows the customs and life-
style of Iceland at the turn of the century.   3630

_____. Paradise Reclaimed. (tr.) Crowell, 1962. Experi-
ences and observations of an Icelandic farmer who is persuaded by a Mormon preacher to make the long pilgrimage
to Utah.   3631

McDonald, Julie. Amalie's Story. S. & S., 1970. The story
of a Danish couple who grow up, fall in love and marry in
Denmark, and finally emigrate to America.   3632

Moberg, Vilhelm. The Emigrants. (tr.) S. & S., 1951.
A peasant family in Sweden and their voyage to America in
1850. (followed by Unto a Good Land)   3633

Sorensen, Virginia. Kingdom Come. Harcourt, 1960. Portrays the deep religious convictions which drove many

Scandinavians to emigrate to America.   3634

Strindberg, August. The Natives of Hemsö. (tr.) Eriksson,
    1965. (written in 1887) Struggle for survival against nat-
    ural elements and other influences in a small community
    on a rocky island off the coast of Sweden.   3635

_____. The Scapegoat. (tr.) Eriksson, 1967. (orig. pub.
    in 1906) A young lawyer beset by the past seeks to carve
    out a new life for himself in a Swedish mountain village. 3636

Wright, Theon. The Knife. Gilbert Press, 1955. The steel-
    bladed knife introduces civilization to the primitive Eskimos in
    mid-nineteenth century Greenland.   3637

    c) Southern Europe

    1) Iberian Peninsula

Alarcón, Pedro Antonio de. The Infant With the Globe. (tr.)
    T. Yoseloff, 1959, c.1955. Broken hearts and bloody deaths
    in Spain in 1840.   3638

_____. The Three-Cornered Hat. (tr.) Cassell, 1891. Ro-
    mance in an Andalusian village based on folk tales.   3639

Bailey, H.C. The Young Lovers. Methuen, 1918. A story
    of some of the battles in the Peninsular War.   3640

Baroja y Nessi, Pio. The Restlessness of Shanti Andia. (tr.)
    Univ. of Mich. Pr., 1959. A novel and a collection of
    shorter works concerning nineteenth century Basques in
    Spain.   3641

Braider, Donald. Rage in Silence. Putnam, 1969. The later
    years of the great artist Goya and his attachment for the
    Duchess of Alba and, after her death, for his mistress.   3642

Champion de Crespigny, Rose. The Spanish Prisoner. by Mrs.
    Philip Champion de Crespigny. Nash, 1907. A romance,
    interrupted by the war with England, results in adventure in
    disguise.   3643

Conrad, Joseph. The Arrow of Gold. Doubleday, 1920. Story
    of a strange, mysterious woman told by the man who loved
    her.   3644

Craigie, Mrs. Pearl Mary. The School for Saints. by John
    Oliver Hobbes, pseud. Stokes, 1897. An Englishman in-
    volved with Marshal Prim and the Carlist outbreak in Spain.
    (followed by Robert Orange)   3645

Crockett, Samuel R. The Firebrand. McClure, 1901. Story
of Queen Christina during the Carlist Wars.   3646

Daudet, Ernest. Rafael. (tr.) Low, 1895. Napoleon and
Charles IV of Spain figure in this tale of the Iberian Peninsula.   3647

Eça de Queiroz, José María de. The City and the Mountains.
(tr.) Ohio Univ. Pr., 1967. (first pub. in 1901) A profli-
gate young Portuguese nobleman is called away from the rev-
elries of Paris to the rural countryside of his ancestors. 3648

_____. Illustrious House of Ramires. (tr.) Ohio Univ. Pr.,
1968. (written in 1900) The effort of Gonzalo Ramires to
obtain a political office without losing his family honor.   3649

_____. The Maias. (tr.) St. Martin's, 1965. A novel of
high society in Lisbon in which a young man unwittingly falls
in love with his long-lost sister.   3650

_____. The Sin of Father Amaro. (tr.) St. Martin's,
1963, c.1962. (orig. pub. in 1874) The corruption of a
Portuguese clergyman destroys his associates.   3651

Forester, C.S. The Gun. Little, 1933. A story of the Peninsular War and the part played by a particular gun.   3652

Fortescue, John W. The Drummer's Coat. Macmillan, 1899.
A novel concerning the Peninsular War.   3653

Gregg, Hilda Caroline. A Young Man Married. by Sydney C.
Grier, pseud. Blackwood, 1909. A Spanish girl and an
English soldier in Spain during the Peninsular War.   3654

Hewlett, Maurice. The Spanish Jade. Doubleday, 1908. Romance of an Englishman in Spain.   3655

Heyer, Georgette. The Spanish Bride. Bantam Bks., 1970,
c.1940. Romance of an English officer and a Spanish
lady.   3656

Hodge, Jane Aiken. The Winding Stair. Doubleday, 1969, c.1968.
A young Englishwoman comes to live with her grandmother in
Portugal and joins in that lady's spying activities during the
Napoleonic Wars.   3657

Lever, Charles. Charles O'Malley. Little, 1841. Battles,
duels, and travels during the Peninsular War.   3658

_____. Tom Burke of Ours. Macmillan, 1844. The career
of an Irishman in Napoleon's service during victories, conspiracies, and defeats.   3659

Oldmeadow, Ernest J. Antonio. Century, 1909. A young
    monk affected by the suppression of monasteries in Portu-
    gal.   3660

Pérez-Galdós, Benito. Saragossa. (tr.) Little, 1899. A
    novel based on the siege of Saragossa in 1808.   3661

_____. Trafalgar. (tr.) Gottsberger, 1884. Strategy of
    Villeneuve and Nelson in their decisive naval encounter.   3662

Sabatini, Rafael. The Snare. Lippincott, 1917. Revolves
    around Wellington's action against the French in Portugal. 3663

Scott, Hugh S. In Kedar's Tents. by H. Seton Merriman,
    pseud. Dodd, 1897. Struggle for power in Spain between
    Don Carlos and the Queen Regent, Christina.   3664

_____. The Velvet Glove. by H. Seton Merriman, pseud.
    Dodd, 1901. Political unrest in Spain during the Carlist
    War is the background for an exciting romance.   3665

Sprague, Rosemary. Fife and Fandango. Walck, 1961. Trials
    at home and in England of a naive, aristocratic Spanish
    señorita who marries a British officer during the Peninsular
    War.   3666

Woods, Margaret L. The King's Revoke. Dutton, 1905. Po-
    litical affairs in Spain under Napoleon's brother, Joseph
    Bonaparte.   3667

_____. Sons of the Sword. McClure, 1901. Romance of
    an Irish girl during the Peninsular War.   3668

_____. The Spanish Lady. Cape, 1927. The various effects
    of a romance between Wellington and a lovely Spanish lady.
                                                               3669

    2) Italy and Adjacent Islands

Bailey, H.C. The Pillar of Fire. Methuen, 1918. England,
    France, and Italy in the 1850s--Napoleon III, Victor Em-
    manuel, and Garibaldi.   3670

_____. The Rebel. Methuen, 1923. Includes accounts of
    Garibaldi's defeat at Mentana and the Franco-Prussian War.
                                                               3671
Beyle, Marie Henri. The Charterhouse of Parma. by Stendhal,
    pseud. Boni & Liveright, 1925. Life of a veteran of Water-
    loo in Italy in the post-Napoleonic age of petty despots. 3672

Bickerstaffe-Drew, Francis. Marotz. by John Ayscough,
    pseud. Putnam, 1908. Sicily during the time of Victor

Emmanuel III and Pope Leo XIII.   3673

Brady, Charles Andrew. Crown of Grass. Doubleday, 1964.
The amorous involvements of Chateaubriand as French Ambassador to Rome jeopardize both his career and his life. 3674

Brown, Beatrice Curtis. For the Delight of Antonio. Houghton, 1932. Involvement of an English youth and an aristocratic Venetian in the revolt against Austria.   3675

Conrad, Joseph. Suspense. Doubleday, Page, 1925. The
shifting moods of Europe after Napoleon had been imprisoned
at Elba.   3676

Crawford, F. Marion. (1) Saracinesca. Macmillan, 1887.
(2) Sant' Ilario (sequel). Macmillan, 1889. (3) Don Orsino (sequel). Macmillan, 1892. (4) Corleone (sequel).
Macmillan, 1898. Panoramic view of social, political and
economic aspects of Roman life in the last half of the century.   3677-80

Crockett, Samuel R. The Silver Skull. Smith & Elder, 1901.
Ferdinand I's rule in the Kingdom of the Two Sicilies after
the Congress of Vienna.   3681

Deeping, Warwick. The Lame Englishman. Cassell, 1911.
Spirited story of an Englishman in the service of the revo-
lutionist Garibaldi.   3682

Denti di Pirajno, Alberto. Ippolita. Doubleday, 1961. Driving
ambition and acquisitiveness of an Italian peasant woman who
married a baron during the period of Italy's unification. 3683

Fogazzaro, Antonio. (1) The Patriot. (tr.) Putnam, 1906.
(2) The Sinner. (tr.) [En. title: The Man of the World]
Putnam, 1907. (3) The Saint. (tr.) Putnam, 1906. Trilogy
dealing with social and religious conditions in Italy and including romance, politics, and domestic affairs.   3684-6

Gavin, Catherine Irvine. The Moon Into Blood. Hodder,
1966. A bomb, meant for Napoleon III, wounds a young
woman and involves her in political intrigue.   3687

Giono, Jean. The Straw Man. (tr.) Knopf, 1959. A hussar
colonel in the 1848 Italian revolt against Austria.   3688

Gregg, Hilda Caroline. One Crowded Hour. by Sydney C.
Grier, pseud. Blackwood, 1912. Two Englishmen fight
along with Garibaldi for Italian freedom.   3689

Hansard, Luke J. The Flame in the South. Hutchinson, 1925.
Impact of revolutionary activities leading to the unification
of Italy.   3690

Hartley, M. Beyond Man's Strength. Heinemann, 190 9.
Life of a couple in Italy against a background of political
developments in early and mid-century.   3691

Hood, Alexander Nelson. Adria. Murray, 1902. An Englishman in Venice during the revolt against the Austrians.   3692

Hopkins, Tighe. For Freedom. Chatto, 1899. Garibaldi and
the War of Italian Liberation in 1859.   3693

Hutton, Edward. Frederic Uvedale. Blackwood, 1901. The
spiritual life of a youth educated in England and living in
Italy.   3694

Kazantzakēs, Nikos. Freedom or Death. S. & S., 1956.
Emotions flare as Cretans fight to throw off the bondage of
Turkey.   3695

Kingsley, Henry. Silcote of Silcotes. Longmans, 1867.
Scenes of battle in the Italian War of Liberation.   3696

Komroff, Manuel. Magic Bow. Harper, 1940. Career of the
great Italian violinist, Paganini, during the Napoleonic period.   3697

Lampedusa, Giuseppe Di. The Leopard. (tr.) Pantheon,
1960. The fortunes of the Sicilian House of Salina in the
latter half of the century.   3698

Lever, Charles. The Daltons. Routledge, 1852. Incidents in
the Italian fight for independence from Austria.   3699

_____. Gerald Fitzgerald the Chevalier. Harper, 1899.
The adventures of a son of the Young Pretender.   3700

Maxwell, Anna. Pietro the Garibaldian. Parsons, 1925.
The War of Italian Liberation with Garibaldi, Cavour, Mazzini, and Victor Emmanuel as prominent figures.   3701

Meredith, George. Vittoria. Scribner, 1866. A young opera
singer against a background of contemporary political affairs,
with a good picture of Mazzini.   3702

Murray, Paul. Heart Is a Stranger. Harper, 1949. The inevitable complications of a political marriage between rival
Vienna and Florence.   3703

Roberto, Federico de. The Viceroys. (tr.) Harcourt, 1962.
(first pub. in 1894) A ruthless matriarch, Donna Teresa,
guides the lives and fortunes of the Uzeda family in a
struggle for land, power, and wealth.   3704

Roberts, Cecil. The Remarkable Young Man. Macmillan,

1954. About Joseph Severn, who nursed Keats during his
final illness in Rome.   3705

Sciasaia, Leonardo. The Council of Egypt. (tr.) Knopf, 1966,
c. 1963. A forgery of an historical work brings the author
a measure of social and political influence as his writing in-
timidates some men and inflames others.   3706

Scott, Hugh S. The Isle of Unrest. by H. Seton Merriman,
pseud. Dodd, 1900. Romance in Corsica during the Franco-
Prussian War.   3707

Scott, James Maurice. The Lady and the Corsair. Dutton,
1958. A Sicilian pirate captures and harasses an English
ship, thus arousing the ire of a lady passenger.   3708

Spender, E. A Soldier for a Day. White, 1901. Adventures
in the Italian insurrection of 1848.   3709

Stubbs, Jean. Eleanora Duse. Stein & Day, 1970. Based on
the life of the great Italian actress Eleanora Duse, her rivalry with Sarah Bernhardt and her affair with playwright-ad-
venturer D'Annunzio.   3710

Thomas, Henry Wilton. The Sword of Wealth. Putnam, 1906.
The Bread Riots and the assassination of King Humbert at
the close of the century.   3711

Trease, Geoffrey. So Wild the Heart. Vanguard, 1959. An
Oxford University student takes a trip to Italy to do scholarly
research, but finds romance and adventure instead.   3712

_____. A Thousand for Sicily. Vanguard, 1966. YA. Ad-
ventures of a journalist and an artist following Garibaldi
through Sicily.   3713

Ward, Mary Augusta. Eleanor. by Mrs. Humphry Ward.
Harper, 1900. Reflects the political, social, and religious
thought of the time.   3714

Werfel, Franz. Verdi. (tr.) S. & S., 1925. Venice in the
1880s with Verdi, Wagner, and Boito.   3715

White, William Hale. Clara Hopgood. by Mark Rutherford,
pseud. Dodd, 1896. Revolutionary ferment in Italy with
Mazzini as a minor character.   3716

Whiting, Mary B. The Torchbearers. Dent, 1904. Political issues and the Bread Riots of 1898.   3717

d) Eastern Europe (including Russia and the
    Balkans), the Near East, and North Africa

Almedingen, Martha Edith von. The Ladies of St. Hedwig's.
by E. M. Almedingen. Vanguard, 1967, c. 1965. Polish
nuns in a convent in Russia are harassed by the Russians
during the Polish Rebellion of 1863.   3718

Armstrong, Thomas. A Ring Has No End. Sloane, 1958. A
four-generation story of a family in Russia from the Crimean
War until after the First World War.   3719

Barr, Amelia E. An Orkney Maid. Appleton, 1918. A story
of the Crimean War showing the founding of the Red Cross.
                                                            3720

Bartos-Höppner, B. Storm Over the Caucasus. (tr.) Walck,
1968. YA. A shepherd boy acting as a messenger becomes
involved in conflict between Russians and Moslems.   3721

Beddoe, David M. The Honour of Henri de Valois. Dent,
1905. The background for this romantic novel is the capture of Syria by Ibrahim.   3722

Benson, Edward Frederic. (1) The Vintage. Harper, 1898.
(2) The Capsina (sequel). Harper, 1899. Battles, sieges,
massacres in the Greek War of Independence, told from the
Christian viewpoint.   3723-4

Bikelas, Demetrios. Loukis Laras. (tr.) Macmillan, 1881.
Adventures of a merchant in the bloody Greek War of Independence.   3725

Blech, William James. The Angel. by William Blake, pseud.
Doubleday, 1950. The fate of the visionary Emperor Alexander I.   3726

Bryant, Marguerite and George H. McAnnally. Chronicles of
a Great Prince. Duffield, 1924. About Prince Paul d'Aren-
zano of a small Balkan principality, based on family letters
and reports.   3727

Cahan, Abraham. The White Terror and the Red. Barnes,
1905. Plots against Czar Alexander II and anti-Jewish
riots under Czar Alexander III.   3728

Carling, John R. By Neva's Waters. Little, 1908. "An
episode in the secret history of Alexander the First, Czar
of all the Russias."   3729

Coulter, Stephen. The Devil Inside. Doubleday, 1960. Dostoev-
sky's compulsive gambling and romance after the death of his
father, showing how his own life figured in his writings.   3730

Czajkowski, Michael. The Black Pilgrim. (tr.) Digby & Long, 1900. A tale of the struggle for faith and freedom in the Balkan Peninsula. 3731

Danilevski, Grigovii P. Moscow in Flames. (tr.) Brentano's, 1917. Attack on Moscow by Napoleonic forces in 1812. 3732

Delves-Broughton, Josephine. Officer and Gentleman. McGraw, 1951. Story of a father and son in the Crimean War. 3733

Dilas, Milovan. Under the Colors. (tr.) by Milovan Djilas. Harcourt, 1971. A clan of Christian Serbs revolts against the Turks in an effort to join the newly independent state of Montenegro in 1879. 3734

Dostoevskii, Fedor. Buried Alive. (tr.) Munro, 1881. The author's own imprisonment is reflected in this novel which is sub-titled, "Ten Years' Penal Servitude in Siberia." 3735

_____. Crime and Punishment. (tr.) Crowell, 1886? Life amidst the lower stratum of mid-nineteenth century St. Petersburg. 3736

_____. House of the Dead. (tr.) Dutton, 1911. Penal servitude in Siberia, based on the author's own experiences. 3737

_____. Poor Folk. (tr.) Roberts, 1894. Realistic account of the living conditions of the masses. 3738

_____. The Possessed. (tr.) Macmillan, 1913. Revolutionary Nihilism in provincial Russia. 3739

Dumitriu, Petru. Family Jewels. (tr.) Pantheon, 1961. Dynasty of Roumanian aristocrats plot and scheme to attain financial and political success, with often tragic results. 3740

Gavin, Catherine Irvine. The Fortress. Doubleday, 1964. Romance of a Yankee sea-captain and a Russian-Finnish noblewoman during Baltic operations in the Crimean War. 3741

Gontcharov, Ivan A. A Common Story. (tr.) Heinemann, 1894. Reflects the unequal class system and the need for social and political reform. 3742

Gordon, Samuel. The Ferry of Fate. Duffield, 1906. The persecution of the Jews in Czarist Russia. 3743

Graham, Winifred. The Zionists. Hutchinson, 1902. Deals with the romance of a Christian and a Jew. 3744

Grant, James. Lady Wedderburn's Wish. Dutton, 1870. Romance against the background of the Crimean War. 3745

_____ . Laura Everingham. Dutton, 1870. Regimental
life and romance in the war in the Crimea.   3746

_____ . The Lord Hermitage. Dutton, 1878. The Crimean
War is the setting for romance and heroics.   3747

_____ . One of the Six Hundred. Dutton, 1875. A vigorous story of action in the Crimean War.   3748

Gregg, Hilda Caroline. (1) An Uncrowned King. Blackwood,
1896. (2) A Crowned Queen (sequel). Blackwood, 1898.
both by Sydney C. Grier, pseud. Two romances of court
politics and intrigue in the imaginary kingdom of Thracia
in the Balkans.   3749-50

Hawkins, Anthony Hope. Phroso. by Anthony Hope, pseud.
Stokes, 1897. A melodramatic tale of the adventures of
an Englishman on a Greek island.   3751

Jefferies, Ian. The Rake and the Rebel. [En. title: The
Troika Belle] by Ira J. Morris, pseud. Morrow, 1967.
Adventures of a young Russian nobleman who is forced to
flee because of an unintentional killing in the Napoleonic
era.   3752

Jennings, John. Banners Against the Wind. Little, 1954.
About Samuel Gridley Howe's part in the fight for Greek
independence.   3753

Jókai, Maurus. The Green Book. (tr.) Harper, 1897. Court
and common life in Russia during the revolutionary 1820s. 3754

_____ . The Lion of Janina. (tr.) Harper, 1898. An
action-jammed story of massacre and bloodshed, telling of
the killing of the Janissaries.   3755

Kane, Harnett T. with Victor Leclerc. The Scandalous Mrs.
Blackford. Messner, 1951. A clergyman's daughter from
Philadelphia becomes the toast of Paris and the envied
darling of a Grand Duke of Russia.   3756

Kay, Mara. Masha. Lothrop, 1968. Glimpses of school days
at the aristocratic Smolni Institute for Noble Girls founded in
Russia by Catherine the Great.   3757

Korolenko, Vladimir. In Two Moods. (tr.) Munro, 1892. A
sympathetic account of the Nihilist movement of the 1870s.
                                                               3758
_____ . The Saghalien Convict. (tr.) Unwin, 1892. A
novel based on the author's banishment for refusing to take
an oath to Alexander III.   3759

Kraszewski, Józef I. The Jew. (tr.) Heinemann, 1890.

A novel of the insurrection of 1860 written by an author
who was exiled in its course.   3760

Lagerlöf, Selma. Jerusalem. Heinemann, 1903. Tragic
story of a Zionist colony in Palestine.   3761

Lambe, John Lawrence. By Command of the Prince. Unwin,
1901. Account of a Bulgarian murder trial.   3762

Landau, Mark Aleksandrovich. Before the Deluge. (tr.) by
M. A. Aldanov, pseud. Scribner, 1947. The period of the
assassination of Alexander II of Russia.   3763

Law, Margaret Lathrop. Aimée. Funk, 1956. A young girl,
captured by pirates and sent to the Turkish court, comes
to enjoy her life there.   3764

Leont'ev, Konstantin. The Egyptian Dove. (tr.) Weybright
and Talley, 1969. About the life and the great love of the
Russian diplomat Leont'ev in Greece and Turkey.   3765

Longard de Longgarde, Dorothea Gerard. The Red-Hot Crown.
by Dorothea Gerard. Long, 1909. Based on the tragedy
which befell Queen Draga of Serbia.   3766

McLaws, Lafayette, i.e., Emily Lafayette McLaws. The Maid
of Athens. Little, 1906. This romantic novel is concerned
chiefly with Lord Byron's visit to Athens.   3767

Mayo, Mrs. J. R. A Daughter of the Klephts. Dutton, 1897.
The war of Greek independence.   3768

Merezhkovsky, Dmitri. December the Fourteenth. (tr.) Cape,
1923. The accession of Czar Nicholas I amidst revolutionary
upheaval and his harsh rule.   3769

Morton, Benjamin A. The Veiled Empress. Putnam, 1923.
A Creole girl is captured by pirates and sent to Turkish
Constantinople as a wife to the Sultan.   3770

Murray, David Leslie. Trumpeter, Sound! Knopf, 1934. Two
English half-brothers, in love with the same dancing girl,
serve in the Crimean War.   3771

Oxenham, John, pseud. for William Arthur Dunkerley. The
Coil of Carne. Lane, 1911. The sufferings of troops in
the Crimean War and the ministrations of Florence Nightingale.   3772

_____. Hearts in Exile. Macmillan, 1904. A narrative
about political exiles in Siberia in the latter part of the
century.   3773

_____. The Long Road. Macmillan, 1907. Russia's
harsh treatment of her political prisoners in Siberia.   3774

Pemberton, Max. The Great White Army. Cassell, 1915.
Napoleon's invasion of deserted Moscow and the disastrous
retreat of the French army in the brutal Russian winter.   3775

Pickthall, Marmaduke. Said the Fisherman. Methuen, 1903.
A good picture of the customs and beliefs of the Orient in
this tale of a fisherman turned merchant.   3776

Potter, Margaret Horton. The Genius. Harper, 1906. Based
roughly on the life of the composer, Tschaikowsky, with
many scenes from Russian life.   3777

Prokosch, Frederic. The Missolonghi Manuscript. Farrar,
1968. Fictional reconstruction of episodes in the life of
Lord Byron during his final days in Greece.   3778

Rabinowitz, Shalom. The Adventures of Menahem-Mendl. (tr.)
by Sholom Aleichem. Putnam, 1969. (orig. pub. in Yiddish
in 1909 in Russia) Jewish life in Russia is shown in the letters between a man seeking his fortune in the city and his
wife keeping their family in their native village.   3779

Ropes, Arthur R. and Mary E. On Peter's Island. Murray,
1901. Secret police versus the underground in the Nihilist
movement.   3780

Schultz, Barbara. The Secret of the Pharaohs. Bobbs, 1966.
YA. Archeological findings and robbery from the Pharaohs'
tombs in Egypt in 1881.   3781

Sladen, Douglas. The Curse of the Nile. Paul, 1913. The
siege and fall of Khartum and the fate of white prisoners. 3782

Solomon, Ruth Freeman. The Eagle and the Dove. Putnam,
1971. The dramatic story of tempestuous love and of a
powerful Jewish family during the latter part of the nineteenth
century in Russia.   3783

Stephens, Eve. Far Flies the Eagle. by Evelyn Anthony,
pseud. Crowell, 1955. Based on the eventful life of the
idealistic Czar Alexander I to his thirty-ninth year.   3784

Terrot, Charles. The Passionate Pilgrim. Harper, 1948.
One of Florence Nightingale's nurses and her shocking
report of field hospitals in the Crimean War.   3785

Tolstoy, Leo. The Cossacks. (tr.) Scribner, 1878. Romance of a Russian gentleman and a simple, primitive
girl.   3786

_____. War and Peace. (tr.) Harper, 1886. A classic
account of life in Russia and of Napoleon's invasion attempt.   3787

Tur, Eugenia, pseud. The Shalonski Family. (tr.) Remington,
1882. Country life in Russia at the time of the Napoleonic
invasion.   3788

Turgenev, Ivan S. Fathers and Sons. (tr.) [En. title:
Fathers and Children] Holt, 1872. The old and the new
contrasted in this view of Russian social and political life. 3789

_____. On the Eve. (tr.) Macmillan, 1895. The end of
the reign of Czar Nicholas I.   3790

_____. Rudin. (tr.) Macmillan, 1894. Shows the inef-
fectuality of Liberalism in contemporary Russia.   3791

_____. Smoke. (tr.) Macmillan, 1896. A novel of char-
acter and romance with the portrait of a complex woman.   3792

_____. The Torrents of Spring. (tr.) Farrar, 1960,
c. 1959. (first pub. in Russia in 1871) A young Russian
falls in love with one girl, becomes involved with another,
and reaps the unhappy reward of his infidelity.   3793

_____. Virgin Soil. (tr.) Macmillan, 1896. A pessi-
mistic view of social and political thought in Russia.   3794

Underwood, Edna. The Penitent. Houghton, 1922. Alexander I
and the beginnings of the Russian struggle for national freedom.   3795

Vazov, Ivan. Under the Yoke. (tr.) Heinemann, 1893. A
searching novel of the attempted revolt of the Bulgarians
from Turkey.   3796

Whishaw, Frederick J. Moscow. Longmans, 1906. A story
of lovers during the Russian resistance to Napoleon.   3797

Whyte-Melville, George John. The Interpreter. Longmans,
1858. International intrigue during Omar Pasha's Turkish
resistance to Russia and the Crimean War.   3798

e)   Overseas Exploration, Enterprise,
     and Expansion

Alderman, Clifford L. Wooden Ships and Iron Men. Walker,
1964. YA. The adventures of a young sailor who fought
with first the British, then the American navy, gives a
picture of the battles in the War of 1812.   3799

Collins, Wilkie. The Frozen Deep. ed. by Robert L. Brannan. Cornell Univ., 1966. Play written by Collins and revised and produced by Charles Dickens (in 1857) concerning
the Arctic Expedition of Sir John Franklin.   3800

Conrad, Joseph and Ford Madox Hueffer. Romance. Smith &
Elder, 1903. A land-and-sea adventure story of England
and the West Indies.   3801

Crisp, Frank. The Treasure of Barby Swin. Coward, 1955.
YA. An English boy has many hair-raising adventures with
a former slave trader, on a whaling voyage, and in search
of treasure.   3802

Daly, Robert Welter. Broadsides. Macmillan, 1940. Sea experiences of an Irishman in the British navy during the Napoleonic Wars.   3803

_____. Soldier of the Sea. Morrow, 1942. Sea-faring ad-
venture and naval warfare of the British marines in the Napoleonic Wars.   3804

Forester, C.S. Admiral Hornblower in the West Indies. Little,
1958. Hornblower's rousing adventures--including the attempted rescue of Napoleon from St. Helena.   3805

_____. Beat to Quarters. Little, 1937. The admirable
Captain Hornblower engages successfully in naval war off
the eastern coast of Central America.   3806

_____. Captain Horatio Hornblower. Little, 1939. A vol-
ume containing three of the Hornblower stories: Beat to
Quarters; Ship of the Line; and Flying Colours (see separate listings).   3807

_____. Commodore Hornblower. Little, 1945. The Com-
modore is assigned to enlist Sweden and Russia on the
British side in the Napoleonic Wars.   3808

_____. Flying Colours. Little, 1939. Captain Hornblower
escapes as he is being taken by the French to a trial for
piracy.   3809

_____. Hornblower and the Atropos. Little, 1953. Among
other activities, Hornblower crosses England by canal and
attends Nelson's funeral.   3810

_____. Hornblower During the Crisis, and Two Stories.
Little, 1967. Forester's last book about Hornblower, unfinished at his death, and his notes on the outcome; also
two stories: "Hornblower's Temptation" and "The Final
Encounter."   3811

_____. Hornblower Goes to Sea. (v. 1) Little, 1965.
YA. Excerpts from Mr. Midshipman Hornblower and
Lieutenant Hornblower (listed separately), especially
selected for young people. 3812

_____. Hornblower in Captivity. (v. 3) Little, 1965. YA.
Excerpts from A Ship of the Line and Flying Colours (listed
separately), especially selected for young people. 3813

_____. Hornblower Takes Command. (v. 2) Little, 1965.
YA. Excerpts from Hornblower and the Atropos and Beat
to Quarters (listed separately), especially selected for
young people. 3814

_____. Hornblower's Triumph. (v. 4) Little, 1965. YA.
Excerpts from Commodore Hornblower and Lord Hornblower
(listed separately), especially selected for young people. 3815

_____. The Indomitable Hornblower. Little, 1963. An
omnibus volume containing Commodore Hornblower, Lord
Hornblower, and Admiral Hornblower in the West Indies
(listed separately). 3816

_____. Lieutenant Hornblower. Little, 1952. Hornblower
has the new experience of playing whist for a living. 3817

_____. Lord Hornblower. Little, 1946. A tale of sea
battles and ships during the Napoleonic Wars; Hornblower
is raised to the peerage. 3818

_____. Mr. Midshipman Hornblower. Little, 1950. Horn-
blower's rise from midshipman to lieutenant. 3819

_____. A Ship of the Line. Little, 1942. Hornblower
commands a ship blockading the Spanish coast in the Napoleonic Wars. 3820

Forman, James. So Ends This Day. Farrar, 1970. YA. The
children of a whaling captain sail with him in the period when
whaling was on the decline and slave-trading on the upswing.
3821

Foster, John T. Rebel Sea Raider. Morrow, 1965. YA. The
story of Raphael Semmes, who commanded the C.S.S. Alabama in naval battle action in the American Civil War. 3822

Gendron, Val. Outlaw Voyage. World, 1955. YA. A young
man works on a disreputable slave ship to earn a livelihood
for his foster mother and, by his industry, earns a place
on a better ship. 3823

Goudge, Elizabeth. Green Dolphin Street. Coward, 1944.
The romantic triangle of two sisters in love with the
same sailor. 3824

Haugaard, Erik Christian. Orphans of the Wind. Houghton,
1966. YA. A deckboy on an English brig during the American Civil War.   3825

Hawes, Charles Boardman. The Mutineers. Little, 1948. YA.
(first pub. in 1920) A boy grows up during a sea voyage
from Salem to Canton in 1809.   3826

Jennings, John. Chronicle of the Calypso, Clipper. Little,
1955. A race to California between two clipper ships and
romance among the ship's doctor, the captain's wife, and
other feminine passengers.   3827

Kipling, Rudyard. Captains Courageous. Bantam Bks., 1963,
c.1896. A lively story of the Gloucester fishermen who
sailed from the New England coasts to the Grand Banks to
catch their cargoes of fish.   3828

Longstreet, Stephen. Masts to Spear the Stars. Doubleday,
1967. Sea-faring to the Orient aboard a giant American
clipper ship in the 1840s.   3829

Marryat, Frederick. Mr. Midshipman Easy. Burt, 1917.
Pictures naval life in the early nineteenth century.   3830

Masefield, John. Bird of Dawning. Macmillan, 1933. Race
between two clippers for the tea trade between China and
England.   3831

Mason, Van Wyck. Harpoon in Eden. Doubleday, 1969. Whaling and trading ventures of a young New Englander who
eventually establishes himself among the Maoris of New Zealand.   3832

Meader, Stephen W. The Voyage of the Javelin. Harcourt,
1959. YA. A ship's boy on a speedy clipper ship sees
life in many countries and rises to the status of fourth
mate.   3833

Nicholls, Frederick Francis. The Log of the Sardis. Norton,
1963, c.1962. YA. Damage to a navigational instrument
figures in a shipwreck and haunts the man involved until he
confesses his responsibility.   3834

Roark, Garland. The Lady and the Deep Blue Sea. Doubleday,
1958. YA. Wild, exciting race between two swift clipper
ships, the Calcutta Eagle and the Emperor, from Melbourne
to Boston.   3835

Robertson, Keith. Ice to India. Viking, 1955. With their
trading business all but ruined by the War of 1812, the
Mason family gambles on taking a load of ice from Philadelphia to India.   3836

_____. The Wreck of the Saginaw. Viking, 1954. YA.
A shipwrecked crew attempts a hazardous 1500-mile voyage across the uncharted Pacific to the safety of Hawaii.   3837

Ross, Sutherland. Freedom Is the Prize. Walker, 1964.
YA. Naval action in the War of 1812 shown in the life of
a young American sailor impressed into British service.   3838

Rowland, Henry Cottrell. Hirondelle. Harper, 1922. About
an Irish lord engaged in slaving and piracy in the War of
1812.   3839

Sperry, Armstrong. Black Falcon. Winston, 1949. YA. A
youth, escaping the English frigate that captured his father's
ship, joins the band of pirate Jean Lafitte.   3840

_____. Storm Canvas. Holt, 1944. YA. A United States
frigate bound for Haiti during the War of 1812 encounters
enemy fighting and hurricane weather.   3841

Steelman, Robert. Call of the Arctic. Coward, 1960. The
intrepid explorer Charles Francis Hall and his three daring
voyages to the Arctic North in the last century.   3842

Steward, Davenport. Black Spice. Dutton, 1959. An American
turns to a career in trading with the Spice Islands after having been a privateer during the War of 1812.   3843

Stuart, Vivian, pseud. The Brave Captains. Hale, 1968.
The daring exploits of a naval captain during the sea and
land action at Balaclava during the Crimean War.   3844

Styles, Showell. Frigate Captain. Vanguard, 1955. Captain
Lord Cochrane's exploits during the Napoleonic Wars.   3845

Subercaseaux, Benjamin. Jemmy Button. (tr.) Macmillan,
1954. A novel based on diaries and logs of two voyages of
the Beagle telling of Commander Robert Fitz-Roy's attempt
to civilize natives.   3846

Sundman, Per Olof. The Flight of the Eagle. (tr.) Pantheon,
1970. The attempt of three Swedish scientists to reach the
North Pole in a gas balloon in 1897; written from notes found
in 1930 at their last camp.   3847

Webb, Christopher. Quest of the "Otter." Funk, 1963. YA.
Mid-nineteenth century whaling is background for a boy's
search for his father, a whaler lost at sea.   3848

Young-O'Brien, Albert Hayward. Windship Boy. by Brian
O'Brien, pseud. Dutton, 1961. YA. Two years of appren-
ticeship aboard a clipper ship with adventure in foreign ports,
illustrated with drawings of sailing ships.   3849

B. ASIA, AFRICA, AND OCEANIA
IN MODERN TIMES (c. 1500-1900)

1. ASIA IN MODERN TIMES

a) India

1) Pre-British to 1600

Bothwell, Jean. Dancing Princess. Harcourt, 1965. YA. An
orphaned princess decides to pick her own husband when she
visits the Emperor's court at Agra.   3850

_____. Defiant Bride. Harcourt, 1969. YA. A girl re-
fuses the marriages her father arranges for her, but the
Emperor's intervention solves the conflict.   3851

_____. Promise of the Rose. Harcourt, 1958. YA. Ro-
mance of Aruna, the Indian Emperor's ward, who falls in
love with one of his agents, although she was to be the
bride of a nobleman.   3852

_____. Ride, Zarina, Ride. Harcourt, 1966. YA. The
daughter of a treasury official becomes involved in an attempt to solve a gold theft.   3853

Eaubonne, Francoise d'. A Flight of Falcons. (tr.) McGraw,
1951. The broken heart of a Spanish-Dutch painter who goes
to India in the late sixteenth century.   3854

Forrest, R. E. The Ruby of Rajast'han. East & West Ltd.,
1914. A romance of Hindustan and Akbar in the sixteenth
century.   3855

Steel, Flora Annie. A Prince of Dreamers. Doubleday, 1908.
Interesting story of Indian life and manners under the gifted
Emperor Akbar.   3856

Taylor, Philip Meadows. A Noble Queen. Kegan Paul, 1878.
India in the last decade of the sixteenth century under brave
Queen Chand Beebee.   3857

2) Seventeenth and Eighteenth Centuries

Bañkimachandra Chattopadhyaya. Chandra Shekhar. (tr.)
Luzac & Co., 1904. Adventures of a young girl un-
happily married to an older man.   3858

Compton, Herbert. A Free Lance in a Far Land. Cassell,
1895. Adventures among the Mahrattas of west central
India at the end of the eighteenth century.   3859

Du Bois, Theodora M. Tiger Burning Bright. Farrar, 1964.
YA. Their flight across the Indian desert made a common
bond between refugees from the Sepoy Rebellion.   3860

Gamon, Richard B. Warren of Oudh. Macdonald, 1926.
India during Warren Hasting's governorship in the mid-eighteenth century.   3861

Gregg, Hilda Caroline. The Great Proconsul. by Sydney C.
Grier, pseud. Blackwood, 1904. Written as a diary by a
member of Warren Hasting's family telling of his work in
India.   3862

_____. In Furthest Ind. by Sydney C. Grier, pseud.
Blackwood, 1894. Travels and experiences during the
early years of the East India Company.   3863

_____. Like Another Helen. by Sydney C. Grier, pseud.
Blackwood, 1899. A young lady's experiences in Calcutta
during the scandalous period of the Black Hole horrors.   3864

Masters, John. Coromandel! Viking, 1955. Barbaric splendor
and power reward young Jason Savage's journey to India.   3865

Payne, Robert. Blood Royal. Prentice-Hall, 1952. Struggle
for royal power, as told by an Englishman who married a
Persian princess.   3866

_____. Young Emperor. [En. title: The Great Mogul]
Macmillan, 1950. India during the time of Shahjahan,
prince and emperor, in the first half of the seventeenth
century.   3867

Penny, Mrs. F. E. Diamonds. Hodder & Stoughton, 1920.
Native customs and traditions are reflected in this account
of the young East India Company.   3868

Pollard, Eliza F. The Silver Hand. Blackie, 1908. About
Warren Hastings, the Mahratta Wars, Tippoo Sahib, and
an ancient prophecy.   3869

Prokosch, Frederic. The Dark Dancer. Farrar, 1964. The
struggle for power of Prince Shahjahan, eventually Mogul
Emperor, and his love of the enigmatic princess for whom
he later built the Taj Mahal as a tomb.   3870

Scott, Sir Walter. The Surgeon's Daughter. Munro, 1885.
A young man brings his fiancée from Scotland to India and
sells her to Tippoo Sultan.   3871

Sell, Frank R. Bhim Singh. Macmillan, 1926. The Rajput
War in India featuring Emperor Aurangzib and his son.   3872

Steel, Flora Annie. Mistress of Men. Stokes, 1918. The
   unwanted girl baby who lived to become Empress Nurjahan
   of India in the early 1600s.   3873

Taylor, Philip Meadows. Ralph Darnell. by Meadows Taylor.
   Kegan Paul, 1865. Struggle for control between the British
   and the native Indians in 1757. (followed by Seeta)   3874

_____. Tara. by Meadows Taylor. Paul, 1863. Uprising
   of the Mahrattas against the ruling Mohammedans in 1657.
   (followed by Ralph Darnell)   3875

_____. Tippoo Sultaun. by Meadows Taylor. Kegan Paul,
   1840. Conflict for supremacy between England and France,
   1788-89.   3876

Tracy, Louis. The Great Mogul. [En. title: Heart's Delight]
   Clode, 1905. Two Englishmen visit India in the early seventeenth century.   3877

Upward, Allen. Athelstane Ford. Pearson, 1899. The British
   conquest of India including an account of the infamous Black
   Hole of Calcutta.   3878

3) Nineteenth Century

Arnold, William Delafield. Oakfield. Longmans, 1853. A
   young Oxford graduate in India has difficulty adjusting to
   the realities of life.   3879

Blanch, Lesley. The Nine-Tiger Man. Atheneum, 1965. A
   lady and her housemaid become competitors for the heart of
   a handsome Indian prince.   3880

Chatterji, Bankim Chandra. Krishnakanta's Will. (tr.) by
   Bankim-chandra Chatterjee. New Directions, 1962. Tragedy
   resulting from marital infidelity in Victorian India.   3881

Chesney, G. T. The Dilemma. Harper, 1876. Efforts of Englishmen to defend their homes in the Indian Mutiny of the
   1850s.   3882

Diver, Maud. Candles in the Wind. Lane, 1909. India during the latter part of the century.   3883

_____. (1) Captain Desmond, V.C. Lane, 1907. (2)
   Desmond's Daughter. Putnam, 1916. Both books deal with
   English life in India in the late 1800s.   3884-5

_____. The Great Amulet. Lane, 1908. A romance of the
   Indian border depicting military conflicts, bouts with cholera,
   and the people themselves.   3886

_____. (1) The Hero of Herat. Putnam, 1913. (2) The
Judgment of the Sword (sequel). Putnam, 1913. Two good
stories of exploration and of the Afghan Wars of the 1830s
and '40s.   3887-8

Durand, Henry Mortimer. Helen Treveryan. Macmillan, 1892.
The second Afghan War and relations of the British with the
people of India.   3889

Forrest, R. E. Eight Days. Smith & Elder, 1891. The eight
days depicted are the period in May, 1857, in which the Sepoy Mutiny started.   3890

_____. The Sword of Azrael. Methuen, 1903. An English
officer escapes from the Mutiny of the Sepoys in 1857.   3891

Greenhow, H. M. Brenda's Experiment. Jarrold & Sons,
1896. Indian customs and religion figure in the tale of an
English girl married to a Mohammedan.   3892

Gregg, Hilda Caroline. The Advanced Guard. by Sydney C.
Grier, pseud. Blackwood, 1903. The Indian frontier just
prior to the Mutiny, with an account of native dungeons and
torture practices.   3893

_____. The Warden of the Marches. by Sydney C. Grier,
pseud. Blackwood, 1901. The precarious peace of the
frontier is upset when a new commissioner's policies bring
war.   3894

Griffiths, Arthur. Before the British Raj. Everett, 1903.
Adventures of a soldier in India about 1800.   3895

Hamilton, Lillias. A Vizier's Daughter. Murray, 1900. The
rugged life of the race of people called Hazaras in Afghan-
istan in the latter part of the nineteenth century.   3896

Harcourt, A. F. P. Jenetha's Venture. Cassell, 1899. A
story of the siege of Delhi depicting most of the important
personages in that event.   3897

_____. The Peril of the Sword. Skeffington, 1903. Mili-
tary action at Cawnpore and Lucknow during the Indian
Mutiny.   3898

Hockley, William Browne. Pandurang Hari. Chatto, 1891.
Account of a Hindu early in the century, giving much information about the Mahrattas.   3899

Hunter, William Wilson. The Old Missionary. Frowde, 1895.
Sympathetic picture of India in the early nineteenth century.
                                                              3900
Irwin, H. C. With Sword and Pen. Unwin, 1904. Native

customs in India in mid-nineteenth century.   3901

Kaye, Mary Margaret. Shadow of the Moon. Messner, 1957.
Story of the Sepoy Rebellion.   3902

Lang, John. The Wetherbys. Chapman & Hall, 1853. Satiric
comment on English-Indian relations preceding the Mutiny. 3903

MacMunn, George Fletcher. A Freelance in Kashmir. Dutton, 1914. Kashmir in 1804 is the scene of this tale of romance and adventure.   3904

Masters, John. The Deceivers. Viking, 1952. Thrilling tale
concerning the cult of the goddess Kali.   3905

_____. Nightrunners of Bengal. Viking, 1951. Suspense
during the Sepoy Rebellion in the nineteenth century.   3906

Mundy, Talbot. Rung Ho! Scribner, 1914. Vivid account of
a young officer's introduction to Indian people and customs.
                                                              3907

Oliphant, Philip Laurence. Maya. Constable, 1908. The
daughter of an English officer and her Indian childhood. 3908

Ollivant, Alfred. Old For-Ever. Doubleday, Page, 1923.
Experiences during the Afghan War period including an outbreak of cholera.   3909

Pearce, Charles E. Love Besieged. Paul, 1909. Has as
historical background the siege of Lucknow.   3910

_____. Red Revenge. Paul, 1911. The siege and capture
of Cawnpore during the Mutiny in 1857.   3911

_____. A Star of the East. Paul, 1912. The Mutiny of
1857 and the events leading up to it.   3912

Scott, Hugh S. Flotsam. by H. Seton Merriman, pseud.
Longmans, 1896. Based chiefly in India during the rebellious years of the mid-nineteenth century.   3913

Steel, Flora Annie. On the Face of the Waters. Macmillan,
1896. A vivid re-creation of the Mutiny period with emphasis on the siege and capture of Delhi.   3914

Sutherland, Joan. The Edge of Empire. Mills & Boon, 1916.
Social life in Kashmir and the expedition of 1895 to Chitral.
                                                              3915

Taylor, Philip Meadows. Confessions of a Thug. by Meadows
Taylor. Bentley, 1839. Incidents of local color told by an
Indian officer.   3916

_____. Seeta. by Meadows Taylor. Kegan Paul, 1873.

   Picture of the Indian Mutiny of 1857 against the English.   3917

Thorburn, Septimus S. His Majesty's Greatest Subject. Appleton, 1897. A political story of the British in India.   3918

Tracy, Louis. The Red Year. Clode, 1908. A vivid, realistic
   story of the Indian Mutiny of 1857.   3919

Tuttiett, Mary Gleed. In the Heart of the Storm. by Maxwell
   Gray, pseud. Appleton, 1891. A novel of India during the
   Great Mutiny.   3920

Wallis, Henry M. An Old Score. by Ashton Hilliers, pseud.
   Ward & Lock, 1906. The righting of a wrong after two
   generations.   3921

Wentworth, Patricia. The Devil's Wind. Putnam, 1912. A
   view of official circles during the Mutiny in the 1850s.   3922

   b)   China

Buck, Pearl. Imperial Woman. Day, 1956. Compelling story
   of Tzu-hsi, last and most powerful Empress of China.   3923

_____. Peony. Day, 1948. Romance of a Chinese bonds-
   maid and the son of her wealthy Jewish master in the nineteenth century.   3924

Clift, Charmain and George Henry Johnston. The Big Chariot.
   Bobbs, 1953. Tale of excitement with brother against brother
   during seventeenth century warfare.   3925

Coates, Austin. City of Broken Promises. Day, 1968, c.1967.
   A Chinese orphan girl who is raised in a convent and sold
   into concubinage becomes one of the richest women on the
   waterfront.   3926

Gardner, Mona. Hong Kong. Doubleday, 1958. The Opium
   War and the Chinese effort to evict foreigners.   3927

Hunter, Bluebell Matilda. The Manchu Empress. Dial, 1945.
   Oriental court splendor and ruthless cruelty under China's
   last Empress.   3928

Jernigan, Muriel Molland. Forbidden City. Crown, 1954.
   Tzu-hsi, last Empress of China, with a good picture of
   Peking life.   3929

Lee, Virginia. The House That Tai Ming Built. Macmillan,
   1963. Four-generation story of a Chinese family with part
   of the action in China and part in California.   3930

Lin, Yutang. The Red Peony. World, 1961. Love affairs of
an unconventional young Chinese widow in nineteenth century
Peking, told with good historical background.   3931

Mackay, Margaret. Valiant Dust. Day, 1941. Chinese life
in the later nineteenth century is the background for the
story of a Scotch family.   3932

Payne, Robert. House in Peking. Doubleday, 1956. Intrigue
and romance at the court of Manchu Emperor Ch'ien Lung
in the eighteenth century.   3933

Wright, Constance. Their Ships Were Broken. Dutton, 1938.
Opium smuggling in nineteenth century China.   3934

Yaukey, Grace. China Trader. by Cornelia Spencer, pseud.
Day, 1940. An American trader and his wife in a Portu-
guese-held town in the late eighteenth century.   3935

c) Japan and Korea

Adams, J. William. Shibesawa; or, The Passing of Old Japan.
Putnam, 1906. The end of the Shogunate and the beginning
of Japan's mingling with the West.   3936

Bennet, Robert Ames. The Shogun's Daughter. McClurg,
1910. Commodore Perry's trip to Japan when the Shogun,
as military dictator, ruled the country, then closed to
foreigners.   3937

Blaker, Richard. The Needle-Watcher. Doubleday, 1932.
Forceful story of a seventeenth century English seaman who,
through his knowledge of the compass, became a friend of
the Shogun.   3938

Butler, William. The Ring in Meiji. Putnam, 1965. Japanese feudal rivalries and the settling of two Americans during the early days of Westernization in Japan.   3939

Fraser, Mary Crawford. The Stolen Emperor. by Mrs. Hugh
Fraser. Long, 1903. Japan during its feudal era in mid-
nineteenth century.   3940

Hayashi, Viscount, ed. For His People. Harper, 1903.
Based on an old Japanese play, this story gives a good
picture of seventeenth century feudalism.   3941

Ihara, Saikaku. The Life of an Amorous Woman and Other
Writings. (tr.) New Directions, 1963. Japanese classic
reflecting conditions in the seventeenth century.   3942

Lancaster, Bruce. Venture in the East. Little, 1951.

The Dutch East India Company in medieval seventeenth century Japan.   3943

Longstreet, Stephen and Ethel. Geisha. Funk, 1960. An American surgeon saves the life of the Shogun and enters an ill-fated romance with a beautiful geisha.   3944

Lund, Robert. Daishi-San. Day, 1961. About shipbuilder Will Adams, first Englishman in Japan, who settled there permanently about 1600.   3945

Maclay, A.C. Mito Yashiki. Putnam, 1889. A novel of Japan in the mid-nineteenth century.   3946

Mori, Ogai. The Wild Geese. (tr.) Tuttle, 1959. (orig. pub. in 1911-13) The life of the city and of the main characters in Tokyo in the 1880s.   3947

Nagayo, Yoshiro. Bronze Christ. (tr.) Taplinger, 1959. The use in the seventeenth century of a statue of Christ to detect Christians, who were then executed.   3948

Natsume, Soseki. Grass on the Wayside. (tr.) Univ. of Chicago Pr. , 1969. (written before 1916) Autobiographical novel concerning a difficult period in the life of the author, who was born in 1867.   3949

Price, Willard de Mille. Barbarian. Day, 1941. Shows American trade relations with Japan shortly after Perry's visit.
3950

d) Other Asiatic Peoples

Clavell, James. Tai-Pan. Atheneum, 1966. The head of an English trading company encounters numerous difficulties trying to develop business with Hong Kong.   3951

Landon, Margaret. Anna and the King of Siam. Day, 1944. An English governess to the many children of the King of Siam (Thailand).   3952

Lofts, Norah. Scent of Cloves. Fawcett, 1971, c.1957. The daughter of English nobility, orphaned as a small child, eventually becomes a "Company's Daughter" of the Dutch East India Company and goes as a bride into a bizarre situation.   3953

_____. Silver Nutmeg. Pyramid Bks. , 1967, c.1947. Passionate romance and Dutch colonial enterprise in the East Indies in the mid-seventeenth century.   3954

Meacham, Ellis K. The East Indiaman. Little, 1968. A naval Captain of the East India Company deals with the

pirate Barbarossa, the Vellore Mutiny, Chinese truculence,
and political intrigues.   3955

Monsarrat, Nicholas. The White Rajah. Sloane, 1961. A
baronet's son turned buccaneer marries a Rajah's daughter
and later assumes the throne himself.   3956

Morrow, Honoré. Splendor of God. Morrow, 1929. Missionaries in Burma encounter a conflict between Christian
and Buddhist philosophies.   3957

Palgrave, W. Gifford. Hermann Agha. King, 1872. Oriental
splendor provides background for an Englishman's life in the
service of an Asian ruler.   3958

2. AFRICA IN MODERN TIMES

Abrahams, Peter. Wild Conquest. Harper, 1950. The northward trek of the Boers in the 1830s.   3959

Bryden, H. A. The Exiled Scot. New Amsterdam Bk. Co.,
1899. A Jacobite refugee in the employ of the Dutch East
India Company in Africa.   3960

Charters, Zelda. Barbary Brew. Stackpole Sons, 1937. A
young American doctor is captured by pirates and sold as a
slave in Tripoli.   3961

Cialente, Fausta. The Levantines. (tr.) Houghton, 1963,
c. 1962. A picture of the rich Levantine society of Alexandria
from 1869 until World War II.   3962

Cloete, Stuart. The Fiercest Heart. Houghton, 1960. The
trip by wagon of a group of Boer farmers seeking a lost
freedom in the wilds of South Africa.   3963

_____. The Hill of Doves. Houghton, 1941. Boer families
in the Transvaal in 1880.   3964

_____. The Mask. Houghton, 1957. Features the war be-
tween the Boers and the Kaffirs during 1852-54.   3965

_____. Rags of Glory. Doubleday, 1963. A novel of the
Boer War between the English and Dutch in South Africa,
in which several famous historical figures appear.   3966

_____. The Turning Wheels. Houghton, 1937. The over-
land journey of the Boers from Cape Colony to the Trans-
vaal.   3967

_____. Watch for the Dawn. Houghton, 1939. A young
Boer tries to build a new life in the unexplored African

veldt.   3968

Cobban, J. MacLaren. Cease Fire! Methuen, 1900. "A
story of the Transvaal War of 1881."   3969

_____. The Red Sultan. Rand McNally, 1893. Fast-
moving, colorful story of Morocco late in the eighteenth
century.   3970

Corder, Eric. Slave Ship. McKay, 1969. The bloody, de-
humanizing trade of those brutal men who earned their living
by selling African Negroes into slavery.   3971

Cripps, Arthur S. (1) A Martyr's Servant. Duckworth, 1915.
(2) A Martyr's Heir (sequel). Duckworth, 1916. Told as
first-hand accounts of Jesuit missionary work in Africa in
the sixteenth century.   3972-3

Cullum, Ridgwell. The Compact. Doran, 1909. A romantic
triangle in South Africa during the Transvaal War of 1881.
                                                                 3974

De Kalb, Eugenie. Far Enough. Stokes, 1935. The Great
Trek of the Boers in 1836 and the effect it had on a woman's
life.   3975

Divine, Arthur Durham. Golden Fool. by David Divine,
pseud. Macmillan, 1954. The discovery of gold and
other background causes of the Boer War.   3976

Doyle, Sir Arthur Conan. The Tragedy of the Korosko.
Smith & Elder, 1898. A pleasure-seeking group of Euro-
peans finds more danger and adventure than expected in a
trip to Africa.   3977

Eden, Dorothy. Siege in the Sun. by Mary Paradise, pseud.
Coward, 1967. The story of various personages caught in
the long siege of Mafeking in South Africa.   3978

Fairbridge, Dorothea. That Which Hath Been. Low, 1913.
A story of the Dutch East India Company in Africa about
1700.   3979

Gartner, Chloe. Drums of Khartoum. Morrow, 1967. Romance set in Khartoum on the Nile during its siege and
fall in 1884-5, showing life in an army outpost surrounded
by desert.   3980

Golon, Sergeanne, pseud. for Serge and Anne Golon.
Angélique in Barbary. (tr.) [En. title: Angélique and
the Sultan] Bantam Bks., 1968, c.1960. Countess Angélique, in quest of her husband, is twice captured by pirates
and sold into slavery among the Moslems of North Africa.
                                                                 3981

Haggard, H. Rider. Child of Storm. Longmans, 1913. Mid-
nineteenth century quarrel in Zululand between two Princes.
(followed by Finished)   3982

_____. Finished. Longmans, 1917. Events prior to, dur-
ing, and after the Zulu War.   3983

_____. Marie. Cassell, 1912. An exciting, interesting
story of the Great Trek in South Africa, as the Boers sought
freedom from oppression. (followed by Child of Storm)   3984

_____. Swallow. Longmans, 1899. The Great Trek of the
Dutch settlers who left Cape Colony to escape unpopular
British rule.   3985

Hawes, Charles Boardman. Great Quest. Little, 1921. Adventures of New Englanders in Africa in the 1820s.   3986

Hervey, Harry. Barracoon. Putnam, 1950. A bride arrives
in Portuguese Guinea to learn belatedly that her husband is
a slave trader.   3987

Howarth, Anna. Katrina. Smith & Elder, 1898. The effect
of a smallpox epidemic on daily life in mid-nineteenth century South Africa.   3988

_____. Nora Lester. Smith & Elder, 1902. Relations be-
tween English and Dutch farmers in South Africa in the
1890s.   3989

_____. Sword and Assegai. Smith & Elder, 1899. The
historical setting is the Kaffir risings of 1846 and 1851 in
South Africa.   3990

Juta, Rene. Cape Currey. Holt, 1920. Cape Town in the
1820s--a romantic story which includes much political history.   3991

Kaye, Mary Margaret. Trade Wind. Coward, 1964, c.1963.
Romance of an American girl in Zanzibar with a renegade
British slave-trader.   3992

Krepps, Robert Wilson. Earthshaker. Macmillan, 1958. An
American and a Boer each try to steal a fabulous diamond
horde from an African king.   3993

_____. Tell It on the Drums. Macmillan, 1955. A descrip-
tion of life, hunting, and landscape as four diamond thieves
and an innocent companion flee across the South African veldt
in the 1880s.   3994

Lee, Jonathan. The Fate of the Grosvenor. [En. title:
Wreck of the Grosvenor] Covici, 1938. The wreck of an

East Indian trading vessel off the coast of South Africa and
the experiences of its survivors as they seek to make their
way to Capetown.   3995

Lytton, David.   The Paradise People.   S. & S. , 1962.   Hardy
Dutch pioneers in a Boer community among the natives of
northern South Africa.   3996

Mason, A. E. W.   The Four Feathers.   Macmillan, 1902.   A
youth proves he is not a coward in nineteenth century
Africa.   3997

Millin, Sarah Gertrude.   The Burning Man.   Putnam, 1952.
An unhappy man's effort to find solace as a missionary to
Africa.   3998

_____.   King of the Bastards.   Harper, 1949.   Early white
settlers in South Africa.   3999

Mitford, Bertram.   Aletta.   White, 1900.   An Englishman and
his Dutch wife just before and during the Boer War.   4000

_____.   The Gun Runner.   Fenno, 1893.   A romance of
Zululand in the late 1870s.   4001

_____.   The Induna's Wife.   White, 1898.   The wars of
the South African colonies at the time of the Great Trek.   4002

_____.   The King's Assegai.   Fenno, 1894.   A story of
the Matabele rising, suppressed by the British in 1896.   4003

_____.   The Luck of Gerald Ridgeley.   Chatto, 1893.   A
tale of the Zulu border in the 1870s.   4004

_____.   A Romance of the Cape Frontier.   Heinemann,
1891.   Exciting story of the Kaffir Rising in the late
1870s.   4005

_____.   The Sign of the Spider.   Dodd, 1896.   Fighting
and romance in South Africa toward the end of the nineteenth century.   4006

_____.   'Tween Snow and Fire.   Cassell, 1892.   Frontier
warfare with Kaffirs combined with romance.   4007

_____.   The Word of the Sorceress.   Hutchinson, 1902.
Vivid account of Zululand and of fighting with the British. 4008

Montupet, Jeanne.   The Red Fountain.   (tr.)   St. Martin's,
1961.   A French family struggles to establish its home and
fortune in nineteenth century Algeria despite natural disasters and hostile natives.   4009

Rabie, Jan. A Man Apart. (tr.) Macmillan, 1969. Growing conflict between Dutch and Hottentots in South Africa is
intensified by new arrivals.   4010

Ralli, Constantine S. The Strange Story of Falconer Thring.
Hurst & Blackett, 1907. Based on the Zulu War of the
1870s.   4011

Roberts, Morley. The Colossus. Harper, 1899. A story of
plans to exploit the wealth of South Africa.   4012

Rooke, Daphne. Diamond Jo. Reynal, 1965. A Jewish diamond
buyer during the Transvaal diamond rush in the 1860s and his
love for a dancehall girl.   4013

_____. Mittee. Houghton, 1951. Romance and social life
in a South African community in the 1890s and the friendship between a Boer lady and her African servant.   4014

_____. Wizards' Country. Houghton, 1957. The life, be-
liefs, and customs of the Tshanini, a Zulu tribe.   4015

Rooney, Philip. Golden Coast. Duell, 1949. A sea yarn of
a sailing ship's voyages and encounters with Barbary
pirates.   4016

Russell, George Hansby. Under the Sjambok. Murray, 1899.
The Transvaal just before the South African War.   4017

Scholefield, Alan. Great Elephant. Morrow, 1968. Adventures of the white family of a fugitive who takes refuge
among the Zulus of South Africa in the early nineteenth
century.   4018

_____. A View of Vultures. Doubleday, 1966. A Scots-
man persistently seeks revenge against three fellow ex-con-
victs in South Africa who, ten years earlier, had chopped
off his manacled hand to free themselves.   4019

_____. Wild Dog Running. Morrow, 1971. The tragic im-
migration of a poverty-stricken English family to the supposed land of plenty, South Africa.   4020

Sinclair, Kathleen H. The Covenant. by Brigid Knight, pseud.
Crowell, 1943. Differences between English and Dutch factions in South Africa during the Boer War.   4021

_____. Walking the Whirlwind. by Brigid Knight, pseud.
Crowell, 1941. A family in nineteenth century South Africa.   4022

_____. Westward the Sun. by Brigid Knight, pseud.
Crowell, 1942. The discovery of gold and increasing

tension between English and Boers.   4023

Skelton, Gladys. Dominion. by John Presland, pseud.
Stokes, 1925. Political career of Cecil Rhodes, premier
of Cape Colony.   4024

Slaughter, Frank G. The Deadly Lady of Madagascar. by C.
V. Terry, pseud. Doubleday, 1959. Fate of an East India
Company ship commissioned to destroy a pirate in the
1700s.   4025

Smith, Wilbur A. When the Lion Feeds. Viking, 1964. A
tale of the gold fields and the Zulu War in Africa in the
1860s.   4026

Steen, Marguerite. The Sun Is My Undoing. Viking, 1941.
Adventures of an eighteenth century English slave trader,
temporarily a prisoner of Barbary pirates. (followed by
Twilight on the Floods)   4027

_____. Twilight on the Floods. Doubleday, 1949. English
colonization and problems on the Gold Coast in the 1890s. 4028

Thesen, Hjalmar. The Echoing Cliffs. McKay, 1964. Adventures of a young African who is the sole survivor of a
hostile attack which destroyed the rest of his tribe.   4029

Watt, Lauchlan Maclean. The House of Sands. Secker, 1913.
Experiences of a Scotsman with the Moors of the Barbary
coast in the seventeenth century.   4030

Yerby, Frank. The Dahomean. Dial, 1971. How native customs and traditions of Africans were changed by the cruel,
greedy slave trade and by encroaching colonialism.   4031

Young, Francis Brett. (1) They Seek a Country. Reynal,
1937. (2) City of Gold. Reynal, 1939. English colonists
in South Africa during the nineteenth century take part in
developing the country.   4032-3

3. OCEANIA IN MODERN TIMES

   a) Australia and New Zealand

Andrews, Mrs. T.R. Stephen Kyrle. Unwin, 1901. Immigrants to Australia in the 1860s.   4034

Becke, Louis. Helen Adair. Lippincott, 1903. Helen's father
is sent to Botany Bay in the 1770s, so she devises a drastic
scheme to follow him.   4035

_____ and Walter Jeffery. A First Fleet Family. Mac-

millan, 1896. The voyage of exiled convicts to the new
settlements in New South Wales in the late eighteenth
century.   4036

Blunden, Godfrey. Charco Harbour. Vanguard, 1968. Exciting experiences of Captain James Cook and his crew following shipwreck as they take refuge in a lonely harbour in the
South Seas.   4037

Boyd, Martin. Cardboard Crown. Dutton, 1953, c.1952. A
tale of upper-class Victorian Australia.   4038

_____. A Difficult Young Man. Reynal, 1956, c.1955.
An account of an English-Australian family with Spanish
ancestors in Australia, 1892-1911.   4039

Browne, Thomas A. Nevermore. by Rolf Boldrewood, pseud.
Macmillan, 1892. Excitement in Australia in mid-nineteenth
century caused by the discovery of gold.   4040

_____. (1) Robbery Under Arms. Macmillan, 1888.
(2) The Miner's Right. Macmillan, 1890. (3) A Colonial
Reformer. Macmillan, 1890. (4) A Sydney-Side Saxon.
Macmillan, 1891. (5) Babes in the Bush. Macmillan,
1900. all by Rolf Boldrewood, pseud. These independent
novels give attractive pictures of the life of settlers of
Australia in the mid-nineteenth century.   4041-5

_____. The Squatter's Dream. by Rolf Boldrewood, pseud.
Macmillan, 1890. Sheep raising in colonial Australia in the
1800s.   4046

_____. War to the Knife. by Rolf Boldrewood, pseud.
Macmillan, 1899. Fighting in the Maori War in New Zealand
in the 1860s.   4047

Bruce, Robert. Benbonuna. Long, 1904. Life in the Australian bush in the middle of the nineteenth century.   4048

Burton, Hester. No Beat of Drums. World, 1967, c.1966.
YA. Penal colony life in Tasmania in the 1830s as the
prisoners worked to develop the frontier country.   4049

Clark, Mavis Thorpe. Blue Above the Trees. Meredith,
1968. YA. A pioneer family settles in a rain forest area
of Australia in 1877.   4050

Close, Robert Shaw. Eliza Callaghan. Doubleday, 1958.
Irish girl escapes an Australian penal colony and makes
a good marriage with a founder of Melbourne.   4051

Couvreur, Jessie C. Uncle Piper of Piper's Hill. by Tasma,
pseud. Trübner, 1888. Australian life in nineteenth cen-

tury Victoria. 4052

Cowan, James. The Adventures of Kimble Bent. Whitcombe
& Tomba, 1911. Story of a man who lived for thirteen
years with the wild cannibals of the New Zealand bush. 4053

Dark, Eleanor. Storm of Time. McGraw, 1950. The flavor
of early Australia with its mingling of English settlers, convicts, and aborigines. 4054

_____. The Timeless Land. Macmillan, 1941. Early diffi-
culties of establishing a stable community in Australia with
its many convicts. 4055

Doudy, Henry A. Magic of Dawn. Hutchinson, 1924. Exploration and settlement of Australia in the 1840s. 4056

Dyson, Edward. In the Roaring 'Fifties. Chatto, 1906. An
account of the Australian gold rush of the 1850s. 4057

Eden, Dorothy. Sleep in the Woods. Coward, 1961. Two
girls go husband-hunting in New Zealand in the time when
settlers still had to battle savage.natives. 4058

_____. The Vines of Yarrabee. Coward, 1969. Gentle
English lady finds life at the Australian plantation, Yarrabee, wilder and harder than she had expected. 4059

Gaskin, Catherine. I Know My Love. Doubleday, 1962.
Competition for wealth and love in nineteenth century Australia, as two women love one man in the midst of the gold
rush. 4060

_____. Sara Dane. Lippincott, 1955. Romance and life of
a naval officer and a former prisoner in late eighteenth century Australia. 4061

Goldsmith, Henry. Euancondit. Sonnenschein, 1895. Life
in Australia during the 1860s. 4062

Hay, William. Herridge of Reality Swamp. Unwin, 1907.
The hardships of convicts banished to uncivilized New
South Wales. 4063

Heney, Helen. Dark Moon. Crowell, 1954. Absorbing story
of a girl who, just before her marriage, was shipwrecked
and believed dead for six years. 4064

Hornung, Ernest William. Denis Dent. Isbister, 1903. Adventures in the mid-nineteenth century Australian gold
fields. 4065

_____. The Rogue's March. Scribner, 1896. Abuses

heaped on the convicts at the penal colony at New South
Wales.   4066

Keneally, Thomas. Bring Larks and Heroes. Viking, 1968,
c. 1967. A scholarly corporal in the British army at a
penal colony in Australia is confronted with appalling brutality and difficult choices.   4067

Kingsley, Henry. The Recollections of Geoffrey Hamlyn.
Longmans, 1859. The life of mid-nineteenth century Australia, with much of the story concerning an exiled convict.   4068

Lyttleton, Edith J. Promenade. by G.B. Lancaster, pseud.
Reynal, 1938. Pioneer life in colonial New Zealand in the
nineteenth century.   4069

Nordhoff, Charles and James Norman Hall. Botany Bay.
Little, 1941. A highwayman, Hugh Tallant, is sent to the
penal colony in Australia.   4070

Outhwaite, R. L. and C. H. Chomley. The Wisdom of Esau.
Unwin, 1901. Controversy over land ownership in Australia
in the later nineteenth century.   4071

Park, Ruth. The Frost and the Fire. Houghton, 1958. A
wide range of people came to New Zealand in the 1860s to
search for gold.   4072

Satchell, William. The Greenstone Door. Sidgwick & Jackson,
1914. Exciting events in New Zealand during the middle of
the nineteenth century.   4073

Simpson, Helen de Guerry. Under Capricorn. Macmillan,
1938. Life among the upper classes in Australia during
the 1830s.   4074

Stringfellow, Olga. The Fresh and the Salt. [En. title:
Mary Bravender] Doubleday, 1959. Romances and adventures await a Scottish girl who comes to New Zealand to
marry a man she knows only slightly.   4075

White, Patrick. Voss. Viking, 1957. Ill-fated trek of the
German explorer Voss across the Australian desert.   4076

Whitney, Janet. Jennifer. Morrow, 1940. Life in an English prison colony in Australia in the early 1800s.   4077

b) The Philippines, Indonesia, and
    Other Islands of the Pacific

Becke, Louis and Walter Jeffery. The Mutineer. Lippin-

cott, 1898. The mutiny of the seamen on the Bounty and
their settling on Pitcairn Island in 1790.   4078

Bushnell, Oswald Andrew. Molokai. World, 1963. Various
types of persons find fulfillment in both earthly and divine
love at the leper colony of the devoted Father Damien.   4079

Clarke, Marcus A. H. For the Term of His Natural Life.
Munro, 1874. A grim account of the almost unbelievably
cruel treatment accorded convicts at the penal colony in
nineteenth century Tasmania.   4080

Conrad, Joseph. Almayer's Folly. Macmillan, 1895. Married life of a civilized European and a semi-savage Malayan
in Borneo.   4081

Cronin, Bernard. The Coastlanders. Hodder & Stoughton,
1918. Opposition of older settlers to new ways and developments in nineteenth century Tasmania.   4082

Dick, Isabel. Country Heart. Crowell, 1946. Girl descended from Tasmanian pioneers marries a Boer War
veteran and lives for a time in Africa.   4083

_____. Wild Orchard. Crowell, 1945. Emigrants from
Victorian England become pioneers in Tasmania in the 1840s.
(followed by Country Heart)   4084

Foreman, Russell. Long Pig. McGraw, 1958. Thirteen
survivors of a nineteenth century shipwreck land on a can-
nibal isle in the Fijis.   4085

Gerahty, Digby George. Bonin. by Robert Standish, pseud.
Macmillan, 1944. Life of shipwrecked English seamen on
the Bonin Islands, whose ownership was disputed.   4086

Harrison, Samuel Bertram. White King. Doubleday, 1950.
A medical missionary and his work in Hawaii in the second
quarter of the nineteenth century.   4087

Hay, William. Captain Quadring. Unwin, 1912. The penal
colony in nineteenth century Tasmania.   4088

_____. The Escape of the Notorious Sir William Heans.
Unwin, 1918. A romance depicting the convict period of
Tasmania.   4089

Hoyt, Helen P. The Jeweled Cross. Doubleday, 1964. YA.
In 1882 orphaned Samantha Allen goes to live in the little-
known, mysterious Hawaiian Islands.   4090

Hyne, C.J. Cutcliffe. Sandy Carmichael. Lippincott, 1908.
Adventures of two fugitives among cannibal-infested Pacific

islands in the eighteenth century.   4091

Lyttleton, Edith J. Pageant. by G.B. Lancaster, pseud.
Century, 1933. The aristocratic families who were the
foundation of colonization of Tasmania.   4092

McGinnis, Paul. Lost Eden. McBride, 1947. The care-free
life of one of Cook's sailors who jumped ship at Hawaii.   4093

Melville, Herman. Typee. Wiley & Putnam, 1846. Sailors'
adventures among the cannibalistic natives of the Marquesas
Islands.   4094

Nielsen, Virginia. The Whistling Winds. McKay, 1964. YA.
A young whaler, injured in a fight, is left at the Hawaiian
Islands to recuperate in the company of a missionary
couple.   4095

Nordhoff, Charles and James Norman Hall. The Bounty Trilogy.
Little, 1936. Contains Mutiny on the Bounty, Men Against
the Sea, and Pitcairn's Island (see separate listings).   4096

_____. Men Against the Sea. Little, 1934. The story of
Captain Bligh and his faithful sailors who were set adrift by
mutineers in 1789. (followed by Pitcairn's Island)   4097

_____. Mutiny on the Bounty. Little, 1932. Causes and
results of the mutiny on the ship Bounty on its return voyage
from the South Pacific. (followed by Men Against the Sea)
                                                            4098
_____. Pitcairn's Island. Little, 1934. The mutineers
and a group of Polynesians reach Pitcairn's Island and destroy the Bounty.   4099

O'Connor, Richard. Officers and Ladies. Doubleday, 1958.
Adventures during the American occupation of the Philippines
in the 1890s.   4100

Oxenham, John, pseud. for William Arthur Dunkerley. White
Fire. Hodder, 1905. Life on a South Sea island in the
1800s.   4101

Rizal, José. The Lost Eden. (tr.) Ind. Univ. Pr., 1961.
(orig. pub. in 1887 as Noli Me Tangere) Vignettes of
Filipino life and the evils of Spanish colonization, written
by a Filipino hero who was executed for his patriotic and
political activities.   4102

Teilhet, Darwin Le Ora. Mission of Jeffery Tolamy. Sloane,
1951. Russian attempt to occupy Hawaii in the early nineteenth century.   4103

Wilson, Hazel. Last Queen of Hawaii: Liliuokalani. Knopf,

1963. YA. A fictional biography of the last queen of Hawaii just before it became a territory of the United States in the administration of McKinley. 4104

C. THE WESTERN HEMISPHERE
IN MODERN TIMES (c. 1500-1900)

1. THE UNITED STATES

a) Colonial Period to 1763

Alderman, Clifford L. To Fame Unknown. Appleton, 1954. A novel of war and romance during the last part of the French and Indian Wars. 4105

Alfriend, Mary Bethell. Juan Ortiz. Chapman & Grimes, 1941. Spanish explorer who lived ten years with Indians in Florida, then became a guide for De Soto. 4106

Allen, Hervey. Bedford Village. Rinehart, 1944. Indian-reared Salathiel Albine works to adapt himself to white man's customs. (followed by Toward the Morning) 4107

_____. The City in the Dawn. Rinehart, 1950. An abridgement of Salathiel Albine's adventures as told in The Forest and the Fort, Bedford Village, and Toward the Morning, with a concluding chapter, "The City in the Dawn" (see separate listings) 4108

_____. The Forest and the Fort. Farrar, 1943. Salathiel Albine, raised by Shawnee Indians, returns to the world of the white man. (followed by Bedford Village) 4109

_____. Toward the Morning. Rinehart, 1948. Pioneer life in Pennsylvania before the Revolution, featuring Salathiel Albine and his common-law wife, Melissa. 4110

Aswell, Mary Louise. Abigail. Crowell, 1959. Lively, worldly Abigail rebels against the quiet life of her Quaker parents. 4111

Austin, Jane Goodwin. Betty Alden; The First Born Daughter of the Pilgrims. Houghton, 1891. Life of the Pilgrims in Massachusetts after the first hard winter was over. 4112

Babcock, William Henry. The Tower of Wye. [same as The Brides of the Tiger] Coates, 1901. Early colonists along the Atlantic coast. 4113

Bacheller, Irving. Candle in the Wilderness. Bobbs, 1930. A vivid, picturesque story of Indians and colonists in the early days of New England. 4114

Barker, Shirley. The Last Gentleman. Random, 1960. The
English loyalty of the New Hampshire governor, Sir John
Wentworth.   4115

_____. Peace, My Daughters. Crown, 1949. A novel of
the infamous witchcraft trials in Salem with the devil disguised as a shoemaker.   4116

_____. Rivers Parting. Crown, 1950. English colonists
in the New World find their loyalties divided between their
old and new homes.   4117

_____. Strange Wives. Crown, 1963. Tension resulting
from intermarriage between a Christian girl and an orthodox
Jew in colonial Rhode Island, showing Jewish customs.   4118

_____. Tomorrow the New Moon. Bobbs, 1955. Three
cousins from the Isle of Man who settled on Martha's Vineyard.   4119

Barr, Amelia E. The Bow of Orange Ribbon. Dodd, 1888.
Contrast between the simple New York Dutch and the dash-
ing British soldiers. (followed by The Maid of Maiden
Lane)   4120

_____. The House on Cherry Street. Dodd, 1909. Politi-
cal controversy in British colonial New York.   4121

_____. A Maid of Old New York. Dodd, 1911. New Am-
sterdam in the days of Peter Stuyvesant.   4122

Barrett, Wilson and E.A. Barron. In Old New York. Macqueen, 1900. A view of life in colonial New York before
the Revolution.   4123

Belden, Jessie Van Zile. Antonia. Page, 1901. Story of
Dutch colonists in the Hudson River Valley.   4124

Best, Allena. Seven Beaver Skins. by Erick Berry, pseud.
Winston, 1948. YA. The story of a Dutchman skilled in
falconry and fur-trading in New Amsterdam.   4125

_____. Valiant Captive. by Erick Berry, pseud. Chilton,
1962. YA. Captured in Massachusetts by marauding Indians,
young Margaret Eames is eventually ransomed by the French
in Quebec.   4126

Blacker, Irwin R. Taos. World Pub., 1959. Rebellion of the
Pueblo Indians of New Mexico against Spanish oppression in
the 1680s.   4127

Blake, Forrester. The Franciscan. Doubleday, 1963. A
Spanish missionary among the Pueblo Indians in seventeenth

century New Mexico is confronted by difficulties and dilem-
mas.   4128

Bloundelle-Burton, John. The Land of Bondage. White, 1904.
Adventures of indentured servants in colonial Virginia.   4129

Borden, Lucille Papin. King's Highway. Macmillan, 1941.
Story of the Starforths, refugees from Elizabethan England,
who seek religious freedom in the New World.   4130

Borland, Barbara Dodge. The Greater Hunger. Appleton,
1962. Love and trials of an English country girl who is a
gardening enthusiast and a young divine who is an idealist,
in the Massachusetts Bay Colony of 1629.   4131

Bowen, Marjorie, pseud. for Gabrielle Campbell Long. Mr.
Washington. Appleton, 1915. Washington's career as a
soldier in the French and Indian Wars and during the Revolution.   4132

Boyce, Burke. Morning of a Hero. Harper, 1963. Early career of George Washington as surveyor and soldier, occupations which prepared and matured him for future tasks.   4133

Boyd, Thomas Alexander. Shadow of the Long Knives. Scribner, 1928. Adventures of an Indian-reared scout who attempts
to achieve peace between British and Indians.   4134

Bradbury, Bianca. Goodness and Mercy Jenkins. Washburn,
1963. YA. Mercy Jenkins, a spirited teen-aged orphan,
scandalizes her staid Puritan town by her unconventional actions.   4135

Breslin, Howard. Bright Battalions. McGraw, 1953. Fighting and romance in the French and Indian Wars.   4136

_____. The Silver Oar. Crowell, 1954. A story of colonial
America ending with the Boston uprising of 1689.   4137

Buchan, John. Salute to Adventurers. Doran, 1917. A Scotsman who comes to Virginia to manage an estate finds adventure in the wild, new country.   4138

Burke, Wilfrid L. Naked Days of the Lost Moon. Vantage,
1970. The explosive atmosphere in western Pennsylvania
resulting from friction between English and French settlers,
Indians, militia, and Quakers.   4139

Bynner, Edwin Lassetter. Agnes Surriage. Houghton, 1886.
Romance of the collector of the port of Boston and a servant,
the daughter of a poor fisherman.   4140

_____. The Begum's Daughter. Little, 1890. Customs

and life in New Amsterdam during the 1689-91 rebellion
and the, rule of Jacob Leisler.   4141

_____. Penelope's Suitors. Houghton, 1887. Diary of the
romances of Penelope Pelham, later the wife of Massachusetts Governor Buckley.   4142

Cannon, LeGrand. Come Home at Even. Holt, 1951. Quest
of freedom and happiness in America in the Puritan colony
of Salem.   4143

Carlisle, Helen G. We Begin. Smith, 1932. A story of Pilgrim founders of our country with emphasis on personali-
ties.   4144

Chalmers, Harvey. Drums Against Frontenac. R.R. Smith,
1949. The capture of Fort Frontenac by British General
Bradstreet and his troops.   4145

Clapp, Patricia. Constance. Lothrop, 1968. YA. The difficulties facing the Mayflower Pilgrims challenge a young girl
to grow up quickly.   4146

Clark, Imogen. The Domine's Garden. Murray, 1901. Social
life among the Dutch in colonial New York.   4147

Clark, Mary Higgins. Aspire to the Heavens. Meredith, 1969,
c.1968. YA. The youth of George Washington, the influence
of his mother, and his marriage to Martha Custis.   4148

Clarke, Mary Stetson. The Iron Peacock. Viking, 1966. YA.
A young woman, unable to pay for her ocean passage, becomes an indentured worker for the owner of an iron works.
                                                                  4149

Coatsworth, Elizabeth. Sword of the Wilderness. Macmillan,
1936. YA. Through a long, hard winter, captured Seth
Hubbard comes to know and understand the Indian way of
life.   4150

Cochran, Hamilton. Silver Shoals. Bobbs, 1945. A tale of
hunting for sunken treasure.   4151

Colver, Alice. The Measure of the Years. Dodd, 1954. First
families of Indian Village, now known as Stockbridge, Massachusetts. (followed by There Is a Season)   4152

_____. There Is a Season. Dodd, 1957. A girl's elope-
ment with a romantic peddler, and her later, more solid,
marriage.   4153

Constantin-Weyer, Maurice. The French Adventurer. Macaulay,
1931. A fictional account of the famous explorer La Salle.
                                                                  4154

Cooke, Grace MacGowan and Alice MacGowan. Return.
Page, 1905. Georgia in the days following its founding
by Oglethorpe.   4155

Cooke, John Esten. My Lady Pokahontas. Houghton, 1879.
Concerns John Smith and the Indian princess Pocahontas--his
problems in settling Jamestown; her marriage and life in
England.   4156

Cooke, Rose. Steadfast. Houghton, 1889. This is the story
of a young New England minister.   4157

Coolidge, A.C. Prophet of Peace. Hungerford-Holbrook, 1907.
The romance of a Quaker and a Puritan is opposed by rela-
tives.   4158

Cooper, James Fenimore. The Leather-Stocking Tales: (1)
The Deerslayer. Lea & Blanchard, 1841. The famous
backwoodsman, Hawkeye, as a youth. (2) The Last of the
Mohicans. Carey & Lea, 1826. Incidents of the Old French
War. (3) The Pathfinder. Bentley, 1840. Romance comes
to Hawkeye. (4) The Pioneers. Colburn & Bentley, 1832.
Seventy-year-old Hawkeye in his boyhood home. (5) The
Prairie. Colburn, 1827. The eighty-year-old woodsman goes
to the Upper Missouri to escape the advance of civilization.
                                                                     4159-63
Cooper, Jamie Lee. Shadow of a Star. Bobbs, 1965. Three
Basque brothers become a fur-trader, an outlaw, and a
priest among the American Indians in the 1680s.   4164

Cooper, Kent. Anna Zenger: Mother of Freedom. Farrar,
1946. Struggle for freedom of the press with the first news-
paperwoman in a prominent part.   4165

Cross, Ruth. Soldier of Good Fortune. Banks Upshaw, 1936.
Adventures of a French nobleman in the American South-
west.   4166

Crowley, Mary Catherine. The Heroine of the Strait. Little,
1902. Pontiac's Conspiracy with the French against the
British.   4167

Davidson, L.S. The Disturber. Macmillan, 1964. Story of
Thomas Morton who aroused Puritan opposition by his colony
of Merry Mount near Plymouth.   4168

Devon, John Anthony. O Western Wind. Putnam, 1957. The
Mayflower Pilgrims and the settlement of Plymouth.   4169

Dickson, Harris. The Black Wolf's Breed. Bobbs, 1900.
Louisiana in the French colonial period before the outbreak
of the Seven Years War.   4170

_____. Gabrielle Transgressor. Lippincott, 1906. Ro-
mance of a Turkish prince and a French girl in colonial
New Orleans.   4171

_____. The Siege of Lady Resolute. Harper, 1902.
Legend of the rich merchant who wished to become Prince
of Louisiana.   4172

Dix, Beulah M. The Making of Christopher Ferringham. Macmillan, 1901. The strictness of the Puritan founders of
Massachusetts and their attitude toward Quakers.   4173

_____. Mistress Content Cradock. Barnes, 1899. A story
of some who sought religious freedom in the New World.   4174

_____ and Carrie A. Harper. The Beau's Comedy. Harper,
1902. A Londoner in the American colonies is falsely suspected of being an Indian spy.   4175

Dodge, Constance. In Adam's Fall. Macrae Smith, 1946.
Witch hunt in Puritan Salem.   4176

Dowdey, Clifford. Gamble's Hundred. Little, 1939. The romance of a surveyor near Williamsburg, Virginia.   4177

Du Bois, Theodora M. Freedom's Way. Funk, 1953. A young
English gentlewoman is unjustly sent as an indentured slave
to America.   4178

Edmonds, Walter D. They Had a Horse. Dodd, 1962. A
struggling young pioneer couple in upstate New York manages to buy a surprising horse.   4179

Ehle, John. The Land Breakers. Harper, 1964. Diverse and
interesting persons figure in the hard pioneer life of the
mountains along the Carolina-Tennessee frontier.   4180

Ethridge, Willie Snow. Summer Thunder. Coward, 1959.
Colonization of Georgia, an attempted Spanish invasion,
and the career of James Oglethorpe.   4181

Faulkner, Nancy. Tomahawk Shadow. Doubleday, 1959. YA.
The hero is a sixteen-year-old boy who gains an insight into
the beliefs of Roger Williams and the circumstances surrounding King Philip's War.   4182

Flannagan, Roy Catesby. Forest Cavalier. Bobbs, 1952.
Beginnings of American national feeling in Jamestown in
1676.   4183

Fletcher, Inglis. Bennett's Welcome. Bobbs, 1950. A captain in Charles II's army comes to Carolina as an indentured servant and builds a new life.   4184

_____. Cormorant's Brood. Lippincott, 1959. Friction between British governor and colonists in North Carolina. 4185

_____. Lusty Wind for Carolina. Bantam Bks., 1971, c. 1944. Huguenot settlers find excitement, romance, and opportunity in the New World.   4186

_____. Men of Albemarle. Bobbs, 1942. English settlers in colonial North Carolina and a turbulent political battle. 4187

_____. Roanoke Hundred. Bobbs, 1948. The expedition of Grenville's group to Roanoke Island in 1585.   4188

_____. Rogue's Harbor. Bobbs, 1964. Effort of North Carolina colonists to obtain a measure of freedom from their Lords Proprietors, spiced by romance.   4189

_____. The Scotswoman. Bobbs, 1954. Flora MacDonald saves Bonnie Prince Charlie and is forced to fly to the New World.   4190

_____. The Wind in the Forest. Bobbs, 1957. Conflict between fiercely independent pioneer farmers and plantation owners loyal to England.   4191

Foote, Mary. The Royal Americans. Houghton, 1910. This story spans the period from Montcalm's capture of Oswego to the Revolution.   4192

Forbes, Esther. A Mirror for Witches. Houghton, 1928. Compelling story of a fear-crazed girl accused and imprisoned as a witch.   4193

_____. Paradise. Harcourt, 1937. Story of an estate (named Paradise) twenty miles from Boston.   4194

Forbes-Lindsay, C. H. John Smith, Gentleman Adventurer. Lippincott, 1907. The difficulties and successes of the early settlers in Virginia.   4195

Fraser, Mary Crawford. In the Shadow of the Lord. by Mrs. Hugh Fraser. Holt, 1906. A tale of George Washington's parents and of his childhood near Fredericksburg.   4196

Frey, Ruby. Red Morning. Putnam, 1946. Adventures of Jane Bell in Ohio in 1750, including capture by the Indians.
4197

Fuller, Hulbert. Vivian of Virginia. Page, 1900. Bacon's Rebellion, brought on by the British governor's failure to provide adequate defense against Indians.   4198

Fuller, Iola. Gilded Torch. Putnam, 1957. La Salle's expedition which resulted in the discovery of the Mississippi. 4199

Garnett, David. Pocahontas. Harcourt, 1933. The childhood of Pocahontas, her rescue of John Smith, and her
subsequent marriage and life in England.   4200

Gay, Margaret Cooper. Hatchet in the Sky. S. & S., 1954.
The Detroit area during the French and Indian Wars and the
Pontiac Conspiracy.   4201

Gebler, Ernest. The Plymouth Adventure. Doubleday, 1950.
Sympathetic account of the Mayflower Pilgrims--their voyage
and first winter in the New World.   4202

Gerson, Noel B. Daughter of Eve. Doubleday, 1958. Indian
customs and English life are background for the story of
Pocahontas.   4203

_____. Forest Lord. by Samuel Edwards, pseud. Double-
day, 1955. An English nobleman, shanghaied aboard a British ship, comes to America.   4204

_____. The Highwayman. Doubleday, 1955. Melodramatic
tale of colonial life during King George's War.   4205

_____. The Impostor. Doubleday, 1954. Swords and guns
flash as a conspiracy to betray the American colonies is defeated.   4206

_____. King's Messenger. by Samuel Edwards, pseud.
Farrar, 1956. A seventeenth century British spy saves
the American colonies from the French.   4207

_____. The Land Is Bright. Doubleday, 1961. About
William Bradford and the early years of the hard-pressed
Plymouth Colony.   4208

_____. Roanoke Warrior. by Carter A. Vaughan, pseud.
Doubleday, 1965. A fugitive from an English debtors' prison
becomes a colonial leader in attacking the Tuscarora Indians.
                                                            4209

_____. Savage Gentleman. Doubleday, 1950. Life and ro-
mance amid the wilderness fighting of the French and Indian
wars.   4210

_____. The Seneca Hostage. by Carter A. Vaughan, pseud.
Doubleday, 1969. A pleasure-loving visitor to America is
captured and held hostage by the Seneca Indians.   4211

_____. The Silver Saber. By Carter A. Vaughan, pseud.
Doubleday, 1967. Rise of an ex-convict who comes to America as an indentured servant and becomes a member of
the military.   4212

_____. The Wilderness. by Carter A. Vaughan, pseud.

Doubleday, 1959. Handsome Paul Ferrand was a spy for
the French and a counterspy for the English in New England
in 1745.   4213

Gibbs, Alonzo. The Fields Breathe Sweet. Lothrop, 1963.
YA. Tale of Quaker homesteaders on Long Island tells of
their way of life and of the two romances of the eighteen-
year-old daughter.   4214

Gibbs, George. The Love of Mademoiselle. [formerly In
Search of Mademoiselle] Appleton, 1926. Rivalry between
French and Spanish colonists in early Florida.   4215

Goodwin, Maud W. The Head of a Hundred in the Colony of
Virginia. Little, 1895. The settling of Virginia and fighting
with the Indians, told in autobiographical form.   4216

_____. Sir Christopher. Little, 1904. "A romance of a
Maryland manor in 1644."   4217

_____. White Aprons. Little, 1896. Story of Bacon's Re-
bellion, in which women formed a line to delay the enemy.
                                                                  4218
Gordon, Caroline. The Green Centuries. Scribner, 1941.
Lives of two pioneer brothers--one is captured by Indians,
the other becomes an Indian fighter.   4219

Grant, Dorothy. Margaret Brent, Adventurer. Longmans,
1944. The fight of a devout Catholic woman for religious
freedom in Maryland.   4220

_____. Night of Decision. Longmans, 1946. Colonial New
York under Stuart-appointed governor Colonel Thomas Don-
gan.   4221

Gregory, Jackson. Lords of the Coast. Dodd, 1935. California in the rough, ready days of early settlement.   4222

Griffin, Henry Farrand. The White Cockade. Greystone,
1941. Adventures of a roving Yankee sea captain and the
French Royalist whom he rescues.   4223

Hall, Ruth. The Golden Arrow. Houghton, 1901. Story of
the indomitable Anne Hutchinson, New England religious
leader who, banished from one colony, founded another.   4224

Hamilton, Harry. Thunder in the Wilderness. Bobbs, 1949.
Story of French traders and Indians in the Mississippi
Valley.   4225

Hammand, Esther Barstow. Road to Endor. Farrar, 1940.
A Salem minister attempts to do away with witchcraft.   4226

Harding, Newman. The Eternal Struggle. Long, 1912.
Adventure and love in Puritan Massachusetts.   4227

Hawthorne, Nathaniel. The Scarlet Letter. Ticknor, Reed and
Fields, 1850. Effects of sin in the lives of three people in
rigid Puritan Massachusetts.   4228

Hersch, Virginia. Seven Cities of Gold. Duell, 1946. Coronado's second expedition in search of gold--to Mexico, Texas, Kansas.   4229

Hinsdale, Harriet. Be My Love. Farrar, 1950. Social life
and customs of Boston in colonial times.   4230

Holland, Josiah Gilbert. The Bay Path. Scribner, 1857. New
England colonial life and character.   4231

Howard, Elizabeth. Verity's Voyage. Morrow, 1964. YA. A
girl takes a trip to Boston in an effort to avoid an arranged
marriage.   4232

Hughes, Rupert. Stately Timber. Scribner, 1939. Adventures
of a young man in Puritan New England.   4233

Irving, Washington. Rip Van Winkle and The Legend of Sleepy
Hollow. Macmillan, 1963. Two classic tales--one about the
lazy man who slept twenty years; the other about a frightening race with the Headless Horseman, both of which reflect
the thoughts and customs of the time.   4234

Jennings, John. Gentleman Ranker. Reynal, 1942. An English playboy becomes a man in the army in colonial Virginia.   4235

_____. Next to Valour. Macmillan, 1939. A Scotsman who
settles in New England becomes involved in the French and
Indian Wars.   4236

Johnston, Mary. Audrey. Houghton, 1902. A girl of the
Virginia backwoods loses her family and home at the hands
of the Indians.   4237

_____. Croatan. Little, 1923. The English settlers on
Roanoke Island, attacked by hostile Indians, are aided by
friendly ones.   4238

_____. The Great Valley. Little, 1926. A minister and
his family migrate from Scotland to the Shenandoah Valley.
                                                                4239
_____. Prisoners of Hope. Houghton, 1898. Political
unrest in Virginia when Britain sent convicts as colonists. 4240

_____. The Slave Ship. Little, 1924. A vividly told tale

of slave traffic between Africa and Virginia.   4241

_____. To Have and to Hold. [En. title: By Order of
the Company] Houghton, 1900. Lovely English girl flees
to the colonies to preserve her honor.   4242

Jordan, Mildred A. Echo of the Flute. Doubleday, 1958. A
family's experiences in Pennsylvania, with a vivid description of the yellow fever epidemic of 1793.   4243

_____. One Red Rose Forever. Knopf, 1941. A romance
of the early American glassmaker, German immigrant Baron
Stiegel.   4244

Kennedy, John P. Rob of the Bowl: A Legend of St. Inigoes.
Lea & Blanchard, 1838. "A story of the early days of
Maryland."   4245

Kennedy, Sara Beaumont. The Wooing of Judith. Doubleday,
1902. A romance of Virginia during the period of British
colonization.   4246

Kenyon, Theda. Golden Feather. Messner, 1943. Romance
of English colonists in Virginia.   4247

Kester, Vaughan. John O' Jamestown. McClure, 1907. Captain John Smith and the first permanent English settlement
in America.   4248

King, Grace Elizabeth. La Dame de Sainte Hermine. Macmillan, 1924. Adjustment of a cultured French girl to
wilderness life during the settlement of New Orleans.   4249

Knipe, Emilie Benson and Alden Arthur Knipe. The Shadow
Captain. Dodd, 1925. An account of the activities of an
Englishman in the town of New York in 1703.   4250

Knowles, Mabel Winifred. The Witch-Finder. by May Wynne,
pseud. Jarrolds Ltd., 1923. A tale of witch hunts, trials,
and executions in Massachusetts.   4251

Knox, Dorothea H. The Heart of Washington. Neale, 1909.
Recounts an early romance of George Washington.   4252

Lathrop, West. Black River Captive. Random House, 1946.
YA. A boy and his dog are captured by Indians in New
Hampshire during the French and Indian Wars.   4253

Lauritzen, Jonreed. Rose and the Flame. Doubleday, 1951.
Spaniards and Indians vie for control of the Southwest.   4254

Lee-Hamilton, Eugene. The Romance of the Fountain. Fisher
Unwin, 1905. Ponce de Leon's search for the fountain of

youth resulting in the discovery of Florida.   4255

Lide, Alice and Margaret Johansen. <u>Dark Possession.</u> Appleton, 1934. Colonial South Carolina when English settlers
and indentured servants faced a primitive life and a hostile
land.   4256

Lincoln, Victoria. <u>A Dangerous Innocence.</u> Rinehart, 1958.
A tangle of romance and jealousy causes involvement in the
Salem witchcraft trials.   4257

Linderholm, Helmer. <u>Land of the Beautiful River.</u> (tr.) St.
Martin's, 1963. Early Swedish colonization in the Delaware
region reflecting political schemes, Indian attacks, and the
determination of the settlers to survive.   4258

Lofts, Norah. <u>Blossom Like the Rose.</u> Knopf, 1939. A
crippled boy seeks happiness in the New World.   4259

Longstreet, Stephen. <u>War in the Golden Weather.</u> Doubleday,
1965. Adventures and campaigns in the company of George
Washington on the Virginia frontier during the French and
Indian Wars.   4260

Lovelace, Maud Hart. <u>The Charming Sally.</u> Day, 1932. Romance between a Quaker boy and a girl of the first theatrical company to come to the colonies.   4261

_____. <u>Early Candlelight.</u> U. of Minn., 1929. Frontier
life on the Upper Mississippi including soldiers, Indians,
trappers, and missionaries.   4262

McLaws, Lafayette, i.e., Emily Lafayette McLaws. <u>When
the Land Was Young.</u> Lothrop, 1902. Romance of Antoinette Huguenin and Captain Jack Middleton in the days
of Caribbean buccaneers.   4263

MacPhail, Andrew. <u>The Vine of Sibmah.</u> Macmillan, 1906.
Adventures of an English captain in his search for a Londoner's daughter in the colonies.   4264

Malkus, Alida Sims. <u>There Really Was a Hiawatha.</u> Grosset,
1963. YA. About the Onondaga warrior, Great White Eagle,
who helped bring about the Iroquois Confederacy and who
was the "Hiawatha" of Longfellow's poem.   4265

Mann, Helen R. <u>Gallant Warrior.</u> Eerdmans, 1954. Concerns a pioneer woman and her baby who were captured
by Indians.   4266

Marsh, George Tracy. <u>Ask No Quarter.</u> Morrow, 1945.
Yarn of a Newport man who battles Indians, pirates, and
poverty.   4267

Marshall, Edison. The Lost Colony. Doubleday, 1964. A
fictional unravelling of the fate of the second Fort Raleigh
colony as related to mysterious murders in England.   4268

Mason, Van Wyck. Rascals' Heaven. Doubleday, 1964. Although many of its first settlers were from English debtors'
prisons, Georgia, founded by General Oglethorpe, became a
worthy member of the original thirteen colonies.   4269

_____. The Young Titan. Doubleday, 1959. Stir-
rings of unity and independence in the New World exempli-
fied in the siege of Louisbourg.   4270

Matschat, Cecile Hulse. Tavern in the Town. Farrar & Rinehart, 1942. A story of everyday life and love in Tidewater
Virginia.   4271

Miers, Earl Schenck. Valley in Arms. Westminster, 1943.
Struggles of a pioneer couple with Indians and frontier hardships.   4272

Miller, Helen Topping. Dark Sails. Bobbs, 1945. Oglethorpe
leads a group of English settlers to St. Simons Island.   4273

_____. Proud Young Thing. Appleton, 1952. Romantic
novel which takes place in Charleston, South Carolina.   4274

Monroe, Forest. Maid of Montauks. Jenkins, 1902. Contacts
of the Montauk Indian tribe with the British in New York.   4275

Montgomery, K. L., pseud. for Kathleen and Letitia Montgomery. Maids of Salem. Long, 1915. The witch hunt
craze, influenced by Cotton Mather, in Salem and Boston.   4276

Moore, Ruth. A Fair Wind Home. Morrow, 1953. This
novel concerns Maine and the early history of her sea-
faring ventures.   4277

Morton, Stanley, pseud. for Stanley and Morton Freedgood.
Yankee Trader. Sheridan, 1947. A sea captain and trader
whose ambitions are wealth and power.   4278

Motley, John Lothrop. Merry Mount. Munroe, 1849. Reflects the cheerlessness and gloom prevalent among the
Puritans in the Plymouth colony.   4279

Mott, Michael. Master Entrick, an Adventure. Delacorte,
1966, c. 1965. YA. The work and wanderings of an English boy who is kidnapped and sent as a bond servant to
America in 1754.   4280

Murfree, Mary Noailles. The Amulet. by Charles Egbert
Craddock, pseud. Macmillan, 1906. Fighting between the

English and Cherokees in Tennessee.   4281

_____. A Spectre of Power. by Charles Egbert Crad-
dock, pseud. Houghton, 1903. The Mississippi Valley
during the conflicts between England and France.   4282

_____. The Story of Old Fort Loudon. by Charles Egbert
Craddock, pseud. Macmillan, 1899. An aspect of the Seven
Years War--the Cherokee attack on Fort Loudon.   4283

Murphy, Edward F. Bride for New Orleans. Hanover, 1955.
The work of priests and nuns with the Casket girls, who
came to New Orleans to marry.   4284

Neilson, Winthrop and Frances. Edge of Greatness. Putnam,
1951. Benjamin Franklin and the day of Braddock's defeat.
                                                        4285

Newton, John Edward. The Rogue and the Witch. Abelard,
1955. Temporary exile of a Puritan minister accused of
witchcraft.   4286

Oemler, Marie. The Holy Lover. Boni & Liveright, 1927.
The strict moral principles of John and Charles Wesley
and John's reaction to his own great romance.   4287

O'Leary, Thomas V. The Mark of the Turtle. Chilton, 1961.
YA. Chris O'Shea is captured and later adopted by Seneca
Indians, and must later choose to remain with the Indians
or return to his white family.   4288

O'Meara, Walter. The Spanish Bride. Putnam, 1954. An
actress journeys from Castile to frontier New Mexico.   4289

Page, Elizabeth. Wilderness Adventure. Rinehart, 1946.
Frontiersmen to the rescue of a girl captured by Indians. 4290

Pangborn, Edgar. Wilderness of Spring. Rinehart, 1958.
The rising fortunes of two brothers--one in sailing, the
other in medicine.   4291

Paradise, Jean. The Savage City. Crown, 1955. Action-
packed novel of New York in the violent 1740s.   4292

Parrish, Randall. A Sword of the Old Frontier. McClurg,
1905. Indian Wars at the time of the Pontiac Conspiracy
around Fort Chartres, Illinois, and Detroit, Michigan. 4293

Patterson, Burd Shippen. The Head of Iron. Walker, 1908.
General Braddock's defeat and the British attack on Fort
Duquesne.   4294

Pawle, Kathleen. Mural for a Later Day. Dodd, 1938. A
novel of the founding of New Sweden, a settlement on the

Delaware River.   4295

Payson, William Farquhar. John Vytal. Harper, 1901. What
happened to the English settlement at Roanoke?   4296

Pendexter, Hugh. The Red Road. Bobbs, 1927: Events surrounding the battle which resulted in Braddock's defeat.   4297

_____. Wife-Ship Woman. Bobbs, 1926. Story of a girl
who came from France to marry in colonial Louisiana.   4298

Peterson, Henry. Dulcibel. Winston, 1907. Trials and sen-
tences of a number of people accused of witchcraft in Salem.
                                                                 4299
Petry, Ann. Tituba of Salem Village. Crowell, 1964. The
hysteria and superstition of the Salem witch trials condemned Tituba, who was black and a slave.   4300

Phillips, Alexandra. Forever Possess. Dutton, 1946. Leisler's Rebellion and daily life on Hudson River Valley estates.   4301

Pier, Arthur S. Young Man From Mount Vernon. Stokes,
1940. Fictional account of the youth of George Washington.   4302

Pinckney, Josephine. Hilton Head. Farrar & Rinehart, 1941.
Tells of a young English surgeon, Henry Woodward, who
came to Carolina.   4303

Pound, Arthur. Hawk of Detroit. Reynal, 1939. A novel
of the founding of Detroit and of the French background of
that city.   4304

Provan, Eldoris A. Drummer for the Americans. Chilton,
1965. YA. Adventures of a young drummer with the Royal
American troops in the Ohio Valley during the French and
Indian Wars.   4305

Pryor, Elinor. The Double Man. Norton, 1957. A British
boy brought up as a Cherokee Indian in South Carolina.   4306

Quiller-Couch, Arthur T. Lady Good-For-Nothing. Scribner,
1910. Mid-eighteenth century romance of a gentleman and
a servant girl.   4307

Rayner, Emma. The Dilemma of Engeltie. Cassell, 1912.
Incident between New Englanders and Dutch colonists at
Christmas, 1702.   4308

_____. Doris Kingsley, Child and Colonist. Dillingham,
1901. Oglethorpe's colony in Georgia, a haven for religious
refugees and poor debtors.   4309

_____. Free to Serve. Small, Maynard, 1897. An
English lady becomes a bond-servant in a Dutch home
in New York.   4310

_____. In Castle and Colony. Stone, 1899. The rivalry
between Swedish and Dutch colonies on opposite sides of
the Delaware River.   4311

Rees, Gilbert. I Seek a City. Dutton, 1950. Portrays Roger
Williams, who sought emotional and religious peace in the
New World.   4312

Reid, Mildred I. Over Fool's Hill. Humphries, 1964. The
medical practice and stormy romance of a young doctor in
Salem, Massachusetts.   4313

Richardson, John. Wacousta. McClurg, 1882. Successes of
the Indians under Pontiac in attacking unsuspecting garri-
sons; their failure against Detroit.   4314

Riggs, Sidney H. Arrows and Snakeskins. Lippincott, 1962.
YA. A captured boy joins the Pequot Indian tribe and is
captured in turn by the British when the tribe is defeated. 4315

Roberts, Kenneth. Boon Island. Doubleday, 1956. Shipwreck on a small island off the coast of New Hampshire. 4316

_____. Northwest Passage. Doubleday, 1937. Thrilling
story of Rogers' expedition against the Indians and his
search for an overland route to the Pacific.   4317

Robinson, Gertrude. Sign of the Golden Fish. Winston, 1949.
YA. The adventures of a teen-aged boy with Cornish fishermen in Maine.   4318

Safford, Henry B. Tristram Bent. Coward, 1940. An Englishman raised in Holland spies on the Dutch in the New
World.   4319

Sass, Herbert R. Emperor Brims. Doubleday, 1941. Colorful story of Indian uprising against settlers in South Carolina.   4320

Savage, Les. Royal City. Hanover House, 1956. Tragic
revolt of the Pueblo Indians in Santa Fe in 1680.   4321

Schachner, Nathan. The King's Passenger. Lippincott, 1942.
An associate of Bacon in the Rebellion of 1676.   4322

Schaefer, Jack W. The Canyon. Houghton, 1953. A young
Cheyenne Indian of the Great Plains dislikes war and tries
living apart from his tribe in a sheltered canyon.   4323

Schofield, William Greenough. Ashes in the Wilderness.
Macrae Smith, 1942. A story of King Philip's War, 1675-
76.   4324

Schumann, Mary. Strife Before Dawn. Dial, 1939. About a
young Quaker colonist and the two women who love him.   4325

Scruggs, Philip Lightfoot. Man Cannot Tell. Bobbs, 1942.
An indentured servant finds love and adventure during
Bacon's Rebellion.   4326

Seifert, Shirley. By the King's Command. Lippincott, 1962.
In 1773, when Texas was a Spanish province, King Charles
III ordered the residents of the village of Los Adaes to move
to the new capital, San Antonio de Bexar.   4327

_____. River Out of Eden. Mill, 1940. A young boatman
on the lower Mississippi in 1763.   4328

Sessler, Jacob John. Saints and Tomahawks. Pyramid Press,
1940. Dramatic story of Moravian colonists and mission-
aries.   4329

Seton, Anya. The Winthrop Woman. Houghton, 1958. About
Governor Winthrop's niece from England and her adjustment
to colonial life.   4330

Seton, William. Romance of the Charter Oak. O'Shea, 1871.
The hiding of the Connecticut charter from the hated British
governor in an oak tree in Hartford.   4331

Shafer, Donald Cameron. Smokefires in Schoharie. Longmans, 1938. A settlement in the Schoharie Valley survives
attacks by Indians.   4332

Shaw, Adele Marie. The Coast of Freedom. Doubleday, 1903.
The infamous witch hunts in Massachusetts, during which the
governor's wife was accused.   4333

Shaw, Margaret. Inherit the Earth. Bobbs, 1940. Adventures
of an English girl who comes to America as an indentured
servant.   4334

Shelton, Jess. Martin's Land. Chilton, 1961. An early settler
in Osage country raised an Indian family, and later a white
family, thus setting the stage for tragedy.   4335

Simms, W. Gilmore. The Yemassee. Harper, 1835. The
grim war between white men and Creek and Cherokee Indi-
ans.   4336

Simons, Katherine D. M. Always a River. by Drayton Mayrant, pseud. Appleton, 1956. A Puritan schoolmaster

seeks peace in French Huguenot Carolina.   4337

Singmaster, Elsie. High Wind Rising. Houghton, 1942. The
hard-working German settlers of Pennsylvania during the
French and Indian Wars.   4338

_____. I Heard of a River. Winston, 1948. YA. Search-
ing for religious freedom and a decent livelihood, German
Lutherans come to Pennsylvania in the seventeenth century.
                                                           4339

Smith, Alice Prescott. Kindred. Houghton, 1925. An English spy among the French and the Indians in the Seven
Years War.   4340

Smith, Arthur D. Howden. Beyond the Sunset. Brentano's,
1923. Adventures with the Indians in mid-eighteenth century New York.   4341

Smith, Ruel Perley. Prisoners of Fortune. Page, 1907.
Story of the Massachusetts Bay Colony involving pirates
and a treasure search.   4342

Snedeker, Caroline Dale. Uncharted Ways. Doubleday, Doran,
1935. The persecution of Quakers in Massachusetts.   4343

Speare, Elizabeth George. The Prospering. Houghton, 1967.
Attempt to establish an Indian mission at Stockbridge,
Massachusetts, during the bloody French and Indian Wars. 4344

_____. The Witch of Blackbird Pond. Houghton, 1958. YA.
A friendly girl from the Bahamas finds the beliefs of her
Puritan aunt in Connecticut too confining for her.   4345

Spector, Robert M. The Greatest Rebel. Walck, 1969. YA.
Pictures the unrest and resentment in the Virginia Colony
that led to Bacon's Rebellion in the 1670s.   4346

Stevens, Sheppard. The Sword of Justice. Little, 1899.
Florida during the struggle between French and Spanish.   4347

Stimson, Frederic Jesup. King Noanett. by J.S. of Dale,
pseud. Scribner, 1897. About Devon settlers in Virginia
and Massachusetts.   4348

Stouman, Knud. L. Baxter, Medicus. Greystone, 1941. The
studies of an American doctor abroad and his practice in
New York.   4349

_____. With Cradle and Clock. Harper, 1946. Practice
of medicine in New York City by an English doctor.   4350

Stover, Herbert Elisha. Song of the Susquehanna. Dodd,
1949. Trading in Pennsylvania during the French and

Indian Wars.   4351

Stuart, H. Longan. Weeping Cross. Doubleday, 1908. An
Indian massacre at Long Meadow, Massachusetts.   4352

Sublette, Clifford. The Bright Face of Danger. Little, 1926.
The vengeful hero joins Bacon's Rebellion.   4353

_____. The Scarlet Cockerel. Little, 1925. Rapidly mov-
ing tale of the French Huguenot colonization of Carolina.   4354

Swanson, Neil. The Judas Tree. Putnam, 1933. Indian attack on Fort Pitt (Pittsburgh) during the Pontiac Conspiracy.
(followed by The Silent Drum)   4355

_____. The Silent Drum. Bantam Bks., 1970, c.1940.
Friction between settlers and traders in the Fort Pitt
area.   4356

_____. The Unconquered. Doubleday, 1947. Frontier life
at the time of the Indian uprising known as the Pontiac Conspiracy.   4357

Taylor, Mary Imlay. Anne Scarlet. McClurg, 1901. A witch
hunt in Salem in which Cotton Mather figures.   4358

Tebbel, John William. Conqueror. Dutton, 1951. Story of
Sir William Johnson and his dealings with the Indians.   4359

_____. Touched With Fire. Dutton, 1952. La Salle's ex-
plorations in the Mississippi Valley.   4360

Thackeray, William Makepeace. The Virginians. Lippincott,
1879. About two grandsons of Englishman Henry Esmond
who migrate to America.   4361

Tracy, Don. Carolina Corsair. Dial, 1955. Blood and thunder
story of the infamous Blackbeard.   4362

_____. Chesapeake Cavalier. Dial, 1949. Rise of an Eng-
lish indentured servant.   4363

_____. Roanoke Renegade. Dial, 1954. A story of Raleigh's
lost Roanoke colony.   4364

Vance, Marguerite. The Beloved Friend. Holt, 1963. YA.
Sally Carey, beautiful and charming lady of Virginia, and
her husband, George William Fairfax, were friends of the
young George Washington.   4365

Watson, Sally. The Hornet's Nest. Holt, 1968. YA. Two
Scots flee to the American colonies to escape persecution,
only to find similar conditions exist there also.   4366

Webster, J. Provand. Children of Wrath. Routledge, 1899.
    Colonists in Virginia near the end of the seventeenth cen-
    tury.   4367

Wellman, Paul I. Ride the Red Earth. Doubleday, 1958.
    A Frenchman's adventures in Spanish-held Texas and Mex-
    ico.   4368

Westley, George Hembert. The Maid and the Miscreant.
    Mayhew, 1906. Exploits of an English rogue disapproved of
    by the Puritan colonists.   4369

Whalen, Will Wilfrid. Golden Squaw. Dorrance, 1926. The
    life among Indians of a bride captured on the morning of
    her marriage.   4370

Whitson, Denton. Governor's Daughter. Bobbs, 1953. Ro-
    mance in New York during the French and Indian Wars.   4371

Widdemer, Margaret. The Golden Wildcat. Doubleday, 1954.
    Bitter rivalry of the French and British for Indian support.
                                                                   4372

_____. Lady of the Mohawks. Doubleday, 1951. Romance
    of Molly Brant and Colonel Johnson during the French and
    Indian Wars.   4373

_____. Red Cloak Flying. Doubleday, 1950. An Irish
    girl in exile is loved by two men.   4374

Wilkins, Mary Eleanor. The Heart's Highway. Doubleday,
    1900. Unrest and tobacco riots in Virginia following
    Bacon's Rebellion.   4375

Winwar, Frances. Gallows Hill. Holt, 1937. A narrative of
    Salem during the witchcraft trials.   4376

Zara, Louis. Blessed Is the Land. Crown, 1954. Story of
    Jews who came as pioneers to New Amsterdam in 1654.   4377

b) Revolutionary Era (1763-1789)

Adams, Marshall. They Fought for Liberty. Dodge, 1937.
    Account of a young patriot who returned to America from
    England at the start of the Revolution.   4378

Alderman, Clifford L. Arch of Stars. Appleton, 1950.
    Effect of the war on people in Vermont.   4379

Allen, Merritt Parmelee. Battle Lanterns. McKay, 1949.
    YA. The importance of young people and Negroes in the
    Revolution in support of the Swamp Fox is noted in this
    novel.   4380

Allis, Marguerite. Not Without Peril. Putnam, 1941. Life
in Vermont of a spirited pioneer woman, Jemima Sart-
well.   4381

Atkinson, Eleanor. Johnny Appleseed. Harper, 1915. A
warm account of a man whose life became a legend--
John Chapman.   4382

Bacheller, Irving. In the Days of Poor Richard. Bobbs, 1922.
Important figures in the Revolution and scenes in both England and America.   4383

_____. The Master of Chaos. Bobbs, 1932. The war ex-
periences and romance of a young secretary to General
Washington.   4384

Barker, Shirley. Fire and the Hammer. Crown, 1953. Swift-
paced story of Quaker brothers and their Tory activities in
Pennsylvania.   4385

Barr, Amelia E. A Song of a Single Note. Dodd, 1902. A
story of New York during the Revolutionary War.   4386

_____. The Strawberry Handkerchief. Dodd, 1908. New
York at the time of the controversial Stamp Act.   4387

Barry, Jane. The Carolinians. Doubleday, 1959. Loyalist
family in South Carolina shelters a wounded officer of Morgan's Raiders.   4388

_____. The Long March. Appleton, 1955. Action-packed
report of General Dan Morgan and the Battle of Cowpens. 4389

Beebe, Elswyth Thane. The Dawn's Early Light. by Elswyth
Thane. Duell, 1943. Williamsburg is the setting for this
novel of Revolutionary times. (followed by Yankee Stranger)
                                                        4390
Beers, Lorna. The Crystal Cornerstone. Harper, 1953. YA.
Service in Washington's army was difficult for a sixteen-
year-old.   4391

Bellamy, Edward. The Duke of Stockbridge. Silver, 1900.
The main event here is Shays's Rebellion.   4392

Benét, Stephen Vincent. Spanish Bayonet. Doran, 1926.
Oppression of indentured laborers on a Florida plantation.   4393

Beverley-Giddings, Arthur Raymond. The Rival Shores. Morrow, 1956. Loyalist refugees in eastern Maryland and Delaware just prior to the outbreak of the war.   4394

Beyer, Audrey White. Dark Venture. Knopf, 1968. YA. A

young African boy is captured by slave traders and brought
to a home in Rhode Island.   4395

_____. Katherine Leslie. Knopf, 1963. YA. A girl, con-
demned unjustly to a long prison sentence, escapes and flees
to the New World.   4396

Boyce, Burke. Man From Mt. Vernon. Harper, 1961. Portrays George Washington as a man and a soldier.   4397

_____. The Perilous Night. Viking, 1942. Family life on
a Hudson River farm with a beautiful girl and her suitors. 4398

Boyd, James. Drums. Scribner, 1956, c.1925. YA. Scots
in North Carolina and naval action during the Revolutionary
War.   4399

Brady, Cyrus Townsend. The Blue Ocean's Daughter. Moffat,
1907. Encounters of an American privateer and British
frigates result in excitement for a captain's daughter.   4400

_____. The Grip of Honour. Scribner, 1900. Features
John Paul Jones, revolutionary hero.   4401

Breslin, Howard. Shad Run. Crowell, 1955. A fisherman's
daughter in the Hudson River Valley at the time the Consti-
tution was ratified.   4402

Brick, John. Captives of the Senecas. Duell, 1964. YA. Adventure and excitement as two young hunters are captured by
Seneca Indians.   4403

_____. Eagle of Niagara. Doubleday, 1955. David Harper,
Continental soldier, captured by Indian Joseph Brant.   4404

_____. The King's Rangers. Doubleday, 1954. A group of
woodsmen, led by Colonel Butler, fight for the King in New
York State.   4405

_____. The Raid. Farrar, 1951. Indian raids and captivity
spice a vivid account of life in the Hudson River Valley. 4406

_____. The Rifleman. Doubleday, 1953. Activities of rough-
and-ready Tim Murphy, frontiersman.   4407

_____. The Strong Men. Doubleday, 1959. A professional
soldier, Baron von Steuben, forms an army from raw colonial volunteers at Valley Forge.   4408

Bristow, Gwen. Celia Garth. Crowell, 1959. Absorbing tale
of love and war with an orphaned twenty-year-old seamstress
as heroine.   4409

Burt, Katherine N. Close Pursuit. Scribner, 1947. Romantic novel of an English governess on a Tidewater Virginia plantation.   4410

Cannon, LeGrand. Look to the Mountain. Holt, 1942. Young
newlyweds build a home and future in the New Hampshire
mountains.   4411

Carter, Jefferson. Madam Constantia. Longmans, 1919. An
Englishman's experiences as an American prisoner-of-war. 4412

Cavanna, Betty. A Touch of Magic. Westminster Pr., 1961.
YA. Contrasting lives and loves of wealthy Philadelphia
girls and the daughter of their seamstress.   4413

Chambers, Robert W. (1) Cardigan. Harper, 1901. (2) The
Maid-At-Arms. Harper, 1902. Stories of the Johnson fam-
ily showing strained relations between British, colonists, and
Indians.   4414-5

_____. The Little Red Foot. Doran, 1921. Indian and
Tory warfare in northern New York State.   4416

_____. Love and the Lieutenant. Appleton, 1935. Includes
British recruiting of Hessian soldiers in Germany and the
Burgoyne campaign.   4417

_____. The Painted Minx. Appleton, 1930. Romance of a
Tory actress who waits throughout the War for her colonial
lover.   4418

_____. The Reckoning. Appleton, 1905. Effects of the
Revolution on the wealthy landowners of New York State.   4419

Chapman, Ann S. Mary Derwent. Burt, 1909. A tale of
the Wyoming Valley, scene of a devastating Indian massacre.   4420

Chapman, Maristan, pseud. for Mary and Stanton Chapman.
Rogue's March. Lippincott, 1949. Realistic picture of the
southern backwoods and account of the Battle of Kings Mountain.   4421

_____. Tennessee Hazard. Lippincott, 1953. Frontier
life in Tennessee at the time of the conspiracy to surrender
frontier lands to the Spaniards.   4422

Churchill, Winston. Richard Carvel. Macmillan, 1899. A
Maryland patriot is a friend of and a sailor under John
Paul Jones.   4423

Coffin, Charles C. Daughters of the Revolution and Their
Times. Houghton, 1895. The start of the Revolution--

the Boston Tea Party and the Battle of Lexington.   4424

Cooke, John Esten.   (1) The Virginia Comedians. Appleton,
1854.   (2) Henry St. John, Gentleman. Appleton, 1883.
Social and cultural life in Virginia in the last half of the
century.   4425-6

Cooper, James Fenimore. Red Rover. Colburn, 1828. A former pirate fights for his country in the Revolutionary War.
                                                       4427
_____. The Spy. Lea & Carey, 1829. Harvey Birch is the
hero in this classic of the Revolution.   4428

Cormack, Maribelle and William P. Alexander. Land for My
Sons. Appleton, 1939. A Scotch-Irish scout and surveyor
leaves roadbuilding to join Washington's army.   4429

Crabb, Alfred Leland. Journey to Nashville. Bobbs, 1957. Description of the journey to and the founding of Nashville. 4430

Crownfield, Gertrude. Where Glory Waits. Lippincott, 1934.
The unhappy romance of Anthony Wayne and Mary Vining. 4431

Davis, Burke. The Ragged Ones. Rinehart, 1951. Swift-
moving narrative of the attacks upon Cornwallis by Generals
Morgan and Greene.   4432

_____. Yorktown. Rinehart, 1952. A soldier's experi-
ences during the final years of the Revolution.   4433

Davis, William Stearns. Gilman of Redford. Macmillan, 1927.
Story of Boston on the brink of war as related by a student
at Harvard.   4434

Decker, Malcolm. The Rebel and the Turncoat. McGraw,
1949. A youth's indecision as to which side he should
take in the Revolution.   4435

Degenhard, William. The Regulators. Dial, 1943. A vivid
picture of the significant Shays's Rebellion.   4436

De Haven, Aubrey. The Scarlet Cloak. Blackwood, 1907.
A son searches for his runaway mother during the war. 4437

Devereux, Mary. From Kingdom to Colony. Little, 1899.
Shows the determination and sacrifices that made the American Revolution successful.   4438

Dodge, Constance. The Dark Stranger. Penn, 1940. An immigrant from Scotland seeks his fortune in the New World--
land of opportunity.   4439

_____. Weathercock. Dodd, 1942. Southern aristocrat's

struggle to reconcile the justice of his own wealth with
the poverty of others. 4440

Doughty, W. Dyre. Crimson Mocassins. Harper, 1966. YA.
A story which involves a history of the Miami Indians and
George Rogers Clark's action against them. 4441

Eastman, Edward Roe. The Destroyers. Am. Agriculturist,
Inc., 1946. Attack on Cherry Valley by Tories and Indians. 4442

Eaton, Evelyn. Give Me Your Golden Hand. Farrar, 1951.
An unacknowledged son of George III chooses to be a bonded
servant in revolutionary America. 4443

Edmonds, Walter D. Drums Along the Mohawk. Little, 1936.
Indian attacks on a farming community's fortress in the Mohawk Valley. 4444

_____. In the Hands of the Senecas. Little, 1947. Attack
by Seneca Indians on settlers in Dygartsbush, New York, in
1778. 4445

_____. Wilderness Clearing. Dodd, 1944. Romance in
the Mohawk Valley under threat of attacks from Indians
and British alike. 4446

Eggleston, George Cary. A Carolina Cavalier. Lothrop,
1901. Activities of guerrillas in the Carolinas. 4447

Ellsberg, Edward. Captain Paul. Dodd, 1941. John Paul
Jones battles both with British ships and with a massive,
enraged whale. 4448

_____. "I Have Just Begun to Fight." Dodd, 1964, c.1942.
YA. A retelling for the Young Adult audience of the author's
book about John Paul Jones, Captain Paul (listed above). 4449

Erskine, John. Give Me Liberty. Stokes, 1940. A young
Virginian's contacts with Patrick Henry. 4450

Farmer, James Eugene. Brinton Eliot: From Yale to Yorktown. Macmillan, 1902. A student at Yale joins the American Revolutionary Army. 4451

Farrar, Rowena Rutherford. Bend Your Heads All. Holt,
1965. A pioneer family yields to the urge to move ever
onward, finding still another new frontier, this one in
Tennessee. 4452

Fast, Howard. April Morning. Bantam Bks., 1968, c.1961.
A youth attains maturity as a soldier in the colonial militia. 4453

_____. Citizen Tom Paine. Duell, 1943. Activities of
a revolutionary writer in England, France, and the United
States.   4454

_____. Conceived in Liberty. S. & S., 1939. Persever-
ance of the determined American army during the cruel
winter at Valley Forge.   4455

_____. The Proud and the Free. Little, 1950. Little-
known revolt of the Eleventh Regiment of the Pennsylvania
Line on New Year's Day, 1781.   4456

_____. The Unvanquished. Duell, 1942. The development
of Washington from a Virginia gentleman into a national
leader.   4457

Finlay, Lucile. The Coat I Wore. Scribner, 1947. British
sympathizers in Louisiana during the war.   4458

Fleming, Thomas J. Now We Are Enemies. St. Martins,
1960. The story of colonial entrenchment and resistance
at Bunker Hill.   4459

Fletcher, Inglis. Raleigh's Eden. Bantam Bks., 1970, c.1940.
A plantation in North Carolina before and during the Revolution.   4460

_____. Toil of the Brave. Bobbs, 1946. The contest be-
tween a Continental and a Britisher for a lady's favor in
revolutionary North Carolina.   4461

_____. Wicked Lady. Bobbs, 1962. The alluring English
wife of a German landowner in North Carolina uses her wiles
to oppose the Revolution.   4462

Flood, Charles Bracelen. Monmouth. Houghton, 1961. Story
of a courier and spy who harassed the British in the winter
of 1778, as the American colonists fought for independence.
                                                             4463

Forbes, Esther. The General's Lady. Harcourt, 1938. Beautiful Tory girl marries an American general to protect her
family, then falls in love with a British officer.   4464

_____. Johnny Tremain. Houghton, 196?, c.1943. An
eager, intelligent apprentice lives in Boston and is involved
in the events leading to the Revolution, including the Boston
Tea Party.   4465

Forbes-Lindsay, C.H. Daniel Boone. Lippincott, 1908. Adventures of this noted frontiersman in Kentucky.   4466

Ford, Paul Leicester. Janice Meredith. Dodd, 1899. A
romance of New Jersey and New York during the Revo-

lution.   4467

Forman, James. The Cow Neck Rebels. Farrar, 1969. YA.
The effects of the imminent war on the Cameron family in
the days preceding the Battle of Long Island in 1776.   4468

Fox, John, Jr. Erskine Dale, Pioneer. Scribner, 1920.
The two facets of the life of a youth, raised among Indians,
who inherits a Virginia estate.   4469

Frederic, Harold. In the Valley. Scribner, 1890. Life in the
Mohawk Valley from the viewpoint of Dutch settlers who
hated the British.   4470

French, Allen. The Colonials. Doubleday, 1902. "Chiefly connected with the siege and evacuation of the town of Boston in
New England."   4471

Fritz, Jean. Early Thunder. Coward, 1967. YA. A Tory
boy in Salem, Massachusetts begins to understand the feelings of the colonists and to question the ideals of his family.   4472

Frye, Pearl. Gallant Captain. Little, 1955. Compelling tale
of the Bon Homme Richard and her gallant captain, John
Paul Jones.   4473

Gerson, Noel B. Dragon Cove. by Carter A. Vaughan, pseud.
Doubleday, 1964. Privateering and blockade-running in the
Newport area by a patriotic captain aided by local girls.   4474

_____. Fortress Fury. by Carter A. Vaughan, pseud.
Doubleday, 1966. Frontier fighting against both British and
Indians and a woodsman's perilous spying assignment to
British-held Fort Detroit.   4475

_____. Give Me Liberty. Doubleday, 1966. The stirring
story of Patrick Henry who was very prominent in the early
American Revolution but later retired from public life.   4476

_____. I'll Storm Hell. Doubleday, 1967. A rousing ac-
count of "Mad Anthony" Wayne, whose emergence as a military leader typified the growth of the colonies into a nation.
                                                               4477
_____. Scoundrel's Brigade. by Carter A. Vaughan, pseud.
Doubleday, 1962. Pursuit of British counterfeiters who
worked to depreciate colonial money during the Revolutionary
War.   4478

_____. The Swamp Fox, Francis Marion. Doubleday, 1967.
Marion's hit-and-run tactics in South Carolina during the
Revolution so harassed the British that they put a price on
his head.   4479

_____. Yankee Doodle Dandy. Doubleday, 1965. The
rise in business and politics of John Hancock who became
one of the founding fathers of the American Republic.   4480

_____. The Yankee Rascals. by Carter A. Vaughan,
pseud. Doubleday, 1963. A daring colonial officer is captured by the British in New York, rescued by Continental
spies, and returns to plan a prisoner-of-war rescue.   4481

Gessner, Robert. Treason. Scribner, 1944. One of Benedict
Arnold's aides learns, to his disillusionment, of his hero's
treason.   4482

Giles, Janice Holt. The Kentuckians. Houghton, 1953. A
novel of Kentucky when it was part of Virginia and of the
land speculators who operated there.   4483

Gordon, Charles William. The Rebel Loyalist. by Ralph Connor,
pseud. Dodd, 1935. Adventures of a loyalist among rebels
during the struggle between England and her colonies.   4484

Gray, Stanley. Half That Glory. Macmillan, 1941. A young
Virginian who runs away to sea eventually becomes involved
in diplomatic relations.   4485

Groh, Lynn. The Culper Spy Ring. Westminster, 1969. YA.
Early Army intelligence at work is the theme for this novel
of spying in the American Revolution.   4486

Haines, Edwin Irvine. The Exquisite Siren. Lippincott, 1938.
The Tory wife of Benedict Arnold and her secret love for
another.   4487

Haislip, Harvey. The Prize Master. Doubleday, 1959. Adventures of a teen-aged midshipman who brings a captured
British ship to port. (followed by Sea Road to Yorktown) 4488

_____. A Sailor Named Jones. Doubleday, 1957. Narra-
tive of John Paul Jones written by a retired Navy captain.
(followed by The Prize Master)   4489

_____. Sea Road to Yorktown. Doubleday, 1960. Young Am-
erican seaman Thomas Potter serves with the French fleet
of De Grasse in the Caribbean and at Yorktown. (completes
trilogy)   4490

Hall, Marjory. A Hatful of Gold. Westminster, 1964. YA.
A fictionalized account of the heroine Molly Pitcher, whose
bravery has become legendary.   4491

Harris, Cyril. Richard Pryne. Scribner, 1941. Suspense-
filled tale of a civilian spy for Washington.   4492

_____. Trumpets at Dawn. Scribner, 1938. How war
affected social relationships, traditions, and economic
balance.   4493

Havighurst, Walter. Proud Prisoner. Holt, 1964. YA. The
part Henry Hamilton, the "Hair Buyer," played in campaigns
in the West and his capture at Vincennes by the George
Rogers Clark expedition.   4494

Haycox, Ernest. Winds of Rebellion. Criterion, 1964. YA.
Three adventure stories of spying and soldiering during the
Revolution.   4495

Henri, Florette. Kings Mountain. Doubleday, 1950. Pictures
leaders of the American and British sides in the Battle of
Kings Mountain.   4496

Hopkins, Joseph G. E. Patriot's Progress. Scribner, 1961.
Difficult decisions are forced upon a young Massachusetts
physician whose own political leanings are opposed to those
of his mother and his girl friend. (followed by Retreat
and Recall)   4497

_____. Retreat and Recall. Scribner, 1966. A doctor
from Massachusetts gathers information for the Continental
Army in Tory New York.   4498

Horan, James David. The King's Rebel. Crown, 1953. A
British officer, in sympathy with the struggling colonists,
resigns his army commission.   4499

Horne, Howard. Concord Bridge. Bobbs, 1952. Romance of a
girl spy at the start of the War.   4500

Hough, Frank Olney. If Not Victory. Lippincott, 1939. Exploits of a Quaker boy who becomes a soldier in the Continental Army.   4501

_____. The Neutral Ground. Lippincott, 1941. Efforts
of two Westchester County, New York, men to win their
neighbors' votes in a political fight.   4502

_____. Renown. Lippincott, 1938. A sympathetic portrait
of Benedict Arnold.   4503

Hubbard, Lindley Murray. An Express of '76. Little, 1906.
"A chronicle of the town of York in the War of Independ-
ence."   4504

Jacobs, Helen Hull. Storm Against the Wind. Dodd, 1944.
Tidewater Virginia while colonial resistance to British
rule was stiffening.   4505

Jahoda, Gloria. Delilah's Mountain. Houghton, 1963.
Hardships and danger as well as love and devotion among
English pioneers in mountainous western Virginia.   4506

Jennings, John. The Sea Eagles. Doubleday, 1950. The
young American Navy during the Revolution--its ships, its
men, and the women they left behind.   4507

_____. The Shadow and the Glory. Reynal, 1943. A New
Hampshire boy runs away to join the army.   4508

Jewett, Sarah Orne. The Tory Lover. Houghton, 1901. A
novel introducing the hero John Paul Jones.   4509

Johnston, Mary. Hunting Shirt. Little, 1931. A frontiersman's
two-year search in Indian territory for his sweetheart's stolen
necklace.   4510

Johnston, Norma. The Bridge Between. Funk, 1966. YA. A
teen-ager is the mainstay of her family during the illness of
her mother and the intrigues of the Revolution.   4511

Jones, Peter. Rebel in the Night. Dial, 1971. A Long Island
farmboy takes a dim view of the fighting, hardships, and
dangers involved in service in the Continental Army.   4512

Karig, Walter and Horace V. Bird. Don't Tread on Me.
Rinehart, 1954. The vigorous adventures of John Paul
Jones.   4513

Kennedy, John P. Horseshoe Robinson. Putnam, 1835. South
Carolina and its strong Tory feelings during the Revolution.
                                                           4514
Kennedy, Sara Beaumont. Joscelyn Cheshire. Doubleday,
1901. Life at Hillsboro, N.C., and aboard a British prison
ship during the Revolutionary War.   4515

Lancaster, Bruce. The Big Knives. Little, 1964. A young
merchant accompanies the George Rogers Clark expedition
against the British and gives some military, political, and
economic insights into the period.   4516

_____. The Blind Journey. Little, 1953. Secret mission
of Benjamin Franklin's messenger from France to America.
                                                           4517
_____. Guns of Burgoyne. Stokes, 1939. Burgoyne's de-
feat at Saratoga.   4518

_____. The Phantom Fortress. Little, 1950. The military
tactics of Francis Marion, the Swamp Fox, and the romance
of one of his men.   4519

_____. The Secret Road. Little, 1952. Suspense and

thrills as General Washington's "secret service" collects
information.   4520

_____. Trumpet to Arms. Little, 1944. The forming
of individualistic Americans into the army which won our
freedom.   4521

Leland, John Adams. Othniel Jones. Lippincott, 1956. A
young Cherokee fights with the Swamp Fox, Francis Marion,
in Tennessee.   4522

Levy, Mimi C. Whaleboat Warriors. Viking, 1963. YA. Concerns the use of whaleboats to carry messages and supplies
for the American troops.   4523

Linington, Elizabeth. The Long Watch. Viking, 1956. A
newspaperman is hero in this report of New York's reactions to revolt.   4524

Longstreet, Stephen. Eagles Where I Walk. Doubleday, 1961.
Experiences of a young upper class doctor in the colonial
army in New York State with glimpses also of colonial high
society.   4525

_____. A Few Painted Feathers. Doubleday, 1963. A
New York surgeon and an English-educated Indian chief accompany the colonial army in the south during the Revolutionary War.   4526

Lynde, Francis. Mr. Arnold. Bobbs, 1923. Benedict Arnold's
activities in Virginia in 1780.   4527

MacDonald, Carolyn. Thunder on the Wind. Pocket Bks.,
1972. The romance of a widow with an eight-year-old son
and a Scottish preacher in North Carolina.   4528

McDowell, Robert E. Tidewater Sprig. Crown, 1961. A
landed aristocrat, having exhausted his family's patience
by too many escapades, finds he must work to eat and becomes a successful businessman.   4529

McIntyre, John Thomas. Drums in the Dawn. Doubleday,
Doran, 1932. A romance which touches on the rebelling
colonies' needs for financial support.   4530

McLean, Sydney. A Moment of Time. Putnam, 1945. The
steadfastness and courage of a New England woman and her
family.   4531

Mason, Van Wyck. Eagle in the Sky. Lippincott, 1948. A
story of sailors and doctors in the American Revolution.   4532

_____. Rivers of Glory. Lippincott, 1942. Adventures

in the naval war of the Revolution, especially the siege
of Savannah. (followed by Eagle in the Sky)   4533

_____. Stars on the Sea. Lippincott, 1940. Story of
privateering in the opening years of the war. (followed by
Rivers of Glory)   4534

_____. Three Harbours. Lippincott, 1938. Naval action
during the Revolution in the three harbors of Boston, Bermuda, and Norfolk. (followed by Stars on the Sea)   4535

_____. Valley Forge: 24 December, 1777. Doubleday,
1950. Touching account of the Christmas of Washington's
suffering troops.   4536

_____. Wild Horizon. Little, 1966. Cruel, tragic battles
in the last years of the Revolution, when some -Americans
crossed the Allegheny Mountains in search of peace and
freedom.   4537

Melville, Herman. Israel Potter. Putnam, 1855. Experiences
of an American sailor captured by the British.   4538

Mercer, Charles E. Enough Good Men. Putnam, 1960. Effects of the Revolution on the lives of a small group.   4539

Millard, Joseph. The Incredible William Bowles. Chilton,
1966. A Tory planter fights with the British, is adopted
by Indians in Florida, and spends the rest of his life fighting for Indian rights against the white man.   4540

Miller, Helen Topping. Christmas at Mount Vernon. Longmans, 1957. The Washingtons' first Christmas at home
after the close of the war.   4541

_____. Slow Dies the Thunder. Bobbs, 1955. War-time
activities in South Carolina--Charleston and Kings Mountain.   4542

_____. The Sound of Chariots. Bobbs, 1947. Life and
war on the Georgia and Tennessee frontiers.   4543

_____. Trumpet in the City. Bobbs, 1948. The early
phase of the war as it appeared to the residents of Savannah.   4544

Mills, Weymer Jay. The Van Rensselaers of Old Manhattan.
Stokes, 1907. Romance with New York as background.   4545

Minnigerode, Meade. The Black Forest. Farrar, 1937.
Two generations of pioneers in the area west of the Allegheny Mountains.   4546

Mitchell, S. Weir. Hugh Wynne, Free Quaker. Century,
1897. The Quaker practice of friendship contrasted with
the war.   4547

Morrow, Honoré. Beyond the Blue Sierra. Morrow, 1932.
The Mexican settlement of California and the founding of
San Francisco.   4548

Muir, Robert. Sprig of Hemlock. Longmans, 1957. Story of
the ill-fated Shays's Rebellion of 1786-87.   4549

Nutt, Frances Tysen. Three Fields to Cross. Stephen-Paul,
1947. Staten Island during the Revolution.   4550

Orrmont, Arthur. Diplomat in Warpaint. Abelard, 1968. YA.
The well-educated Alexander McGillivray, of mixed Scottish
and Indian blood, becomes a Creek Chief and helps to keep
that tribe neutral during the Revolution.   4551

Osgood, Grace Rose. At the Sign of the Blue Anchor. Clark,
1909. A story of 1776.   4552

Page, Elizabeth. Tree of Liberty. Farrar, 1939. About an
American family friendly with Thomas Jefferson.   4553

Paradise, Viola I. Tomorrow the Harvest. Morrow, 1952.
Story of two women in a small Maine village just after the
Revolution.   4554

Parrish, Randall. My Lady of Doubt. McClurg, 1911. A
Maryland officer in a British uniform spies for Washington.
                                                               4555
_____. Prisoners of Chance. McClurg, 1908. Set in the
lower Mississippi Valley during the French occupation.   4556

Pendexter, Hugh. Red Belts. Doubleday, 1920. Frontier adventures and Indian fighting during the formation of the state
of Tennessee.   4557

Pridgen, Tim. Tory Oath. Doubleday, 1941. Scots settlers
in North Carolina at the time of the Revolution.   4558

Quinby, Alden W. Valley Forge. Eaton & Mains, 1906. Contrasts Washington's ill-equipped troops during the harsh
winter with the British in comfort in Philadelphia.   4559

Raddall, Thomas. The Governor's Lady. Doubleday, 1960.
Governor Wentworth, his ambitious wife, and what befell
them because of the Revolution.   4560

Rayner, William. The World Turned Upside Down. Morrow,
1970. A British major, disguised as a slave while trying
to return to his own lines, is apprehended and falsely ac-

cused of a crime.   4561

Richter, Conrad. A Country of Strangers. Knopf, 1966. A
white girl who has been captured and reared by Indians
finds life unbearable when she is restored to her white
home. (companion novel to The Light in the Forest)   4562

_____. Free Man. Knopf, 1943. A German immigrant
sold as an indentured servant escapes to freedom.   4563

_____. The Light in the Forest. Knopf, 1953. How a
white boy raised by Delaware Indians reacts to rescue.   4564

Ripley, Clements. Clear for Action. Appleton, 1940. An
account of the sea battle in which John Paul Jones said, "I
have not yet begun to fight."   4565

Rives, Hallie Erminie. Hearts Courageous. Bobbs, 1902.
The fight for American independence with Patrick Henry as
one of the leaders.   4566

Roberts, Kenneth. Arundel. Doubleday, 1930. "A chronicle
of the province of Maine and of the secret expedition of
Benedict Arnold against Quebec."   4567

_____. Oliver Wiswell. Fawcett, 1963, c.1940. The
Tory side of the American War of Independence.   4568

_____. Rabble in Arms. Doubleday, 1933. The leader-
ship of Benedict Arnold is emphasized with the American
Congress as "villain."   4569

Sabatini, Rafael. The Carolinian. Houghton, 1925. Vivid
story of the conflict between British and colonials in South
Carolina.   4570

Safford, Henry B. Tory Tavern. Penn, 1942. A Tory boy,
after three years in the British navy, becomes a spy for
the Americans.   4571

St. George, Judith. Turncoat Winter, Rebel Spring. Chilton,
1970. YA. A patriotic boy is faced with a dilemma when
he learns that the friend who saved his life is spying against
his country.   4572

Savage, Josephine. Daughter of Delaware. Day, 1964. YA.
Young Polly Lawson, journeying to France to present her
horse to the French Queen, proves herself brave and
loyal.   4573

Schindall, Henry. Let the Spring Come. Appleton, 1953.
Colorful story of Virginia at the end of the war.   4574

Schneider, Benjamin. Winter Patriot. Chilton, 1967. YA.
Son of a blacksmith killed during the war joins the colonists harassing the British forces.   4575

Schoonover, Lawrence. The Revolutionary. Little, 1958. Sea
action of John Paul Jones and his Bon Homme Richard,
named for Benjamin Franklin.   4576

Scollard, Clinton. The Son of a Tory. Badger, 1901. The
siege of Fort Stanwix by the British.   4577

Scott, John Reed. The Make-Believe. Lippincott, 1911. Life
in high society circles in colonial Maryland.   4578

Sears, Margaret L. Menotomy: A Romance of 1776. Badger,
1908. Massachusetts in the early stages of the Revolution.
                                                        4579
Seifert, Shirley. Let My Name Stand Fair. Lippincott,
1956. Story of Nathanael and Catherine Greene during the
Revolution.   4580

_____. Never No More. Lippincott, 1964. The winter of
1773 was a hard one for Daniel and Rebecca Boone, following the death of a son in an Indian attack.   4581

_____. Waters of the Wilderness. Lippincott, 1941.
George Rogers Clark's holding of Kaskaskia and Vincennes
during the war.   4582

Simms, W. Gilmore. (1) The Partisan. Harper, 1935. (2)
Mellichampe. Harper, 1836. (3) Katherine Walton. Hart,
1851. (4) The Scout. Redfield, 1854. (5) The Forayers.
Redfield, 1855. (6) Eutaw. Redfield, 1856. A series of
novels picturing South Carolina during the Revolution and
presenting major military events, prominent people, outlaw activities, and social functions.   4583-88

Simons, Katherine D. M. The Red Doe. by Drayton Mayrant,
pseud. Appleton, 1953. Francis Marion, the Swamp Fox
of Revolutionary War fame.   4589

Sinclair, Harold. Westward the Tide. Doubleday, 1940. The
early life of George Rogers Clark and his expedition to
Vincennes.   4590

Slaughter, Frank G. Flight From Natchez. Doubleday, 1955.
Doctor's career after dishonorable discharge from British
army.   4591

_____. Sangaree. Doubleday, 1948. Practice of a doctor
on a Georgia plantation after the Revolutionary War.   4592

Spicer, Bart. Brother to the Enemy. Dodd, 1958. Danger-

ous assignment to enter the British garrison and capture
traitor Benedict Arnold.   4593

_____. The Day Before Thunder. Dodd, 1960. Young
member of a banking house finds that there is fraud and
conspiracy within the business related to the coming Revolution.   4594

Stackpole, Edouard A. Nantucket Rebel. Washburn, 1963.
Members of a Quaker whaling community on Nantucket Island become involved in the Revolution as privateers harassing British shipping.   4595

Stanley, Edward. Thomas Forty. Duell, 1947. A young printer,
at first undecided, joins the American Army.   4596

Stephens, Robert Neilson. The Continental Dragoon. Page,
1901. A romance of the area between British and American lines.   4597

_____. Philip Winwood. Page, 1900. Domestic crisis of
an American captain whose wife has Loyalist sympathies. 4598

Stevenson, Burton E. A Soldier of Virginia. Houghton, 1901.
The early campaigns of Washington and the defeat of Braddock.   4599

Stimson, Frederic Jesup. My Story. by J. S. of Dale, pseud.
Scribner, 1917. Purported autobiography of Benedict Arnold.   4600

Stover, Herbert Elisha. Eagle and the Wind. Dodd, 1953.
A tale of Pennsylvania during the American Revolution.   4601

_____. Men in Buckskin. Dodd, 1950. British-inspired
Indian raids in Pennsylvania.   4602

_____. Powder Mission. Dodd, 1951. Expedition down
the Mississippi for powder for Washington's army.   4603

Swanson, Neil. The First Rebel. Farrar, 1937. About Scotch-
Irish colonists and their insistence on freedom.   4604

_____. The Forbidden Ground. Farrar, 1938. Depicts
fur trading in and around Detroit.   4605

Taylor, David. Farewell to Valley Forge. Lippincott, 1955.
Adventures of two young people who spy for Washington.   4606

_____. Lights Across the Delaware. Lippincott, 1954.
Washington's capture of Trenton at Christmas, 1776.   4607

_____. Mistress of the Forge. Lippincott, 1964. The

burgeoning Pennsylvania iron industry is the setting for
this tale of Tory uprising and a girl who inherits a
forge.   4608

_____. Storm the Last Rampart. Lippincott, 1960. Wash-
ington's secret intelligence system in the last phase of the
Revolution.   4609

_____. Sycamore Men. Lippincott, 1958. The men who
fought the British under the command of Francis Marion in
the swamps and underbrush of the Carolinas.   4610

Taylor, Mary Imlay. A Yankee Volunteer. McClurg, 1899.
The early days of the Revolution with Generals Washington,
Putnam, and Howe.   4611

Teilhet, Darwin Le Ora. The Road to Glory. Funk, 1956.
Father Junipero Serra and his missionary work among the
Indians in California.   4612

Thompson, Daniel P. The Green Mountain Boys. Caldwell,
1840. Contains accounts of land controversies and war in
Vermont under the leadership of Ethan Allen.   4613

Thompson, Maurice. Alice of Old Vincennes. Bobbs, 1901.
The patriotism of a lady in old French Vincennes, Indiana.
                                                                        4614
Thompson, N.P. The Rangers. Nichols & Hall, 1851.
George Rogers Clark's campaigns in the West.   4615

Tilton, Dwight, pseud. for George Tilton Richardson and
Wilder Dwight Quint. My Lady Laughter. Clark, 1904.
Growing tension between British and colonists and the
siege of Boston.   4616

Todd, A.L. Richard Montgomery. McKay, 1967. YA. A
little-known American military leader who was instrumental
in the defense of New York and the attacks on St. John's,
Montreal, and Quebec.   4617

Toepfer, Ray Grant. Liberty & Corporal Kincaid. Chilton,
1968. Activities of a militia company in Virginia in 1781
including the prevention of an attempt to capture Governor
Thomas Jefferson.   4618

Townsend, Frank Sumner. Hugh Graham. Abingdon, 1916.
Pioneer life and Indian fighting in western Pennsylvania
just before the Revolution.   4619

Turnbull, Agnes. The Day Must Dawn. Macmillan, 1942.
Everyday events in a frontier town threatened by Indian
attack.   4620

Tyson, J. Audrey. The Stirrup Cup. Appleton, 1903. A
story of Aaron Burr in New York and Pennsylvania.   4621

Van de Water, Frederic. Catch a Falling Star. Duell, 1949.
Romance of Vermont with Ethan Allen as a character.
(followed by Wings of the Morning)   4622

_____. Day of Battle. Washburn, 1958. The battle of
Bennington and the romance of an American soldier with a
Tory girl.   4623

_____. The Reluctant Rebel. Duell, 1948. Ethan Allen
and the Green Mountain Boys fight for liberty. (followed by
Catch a Falling Star)   4624

_____. Wings of the Morning. Washburn, 1956. The fight
for independence in eastern Vermont. (followed by Day of
Battle)   4625

Van Every, Dale. Bridal Journey. Messner, 1950. Occurs
in the Ohio River Valley during the seething times near the
end of the Revolution.   4626

_____. Captive Witch. Messner, 1951. A tale of the west-
ern frontier, then Virginia and Kentucky, combining romance
and Indian fighting.   4627

_____. The Voyagers. Holt, 1957. The American frontier
in the late eighteenth century.   4628

Vining, Elizabeth Gray. The Virginia Exiles. by Elizabeth J.
Gray. Lippincott, 1955. The conviction and dignity of the
Quaker spirit in the upset times of the Revolution.   4629

Wallace, Willard M. East to Bagaduce. Regnery, 1963. The
disastrous naval siege of British-held Bagaduce, Maine, in
the summer of 1779 is the setting for this novel.   4630

Wellman, Manly Wade. Clash on the Catawba. Washburn,
1962. YA. Carolina militiaman Zack Harper participates
in the action at Cowpens and the Catawba.   4631

Wells, Evelyn. A City for Saint Francis. Doubleday, 1967.
The wife of a Spanish aristocrat finds true love amidst the
rigors of De Anza's expedition from Mexico to the present
San Francisco.   4632

Westcott, Jan. Captain Barney. Crown, 1951. Action-filled
story of a noted naval officer, Joshua Barney.   4633

Wheelwright, Jere Hungerford. Kentucky Stand. Scribner,
1951. Indian warfare and pioneer life in Kentucky.   4634

White, Helen C. Dust on the King's Highway. Macmillan,
1947. Work of Father Garcés and other missionaries
among Indians in California and Mexico.   4635

White, Stewart Edward. Daniel Boone, Wilderness Scout.
Doubleday, Doran, 1935. Adventures of Long Knife, who
first blazed the Wilderness Trail to Kentucky.   4636

Wibberley, Leonard. John Treegate's Musket. Farrar, 1959.
YA. John Treegate was a loyal subject of George III and opposed rebellion--until finally even he felt British oppression
was too much to bear. (followed by Peter Treegate's War)
                                                               4637
_____. Peter Treegate's War. Farrar, 1960. YA. Six-
teen-year-old Peter Treegate fights as well as a man in
the Battle of Bunker Hill and is torn between his father and
his foster-father. (followed by Sea Captain From Salem) 4638

_____. Sea Captain From Salem. Farrar, 1961. YA.
A Salem fisherman sails his sloop-of-war, Hornet, on a
mission for Benjamin Franklin. (followed by Treegate's
Raiders)   4639

_____. Treegate's Raiders. Farrar, 1962. YA. Young
Captain in the colonial army takes part in action at Kings
Mountain, Cowpens, and Yorktown. (4th in Treegate series)
                                                               4640

Widdemer, Margaret. Buckskin Baronet. Doubleday, 1960.
An English baronet comes to America as an observer, becomes involved in several romances, is captured by Indians,
and learns startling facts about his own past.   4641

Wiener, Willard. Morning in America. Farrar, 1942. Experiences of an American soldier who served under Charles
Lee.   4642

Williams, Ben Ames. Come Spring. Houghton, 1940. The
building of a home in frontier Maine during the Revolution.
                                                               4643
Winn, Mary P. and Margaret Hannis. The Law and the
Letter. Neale, 1907. The coming to New Orleans of young
girls as the brides of French soldiers.   4644

Wyckoff, Nicholas E. Braintree Mission. Macmillan, 1957.
Boston in the 1770s and a suggestion to preserve peace by
seating representative American colonists in Parliament. 4645

Yerby, Frank. Bride of Liberty. Doubleday, 1954. A romantic triangle of two sisters and the man they both love. 4646

Ziegler, Isabelle Gibson. The Nine Days of Father Serra. Longmans, 1951. Missionary work in early Spanish California.   4647

c) National Period (1789-1861)

Abbott, Jane Ludlow. River's Rim. Lippincott, 1950.
American patriot's loyalty is suspected because of relatives' leanings in the War of 1812.   4648

Adams, Samuel Hopkins. Banner by the Wayside. Random,
1947. A touring theatrical group in the Erie Canal region.
                                                                  4649

_____. Canal Town. Random, 1944. A crusading doctor
attacks disease in an Erie Canal town--Palmyra, New York.
                                                                  4650

_____. The Gorgeous Hussy. Houghton, 1934. Peggy
O'Neale leads an active life in Washington's political and
social circles.   4651

_____. Sunrise to Sunset. Random, 1950. Life in the cot-
ton mill town of Troy, New York, when employees sought
better working conditions.   4652

Ainsworth, Edward Maddin. Eagles Fly West. Macmillan,
1946. Story of a newspaperman and pioneer settlements,
the gold rush, and the Spanish-Mexican culture in early
California.   4653

Aldrich, Bess Streeter. Song of Years. Grosset, 1961,
c.1939. Story of the lives and emotions of Iowa pioneers
revolving around a family of nine children.   4654

Allen, Henry. The Gates of the Mountains. by Will Henry,
pseud. Random House, 1963. A half-breed Indian finds
both adventure and romance on the famous Lewis and Clark
expedition to the Pacific Northwest.   4655

Allen, James Lane. The Choir Invisible. Macmillan, 1897.
Story of a hopeless romance in Kentucky after the Revolutionary War.   4656

Allen, Merritt Parmelee. East of Astoria. Longmans, 1956.
YA. The adventures of men who work for Astor's fur com-
pany and the attempted settlement of a community named
Astoria.   4657

Allen, T.D., pseud. for Terry D. and Don B. Allen. Doctor
in Buckskin. Harper, 1951. Medical missionary to frontier
Oregon.   4658

_____. Troubled Border. Harper, 1954. John McLoughlin,
superintendent of Hudson's Bay Company at Fort Vancouver
on the Columbia River.   4659

Allis, Marguerite. All in Good Time. Putnam, 1944. A

Connecticut clockmaker who foresaw mass production.   4660

_____. Brave Pursuit. Putnam, 1954. Pioneer life in the
early days of Ohio statehood showing the status of women. 4661

_____. Charity Strong. Putnam, 1945. Connecticut lady
with the convention-defying ambition to be an opera singer. 4662

_____. The Law of the Land. Putnam, 1948. Experi-
ences of a Connecticut woman early in the fight for woman
suffrage.   4663

_____. Now We Are Free. Putnam, 1952. Post-Revolu-
tion migration of settlers from Connecticut to Ohio. (followed by To Keep Us Free)   4664

_____. The Splendor Stays. Putnam, 1942. Domestic and
political life in Connecticut at the inception of the Monroe
Doctrine; centered on the lives of seven sisters.   4665

_____. To Keep Us Free. Putnam, 1953. A reconstruc-
tion of early life on the Ohio frontier.   4666

_____. Water Over the Dam. Putnam, 1947. The effects
of the Farmington, Connecticut Canal on the lives of the
people in the area.   4667

Andrews, Robert. Great Day in the Morning. Coward, 1950.
Attempt to draw Colorado into the Civil War as a Confederate
state and to use her gold for the southern cause.   4668

Anness, Milford E. Song of Metamoris. Caxton, 1964. Tecumseh and his brother, Metamoris, led a crusade to protect Indian lands from the encroachment of the white man,
but suffered a decisive defeat at Tippecanoe.   4669

Arnold, Elliott. Time of the Gringo. Knopf, 1953. Exciting
narrative of New Mexico in the time before the Mexican
War.   4670

_____. White Falcon. Knopf, 1955. John Tanner's life
with the Ottawa and Chippewa Indians.   4671

Atherton, Gertrude. The Conqueror. Macmillan, 1901. A
novel based on the career of Alexander Hamilton, written
in a sympathetic vein.   4672

_____. The Doomswoman. Continental, 1901. Depicts
Spanish life in old California in the 1840s.   4673

_____. Rezánov. Cupples, 1906. Manners and trade af-
fairs in San Francisco in 1806, when the Russians were attempting to gain a foothold in California.   4674

_____. The Valiant Runaways. Dodd, 1899. Turmoil in
California in the period when Mexican power was declin-
ing.   4675

Atkinson, Eleanor. Hearts Undaunted. Harper, 1917. A girl
raised by Indians returns to her white mother and becomes
a frontier wife.   4676

Atkinson, Oriana. The Golden Season. Bobbs, 1953. Robust
story of Dutch settlers in the Catskill region.   4677

_____. The Twin Cousins. Bobbs, 1951. Family life at an
inn on the Susquehanna Turnpike at Catskill, New York. (followed by The Golden Season)   4678

Austin, Mary. Isidro. Houghton, 1905. Indians and Spanish
settlers in California at the time of the missions.   4679

Babcock, Mrs. Bernie. Little Abe Lincoln. Lippincott, 1926.
The childhood, in Kentucky and Indiana, of Lincoln and his
sister, Sarah.   4680

_____. The Soul of Ann Rutledge. Lippincott, 1919. The
romance of Ann Rutledge and Abraham Lincoln which influenced him even after her death.   4681

Bacheller, Irving. D'ri and I. Harper, 1901. A story of
America during the War of 1812 featuring vivid descriptions
of the St. Lawrence Valley.   4682

_____. Eben Holden. Lothrop, 1900. Story of a beloved
servant in the Adirondacks, with Horace Greeley and Abraham Lincoln as characters.   4683

_____. The Light in the Clearing. Bobbs, 1917. A tale
of the north country in the time of Silas Wright, a governor
of New York.   4684

_____. A Man for the Ages. Bobbs, 1919. Story of a fam-
ily in New Salem, Illinois, during Lincoln's young manhood.
                                                        4685
Bailey, Paul Dayton. Claws of the Hawk. Westernlore, 1966.
A biographical novel of Wahker the Ute, horsethief and war
chief.   4686

Baker, Karle Wilson. Star of the Wilderness. by Charlotte
Wilson, pseud. Coward, 1942. A Cincinnati couple seek
their fortune in Texas.   4687

Baldwin, Leland Dewitt. The Delectable Country. Furman,
1939. A young riverman's adventures in the Ohio Valley in
"the pursuit of happiness."   4688

Ball, Zachary.   Pull Down to New Orleans.   Crown, 1946.
Romance with the Ohio and Mississippi Rivers as setting.   4689

Ballard, Willis Todhunter.   Gold in California!   Doubleday,
1965.   An Ohio newspaperman and his family move to California during the Gold Rush, experiencing life in a wagon
train and in mining camps.   4690

Banks, Nancy H.   Oldfield.   Macmillan, 1902.   Rural life in
Kentucky in mid-century.   4691

_____.   Round Anvil Rock.   Macmillan, 1903.   A romance
of early Kentucky.   4692

Banks, Polan.   Black Ivory.   Harper, 1926.   Pirate Jean Lafitte's career as a   slave trader in New Orleans.   4693

Barnes, Percy Raymond.   Crum Elbow Folks.   Lippincott,
1938.   A charming picture of life in a Quaker settlement
in New York.   4694

Barney, Helen Corse.   Fruit in His Season.   Crown, 1951.
Quaker pioneers, objecting to slavery, leave Virginia for
Ohio.   4695

Barr, Amelia E.   The Belle of Bowling Green.   Dodd, 1904.
The wealthy New York Dutch, who disdained to let the war
interfere with their social life.   4696

_____.   The Maid of Maiden Lane.   Dodd, 1900.   Should New
York or Philadelphia be the capital of the young United
States?   4697

_____.   Remember the Alamo.   Dodd, 1888.   The dramatic
attack on the Alamo in the Texan War for independence from
Mexico.   4698

_____.   She Loved a Sailor.   Warne, 1899.   A romance of
the administration of President Andrew Jackson.   4699

_____.   Trinity Bells.   Dodd, 1899.   Quiet tale of peaceful
family life in New York in the early nineteenth century.   4700

Barrett, Monte.   Sun in Their Eyes.   Bobbs, 1944.   Life in
Texas when there was friction with the Spanish.   4701

_____.   Tempered Blade.   Bobbs, 1946.   Texas at the time
of the break from Mexico, with Jim Bowie as hero.   4702

Bartlett, Jenniebelle.   Cry Above the Winds.   Morrow, 1951.
Pictures Monterey in the 1830s and deals with Indians,
Mexicans, and settlers.   4703

Bartlett, Lanier. Adios! Morrow, 1929. Armed resistance
of Spanish Californians to acquisition of the area by the
United States.   4704

Bartlett, Virginia Stivers. Mistress of Monterey. Bobbs,
1933. Social and political controversy in California as reflected in the lives of Governor Fages and his wife.   4705

Bates, Morgan. Martin Brook. Harper, 1901. A report of
conditions which resulted in the Abolitionist point of view. 4706

Baume, Frederic E. Yankee Woman. Dodd, 1945. A New
England widow sails her husband's ship to California during
the gold rush.   4707

Beach, Rex. The World in His Arms. Putnam, 1946. A
Boston fur-poacher in Alaska.   4708

Bean, Amelia. The Fancher Train. Doubleday, 1958. A
stirring account of the tragic Mountain Meadow Massacre--
the slaughter of an entire wagon train.   4709

Beebe, Ralph. Who Fought and Bled. Coward, 1941. Action
of the War of 1812 with General Hull near Detroit.   4710

Beecher, Henry Ward. Norwood. Fords, Howard & Hulbert,
1866. The gossip and romance of a prosperous small town
in New England.   4711

Bell, Sallie. Marcel Armand. Page, 1935. A three-sided romance with one of Jean Lafitte's pirates as hero.   4712

Benezra, Barbara. Gold Dust and Petticoats. Bobbs, 1964.
YA. Marcy Miller and her family find many adventures in
San Francisco after an eventful wagon train trip.   4713

Bennet, Robert Ames. A Volunteer With Pike. McClurg,
1909. A tale of the Louisiana Purchase and Zebulon Pike's
journey westward, including the discovery of Pike's Peak. 4714

Benson, Ramsey. Hill Country. Stokes, 1928. Early Swed-
ish settlers in Minnesota.   4715

Berry, Don. Moontrap. Viking, 1962. A mountain man who
attempts to settle down and farm in pioneer Oregon with his
Indian wife encounters difficulties.   4716

_____. To Build a Ship. Viking, 1963. An isolated com-
munity on the Oregon coast becomes absorbed in the task of
building a ship as a lifeline of communication.   4717

_____. Trask. Viking, 1960. The customs and beliefs
of Oregon Indians discovered by a pioneer travelling through

their territory.   4718

Best, Allena. Homespun. by Erick Berry, pseud. Lothrop,
1937. A story of pioneers in such daily occupations as
hunting, spinning, and weaving.   4719

Best, Herbert. Young'un. Macmillan, 1944. Warm, refreshing story of three children left to shift for themselves on a
small northern farm.   4720

Binns, Archie. The Land Is Bright. Scribner, 1939. A wagon
train journeys from Illinois to Oregon and encounters incredible hardships.   4721

_____. Mighty Mountain. Scribner, 1940. A New England
Yankee settles in the Washington Territory.   4722

Bird, Robert Montgomery. Nick O' the Woods; or, The Jibbe-
nainosay. Armstrong, 1837. Indian warfare in Kentucky
with the capture of hero and heroine and its results.   4723

Birney, Hoffman. Eagle in the Sun. Putnam, 1935. An exciting tale of Santa Fe during the Mexican War.   4724

_____. Grim Journey. Minton, Balch, 1934. Tale told by
a survivor of the terrible sufferings of the Donner Party,
caught in mountain snowstorms.   4725

Bischoff, Ilse. Proud Heritage. Coward, 1949. The life of
Gilbert Stuart, who became an outstanding painter.   4726

Blake, Forrester. Johnny Christmas. Morrow, 1948. A
story of Indians and Mexicans in the American Southwest
in the 1830s and '40s.   4727

Boden, Clara Nickerson. The Cut of Her Jib. Coward, 1953.
Depicts life in a Massachusetts coastal town in the 1850s as
reflected in the diary of the author's grandmother.   4728

Bogue, Herbert Edward. Dareford. Clark, 1907. A novel
with interesting references to laws just before the Civil
War, especially the fugitive slave laws.   4729

Bonner, Geraldine. The Emigrant Trail. Duffield, 1910. The
overland route to California via Missouri.   4730

Bonney, Edward. The Banditti of the Prairies. Univ. of Okla.
Pr., 1963. A bounty hunter explains why he rounded up a
band of outlaws.   4731

Bontemps, Arna. Black Thunder. Macmillan, 1936. The
"Gabriel Insurrection": a mob of slaves attempt to capture Richmond about 1800.   4732

Boyd, James. The Long Hunt. Scribner, 1930. Realistic
story of a rugged frontiersman well-versed in forest-
craft.   4733

Boyles, C.S. Nameless Breed. by Will C. Brown, pseud.
Macmillan, 1960. A son seeks to rescue his father who is
held captive by the Comanches.   4734

Boyles, Kate and Virgil D. Boyles. Langford of the Three
Bars. McClurg, 1907. Cattle ranching in South Dakota when
rustling was prevalent and law enforcement poor.   4735

Brady, Cyrus Townsend. In the Wasp's Nest. Scribner, 1902.
"A story of a sea-waif in the War of 1812."   4736

Brand, Anna. Thunder Before Seven. Doubleday, 1941. A
tale of the Texan revolt against Mexico.   4737

Breslin, Howard. Concert Grand. Dodd, 1963. Romances
and musical successes of the brilliant New Orleans-born
composer, Louis Moreau Gottschalk.   4738

_____. The Tamarack Tree. McGraw, 1947. Effects on
Vermont residents of a Whig rally addressed by Daniel Web-
ster.   4739

Brick, John. Rogues' Kingdom. Doubleday, 1965. Romance
proves both the undoing and the salvation of a prosperous
family of horsethieves in upstate New York.   4740

Brigham, Johnson. The Sinclairs of Old Fort Des Moines.
Torch Press, 1927. Pioneer life in Iowa in the 1840s.   4741

Bristow, Gwen. Calico Palace. Pocket Bks., 1971, c. 1970.
A girl of nineteen finds hardships and thrills in California
during gold rush days as her determination aids her in busi-
ness and romance.   4742

_____. Deep Summer. Crowell, 1937. Love blossoms be-
tween a northern Puritan girl and a southern aristocrat in
Louisiana. (followed by The Handsome Road)   4743

_____. The Jubilee Trail. Crowell, 1950. Adventures of
a quiet New York girl on the Santa Fe Trail after she leaves
finishing school   4744

Browin, Frances Williams. Looking for Orlando. Criterion,
1961. YA. Young Southerner visiting his Quaker grand-
parents in Pennsylvania has to decide whether to aid in the
escape of a runaway slave.   4745

Brown, Charles B. Arthur Mervyn. McKay, 1800. Life in
Philadelphia during the yellow fever outbreak of 1793. 4746

Brown, Dee. Wave High the Banner. Macrae Smith, 1942.
Davy Crockett, famous frontiersman and hero of the Alamo.
4747

Brown, Joe David. The Freeholder. Morrow, 1949. An English boy, raised in an orphan asylum, comes to America in
quest of freedom and success.   4748

Brown, Katharine Holland. Diane. Doubleday, Page, 1904.
Dealings in runaway slaves in a French community in Mississippi and the Underground Railroad.   4749

_____. The Father. Day, 1928. A father's abolitionist cru-
sading and his daughter's romance are subjects for this lively
novel in which Lincoln appears.   4750

Brown, Marion Marsh. Broad Stripes and Bright Stars. Westminster Pr., 1955, c.1954. YA. The story of Francis Scott
Key, showing how the patriotism he felt as a boy culminated
in his writing of "The Star-Spangled Banner" at the Battle of
Fort McHenry.   4751

Brown, Theron. Under the Mulberry Trees. Badger, 1909.
William Miller's claim that the Second Advent was at hand
caused great excitement in the Connecticut countryside.   4752

Brown, William Garrott. A Gentleman of the South. Macmillan,
1903. Heartbreak caused by the so-called code-of-honor
which settled differences by dueling.   4753

Bryan, Jack Yeaman. Come to the Bower. Viking, 1963.
Romantic conflict and the Texas war for independence from
Mexico as seen in the story of a young lawyer.   4754

Burgess, Jackson. Pillar of Cloud. Putnam, 1957. Pioneers
blazing a trail from Kansas to the western mountains.   4755

Burgoyne, Leon E. Ensign Ronan. Winston, 1955. Youth
seeks revenge on Indians but finds romance instead.   4756

Burman, Ben Lucien. Steamboat Round the Bend. Farrar &
Rinehart, 1933. Gentle love story of a southern couple
against the colorful background of river and bayou country.
4757

Burnett, Frances Hodgson. In Connection With the De Willoughby
Claim. Scribner, 1899. A rural area of Tennessee before
the outbreak of the Civil War.   4758

Burr, Anna. The Golden Quicksand. Appleton, 1936. A
young easterner seeks his missing brother in Santa Fe.   4759

Butler, Beverly. Feather in the Wind. Dodd, 1965. YA.
How a pioneer family and a doctor from Scotland react to
Indian attacks and other hardships.   4760

_____. The Fur Lodge. Dodd, 1959. YA. A boy takes
his place with the men on a demanding, rugged fur-trading
trip.   4761

_____. The Silver Key. Dodd, 1961. YA. A young lady
who settles in a Welsh farming community in Wisconsin becomes involved in the Abolitionist movement.   4762

_____. Song of the Voyageur. Dodd, 1955. YA. A girl
faces the difficult choice of two ways of life as she must
choose between two suitors--one an Easterner, one a west-
ward-facing pioneer.   4763

Bynner, Edwin Lassetter. Zachary Phips. Houghton, 1892.
Adventures of a Boston boy who joined Aaron Burr's expedition.   4764

Byrd, Sigman and John Sutherland. The Valiant. Jason Press,
1955. Stand of the Nez Percé Indians against the inroads of
the white man in Oregon.   4765

Cable, George Washington. Dr. Sevier. Scribner, 1884. A
tale of life in thriving New Orleans at mid-century.   4766

_____. The Grandissimes. Scribner, 1880. A novel of
the Creole inhabitants of New Orleans.   4767

Caldwell, Taylor (full name: Janet Taylor Caldwell). The
Turnbulls. Scribner, 1943. An English immigrant becomes
a powerful figure in the New York financial world.   4768

_____. The Wide House. Scribner, 1945. Life of a family
amidst religious and racial intolerance in upstate New York.
                                                           4769
Cameron, Margaret. Johndover. -Harper, 1924. A disillusioned widow, an escaped convicted murderer, and a youth
whose Puritan conscience demands justice.   4770

Campbell, Patricia. Cedarhaven. Macmillan, 1965. Experiences of three sisters transplanted from old Virginia to
frontier life in Washington Territory in 1859.   4771

_____. The Royal Anne Tree. Macmillan, 1956. A young
girl is orphaned soon after her arrival as a settler in Washington territory.   4772

Campbell, Walter Stanley. 'Dobe Walls. by Stanley Vestal,
pseud. Houghton, 1929. Mexicans, Indians, and pioneers
figure in this tale of a fort on the Santa Fe Trail in Kit
Carson's time.   4773

_____. Revolt on the Border. by Stanley Vestal, pseud.
Houghton, 1938. Adventure on the Santa Fe Trail at the

time of the annexation of New Mexico.   4774

Canfield, Chauncey L. The City of Six. McClurg, 1910.
California placer miners in the gold rush of '49.   4775

_____. The Diary of a 'Forty-Niner. Morgan Shepard,
1906. Digging for gold, miners' quarrels, and land disputes
in early California.   4776

Cannon, Cornelia James. Red Rust. Little, 1928. A young
Swedish farmer experiments to produce a better variety of
wheat.   4777

Cannon, LeGrand. A Mighty Fortress. Farrar, 1937. Inspiring, entertaining story of a New England farmer who
became a preacher.   4778

Capps, Benjamin. The Brothers of Uterica. Meredith, 1967.
A cosmopolitan band of idealists seeks to found a utopia in
the American midwest at mid-century.   4779

_____. A Woman of the People. Duell, 1966. Two ab-
ducted white girls are raised as Indians of the Comanche
tribe.   4780

Carhart, Arthur Hawthorne. Drum Up the Dawn. Dodd, 1937.
About Zebulon Pike's expedition westward.   4781

Carmer, Carl. Genesee Fever. Farrar, 1941. A gentleman
schoolteacher with strong political ideas.   4782

Carnahan, Walter. Hoffman's Row. Bobbs, 1963. Romanticized story of an incident in Abraham Lincoln's life as a
young lawyer in Springfield, Illinois.   4783

Carpenter, Edward Childs. Captain Courtesy. Jacobs, 1906.
The struggle for control of California, culminating in victory
for the United States.   4784

_____. The Code of Victor Jallot. Jacobs, 1907. New
Orleans at the time of the Louisiana Purchase.   4785

Case, Josephine. Written in Sand. Houghton, 1945. Yankee
General William Eaton leads an invasion of Tripoli in 1805.
                                                                  4786

Case, Victoria. A Finger in Every Pie. Doubleday, 1963.
Reminiscences concerning settlers and Indians, good and
bad, in the old Oregon Territory, as told by a spirited
spinster.   4787

Cather, Willa. Death Comes for the Archbishop. Knopf, 1927.
The growth and development of the southwest reflected in
the story of the Archbishop of Santa Fe.   4788

_____. My Antonia. Houghton, 1918. An immigrant Bo-
hemian girl is confronted by the trials of rugged frontier
life.   4789

_____. Sapphira and the Slave Girl. Knopf, 1940. An in-
valid Virginia lady who "married beneath herself" and her
jealousy toward a slave girl.   4790

Catherwood, Mary H. Lazarre. Bowen-Merrill, 1901. Based
on the story of the French Dauphin's supposed escape to Am-
erica in a temporary state of insanity.   4791

Catto, Max. Charlie Gallagher, My Love! by Simon Kent,
pseud. Macmillan, 1961, c.1960. The Wild West of 1868
takes its toll of the members of a small Italian circus en
route to Texas.   4792

Caudill, Harry M. Dark Hills to Westward. Little, 1969.
A brave frontier woman, Jennie Wiley, is abducted from
her western Virginia cabin by Indians in 1789.   4793

Chambers, Robert W. The Happy Parrot. Appleton, 1929.
Lively adventures of a schooner engaged in the slave trade
during the War of 1812.   4794

_____. The Rake and the Hussy. Appleton, 1930. Vivid
and detailed sketches of people and events during the de-
fense of New Orleans.   4795

Chase, Mary Ellen. Silas Crockett. Macmillan, 1935. A
four-generation story of Maine seafarers.   4796

Chidsey, Donald Barr. Stronghold. Doubleday, 1948. Love,
romance, and murder against a backdrop of the War of 1812
and the Embargo Act.   4797

Churchill, Winston. Coniston. Macmillan, 1906. Social and
political life and developments in Boston and Washington at
mid-century. (followed by Mr. Crewe's Career)   4798

_____. The Crisis. Macmillan, 1901. St. Louis is pre-
sented as a forum for the conflicting views which led to the
Civil War.   4799

_____. The Crossing. Macmillan, 1904. Exploration of
the Midwest, wilderness life, and the relations of white
men and Indians on George Rogers Clark's expedition.   4800

Cicchetti, Janet. O Genesee. Lippincott, 1958. Pioneering
in New York State with the added hazard of the War of
1812.   4801

Clagett, John. Wilderness Virgin. Pop. Lib., 1962. (pub.

in 1954 as Buckskin Cavalier) A Virginia cavalier searches
for his beloved, who had been captured by Indians.   4802

Clark, Howard. The Mill on Mad River. Little, 1948. A
story of the brass and clock-making industries in Connecticut.   4803

Clarke, Mary Stetson. The Glass Phoenix. Viking, 1969. YA.
The making of the famous Sandwich glass is told in the story
of a boy who worked in the glass factory.   4804

_____. The Limner's Daughter. Viking, 1967. YA. A
teen-aged girl assumes responsibility for her injured, widowed
father and her small brother.   4805

Cleghorn, Sarah N. A Turnpike Lady. Holt, 1907. A novel
of daily life in the Vermont country-side during the War of
1812.   4806

Cochran, Louis. The Fool of God. Duell, 1958. The story
of Alexander Campbell, a Scotch-Irishman who came to America in 1809 and became a religious and political leader. 4807

_____. Raccoon John Smith. Duell, 1963. Based on the
career of the colorful itinerant preacher known as "Raccoon
John" who preached of the love of God and favored Christian unity.   4808

Coffin, Robert Peter. John Dawn. Macmillan, 1936. The
Maine seacoast and the shipbuilding industry which flourished there.   4809

Coker, Elizabeth Boatwright. Daughter of Strangers. Dutton,
1950. The live-happily-ever-after tale of an octoroon girl
on a South Carolina plantation.   4810

Colby, Merle. All Ye People. Viking, 1931. Panoramic
picture of American pioneers in the East, South, and West
in the year 1810.   4811

_____. The New Road. Viking, 1933. The growth of a
frontier town in early Ohio.   4812

Colver, Anne. Listen for the Voices. Farrar, 1939. The
Concord literary circle, with Emerson, Thoreau, and Alcott.   4813

_____. Theodosia. (rev. ed.) Holt, 1962, c.1941. YA.
The courageous daughter of Aaron Burr stood by her father
during his successes, the aftermath of his duel with Hamilton, and his trial for treason.   4814

Comfort, Will. Apache. Dutton, 1931. A dramatically told

story of Mangus Colorado, Apache chief who tried to
drive away the white intruders.   4815

Conrader, Constance Stone. Blue Wampum. Duell, 1958.
YA. A boy of French-Indian-American parentage sees the
paths of white men and Indians diverging in pioneer Wisconsin as he lives among the Winnebagoes.   4816

Conway, Moncure Daniel. Pine and Palm. Holt, 1887.
Friends from the North and the South differ on the slavery
issue, and each agrees to spend a year in the other's
home.   4817

Cook, Roberta. Thing About Clarissa. Bobbs, 1958. Humorous account of two young ladies just returned from a fashionable finishing school.   4818

Coolidge, Dane. Gringo Gold. Dutton, 1939. The activities
of Mexican bandit Joaquin Murrieta during the California
gold rush.   4819

Cooper, Courtney Ryley. The Golden Bubble. Little, 1928.
A Kansas City man joins the Colorado gold rush and finds
romance as well as success.   4820

_____. The Pioneers. Little, 1938. A wagon train led by
Kit Carson journeys on the Oregon Trail.   4821

Cooper, James Fenimore. Afloat and Ashore. Hurd & Houghton, 1867. Seafaring life of an American in the Atlantic and
Pacific in the early national period.   4822

Cooper, Jamie Lee. The Horn and the Forest. Bobbs, 1963.
The son of a backwoods doctor and a part-Indian mother
feels divided loyalties when his Indian relatives ally with
the British.   4823

Courlander, Harold. The African. Crown, 1967. An African,
enslaved and transported to America, seeks to recover his
freedom and dignity.   4824

Cowdrey, A.E. Elixir of Life. Doubleday; 1965. The yellow
fever epidemic of the 1850s led to the flight from New Orleans of the "best families"; this is the story of those who
stayed.   4825

Crabb, Alfred Leland. Home to Kentucky. Bobbs, 1953.
Henry Clay's career as a lawyer, closing with his famous
Cumberland Gap speech.   4826

_____. Home to the Hermitage. Bobbs, 1948. A novel of
Andrew Jackson and his wife, Rachel.   4827

Cranston, Paul. To Heaven on Horseback. Messner, 1952.
Story of Narcissa and Marcus Whitman, pioneer missionaries to Oregon, based on a journal she kept.   4828

Cronyn, George W. '49; A Novel of Gold. Dorrance, 1925.
Vivid story of westward expansion speeded by the lust for
gold.   4829

Crowley, Mary Catherine. Love Thrives in War. Little,
1903. Brock's taking of Detroit and fighting in the War
of 1812.   4830

Crownfield, Gertrude. Conquering Kitty. Lippincott, 1935.
Exploits of the jilted Kitty Knight, who determined to break
men's hearts during the War of 1812.   4831

Culp, John H. The Men of Gonzales. Sloane, 1960. Thirty-
two men who came from Gonzales to aid in the defense of
the Alamo.   4832

_____. Oh, Valley Green! Holt, 1972. The story of Am-
erica's westward expansion and of political efforts to annex
Texas and California.   4833

Curwood, James O. The Courage of Captain Plum. Bobbs,
1908. A young officer is commissioned to investigate a
Mormon settlement and report on the marriage problem. 4834

Dahl, Borghild. Stowaway to America. Dutton, 1959. YA. A
Norwegian kitchen maid comes to New York in 1825 as a
stowaway.   4835

Dana, Richard Henry. Two Years Before the Mast. Houghton,
1840. Spirited account of a voyage on a merchant sailing
vessel.   4836

Daniels, Harriet. Muller Hill. Knopf, 1943. A mysterious
French aristocrat makes a temporary home in New York
State.   4837

David, Evan John. As Runs the Glass. Harper, 1943. Seagoing yarn of a Maine family in the period following the
Revolution.   4838

Davidson, Louis B. and Edward J. Doherty. Captain Marooner.
Crowell, 1952. Mutiny on a whaling ship out of Nantucket.
                                                        4839

Daviess, Maria Thompson. The Matrix. Century, 1920. Romance of Thomas Lincoln and Nancy Hanks, parents of Abraham Lincoln.   4840

Davis, Dorothy Salisbury. Men of No Property. Scribner,
1956. Arrival of Irish immigrants in New York and their

Americanization.   4841

Davis, Harold Lenoir. Beulah Land. Morrow, 1949. A
young couple's search for happiness in a journey westward
to Oregon.   4842

Davis, J. Frank. The Road to San Jacinto. Bobbs, 1936.
Tangled Texas-Mexican politics and the leadership of Houston are the background.   4843

Davis, Julia. Cloud on the Land. Rinehart, 1951. Adjustment
of a girl who opposes slavery in her marriage to a slave-
holder.   4844

_____. Eagle on the Sun. Rinehart, 1956. Lucy MacLeod
manages the family plantation while the men fight in the Mexican War.   4845

De Forest, John W. Kate Beaumont. Estes, 1871. The South
before the Civil War--social life and the attitude toward
slavery.   4846

De Leeuw, Cateau. Give Me Your Hand. Little, 1960. YA.
A young girl in pioneer Ohio has to choose between a stranger
from the East and a young farmer.   4847

Dell, Floyd. Diana Stair. Farrar, 1932. The heroine is a
reformer in Boston in the 1840s.   4848

Delmar, Viña. Beloved. Harcourt, 1956. The romance of
Judah Philip Benjamin, lawyer who came to be known as "the
brains of the Confederacy."   4849

Derleth, August. Bright Journey. Scribner, 1940. Fur trading
in the wild, lovely Northwest Territory, told by a poet-novel-
ist. (followed by The House on the Mound)   4850

_____. Hills Stand Watch. Duell, 1960. A Wisconsin
lead-mining village and a girl discontented with her marriage.   4851

_____. The House on the Mound. Duell, 1958. A fur
trader's attempt to gain custody of his illegitimate son. 4852

_____. Restless Is the River. Scribner, 1939. A Hungar-
ian exile who settles in Wisconsin raises grapes for wine. 4853

_____. The Wind Leans West. Candlelight Pr., 1969.
Problems of pioneer real estate and financial promotion
in early Milwaukee as the Wisconsin territory expands.   4854

_____. Wind Over Wisconsin. Scribner, 1938. Indian
wars in Wisconsin with special emphasis on the natural

beauty of the region.   4855

Desmond, Alice Curtis. Bewitching Betsy Bonaparte. Dodd,
1958. About the Baltimore girl whose marriage to Jerome
Bonaparte was opposed by his brother Napoleon.   4856

Dickson, Harris. House of Luck. Small, 1916. Speculation
in land in lower Mississippi.   4857

Dillon, Mary C. In Old Bellaire. Century, 1906. A conscientious teacher faces conflict between her own beliefs and
those of the people among whom she works.   4858

_____. The Patience of John Morland. Doubleday, Page,
1909. American politics and politicians under Presidents
Monroe, Adams, and Jackson.   4859

_____. The Rose of Old St. Louis. Century, 1904. St.
Louis, Washington, and Paris in the days of the early
Chouteaus, Jefferson, and Napoleon.   4860

Dobler, Lavinia. Black Gold at Titusville. Dodd, 1959. YA.
The finding of the first oil well in Pennsylvania in 1859. 4861

Dodge, Louis. The American. Messner, 1934. An unsuccessful Illinois farmer seeks fortune in the western gold fields. 4862

Dolbier, Maurice. Benjy Boone. Dial, 1967. A young man
from Maine tours the United States with an itinerant theatrical troupe in quest of his actor-father in 1839.   4863

Dooley, Sallie May. Dem Good Ole Times. by Mrs. James
H. Dooley. Doubleday, Page, 1906. The life of a slave
on a southern plantation as related to his granddaughter. 4864

Dougall, Lily. The Mormon Prophet. Appleton, 1899.
Joseph Smith--his founding of Mormonism, the persecution of the sect, and Smith's death at the hands of a mob. 4865

Dowdey, Clifford. Tidewater. Little, 1943. Virginia landowner who moved his household to the Mississippi Valley. 4866

Downes, Anne Miller. The Pilgrim Soul. Lippincott, 1952.
Hardships and joys of a pioneer couple settling in the New
Hampshire mountains.   4867

_____. The Quality of Mercy. Lippincott, 1959. A Phila-
delphia family become pioneers in the wild country beyond
the Cumberlands.   4868

Drago, Harry Sinclair. Boss of the Plains. by Will Ermine,
pseud. Morrow, 1940. A driver on the Great Plains when
wagon freighting and Pony Express linked the coasts.   4869

Duffus, Robert. Jornada. Covici, 1935. A romance is
nearly engulfed in the fighting which involves Indians, Mexicans, and Americans.   4870

Duncan, Thomas W. Big River, Big Man. Lippincott, 1959.
Panoramic view of territorial and business growth dealing
largely with upper Mississippi lumbering.   4871

Duval, John C. Early Times in Texas. Steck, 1935. Pioneer
life on the frontier and the Texan revolution of 1835-36.   4872

Dye, Eva. Conquest. Doubleday, 1922. The expedition of
Lewis and Clark and the rush of immigrants into the newly
opened West.   4873

Eaton, Evelyn and Edward R. Moore. Heart in Pilgrimage.
Harper, 1948. Elizabeth Seton's role as wife and mother
and her later founding of the Sisters of Charity.   4874

Edmonds, Walter D. Chad Hanna. Little, 1940. The rollick-
ing tale of an orphan boy who ran away and joined the circus
in the Mohawk Valley.   4875

_____. Erie Water. Little, 1933. The building of the
Erie Canal and the romance of a carpenter who worked on
it.   4876

_____. Rome Haul. Little, 1929. A farm lad starts as a
driver on the Erie Canal and manages to make good.   4877

_____. The Wedding Journey. Little, 1947. A husband
who gambled away their honeymoon money and the bride
who stood by him.   4878

_____. Young Ames. Little, 1942. A country boy who
sought success in the big city.   4879

Edwards, E. J. and Jeanette E. Rattray. "Whale Off!" Stokes,
1932. American shore whaling, particularly small boat whaling off Long Island.   4880

Eggleston, Edward. The Circuit Rider. Scribner, 1874.
Ohio at the time of the War of 1812, showing the moral and
social influence of the circuit riders.   4881

_____. The Faith Doctor. Appleton, 1891. A story of
faith healing, which had recently become a popular idea in
New York.   4882

_____. The Graysons. Century, 1888. Pioneer life in
Illinois, showing Lincoln as a lawyer in a murder trial.   4883

_____. The Hoosier Schoolboy. Warne, 1882. A story

of early settlers in Indiana reflecting the status of education.   4884

_____. The Hoosier Schoolmaster. Judd, 1871. Experi-
ences of an Indiana school teacher who boards with the
families of his pupils.   4885

_____. Roxy. Scribner, 1878. Events in a southern Indiana
town near the scene of the battle of Tippecanoe.   4886

Eggleston, George Cary. Dorothy South. Lothrop, 1902. A
romance of Virginia just before the Civil War.   4887

_____. Irene of the Mountains. Lothrop, 1909. A romance
of old Virginia during a political race for governor.   4888

_____. Two Gentlemen of Virginia. Lothrop, 1908. The
"old regime" in Virginia just before the Civil War.   4889

Ehle, John. The Journey of August King. Harper, 1971. A
North Carolina farmer decides to help a fugitive slave girl
escape.   4890

Ehrlich, Leonard. God's Angry Man. S. & S., 1932. A
powerful account of John Brown's firm conviction that
slavery should be abolished.   4891

Eifert, Virginia S. The Buffalo Trace. Dodd, 1966, c.1955.
YA. About Abraham Lincoln's grandfather who followed
Daniel Boone to Kentucky and about the marriage of Lin-
coln's parents. (followed by Out of the Wilderness)   4892

_____. Out of the Wilderness. Dodd, 1966, c.1956. YA.
Set in Kentucky and Illinois, this tells of the first twenty-
two years of Lincoln's life and his desire for an education.
(followed by Three Rivers South)   4893

_____. Three Rivers South. Dodd, 1966, c.1953. YA. Abe
Lincoln's life as a riverboat pilot.   4894

Ellerbe, Rose Lucile. Ropes of Sand. Fischer, 1925. A
vivid story of the American settlement of southern California, and a man's search for his Indian son.   4895

Ellis, William D. The Bounty Lands. World Pub., 1952.
Westward movement caused when Revolutionary War veter-
ans were granted land in Ohio. (followed by Jonathan
Blair, Bounty Lands Lawyer)   4896

_____. The Brooks Legend. Crowell, 1958. Surgeon's
mate's attempt, after the War of 1812, to acquire an
M.D. degree.   4897

_____. Jonathan Blair, Bounty Lands Lawyer. World
Pub., 1954. An eastern lawyer on the Ohio frontier.
(followed by The Brooks Legend)   4898

Embree, Charles Fleming. A Dream of a Throne. Little,
1900. A story of the war between the United States and
Mexico.   4899

Emmons, Della F.G. Sacajawea of the Shoshones. Binfords,
1943. Sacajawea, the "Bird Woman" of the Lewis and
Clark expedition.   4900

Erdman, Loula Grace. The Wind Blows Free. Dodd, 1952.
The struggles of homesteaders in the Texas Panhandle.   4901

Ertz, Susan. No Hearts to Break. Appleton, 1937. Elizabeth
Patterson, a Baltimore girl, marries Jerome Bonaparte,
Napoleon's brother.   4902

Evansen, Virginia B. Nancy Kelsey. McKay, 1965. YA.
About the first American woman to make the journey overland by wagon-train and on foot from Missouri to California
in 1841.   4903

_____. Sierra Summit. McKay, 1967. The first success-
ful crossing of the Sierra Nevada Mountains was achieved
at great expense in effort and suffering in 1844.   4904

Evarts, Hal. Fur Brigade. Little, 1928. A fur trapper and
his girl in the Indian-dominated early West.   4905

Faherty, William B., S.J. A Wall for San Sebastian. Academy
Guild, 1962. Missionary, once a soldier, is torn between
religious and military methods to aid his town.   4906

Faulknor, Cliff. The White Calf. Little, 1965. YA. The
customs and culture of the Blackfoot Indians are reflected
in this tale of young Eagle Child who finds an amazing white
buffalo calf.   4907

Faust, Frederick. The Long Chance. by Max Brand, pseud.
Dodd, 1941. A young frontiersman and a cowardly southerner
in the Old West.   4908

Field, Rachel L. All This, and Heaven Too. Macmillan,
1938. After innocent involvement in a French murder trial,
"Mlle. D" comes to America and begins a new life.   4909

Fierro Blanco, Antonio de. The Journey of the Flame. (tr.)
Houghton, 1933. A Spanish Inspector General's trip through
California told in a tale filled with authentic Mexican and
Spanish folklore.   4910

Finger, Charles Joseph. When Guns Thundered at Tripoli.
Holt, 1937. A rousing tale of American merchant shipping
during the Tripolitan War.   4911

Finney, Gertrude E. Stormy Winter. Longmans, 1959. YA.
San Juan Island, in Puget Sound, claimed by both Great
Britain and the U.S. and harassed by the Haida Indians,
was a precarious locale for colonists.   4912

Fisher, Aileen Lucia. My Cousin Abe. Nelson, 1962. YA.
The story of Abraham Lincoln, as though told in the words
of his cousin, Dennis Friend Hanks.   4913

Fisher, Anne. Oh Glittering Promise! Bobbs, 1949. A Pennsylvania coal miner becomes a California gold miner.   4914

Fisher, Vardis. Children of God. Harper, 1939. The beginnings, growth, and quest for peace of the Mormons, 1820-
90.   4915

_____. City of Illusion. Harper, 1941. The Comstock
Lode in Nevada and the brief flourishing of Virginia City. 4916

_____. The Mothers. Vanguard, 1943. Tragic story of
the Donner Party told from the viewpoint of mothers involved.   4917

_____. Mountain Man. Morrow, 1965. The affection of
a hardy Rocky Mountain fur-trapper for an Indian girl eventually converts him into a deadly foe of Indians when her
own people kill her.   4918

_____. Tale of Valor. Doubleday, 1958. The grueling eight
thousand mile trip of exploration of Lewis and Clark to the
Pacific Northwest.   4919

Fleischmann, Glen. While Rivers Flow. Macmillan, 1963.
Much against his will, a young army officer is ordered to
force the Cherokees from their territory in Georgia and
Tennessee.   4920

Fletcher, Inglis. The Queen's Gift. Bobbs, 1952. Plantation
life after British surrender at Yorktown.   4921

Footner, Hulbert. The Furbringers. McCann, 1920. A young
trader is forced to take a stand against the domineering
father of the girl he loves.   4922

Forbes, Esther. O Genteel Lady! Houghton, 1926. The literary circle of Boston and Concord with Longfellow, Emerson, Thoreau, and Whittier.   4923

_____. Rainbow on the Road. Houghton, 1954. A light-hearted itinerant portrait painter in Puritan New England. 4924

_____. The Running of the Tide. Houghton, 1948. Salem,
Massachusetts, in the flourishing period of her merchant
ships.   4925

Foreman, Leonard L. The Road to San Jacinto. Dutton, 1943.
The defense of the Alamo as a step on the road to victory
at San Jacinto; Davy Crockett figures.   4926

Forester, C.S. The Captain From Connecticut. Little, 1941.
Fast-sailing yarn of naval encounters between Americans
and British in the War of 1812.   4927

Forrest, Williams. Trail of Tears. Crown, 1959. Forced
removal of the Cherokees from their Georgia home to far-
off Oklahoma.   4928

Fort, John. God in the Straw Pen. Dodd, 1931. The powerful impact of a camp meeting on the people of a poor
Georgia community.   4929

Franchere, Ruth. Hannah Herself. Crowell, 1964. YA. A
girl from Connecticut journeys by stagecoach to visit her
sister in Illinois and finds that the frontier town is a whole
different world for her.   4930

Frazee, Steve. Year of the Big Snow. Holt, 1962. The fourth
expedition of John Charles Fremont in 1848, to see about a
railroad from St. Louis to California.   4931

Frazier, Neta Lohnes. Sacajawea. McKay, 1967. YA. Story
of the Indian girl who was the guide for the Lewis and Clark
Expedition of 1804-05.   4932

Frederick, John. The Bronze Collar. Putnam, 1925. A
French soldier and an English nobleman in Spanish California.   4933

Friermood, Elisabeth. The Wild Donahues. Doubleday, 1963.
YA. Lawlessness, slave-running, and a tragic marriage
provide the action in this novel of pre-Civil War Indiana. 4934

Frost, Elizabeth H. This Side of Land. Coward, 1942.
Life on the island of Nantucket in the early 1800s.   4935

Frost, Thomas G. The Man of Destiny. Grammercy Pub.,
1909. This novel is based on the career of Ulysses S.
Grant at West Point and in the Mexican and Civil Wars. 4936

Fuller, Edmund. A Star Pointed North. Harper, 1946.
Frederick Douglass, born a slave, escapes to become
an Abolitionist leader and noted orator.   4937

Fuller, Iola. The Loon Feather. Harcourt, 1940. Story of
Mackinac Island and of the marriage of Tecumseh's daughter to a French trader.   4938

_____. The Shining Trail. Duell, 1943. The first Black
Hawk War results when the Sauk Indians seek to defend their
lands.   4939

Furnas, Joseph Chamberlain. The Devil's Rainbow. Harper,
1962. A novel, irreverent at times, concerning the character and career of Mormon Prophet Joseph Smith and some
of his followers.   4940

Furnas, Marthedith. The Far Country. Harper, 1947. Journal kept by a Kentucky storekeeper on his overland trip to
California.   4941

Gabriel, Gilbert W. I, James Lewis. Doubleday, 1932.
John Jacob Astor's fur-trading expedition to the Pacific
Northwest.   4942

_____. I Thee Wed. Macmillan, 1948. The planning of
an American refuge for Marie Antoinette, and the French
seamstress who was prepared to be her double.   4943

Gaither, Frances. Double Muscadine. Macmillan, 1949. The
dramatic story behind a Negro slave's trial for murder.   4944

_____. The Red Cock Crows. Macmillan, 1944. An at-
tempted slave rebellion in Mississippi in the 1830s involves
a youth sympathetic to the slaves.   4945

Gant, Matthew, pseud. The Raven and the Sword. Coward,
1960. Action-packed early life of Sam Houston including
his adventures among the Cherokees, as a Congressman,
and as Governor of Tennessee.   4946

Garland, Hamlin. Trail-Makers of the Middle Border. Macmillan, 1927. Pioneer life during the westward expansion,
the building of railroads, and the Civil War.   4947

Gerson, Noel B. Clear for Action. Doubleday, 1970. A biographical novel of David Farragut which follows his career
from boyhood through the War of 1812 and the Civil War. 4948

_____. The Cumberland Rifles. Doubleday, 1952. Post-
Revolution events in Tennessee before the acquisition of
statehood.   4949

_____. The Golden Eagle. Doubleday, 1953. Fast-moving
adventure and romance in the Mexican War.   4950

_____. Old Hickory. Doubleday, 1964. The life of fiery

Andrew Jackson, seventh President of the U.S., show-
ing the influence of women on his career.   4951

_____. The River Devils. by Carter A. Vaughan, pseud.
Doubleday, 1968. A versatile New Englander joins the
"river pirate" who expedited and protected American trade
on the Mississippi prior to the Louisiana Purchase.   4952

_____. Sam Houston. Doubleday, 1968. Fast-moving story
of Sam Houston including his political, military, and romantic
life and his three years with the Cherokee Indians.   4953

_____. The Slender Reed. Doubleday, 1965. James Knox
Polk grew from a sickly farm boy to be the courageous
President who wrested Texas from Mexico.   4954

_____. The Yankee From Tennessee. Doubleday, 1960.
Fictionalized biography of the driving and explosive Andrew
Jackson, who became a famous general and President of the
United States.   4955

Gibbs, Alonzo. The Least Likely One. Lothrop, 1964. YA. A
youth goes on fowling expeditions through Pennsylvania and
New Jersey to aid his father in the business of running a
bird shop.   4956

_____. A Man's Calling. Lothrop, 1966. YA. Surveyor's
foster-daughter searches for her true identity as she fills a
man's job--surveyor's assistant.   4957

Giles, Janice Holt. The Believers. Houghton, 1957. Story of
a husband who accepted the Shaker beliefs and of his wife
who could not.   4958

_____. The Great Adventure. Houghton, 1966. Perilous
travel through the western mountains in the face of sickness,
violence, Indian attack, and mid-winter weather.   4959

_____. Johnny Osage. Houghton, 1960. Johnny Fowler,
white friend of the Osage Indians, falls in love with a mission worker. (followed by Voyage to Santa Fe)   4960

_____. The Land Beyond the Mountains. Houghton, 1958.
A story of the settling of Kentucky and James Wilkinson's
attempts to set up an empire in the west.   4961

_____. Savanna. Houghton, 1961. The granddaughter of
Hannah Fowler, widowed in her youth, fights to preserve her
independent way of life in the Arkansas Territory in 1824. 4962

_____. Six-Horse Hitch. Houghton, 1969. Story of the
early overland stage in Colorado as told by a young stagecoach driver.   4963

_____. Voyage to Santa Fe. Houghton, 1962. The wife of Johnny Osage is introduced to the perils and adventures of the Old West as they travel to Santa Fe in a wagon train.   4964

Goodrich, Arthur. The Sign of Freedom. Appleton, 1916. About a "bound boy" who ultimately finds freedom and achievement as a soldier in the Civil War.   4965

Gorman, Herbert Sherman. The Wine of San Lorenzo. Farrar, 1945. The Mexican War--the battle of the Alamo and the surrender of Santa Anna.   4966

Graham, Shirley. There Once Was a Slave. Messner, 1947. Frederick Douglass, the slave who escaped, obtained an education, and became a leading Abolitionist.   4967

Grant, Blanch. Doña Lona. Funk, 1941. A noble Spanish lady runs a gambling saloon in Santa Fe.   4968

Gray, J. Thompson. A Kentucky Chronicle. Neale, 1906. Features the settling of Kentucky, particularly the founding and development of Louisville.   4969

Grebenc, Lucile. The Time of Change. Doubleday, 1938. New England farm life for a young widow and her infant son.   4970

Greer, Herb. The Short Cut. Roy, 1965. The desperate plight of the Donner Party while taking a short cut in their trek to California.   4971

Greve, Alice Wheeler. From Out This House. Binfords, 1945. "A novel of the wagon train of 1847 and the tragic Whitman mission."   4972

_____. Shadow on the Plains. Binfords, 1944. Indian attacks and massacre on the old Oregon Trail.   4973

Grey, Zane. The Border Legion. Harper, 1916. A maiden is captured by a band of desperadoes in southern Idaho.   4974

_____. Desert Gold. Harper, 1913. Border fighting between the United States and Mexico.   4975

_____. Fighting Caravans. Harcourt, 1929. Struggle for peace and a pioneer's romance along the old Santa Fe Trail.   4976

Grossman, Adrienne and Valerie Beardwood. Trails of His Own. Longmans, 1961. YA. The story of John Muir, who made conservation of our forests and natural resources his life work before the Civil War and greatly furthered the National Park program.   4977

Grubb, Davis. The Golden Sickle. World, 1968. A river
pirate and a robber's son compete in a quest for hidden
treasure along the Ohio River.   4978

Gulick, Grover C. Bend of the Snake. by Bill Gulick, pseud.
Houghton, 1950. Vigorous early competition among business-
men in the Washington Territory.   4979

_____. The Land Beyond. by Bill Gulick. Houghton, 1958.
About a mountain man who lives with the Nez Percé Indians,
trapping and exploring in the Northwest.   4980

Guthrie, Alfred Bertram. The Big Sky. Sloane, 1947. The
coming of the white man to the West--his dreams and determination.   4981

_____. The Way West. Sloane, 1949. Adventures and
hardships of an overland trek from Missouri to Oregon.   4982

Hackney, Louise. Wing of Fame. Appleton, 1934. A story
of James Smithson, who provided for the founding of the
Smithsonian Institution.   4983

Hale, Edward Everett. The Man Without a Country. Watts,
1960. (first pub. in 1863) The classic story of Philip
Nolan, whose hasty wish never to hear of his country again
tragically came true.   4984

Hall, Marjory. Drumbeat on the Shore. Westminster, 1965.
YA. Two girls, Abigail and Nabby Bates, help a soldier
on a secret mission deceive the British during the War of
1812.   4985

Hall, Rubylea. The Great Tide. Duell, 1947. A yellow fever
epidemic and a torrential hurricane ravage St. Joseph,
Florida.   4986

Hallet, Richard M. Michael Beam. Houghton, 1939. Tale
of a frontiersman and his two loves--one for an Indian
maid.   4987

Ham, Tom. Give Us This Valley. Macmillan, 1952. The
hardships of a young couple from Pennsylvania who settle
in Georgia.   4988

Hancock, Albert E. Bronson of the Rabble. Lippincott, 1909.
The romance and military exploits of a blacksmith's son
who marries a senator's daughter.   4989

Hargreaves, Sheba. The Cabin at the Trail's End. Harper,
1928. An interesting, well-told tale of early pioneers in
Oregon.   4990

_____. Heroine of the Prairies. Harper, 1930. Clear
picture of a frontier settlement on the Oregon Trail.   4991

Harper, Robert S. Trumpet in the Wilderness. Mill, 1940.
A young man goes west to make his fortune and becomes
involved in the War of 1812.   4992

Harris, Cyril. Street of Knives. Little, 1950. The story of
Aaron Burr's trip to Mexico and his arrest for treason.   4993

_____. The Trouble at Hungerfords. Little, 1953. Labor
trouble in Peekskill, New York in mid-nineteenth century,
as workers were beginning to make demands on employers.
                                                               4994
Harris, Laura B. Bride of the River. Crowell, 1956. A
plantation girl adjusts to life as the bride of a Mississippi
riverboatman.   4995

Harris, Margaret and John. Chant of the Hawk. Random,
1959. A strong novel of mountain men and trappers along
the Oregon Trail.   4996

Havighurst, Walter. The Winds of Spring. Macmillan, 1940.
A refreshing story of Wisconsin with a pioneer ornitholo-
gist as hero.   4997

Hawkins, Anne. To the Swift. Harper, 1949. The heroic devotion to duty of the Pony Express riders.   4998

Hawthorne, Nathaniel. The Blithedale Romance. Houghton,
1852. Story of two girls at Brooks Farm based on incidents
in Hawthorne's participation in that experiment in communal
living.   4999

_____. The House of the Seven Gables. Ticknor, Reed &
Fields, 1851. Eccentric individuals in the last generation
of a decaying family.   5000

Haycox, Ernest. Canyon Passage. Little, 1945. Misplaced
loyalty and an Indian uprising on the Oregon-California
trail interrupt the course of love.   5001

_____. The Earthbreakers. Little, 1952. A group of
sturdy pioneers cross plains and mountains to settle in the
Oregon Territory.   5002

Hazelton, George C., Jr. The Raven. Appleton, 1909. The
unhappy life, the romance, and the tragic death of the famed
poet, Edgar Allan Poe.   5003

Henkle, Henrietta. Deep River. by Henrietta Buckmaster,
pseud. Harcourt, 1944. An anti-slavery mountaineer from
Georgia leads in the fight for the Union.   5004

_____. Fire in the Heart. by Henrietta Buckmaster,
pseud. Harcourt, 1948. Based on the life and career
of the famous theater star, Fanny Kemble.   5005

Hepburn, Andrew. Letter of Marque. Little, 1959. American sailors, impressed into British service, escape and
turn privateer.   5006

Hergesheimer, Joseph. Balisand. Knopf, 1924. A duel over
a girl's love is interrupted by her death, but is fought sixteen years later.   5007

_____. Java Head. Knopf, 1919. The seafaring traders of
Salem, one of whom brings home an Oriental wife.   5008

Hinckley, Helen. The Mountains Are Mine. Vanguard, 1946.
A young Mormon girl is involved in a polygamous marriage.   5009

Hodge, Jane Aiken. Here Comes a Candle. Doubleday, 1967.
A young Englishwoman, fleeing unpleasant memories, becomes the companion of a deeply disturbed little girl in America during the War of 1812.   5010

_____. Savannah Purchase. Doubleday, 1971. A girl takes
her look-alike cousin's place as wife of a planter and mistress of a southern plantation while the cousin goes to help
rescue their friend Napoleon from St. Helena.   5011

Hoffmann, Margaret Jones. My Dear Cousin. by Peggy Hoffmann. Harcourt, 1970. Romance of a British diplomat and
a Baltimore lady during the embittered Anglo-American relations preceding the War of 1812 (based on actual letters
and diaries).   5012

Hogan, Pendleton. The Dark Comes Early. Washburn, 1934.
Romance set during the Texans' struggle for independence
from Mexico.   5013

Holland, Josiah Gilbert. Miss Gilbert's Career. Scribner,
1860. Life in a Yankee factory town.   5014

Holt, Felix. Dan'l Boone Kissed Me. Dutton, 1954. Warm
story of young love and western Kentucky life.   5015

_____. The Gabriel Horn. Dutton, 1951. A tale of set-
tlers of the West, narrated by a little boy.   5016

Horan, James David. The Shadow Catcher. Crown, 1961. A
fugitive from New York participates in a hazardous expedition into Oregon Territory to establish a trading post on the
Columbia River.   5017

Hough, Emerson. Tne Covered Wagon. Appleton, 1922.
Part of a wagon caravan bound for Oregon is deflected
to California by news of gold.   5018

_____. 54-40 or Fight. Bobbs, 1909. The controversy
between the young United States and Great Britain over the
northwest boundary.   5019

_____. The Magnificent Adventure. Appleton, 1916. The
Lewis and Clark expedition, Theodosia Burr, and the Louisiana Purchase.   5020

_____. The Purchase Price. Bobbs, 1910. Impact of the
Slavery Question on mid-century politics and life.   5021

_____. The Way of a Man. Methuen, 1907. Conflict of
political ideals and commercial interests in the South just
prior to the Civil War.   5022

Hough, Henry B. Long Anchorage. Appleton, 1947. New
Bedford when the whaling industry was thriving and the textile industry growing.   5023

Howard, Elizabeth. Winter on Her Own. Morrow, 1968. YA.
A glimpse of early home manufacturing and the peddlers'
trade as an artistic country girl leaves her home to spend
the winter painting designs on tinware.   5024

Howe, E.W. The Story of a Country Town. Harvard Univ.
Pr., 1961. (orig. pub. in 1883) An autobiographical novel
which depicts life as it was in the midwest in the 1850s. 5025

Howells, William Dean. Leatherwood God. Century, 1916.
Joseph Dylks claims to be a god in a pioneer Ohio community about 1830.   5026

Hubbard, Elbert. Time and Chance. Putnam, 1901. This
story tells of Capt. John Brown of the Harper's Ferry incident.   5027

Hubbard, Lucien. Rivers to the Sea. S. & S., 1942. A
story of steamboating between Pittsburgh and New Orleans--
full of action and suspense.   5028

Hueston, Ethel. The Man of the Storm. Bobbs, 1936. In-
corporation of St. Louis, as part of the Louisiana Purchase,
into the United States, and adventures of explorer John
Colter.   5029

_____. Star of the West. Bobbs, 1935. An account of
the Lewis and Clark Expedition to the Pacific Northwest.   5030

Hughes, Rupert. The Golden Ladder. Harper, 1924. A

romance of Aaron Burr and his second wife, telling of his
duel with Hamilton.   5031

Hutchens, Jane. Timothy Larkin. Doubleday, 1942. Missouri family, abandoned by the father, in the decade before
the Civil War.   5032

Jackson, Helen Hunt. Ramona. Avon Bks., 1970, c.1884.
The cruelty of the white man toward the Indian in early
California.   5033

Janet, Lillian, pseud. for Janet Cicchetti and Lillian Ressler
Groom. Touchstone. Rinehart, 1947. Romantic triangle
in California after the gold rush.   5034

Jennings, John. River to the West. Doubleday, 1948. A
novel of John Jacob Astor's fur business in the Pacific
Northwest.   5035

_____. The Salem Frigate. Doubleday, 1946. Adventure
on the frigate Essex in action against the Barbary pirates. 5036

_____. Shadows in the Dusk. Little, 1955. Indians and
Mexicans take over the government of Santa Fe by force. 5037

_____. The Tall Ships. McGraw-Hill, 1958. About Am-
erican privateers who harass British shipping in the War
of 1812.   5038

_____. Tide of Empire. by Bates Baldwin, pseud. Holt,
1952. About a young South Carolinian who has some contact
with Jerome Bonaparte and his American wife.   5039

Johnson, Annabel and Edgar. Torrie. Harper, 1960. YA.
A fourteen-year-old girl grows up as her family joins a
wagon train migration west from St. Louis.   5040

_____. Wilderness Bride. Harper, 1962. YA. A teen-
aged Mormon bride, who prefers shooting to cooking, travels
the long road to Utah in search of a life free from persecution.   5041

Johnston, Mary. Lewis Rand. Houghton, 1908. Burr's conspiracy figures in this tale of a French lawyer in Virginia
during Jefferson's administration.   5042

_____. Miss Delicia Allen. Little, 1933. Gracious, cul-
tured life on a Virginia plantation before and during the
Civil War.   5043

Jones, Idwal. Vermilion. Prentice-Hall, 1947. A celebrated
cinnabar mine in California and several generations of
owners.   5044

Jones, Madison. Forest of the Night. Harcourt, 1960. A conscientious schoolteacher attempts to bring education to a backward Tennessee frontier village. 5045

Jones, Nard. Scarlet Petticoat. Dodd, 1941. Fur trading on the Columbia River. 5046

_____. Swift Flows the River. Dodd, 1940. Rugged pioneering in the magnificent Columbia River Valley. 5047

Jordan, Mildred A. Asylum for the Queen. Knopf, 1948. Pennsylvania is considered as a refuge for the Queen during the French Revolution. 5048

Kane, Harnett T. The Gallant Mrs. Stonewall. Doubleday, 1957. The marriage of Anna and Thomas Jackson and his rise to fame in the Civil War. 5049

_____. Lady of Arlington. Doubleday, 1953. Story of Robert E. Lee's wife, Mary Custis Lee. 5050

_____. New Orleans Woman. Doubleday, 1946. Courageous Myra Clark Gaines, who fought for her mother's reputation and her own inheritance. 5051

_____. Pathway to the Stars. Doubleday, 1950.` The financial success of a Baltimore man in New Orleans. 5052

Kantor, MacKinlay. Spirit Lake. World, 1961. Frontier life and relations of whites and Indians in early Iowa with the massacre of thirty settlers in 1857 by a band of outlaw Indians. 5053

Kelland, Clarence Budington. Hard Money. Harper, 1930. Story of a young Dutchman who establishes a successful bank in New York. (followed by Gold) 5054

Kelley, Welbourn. Alabama Empire. Rinehart, 1957. Adventures of a Scots doctor who came to practice medicine in the young United States. 5055

Kendrick, Baynard Hardwick. The Flames of Time. Scribner, 1948. Florida at the time it passed from the Spanish flag to the American. 5056

Kennedy, John P. Swallow Barn. Putnam, 1832. Happy, peaceful life of southern hospitality in pre-Civil War Virginia. 5057

Kennedy, Lucy. Mr. Audubon's Lucy. Crown, ´1957. The story of John James Audubon and his wife Lucy, who married despite her father's opposition. 5058

Kester, Vaughan. Prodigal Judge. Bobbs, 1911. Rambling
tale with a disreputable judge as hero.   5059

Keyes, Frances Parkinson. The Chess Players. Farrar, 1960.
Career of a great chess player of New Orleans who may
have been a Confederate agent.   5060

Kirkland, Elithe. Divine Average. Little, 1952. Combines
adventure with a study of relations between Texans, Indians,
and Mexicans.   5061

_____. Love Is a Wild Assault. Doubleday, 1959. Fic-
tional biography of a Texas pioneer woman who married
three   times and had eighteen children.   5062

Kirkland, Joseph. The McVeys. Houghton, 1888. The day-to-
day struggles of people who settled on the Illinois plains. 5063

_____. Zury, the Meanest Man in Spring County. Hough-
ton, 1887. Pioneer life on the Illinois prairie.   5064

Kirkman, Marshall Monroe. The Romance of Gilbert Holmes.
Simpkin, 1902. A story with Lincoln and Jefferson Davis
as young men.   5065

Knight, Ruth Adams. Certain Harvest. Doubleday, 1960. The
story of Peter Cooper, inventor and industrialist, during the
growth of New York.   5066

Koob, Theodora. Surgeon's Apprentice. Lippincott, 1963. YA.
Pictures the practice of medicine in rural Virginia as a boy
becomes his doctor-father's assistant.   5067

Krause, Herbert. The Oxcart Trail. Bobbs, 1954. Adventures of a young man involved in a killing on the Underground Railroad.   5068

Krey, Laura Lettie. On the Long Tide. Houghton, 1940. A
story of Texas during its struggles for independence and
statehood.   5069

Kroll, Harry Harrison. Fury in the Earth. Bobbs, 1945.
The effects on people and land of the New Madrid earthquake in the Mississippi Valley.   5070

_____. Rogue's Companion. Bobbs, 1943. The checkered
career of a Mississippi Valley speculator.   5071

Krueger, Carl. Saint Patrick's Battalion. Dutton, 1960.
Irish immigrants enlisted in the U.S. Army label the Mexican War one of aggression and transfer to the Mexican
side.   5072

Kyne, Peter B. Tide of Empire. Cosmopolitan Bk., 1928.
A young Irishman's romance in gold rush California.   5073

La Farge, Oliver. The Long Pennant. Houghton, 1933. A
privateer's capture of a British ship in the Caribbean in
the War of 1812.   5074

Laing, Alexander Kinnan. Jonathan Eagle. Duell, 1955.
Land and sea exploits in a New England setting.   5075

_____. Matthew Early. Duell, 1957. A New England
sea captain's pursuit of romance.   5076

Laird, Charlton Grant. Thunder on the River. Little, 1949.
Romance of a white captive and an Indian girl during the
Black Hawk War in Illinois.   5077

_____. West of the River. Little, 1953. Absorbing view
of fur trading on the upper Mississippi.   5078

Lampman, Evelyn Sibley. Half-Breed. Doubleday, 1967. YA.
A young half-breed leaves his Crow Indian home to search
for his white father in the Oregon territory.   5079

Lancaster, Bruce. For Us, the Living. Stokes, 1940. Pioneer life in Indiana, Illinois, and Kentucky, with young Abe
Lincoln as a character.   5080

Lane, Carl D. The Fleet in the Forest. Coward, 1943.
Perry's ships for the Battle of Lake Erie were built in
the Pennsylvania forests.   5081

Lane, Elinor Macartney. The Mills of God. Appleton, 1901.
People and events in Virginia and Europe at the end of the
century.   5082

Lathrop, West. Keep the Wagons Moving! Random House,
1949. YA. Two brothers travel from Independence, Missouri, to Oregon in the summer of 1846.   5083

Laughlin, Ruth. The Wind Leaves No Shadow. McGraw, 1948.
The colorful days in New Mexico just before the Mexican
War.   5084

Lauritzen, Jonreed. Captain Sutter's Gold. Doubleday, 1964.
The ambition of Johann Sutter, a Swiss immigrant, was to
establish an empire of his own in California.   5085

_____. The Everlasting Fire. Doubleday, 1962. The diffi-
cult migration of the harassed early Mormons from Illinois
in their search for a Promised Land under the leadership of
Brigham Young.   5086

Leahy, Jack Thomas. Shadow on the Waters. Knopf, 1960.
Changes due to encroaching settlement by the white man
are the theme for this story of a northwest Indian village. 5087

Lee, Chin-Yang. The Land of the Golden Mountain. Meredith, 1967. Adventures, hardships, and romance of a
seventeen-year-old Chinese girl who comes to California
in gold rush days disguised as a boy.   5088

Le May, Alan. Pelican Coast. Doubleday, 1929. Piracy and
smuggling in old New Orleans in the early 1800s.   5089

Lewis, Alfred Henry. The Throwback. Cassell, 1906. Ranching in Texas in the 1850s included clashes with Indians.   5090

Lewis, Janet. The Invasion. Harcourt, 1932. About the
Johnston family of Michigan and the Ojibway tribe it married into.   5091

Lewis, Sinclair. The God-Seeker. Random, 1949. The story
of a carpenter in St. Paul and his efforts to organize labor.
                                                              5092

Lewisohn, Ludwig. The Island Within. Harper, 1928. A
Jewish family, immigrating from Poland, comes into contact with American civilization.   5093

Lighton, W. Rheem. The Shadow of a Great Rock. Putnam,
1907. A tale of settlers in Nebraska who battled fierce
Sioux to establish homes.   5094

Lillibridge, William Otis. Where the Trail Divides. Dodd,
1907. Dakota frontier life with cowboys and Indians.   5095

Lincoln, Joseph and Freeman. The New Hope. Coward, 1941.
A Cape Cod privateer slips through the British blockade in
the War of 1812.   5096

Linderman, Frank Bird. Beyond Law. Day, 1933. Indians
and fur traders in the far West.   5097

Linney, Romulus. Heathen Valley. Atheneum, 1962. An
Episcopal bishop, assisted by a tramp, tries to establish a
church among the people of a North Carolina mountain valley.   5098

Lion, Hortense. Mill Stream. Houghton, 1941. Rhode Island during conflict over home industry or foreign trade.   5099

Lloyd, J. Uri. Stringtown on the Pike. Dodd, 1900. Kentucky just before the Civil War with a superstitious Negro
the most notable character.   5100

Lofts, Norah. Winter Harvest. Doubleday, 1955. Study of

four diverse people in the Donner party.   5101

Longstreth, Thomas. Two Rivers Meet in Concord. Westminster, 1946. A novel which reflects Thoreau's strong
social and political philosophy.   5102

Loomis, Noel M. Short Cut to Red River. Macmillan, 1958.
The establishment of a commercial wagon route from Mexico to Arkansas by the Connelly Expedition in 1839.   5103

_____. The Twilighters. Macmillan, 1955. A brutal and
bloody story of migrants to Texas slaughtered by bandits. 5104

Lovelace, Maud Hart. The Black Angels. Day, 1926. A
travelling concert company, the Angel Family Concert
Troupe, touring the Midwest.   5105

_____ and Delos Wheeler Lovelace. One Stayed at Welcome.
Day, 1934. Romance and pioneering in Minnesota after the
Mexican War.   5106

Lutes, Della. Gabriel's Search. Little, 1940. Community
life in Michigan among the sturdy pioneers who settled the
territory.   5107

Lyle, Eugene P. The Lone Star. Page, 1907. The revolt of
Texas Americans against Mexico, featuring Houston, Bowie,
and Crockett.   5108

Lynn, Margaret. Free Soil. Macmillan, 1920. Struggles of
free-soilers to build homes in frontier Kansas.   5109

Lytle, Andrew Nelson. The Long Night. Bobbs, 1936. A
boy's quest to revenge the murder of his father by Alabama
gangsters.   5110

Mabie, Mary Louise. The Long Knives Walked. Bobbs, 1932.
Journey of a covered wagon on the Oregon Trail.   5111

McCarter, Margaret. Vanguards of the Plains. Harper, 1917.
The part played by commercial enterprise in the development of the West.   5112

McCoy, Samuel. Tippecanoe. Bobbs, 1916. An English immigrant to Indiana fights for the United States against Indians
at Tippecanoe.   5113

McCulley, Johnston. Captain Fly-By-Night. Watt, 1926. Adventure in Mexican California during the second quarter of
the nineteenth century   5114

McCutcheon, George Barr. Viola Gwyn. Dodd, 1922. A
young lawyer comes to Indiana full of hatred and finds love. 5115

McElfresh, Adeline. To Each Her Dream. Bobbs, 1961.
YA. A girl of the 1840s is unsuccessful in entering medical school, but proves very capable in aiding her doctor
father and in continuing his work after his death.   5116

McIntyre, Marjorie. The River Witch. Crown, 1955. A
young girl has her own boat on the Mississippi and Missouri
Rivers.   5117

McKee, Ruth E. Christopher Strange. Doubleday, 1941. A
young lawyer, raised and educated in the East, becomes a
settler in California.   5118

McKeown, Martha Ferguson. Mountains Ahead. Putnam, 1961.
Recently married woman matures among Kentuckians in a
wagon train bound for Oregon in 1847.   5119

MacKinnon, Mary Lineham. One Small Candle. Crown,
1956. Touching tale of a second wife's struggle for her
husband's love.   5120

McMeekin, Clark, pseud. for Dorothy Clark and Isabel Mc-
Meekin. Reckon With the River. Appleton, 1941. An
eighty-year-old pioneer woman and her family in the Ohio
Valley.   5121

_____. Red Raskall. Appleton, 1943. An English girl
who sails for America is shipwrecked off the coast of Virginia.   5122

McNeilly, Mildred Masterson. Each Bright River. Morrow,
1950. A courageous southern girl is left alone in rugged
Oregon when her fiancé commits suicide.   5123

_____. Heaven Is Too High. Morrow, 1944. A Russian
aristocrat, fleeing the wrath of Empress Catherine, finds
opportunity in the Pacific Northwest.   5124

Malkus, Alida Sims. Caravans to Santa Fe. Harper, 1928.
A young couple is beset by the cultural differences between
Spanish grandees and American traders.   5125

Mally, Emma Louise. Abigail. Appleton, 1956. A Yankee
abolitionist girl, her Louisiana cousin, and the Underground
Railroad.   5126

Malm, Dorothea. The Woman Question. Appleton, 1958.
The fight of Susan B. Anthony and Lucy Stone to secure
woman suffrage.   5127

Malvern, Gladys. Mamzelle. Macrae Smith, 1955. Romance
of a Louisiana girl in Washington in the company of Dolly
Madison, wife of the President.   5128

Manfred, Frederick. Lord Grizzly. McGraw, 1954. Hugh
   Glass, injured by a bear, sought revenge on men he
   thought had deserted him.   5129

Markey, Gene. That Far Paradise. McKay, 1960. "Mad"
   Anthony Wayne and migration from Virginia to the Kentucky
   wilderness.   5130

Marshall, Edison. Yankee Pasha. Farrar, 1947. Jason Star-
   buck's pursuit of romance and adventure.   5131

Masters, Edgar Lee. Children of the Market Place. Macmillan, 1922. An English youth inherits an estate in Illinois, where he comes to know Stephen Douglas.   5132

Maule, Mary Katherine. Prairie-Schooner Princess. Lothrop,
   1920. Story of a child orphaned during the crossing of the
   plains and adopted by a Quaker family.   5133

Meeker, Arthur. Far Away Music. Houghton, 1945. Family
   life in Chicago in the 1850s.   5134

Meigs, Cornelia. Call of the Mountain. Little, 1940. A Vermont boy's struggles to make his mountain farm productive.
                                                            5135
Melville, Herman. Moby Dick. Harper, 1851. Classic tale
   of American whaling; Captain Ahab's mad obsession to kill
   the white whale which had injured him.   5136

Miller, Caroline. Lamb in His Bosom. Harper, 1933. Backwoods Georgia is the setting for this tale rich in local
   color.   5137

_____. Lebanon. Doubleday, 1944. The picturesque back-
   woods of Georgia and a lovely girl who lived there.   5138

Miller, Heather Ross. Gone a Hundred Miles. Harcourt,
   1968. A stoical German country doctor in North Carolina
   and the three women in his life: his frail French wife, a
   wilful river girl, and his determined daughter.   5139

Miller, Helen Topping. Born Strangers. Bobbs, 1949. Pictures two families (the author's ancestors) in nineteenth
   century Michigan.   5140

_____. Her Christmas at the Hermitage. Longmans, 1955.
   A Christmas celebration of Rachel and Andrew Jackson before his presidential campaign.   5141

Minnigerode, Meade. Cockades. Putnam, 1927. Based on
   the legend of the French Dauphin's escape to America after
   the French Revolution.   5142

Mitchell, S. Weir. Far in the Forest. Century, 1889.
About the courageous men who wrested their living from
the wild forests of Pennsylvania.   5143

_____. The Red City. Century, 1908. Washington's sec-
ond term as President in Philadelphia, then the capital.   5144

_____. Westways. Century, 1913. Bitter controversy in
a small northern village before the Civil War.   5145

Moberg, Vilhelm. The Last Letter Home. (tr.) S. & S.,
1961. About the Swedish Nilsson family and the home they
establish in the Minnesota wilderness. (completes trilogy) 5146

_____. Unto a Good Land. (tr.) S. & S., 1954. The
Swedish immigrants who came by sailboat, wagon, riverboat,
and on foot to settle in Minnesota. (followed by The Last
Letter Home)   5147

Moore, John Trotwood. Hearts of Hickory. Cokesbury, 1926.
Exploits of Davy Crockett and Andrew Jackson in the War of
1812.   5148

Morgan, George. The Issue. Lippincott, 1904. Political and
social aspects of the slavery question in the South.   5149

Morrow, Honoré. Black Daniel. Morrow, 1931. Daniel Webster, his second wife, Caroline, and their circle.   5150

_____. On to Oregon! Morrow, 1954, c.1926. A thirteen-
year-old boy grows up fast as tragedy strikes his family on
their journey to Oregon.   5151

_____. We Must March. Stokes, 1925. Narcissa Whitman
and a band of pioneer missionaries journey across the
Rockies to Oregon.   5152

Mudgett, Helen Parker. The Seas Stand Watch. Knopf, 1944.
The recovery of sea trade after the Revolutionary War.   5153

Mulford, Clarence E. Bring Me His Ears. McClurg, 1922.
The American West of the Missouri River and the Santa
Fe Trail.   5154

Muller, Charles Geoffrey. Hero of Champlain. Day, 1961.
YA. A young midshipman serves his country well in the
Battle of Lake Champlain during the War of 1812.   5155

Mulvihill, William. Night of the Axe. Houghton, 1972. A
small band emigrating to California discovers a giant tree
which has strange and disturbing effects on them.   5156

Murray, Charles A. The Prairie Bird. Routledge, 1844.

The Indians in the Ohio Valley several years after their
defeat by General Wayne.   5157

Myers, John. I, Jack Swilling, Founder of Phoenix, Arizona.
Hastings, 1961. A story of the little-known man whose reconstruction of a prehistoric irrigation system helped in the
development of the Southwest.   5158

_____. The Wild Yazoo. Dutton, 1947. Rough-and-ready
pioneer life along the Yazoo River in Mississippi.   5159

Nathan, Leonard. Wind Like a Bugle. Macmillan, 1954. Conflict between Abolitionists and the pro-slavery faction in
Kansas.   5160

Neihardt, John G. Splendid Wayfaring. Macmillan, 1920.
Vivid story of a frontiersman who explored the central
overland route to the West.   5161

Nelson, Truman. The Sin of the Prophet. Little, 1952. The
story of a runaway slave who was sent back into slavery. 5162

_____. The Surveyor. Doubleday, 1960. John Brown's
political activities in Kansas during its fight over admission
as slave or free state.   5163

Nicholson, Meredith. The Cavalier of Tennessee. Bobbs,
1928. A novel of Andrew Jackson--his romance, pioneering
efforts, and election to the Presidency.   5164

Nickerson, Jan. Bright Promise. Funk, 1965. YA. An ambitious girl seeks an education although this was rare for
girls in the early nineteenth century.   5165

Niles, Blair. East by Day. Farrar, 1941. Account of the
Amistad case--a sailing ship on which a slave crew had
seized control.   5166

Noble, Iris. Courage in Her Hands. Messner, 1967. YA. A
girl is confronted with strange and trying situations when her
father brings her to an American-Russian fur-trading post in
California.   5167

O'Dell, Scott. Hill of the Hawk. Bobbs, 1947. Relations of
Kit Carson and a frontiersman in early California.   5168

_____. The Island of the Blue Dolphins. Houghton, 1960.
YA. Fate of a young Indian girl after tragedy strikes her
tribe.   5169

_____. Woman of Spain. Houghton, 1934. A Spanish
señorita in early California is wooed by two Americans. 5170

Olsen, Theodore V. There Was a Season. Doubleday, 1972.
Jefferson Davis as a young graduate of West Point and his
tragic romance with Sarah Knox Taylor, whose father was
Davis' superior officer and later President.   5171

O'Neal, Cothburn. The Very Young Mrs. Poe. Crown, 1956.
A fictionalized biography of Virginia Clemm, who married
her talented but moody cousin, Edgar Allen Poe, when she
was only thirteen.   5172

O'Neill, Charles Kendall. Morning Time. S. & S., 1949.
Post-Revolution life and Wilkinson's conspiracy with the
Spanish.   5173

O'Rourke, Frank. The Far Mountains. by Frank O'Malley,
pseud. Morrow, 1959. The decline of Spanish influence
in the territory that became New Mexico and Texas.   5174

Orr, Myron David. The Citadel of the Lakes. Dodd, 1952.
Astor's attempt to monopolize the fur trade on Mackinac
Island.   5175

_____. Mission to Mackinac. Dodd, 1956. Relations be-
tween the English and the French before the outbreak of the
War of 1812.   5176

Page, Elizabeth. Wagons West. Farrar & Rinehart, 1930.
Based on letters recounting a journey along the Oregon
Trail to California.   5177

Palmer, Bruce and John C. Giles. Horseshoe Bend. S. & S.,
1962. Half-breed William Weatherford leads the Creek Indians against Andrew Jackson in resistance to white advances.
                                                                   5178
Parker, Cornelia Stratton. Fabulous Valley. Putnam, 1956.
Transformation of a quiet Pennsylvania farming town into a
rowdy oil boom town.   5179

Parrish, Anne. A Clouded Star. Harper, 1948. An ex-slave
guides a small group northward on the Underground Railroad.   5180

Parrish, Randall. The Devil's Own. McClurg, 1917. Exciting tale of the Black Hawk War of 1832 against white settlement of Indian land.   5181

_____. When Wilderness Was King. McClurg, 1904.
A story of the Illinois frontier and the massacre at Fort
Dearborn.   5182

Partridge, Bellamy. The Big Freeze. Crowell, 1948. The
main historical event is the building of the Croton aqueduct
in New York City.   5183

Pearce, Richard Elmo. The Impudent Rifle. Lippincott, 1951.
A West Point lieutenant campaigns for fair treatment for the
Indians in Arkansas Territory.   5184

_____. The Restless Border. Lippincott, 1953. Captain
Alexander Prince versus Santa Anna and the Comanches on
the Texas border.   5185

Peattie, Donald Culross. Forward the Nation. Putnam, 1942.
The Lewis and Clark Expedition and the Indian Bird Woman,
Sacajawea, who guided it.   5186

Peeples, Samuel A. The Dream Ends in Fury. Harper, 1949.
An abused Mexican, Joaquin Murrieta, turns bandit in California during the gold rush.   5187

Pendexter, Hugh. Harry Idaho. Bobbs, 1926. Tale of a lost
gold mine, Mormon fanatics, Indian allies, and romance. 5188

_____. Kings of the Missouri. Bobbs, 1921. The "kings"
headed rival fur companies in the trade area around St.
Louis.   5189

_____. Old Misery. Bobbs, 1924. California in the rough,
roaring days following the discovery of gold.   5190

_____. A Virginia Scout. Bobbs, 1922. The dangers and
thrills of scouting frontier country with capture by Indians.
                                                                 5191

Perling, Joseph Jerry. A President Takes a Wife. Denlinger,
1959. Biographical novel of Julia Gardiner Tyler, whose
husband was President during the bitter controversy over
the annexation of Texas.   5192

Pidgin, Charles Felton. Blennerhassett. Clark, 1902. Tells
of the Blennerhassett-Burr conspiracy to conquer Texas and
establish an independent empire.   5193

Pittman, Hannah D. The Heart of Kentucky. Neale, 1908.
Factually based story of a murderer brought to justice in
Kentucky.   5194

Pole, James T. Midshipman Plowright. Dodd, 1969. YA.
A young graduate of the new United States Naval Academy
is captured while serving on shipboard in the Mexican
War.   5195

Poole, Ernest. The Nancy Flyer. Crowell, 1949. The
thrills of stagecoach driving in New England.   5196

Pope, Edith. River in the Wind. Scribner, 1954. A spirited account of the Seminole War in Florida.   5197

Post, Waldron K. Smith Brunt. Putnam, 1899. A tale of
the naval engagement in which Captain James Lawrence
gave his famous command, "Don't give up the ship."   5198

Powers, Alfred. Long Way to Frisco. Little, 1951. Tale
of California and Oregon centered on a bankrupt miner's
contract to deliver fourteen hundred hogs to San Francisco.
                                                             5199

Powers, Anne. Ironmaster. Bobbs, 1951. The political and
financial career of an early industrialist.   5200

Prescott, John. Journey by the River. Random, 1954. Westward journey of a pioneer wagon train.   5201

Price, Eugenia. New Moon Rising. Bantam Bks., 1970,
c. 1969. By dint of hard work a Southerner acquires a
plantation and slaves on St. Simon's Island, Georgia, only
to lose them in the Civil War.   5202

Pridgen, Tim. West Goes the Road. Doubleday, 1944. The
Midwest shortly after the Revolution.   5203

Pryor, Elinor. And Never Yield. Macmillan, 1942. Mormons in Missouri and Illinois confronted by neighbors'
hatred as well as by wilderness hardships.   5204

Pryor, Sara Agnes. Colonel's Story. by Mrs. Roger A.
Pryor. Macmillan, 1911. A southern colonel on a hospitable plantation in ante-bellum Virginia.   5205

Putnam, George Palmer. Hickory Shirt. Duell, 1949. Two
young men fight against each other and against the dangers
of Death Valley.   5206

Putnam, Nina. The Inner Voice. Sheridan, 1940. This novel
of a Quaker in the south gives an insight into the Quaker
way of life.   5207

Pyle, Howard. Within the Capes. Scribner, 1885. A sailor's
adventures at sea and his romance at home.   5208

Quick, Herbert. The Hawkeye. Bobbs, 1923. The growth of
a new nation, represented here by persevering Iowa pioneers. (followed by The Invisible Woman)   5209

_____. Vandemark's Folly. Bobbs, 1922. An Erie Canal
boatman searching for his lost mother eventually settles in
Iowa. (followed by The Hawkeye)   5210

Ratigan, William. Adventures of Captain McCargo. Random,
1956. Picaresque story of a hardy captain on the Great
Lakes.   5211

Rayford, Julian Lee. Child of the Snapping Turtle, Mike Fink. Abelard, 1951. Frontier and river adventures of a famous scout, trapper, and boatman. 5212

Raynolds, Robert. Brothers in the West. Harper, 1931. Wanderings of two brothers in the Old West in mid-century. 5213

Read, Opie. By the Eternal. Laird & Lee, 1906. Adventure in New Orleans centering around Andrew Jackson. 5214

Reed, Myrtle. The Shadow of Victory. Putnam, 1903. Indian warfare and the massacre at Fort Dearborn. 5215

Reed, Warren. She Rode a Yellow Stallion. Bobbs, 1950. Three generations of a Scottish-American family in Wisconsin. 5216

Rhodes, James A. and Dean Jauchius. The Court-Martial of Commodore Perry. Bobbs, 1961. Fictional account of the trial of Oliver Hazard Perry over a question of naval competency. 5217

Richardson, Norval. The Lead of Honour. Page, 1910. The setting is Mississippi in the 1830s. 5218

Richter, Conrad. The Awakening Land. Knopf, 1966. An omnibus volume containing The Trees, The Fields, and The Town (listed separately). 5219

_____. The Fields. Knopf, 1946. Marriage of a pioneer girl to a Boston lawyer in early Ohio. (followed by The Town) 5220

_____. The Town. Knopf, 1950. Pioneer town which has grown gradually from a once dense forest in Ohio. 5221

_____. The Trees. Knopf, 1940. Pioneers in Ohio clear a homesite in the forest. (followed by The Fields) 5222

Rickert, Edith. Out of the Cypress Swamp. Baker & Taylor, 1902. Pirates, war against the British, and a color-line marriage problem in New Orleans around 1812. 5223

Ridle, Julia B. Mohawk Gamble. Harper, 1963. YA. Recaptured after an attempted escape from the Mohawks, a youth bides his time patiently while waiting another opportunity (based on an actual journal). 5224

Roark, Garland. Rainbow in the Royals. Doubleday, 1950. Sailing ships and seamanship during the California gold rush. 5225

_____. Star in the Rigging. Doubleday, 1954. "A novel

of the Texas navy in their struggle for freedom. "   5226

_____ and Charles Thomas. Hellfire Jackson. Doubleday,
1966. Saga of a dynamic preacher who took part in the
Texan War for Independence.   5227

Roberts, Charles H. Down the O-hi-o. McClurg, 1891.
Quaker life in the Ohio Valley before the Civil War.   5228

Roberts, Elizabeth Madox. The Great Meadow. Viking, 1930.
Migration of pioneers from Virginia to Kentucky describing
the beauty of the country.   5229

Roberts, Kenneth. Captain Caution. Fawcett, 1970, c.1934.
A young first mate takes command of his ship on the death
of his captain early in the War of 1812.   5230

_____ . The Lively Lady. Doubleday, 1931. When his ship
is captured in the War of 1812, the captain is imprisoned
at Dartmoor for a time.   5231

_____ . Lydia Bailey. Doubleday, 1947. A young couple
is caught up in the Haiti Revolution and the Tripolitan
War.   5232

Roberts, Walter Adolphe. Royal Street. Bobbs, 1944. Rise
of a young man, skilled in fencing and politics, in New Orleans in the 1840s.   5233

Robertson, Constance. Fire Bell in the Night. Holt, 1944.
Love of a girl for two men--one who favored the Underground Railroad, one who opposed it.   5234

Robison, Mabel Otis. Pioneer Panorama. Denison, 1957.
Growing pains of Minnesota in the years from 1853 to
1866.   5235

Roe, Virginia. The Splendid Road. Cassell, 1925. Pioneers on
the Oregon Trail and in the Sacramento Valley.   5236

Rogers, Cameron. The Magnificent Idler. Doubleday, Page,
1926. Follows the life and career of the great American
poet, Walt Whitman.   5237

Rogers, Robert C. Will O' the "Wasp." Putnam, 1896. A
sea story of the War of 1812 against England.   5238

Root, Corwin. An American, Sir. Dutton, 1940. A youth
is persuaded by a pretty girl to fight in the War of 1812.   5239

Ross, Zola Helen. Land to Tame. Bobbs, 1956. Trouble
between Indians and whites over "ceding" tribal lands.   5240

Ryan, Don. Devil's Brigadier. Coward, 1954. Two
brothers seek revenge for their father's murder in post-
Revolutionary politics.   5241

Ryan, Marah Ellis. For the Soul of Rafael. McClurg, 1906.
A romantic triangle involving a Spanish family in California
in the 1840s.   5242

Sabin, Edwin Legrand. White Indian. Jacobs, 1925. An Englishman becomes a fur trapper and marries an Indian
girl.   5243

Sass, Herbert R. Look Back to Glory. Bobbs, 1933. Tidewater South Carolina in the seething period before seces-
sion.   5244

Savage, Les. Doniphan's Ride. Doubleday, 1959. A young
soldier with Colonel Doniphan's First Missouri Volunteers
in the Mexican War of 1846.   5245

Schachner, Nathan. The Sun Shines West. Appleton, 1943.
Romance in Kansas just before the Civil War.   5246

Schaeffer, Evelyn Schuyler. Isabel Stirling. Scribner, 1920.
A woman's life in New England and Arizona from the 1850s
to the 1870s.   5247

Schumann, Mary. My Blood and My Treasure. Dial, 1941.
Lovers find themselves on opposing sides in the War of
1812.   5248

Scott, Reva. Samuel Brannan and the Golden Fleece. Mac-
millan, 1944. Early days of the California Gold Rush.   5249

Sedgwick, Catharine Maria. Hope Leslie. Harper, 1842.
Life on a New England homestead.   5250

Seifert, Shirley. Captain Grant. Lippincott, 1946. About
Grant's military service and marriage to the start of the
Civil War.   5251

_____. The Medicine Man. Lippincott, 1971. Based on
the life of Dr. Antoine Saugrain, who served as an army
doctor, and his search for a way to handle the perishable
smallpox vaccine.   5252

_____. Proud Way. Lippincott, 1948. Varina Howell
during the two years before her marriage to Jefferson
Davis.   5253

_____. The Senator's Lady. Lippincott, 1967. The able,
underrated Senator Stephen A. Douglas of Illinois and his
helpmate, Adele Cutts Douglas, with a surprising view of

Lincoln.   5254

_____. Those Who Go Against the Current. Lippincott,
1943. Exploration of the Missouri River and the founding
of St. Louis.   5255

_____. The Three Lives of Elizabeth. Lippincott, 1952.
The heroine's marriages and life in Missouri, in Washington,
D.C., and in New York.   5256

_____. The Turquoise Trail. Lippincott, 1950. Based on
a bride's diary of a trip from Missouri to Mexico during the
Mexican War.   5257

Selby, John. Elegant Journey. Rinehart, 1944. A Maryland
landowner frees his slaves and moves his family to Wisconsin where he founds a town.   5258

Seton, Anya. Dragonwyck. Pocket Bks., 1970, c.1943. Discoveries of a poor New England girl who goes to live with
her wealthy New York cousins.   5259

_____. My Theodosia. Houghton, 1941. Romantic life and
mysterious death of Aaron Burr's daughter.   5260

Settle, Mary Lee. Know Nothing. Viking, 1960. Ante-bellum
novel of plantation owners in what became West Virginia.   5261

_____. O Beulah Land. Viking, 1956. A war veteran claims
his bounty land on the Virginia frontier. (followed by Know
Nothing)   5262

Shaftel, George Armin. Golden Shore. Coward, 1943. Conflict and romance during the American conquest of California.   5263

Shelton, Jess. Brood of Fury. Chilton, 1959. A violent tale
of the blind loyalty which made frontier family feuds so
bloody and destructive.   5264

_____. Hangman's Song. Chilton, 1960. Realistic story
of a man who hunts through Missouri, Arkansas, and Indian
Territory to revenge himself on the man he blames for his
mother's death.   5265

Shepard, Odell and Willard Odell Shepard. Holdfast Gaines.
Macmillan,. 1946. Tale of an Indian boy raised by a white
family during the last part of the eighteenth century.   5266

Sherburne, James. Hacey Miller. Houghton, 1971. Conflict
between pro-slavery and abolitionist sentiments in pre-Civil
War Kentucky. (followed by The Way to Fort Pillow)   5267

Simms, W. Gilmore. Voltmeier. Univ. of S.C. Pr., 1969. (first pub. in serial form in 1869) Voltmeier's dual life as an intellectual American landowner and an enigmatic frontier outlaw in the Carolinas in the 1830s.   5268

Sinclair, Harold. American Years. Doubleday, 1838. Story of a small town, probably patterned on Bloomington, Illinois.   5269

Singmaster, Elsie. I Speak for Thaddeus Stevens. Houghton, 1947. About the lawyer and statesman who wielded so much influence in Congress.   5270

Slaughter, Frank G. Fort Everglades. Doubleday, 1951. A doctor in the Florida Everglades during the second Seminole War.   5271

_____. The Golden Isle. Doubleday, 1947. A slave trader in Florida kidnaps a doctor to care for the slaves.   5272

_____. The Warrior. [En. title: The Flaming Frontier] Doubleday, 1956. A white man adopted by Osceola tells of the Seminole War in Florida in 1835.   5273

Small, Sidney. The Splendid Californians. Bobbs, 1928. Spanish settlers in California fight Indians and Mexicans, as well as nature.   5274

Smith, Francis Hopkinson. The Fortunes of Oliver Horn. Scribner, 1902. Social and artistic life in Washington, New York, and the South.   5275

_____. Kennedy Square. Scribner, 1911. Life in Maryland with frequent references to literary figures such as Longfellow and Poe.   5276

Snedeker, Caroline Dale. Seth Way. by Caroline Dale Owen. Houghton, 1917. New Harmony, Indiana: an experiment in communal living.   5277

Snow, Charles H. Argonaut Gold. Macrae Smith, 1936. A wagon train trip westward through Wyoming and Nevada.   5278

Sorensen, Virginia. A Little Lower Than the Angels. Knopf, 1942. The Mormons' settlement at Nauvoo, Illinois, and the start of their move to Utah.   5279

Spearman, Frank H. Carmen of the Rancho. Doubleday, 1937. Romance of a lovely Spanish girl and a Texas scout in early California.   5280

Sperry, Armstrong. No Brighter Glory. Macmillan, 1942. Concerns the Northwest when John Jacob Astor was building his fur trading empire.   5281

Spicer, Bart. The Wild Ohio. Dodd, 1953. Refugees from
the French Revolution face hardships in frontier Ohio.   5282

Stanford, Alfred Boller. The Navigator. Morrow, 1927. The
daring seamen of Salem and the achievements of navigator
Nathaniel Bowditch.   5283

Stanley, Edward. The Rock Cried Out. Duell, 1949. The
Blennerhassetts and the treason of Aaron Burr.   5284

Stern, Philip Van Doren. The Drums of Morning. by Peter
Storme, pseud. Doubleday, 1942. The son of a murdered
Abolitionist grows up to continue his father's fight.   5285

Sterne, Emma Gelders. Some Plant Olive Trees. Dodd, 1937.
The colony in Alabama established by Bonapartist refugees
from France.   5286

Stevens, Sheppard. In the Eagle's Talon. Little, 1902. America and Paris before the Louisiana Purchase.   5287

Stevenson, Burton E. The Heritage. Houghton, 1902. The
courage of early Ohio settlers defending their new homes
against Indians.   5288

Stevenson, Janet. The Ardent Years. Viking, 1960. The
theatrical life and marriage of English actress Fanny
Kemble and American Pierce Butler.   5289

_____. Sisters and Brothers. Crown, 1966. Moving story
of two Abolitionist orators, Sarah and Angelina Grimké,
whose beliefs are put to the test when they find two nephews
who are black.   5290

Steward, Davenport. Rainbow Road. Tupper, 1953. The discovery of gold in Georgia brings a rush of fortune seekers.
                                                                   5291
_____. They Had a Glory. Tupper, 1952. Frontier hard-
ships of a Revolutionary War veteran.   5292

Stewart, George Rippey. East of the Giants. Holt, 1938.
New England ship captain's daughter meets a Spanish
rancher in California.   5293

_____. Ordeal by Hunger. Holt, 1936. The endurance
and perseverance of the Donner wagon train against over-
powering hazards.   5294

Stone, Irving. Immortal Wife. Pocket Bks., 1966, c.1944.
The heroine is Jessie Benton Fremont, whose husband
was once a presidential candidate.   5295

_____.   Love Is Eternal. Doubleday, 1954. A novel about Mary Todd and Abraham Lincoln and the transition from Springfield, Illinois, to Washington, D.C.   5296

_____.   The President's Lady. Doubleday, 1951. Based on the lives of Rachel and Andrew Jackson.   5297

Stong, Philip. Buckskin Breeches. Farrar, 1937. Account of a family from Ohio on the Iowa frontier.   5298

_____.   Forty Pounds of Gold. Doubleday, 1951. Two young men from Ohio head west in search of gold.   5299

Stowe, Harriet Beecher. Dred. Houghton, 1896. An attack on the evils and intolerance of slavery.   5300

_____.   The Minister's Wooing. Houghton, 1859. Life and religion in New England at the end of the eighteenth century.
5301
_____.   Uncle Tom's Cabin. Houghton, 1852. Classic, impassioned tale of the brutality of slavery, which was used for the emancipation cause.   5302

_____.   Uncle Tom's Cabin. (adapted by Ann Terry White) Braziller, 1966. (first pub. in 1852) The classical, contro- versial book about slavery re-written in modern language for everyone from Junior High to adults.   5303

Strachey, Rachel. Marching On. by Ray Strachey, pseud. Harcourt, 1923. The story of a young woman caught up in the Abolitionist movement.   5304

Street, James Howell. Oh, Promised Land. Dial, 1940. An orphaned brother and sister in Georgia, Alabama, and Mississippi.   5305

Stuart, Charles Duff. Casa Grande: A California Pastoral. Holt, 1906. Land disputes in California resulting from the change in government.   5306

Styron, William. The Confessions of Nat Turner. Random House, 1967. A condemned slave who had led a bloody Negro uprising in Virginia in 1831 reflects on his life.   5307

Suckow, Ruth. Country People. Knopf, 1924. Three genera- tions of a German family who settled in Iowa.   5308

Summers, Richard Aldrich. Vigilante. Duell, 1949. A California politician is the object of the Vigilantes' pur- suit.   5309

Swanson, Neil. The Phantom Emperor. Putnam, 1934. James Dickson, calling himself Montezuma II, attempted to win a kingdom in the West.   5310

_____. The Star-Spangled Banner. Holt, 1958. YA. The
story of a teen-aged boy who was becoming a soldier at the
time Francis Scott Key was inspired to write "The Star
Spangled Banner."   5311

Sweeny, Sarah L. Harvest of the Wind. Caxton, 1935. Pioneer Kansas in the period between the Kansas-Nebraska
Bill and the Civil War.   5312

Swift, Hildegarde Hoyt. The Railroad to Freedom. Harcourt,
1960, c.1932. YA. Harriet Tubman, born a slave in
Maryland, escapes and works on the Underground Railroad.
                                                                 5313

Tate, Allen. The Fathers. Putnam, 1938. Decline of a large
estate in Virginia just before the Civil War.   5314

Taylor, Robert Lewis. Travels of Jaimie McPheeters. Doubleday,
1958. Adventures of a doctor and his son on their way to California during the Gold Rush of 1849.   5315

_____. Two Roads to Guadalupe. Doubleday, 1964. Two
half-brothers serve as soldiers during the Mexican War,
going separate ways and reacting differently to their experiences.   5316

Tebbel, John William. Voice in the Streets. Dutton, 1954.
A poor Irishman attains success in New York City.   5317

Teilhet, Darwin Le Ora. Steamboat on the River. Sloane,
1952. Eventful journey of a steamboat on the Sangamon
with the youthful Abe Lincoln included.   5318

Terhune, Mary Virginia. Carringtons of High Hill. by Marion
Harland, pseud. Scribner, 1919. An old southern family
and its perplexing mystery.   5319

Terrell, John Upton. Plume Rogue. Viking, 1942. Pioneers
follow the route of Lewis and Clark from St. Louis to the
Columbia River.   5320

Tiernan, Mary Spear. Homoselle. Fenno, 1881. Rich picture of southern life on the James River.   5321

_____. Suzette. Holt, 1885. Richmond family life in a
society founded on slavery.   5322

Titus, Harold. Black Feather. Macrae Smith, 1936. Action-
packed story of a fur trader in Michigan.   5323

Todd, Helen. So Free We Seem. Reynal, 1936. A courageous
mother, deserted by her husband, is left to manage their

Missouri farm.   5324

Tracy, Don. Cherokee. Dial, 1957. White man's mistreat-
ment of the Cherokees in the Great Smokies.   5325

_____. Crimson Is the Eastern Shore. Dial, 1953. The
War of 1812 on the eastern coast of Maryland.   5326

_____. The Last Boat Out of Cincinnati. Trident Pr.,
1970. A stableboy, posing as a gentleman, goes to Cincinnati just at the outbreak of the Civil War to buy horses and
finds wild adventure.   5327

Troyer, Howard W. The Salt and the Savor. Wyn, 1950.
Frontier life in Ohio from the 1840s through the Civil War.
                                                                5328

Tufts, Anne. Rails Along the Chesapeake. Holt, 1957. YA.
A young New Englander helps in the building of Peter Cooper's
Tom Thumb, the first steam locomotive in America to carry
passengers.   5329

Tupper, Edith S. Hearts Triumphant. Appleton, 1906. A
romance set in New York with Aaron Burr and Jerome
Bonaparte as figures.   5330

Twain, Mark, pseud. for Samuel L. Clemens. The Adventures
of Huckleberry Finn. Harper, 1951. YA. (first pub. 18--)
The adventures of a runaway boy and an escaping slave on a
raft trip down the Mississippi River.   5331

_____. The Adventures of Tom Sawyer. World, 1946. YA.
(first pub. 1876) The classic tale of a boy in Hannibal,
Missouri, a small town on the Mississippi River, based
on the author's life.   5332

Upchurch, Boyd. The Slave Stealer. Weybright & Talley,
1968. Jewish peddler accepts a commission to steal and
escort a young slave to a man who wants her as a wife.   5333

Vachell, Horace Annesley. John Charity. Dodd, 1901. A
story of romance and political activity in England and California in the 1830s.   5334

Valentine, Edward Abram Uffington. Hecla Sandwith. Bobbs,
1905. The Quakers who settled in Pennsylvania in the
1850s.   5335

Van Every, Dale. Our Country Then. Holt, 1958. Excerpts
from the author's various writings are woven together to
give a picture of American frontier life from the Revolution
until the early nineteenth century.   5336

_____. The Scarlet Feather. Holt, 1959. Families with

different cultural backgrounds adjust to Kentucky pioneer
life.   5337

_____. The Shining Mountains. Messner, 1948. The ex-
tension of our country's frontiers with the Lewis and Clark
Expedition.   5338

_____. The Trembling Earth. Messner, 1953. The New
Madrid earthquake in lead-mining southeastern Missouri.   5339

_____. Westward the River. Putnam, 1945. An Ohio
Valley romance showing international influences in the
young American nation.   5340

Venable, Clarke. All the Brave Rifles. Reilly & Lee, 1929.
Life in frontier Texas, including fighting at the Alamo and
claim jumping.   5341

Vining, Elizabeth Gray. Jane Hope. by Elizabeth J. Gray.
Viking, 1962, c.1933. YA. Home life at Chapel Hill,
North Carolina, just before the Civil War.   5342

Wallace, Willard M. Jonathan Dearborn. Little, 1967. The
son of a minister during the War of 1812 when New England
seamanship was a force to be reckoned with.   5343

Walz, Jay and Audrey. Undiscovered Country. Duell, 1958.
The touching, scandalous love of Arctic explorer Elisha
Kent Kane and spiritualist Maggie Fox.   5344

Ward, Christopher. Strange Adventures of Jonathan Drew.
S. & S., 1932. A wandering New England peddler in the
1820s. (followed by A Yankee Rover)   5345

_____. A Yankee Rover. S. & S., 1932. An itinerant
New England peddler in the Southwest.   5346

Warren, Lella. Foundation Stone. Knopf, 1940. About a
southern family from the 1820s through the Civil War.   5347

Warren, Robert Penn. World Enough and Time. Random,
1950. Famous Kentucky trial of Jeremiah Beaumont,
charged with a Colonel's murder.   5348

Waters, Gladys. Fairacres. Waters Press, 1952. Spirited
tale of slave running and of the founding of Independence,
Missouri.   5349

Watkin, Lawrence Edward. Gentleman From England. Knopf,
1941. Life in America when freedom and independence
were new, exciting possessions.   5350

Webb, Christopher. Mark Toyman's Inheritance. Funk,

1960. YA. A young Kansan travels to California by wagon train and then returns to fight at Shiloh and Vicksburg.   5351

Weld, John. Don't You Cry for Me. Scribner, 1940. The determination of a wagon train to California, based largely on the Donner party tragedy.   5352

Wellman, Paul I. The Buckstones. Trident Pr., 1967. The spunky daughter of a braggart journeys to Washington to ask President Jackson to release her father from a debtors' prison.   5353

_____. The Comancheros. Doubleday, 1952. A New Orleans gambler becomes a Texas Ranger and fights the Comancheros.   5354

_____. The Iron Mistress. Doubleday, 1951. About a famous fighter of the Old West, Jim Bowie, whose favorite weapon was a bowie knife.   5355

_____. Magnificent Destiny. Doubleday, 1962. The intertwined lives of Andrew Jackson and Samuel Houston and their efforts in the territorial expansion of the United States.   5356

Welty, Eudora. The Robber Bridegroom. Doubleday, 1942. Imaginative story of a bandit and a beautiful girl.   5357

West, Jessamyn. Except For Me and Thee. Avon Bks., 1970, c.1949. Quakers Jess and Eliza Birdwell move from Pennsylvania to Indiana--he is a nurseryman and she a minister. (followed by The Friendly Persuasion)   5358

_____. Leafy Rivers. Avon Bks., 1972, c.1967. Married to an inefficient teen-aged schoolteacher on the Ohio frontier, a young bride takes on the responsibility for her family.   5359

Wetherell, June. The Glorious Three. Dutton, 1951. The hard trip across the wilderness from Connecticut to Oregon.   5360

Wheeler, Sessions S. Paiute. Caxton, 1965. Concerns the Paiute Indians and discoveries of gold and silver in Nevada in 1859 and 1860.   5361

White, Stewart Edward. The Blazed Trail. McClure, 1902. A vivid story of the lumber industry in Michigan.   5362

_____. Folded Hills. Doubleday, 1934. An American man, his Spanish-American wife, and their small son on their southern California ranch.   5363

_____. Gold. Doubleday, Page, 1913. The wild, rough
life in California following the gold strike of '49. (followed by The Gray Dawn)   5364

_____. The Gray Dawn. Doubleday, Page, 1915. San
Francisco in the wild 1850s when decent citizens banded together as Vigilantes. (followed by Rose Dawn)   5365

_____. The Long Rifle. Doubleday, Doran, 1932. Trap-
ping in the Rockies and life with Blackfoot Indians of a youth
who inherited Daniel Boone's rifle.   5366

_____. Ranchero. Doubleday, 1933. Andy Burnett settles
in California and courts a Spanish girl.   5367

_____. The Riverman. McClure, 1908. Michigan's rugged
lumberjacks and the thriving timber business.   5368

_____. Stampede. Doubleday, 1942. Action-packed story
of the feud between ranchers and squatters in California.   5369

Whitlock, Brand. The Stranger on the Island. Appleton, 1933.
An outsider's love for a member of a religious sect which
practices polygamy.   5370

Whitney, Janet. Intrigue in Baltimore. Little, 1951. Irish-
educated youth claims his Baltimore estate.   5371

_____. Judith. Morrow, 1943. Tangled romances of a
young doctor amid Philadelphia's yellow fever epidemic.   5372

Whitney, Phyllis A. Skye Cameron. Appleton, 1957. YA.
A period romance of a red-haired beauty in New Orleans
who finds herself very much attracted to her brother-in-
law.   5373

Widdemer, Margaret. Red Castle Women. Doubleday, 1968.
The secrets of three generations of inhabitants of a great
Hudson River mansion are unlocked by a young bride.   5374

Wilder, Robert. Bright Feather. Putnam, 1948. The war
which resulted from the attempt to force the Seminole Indians to leave their homes.   5375

Williams, Ben Ames. Strange Woman. Houghton, 1941. A
wicked, though beautiful, woman destroys her admirers.   5376

_____. Thread of Scarlet. Houghton, 1939. The War of
1812 around the island of Nantucket with an account of a
naval engagement.   5377

Williams, Cecil B. Paradise Prairie. Day, 1953. Saga of
Oklahoma in pioneer times.   5378

Williams, Mary Floyd. Fortune, Smile Once More! Bobbs,
1946. An Australian convict and an English lady's maid
in San Francisco.   5379

Williamson, Joanne S. And Forever Free.... Knopf, 1966.
YA. A young newspaper reporter from Germany works in
New York and observes the events prior to the Civil War. 5380

Wills, Grace E. Murphy's Bend. Westminster, 1946. Pioneer settlers in the Susquehanna River Valley early in the
nineteenth century.   5381

Willsie, Honoré McCue. Benefits Forgot. Stokes, 1917. A
loving mother sacrifices everything for her unappreciative
son.   5382

Wilson, Charles M. The Great Turkey Drive. McKay, 1964.
YA. Concerns the tedious and hazardous method of getting
turkeys to market in the early nineteenth century--herding
them on foot cross-country.   5383

Wilson, Harry Leon. The Lions of the Lords. Lothrop, 1903.
Brigham Young's Mormon settlement at Salt Lake.   5384

Wilson, William E. Abe Lincoln of Pigeon Creek. McGraw,
1949. Fictional story of the young Abraham Lincoln in
Indiana.   5385

Woolson, Constance Fenimore. East Angels. Harper, 1886.
Peaceful Georgia before the Civil War changed its way of
life.   5386

Wormser, Richard Edward. Battalion of Saints. McKay, 1961.
Young mountain man guides a battalion of Mormons along
the Santa Fe Trail in an aura of mutual distrust and dislike, with one romantic exception.   5387

Wyckoff, Nichols E. The Corinthians. Macmillan, 1960.
The two different households of a Mormon, one in Illinois
and one in Missouri.   5388

Yates, Elizabeth. Hue and Cry. Coward, 1953. An organiza-
tion to catch horse thieves in New Hampshire.   5389

Yerby, Frank. Fairoaks. Dial, 1957. A vast southern plantation and the controversial slave trade.   5390

_____. The Foxes of Harrow. Dial, 1946. Stephen Fox,
who rose from poverty to establish a great plantation.   5391

_____. The Treasure of Pleasant Valley. Dial, 1955. A
man settles in California during the Gold Rush.   5392

Young, Gordon Ray. Days of '49. Doran, 1925. A man's
search for his brother's runaway wife reveals a cross-
section of gold-rush California.   5393

Young, Stark. Heaven Trees. Scribner, 1926. Luxurious
life on a gracious, hospitable Mississippi plantation.   5394

Zelley, Frankie Lee. Farewell the Stranger. by Saliee
O'Brien, pseud. Morrow, 1956. Devora Griggs' fight for
her marriage was harder than her fights with Indian
raiders.   5395

d) Civil War Period (1861-1865)

Alcott, Louisa May. Little Women. Little, 1968. YA.
(first pub. in 1868) One-hundredth anniversary publication
of the classic tale of four sisters and their family life.
(followed by Little Men)   5396

Allen, Henry. Journey to Shiloh. by Will Henry, pseud.
Random House, 1960. The hardships of war as seen by
several untried young soldiers in the Confederate Army under General Bragg.   5397

_____. One More River to Cross. by Will Henry, pseud.
Random House, 1967. An emancipated Arkansas Negro
who seeks full freedom in the West finds it only in spiritual virtue.   5398

Allen, Hervey. Action at Aquila. Farrar, 1938. A Civil War
romance centering on the battle at Aquila.   5399

Allen, James Lane. The Sword of Youth. Century, 1915. A
youth, longing to be a soldier, is torn between duty to a dying mother and patriotism.   5400

Allen, Merritt Parmelee. Blow, Bugles, Blow. McKay, 1956.
YA. A young orphan joins the Union Army and learns about
war and human nature.   5401

Allis, Marguerite. The Rising Storm. Putnam, 1955. Opposing views of slavery held by twin brothers cause conflict; operation of the Underground Railroad.   5402

Andrews, Mary R.S. The Perfect Tribute. Scribner, 1956,
c.1906. YA. The character and magnetism of Lincoln win
the respect of a dying Confederate officer.   5403

Appell, George Charles. Man Who Shot Quantrill. Doubleday,
1957. Curtis Blakeman of the Union Army, who pursued
Quantrill's guerrillas.   5404

Ashley, Robert. The Stolen Train. Winston, 1953. A story
of the Andrews Raiders. 5405

Babcock, Mrs. Bernie. Soul of Abe Lincoln. Lippincott,
1923. Romance of two young people caught up in the swirl
of war and influenced greatly by Lincoln. 5406

Babcock, William Henry. Kent Fort Manor. Coates, 1902.
A story of civilian life in and around war-time Washington.
5407

Bacheller, Irving. Father Abraham. Bobbs, 1925. Conflict
between a northern boy and his southern relatives, with
Lincoln introduced as a hero of youth. 5408

Barney, Helen Corse. Green Rose of Furley. Crown, 1953.
A Quaker station on the Underground Railroad. 5409

Basso, Hamilton. The Light Infantry Ball. Doubleday, 1959.
Deterioration of southern society in the conflict of beliefs
and arms. 5410

Bechdolt, Frederick Ritchie. Bold Raiders of the West.
Doubleday, 1940. New Mexico in the wild, rough times
when the West was still young. 5411

Becker, Stephen D. When the War Is Over. Random House,
1969. A young rebel guerrilla who has shot a Union officer
suffers from the mass hysteria which follows Lincoln's assassination. 5412

Beebe, Elswyth Thane. Yankee Stranger. · by Elswyth Thane.
Duell, 1944. Civilian life behind the front lines during hostilities. (followed by Ever After) 5413

Bell, John. Moccasin Flower. Bk. Masters, 1935. The
Sioux uprising near St. Paul in 1862. 5414

Bellah, James Warner. The Valiant Virginians. Ballantine,
1953. Courage of the Virginia cavalry under Early and its
battle with Sheridan. 5415

Benadum, Clarence Edward. Bates House. Greenberg, 1951.
Civil War story of a southern girl and a Yankee lawyer. 5416

Bennett, John Henry. So Shall They Reap. Doubleday, 1944.
Two groups of southerners carry on their traditional family
feud despite the war. 5417

Benson, Blackwood Ketcham. Bayard's Courier. Macmillan,
1902. Story of a cavalryman's love and adventure. 5418

_____. A Friend With the Countersign. Macmillan, 1901.
Both sides of the war as seen by a Union spy. 5419

_____ . Old Squire. Macmillan, 1903. The adventures of
a Negro who takes part in the Gettysburg campaign.   5420

_____ . Who Goes There? Macmillan, 1900. A Federal
spy, who has lost his memory, serves with the Rebel
army. (followed by A Friend With the Countersign)   5421

Blech, William James. The Copperheads. by William Blake,
pseud. Dial, 1941. Effects of the war on New York City
and on the romance of a German immigrant's daughter.   5422

Borland, Hal. The Amulet. Lippincott, 1957. Young Coloradan delays his wedding to fight for the Confederacy in Missouri.   5423

Boyd, James. Marching On. Scribner, 1927. Experiences
of a southern soldier and prisoner-of-war.   5424

Boyd, Thomas Alexander. Samuel Drummond. Scribner,
1925. The plight of an industrious Iowa farmer caught
in the conflict and aftermath of war.   5425

Bradbury, Bianca. Flight into Spring. Washburn, 1965. YA.
Romance of a Southern belle and a Northern man during the
Civil War.   5426

Bradford, Roark. Kingdom Coming. Harper, 1933. Southern
Negro's viewpoint of plantation life, the Civil War, and post-
bellum changes.   5427

_____ . Three-Headed Angel. Harper, 1937. A southern
family's struggle for material wealth which was their criterion of success.   5428

Brady, Cyrus Townsend. The Patriots. Dodd, 1906. Hardships of the final years of the war; Lee's surrender to
Grant at Appomattox.   5429

_____ . The Southerners. Scribner, 1903. Scene of this
Civil War story is Mobile, Alabama.   5430

Branch, Houston and Frank Waters. Diamond Head. Farrar,
1948. The southern cruiser Shenandoah pursues New England whalers.   5431

Branson, H.C. Salisbury Plain. Dutton, 1965. A novel about
a group of people--men and women--during the War and of
the results of their own character differences and the pres-
sure of combat.   5432

Breslin, Howard. A Hundred Hills. Crowell, 1960. A Confederate family in besieged Vicksburg and their varied reactions to war.   5433

Brick, John. Jubilee. Doubleday, 1956. Sherman's famous--
or infamous--"March to the Sea." 5434

_____. The Richmond Raid. Doubleday, 1963. The attempt
to raid Richmond and thus to deal a crippling blow to the Confederacy suffers from Southern opposition and Northern inade-
quacies. 5435

_____. Troubled Spring. Farrar, 1950. Union soldier re-
turns from Andersonville prison to find his brother married
to his sweetheart. 5436

Brier, Royce. Boy in Blue. Appleton, 1937. A Union soldier's experiences in the Cumberland Valley and at the
Battle of Chickamauga. 5437

Bristow, Gwen. The Handsome Road. Crowell, 1938. Concerns two southern women--one an aristocrat, the other
from the "poor white" class. 5438

Brooks, Asa Passavant. The Reservation. Brooks, 1908.
"A romance of the pioneer days of Minnesota and of the
Indian Massacre of 1862." 5439

Brown, Karl. Cup of Trembling. Duell, 1953. Frederick
Stowe, son of Harriet Beecher Stowe. 5440

Bryant, Will. The Big Lonesome. Doubleday, 1971. Failing
to find gold in California, a father and soon seek it in Idaho,
where they encounter bears, Indians, and claim-jumpers. 5441

Buckley, R. Wallace. The Last of the Houghtons. Neale,
1907. The strain and breaking of family ties resulting from
opposing loyalties in the war. 5442

Burchard, Peter. Jed. Coward, 1960. YA. A hardened sixteen-year-old Union soldier proves he has a heart by being
kind to an injured Confederate boy. 5443

Burchell, Sidney Herbert. The Shepherd of the People. Gay
& Hancock, 1924. Social life in the nation's capital during
the opening years of the war. 5444

Burnett, William Riley. The Dark Command. Knopf, 1938.
Kansas and Missouri during the war. 5445

Burress, John. Bugle in the Wilderness. Vanguard, 1958.
Domestic problems of a rural Missouri family are intensified by wartime stress. 5446

Buster, Greene B. Brighter Sun. Pageant, 1954. Escape
from a Kentucky plantation via the Underground Railroad. 5447

Cable, George Washington. The Cavalier. Scribner, 1903.
The Confederate view of the war in Mississippi in the
early years.   5448

_____. Kincaid's Battery. Scribner, 1908. New Orleans
at the start of the war, with a young artillery officer as
hero.   5449

Cain, James Mallahan. Mignon. Dial, 1962. A Union war
veteran is attracted by a fortune-hunting southern widow and
drawn into the contraband cotton trade.   5450

Campbell, Marie. A House With Stairs. Rinehart, 1950.
Story of two girls, one white, one Negro, on a southern
plantation.   5451

Campbell, Thomas B. Old Miss. Houghton, 1929. The happy
childhood and tranquil early married life of a Virginia lady
is tragically interrupted by the war.   5452

Carrighar, Sally. The Glass Dove. Doubleday, 1962. A young
lady operates her farm home as a station on the Underground
Railroad when her father joins the Union Army.   5453

Castor, Henry. The Spanglers. Doubleday, 1948. A Pennsylvania Dutch family and a brief look at unspeakably horrible
Andersonville prison.   5454

Catto, Max. King Oil. S. & S., 1970. The stormy marriage
of a Texas landowner and a Spanish lady.   5455

Catton, Bruce. Banners at Shenandoah. Doubleday, 1955. YA.
The action seen by a youthful standard bearer with Sheridan's
fighting cavalry.   5456

Chambers, Robert W. Ailsa Paige. Appleton, 1910. New
York during the firing on Fort Sumter and the gay quality
of the first wave of war enthusiasm.   5457

_____. Secret Service Operator 13. Appleton, 1934. An
account of the devious methods of obtaining and passing information during the war.   5458

_____. Whistling Cat. Appleton, 1932. Two young Texans
serve as telegraphers for the Union Army.   5459

Cochran, Hamilton. The Dram Tree. Bobbs, 1961. Blockade-
running, intense romantic rivalry between two girls, and the
legend of the "dram tree" fill this novel of the Civil War. 5460

Cochran, John Salisbury. Bonnie Belmont. Cochran, 1907.
"Historical romance of the days of slavery and the Civil
War" in Ohio.   5461

Coker, Elizabeth Boatwright. La Belle. Dutton, 1959.
Based on the life of a famous southern beauty who, with
her mother, became a camp-follower to Sherman's troops. 5462

Cooke, John Esten. Mohun. Dillingham, 1869. The Army
of North Virginia and wretched condition of Lee's soldiers,
ending with the surrender at Appomattox.   5463

_____. Surry of Eagle's Nest. Dillingham, 1866. A
Confederate view of the war, with pictures of Jackson and
Jeb Stuart.   5464

Corbett, Elizabeth. Faye's Folly. Appleton, 1941. Political,
social, and romantic events at Fay's Folly, an Illinois
farm.   5465

Corrington, John William. And Wait for the Night. Putnam,
1964. Pictures oppression of southerners at Shreveport,
Louisiana, during the final period of the Civil War.   5466

Crabb, Alfred Leland. Dinner at Belmont. Bobbs, 1942. A
story of captured Nashville.   5467

_____. Home to Tennessee. Bobbs, 1952. Emphasis is
on the strategy of war in an effort to recapture Nashville. 5468

_____. Lodging at the Saint Cloud. Bobbs, 1946. Tale of
occupied Nashville with Yankee soldiers seeking southern
spies.   5469

_____. A Mockingbird Sang at Chickamauga. Bobbs, 1949.
A tale of embattled Chattanooga, told from the Confederate
viewpoint.   5470

_____. Peace at Bowling Green. Bobbs, 1955. A novel
about life in Kentucky.   5471

Crane, Stephen. The Red Badge of Courage. Appleton, 1895.
The growth and maturing of an inexperienced soldier in the
Civil War, especially at the Battle of Chancellorsville.   5472

Cullinan, Thomas. The Beguiled. Horizon Pr., 1966. Varying views of students and teachers as to what happened during the stay of a wounded Union soldier at a southern school
for girls.   5473

Dahlinger, Charles W. Where the Red Volleys Poured. Dillingham, 1907. Battles and campaigns of the war including Centreville, Fredericksburg, and Gettysburg.   5474

Davis, Clyde Brion. Nebraska Coast. Farrar, 1939. A
farm family moves west to avoid the Civil War and builds
a full life in Nebraska.   5475

Davis, Julia. Bridle the Wind. Rinehart, 1953. A Virginia lady achieves reconciliation with her husband after
helping a fugitive slave escape.   5476

Davis, Maggie. The Far Side of Home. Macmillan, 1963.
The feelings of small town, non-slave-owning Southerners
are explored in this story of a Confederate who married
in haste while on leave.   5477

De Forest, John W. Miss Ravenel's Conversion From Seces-
sion to Loyalty. Harper, 1867. A contemporary novel reflecting American sentiments at the time.   5478

Deland, Margaret. The Kays. Harper, 1926. The unpopular-
ity of a pacifist mother and her conscientious objector son.
                                                         5479

Demarest, Phyllis Gordon. Wilderness Brigade. Doubleday,
1957. A Union soldier, an escaped prisoner-of-war, is
rescued by and later marries a southern girl.   5480

Devon, Louis. Aide to Glory. Crowell, 1952. Story of
General Grant's aide-de-camp and subsequent Secretary of
War, John Rawlins.   5481

Divine, Arthur Durham. Thunder on the Chesapeake. by
David Divine, pseud. Macmillan, 1961. Crucial duel between the two ironclads, the Monitor and the Merrimac,
together with divided allegiance and light romance.   5482

Dixon, Thomas. The Man in Gray. Appleton, 1921. Southern
view of the war, preceding events, and prominent people,
especially John Brown and Robert E. Lee.   5483

_____. The Southerner. Appleton, 1925. A novel empha-
sizing Lincoln's sympathies for the South.   5484

_____. The Victim. Appleton, 1914. The career of Jeffer-
son Davis from his service in the U.S. Army to his Presidency of the Confederacy.   5485

Doneghy, Dagmar. The Border. Morrow, 1931. A saga of
Missouri-Kansas border conflict as it affects a mother and
her six small sons.   5486

Dowdey, Clifford. Bugles Blow No More. Little, 1937. An
intense account of conditions in Richmond between 1861 and
1864.   5487

_____. The Proud Retreat. Doubleday, 1953. Interesting
picture of the defeated Confederacy trying to save its treasury.   5488

_____. Where My Love Sleeps. Little, 1945. The fight-

ing around Richmond and Petersburg near the end of the
war.   5489

Drago, Harry Sinclair. Stagecoach Kingdom. Doubleday,
1943. The Midwest during the Civil War.   5490

Edgerton, Lucile. Pillars of Gold. Knopf, 1941. The Arizona gold rush of the 1860s with good descriptions of the
Southwest.   5491

Edmonds, Walter D. The Big Barn. Little, 1930. A romantic triangle is the plot in this well-told story of farm
life in the Erie Canal region.   5492

_____. Cadmus Henry. Dodd, 1949. YA. A Confederate
youth with aspirations to a cavalry post becomes a balloon-
ist for the army.   5493

Edwards, Amelia A. B. Debenham's Vow. Hurst & Blackett,
1870. Exciting account of blockade running at Charleston. 5494

Eggleston, George Cary. Bale Marked Circle X. Lothrop,
1902. Adventures of blockade runners who defied danger
for financial gain.   5495

_____. Master of Warlock. Lothrop, 1903. A romance
of war-torn Virginia in the early part of the hostilities. 5496

_____. The Warrens of Virginia. Dillingham, 1908.
Both the North and the South are shown suffering the effects of war.   5497

Ehle, John. Time of Drums. Harper, 1970. Realistic picture of the brutality of civil war and insights into the characters of people in the army and at home.   5498

Eliot, George Fielding. Caleb Pettengill, U.S.N. Messner,
1956. About a Union gunboat commander blockading southern
ports.   5499

Erdman, Loula Grace. Another Spring. Dodd, 1966. Ordeals
of three refugee families from southwestern Missouri who
are driven from their homes by Union vengeance against
Quantrill's Raiders.   5500

_____. Many a Voyage. Dodd, 1960. The wife of a cru-
sading newspaperman views the troubled Midwest.   5501

Fairbank, Janet Ayer. Bright Land. Houghton, 1932. A New
England girl who runs away from home finds fulfillment in
frontier Illinois.   5502

_____. The Cortlandts of Washington Square. Bobbs,

1922. A determined young lady from New York becomes
a war nurse against family objections.   5503

Farrell, Cliff. Trail of the Tattered Star. Doubleday, 1961.
The efforts of active Confederates in San Francisco to win
California to the southern cause.   5504

Ferrel, Elizabeth and Margaret. Full of Thy Riches. Mill,
1944. A Quaker girl and her elderly husband move south,
where she falls in love.   5505

Feuille, Frank. The Cotton Road. Morrow, 1954. Running
southern cotton to English markets through the Union blockade.   5506

Foote, Shelby. Shiloh. Dial, 1952. Battle of Shiloh as it affects six soldiers--Union and Confederate.   5507

Fox, John, Jr. The Little Shepherd of Kingdom Come. Scribner, 1903. A story of the Kentucky mountains and divided
loyalties in the war.   5508

Frothingham, Jessie P. Running the Gauntlet. Appleton,
1906. Based on the life of William B. Cushing, the naval
hero who destroyed the southern ship Albemarle.   5509

Gaither, Frances. Follow the Drinking Gourd. Macmillan,
1940. The drinking gourd in this tale of an Alabama plantation is the Big Dipper, which guided runaway slaves northward.   5510

Gardiner, Dorothy. The Great Betrayal. Doubleday, 1949.
Wanton massacre of friendly Indians by Colonel Chivington,
whose ruthlessness was caused by ambition to a Congres-
sional seat.   5511

Garth, David. Gray Canaan. Putnam, 1947. The loss of a
secret Confederate plan and attempts to recover it.   5512

Giles, Janice Holt. Run Me a River. Houghton, 1964. Riverboat workers and passengers have a confusing, frightening
time as they hurry to get safely past the newly-arrived gun-
boats in the early part of the Civil War.   5513

Glasgow, Alice. Twisted Tendril. Stokes, 1928. A novel
of the ironic life of John Wilkes Booth and his twisted
ideals.   5514

Glasgow, Ellen. The Battle Ground. Doubleday, Page, 1902.
Virginia in the prosperous era before the war and the
tragedy brought by the fighting.   5515

Gordon, Caroline. None Shall Look Back. Scribner, 1937.

Story of a wealthy Kentucky family and of General Nathan
Bedford Forrest of the Confederate Cavalry.   5516

Greene, Homer. A Lincoln Conscript. Houghton, 1909. A
much-misunderstood conscientious objector receives the
friendship of the wise President.   5517

Gruber, Frank. Buffalo Grass. Rinehart, 1956. A picture
of Kansas near the end of the Civil War.   5518

Gulick, Grover C. They Came to a Valley. by Bill Gulick.
Doubleday, 1966. Early settlers in the Idaho Territory and
their various occupations, loyalties, and experiences.   5519

Haas, Ben. The Foragers. S. & S., 1962. The unpleasant
duty of a Confederate officer is to plunder and pillage in order to supply food to his desperately hungry men.   5520

Harben, Will N. The Triumph. Harper, 1917. Experiences of
an Abolitionist and his family in Georgia.   5521

Harris, Joel Chandler. A Little Union Scout. Duckworth,
1905. A Federal scout proves to be a charming lady in
disguise.   5522

Harrison, Constance. The Carlyles. Appleton, 1905. Grant's
capture of Richmond and Lincoln's visit to the Confederate
capital.   5523

Hart, Scott. Eight April Days. Coward, 1949. Spirit of
the Confederate Army during the retreat from Petersburg
to Appomattox.   5524

Havighurst, Marion Boyd. The Sycamore Tree. World, 1960.
YA. Families and friends are divided and set against one
another by the Civil War.   5525

Havill, Edward. Big Ember. Harper, 1947. Fresh account
of Norwegian settlers in Minnesota and their fights with the
Sioux.   5526

Hawthorne, Hazel. Three Women. Dutton, 1938. The lives
of three women who grew up together on Cape Cod.   5527

Haycox, Ernest. The Long Storm. Little, 1946. Action of
Copperheads in Oregon as the Civil War has far-flung
repercussions.   5528

Heyward, Du Bose. Peter Ashley. Farrar, 1932. Concerns
traditions of the Old South and the hero's struggle with his
conscience at the outbreak of war.   5529

Hicks, John. The Long Whip. McKay, 1969. The plight of

Negro slaves, their military service in the Civil War,
and their treatment in the South after the War, reflected
in the life of one man who tried to improve his lot.   5530

Honig, Donald. Walk Like a Man. Sloane, 1961. A youth
of sixteen tries to bring his scoundrel uncle to face up to
his duties.   5531

Horan, James David. Seek Out and Destroy. Crown, 1958.
The CSS Lee's attempt to wound the North economically by
destroying the New Bedford whaling fleet.   5532

Horsley, Reginald. Stonewall's Scout. Harper, 1896. A
story of the Civil War, including an account of Gettysburg.   5533

Howard, J. Hamilton. In the Shadow of the Pines. Eaton &
Mains, 1906. A tale about the Great Dismal Swamp in
Virginia.   5534

Hunt, Irene. Across Five Aprils. Follett, 1964. YA. Emphasizes how the daily lives of rural people continue and
are changed by war, as a young boy must assume responsibility for his family.   5535

Jacobs, Thornwell. Red Lanterns on St. Michael's. Dutton,
1940. A well-documented story of Charleston during the
War between the States.   5536

Johnston, Mary. Cease Firing. Houghton, 1912. Vivid pictures of the disasters and horrors of war.   5537

_____. Drury Randall. Little, 1934. A southern gentle-
man's search for spiritual peace and happiness.   5538

_____. The Long Roll. Houghton, 1911. A detailed story
of the Shenandoah Valley campaign with Stonewall Jackson
prominent.   5539

Jordan, Jan. Dim the Flaring Lamps. Prentice-Hall, 1972.
A biographical novel of John Wilkes Booth, whose turbulent
youth and intense feelings led to his assassination of Lincoln.   5540

Kane, Harnett T. Bride of Fortune. Doubleday, 1948. The
first lady of the Confederacy--Mrs. Jefferson Davis.   5541

_____. The Smiling Rebel. Doubleday, 1955. The Con-
federacy's seventeen-year-old spy, spirited Belle Boyd.   5542

Kantor, MacKinlay. Andersonville. World Pub., 1955. Life
and death in and around notorious Andersonville prison.   5543

_____. Arouse and Beware. Coward, 1936. Two Federal soldiers escape from the infamous Confederate prison of Belle Island. 5544

_____. Long Remember. Coward, 1955. A panoramic story of the Battle of Gettysburg. 5545

Kelland, Clarence Budington. Arizona. Harper, 1939. A woman combines the talents of shooting and cooking to earn a living in the Wild West by baking pies. 5546

Kelly, Eleanor. Richard Walden's Wife. Bobbs, 1950. A southern lady and her household join her husband in pioneer Wisconsin. 5547

Kennedy, Sara Beaumont. Cicely. Doubleday, 1911. A tale of Sherman's March through Georgia with the capture and burning of Atlanta. 5548

Kennelly, Ardyth. The Spur. Messner, 1951. John Wilkes Booth reviews his life in the six days between his assassination of Lincoln and his own death. 5549

Keyes, Frances Parkinson. Madame Castel's Lodger. Farrar, 1962. The life and career of a professional soldier, General Pierre Beauregard, telling some of his frustrations and successes. 5550

King, Charles. Between the Lines. Harper, 1889. A reliable account of the action of the Army of the Potomac. 5551

_____. The General's Double. Lippincott, 1897. A story of the Army of the Potomac, stressing McClellan's campaign in Maryland. 5552

_____. Norman Holt. Dillingham, 1901. The military exploits of the Army of the Cumberland. 5553

_____. The Rock of Chickamauga. Dillingham, 1907. The defense of Chickamauga, where General Thomas won the nickname "Rock." 5554

Kjelgaard, James Arthur. The Land Is Bright. Dodd, 1958. YA. The effects on Virginians of the division between those who would stand by the Union and those who would secede. 5555

Kroll, Harry Harrison. The Keepers of the House. Bobbs, 1940. A rebellious youth discovers he is the illegitimate son of a plantation owner. 5556

Lagard, Garald. Leaps the Live Thunder. Morrow, 1955. Most memorable character is Colonel Turpentine, a yellow, whisky-drinking cat. 5557

_____. Scarlet Cockerel. Morrow, 1948. Love of a
surgeon with Mosby's Raiders for a Union general's
daughter.   5558

Lancaster, Bruce. Night March. Little, 1958. Two officers
attempt to rescue Union soldiers from Libby Prison.   5559

_____. No Bugles Tonight. Little, 1948. In the process
of spying a man learns a cause is more important than an
individual.   5560

_____. Roll, Shenandoah. Little, 1956. A soldier,
wounded at Appomattox, returns to war as a newspaper
reporter.   5561

_____. The Scarlet Patch. Little, 1947. Foreign-born
volunteers who fought for the survival of the Union.   5562

Le May, Alan. By Dim and Flaring Lamps. Harper, 1962.
A young mule-trader in divided Missouri courts the daughter
of a riverboat owner and feuds with a robber-killer.   5563

Lentz, Perry. The Falling Hills. Scribner, 1967. The Fort
Pillow massacre and the disillusionment of both a Union and
a Confederate officer (based on an actual battle in 1864). 5564

Lincoln, Joseph Crosby. Storm Signals. Appleton, 1935.
Life on Cape Cod during the Civil War portrayed in the
story of two sea captains.   5565

Lincoln, Natalie Sumner. The Lost Despatch. Appleton, 1913.
Story of a woman in Washington suspected of being a spy
and a murderess.   5566

Longstreet, Stephen. Gettysburg. Farrar, 1961. Life in the
little town of Gettysburg at the time of the famous battle. 5567

_____. Three Days. Messner, 1947. The three days of
the title are the time of the Battle of Gettysburg.   5568

Love, Edmund G. A Shipment of Tarts. Doubleday, 1967.
A young Union officer assigned to convoy sixty-eight ladies
out of Memphis on a riverboat encounters a plethora of
difficulties.   5569

Lowden, Leone. Proving Ground. McBride, 1946. A frontier
family in Indiana during the war.   5570

Lytle, Andrew Nelson. The Velvet Horn. McDowell, 1957.
Beautifully written story of five young people orphaned
shortly before the war.   5571

McCord, Joseph. Redhouse on the Hill. Macrae Smith,

1938. The personal conflict of a southern sympathizer
who loved a Union soldier. 5572

McGehee, Thomasine. Journey Proud. Macmillan, 1939.
Warm story of a southern family which preserved its ideals
despite misfortunes. 5573

MacGowan, Alice. Sword in the Mountains. Putnam, 1910.
A story which shows suffering and loyalty in the Cumberland
Mountains. 5574

Mackie, Pauline Bradford. The Washingtonians. Page, 1903.
The intrigues of political life in Washington toward the end
of the war. 5575

McLaws, Lafayette, i.e., Emily Lafayette McLaws. The Welding. Little, 1907. Political issues in the preliminary
stages of the Civil War. 5576

McMeekin, Clark, pseud. for Dorothy Clark and Isabel Mc-
Meekin. City of the Flags. Appleton, 1950. Conflicting
loyalties in Louisville when Kentucky was still neutral. 5577

McNeilly, Mildred Masterson. Praise at Morning. Morrow,
1947. International intrigue when the War between the
States brings the Russian fleet to American waters. 5578

Mally, Emma Louise. The Mockingbird Is Singing. Holt,
1944. The loves of two young couples in New Orleans and
Texas. 5579

Manfred, Frederick. Scarlet Plume. Trident Pr., 1964. A
white woman captured by attacking Sioux during a massacre
eventually adapts to the ways of the red man. 5580

Markey, Morris. The Band Plays Dixie. Harcourt, 1927.
The simultaneous friendship and enmity of two imprisoned
Union men who love the same girl. 5581

Mason, Van Wyck. Blue Hurricane. Lippincott, 1954. Melodramatic romance against a background of river war on the
Mississippi. 5582

_____. Hang My Wreath. by Ward Weaver, pseud. Funk,
1941. Fast-moving drama of events leading to the bloody
battle of Antietam. 5583

_____. Our Valiant Few. Little, 1956. A tale of the
Union naval blockade of Savannah and Charleston. 5584

_____. Proud New Flags. Lippincott, 1951. Drama of
building the Confederate fleet. 5585

Meader, Stephen W. The Muddy Road to Glory. Harcourt,
1963. YA. A sixteen-year-old farm boy volunteers as
a Union soldier during the War.   5586

Miller, Helen Topping. Christmas for Tad. Longmans, 1956.
Christmas with Lincoln's family in the White House during
the Civil War.   5587

_____. No Tears for Christmas. Longmans, 1954.
Union troops spend Christmas at a Tennessee plantation.   5588

_____. Shod With Flame. Bobbs, 1946. Romance of
three women in love with the same Rebel soldier.   5589

_____. Sing One Song. Appleton, 1956. Residents of
Kentucky torn between their sympathies for the North and
the South.   5590

Miller, May. First the Blade. Knopf, 1938. Guerrilla action in Missouri; settlement of the San Joaquin Valley in
California.   5591

Minnigerode, Meade. Cordelia Chantrell. Putnam, 1926.
Picture of a charming lady of Charleston.   5592

Mitchell, Margaret. Gone With the Wind. Pocket Bks., 1971,
c. 1936. The tempestuous romance of the wilful Scarlett
O'Hara against the background of the war and its aftermath.
                                                        5593

Mitchell, S. Weir. A Diplomatic Adventure. Century, 1906.
Diplomatic relations with France as both sides in the American dispute seek foreign support.   5594

_____. Roland Blake. Century, 1864. Action and battles
as well as social life in New York and Philadelphia.   5595

Montgomery, James Stuart. Tall Men. Greenberg, 1927.
Action-filled tale of Confederate blockade runners.   5596

Morris, Gouverneur. Aladdin O'Brien. Century, 1902.
A northern story of the Civil War.   5597

Morrison, Gerry. Unvexed to the Sea. St. Martins, 1961.
Centered around the siege of Vicksburg and Sherman's
destructive march to the sea.   5598

Morrow, Honoré. Forever Free. Morrow, 1927. Lincoln's
household in the early years of the war harbored a lovely
southern spy. (followed by With Malice Toward None)   5599

_____. Great Captain. Morrow, 1935. Contains a trilogy
about Lincoln: Forever Free, With Malice Toward None,
and The Last Full Measure (see separate listings).   5600

_____. The Last Full Measure. Morrow, 1930. Dramatic account of the last few months of Lincoln's life; the Booth conspiracy and the assassination.   5601

_____. With Malice Toward None. Morrow, 1928. Lincoln's conflict with Charles Sumner in the last two years of the war. (followed by The Last Full Measure)   5602

Murfree, Mary Noailles. The Storm Centre. by Charles Egbert Craddock, pseud. Macmillan, 1905. The romance of a southern gentlewoman and a wounded Union soldier.   5603

Noble, Hollister. Woman With a Sword. Doubleday, 1948. About Anna Ella Carroll, whose military advice aided Lincoln's cabinet.   5604

Nolan, Jeannette C. Belle Boyd, Secret Agent. Messner, 1967. YA. A true story of a lovely gentlewoman who becomes a daring spy for the Confederacy.   5605

Norton, Alice Mary. Ride Proud, Rebel! by Andre Norton, pseud. World, 1961. YA. Impact of the war upon a young scout as his group of raiders hits the enemy again and again in the last days of the war.   5606

O'Connor, Richard. Company Q. Doubleday, 1957. Deranked officers are banded together to form a new company.   5607

_____. Guns of Chickamauga. Doubleday, 1955. Story of a Chicago newspaperman discharged from the Union Army. 5608

Oldham, Henry. The Man From Texas. Petersen, 1884. The daring exploits of a Confederate guerrilla general.   5609

O'Neal, Cothburn. Untold Glory. Crown, 1957. A Tennessee lady makes friends with Union officers to smuggle medical supplies into Memphis.   5610

Palmer, Bruce. Many Are the Hearts. S. & S., 1961. Four novelettes which tell the real, non-romantic, story of the war--"The Butcher's Bill," "My Brother's Keeper," "The Rooster," and "The Short Straw."   5611

Palmer, Frederick. The Vagabond. Harper, 1903. A romance of Virginia with the war in the background.   5612

Parrish, Randall. My Lady of the North. McClurg, 1904. Adventures of one of General Lee's couriers and action in the Shenandoah Valley.   5613

_____. My Lady of the South. McClurg, 1909. Romance defies a bitter feud between two families.   5614

_____. The Red Mist. McClurg, 1914. Adventures of a
Confederate spy in Maryland.   5615

Pennell, Joseph Stanley. History of Rome Hanks and Kindred
Matters. Scribner, 1944. In learning about his ancestors
a young man discovers much about America as well.   5616

Penney, Kate Mayhew. Cross Currents. Humphries, 1938.
Ohio teacher who marries a southerner comes to under-
stand the southern attitude.   5617

Perényi, Eleanor. The Bright Sword. Rinehart, 1955. Confederate General John Bell Hood, noble soldier of a lost
cause.   5618

Pulse, Charles K. John Bonwell. Farrar, 1952. Vivid story
of life in the Ohio Valley.   5619

Reising, Otto. The Quarrel. by Paul Strahl, pseud. Duell,
1947. A romantic triangle which lasts into the second generation.   5620

Rhodes, James A. and Dean Jauchius. Johnny Shiloh. Bobbs,
1959. Based on the adventures of the youngest soldier to
bear arms throughout a major war.   5621

Richardson, Norval. The Heart of Hope. Dodd, 1905. The
siege of Vicksburg is the main event of this novel.   5622

Roark, Garland. The Outlawed Banner. Doubleday, 1956.
Sea fighting, blockade running, and divided allegiance dur-
ing the War between the States.   5623

Roberts, Richard Emery. The Gilded Rooster. Putnam, 1947.
Conflicts of four people in an unfinished Wyoming fort attacked by the Sioux.   5624

Roberts, Walter Adolphe. Brave Mardi Gras. Bobbs, 1946.
Romance and spying in New Orleans seen from a southern
viewpoint.   5625

Robertson, Constance. The Golden Circle. Random, 1951.
The turmoil of the war reflected both in politics and in
people's lives in Ohio.   5626

_____. Salute to the Hero. Farrar, 1942. The story of
a clever, calculating general who convinced people he was
a hero.   5627

_____. The Unterrified. Holt, 1946. A story about a
group of northerners who dared advocate a peaceful settle-
ment with the South.   5628

Robertson, Don. By Antietam Creek. Prentice-Hall, 1960.
Tells of the men and strategy of one of the bloodiest
battles of the Civil War. 5629

_____. The River and the Wilderness. Doubleday, 1962.
Havoc wrought by the Civil War on both soldiers and civil-
ians, with accounts of the blood-bath of Fredericksburg,
Chancellorsville, and Hooker's Wilderness Campaign. 5630

_____. The Three Days. Prentice-Hall, 1959. Human as-
pect of the struggle between the blue and the gray at Gettysburg. (followed by By Antietam Creek) 5631

Rowell, Adelaide Corinne. On Jordan's Stormy Banks. Bobbs,
1948. About Sam Davis, Confederate scout, who was hanged
as a spy when he was twenty-one. 5632

Sage, William. The Claybornes. Houghton, 1902. The campaigns at Vicksburg and Richmond. 5633

Schachner, Nathan. By the Dim Lamps. Stokes, 1941. New
Orleans and surrounding Louisiana during and following
the war. 5634

Schaefer, Jack W. Company of Cowards. Houghton, 1957.
The "renegade" Company Q has a chance to prove its
bravery. 5635

Seabrook, Phoebe H. A Daughter of the Confederacy. Neale,
1906. Domestic life in the south during the war. 5636

Seawell, Molly Elliot. The Victory. Appleton, 1906. Family
differences caused by divided loyalties. 5637

Seifert, Shirley. Farewell, My General. Lippincott, 1954.
Romance of Flora Cooke and Jeb Stuart and his dramatic
military career. 5638

_____. Look to the Rose. Lippincott, 1960. Wartime ro-
mance of Nelly Gordon, whose daughter, Juliette Low, was
to found the Girl Scouts in the United States. 5639

_____. The Wayfarer. Mill, 1938. A wanderer's adven-
tures with whales, horses, and women. 5640

Sherburne, James. The Way to Fort Pillow. Houghton, 1972.
Hacey Miller, teacher at Berea College, fights with the
Union as the war splits the loyalties of Kentuckians. 5641

Shuster, George Nauman. Look Away. Macmillan, 1939. The
struggle to preserve a marriage beset by conflicting loyalties
in the war. 5642

Simons, Katherine D. M.   The Running Thread.   by Drayton
Mayrant, pseud. Appleton, 1949. An Irish girl falls in
love with a southerner during the war.   5643

Sinclair, Harold. The Cavalryman. Harper, 1958. The
army's expedition against the marauding Sioux Indians in
the Dakotas.   5644

_____. Horse Soldiers. Harper, 1956. A tingling tale
based on the sixteen-day Grierson's Raid. (followed by
The Cavalryman)   5645

Sinclair, Upton. Theirs Be the Guilt. Twayne, 1959. (pub.
in 1904 as Manassas) Events before and during the early
part of the war, including the operation of the Underground
Railroad.   5646

Slaughter, Frank G. In a Dark Garden. Doubleday, 1946.
Young southern surgeon treats the wounded of both sides. 5647

_____. Lorena. Doubleday, 1959. A lovely, courageous
girl prepares to defend her home from the dreaded Sherman
and his march to the sea.   5648

_____. Storm Haven. Doubleday, 1953. Florida cattle
drive during the Civil War.   5649

Smith, Chard Powers. Artillery of Time. Scribner, 1939.
A warm story of family life in upper New York state. (followed by Ladies Day)   5650

Smith, Francis Hopkinson. The Tides of Barnegat. Scribner,
1906. A tale of the everyday life of New Jersey fishermen.   5651

Stacton, David. The Judges of the Secret Court. Pantheon,
1961. Reminiscences of Edwin Booth concerning the per-
sonalities and issues connected with his brother's assassination of President Lincoln.   5652

Stern, Philip Van Doren. The Man Who Killed Lincoln. Random, 1939. A report of the assassination in a thorough
study of John Wilkes Booth.   5653

Sterne, Emma Gelders. No Surrender. Duffield, 1932. Efforts of a southern woman to manage her war-ravaged Alabama plantation.   5654

Stevenson, Janet. Weep No More. Viking, 1957. The mystery
of Elizabeth Van Lew who, protected in her role as the piti-
able "Crazy Bet," worked as a spy for the Union.   5655

Stover, Herbert Elisha. Copperhead Moon. Dodd, 1952.

Sabotage attempts of deserters from the Union Army.   5656

Straight, Michael W. A Very Small Remnant. Knopf, 1963.
The inconsistent military treatment of Indians results in
the notorious Sand Creek Massacre of unsuspecting Chey-
ennes in 1864.   5657

Street, James Howell. By Valour and Arms. Dial, 1944.
The naval war on the Mississippi in which the Confederate
iron-clad, the Arkansas, proved so effective.   5658

_____. Captain Little Ax. Lippincott, 1956. Military ex-
ploits of the young son of a Confederate soldier killed at
Shiloh.   5659

_____. Tap Roots. Dial, 1942. A family in Mississippi
maintains its anti-slavery convictions.   5660

Stribling, Thomas S. The Forge. Doubleday, 1931. A
middle-class Alabama family during and after the war.
(followed by The Store)   5661

Tiernan, Mary Spear. Jack Horner. Fenno, 1890. Romance
in Richmond during the final year of the war.   5662

Toepfer, Ray Grant. Scarlet Guidon. Coward, 1958. The
common soldier in the war, reflected in the experiences
of an Alabama company.   5663

_____. The Second Face of Valor. Chilton, 1966. YA.
Both courage and maturity are needed by a young man who
fights for a losing cause and by the girl who loves him.   5664

Toepperwein, Herman. Rebel in Blue. Morrow, 1963. A
Union banker poses as a Southerner in Texas, and does
his part in defeating the Confederacy.   5665

Tracy, Don. On the Midnight Tide. Dial, 1957. Exploits
of two brothers who are blockade runners out of North Carolina.
                                                            5666

Wagner, Constance. Ask My Brother. Harper, 1959. Revolves around a cold woman who is deceptively lady-like.   5667

Waldman, Emerson. Beckoning Ridge. Holt, 1940. Effects
of the war on a farming community in the Virginia mountains.   5668

Walker, Margaret. Jubilee. Houghton, 1966. The daughter
of a slave and a plantation owner struggles to obtain a better
life for herself and her children (based on the life of the
author's great-grandmother).   5669

Wallace, Willard M. The Raiders. Little, 1970. Adventures

of a Union spy aboard the Confederate raider <u>Alabama</u>
during the Civil War.   5670

Warren, Robert Penn. <u>Band of Angels</u>. Random, 1955.
Problems of a mulatto girl sold into slavery.   5671

———. <u>Wilderness</u>. Random House, 1961. A Bavarian
who comes to fight for the freedom of humanity in the Union
Army is rejected because of lameness, but finds a place in
the army's supply column.   5672

Webber, Everett and Olga. <u>Bound Girl</u>. Dutton, 1949. Life
of Rebecca Whitman on the border between Missouri and
Kansas.   5673

Weber, William. <u>Josh</u>. McGraw, 1969. Riotous adventures
of a sixteen-year-old southern boy in search of his horse,
which has been stolen by Yankees.   5674

Webster, Henry K. <u>Traitor or Loyalist</u>. Macmillan, 1904.
Concerns the Union blockade on cotton shipments which
caused great financial hardship to the South.   5675

West, Jessamyn. <u>The Friendly Persuasion</u>. Avon Bks., 1971,
c.1940. Though they are peace-loving Quakers, Jess and
Eliza Birdwell are both strong-willed people and frequently
disagree.   5676

Wheelwright, Jere Hungerford. <u>Gray Captain</u>. Scribner,
1954. A vivid account of the Army of Northern Virginia. 5677

Whitney, Phyllis A. <u>The Quicksilver Pool</u>. Appleton, 1955.
A loveless marriage and its tortuous course.   5678

Williams, Ben Ames. <u>House Divided</u>. Houghton, 1947. A
long story of Confederate aristocrats related to Lincoln. 5679

Williams, Churchill. <u>The Captain</u>. Lothrop, 1903. The story
of Grant before his assignment to the Army of the Potomac.
                                                                   5680

Williams, Dorothy Jeanne. <u>The Confederate Fiddle</u>. by J.R.
Williams, pseud. Prentice-Hall, 1962. YA. Young boy
goes on a wagon train to sell cotton and bring supplies to
Confederate troops.   5681

Wilson, William E. <u>The Raiders</u>. Rinehart, 1955. An Ohio
River border town is attacked by Confederate Morgan's
Raiders.   5682

Winslow, William Henry. <u>Southern Buds and Sons of War</u>.
Clark, 1907. South Carolina during the upheavals of war. 5683

Wood, Lydia C. <u>The Haydocks' Testimony</u>. Headley, 1891.

Experiences of Quakers in the South as they follow their
teachings against war and slavery. 5684

Yerby, Frank. Captain Rebel. Dial, 1956. A New Orleans
gambler runs the Union blockade. 5685

Young, Rosamond McPherson. The Spy With Two Hats. Mc-
Kay, 1966. YA. A thrilling story of a man who worked
as a Pinkerton operative during the Civil War. 5686

Young, Stark. So Red the Rose. Scribner, 1934. Mississippi
plantation social life before and even during the war. 5687

Zara, Louis. Rebel Run. Crown, 1951. Capture of a train
by Federal troops in an effort to cut communications. 5688

e) Reconstruction and Expansion (1865-1900)

Adams, Andy. The Log of a Cowboy. Houghton, 1903. An
accurate account of a cattle drive from Texas to the Blackfoot Agency in Montana. 5689

_____. The Outlet. Houghton, 1905. A cattle drive in the
1880s, as a rancher delivers the cattle he has sold. 5690

Adams, Henry. Democracy. Holt, 1880. A novel of politics
in the nation's capital. 5691

Adams, Samuel Hopkins. Tenderloin. Random, 1959. New
York's rowdy tenderloin area in the Gay Nineties as seen
by a reporter for The Police Gazette. 5692

Adleman, Robert H. The Bloody Benders. Stein & Day, 1970.
About a family of outlaws who lived in southeastern Kansas
in the late nineteenth century, based on fact, legend, and
speculation. 5693

Alcott, Louisa May. Jo's Boys. Collier Bks., 1962. YA.
(first pub. in 18--) The continued story of the boys of
Plumfield and the children of the "little women" as they
become young men and women. (completes trilogy) 5694

_____. Little Men. Macmillan, 1963. YA. (first pub. in
18--) Jo and her husband, Professor Bhaer, establish a
school for boys. (followed by Jo's Boys) 5695

_____. An Old-Fashioned Girl. Grosset, 1961, c.1911.
YA. (first pub. 1897) A country girl visits friends in the
city. 5696

Aldrich, Bess Streeter. A Lantern in Her Hand. Appleton,
1956. (first pub. in 1928) A courageous young bride faces

with her husband the trials and hardships of a covered
wagon trip to Nebraska and of a homestead there.   5697

_____. The Lieutenant's Lady. Appleton, 1942. Experi-
ences of a soldier's young wife at an army outpost on the
Missouri River, based on an actual diary.   5698

Alexander, Holmes Moss. American Nabob. Harper, 1939. A
story of Virginia and West Virginia in the rebuilding period
following the Civil War.   5699

Allen, Henry. Custer's Last Stand. by Will Henry, pseud.
Chilton, 1966. YA. Carries the story from Custer's de-
struction of the Indian camp on the Washita (1868) to the
Battle of the Little Big Horn (1876) and the death of Crazy
Horse (1877).   5700

_____. From Where the Sun Now Stands. by Will Henry,
pseud. Random House, 1960. When peaceful negotiations
fail, Chief Joseph leads the Nez Percé Indians in an orderly
retreat through the Northwest.   5701

_____. Mackenna's Gold. by Will Henry, pseud. Bantam
Bks., 1969, c.1963. Competitive quest of an abandoned
Arizona gold mine between a half-breed and a cowboy who
learned of the mine from an old, dying Apache.   5702

_____. Niño. by Clay Fisher, pseud. Morrow, 1961.
A story based on the legend of the "Apache Kid."   5703

_____. No Survivors. by Will Henry, pseud. Random
House, 1950. Custer's battles with Indians come to a cli-
max in the tragedy of the Little Big Horn.   5704

_____. Sons of the Western Frontier. by Will Henry,
pseud. Chilton, 1966. YA. A group of short stories
based on actual historical people and events.   5705

_____. Yellowstone Kelly. by Clay Fisher, pseud.
Houghton, 1957. The activities of an Indian scout in the
West in the 1870s.   5706

Ames, Francis H. That Callahan Spunk. Doubleday, 1965.
Ordeals of Irish homesteaders who move from New England
to the Montana frontier, recounted by a younger member. 5707

Anderson, Ada Woodruff. The Heart of the Ancient Firs.
Little, 1908. Life in the Northwest after the completion
of the Northern Pacific Railway.   5708

Andrews, Annulet. Melissa Starke. Dutton, 1935. The adjustment of southerners to the new standards which came
to prevail after the war.   5709

Appel, David. Comanche. World, 1951. The story of
Custer's Last Stand told by the horse, Comanche, who sur-
vived the battle.   5710

Arnold, Elliott. Broken Arrow. Duell, 1954. YA. The
friendship between the Apache Chief Cochise and the Amer-
ican scout Tom Jeffords.   5711

Arthur, Herbert. Freedom Run. by Arthur Herbert, pseud.
Rinehart, 1951. Californians repel a Russian invasion after
the U.S. purchase of Alaska.   5712

Aschmann, Helen Tann. Connie Bell, M.D. Dodd, 1963. YA.
A young woman desirous of becoming a medical doctor is
confronted by deep-rooted prejudices and strenuous opposi-
tion.   5713

Atherton, Gertrude. Senator North. Lane, 1900. Washington
in the late 1890s showing political discussions during the
Spanish-American War.   5714

Aydelotte, Dora. Across the Prairie. Appleton, 1941. A
story of small town people and events in Kansas in the
1890s.   5715

_____. Long Furrows. Appleton, 1935. A narrative of
everyday life in a midwestern rural community in the
1890s.   5716

_____. Measure of a Man. Appleton, 1942. Country store-
keeper and prominent citizen of a small Illinois town near the
end of the century.   5717

_____. Run of the Stars. Appleton, 1940. Friction be-
tween the ranchers who want free range and the "nesters"
who fence their farmland.   5718

_____. Trumpets Calling. Appleton, 1938. A good story
of Oklahoma homesteading in the newly-opened Cherokee
Strip.   5719

Ballard, Willis Todhunter. Westward the Monitor's Roar.
Doubleday, 1963. A Western which tells of the California
mining industry in the late 1800s.   5720

Bandelier, A.F. The Delight Makers. Dodd, 1890. The life
and activities of the Pueblo Indians of New Mexico, based
on ethnological study.   5721

Barber, Elsie Oakes. Hunt for Heaven. Macmillan, 1950.
Community settled in Pennsylvania by a church group
from Chicago.   5722

Barnett, Donald R. A Cross of Gold. Dorrance, 1939.
Frontier Montana during the second half of the nineteenth
century.   5723

Barry, Jane. Maximilian's Gold. Doubleday, 1966. A party
of six, including Missourians and Confederate veterans, set
out on a long quest for gold.   5724

_____. A Shadow of Eagles. Doubleday, 1964. A loyal
cattle-drive boss who loves the ranch and the wilful daughter
of the Spanish rancher figure in this novel of Texas.   5725

_____. A Time in the Sun. Doubleday, 1962. Experiences
of a colonel's daughter who is captured by the Indians during
the Apache campaigns of the 1870s.   5726

Bass, Milton R. Jory. Putnam, 1969. A youth, after killing
the man who had murdered his father, goes to Texas and
earns his way with his guns.   5727

Bean, Amelia. The Feud. Doubleday, 1960. Exciting
account of early Arizona's Graham-Tewksbury feud.   5728

_____. Time for Outrage. Doubleday, 1967. Based on
warfare between local frontiersmen and corrupt officials in
Lincoln County, New Mexico, in 1878.   5729

Beebe, Elswyth Thane. Ever After. by Elswyth Thane.
Duell, 1945. Romance which takes place in Virginia, New
York, England, and Cuba.   5730

Beer, Thomas. Sandoval. Knopf, 1924. A charming scoundrel
from the deep south fascinates New York society.   5731

Bindloss, Harold. The Cattle-Baron's Daughter. Stokes,
1906. The west in the 1870's, when homesteaders were
fencing in parts of former grazing lands.   5732

Binns, Archie. You Rolling River. Scribner, 1947. The
town of Astoria on the Pacific coast at the mouth of the
Columbia River.   5733

Birney, Hoffman. The Dice of God. Holt, 1956. A novel
based on Custer's Seventh Cavalry and its stand at the
Little Big Horn.   5734

Bisno, Beatrice. Tomorrow's Bread. Liveright, 1938. Experiences of a Russian Jewish immigrant in late nineteenth
century Chicago.   5735

Blackburn, Thomas Wakefield. A Good Day to Die. McKay,
1967. Ideals of the Sioux Indians and their last desperate
stand against the encroachments of the advancing white

man, 1890-91.   5736

Blacker, Irwin R., ed. The Old West in Fiction. Obolensky,
1961. A collection of good short stories and excerpts with
a preface concerning literature of the West.   5737

Blake, Forrester. Wilderness Passage. Random, 1953.
Westward expansion into Utah--wagon trains, fur trappers,
and the struggling Mormon settlers.   5738

Bojer, Johan. The Emigrants. (tr.) Appleton, 1925. Trials
of Norwegian settlers in the Red River Valley, North Dakota.   5739

Bontemps, Arna. Chariot in the Sky. Holt, 1951. YA. The
Jubilee Singers, former slave children, perform to raise
money for Fisk University in Tennessee.   5740

Borland, Hal. The Seventh Winter. Lippincott, 1959. A
cattleman's struggle against fierce weather in pioneer
Colorado.   5741

_____. When the Legends Die. Lippincott, 1963. An In-
dian who has experienced both native life close to nature
and that of bronc-busting white men is forced to choose between them.   5742

Bosworth, Allan Rucker. Storm Tide. Harper, 1965. Romance aboard a New England whaling vessel during adventures in the Pacific, when the owner, a young girl, sails
with the ship.   5743

Breneman, Mary Worthy, pseud. of Mary Worthy Thurston and
Muriel Breneman. The Land They Possessed. Macmillan,
1956. Americanization of homesteaders from the Ukraine.
                                                                5744
Bretherton, Vivien. Rock and the Wind. Dutton, 1942.
A girl from Cornwall comes to love her new home in wide,
wild America.   5745

Brink, Carol. Buffalo Coat. Macmillan, 1944. A story of
the doctors of Opportunity, Idaho, in the 1890s.   5746

_____. Snow in the River. Macmillan, 1964. Three
brothers leave their home in Scotland to seek their fortunes
in the great American Northwest.   5747

Brooks, Mansfield. The Newell Fortune. Lane, 1906. A
young American investigates the origin of his inherited fortune, and becomes involved in the slave trade.   5748

Brown, Dee. Yellowhorse. Houghton, 1956. The cavalry on
the western frontier uses a balloon against the Sioux.   5749

Brown, Harry P. The Stars in Their Courses. Knopf,
1960. A Western which involves water rights, romance,
and gunplay.   5750

Buck, Charles Neville. The Code of the Mountains. Watt,
1915. Life in both Kentucky and the Philippines during
the Spanish-American War.   5751

Burchard, Peter. Stranded. Coward, 1967. YA. A Scots
sailor finds New York a surprisingly wicked city in 1875. 5752

Burnett, William Riley. Adobe Walls. Knopf, 1953. "A
novel of the last Apache rising."   5753

_____. Mi Amigo. Knopf, 1959. A story of one of the
Southwest's most notorious killers, Billy the Kid.   5754

_____. Saint Johnson. Dial, 1930. A man's desire to be-
come sheriff of Tombstone, Arizona, is thwarted by his
thirst for revenge.   5755

Busch, Niven. Duel in the Sun. Morrow, 1944. A vigorous
western story of a part-Indian orphan girl.   5756

Cable, George Washington. John March, Southerner. Scribner, 1894. Financial schemes and political quarrels in a
southern town suffering from Civil War ravages.   5757

Caldwell, James Fitz James. The Stranger. Neale, 1907.
A schoolteacher from the North in the Reconstruction
South.   5758

Caldwell, Taylor, pseud. for Janet Taylor Caldwell Reback
and Marcus Reback. Melissa. Pyramid Bks., 1971, c.1948.
A girl, handicapped by the warped set of values given her by
her dead father, tries to find a normal life with her devoted
husband.   5759

_____. A Prologue to Love. Doubleday, 1961. A daughter
follows her father's belief that money is paramount and becomes a wealthy, miserable, unloved woman--until she be-
gins to see her error.   5760

_____. (full name: Janet Taylor Caldwell). This
Side of Innocence. Scribner, 1946. Family discord when
an adventuress married to one brother falls in love with
another.   5761

Capps, Benjamin. Sam Chance. Duell, 1965. A Confederate
veteran establishes himself as a successful rancher in Texas and helps in the economic and political development of
the state.   5762

_____. The Trail to Ogallala. Duell, 1964. The challenge of driving three thousand spooky cattle from Texas to Nebraska brings out the best and the worst in men.   5763

_____. The White Man's Road. Harper, 1969. Dilemma of a young half-breed who loves his Comanche mother and admires his white father.   5764

Carr, Harriet H. Against the Wind. Macmillan, 1955. How a family of determined homesteaders persevered in proving up their land in North Dakota at the turn of the century.   5765

Carr, John Dickson. Papa La-Bas. Harper, 1968. A murder mystery in New Orleans features interesting local characters, including a real person, Judah P. Benjamin, active in the Southern cause during the war.   5766

Carson, Katharine. Mrs. Pennington. Putnam, 1939. Small-town life in Kansas during a chautauqua program one summer.   5767

Carter, Isabel Hopestill. Shipmates. Scott, 1934. A sea captain's wife scorns security ashore to sail with her husband.
                                                                         5768

Castle, Marian. Silver Answer. Morrow, 1960. Melissa's second marriage is threatened when her supposedly dead first husband reappears in a Colorado mining town.   5769

Chay, Marie. Pilgrim's Pride. Dodd, 1961. Seeking opportunity and a new life in a new world, an Italian immigrant family takes up mining in Colorado.   5770

Cheney, Brainard. Lightwood. Houghton, 1939. Difficulties facing southerners trying to hold and rebuild their lands after the war.   5771

Cheshire, Gifford Paul. Thunder on the Mountain. Doubleday, 1960. Chief Joseph leads his Nez Percé Indians on a long trek northward in search of a new home, after being driven from their land.   5772

Chester, George Randolph. Get-Rich-Quick Wallingford. Burt, 1907. A fast-talking swindler aspires to profit at others' expense.   5773

Chevalier, Elizabeth. Drivin' Woman. Macmillan, 1942. A Virginia belle, a river boat gambler, and the rising tobacco industry in the post-Civil War era.   5774

Christie, Robert. The Trembling Land. Doubleday, 1959. Psychological novel of a man of the west who flees a revenging gun for twenty years.   5775

Churchill, Winston. Mr. Crewe's Career. Macmillan, 1908.
The powerful political influence of great financial concerns
such as railroads.   5776

Clark, Walter Van Tilburg. The Ox-Bow Incident. Random,
1940. Rough-and-ready cowboy life in Nevada about
1885.   5777

Clarke, William Kendall. Tomfool's Pike. Holt, 1960. A
derelict engineer assumes leadership in moving a town
threatened by expansion of the New York watershed system.
                                                                      5778
Coburn, Walt. Barb Wire. Century, 1931. Conflict between
cattle ranchers, who wanted open range, and sheep raisers,
who built fences.   5779

Cockrell, Marian. The Revolt of Sarah Perkins. McKay,
1965. A plain New England spinster, chosen because of
her apparent docility, surprises herself and her employers
with her vigorous defense of her ideals.   5780

Coker, Elizabeth Boatwright. India Allan. Dutton, 1953.
Colorful narrative of South Carolina and the hated carpet-
bag government.   5781

Constant, Alberta. Oklahoma Run. Crowell, 1955. Pioneer
life at the opening of the Oklahoma Territory.   5782

Cooke, David C. Post of Honor. Putnam, 1958. An isolated
fort in the Wild West faces an Indian uprising.   5783

Coolidge, Dane. The Fighting Danites. Dutton, 1934. Conflict between the U.S. government and the Mormons in
Utah.   5784

_____. Hidden Water. McClurg, 1910. Conflict between
cattlemen and sheepmen for grazing rights in Arizona.   5785

_____. Long Rope. Dutton, 1935. Long Rope Bowman
backs up his boast of being the best cowboy in the West.   5786

Cooper, Courtney Ryley. The Last Frontier. Little, 1923.
The opening of the West and the building of the Kansas-
Pacific Railroad.   5787

_____. Oklahoma. Little, 1926. The Oklahoma land rush
in 1889 when the Territory was opened to homesteaders.   5788

Corbett, Elizabeth. The Far Down. Appleton, 1939. The
family of a Civil War veteran after his death.   5789

_____. The Langworthy Family. Appleton, 1937. Family
life in the Midwest toward the end of the nineteenth century. 5790

_____. Mr. and Mrs. Meigs. Appleton, 1940. A sympathetic, entertaining story of family life.   5791

_____. She Was Carrie Eaton. Appleton, 1938. Quiet story of domestic life in a small midwestern town.   5792

Corcoran, William. Golden Horizons. Macrae Smith, 1937. Early settlers in western Kansas.   5793

Corle, Edwin. Billy the Kid. Duell, 1953. A story which essays to understand the youthful desperado who committed twenty-one murders.   5794

Crabb, Alfred Leland. Breakfast at the Hermitage. Bobbs, 1945. A novel of Nashville's rebuilding with emphasis on beauty in architecture.   5795

_____. Reunion at Chattanooga. Bobbs, 1950. Yankee ex-soldiers return as peacetime visitors to Grandma Blevins and her family in post-war Kentucky.   5796

_____. Supper at the Maxwell House. Bobbs, 1943. A novel of recaptured Nashville and of the opening of a new restaurant.   5797

Crane, William D. Andrew Johnson. Dodd, 1968. YA. A story of Andrew Johnson, who had the difficult task of following Lincoln as President after the assassination.   5798

Croy, Homer. Lady From Colorado. Duell, 1957. An Irish girl goes to the West as a washerwoman.   5799

Cullum, Ridgwell. The One Way Trail. Jacobs, 1911. Frontier life on a Montana ranch.   5800

_____. The Watchers of the Plains. Jacobs, 1909. Indian uprising in the Nebraska and Dakota region in the 1870s.   5801

Culp, John H. Born of the Sea. Sloane, 1959. A Texas cowboy participates in cattle drives from Texas to Abilene, Kansas, in the 1870s.   5802

_____. The Bright Feathers. Holt, 1965. This novel portrays vividly some of the widely divergent people who founded the Oklahoma Territory.   5803

_____. Timothy Baines. Holt, 1969. Assorted characters in the still wild American West following the Civil War.   5804

_____. A Whistle in the Wind. Holt, 1968. Renegade Indians and whites live in close, not always harmonious contact in a Comanchero camp in Texas.   5805

Cunningham, John M. Warhorse. Macmillan, 1956. "A
  novel of the Old West; ranch life in Montana."   5806

Dahl, Borghild. Karen. Dutton, 1947. YA. A Norwegian
  immigrant in the 1870s rises to a position of social influence in her community.   5807

Davis, Christopher. A Peep Into the Twentieth Century.
  Harper, 1971. A psychological novel of the personal moral
  conflict and the debated feasibility of the method, attending
  the first execution in the electric chair in 1890.   5808

Davis, Clyde Brion. Jeremy Bell. Rinehart, 1947. Experiences of two boys working in a southern lumber camp.   5809

Davis, Hazel H. General Jim. Bethany Pr., 1958. A fictional biography of the twentieth President of the United States,
  James Garfield.   5810

Deasy, Mary. The Corioli Affair. Little, 1954. Tragic romance of a dashing river captain and a young Irish girl. 5811

Derleth, August. The Shadow in the Glass. Duell, 1963.
  Nelson Dewey rises by hard work to become Governor of
  early Wisconsin, but is disappointed in his married life,
  for his wife has more political ambition than he.   5812

_____. Still Is the Summer Night. Scribner, 1937. The
  strong love of a Wisconsin family for their small home
  town on the rolling Sac Prairie.   5813

Dieter, William. The White Land. Knopf, 1970. Clash between a superstitious Montana cattleman and a preacher's
  son who becomes a cowboy.   5814

Dixon, Thomas. The Clansman. Doubleday, Page, 1905.
  The rise to strength of the Ku Klux Klan--the Invisible
  Empire. (followed by The Traitor)   5815

_____. The Leopard's Spots. Wessels, 1908. First book
  in a series about racial conditions in the South following the
  Civil War. (followed by The Clansman)   5816

_____. The Traitor. Doubleday, 1907. The decline and
  dissolution of the Ku Klux Klan.   5817

Doctorow, E. L. Welcome to Hard Times. S. & S., 1960.
  The efforts to maintain law and order in the frontier town
  of Hard Times, Dakota Territory.   5818

Dohrman, Richard. The Last of the Maidens. Holt, 1969. A
  man with larceny on his mind masquerades as a minister
  (with papers stolen from a dead man) in a small southern

town. 5819

Dowdey, Clifford. Last Night the Nightingale. Doubleday,
1962. A love tangle during Reconstruction days in Virginia
on a plantation named Bellevue. 5820

_____. Sing for a Penny. Little, 1941. The financial suc-
cess and social failure of a man who put fortune ahead of all
else. 5821

Downing, J. Hyatt. Hope of Living. Putnam, 1939. A courageous wife takes over the management of a Dakota farm. 5822

_____. Sioux City. Putnam, 1940. An ambitious young
man during the growth of Sioux City. 5823

Drago, Harry Sinclair. Montana Road. Morrow, 1935.
Settlement of the Dakota Territory and efforts of the Indians
to save their land. 5824

_____. Singing Lariat. by Will Ermine, pseud. Morrow,
1939. A Civil War veteran finds bitter fighting as he tries
to stop the sale of whisky and guns to the Indians. 5825

Ducharme, Jacques. The Delusson Family. Funk, 1939.
Warm, simple account of a French-Canadian family in
New England. 5826

Duncan, Thomas W. The Labyrinth. Doubleday, 1967. A
great train wreck in Iowa in the later nineteenth century
occasions a retrospective view of the lives of various passengers. 5827

Dykeman, Wilma. The Tall Woman. Holt, 1962. A strong
North Carolina mountain woman struggles to provide for
herself and her loved ones in harsh post-Civil War days. 5828

East, Fred. Ghost Gold. by Tom West, pseud. Dutton,
1950. Shooting-packed search for $40,000 stolen from the
Sagebrush Bank. 5829

Eberhart, Mignon G. The Cup, the Blade or the Gun. Random
House, 1961. A murder mystery concerning a Connecticut
girl who marries a Confederate officer and encounters hostility and suspicion on his family plantation. 5830

Ehle, John. The Road. Harper, 1967. Natural and human
obstacles confronted by an entrepreneur who tries to build
a railroad through the North Carolina mountains. 5831

Elston, Allan Vaughan. Beyond the Bitterroots. Lippincott,
1960. Gun fighting and vengeance in the Territory of Idaho
in the 1880s. 5832

_____. Forbidden Valley. Lippincott, 1955. A Western
about Wyoming in the 1880s, when train robberies and
gunplay were not uncommon.   5833

_____. Treasure Coach from Deadwood. Lippincott, 1962.
Gold shipments from prosperous mines made tempting tar-
gets for thieves in the wild, lonely Black Hills of South
Dakota.   5834

Elwood, Muriel. Against the Tide. Bobbs, 1950. The marriage of a California rancher and a Spanish girl.   5835

Erdman, Loula. The Edge of Time. Dodd, 1950. A young
married couple homestead in the Texas panhandle before the
advent of the railroad.   5836

_____. The Far Journey. Dodd, 1955. A young mother's
journey by covered wagon to join her husband in Texas.   5837

Ertz, Susan. The Proselyte. Appleton, 1933. Marriage in
London of a Mormon missionary and the romantic crisis
caused by the doctrine of polygamy after the couple returns
to Utah.   5838

Espey, John Jenkins. The Anniversaries. Harcourt, 1963.
Memories of a successful businessman who found his fortune
in southern California in the second half of the nineteenth
century.   5839

Evans; Muriel. Wagons to Tucson. by Ed Newsom, pseud.
Little, 1954. A wagon train journey through Indian lands
to Tucson.   5840

Evarts, Hal. The Shaggy Legion. Little, 1930. Colorful,
realistic picture of the far West and the diminishing of the
buffalo herds.   5841

_____. Tumbleweeds. Little, 1923. The opening and settling
of the Cherokee Strip of Oklahoma.   5842

Fairbank, Janet Ayer. The Smiths. Bobbs, 1925. Parallels
the rise of a family with the growth of a city, Chicago.   5843

Faralla, Dana. Circle of Trees. Lippincott, 1955. Immigrants from Denmark survive a disastrous first year in
building a home in Minnesota.   5844

Fast, Howard. The American. Duell, 1946. Based on the
career of an Illinois politician, John Peter Altgeld.   5845

_____. Freedom Road. Duell, 1944. Thought provoking
novel of race relations and the Ku Klux Klan in the South. 5846

_____. The Last Frontier. Duell, 1941. Cheyenne In-
dians, treated unfairly on an Oklahoma reservation, defy
the army and return to Montana.   5847

Ferber, Edna. Cimarron. Grosset, 1929. The growth of a
town in the newly opened Oklahoma Territory.   5848

_____. Saratoga Trunk. Doubleday, 1941. Society life of
a Texan and an adventuress in New Orleans and Saratoga. 5849

_____. Show Boat. Fawcett, 1971, c.1926. Pictures a
passing aspect of American theater--a Mississippi River
showboat.   5850

Ferber, Richard. The Hostiles. Dell, 1958. The resistance
of the Sioux to reservation·life before the Battle of the Little
Big Horn.   5851

Fergusson, Harvey. The Conquest of Don Pedro. Morrow,
1954. A New York businessman finds health, marriage,
and success in New Mexico.   5852

Finney, Gertrude E. Tne Plums Hang High. Longmans, 1955.
An inexperienced young couple from England learn the arts
of farming and housekeeping in the Midwest.   5853

Fish, Rachel Ann. Running Iron. Coward, 1957. Southern
settlers adjust to life in wild, raw Wyoming Territory.   5854

Fisher, Richard. Judgment in July. Doubleday, 1962. Deadwood, South Dakota, just after Custer's fall, lived in the
shadow of Indian attack and of profiteering from unscrupulous fortune hunters.   5855

Fitzgerald, John D. Uncle Will and the Fitzgerald Curse.
Bobbs, 1961. Tne adventures of a fascinating man who refuses to take seriously a six-generation-old family curse as
he seeks his fortune in the growing West.   5856

Flynn, Robert. North to Yesterday. Knopf, 1967. Quixotic
attempt of an old Texas storekeeper to drive a herd of
cattle north to Trails End with a crew of misfits.   5857

Foote, Mary. The Chosen Valley. Houghton, 1892. Two men
engaged in a system of irrigation in the west.   5858

_____. Coeur d'Alêne. Houghton, 1894. Based on the
Coeur d'Alêne labor riots of 1892 in the west.   5859

Ford, James Lauren. Hot Corn Ike. Dutton, 1923. A picture
of New York City in the tale of a street peddler and minor
politician.   5860

Ford, Paul Leicester. The Honorable Peter Sterling. Holt,
1894. The power and influence of politics, honest and
corrupt, in a democratic society.   5861

Foreman, Leonard L. Decision at Little Big Horn. Belmont
Bks., 1971. (pub. in 1942 as The Renegade) A white man
raised by the Sioux finds his loyalties questioned at the
Battle of the Little Big Horn.   5862

Fox, John, Jr. Crittenden. Scribner, 1905. Participation in
the Cuban War helps a southerner find his own courage and
his loyalty to the United States.   5863

_____. The Kentuckians. Scribner, 1898. Political rivalry
between the Cumberland mountaineers and the lowland landowners.   5864

_____. The Trail of the Lonesome Pine. Scribner, 1908.
Hill folk and town folk differences in Kentucky and Virginia
during the process of industrialization.   5865

Fox, Norman Arnold. Rope the Wind. Dodd, 1958. Chief
Joseph and the migration of the Nez Percé Indians through
the Northwest.   5866

Frederic, Harold. The Lawton Girl. Scribner, 1890. Political, social, and commercial life in a small manufacturing
town.   5867

_____. Seth's Brother's Wife. Scribner, 1887. New York
State country life--farming, journalism, voting.   5868

French, Alice. Expiation. by Octave Thanet, pseud. Scribner, 1890. Reconstruction in Arkansas.   5869

Friermood, Elisabeth. Focus the Bright Land. Doubleday,
1967. YA. A girl and her two brothers are itinerant photog-
raphers in Indiana and Illinois in 1881.   5870

_____. Hoosier Heritage. Doubleday, 1954. YA. An Indi-
ana girl goes by covered wagon to Missouri, where she becomes a schoolteacher, although her family continues on to
Kansas.   5871

_____. Jo Allen's Predicament. Doubleday, 1959. YA.
An orphaned girl is housekeeper for a demanding old lady
in Missouri in the 1800s.   5872

Gabriel, Gilbert W. Brownstone Front. Century, 1924. Re-
vealing picture of New York in the 1890s.   5873

Gage, Joseph H. The Beckoning Hills. Winston, 1951. YA.
A story of Italian immigrants to California and their work in

the vineyards and lumber camps.   5874

Garland, Hamlin.   The Moccasin Ranch.   Harper, 1909.   Hardships of immigrant settlers who built homes on the wild Dakota prairie.   5875

_____.   A Spoil of Office.   Arena Pub., 1892.   The politics
of Iowa, Kansas, and Nebraska in the 1870s.   5876

Garth, David.   Fire on the Wind.   Putnam, 1951.   Action-
packed story of the timber country of Michigan.   5877

Gass, William H.   Omensetter's Luck.   New American Lib.,
1966.   The naive natural goodness of a newcomer stirs comment in a small Ohio town where he settles in the 1890s.   5878

Gerson, Noel B.   TR.   Doubleday, 1970.   Biographical novel
concerning the dramatic, forceful Theodore Roosevelt, twenty-
sixth President of the U. S.   5879

Giles, Janice Holt.   Hannah Fowler.   Houghton, 1956.   A
tender love story of pioneer settlers in Kentucky.   5880

Gipson, Fred.   Savage Sam.   Harper, 1962.   YA.   Thrilling
story of children captured by Indians and rescued with the
help of the faithful dog, Sam.   5881

Glasgow, Ellen.   The Deliverance.   Doubleday, Page, 1904.
Post-bellum life on a large Virginia tobacco plantation.   5882

_____.   The Romance of a Plain Man.   Macmillan, 1909.
The story of a "plain man" of Virginia who dares defy society to love a woman of the "aristocracy."   5883

_____.   The Voice of the People.   Doubleday, Page, 1900.
The rich scenery of Virginia is the setting for this story of
political ambition.   5884

Glidden, Frederick.   And the Wind Blows Free.   by Luke
Short, pseud.   Macmillan, 1945.   Free enterprise of cattlemen in early Oklahoma prior to statehood.   5885

Gordon, Armistead.   Ommirandy.   Scribner, 1917.   Story of
an ex-slave who remained with his former master after the
war.   5886

Grey, Zane.   Heritage of the Desert.   Harper, 1910.   Mormons, Navajos, and cattle thieves on the Arizona desert.   5887

_____.   Riders of the Purple Sage.   Harper, 1912.   The
Mormon settlements in Utah.   5888

_____.   Trail Driver.   Harper, 1936.   A cattle drive from

Texas to Kansas in 1871.   5889

_____. The U. P. Trail. Harper, 1918. Indian massacre, captures, and escapes punctuate this story of the building of the Union Pacific Railroad.   5890

_____. Western Union. Harper, 1939. A story of the development of the American West.   5891

_____. Young Forester. Harper, 1910. A story of the then new science of forestry--the conservation of our national resource.   5892

Gulick, Grover C. The Hallelujah Trail. by Bill Gulick. Doubleday, 1965. (first pub. in 1963 as Hallelujah Train) A wagon train carrying whiskey and champagne to Denver is guarded by an army escort and beset by Indians, thieves, and temperance advocates.   5893

Guthrie, Alfred Bertram. These Thousand Hills. Houghton, 1956. The hard work of a cowboy to achieve his dream-- a ranch of his own.   5894

Hagedorn, Hermann. The Rough Riders. Harper, 1927. Exciting story of Theodore Roosevelt in the Spanish-American War.   5895

Haines, William W. The Winter War. Little, 1961. Fighting with Sioux and Cheyenne warriors in Montana's severe winter after Custer's defeat.   5896

Haldeman-Julius, Emanuel and Marcet. Dust. Brentano's, 1921. The drudgery of Kansas pioneers in a loveless marriage building a farm from empty prairie.   5897

Hale, Arlene. Ghost Town's Secret. Abelard, 1962. YA. Adventure story of the 1870s in which a boy rescues his father from unscrupulous gold-seekers.   5898

Hall, Oakley M. Warlock. Viking, 1958. A partly factual story of the western frontier about Wyatt Earp and Tombstone, Arizona.   5899

Hancock, Albert E. Henry Bourland. Macmillan, 1901. The suffering of the South due to poor government planning after the war.   5900

Harris, Bernice. Janey Jeems. Doubleday, 1946. White and Negro mountaineers in rural North Carolina.   5901

Harris, Corra May. Circuit Rider's Wife. Altemus, 1910. A wife relates the trying ministry of her husband in a widely scattered congregation.   5902

Harris, Frank. The Bomb. Kennerley, 1908. The violent
Haymarket Riot in Chicago in 1886, typifying the labor
problems of the period.   5903

Harris, Leon F. and Frank Lee Beals. Look Away, Dixieland. Speller, 1937. A soldier returns to find that the
war has destroyed his home.   5904

Harris, Margaret and John. Arrow in the Moon. Morrow,
1954. A young easterner becomes involved with love, Indians, and adventure in Nebraska and adjoining territories.   5905

_____. Medicine Whip. Morrow, 1953. A western adven-
ture story set in Wyoming.   5906

Hatcher, Harlan H. The Patterns of Wolfpen. Bobbs, 1934.
Growing industrialism changes the life of a family descended
from Kentucky pioneers.   5907

Havighurst, Walter. Climb a Lofty Ladder. Winston, 1952.
YA. A story of Swedish wheat farmers who settled in
Minnesota in the last part of the nineteenth century.   5908

_____. The Quiet Shore. Macmillan, 1937. The growth
and development of the Lake Erie area from swamp to farming to industrial use.   5909

_____. Song of the Pines. Winston, 1949. YA. An itiner-
ant knife grinder comes from Norway to the United States
and earns a place in the lumbering camps of Wisconsin.   5910

Haycox, Ernest. Action by Night. Little, 1943. The war
waged against cattle rustlers by ranchers.   5911

_____. The Adventurers. Little, 1954. Suspense-filled
story of colonists in the Pacific Northwest.   5912

_____. Bugles in the Afternoon. Little, 1944. The per-
sonal conflict and love of a member of General Custer's
force.   5913

_____. Rim of the Desert. Little, 1941. The bitter range
warfare between ranchers and nesters in the Old West.   5914

_____. Trouble Shooter. Doubleday, 1937. A western
thriller built around the growth of the Union Pacific Railroad.   5915

Heinzman, George. Only the Earth and the Mountains. Macmillan, 1964. Although Ben Kane could live at peace with
either Indians or whites, the brutality with which both sides
fought was alien to his nature.   5916

Herbst, Josephine. Pity Is Not Enough. Harcourt, 1933.
The tragic life of a young man who went into the south as
a carpetbagger.   5917

Hooker, Forrestine. When Geronimo Rode. Doubleday, 1924.
Compelling story of the struggle between white men and Indians.   5918

Horgan, Paul. A Distant Trumpet. Farrar, 1960. A soldier
and his bride live on an army post in Arizona Territory
under threat of Apache warfare.   5919

Hough, Emerson. The Girl at the Half-Way House. Appleton,
1900. A former army captain becomes a frontier settler.   5920

_____. North of 36. Appleton, 1923. The struggle of a
young lady in Texas to rebuild her father's ranch by a
cattle drive to Abilene, Kansas.   5921

Howard, Elizabeth. Before the Sun Goes Down. Doubleday,
1946. All levels of society in a small Pennsylvania town
in the 1880s.   5922

Howells, William Dean. The Rise of Silas Lapham. Ticknor,
1885. A climbing Boston family attempts to break into high
society.   5923

_____. The Vacation of the Kelwyns. Harper, 1920. A
tale of New England life in the middle 1870s.   5924

Hueston, Ethel. Calamity Jane of Deadwood Gulch. Bobbs,
1937. Account of a woman of the lusty gold rush era in
the Black Hills country.   5925

Huffman, Laurie. A House Behind the Mint. Doubleday, 1969.
A notorious stagecoach-robber, Black Bart, turns over a
new leaf through his friendship with a poor family.   5926

Hulme, Kathryn. Annie's Captain. Little, 1961. The transition from graceful sailing ships to the new steamships in a
sea captain's life.   5927

Humphrey, William. The Ordways. Knopf, 1965, c.1964.
Four-generation story of the Ordway family, who move to
Texas after the Civil War and help in its early develop-
ment.   5928

Idell, Albert. Bridge to Brooklyn. Holt, 1948. A warm
tale of family life including the excitement over the completion of the Brooklyn Bridge. (followed by The Great
Blizzard)   5929

_____   Centennial Summer. Holt, 1943. New York dur-

ing the centennial year of 1876. (followed by <u>Bridge to</u>
<u>Brooklyn</u>) 5930

_____. <u>The Great Blizzard</u>. Holt, 1948. The story of the
Rogers family in the blizzard of March, 1888, in New York.
5931
_____. <u>Stephen Hayne</u>. Sloane, 1951. Coal mining and
the development of organized labor. 5932

Irwin, Will. <u>Youth Rides West</u>. Knopf, 1925. A picture of
a Colorado mining camp in the 1870s. 5933

Isham, Frederic S. <u>Black Friday</u>. Bobbs, 1904. Bank
failures caused by wild speculation in farming land in the
expanding West. 5934

Janvier, Thomas Allibone. <u>Santa Fe's Partner</u>. Harper, 1907.
Memories of a small territorial New Mexican railroad town.
5935

Jewett, Sarah Orne. <u>A Country Doctor</u>. Houghton, 1884.
A New England country doctor whose unconventional ward becomes a doctor. 5936

Johnson, Annabel and Edgar. <u>The Bearcat</u>. Harper, 1960.
YA. An adolescent boy matures during the struggle of
Montana coal miners to improve their lot. 5937

_____. <u>The Black Symbol</u>. Harper, 1959. YA. About a
boy who runs away and joins a medicine show in the mining
camps of Nevada and Montana to search for his father. 5938

Johnston, Mary. <u>Michael Forth</u>. Harper, 1919. Economic,
domestic, and religious adjustments of southerners during
the Reconstruction. 5939

Johnston, Norma. <u>The Wishing Star</u>. Funk, 1963. YA. The
social adjustment of a sixteen-year-old girl when her family
moves to a new home in Massachusetts in 1899. 5940

Jones, Jack. <u>Off to Philadelphia in the Morning</u>. Hamilton,
1948. Fictionalized biography of the musician Joseph
Parry. 5941

Kelland, Clarence Budington. <u>Gold</u>. Harper, 1931. The
daughter of a banker puts money management before romance. 5942

_____. <u>The Lady and the Giant</u>. Dodd, 1959. This is a
romance which involves the exposure of fraud and the recovery of stolen money. 5943

_____. <u>Valley of the Sun</u>. Harper, 1940. Pioneering in
the desert country of Arizona. 5944

Kennelly, Ardyth. Good Morning, Young Lady. Houghton,
   1953. The paradoxical loves of a delightful young girl--
   first for a bandit, then for a professor.   5945

_____. The Peaceable Kingdom. Houghton, 1949. The sec-
   ond wife and children of a polygamous tailor in Salt Lake
   City in the 1890s. (followed by Up Home)   5946

_____. Up Home. Houghton, 1955. Story of Mormons in
   Salt Lake City in the 1890s showing the special problems of
   a man's "second family."   5947

Kenyon, Theda. Black Dawn. Messner, 1944. Ancient family
   animosity recurs in the aftermath of the war.   5948

Keyes, Frances Parkinson. Blue Camellia. Messner, 1957.
   The pioneers of the rice industry in Louisiana.   5949

Kinkaid, Mary H. The Man of Yesterday. Stokes, 1908. The
   closing years of the century in the Indian Territory.   5950

Klem, Kaye. Touch the Sun. Doubleday, 1971. Dramatic
   story of the developing of a rich silver mine in Virginia
   City, Nevada, in the 1870s.   5951

Krey, Laura Lettie. And Tell of Time. Houghton, 1938.
   Unrest following the Civil War causes trouble to a young
   couple on a Texas plantation.   5952

Kroninger, Robert H. Sarah & the Senator. Howell-North,
   1964. Incredible activities accompany a woman's litigation
   to validate a marriage contract in 1880 in San Francisco. 5953

Lane, Rose Wilder. Free Land. Longmans, 1938. Hardships
   of early settlers on the plains of the Dakotas.   5954

_____. Let the Hurricane Roar. Longmans, 1933. The
   endurance of western pioneers who lived in a dugout and
   forced a living from a hostile country.   5955

Lanham, Edwin. The Wind Blew West. Longmans, 1935.
   The honest courage of pioneers and the greed of slick
   promoters.   5956

La Scola, Ray. The Creole. Morrow, 1961. Sentimental
   novel about the trials and tribulations of a few society
   people in Reconstruction New Orleans.   5957

Laut, Agnes C. Freebooters of the Wilderness. Moffat,
   1910. The dishonest activities of men attempting to
   steal timber in the West.   5958

Lavender, David Sievert. Red Mountain. Doubleday, 1963.

A hard-working young pioneer builds a road and operates
a freight service during the silver mining boom in Colorado.   5959

Le May, Alan. The Searchers. Harper, 1954. The five-
year search for a girl captured by Comanches.   5960

Leonard, Jonathan. Back to Stay. Viking, 1929. Small New
England community in the 1870s.   5961

Liddon, Eloise S. Some Lose Their Way. Dutton, 1941.
Romance of an English actress who comes to Alabama.   5962

Lipsky, Eleazar. The Devil's Daughter. Meredith, 1969.
Based on a famous California trial in the 1880s concerning
the claim of a young woman that she was the rightful wife
of a wealthy former Senator, William Sharon.   5963

_____. Lincoln McKeever. Appleton, 1953. A New York
lawyer, living in the west, undertakes a land grant case
complicated by racial differences.   5964

Lockridge, Ross Franklin. Raintree County. Houghton, 1948.
A long novel of the Fourth of July, 1892, in Indiana, inter-
spersed with flashbacks.   5965

Lockwood, Sarah. Fistful of Stars. Appleton, 1947. A young
couple in a Wisconsin lumber and mining community.   5966

Loomis, Noel M. A Time for Violence. Macmillan, 1960.
Conflict between ranchers and outlaws in the Texas panhandle in the 1880s.   5967

Lott, Milton. Backtrack. Houghton, 1965. A cowboy who has
befriended a Mexican boy during a cattle drive saves the boy
from a murder charge and clears up a mystery in his own
life.   5968

_____. Dance Back the Buffalo. Houghton, 1959. The
Plains Indians attempt to bring back their old way of life
through ceremonial dancing.   5969

_____. The Last Hunt. Houghton, 1954. A western story
about the last of the buffalo hunters.   5970

Lovelace, Maud Hart. Gentlemen From England. Macmillan,
1937. The experiences of a group of Englishmen who came
to Minnesota to make a fortune raising beans.   5971

McCague, James. The Fortune Road. Harper, 1965. Adventures of a correspondent and a boy during construction of
the Union Pacific Railroad.   5972

McCaig, Robert J. The Burntwood Men. Macmillan, 1961.
A story of life in the Montana Territory in the 1880s.   5973

_____. Crimson Creek. Macmillan, 1963. An exciting
story of Indian activity in the Montana Territory in 1897. 5974

McDonald, Lucile Saunders. Stormy Year. Nelson, 1952.
Account of a difficult year for the family of an Indian agent
in Washington territory, based on letters from 1885.   5975

MacDonald, William Colt. California Caballero. Covici,
1936. When American settlers were beginning to outnumber
the Spanish in California.   5976

MacLeod, Le Roy. The Years of Peace. Century, 1932. Life
in a farming village in the Wabash River Valley of Indiana.
                                                          5977
McMeekin, Clark, pseud., for Clark, Dorothy and Isabel Mc-
Meekin. The Fairbrothers. Putnam, 1961. An orphan
girl's life with a matriarchal horse-racing family from the
end of the Civil War to the first running of the Kentucky
Derby.   5978

_____. The October Fox. Putnam, 1956. Picture of a
Kentucky family dominated by the father.   5979

_____. Tyrone of Kentucky. Appleton, 1954. The task
of rebuilding a war-torn farm confronts a Confederate veteran and his bride.   5980

Mann, E.B. Gunsmoke Trail. Morrow, 1942. Cattle rustling,
shady dealings, and murder in the Old West.   5981

_____. Troubled Range. Morrow, 1940. An eastern belle
wins her man in the West.   5982

_____. With Spurs. Morrow, 1937. Fast-moving, action-
packed western.   5983

Marius, Richard. The Coming of Rain. Knopf, 1969. A
young man in post-war Tennessee tries to get information
about his parents.   5984

Markey, Gene. Kentucky Pride. Random, 1956. Two Civil
War veterans vie for an estate and a lady.   5985

Marquand, John P. The Late George Apley. Random House,
1965, c.1936. This novel in the form of a memoir shows
the narrow standards imposed by Boston "high society."   5986

Matschat, Cecile Hulse. Preacher on Horseback. Farrar,
1940. Based on reminiscences of a circuit rider's wife. 5987

Mayer, Albert I. <u>Follow the River.</u> Doubleday, 1969.
First-person account of a schoolteacher from Philadelphia
who travelled down the Ohio River to spend a year teach-
ing and learning about frontier life.   5988

Meeker, Arthur. <u>Prairie Avenue.</u> Knopf, 1949. Plush living
and fast tempo of Chicago stressing the period from 1885
to 1896.   5989

Meigs, Cornelia. <u>Railroad West.</u> Little, 1937. Tells of some
of the difficulties encountered in building the Northern Pacific
Railroad.   5990

Miller, Helen Markley. <u>The Long Valley.</u> Doubleday, 1961.
YA. A young girl cares for her motherless family in Idaho
in the 1880s, placing their happiness before her own.   5991

Miller, Helen Topping. <u>After the Glory.</u> Appleton, 1958.
Reluctant reunion of brothers who fought on opposing sides
in the Civil War.   5992

_____. <u>Christmas at Sagamore Hill With Theodore Roose-
velt.</u> Longmans, 1960. A book which shows the family life
and Christmas customs of 1898.   5993

_____. <u>Christmas With Robert E. Lee.</u> Longmans, 1958.
A short book telling of the Lee family's first Christmas after the surrender at Appomattox.   5994

_____. <u>Mirage.</u> Appleton, 1949. Romantic novel of Texas
two decades after the Civil War.   5995

_____ and John Dewey Topping. <u>Rebellion Road.</u> Bobbs,
1954. Rebuilding a run-down plantation after the Civil
War.   5996

Mitchell, Faye L. <u>Every Road Has Two Directions.</u> Doubleday,
1960. YA. A fifteen-year-old girl leaves her log cabin
home in the Pacific Northwest to attend school at the new
Territorial University at Seattle.   5997

Moore, John Trotwood. <u>The Bishop of Cottontown.</u> Winston,
1906. Social conditions in a southern cotton mill town with
accounts of child labor and attempted lynching.   5998

Murfree, Mary Noailles. <u>Where the Battle Was Fought.</u>
by Charles Egbert Craddock, <u>pseud.</u> Houghton, 1884.
Romance in a Tennessee town close to a great Civil
War battlefield.   5999

Myrick, Herbert. <u>Cache La Poudre.</u> Paul, 1905. "The romance of a tenderfoot in the days of Custer."   6000

Neilhardt, John G. When the Tree Flowered. Macmillan,
1951. "Autobiography" of a Sioux Indian warrior who
fought both other Indians and the advancing white man, reflecting Sioux history and culture.   6001

Newton, Dwight Bennett. Cherokee Outlet. by Dwight Bennett,
pseud. Doubleday, 1961. A Western about Oklahoma during
the days of the Cherokee Strip land rush.   6002

Norris, Kathleen. Certain People of Importance. Doubleday,
1922. The story of the Crabtree family's move from New
England to California.   6003

North, Sterling. The Wolfling. Dutton, 1969. A boy and his
wolf-dog roam the forests of Wisconsin in this story of a
farm boy interested in nature (based on fact).   6004

Norton, Alice Mary. Rebel Spurs. by Andre Norton, pseud.
World, 1962. A former Confederate scout takes up the
threads of a new life in a frontier town in Arizona.   6005

Nyburg, Sidney. The Gate of Ivory. Knopf, 1920. A man's
great love brings him to assume a woman's guilt and that
of her husband.   6006

Ogden, George W. The Land of Last Chance. McClurg, 1919.
A story of the Oklahoma Territory when it was first opened.
                                                             6007

_____. Sooner Land. Dodd, 1929. The difficulties of
homesteaders fighting to retain their land.   6008

Ogley, Dorothy and Mabel Cleland. Iron Land. Doubleday,
1940. The mining of iron ore in Minnesota.   6009

Older, Cora. Savages and Saints. Dutton, 1936. The rebuilding of a Catholic mission at Santa Lucia, California.   6010

O'Rourke, Frank. Action at Three Peaks. Random, 1948.
Life on a frontier army post in the American West.   6011

Oskison, John. Black Jack Davy. Appleton, 1926. A story
of pioneers in Oklahoma.   6012

_____. Brothers Three. Macmillan, 1935. Concerns three
Oklahoma brothers--a merchant, a cattleman, and a scholar.
                                                             6013

Overholser, Wayne D. Land of Promises. by Joseph Wayne,
pseud. Doubleday, 1962. The hardships and rewards of
settlers in the Ute Indian country in the early 1880s.   6014

Overton, Gwendolen. The Heritage of Unrest. Macmillan,
1901. Unjust government policy toward the Apache Indians
in the Southwest.   6015

Page, Thomas Nelson. Red Riders. Scribner, 1924. A lad
of the home guards, too young for war service, fights later
against carpetbaggers.   6016

_____. Red Rock. Scribner, 1899. Struggle to rebuild a
southern plantation in the days of the carpetbaggers and the
Ku Klux Klan.   6017

Parkhill, Forbes. Troopers West. Farrar, 1945. An un-
biased account of Indian-white relations in Wyoming after
Custer's Last Stand.   6018

Parmenter, Christine. A Golden Age. Crowell, 1942. The
story of a happy family in a small Massachusetts town.   6019

Parrish, Randall. Bob Hampton of Placer. McClurg, 1906.
The battle which ensued when Custer attempted to confine
three thousand unwilling Sioux to a reservation.   6020

_____. Molly McDonald. McClurg, 1912. Romance and
Indian fighting on the Great Plains.   6021

Paterson, Arthur. Son of the Plains. Macmillan, 1895.
The dangerous journey along the Santa Fe Trail before the
advent of the railroad.   6022

Paul, Charlotte. Gold Mountain. Random House, 1953. The
heroine is a pioneer school teacher who leaves Seattle for
a small logging community in the Pacific Northwest.   6023

Payne, Robert. The Chieftain. Prentice-Hall, 1953. The
Nez Percé Indians of Oregon and their Chief Joseph.   6024

Payne, Will. Mr. Salt. Houghton, 1903. The financial
panic of 1893.   6025

Peeples, Samuel A. The Missourian. by Brad Ward, pseud.
Macmillan, 1957. A soldier returns from military service
to find that war has taken a terrible toll of his marriage
and his home.   6026

Pettibone, Anita. Johnny Painter. Farrar, 1944. A fourteen-
year-old lad is left to make his own way in the Washington
Territory.   6027

Pierce, Ovid W. The Devil's Half. Doubleday, 1968. Diverse
reactions of various white and black southerners during the
difficult Reconstruction period.   6028

_____. On a Lonesome Porch. Doubleday, 1960. A Caro-
lina family rebuilds its home and life after the Civil War. 6029

Place, Marian. Hold Back the Hunter. by Dale White, pseud.

Day, 1959. YA. A teen-aged half-breed guides the
Langford-Hayden expedition into the Yellowstone area in
1870-71 before Congress designated it a National Park.   6030

Portis, Charles. True Grit. Signet, 1969, c.1968. A girl,
accompanied by two rough lawmen, goes into Indian Territory in pursuit of her father's murderer in the 1880s.   6031

Prebble, John. The Buffalo Soldiers. Harcourt, 1959. Men
of three races figure in this tale of western action just after
the Civil War.   6032

_____. Spanish Stirrup. Harcourt, 1958. A Western about
a cattle drive enlivened by hostile Indians and a wild stampede.   6033

Price, Eugenia. The Beloved Invader. Lippincott, 1965.
Anson Dodge comes to St. Simon's Island, off the Georgia
coast, in 1879 and eventually becomes a minister.   6034

Quick, Herbert. The Invisible Woman. Bobbs, 1924. Political and cultural growth of the midwest farming area in
the 1890s.   6035

Quimby, Myrtle. White Crow. Criterion, 1970. YA. An
exciting story of Indians and Irishmen with romance, adventure, and tragedy.   6036

Raine, William MacLeod. Arkansas Guns. [En. title: Plantation Guns] Houghton, 1954, c.1945. Reconstruction days on
a plantation in Arkansas.   6037

Rayner, Emma. Visiting the Sin. Small, Maynard, 1900.
Revenge in the Kentucky and Tennessee mountains.   6038

Redgate, John. Barlow's Kingdom. S. & S., 1969. A Civil
War veteran returns to his Montana home to find that he has
changed during his years as a soldier and that the people at
home have changed also.   6039

Reese, John. Jesus on Horseback. Doubleday, 1971. An
ex-convict becomes a preacher in Mooney County, Colorado,
in a time of cattle, homesteading, and railroad building.   6040

Reiners, Perceval. Roses From the South. Doubleday, 1959.
Husband-hunting in West Virginia's White Sulphur Springs
and in New York City.   6041

Richter, Conrad. The Lady. Knopf, 1957. The mountains
and deserts of New Mexico in the 1880s provide the scene
for a story of love, loyalty, and violence.   6042

_____. The Sea of Grass. Knopf, 1936. A novelette of

romance on the southwestern frontier. 6043

Ripley, Clements. Gold Is Where You Find It. Appleton, 1936. Rivalry of farming, fruit growing, and mining as industries in early California. 6044

Roberts, Walter Adolphe. Creole Dusk. Bobbs, 1948. A New Orleans doctor fights the yellow fever epidemic in Panama. 6045

Robertson, Don. Paradise Falls. Putnam, 1968. Life in a small Ohio town dominated by a shrewd, self-made mine owner who mixes in every aspect of life in his quest for wealth and power. 6046

Robinson, Henry Morton. Water of Life. S. & S., 1960. Three generations of an Indiana family of whiskey makers, covering the period from the Civil War until Prohibition. 6047

Roe, Vingie E. The Great Trace. Macrae Smith, 1948. The bitter rivalry between two leaders of a wagon train hampers the difficult journey. 6048

Rølvaag, Ole E. Giants in the Earth. (tr.) Harper, 1927. Norwegian pioneers on the wild Dakota frontier. (followed by Peder Victorious) 6049

_____. Peder Victorious. (tr.) Harper, 1929. Second generation of Norwegians in the Dakotas. 6050

Roripaugh, Robert A. Honor Thy Father. Morrow, 1963. The struggle between cattlemen and homesteaders separates a family when father and son hold opposing views. 6051

Ross, Lillian. The Stranger. Morrow, 1942. The story of a California pioneer couple who met through a matrimonial agency. 6052

Ross, Zola Helen. Cassy Scandal. Bobbs, 1954. Anti-Chinese race riots, a raging fire, and a short-lived marriage. 6053

_____. Green Land. Bobbs, 1952. The Pacific Northwest during the development of the railroads. 6054

Rucker, Helen. Cargo of Brides. Little, 1956. A group of young women sails to Washington State to marry bachelors. 6055

_____. The Wolf Tree. Little, 1960. The love story of two young people parallels the growth of the Pacific Northwest lumber industry and San Francisco society. 6056

Rushing, Jane Gilmore. Walnut Grove. Doubleday, 1964. Formation of a young pioneer's conscience during the

building of the railroad in West Texas with Negro work
gangs.   6057

Salzer, Patricia M. The Montagues of Casa Grande. Pageant
Pr., 1953. Everyday life of prosperous Catholic Ameri-
can settlers in New Mexico.   6058

Sanders, Jacquin. The Fortune Finders. Appleton, 1966. A
young Vermont farmer becomes involved in the Nevada gold
rush.   6059

Sandoz, Mari. Miss Morissa. McGraw, 1955. The resolute
heroine fights prejudice against women doctors in Nebraska.
                                                                                          6060

_____. Son of the Gamblin' Man. C.N. Potter, 1960.
Skillfully contrasts the strong, aggressive gambler-promoter
who founded Cozad, Nebraska, and his sensitive son who became a famous artist and teacher--Robert Henri.   6061

Santee, Ross. Bubbling Spring. Scribner, 1949. Stage-
coaches, Indian fights, buffalo hunts, and cattle drives in
the Old West.   6062

Sayre, Anne. Never Call Retreat. Crowell, 1957. YA. A
Quaker family moves from Pennsylvania to Alabama hoping
to help southerners recover from the war.   6063

Schaefer, Jack W. Monte Walsh. Houghton, 1963. The story
of a ranch hand before and during the time when barbed
wire threatened the open range.   6064

_____. Shane. Houghton, 1949. Soft-spoken Shane helps
a Wyoming homesteader defend his property.   6065

Seawell, Molly Elliot. Throckmorton. Appleton, 1890. Virginia just after the Civil War.   6066

Sedges, John, pseud. The Townsman. Day, 1945. An English immigrant settles in a little town in Kansas.   6067

Seifert, Shirley. Destiny in Dallas. Lippincott, 1958. The
Cockerell family and the town of Dallas, Texas, grew and
prospered together in the last half of the nineteenth cen-
tury.   6068

Selby, John. Island in the Corn. Farrar, 1941. The financial decline of a wealthy family.   6069

Seton, Anya. The Turquoise. Avon Bks., 1970, c.1946. A
girl from Santa Fe with the gift of second sight tries to
find happiness in gay New York.   6070

Shank, Margarethe E. Call Back the Years. Augsburg,

1966. The life of Norwegian immigrants in the Dakotas around the turn of the century. 6071

Shenkin, Elizabeth. Brownstone Gothic. Holt, 1961. Mystery-romance of a poor young widow who serves as a companion for her wealthy aunt on Fifth Avenue in New York. 6072

Shiel, M. P. Contraband of War. Richards, 1899. International politics and finance during the Spanish-American War. 6073

Sims, Marian. Beyond Surrender. Lippincott, 1942. Rebuilding a half-ruined plantation with the aid of a few loyal ex-slaves. 6074

Sinclair, Bertrand W. Raw Gold. Dillingham, 1908. The quest for gold by unscrupulous men in the wild Northwest. 6075

Sinclair, Harold. The Years of Growth. Doubleday, 1940. A small Illinois town in the second half of the last century. 6076

Slaughter, Frank G. The Stubborn Heart. Doubleday, 1950. Doctor's wife converts their plantation into a hospital for whites and Negroes. 6077

Smith, Chard Powers. Ladies Day. Scribner, 1941. Novel of romance and social developments in upstate New York. 6078

Sorensen, Virginia. Many Heavens. Harcourt, 1954. Romance of a Mormon couple at the turn of the century. 6079

Stephenson, Howard. Glass. Kendall, 1933. Contrasts farm and town in late nineteenth century Ohio. 6080

Stewart, Catherine. Three Roads to Valhalla. Scribner, 1948. Violence, romance, and tragedy in Florida following the Civil War. 6081

Stewart, Ramona. Casey. Little, 1968. Rise of a poor Irish Catholic immigrant from gang-fighting in the slums to political power in New York City. 6082

Straight, Michael W. Carrington. Knopf, 1960. The fixing of blame for the Fetterman Massacre by the Sioux in 1866. 6083

Street, James Howell. Tomorrow We Reap. Dial, 1949. Inroads of a northern lumber company in Mississippi in the 1890s. 6084

Stribling, Thomas S. The Store. Doubleday, 1932. The transformation of the Old South during the Reconstruction Era. 6085

Swain, Virginia. The Dollar Gold Piece. Farrar, 1942. A
cattle baron in Kansas City in 1887.   6086

Switzer, Gladys. Abigail Goes West. Morrow, 1963. YA.
Abigail Wheeler and her married sister journey by train
across the country in the 1870s, having interesting experiences to offset the actual discomforts.   6087

Synon, Mary. The Good Red Bricks. Little, 1921. Politics,
horse racing, and prize fighting in Chicago in the 1890s.   6088

Tarkington, Booth. The Gentleman From Indiana. McClure,
1900. A crusading newspaperman in an Indiana town.   6089

Tavo, Gus, pseud. for Martha and Gustave Ivan. Track the
Grizzly Down. Knopf, 1963. YA. A family from Texas
finds a ferocious grizzly bear only one of the obstacles
they face in building a ranch in Wyoming.   6090

Taylor, R.S. In Red Weather. Holt, 1961. Selfish rivalries
and apathy result in a tragic catastrophe in a New England
coastal town in the 1870s.   6091

Taylor, Robert Lewis. A Journey to Matecumbe. McGraw,
1961. Experiences of a boy and his uncle as they wander
from Kentucky to Florida in 1870, including good character-
ization and descriptions of scenery.   6092

Taylor, Ross. Brazos. Bobbs, 1938. Adventures of a young
cowboy, his term in jail, and his work on the railroad.   6093

_____. The Saddle and the Plow. Bobbs, 1942. Prob-
lems of a young married couple raising horses in Texas.   6094

Thomas, Maude Morgan. Sing in the Dark. Winston, 1954.
YA. About the Welsh coal miners who came to America in
the 1870s to work in the coal fields of Pennsylvania.   6095

Thomson, John. Gone to Texas. Scribner, 1937. Romance
and adventure in Texas during post-Civil War years.   6096

Tippett, Thomas. Horse Shoe Bottoms. Harper, 1935. How
wage cuts and labor troubles paved the way for labor unions
in the Illinois mining district.   6097

Tolbert, Frank Xavier. The Staked Plain. Harper, 1958.
A renegade Texas blacksmith and gunsmith joins the
Comanches.   6098

Tourgée, Albion W. Bricks Without Straw. Fords, 1880.
Social and political conditions in the south during Reconstruction.   6099

_____. (1) A Fool's Errand. Fords, 1879. (2) The
Invisible Empire. Fords, 1883. Reconstruction in the
south as seen by a Union officer who settled there.   6100-1

Towne, Charles H. Good Old Yesterday. Appleton, 1935.
Family life in New York in the Gay Nineties.   6102

Train, Arthur Cheney. Tassles on Her Boots. Scribner,
1940. Graft, politics, and the career of Boss Tweed in
New York.   6103

Turnbull, Agnes. Rolling Years. Macmillan, 1936. Three
generations of a family in a Scottish community in Pennsylvania, 1870-1910.   6104

Van de Water, Frederic. Thunder Shield. Bobbs, 1933.
Thunder Shield, the hero, is a white boy adopted by Chey-
ennes.   6105

Van Every, Dale. The Day the Sun Died. Little, 1971. The
desperate, hopeless struggle of the Plains Indians against
the United States Army culminating in the violent massacre
at Wounded Knee in 1890.   6106

Vining, Elizabeth Gray. I, Roberta. Lippincott, 1967. A
woman discovers that her husband, who had left with her
mother's fortune, has lost the money and remarried.   6107

Voelker, John Donaldson. Laughing Whitefish. by Robert
Traver, pseud. McGraw, 1965. A young Michigan lawyer
represents an Indian maiden who is suing a company for her
father's share in a mine (based on an actual case).   6108

Ware, Clyde. The Innocents. Norton, 1969. An old pros-
pector adopts a white girl raised by Indians and seeks to
secure her future in the rough atmosphere of a gold mining
camp.   6109

Warren, Charles M. Only the Valiant. Macmillan, 1943.
Pioneer life and cavalry warfare against the Apaches.   6110

_____. Valley of the Shadow. Doubleday, 1948. U.S.
Cavalry company attacks Deesohay and his Apaches.   6111

Waters, Frank. The Wild Earth's Nobility. Liveright, 1935.
A young man who had lost everything in the Civil War builds
a new life in Colorado.   6112

Watts, Mary Stanbery. The Noon-Mark. Macmillan, 1920.
Warm, realistic account of life in a small midwestern
city.   6113

_____. Van Cleve. Macmillan, 1913. Events of the

Spanish-American War and life at the time.   6114

Weekley, Robert S. The House in Ruins. Random, 1958.
Attacks on the Federal Army of occupation by Rebels who
refused to accept Lee's surrender.   6115

_____. The Spirit and the Flesh. Doubleday, 1959. A
novel inspired and loosely based on the life of the dancer,
Isadora Duncan.   6116

Wellman, Manley Wade. Candle of the Wicked. Putnam, 1960.
Two men seek land between Fort Scott, Kansas, and Independence, Missouri, in 1873.   6117

Wellman, Paul I. Angel With Spurs. Lippincott, 1942. General Jo Shelby and his ex-Confederates who go to fight in
Mexico.   6118

_____. The Bowl of Brass. Lippincott, 1944. Two Kan-
sas communities will stop at nothing to acquire county seat
status.   6119

_____. Broncho Apache. Doubleday, 1950. One of Ger-
onimo's defeated band escapes, returns to Arizona, and becomes a ruthless marauder.   6120

Westcott, Edward Noyes. David Harum. Appleton, 1898.
David Harum is a shrewd Yankee banker.   6121

Wharton, Edith. Age of Innocence. Appleton, 1920. The
smug Four Hundred in New York in the 1870s.   6122

_____. The Buccaneers. Appleton, 1938. High society
life in New York and Newport.   6123

Whipple, Maurine. The Giant Joshua. Houghton, 1941. Warm
story of a Mormon household in the Dixie Mission in Utah.
                                                              6124
White, Leslie Turner. Log Jam. Doubleday, 1959. A tale
of the logging industry in the 1870s.   6125

_____. Profane Junction. Morrow, 1958. Political wrang-
ling and the forces of nature hamper railroad building in
California in the 1870s.   6126

White, Stewart Edward. The Rose Dawn. Doubleday, 1920.
California when large ranches were succumbing to small
farms fed by irrigation.   6127

_____. The Westerners. McClure, 1901. An unscrupulous
half-breed is the central figure in this story of wars with
the Sioux.   6128

_____. Wild Geese Calling. Doubleday, 1940. The forests of the Pacific Northwest come alive in this tale of a lumberjack.   6129

White, William Allen. A Certain Rich Man. Macmillan, 1909. A Civil War veteran attains wealth and heroism.   6130

_____. In the Heart of a Fool. Macmillan, 1918. Kansas in the second half of the nineteenth century.   6131

Whitlock, Brand. J. Hardin & Son. Appleton, 1923. Small town life in Ohio.   6132

Whitney, James H. Father by Proxy. Exposition, 1955. Factually based story of Reconstruction days in Florida.   6133

Whitney, Phyllis A. Creole Holiday. Westminster, 1959. YA. A strictly-raised New England girl goes to New Orleans at carnival time.   6134

_____. Sea Jade. Appleton, 1964. An ambitious sea captain engineers a luckless marriage between two heirs of an import company in an attempt to continue the profitable trade with the Orient.   6135

_____. Thunder Heights. Appleton, 1960. A young woman solves the mystery of her mother's death when she inherits the eerie ancestral home.   6136

_____. Window on the Square. Appleton, 1962. Hired as companion to a problem boy, Megan Kincaid learns that he is not naughty but terrified.   6137

Whittington, Harry. Vengeance Is the Spur. Abelard, 1960. The excitement of cavalry life in the west and their clashes with Geronimo and his Apaches.   6138

Williams, Ben Ames. Owen Glen. Houghton, 1950. Laid in a small Ohio town among Welsh coal miners.   6139

_____. The Unconquered. Houghton, 1953. Politics and romance in post-war New Orleans.   6140

Williams, Dorothy Jeanne. Oh, Susanna! by J.R. Williams, pseud. Putnam, 1963. YA. The hardships and rewards of homesteading just after the close of the Civil War and the relations between ranchers and farmers.   6141

Williams, John Edward. Butcher's Crossing. Macmillan, 1960. Amidst the trials and hardships of an unprofitable buffalo-hunt a young Bostonian learns his own capabilities and limitations.   6142

Wilson, Margaret. The Able McLaughlins. Harper, 1923.
Struggle between justice and charity in a Scottish community in the Middle West.   6143

Winsor, Kathleen. Wanderers Eastward, Wanderers West.
Random House, 1965. Business and personal affairs of Mon-
tana and New York figure in the early development of the
West.   6144

Wise, Evelyn V. Long Tomorrow. Appleton, 1938. The work
of a Catholic priest in a prejudiced Minnesota hamlet.   6145

Wister, Owen. Red Men and White. Harper, 1896. Relations with Indians in the West featuring General George
Crook.   6146

_____. The Virginian. Macmillan, 1902. A cultured
Virginian becomes a cowboy and courts a teacher from
Vermont.   6147

Woods, Edith E. The Spirit of the Service. Macmillan, 1903.
Naval service in the Spanish-American War.   6148

Worth, Kathryn. The Middle Button. Doubleday, 1941. YA.
A young North Carolina girl has the ambition to become a
doctor, but her Scotch parents can only think of a husband
for her.   6149

Wyckoff, James. John Slaughter's Way. Doubleday, 1963. A
Western based on the life of John Horton Slaughter, rancher
and sheriff of Tombstone, Arizona.   6150

Wylie, Ida Alexa Ross. Ho, the Fair Wind. Random, 1945.
Martha's Vineyard in the days of camp meetings and whaling ships.   6151

Yerby, Frank. Garfield Honor. Dial, 1961. An explosive
romantic situation revolves around a Union army veteran,
a fiery Mexican girl, and a Texas rancher's daughter.   6152

_____. Griffin's Way. Dial, 1962. The long, difficult
convalescence of a man who lost his memory during the
war.   6153

_____. Pride's Castle. Dial, 1949. The story of Pride
Dawson, a robber-baron of the 1870s.   6154

_____. The Vixens. Dial, 1947. A southern aristocrat
who had fought for the Union returns home.   6155

Young, Agnes. I Swear by Apollo. by Agatha Young, pseud.
S. & S., 1968. The medical practice of a doctor in Vermont and Ohio in the time when Lister was searching for

the causes of infection in operating rooms. 6156

Young, Bob and Jan. Frontier Scientist Clarence King. Messner, 1968. YA. The adventures of Clarence King, who explored and mapped much of the Southwest. 6157

Young, Gordon Ray. Iron Rainbow. Doubleday, 1942. The building of railroads across the American West. 6158

Zara, Louis. Dark Rider. World, 1961. Fictionalized life and adventures--literary and romantic--of the talented author and reporter Stephen Crane, best remembered for The Red Badge of Courage (listed separately). 6159

Ziegler, Elsie Reif. The Blowing-Wand. Winston, 1955. YA. Concerns Bohemian glass-making in Ohio, with the beginnings of the use of machinery which affronted creative craftsmen. 6160

_____. The Face in the Stone. Longmans, 1959. Old-world stonecutters from Serbia learn to adapt their craft to the demands of growing Chicago in the late nineteenth century. 6161

_____. Light a Little Lamp. Day, 1961. The beginnings of social work in Chicago parallel the life of Mary McDowell, an early social worker. 6162

f) Survey Novels (which include more than two periods)

Allen, Henry. The Last Warpath. by Will Henry, pseud. Random House, 1966. A series of episodes in the lives of the Cheyenne Indians from 1680 to 1896, including their unfair treatment by the white man. 6163

Arnold, Elliott. Blood Brother. Duell, 1947. The Apaches after the Gadsden Purchase and the friendship of Cochise and a government scout. 6164

Babson, Naomi. I Am Lidian. Harcourt, 1951. Account of our country from Massachusetts to Montana charmingly told as memories of her youth by a ninety-year-old lady. 6165

Davis, Paxton. The Seasons of Heroes. Morrow, 1967. Three generations of an old Virginia family from the Civil War to the early twentieth century with the various men's war experiences. 6166

Delmar, Viña. The Big Family. Harcourt, 1961. Various members of the John Slidell family played important parts in America's history over the years from the Revolution to the Civil War. 6167

Edmonds, Walter D. Three Stalwarts. Little, 1961. An omnibus volume containing the novels: Drums Along the Mohawk,
Rome Haul, and Erie Water (listed separately).   6168

Ferber, Edna. American Beauty. Doubleday, 1931. The slow
decadence of a fine old Connecticut farm and family through
two centuries.   6169

Fields, Jonathan, pseud. The Memoirs of Dunstan Barr.
Coward, 1959. A saga of the Barr family from pioneer days
until the Depression of 1929.   6170

Hoffenberg, Jack. Sow Not in Anger. Dutton, 1961. The personal and public lives of the Taylors, who built a plantation,
a town, and a business in Georgia.   6171

Johnson, Gerald White. By Reason of Strength. Minton, 1930.
A North Carolina family from the War of Independence
through the War between the States.   6172

Kelly, Regina Zimmerman. Chicago: Big-Shouldered City.
Reilly, 1962. From an Indian massacre of 1812 to the
World's Columbian Exposition in 1893, this is the story
of successive generations of a Chicago family.   6173

Levin, Benjamin H. To Spit Against the Wind. Citadel Pr.,
1970. Kaleidoscopic career of the famous revolutionary
thinker and writer, Thomas Paine.   6174

Lincoln, Joseph Crosby. Christmas Days. Coward, 1938.
Colorful character sketches of a seagoing Cape Cod family
on three Christmases in the 1850s, 1860s, and 1870s.   6175

McMeekin, Clark, pseud. for Dorothy Clark and Isabel Mc-
Meekin. Show Me a Land. Appleton, 1940. Sixty years
in a woman's life, filled with fun, romance, and fine
horses, and showing Virginia and Kentucky in the nineteenth century.   6176

Millard, Joseph. Cut-Hand, the Mountain Man. Chilton, 1964.
YA. The story of Dick Wootton, whose exploits in frontier
Kentucky and the West won him his Indian nickname.   6177

Sandburg, Carl. Remembrance Rock. Harcourt, 1948. A
long epic novel depicting American history from the Pilgrims' landing until after the Civil War.   6178

Seton, Anya. The Hearth and Eagle. Houghton, 1948. A
Yankee family from the colonial period to the Reconstruction.   6179

Steele, Wilbur. Diamond Wedding. Doubleday, 1950. A hardy
Coloradan who married a gentle New England woman.   6180

Stone, Irving. Those Who Love. Doubleday, 1965. The story of John and Abigail Adams from their meeting, through the eventful years of growing national independence, to the end of his Presidency.   6181

Turnbull, Agnes. The King's Orchard. Houghton, 1963. The story of James O'Hara, who flourished both in business and family life on the frontier and later in Pittsburgh, Pennsylvania.   6182

Watson, Virginia C. Manhattan Acres. Dutton, 1934. Ten generations of a New York family during the growth of Manhattan.   6183

Wiley, John. Addie Was a Lady. St. Martin's, 1962. The machinations of a grandmother who ruled her family with an iron fist in a velvet glove.   6184

Zara, Louis. This Land Is Ours. Houghton, 1940. American history from 1755 to 1835 in the life of one Andrew Benton.   6185

2. LATIN AMERICA

    a) Colonial Period to 1800

Allen, Dexter. Coil of the Serpent. Coward, 1956. Reign and military successes of Nezahual. (followed by Valley of Eagles)   6186

_____. Valley of Eagles. Coward, 1957. Nezahual, monarch of Tezcuco, at the time of Cortez.   6187

Attwood, Adeline. Treasure of the Sun. Houghton, 1954, c.1953. Tells many details of Peruvian Indian life and the greed which a treasure engenders.   6188

Baggett, Samuel Graves. Gods on Horseback. McBride, 1952. The conquest of Mexico by Cortez with scenes from Aztec life.   6189

Baker, Betty. The Blood of the Brave. Harper, 1966. YA. A blacksmith and his son join Cortez in his search for gold and conquest.   6190

Baron, Alexander, name originally Alec Bernstein. The Golden Princess. Washburn, 1954. An exciting account of Cortez' conquest of Mexico and of Marina, the Indian girl who became his concubine and interpreter.   6191

Batchellor, D.O. The Unstrung Bow. Sherman & French, 1910. Experiences of an Englishman in Pizarro's conquest of Peru.   6192

Behn, Aphra. Oroonoko. Pearson, 1871. The capture, revolt, and death of a young Negro chief kidnapped from his
home into slavery.   6193

Bloundelle-Burton, John. A Gentleman Adventurer. Melrose,
1895. The efforts of William Paterson and his party to
make the Isthmus of Darien an English colony.   6194

Clagett, John. Cradle of the Sun. Crown, 1952. Juan de
Moncada escapes the Inquisition and resists the Spanish invasion of Yucatan.   /   6195

Cochran, Hamilton. Windward Passage. Bobbs, 1942. Swashbuckling tale of the pirate Henry Morgan and his raid on
Panama.   6196

Craine, Edith Janice. The Victors. Duffield, 1933. The
struggles of the Incas during the Spanish conquest of Peru. 6197

de Cesco, Federica. The Prince of Mexico. (tr.) Day,
1970, c.1968. YA. Romance of an Aztec prince and the
daughter of Montezuma in sixteenth century Mexico.   6198

Dixon, Thomas. The Sun Virgin. Liveright, 1929. The culture of the Incas is reflected in this romance of Pizarro in
Peru.   6199

Douglas-Irvine, Helen. Fray Mario. Longmans, 1939. Adventures and misadventures of a Spanish vagabond in
Chile.   6200

Duguid, Julian. A Cloak of Monkey Fur. Appleton, 1936.
Early Spanish colonizers search avidly for the fabled treasure
of gold in South America.   6201

_____. Father Coldstream. Appleton, 1938. A Jesuit
priest is the hero of this novel of eighteenth century Paraguay.   6202

Duncombe, Frances Riker. The Quetzal Feather. Lothrop,
1967. YA. A Mexico City youth runs away from home and
joins in the conquest of Guatemala in 1523.   6203

Eliot, Ethel. Roses for Mexico. Macmillan, 1946. Account
of the Virgin Mary's appearance to Juan Diego at Guadalupe.
                                                          6204
Foulke, William D. Maya: A Story of Yucatan. Putnam,
1900. Sixteenth century Yucatan as revealed by explorations, early legends, and contemporary accounts.   6205

Friedenthal, Richard. The White Gods. Harper, 1931.

Cortez's conquest of Mexico and his romance with the Indian
girl, Marina.   6206

Green, Gerald. Sword and the Sun. Scribner, 1953. The
struggle between the Pizarros and Diego de Almagro for
control of Peru.   6207

Griffith, George. The Virgin of the Sun. Pearson, 1898. A
tale of the conquest of Peru and the Incas by Pizarro and
de Soto.   6208

Haller, Adolf. He Served Two Masters. (tr.) Pantheon,
1962. YA. A page to the explorer Cortez develops admiration and loyalty to the Aztec emperor Montezuma and serves
him for a time.   6209

Hays, Hoffman Reynolds. Takers of the City. Reynal, 1946.
Bishop Bartolomé de las Casas opposes the conquistadors'
exploitation of native Mexican Indians.   6210

Hudson, Charles Bradford. The Crimson Conquest. McClurg,
1907. The bloody conquest of the Incas of Peru by the Spanish under Pizarro.   6211

Lea, Tom. The Hands of Cantú. Little, 1964. The story of a
horse-breeding ranch in Mexico and of the quest to recover
stolen horses from the Indians.   6212

Locke, Charles O. Last Princess. Norton, 1954. The Spanish conquest of Peru as it appeared to the native Incas.   6213

Maass, Edgar. Don Pedro and the Devil. Bobbs, 1942. Don
Pedro goes with Pizarro to win a kingdom in the New
World.   6214

Madariaga, Salvador de. The Heart of Jade. Creative Age,
1944. A bright tapestry of Aztec civilization in Mexico
during Montezuma's time.   6215

Maltby, A. Queen--But No Queen. Sisleys, 1907. Philip II
of Spain in Yucatan before his marriage with Queen Mary
of England.   6216

Marshall, Edison. Cortez and Marina. Doubleday, 1963.
The daring Spanish conqueror of opulent Aztec Mexico and
his dependence on his Indian mistress-interpreter.   6217

May, Stella Burke. The Conqueror's Lady. Farrar & Rinehart, 1930. The conquest of Chile by Pedro de Valdivia is
the focal point of this novel.   6218

Millar, George Reid. Orellana Discovers the Amazon. [same
as Crossbowman's Story of the First Exploration of the

Amazon] Heinemann, 1954. First-person narration of
the momentous discovery in the mid-sixteenth century.   6219

Minnigerode, Meade. The Terror of Peru. Farrar & Rinehart, 1940. A young Peruvian adventurer and his pursuit
of a lovely Spanish girl.   6220

Mittelholzer, Edgar. Hubertus. [En. title: The Harrowing
of Hubertus] Day, 1955, c.1954. The family story of the
Van Groenwegels, Dutch planters in British Guiana.   6221

Niggli, Josefina. A Miracle for Mexico. N.Y. Graphic Soc.,
1964. YA. The story of the Virgin of Guadalupe provides
the focus for this exciting story of sixteenth century Mexico.   6222

Niles, Blair. Day of Immense Sun. Bobbs, 1936. A novel
about the Peruvian people at the time of the Spanish conquest.   6223

_____. Maria Paluna. Longmans, 1934. Love of an
Indian maiden for a caballero during the Spanish conquest
of Guatemala.   6224

O'Dell, Scott. The King's Fifth. Houghton, 1966. YA. A
young mapmaker recounts Coronado's quest for gold in
Mexico and the American Southwest.   6225

Shedd, Margaret. Malinche and Cortes. Doubleday, 1971.
About the beautiful Indian woman who became the mistress
of Cortes, conqueror of Mexico.   6226

Shellabarger, Samuel. Captain from Castile. Little, 1945.
A colorful account of the Spanish conquest of Mexico.   6227

Smith, Arthur D. Howden. Conqueror. Lippincott, 1933.
Cortez obtains the aid of an Indian girl in conquering the
Aztecs of Mexico.   6228

Spence, Hartzell. Bride of the Conqueror. Random, 1954.
Aristocratic and beautiful Doña Eloisa in sixteenth century
Peru.   6229

_____. Vain Shadow. McGraw, 1947. A rich, colorful
account of Francisco de Orellana, discoverer of the Amazon River.   6230

Stacton, David. A Signal Victory. Pantheon, 1962, c.1960.
Contrasts native Mayan culture and customs with those of
the Spanish who seek to conquer them.   6231

Stucken, Eduard. The Great White Gods. (tr.) Farrar,
1934. Spanish conquest of Aztec Mexico by Cortez.   6232

Thorpe, Francis Newton. The Spoils of Empire. Little,
1903. Concerns the Spanish Conquest of Mexico.   6233

Wallace, Lew. The Fair God. Houghton, 1873. Pictures
Mexican life and culture at the advent of Cortez.   6234

Wilder, Thornton. The Bridge of San Luis Rey. Boni, 1927.
Review of the lives of five persons who died when an osier
bridge broke near Lima, Peru, in the eighteenth century. 6235

b) Nineteenth Century: Revolutions and Republics

Abrahams, Doris. No Castanets. by Caryl Brahms, pseud.
Macmillan, 1963. The Braganza family of Portugal was
exiled to Brazil during the Napoleonic Wars.   6236

Aguilera Malta, Demetrio. Manuela, La Caballeresa del Sol.
(tr.) Southern Ill. Univ. Pr., 1967. About Simon Boli-
var's mistress and how she helped the Great Liberator.   6237

Baerlein, Henry. The House of the Fighting Cocks. Harcourt, 1923. Story of a Spanish student in Mexico under
Maximilian.   6238

Beals, Carleton. Taste of Glory. Crown, 1956. About
Bernardo O'Higgins, liberator of Chile in the early nineteenth century.   6239

Bellah, James Warner. The Journal of Colonel de Lancey.
Chilton, 1967. English soldier of fortune, after a tragic
romance, joins American filibuster William Walker in his
attempt to unite Central America.   6240

Blest-Gana, Alberto. Martin Rivas. (tr.) Chapman & Hall,
1916. Mid-century life in the Republic of Chile--social,
economic, and political.   6241

Brand, Charles Neville. Mexican Masquerade. by Charles
Lorne, pseud. Dodge, 1938. Mexico in the mid-nineteenth
century when Napoleon III set up Maximilian as Emperor. 6242

Breckenfeld, Vivian Gurney. Maggie. by Vivian Breck, pseud.
Doubleday, 1954. YA. About the impulsive daughter of a
San Francisco family who marries an engineer and lives in
an isolated mountain community in Mexico.   6243

Conrad, Joseph. Nostromo. Harper, 1904. Adventure story
of a wealthy Englishman includes exciting episodes and daring men.   6244

Cook, G. Oram. Roderick Taliaferro. Macmillan, 1903.
The shaky government of Maximilian, made Emperor of

Mexico by Napoleon III of France.   6245

Davis, Richard Harding. Soldiers of Fortune. Scribner,
1897. A mining engineer in a small South American republic seething with revolution.   6246

Dombrowski, Katharina von. Land of Women. Little, 1935.
Violence and Indian customs in Paraguay under Francisco
Solano López.   6247

Escragnolle Taunay, Alfredo de. Innocencia. (tr.) by Sylvio
Dinarnte, pseud. Chapman & Hall, 1889. Love and cruelty
in the backlands of Brazil.   6248

Gaines, Diana. Dangerous Climate. Doubleday, 1960. An
Irish girl becomes a stowaway in an attempt to reach the
California gold fields by way of Panama.   6249

Gavin, Catherine Irvine. The Cactus and the Crown. Beagle
Bks., 1970, c.1962. A Confederate doctor and his sister
come to Mexico and become involved in the desperate attempt of Maximilian and Carlotta to build an empire.   6250

Gleason, Judith. Agotime, Her Legend. Grossman, 1970.
Agotime, former queen of Dahomey, Africa, is sold into
slavery and sent to Brazil, where she establishes worship
to her own gods.   6251

Gorman, Herbert Sherman. The Breast of the Dove. Rinehart, 1950. Romance and tragedy in Mexico while Maximilian was Emperor.   6252

_____. Cry of Dolores. Rinehart, 1947. The struggle of
the Mexicans to throw off the rule of Spain in 1810.   6253

Harding, Bertita. Phantom Crown. Bobbs, 1934. Attempt
of Maximilian and Carlotta, backed by Napoleon III, to rule
Mexico.   6254

Henderson, Daniel M. A Crown for Carlotta. Stokes, 1929.
Tragic romance and adventures of Maximilian and Carlotta
in Mexico.   6255

Hudson, William Henry. Green Mansions. Knopf, 1916. A
poetic interpretation of life in the tropical forests of Vene-
zuela.   6256

Jeffries, Graham Montague. Flames of Empire. by Peter
Bourne, pseud. Putnam, 1949. Concerning the ill-
starred Emperor Maximilian of Mexico.   6257

Jennings, John. Call the New World. Macmillan, 1941.
A court-martialed West Point graduate joins the South

American struggle for freedom in the nineteenth century. 6258

La Farge, Oliver. Sparks Fly Upward. Houghton, 1931.
Social classes in mid-century Central America. 6259

Lea, Tom. The Wonderful Country. Little, 1952. A boy,
after killing his father's murderer, flees to Mexico where
he grows up, later returning to be a Texas Ranger. 6260

Lehrer, James. Viva Max! Duell, 1966. A patriotic Mexican general attempts to recover the Alamo. 6261

Locke, Charles O. The Taste of Infamy. Norton, 1960. A
Texan travels south across the border to avenge the murder
of his brother in Mexico. 6262

Lyle, Eugene P. The Missourian. Doubleday, Page, 1905.
The Mexican War with emissaries from the defeated Confederacy and France as figures. 6263

Machado de Assis, Joaquim María. Dom Casmurro. (tr.)
Noonday Pr., 1953. (first pub. in 1900) A psychological
novel of a jealous man who allowed his obsession to ruin
the lives of his wife and son. 6264

_____. The Hand and the Glove. (tr.) Univ. Pr. of Ken-
tucky, 1970. (first pub. in 1874) A proud and beautiful
Brazilian señorita finally chooses one of three suitors. 6265

Marchal, Lucien. Sage of Canudos. (tr.) Dutton, 1954.
Incident involving a "holy city" in the Brazilian hinter-
lands. 6266

Nicole, Christopher. Ratoon. St. Martin's, 1962. British
Guiana sugar plantations, owned by English colonials and
worked by African slaves, are the scene for the East
Coast Insurrection of 1823. 6267

Niles, Blair. Passengers to Mexico. Farrar, 1943. Ill-
fated French attempt to rule Mexico through Maximilian. 6268

Pearsall, Robert Brainard. Young Vargas Lewis. Houghton,
1968. A young American engineer becomes involved in
bloody Latin American fighting during the War of the Triple
Alliance. 6269

Pilling, William. Ponce de Leon. Laurie, 1910. Argentina in the early nineteenth century, depicting the end of
Spanish influence there. 6270

Pollock, Alyce and Ruth Goode. Don Gaucho. McGraw, 1950.
The pampas of Argentina are the scene of vigorous fighting. 6271

Raynolds, Robert. Paquita. Putnam, 1947. Light-hearted
    romance of a noble Spanish lady in Mexico.   6272

Rego, José Lins do. Plantation Boy. (tr.) Knopf, 1966.
    Difficulties of a young plantation owner in northeast Brazil
    because of his concern for his slaves.   6273

Rosa, Joao Guimaraes. The Devil to Pay in the Backlands.
    (tr.) Knopf, 1963. Story of a former member of a band
    of ruffians in the back country of the Brazilian Northwest
    in the late 1800s.   6274

Rundell, E. Ralph. Color of Blood. Crowell, 1948. Argen-
    tina under dictator Juan Manuel de Rosas.   6275

Sabran, Jean. Vengeance of Don Manuel. (tr.) by Bernard
    Deleuze, pseud. Putnam, 1953. An adventure story about
    Spanish colonial days in Chile.   6276

Strabel, Thelma. Storm to the South. Doubleday, 1944. Two
    cousins involved in emotional conflict and political revolu-
    tion in Spanish California and Peru.   6277

Teilhet, Darwin Le Ora. Lion's Skin. Sloane, 1955. Cali-
    fornian William Walker attempts to gain control over Nica-
    ragua.   6278

_____. Retreat from the "Dolphin." Little, 1943. The
    Chilean Revolution and the good ship Dolphin.   6279

Uslar Pietri, Arturo. The Red Lances. (tr.) Knopf, 1963.
    (first pub. in Spain in 1931) Struggles for personal power
    parallel the national struggle in the Venezuelan War for
    Independence.   6280

Verissimo, Erico. Time and the Wind. (tr.) Macmillan,
    1951. A family in southern Brazil during the period from
    1740 to 1895.   6281

White, Edward Lucas. El Supremo. Dutton, 1916. About the
    dictator of Paraguay from 1814 to 1840, Rodríguez de
    Francia.   6282

White, Leslie Turner. Look Away, Look Away. Random,
    1943. A group of southerners attempts to settle in Brazil
    after the American Civil War.   6283

Wilkins, William Vaughan. The City of Frozen Fire. Mac-
    millan, 1951, c.1950. YA. An adventure story of a
    Welsh family which goes to South America in 1826 to save
    a ruby mine threatened by pirates.   6284

Williams, Dorothy Jeanne. Mission in Mexico. by J. R.

Williams, pseud. Prentice-Hall, 1959. YA. Adventures
of an American boy in quest of his father who is fighting
for Maximilian in war-torn Mexico.   6285

Williams, Joel, pseud. The Coasts of Folly. Reynal, 1942.
South Americans plot to gain their independence in the early
nineteenth century.   6286

3. CANADA AND ALASKA

a) French and British Colonial Periods (to 1867)--Canada

Allen, T.D., pseud. for Terry D. and Don B. Allen. Doctor,
Lawyer, Merchant, Chief. Westminster, 1965. YA. A
doctor counsels fur trappers for the Hudson's Bay Company
in pioneer Canada.   6287

Altrocchi, Julia. Wolves Against the Moon. Macmillan, 1940.
The development of a fur trade by a Canadian and his
French-Indian wife, with glimpses of Ottawa Indian life. 6288

Barr, Robert. In the Midst of Alarms. Stokes, 1894. A
romantic tale of a rural area with the Fenian attempt to
capture Canada as background.   6289

Bedford-Jones, Henry. Star Woman. Dodd, 1924. Rivalry
between English and French for the fur trade of the rich
Hudson's Bay territory.   6290

Brick, John. Ben Bryan, Morgan Rifleman. Duell, 1963.
YA. Adventures of a young rifleman who was captured
in the fall of Quebec in 1775.   6291

Butler, Suzanne. My Pride, My Folly. Little, 1953. A Danish girl in search of love and happiness comes to Boston,
later moves to Canada.   6292

Campbell, Grace MacLennan. The Higher Hill. Duell, 1944.
Homey tale of life in Ontario during the War of 1812. 6293

Campbell, Wilfrid. A Beautiful Rebel. Doran, 1909. Attack
of the Americans on Canada during the War of 1812 and
the Battle of Queenstown Heights.   6294

Capes, Bernard. Love Like a Gipsy. Constable, 1901.
Canada and England during the American War of Independence.   6295

Carr, Mary Jane. Young Mac of Fort Vancouver. Crowell,
1940. YA. The exciting story of the son of an Indian
and a fur-trapper.   6296

Cather, Willa. Shadows on the Rock. Knopf, 1931. Deli-
cate, sensitive reflections of events in Quebec under
Frontenac.   6297

Catherwood, Mary H. The Lady of Fort St. John. Houghton,
1891. Rivalry between the forts of Port Royal and St.
John and the heroism of Lady La Tour.   6298

_____. The Romance of Dollard. Century, 1889. French
Captain Dollard and a handful of loyal followers battle an
overwhelming Iroquois force.   6299

_____. The White Islander. Century, 1893. A good
picture of Indians and their treatment of captives.   6300

Chambers, Robert W. The Drums of Aulone. Appleton,
1927. A French girl's experiences reflect Mme. de
Maintenon's anti-Huguenot influence in the French court.   6301

Coatsworth, Elizabeth. Last Fort. Winston, 1952. YA.
The journey of French fur traders from Canada down the
Mississippi Valley in search of business.   6302

Cody, Hiram Alfred. The King's Arrow. Doran, 1922.
Tory loyalists who flee to Canada during the American
Revolution.   6303

Cooney, Percival John. Kinsmen. Doran, 1916. Rebellion
against a quasi-feudal overlord in Upper Canada.   6304

Costain, Thomas B. High Towers. Doubleday, 1949. Account of an attempt to build a French empire in America
featuring the Le Moyne family of Montreal.   6305

Crowley, Mary Catherine. A Daughter of New France.
Little, 1901. "Account of the gallant Sieur Cadillac and
his colony on the Detroit."   6306

_____. In Treaty With Honour. Little, 1906. French
Canada's fight for responsible government in the 1830s.   6307

Curwood, James O. The Black Hunter. Cosmopolitan Bk.,
1926. The disputed Canadian frontier when both France
and England were colonizing.   6308

_____. The Plains of Abraham. Doubleday, 1928. Vivid
account of French-Canadians orphaned by an Indian massacre.   6309

De La Roche, Mazo. Building of Jalna. Little, 1944.
Philip Whiteoak and his bride migrate to Ontario in mid-
nineteenth century.   6310

_____. Morning at Jalna. Little, 1960. A mother and her four children in Canada during the American Civil War. 6311

Eaton, Evelyn. Quietly My Captain Waits. Harper, 1940. Canada under the French regime. 6312

_____. Restless Are the Sails. Harper, 1941. Exciting trip by land and sea to warn Louisbourg of attack. 6313

_____. The Sea Is So Wide. Harper, 1943. Three Acadians, exiled from Nova Scotia, settle in Williamsburg, Virginia. 6314

Elson, John M. The Scarlet Sash. Dent, 1925. A novel of life during the War of 1812, including an account of the Battle of Queenstown Heights. 6315

Elwood, Muriel. Deeper the Heritage. Scribner, 1946. Eighteenth century life in Montreal and eastern Canada. 6316

_____. Heritage of the River. Scribner, 1945. Indian warfare, political intrigue, and romance in Montreal. 6317

_____. Towards the Sunset. Scribner, 1947. The children and grandchildren of French-Canadian pioneers. 6318

_____. Web of Destiny. Bobbs, 1951. The Marquis de Montcalm and Sir William Johnson appear in this tale of Canada. 6319

Fraser, Hermia H. Tall Brigade. Binfords, 1956. Adventures of a brigade leader for the early Hudson's Bay Company. 6320

French, Maida P. Boughs Bend Over. Doubleday, 1944. Loyalists who seek refuge in Canada face difficulties establishing a home in the forests. 6321

Freuchen, Peter. Law of Larion. (tr.) McGraw, 1952. An absorbing, moving tale of Larion, Alaskan Indian chief in a land of desolate and austere beauty. 6322

_____. Legend of Daniel Williams. Messner, 1956. An escaped slave's experiences in Canada. 6323

Gaspé, Philippe Aubert de. The Canadians of Old. (tr.) [pub. later as: Cameron of Lochiel] Appleton, 1890. A story of French settlers in Canada in the mid-eighteenth century. 6324

Gibbs, George. Flame of Courage. Appleton, 1926. Intrigues and romance of members of the French court in Canada during the Seven Years War.   6325

Golon, Sergeanne, pseud. for Serge and Anne Golon. The
    Countess Angélique. (tr.) Putnam, 1968, c.1967. The
    difficulties and perplexities of Angélique and the Count
    during Indian Wars in the forests of the New World.   6326

_____. The Temptation of Angélique. (tr.) Bantam Bks.,
    1971, c.1969. Exiled from the court to New France,
    Countess Angélique undergoes great perils, including the
    presence of a former lover.   6327

Goodridge Roberts, Theodore. Brothers of Peril. by Theo-
    dore Roberts. Page, 1905. Land and sea adventures when
    British fishermen were struggling for control of Newfound-
    land.   6328

Gordon, Charles William. The Rock and the River. by Ralph
    Connor, pseud. Dodd, 1931. Romance of a young Canadian
    boy and an American girl just prior to the War of 1812. 6329

_____. The Runner. by Ralph Connor, pseud. Doubleday,
    1929. Fighting between Americans, English, Indians, and
    Canadians in the War of 1812.   6330

Harris, Cyril. One Braver Thing. Scribner, 1942. English
    loyalist doctor and family exiled to Nova Scotia at the end
    of the American Revolution.   6331

Haworth, Paul Leland. The Path of Glory. Little, 1911.
    A story of the conquest of Canada including Wolfe's mili-
    tary victory on the Plains of Abraham.   6332

Hayes, John F. The Dangerous Cove. Messner, 1960. YA.
    Two teen-aged boys aid a small Newfoundland settlement es-
    cape destruction by visiting fishermen.   6333

Howard, Elizabeth. North Winds Blow Free. Morrow, 1949.
    YA. A Michigan family whose home is a station on the
    Underground Railroad moves to Canada to found a commu-
    nity for escaped slaves.   6334

Isely, Bliss. Blazing the Way West. Scribner, 1939. Early
    French fur traders and explorers.   6335

Jennings, John. Strange Brigade. Little, 1952. The settle-
    ment of the Canadian West.   6336

Kent, Louise Andrews. He Went With Champlain. Houghton,
    1959. YA. Story of the young interpreter who accom-
    panied the Sieur Samuel de Champlain on the voyage that
    resulted in the founding of Quebec in 1604.   6337

Kirby, William. The Golden Dog. Page, 1897. Quebec
in the 1740s was the scene of colonizing and fur trading. 6338

Lancaster, Bruce. Bright to the Wanderer. Little, 1942.
Loyalist refugees engaged in the political conflict over the
Family Compact. 6339

Laut, Agnes C. Heralds of Empire. Appleton, 1902. "Being
the story of one Ramsay Stanhope, lieutenant to Pierre Radis-
son in the Northern fur trade." 6340

_____. Lords of the North. Heinemann, 1901. Pictures
pioneer life, fur trading, and a woman captured by Indians.
6341

_____. The Story of the Trapper. Appleton, 1902. The
exploits and adventures of a fur trapper who wanders
across the continent. 6342

Lobdell, Helen. The Fort in the Forest. Houghton, 1963.
YA. The tragic expedition to establish and hold a fort near
Niagara Falls to further the French claim in Canada. 6343

Lyman, Olim L. The Trail of the Grand Seigneur. New Am-
sterdam Bk. Co., 1903. Refugees from revolutionary
France who seek a new life in America, settling near Lake
Ontario. 6344

Lyttleton, Edith J. Grand Parade. by G.B. Lancaster, pseud.
Reynal, 1943. Four generations of a prominent colonial
Halifax family. 6345

McCulloch, John H. The Men of Kildonan. Doubleday, Doran,
1926. Travels and trials of settlers who migrated from
Scotland to Canada. 6346

McDowell, Franklin D. The Champlain Road. Macmillan,
1939. Jesuit missionaries and martyrs among the Hurons
in Canada. 6347

McIlwraith, Jean. A Diana of Quebec. Smith & Elder, 1912.
Romance of Quebec late in the century with Nelson as one
of the main characters. 6348

McLennan, William and Jean McIlwraith. The Span O' Life.
Harper, 1899. Jacobite activities in Canada and the capture of Louisbourg. 6349

Marquis, Thomas G. Marguerite de Roberval. Fisher Unwin,
1899. Canada as a French colony; the explorations of
Cartier. 6350

Merwin, Samuel. The Road to Frontenac. Doubleday, 1901.
A party travelling through French Canada is captured by

Indians.   6351

Niven, Frederick. Mine Inheritance. Macmillan, 1940.
Evicted Scots crofters settle in the Red River region.   6352

O'Grady, P.W. and Dorothy Dunn. Dark Was the Wilderness.
Bruce, 1945. Features the North American martyrs--
Jogues, Brébeuf, Lalemant, and Goupil.   6353

Parish, John C. The Man With the Iron Hand. Houghton,
1918. French-Canadian expansion into the Mississippi
Valley.   6354

Parker, Gilbert. The Pomp of the Lavilettes. Appleton, 1897.
A rousing tale of adventure and rebellion under Papineau in
1837.   6355

_____. The Power and the Glory. Harper, 1925. The
northern explorations of Robert La Salle.   6356

_____. The Seats of the Mighty. Appleton, 1896. A
colonial romance ending with the fall of Quebec.   6357

_____. The Trail of the Sword. Appleton, 1896. Fighting
among French, Indians, and British in New France and New
England.   6358

_____. When Valmond Came to Pontiac. Macmillan, 1895.
A romance of a Canadian village, with a supposed son of
Napoleon as chief character.   6359

Parrish, Randall. Beyond the Frontier. McClurg, 1915.
Rivalry between La Salle and Governor La Barre in colonial
Canada.   6360

Patterson, Frances Taylor. The Long Shadow. Sheed, 1956.
Fictional biography of the French Jesuit missionary, St.
Jean de Brébeuf.   6361

_____. White Wampum. Longmans, 1934. Fictional ac-
count of the life of an Indian girl converted to Catholicism.   6362

Quiller-Couch, Arthur T. Fort Amity. Scribner, 1904.
Fighting among British, French, Americans, and Indians
in the Ticonderoga-Quebec area in the 1750s.   6363

Raddall, Thomas. Hangman's Beach. Doubleday, 1966.
Friction between a Nova Scotian shipowner and the British
navy during the Napoleonic Wars.   6364

_____. His Majesty's Yankees. [abridged version: Son
of the Hawk] Doubleday, 1942. Effects on Nova Scotia

of the American War for Independence.   6365

_____. Roger Sudden. Doubleday, 1945. Rivalry between
French and English in the colonization of Nova Scotia.   6366

Ritchie, Cicero T. Willing Maid. Abelard-Schuman, 1957.
Struggle for supremacy in Nova Scotia among British,
French, Indians, and Acadians.   6367

Roberts, Charles G. D. (1) The Forge in the Forest. Silver,
1897. (2) A Sister to Evangeline. Silver, 1900. (1) The
settlement of the Acadians and (2) their expulsion, both accounts influenced by Longfellow's poem Evangeline.   6368-9

_____. The Prisoner of Mademoiselle. Page, 1905. Ro-
mance of a Yankee sea captain and a French girl in
Acadia.   6370

Smith, Alice Prescott. Montlivet. Houghton, 1906. English
and French rivals band together to fight the Indians.   6371

Smith, Arthur D. Howden. The Doom Trail. Brentano's,
1922. Fur trade rivalry with the French diverting English
trade goods to their own use.   6372

Speare, Elizabeth George. Calico Captive. Houghton, 1957.
YA. The adventures of a girl captured by Indians in 1754
and later sold to the French in Montreal.   6373

Spicer, Bart. The Tall Captains. Dodd, 1957. Soldiers,
farmers, townsfolk, and politicians in the final days of New
France.   6374

Stone, Grace. The Cold Journey. Morrow, 1934. A group
of captured villagers is marched through the wilderness to
French settlements in the north.   6375

Sullivan, Alan. The Fur Masters. Coward, 1947. Competitive fur trading in the early nineteenth century as seen by a
Hudson's Bay Company man.   6376

_____. Three Came to Ville Marie. Coward, 1943. A
romance of three settlers to New France.   6377

Taylor, Allan. Morgan's Long Rifles. Putnam, 1965. YA.
Exciting tale of a young rifleman on the long march through
northern New York and the attack on Quebec.   6378

Vaczek, Louis C. River and Empty Sea. Houghton, 1950. A
canoe trip to Hudson's Bay through the Canadian wilderness.
                                                        6379
Wharton, Anne Hollingsworth. A Rose of Old Quebec. Lippincott, 1913. Mary Thompson and Captain Nelson in

Quebec and London, 1780-1790.   6380

White, Leslie Turner. His Majesty's Highlanders. Crown,
    1964. The French and Indian Wars as experienced by a
    Scottish Highlander and his assorted companions fighting
    with Wolfe at Quebec.   6381

White, Stewart Edward. Conjurer's House. McClure, 1903.
    Rivalry as the Hudson's Bay Company tries to gain control
    of the fur trade.   6382

b) The Dominion of Canada (1867-1900)

Appel, Benjamin. A Time of Fortune. Morrow, 1963. The
    first half of the book is a rousing tale of the Klondike gold
    miners in 1897; the second shows New York political life
    in the early twentieth century.   6383

Blacker, Irwin R. Days of Gold. World, 1961. Strained re-
    lationships during survival-of-the-fittest competition in the
    Yukon gold rush showing the rapid growth of Dawson City.   6384

Cameron, William Bleasdell. The War Trail of Big Bear.
    Duckworth, 1927. The connection of Big Bear and other
    Cree Indians with the rebellion of 1885 and the Frog Lake
    Massacre.   6385

Campbell, Grace MacLennan. The Thorn-Apple Tree. Duell,
    1943. Romance of Scotch-Canadian pioneers.   6386

Cody, Hiram Alfred. Fighting-Slogan. Doubleday, Doran,
    1926. Romance and rivalries when the Fenians rebelled
    against England.   6387

Constantin-Weyer, Maurice. The Half-Breed. Macaulay,
    1930. About a man who sometimes disagreed violently
    with government policy.   6388

Cotes, Sara Jeannette. The Imperialist. by Mrs. Everard
    Cotes. Constable, 1904. Life and business interests in
    a Canadian town in the 1870s.   6389

De La Roche, Mazo. Mary Wakefield. Little, 1949. A fam-
    ily of English immigrants at their estate, Jalna.   6390

Franchere, Ruth. Stampede North. Macmillan, 1969. YA.
    A photographer and his son go to the Klondike during the
    gold fever days of 1897.   6391

Hatton, Joseph. Under the Great Seal. Cassell, 1893. Poor
    management of political affairs under the Lorne govern-
    ment in Newfoundland.   6392

Houston, James. The White Dawn. Harcourt, 1971.   Three
white whalers, stranded north of Hudson's Bay and rescued by Eskimos, disrupt the lives of their hosts.   6393

Jarvis, W. H. P.   The Great Gold Rush.   Murray, 1913.   The
rush to the Klondike after the discovery of gold.   6394

Keith, Marian. The Silver Maple. Revell, 1906. A Scots
lumberman joins the expedition to assist Gordon in fighting
Riel's second rebellion.   6395

Laurence, Margaret. The Stone Angel. Knopf, 1964. Reminiscences of an aged woman concerning Canada and her own
mistakes in the latter part of the nineteenth century.   6396

Loomis, Alice F. Ride Out Singing. Whittlesey House, 1951.
YA.   Phyllis Vernon came from England to Canada in the
1880s to keep house for her brother.   6397

Lutz, Giles A.   The Magnificent Failure. Doubleday, 1967.
The tragic attempt of a group of French-Indian descent to
protect their homes against Canadian troops.   6398

MacGregor, Mary E. M. A Gentleman Adventurer. Doubleday,
Doran, 1924.   A young Scotsman in the service of the Hudson's Bay Company is stationed at remote outposts.   6399

Mackie, John. The Prodigal's Brother. Jarrold & Sons, 1899.
The Northwest Province during the Red River Rebellion of
1885.   6400

McNamee, James. My Uncle Joe. Viking, 1963, c. 1962. A
boy and his uncle make a scouting trip along the northwest
Canadian frontier in the 1880s.   6401

O'Hagan, Howard. Tay John. Potter, 1960. The beauty,
majesty, and rigors of the Canadian Rockies as they affected
the trappers and settlers.   6402

White, Stewart Edward. The Silent Places. Hodder, 1904.
Two Hudson's Bay Company men and their journey through
untamed wilderness.   6403

Young, Samuel H. The Klondike Clan. Revell, 1916. The
Klondike Gold Rush of the 1890s.   6404

    c)   Alaska before Statehood

Burnett, William Riley.   The Goldseekers. Doubleday, 1962.
Adventures of four men who travel via the North Pacific,
the Bering Sea, and the Yukon River to the gold-fields of
Alaska.   6405

Clarke, Tom E. No Furs for the Czar. Lothrop, 1962.
   YA. The son of a Russian trader who exploited the people
   in an early Alaskan colony abandons trading to help the
   people.   6406

Downes, Anne Miller. Natalia. Lippincott, 1960. A romance of Alaska in the time when the United States acquired
   the territory from Russia, in the 1860s.   6407

4. THE CARIBBEAN AREA

Alderman, Clifford L. The Silver Keys. Putnam, 1960.
   Sir William Phips' expedition from Maine to the Caribbean
   in search of sunken treasure in the late seventeenth century.   6408

Allen, Henry. San Juan Hill. by Will Henry, pseud. Random
   House, 1962. The Spanish American War in Cuba as seen by
   an Arizona cowboy who joined Theodore Roosevelt's "Rough
   Riders."   6409

Atherton, Gertrude. The Gorgeous Isle. Doubleday, 1908.
   A popular nineteenth century winter resort in the West
   Indies.   6410

Best, Herbert. Diane. Morrow, 1954. Plantation owner's
   death is avenged by his daughter, who takes over management of the estate.   6411

Bloundelle-Burton, John. The Hispaniola Plate. Cassell,
   1895. Sir William Phips' quest for a lost Spanish
   treasure.   6412

Bontemps, Arna. Drums at Dusk. Macmillan, 1939. Toussaint L'Ouverture and the Negro uprising in Haiti during
   the French Revolution.   6413

Brown, Wenzell. They Called Her Charity. Appleton, 1951.
   Pirates, pursued by the British, take refuge in the Virgin
   Islands in the seventeenth century.   6414

Carpentier, Alejo. Explosion in a Cathedral. (tr.) Little,
   1963. (pub. in Mexico in 1962) Victor Hugues, a French
   shopkeeper in Haiti, becomes a rebel during the French
   Revolution and conquers the island of Guadeloupe from
   the British.   6415

_____. Kingdom of This World. Knopf, 1957. Haiti in
   the period of King Henri Christophe.   6416

Castor, Henry. The Year of the Spaniard. Doubleday, 1950.
   The historic year of 1898 when the United States won Cuba,

Puerto Rico, and the Philippines from Spain.   6417

Devereux, Mary. Lafitte of Louisiana. Little, 1902. About
Jean Lafitte, the French pirate who operated largely in the
Gulf of Mexico.   6418

Donovan, Frank R. The Unlucky Hero. Duell, 1963. YA.
The British attempt to trap the Spanish fleet in Santiago
Harbor by sinking a ship at its entrance.   6419

Emerson, Peter Henry. Caóba, the Guerilla Chief. Scribner,
1897. A romance of the Cuban Rebellion against Spain in
the late nineteenth century.   6420

Galván, Manuel de Jesus. The Cross and the Sword. (tr.)
Ind. U. Press, 1954. Early Spanish settlement of the
Caribbean area.   6421

Gaskin, Catherine. Fiona. Fawcett, 1971, c.1970. Scots
girl finds her life and her work as a governess greatly
complicated by her gift of second sight which often causes
her to act erratically.   6422

Hearn, Lafcadio. Youma. Harper, 1890. A story of the
Negro insurrection on Martinique in 1848 and of a slave
who remained loyal.   6423

Heckert, Eleanor. The Golden Rock. Doubleday, 1971.
Trading on St. Eustatius Island in the Dutch West Indies
provided a vital, if precarious, link in the supply line of
Washington's army during the American Revolution.   6424

_____. Muscavado. Doubleday, 1968. Forbidden love of
a plantation owner's daughter and a mulatto slave during
a violent slave revolt in the Virgin Islands.   6425

Hergesheimer, Joseph. The Bright Shawl. Knopf, 1922.
A romantic American youth, inflamed by Cuba's struggle
against Spain, joins the revolution.   6426

Horner, Lance. The Street of the Sun. [En. title: Santiago
Blood] Fawcett, 1967, c.1956. A story of love, slavery,
and high society in Havana in the late nineteenth century. 6427

Husband, Joseph. Citadel. Houghton, 1924. A privateer
captain faces slavery and death to rescue his lady.   6428

Jeffries, Graham Montague. Drums of Destiny. [En. title:
Black Saga] by Peter Bourne, pseud. Putnam, 1947.
A Scotch doctor in Haiti during the revolt of the slaves.   6429

Jennings, John. Rogue's Yarn. Little, 1953. A seafaring
yarn of action among the United States, the pirates, and

the French privateers in the Caribbean.   6430

Jesse, F. Tennyson. Moonraker; or, The Female Pirate and
Her Friends. Knopf, 1927. Contains a rousing sea tale
and a story of Toussaint L'Ouverture.   6431

Lancaster, Bruce and Lowell Brentano. Bride of a Thousand
Cedars. Stokes, 1939. The effect on Bermuda of the
blockade runners during the U.S. Civil War.   6432

MacInnes, Colin. Westward to Laughter. Farrar, 1970,
c. 1969. A young Scotsman, forced into slavery in the
Caribbean in the 1750s, rebels at the calm acceptance of
slavery and is involved in a revolt.   6433

Mackintosh, Elizabeth. The Privateer. by Gordon Daviot,
pseud. Macmillan, 1952. Exciting tale of naval action
in the Caribbean in the days of privateer Henry Morgan.   6434

Martineau, Harriet. The Hour and the Man. Moxon, 1841.
Toussaint L'Ouverture's part in the rebellion on Haiti and
his betrayal.   6435

Mason, Van Wyck. Cutlass Empire. Doubleday, 1949.
Henry Morgan's flight from England, and his bloody career
as pirate of the Caribbean.   6436

_____. The "Sea 'Venture." Doubleday, 1961. Romance
during the voyage of the Virginia Company to Jamestown
in 1609, during which the flagship, Sea 'Venture, is blown
off course to Bermuda, stranding the settlers.   6437

Raddall, Thomas. Pride's Fancy. Doubleday, 1946. A
yarn of privateering between Nova Scotia and the Caribbean.   6438

Rhys, Jean. Wide Sargasso Sea. Norton, 1967, c. 1966. The
girlhood and marriage of the woman who was to become the
mad wife of Mr. Rochester in Jane Eyre (listed separately).   6439

Roberts, Walter Adolphe. Single Star. Bobbs, 1949. Revolutionary days in Cuba in the 1890s.   6440

Rowland, Henry Cottrell. In the Shadow. Appleton, 1906.
An Oxford-educated Negro leads a rebellion in Haiti.   6441

Simons, Katherine D.M. The Land Beyond the Tempest.
by Drayton Mayrant, pseud. Coward, 1960. The Sea
Venture, on an expedition to take supplies to Jamestown,
is stricken by a storm off Bermuda.   6442

Slaughter, Frank G. Buccaneer Surgeon. by C.V. Terry,

pseud. Hanover, 1954. A ship's surgeon of Spanish and English ancestry on the Spanish Main.   6443

_____. Pilgrims in Paradise. Doubleday, 1960. Adventures of Puritans from England who settled on an island in the West Indies.   6444

Smith, Herbert Huntington. His Majesty's Sloop, Diamond Rock. by H. S. Huntington, pseud. Houghton, 1904. British defense of an island near Martinique during the Napoleonic War.   6445

Smith, Minna Caroline. Mary Paget. Macmillan, 1900. England and Bermuda at the time of James I.   6446

Street, James Howell. Mingo Dabney. Dial, 1950. Guerrilla warfare in the Cuban revolt against Spanish rule.   6447

Stuart, Morna. Marassa and Midnight. McGraw, 1967, c.1966. YA. A slave uprising finally aids in reuniting two brothers-- both slaves--who had become separated.   6448

Taylor, Angeline. Black Jade. McBride, 1947. Romantic novel of Haiti at the end of the eighteenth century.   6449

Taylor, James G., Jr. Dark Dawn. Mohawk, 1932. Adventure during the Negro uprising in Haiti in 1791.   6450

Vandercook, John W. Black Majesty. Harper, 1928. Romanticized life of Henri Christophe, the slave who became King of Haiti.   6451

Webb, Barbara. Aletta Laird. Doubleday, 1935. Romance in the Bermudas during the American Revolution.   6452

Wilder, Robert. Wind From the Carolinas. Bantam Bks., 1970, c.1964. A multi-generation story of a Tory family which migrated from Carolina to the Bahamas after the American Revolution and built a new life there.   6453

Yerby, Frank. Golden Hawk. Pocket Bks., 1959, c.1948. Buccaneer captain thrives on violence, passionate romance, and piracy in his quest for revenge.   6454

Yolland, G. Under the Stars. White, 1907. The Jamaica Insurrection of 1865.   6455

Alexander, Holmes Moss
 American Nabob 5699
Alexander, Miriam
 House of Lisronan, The 2548
 Port of Dreams, The 2549
Alexander, William P., see Cor-
 mack, Maribelle and William
 P. Alexander
Alexander, the Glorious 731
Alexander, the God (Druon) 183
Alexander, the God (Payne) 202
Alexis, Wilibald, (pseud.) see
 Häring, Wilhelm
Alfred the King 572
Alfriend, Mary Bethell
 Juan Ortiz 4106
Alice Lorraine 2990
Alice of Old Vincennes 4614
Alien Light, The [Consider the
 Lilies] 3035
Alington, Argentine
 Gentlemen--the Regiment! 2948
Alkibiades 123
All Fools Together 3087
All for the Love of a Lady 1878
All in Good Time 4660
All Men Tall 1004
All the Brave Rifles 5341
All the Golden Gifts 2078
All the Living 1832
All the Queen's Men [Elizabeth] 1439
All the Trumpets Sounded 13
All This, and Heaven Too 4909
All Ye People 4811
Allardyce, Alexander
 Balmoral 2235
Allen, Dexter
 Coil of the Serpent 6186
 Jaguar and the Golden Stag 1260
 Valley of Eagles 6187
Allen, Don B., see Allen, T. D.,
 (pseud.)
Allen, Henry
 Custer's Last Stand 5700
 From Where the Sun Now Stands
  5701
 Gates of the Mountains, The 4655
 Journey to Shiloh 5397
 Last Warpath, The 6163
 Mackenna's Gold 5702
 Niño 5703
 No Survivors 5704
 One More River to Cross 5398
 San Juan Hill 6409
 Sons of the Western Frontier 5705
 Yellowstone Kelly 5706
Allen, Hervey
 Action at Aquila 5399

Anthony Adverse 2916
Bedford Village 4107
City in the Dawn, The 4108
Forest and the Fort, The 4109
Toward the Morning 4110
Allen, James Lane
 Choir Invisible, The 4656
 Sword of Youth, The 5400
Allen, Merritt Parmelee
 Battle Lanterns 4380
 Blow, Bugles, Blow 5401
 East of Astoria 4657
Allen, T. D., (pseud.)
 Doctor in Buckskin 4658
 Doctor, Lawyer, Merchant, Chief
  6287
 Troubled Border 4659
Allen, Terry D., see Allen, T. D.,
 (pseud.)
Allis, Marguerite
 All in Good Time 4660
 Brave Pursuit 4661
 Charity Strong 4662
 Law of the Land, The 4663
 Not without Peril 4381
 Now We Are Free 4664
 Rising Storm, The 5402
 Splendor Stays, The 4665
 To Keep Us Free 4666
 Water over the Dam 4667
Almayer's Folly 4081
Almedingen, E. M., see Almedingen,
 Martha Edith von
Almedingen, Martha Edith von
 Candle at Dusk, A 585
 Golden Sequence, The 593
 Ladies of St. Hedwig's, The 3718
 Young Catherine 2888
 Young Mark 2889
Alone among Men 2633
Altar of the Legion, The 516
Altrocchi, Julia
 Wolves against the Moon 6288
Alturlie 2318
Always a River 4337
Amalie's Story 3632
Amateur Gentleman, The 3078
Amazing Duke, The 1902
Amazing Mrs. Bonaparte, The 3451
Amber Princess, The [Electra] 657
American, The (Dodge) 4862
American, The (Fast) 5845
American Beauty 6169
American in Paris, The 3515
American Nabob 5699
American Prisoner, The 3231
American, Sir, An 5239
American Years 5269

477

481

Barr, Amelia E. (cont.)
Knight of the Nets, A 2973
Maid of Maiden Lane, The 4697
Maid of Old New York, A 4122
Master of His Fate [In Spite of Himself] 2974
Orkney Maid, An 3720
Paper Cap, The 2975
Paul and Christina 2976
Remember the Alamo 4698
She Loved a Sailor 4699
Song of a Single Note, A 4386
Strawberry Handkerchief, The 4387
Trinity Bells 4700
Barr, Gladys
Cross, Sword, and Arrow 848
Barr, Robert
Cardillac 2051
Countess Tekla, The 783
In the Midst of Alarms 6289
Over the Border 1726
Sword Maker, The 1090
Barracoon 3987
Barrett, Frank
Obliging Husband, The 1727
Perfidious Lydia 2977
Set of Rogues, A 1728
Barrett, Monte
Sun in Their Eyes 4701
Tempered Blade 4702
Barrett, Wilson and E. A. Barron
In Old New York 4123
Barricade 3606
Barringer, Daniel Moreau
And the Waters Prevailed 474
Barringer, Leslie
Kay, the Left-Handed 665
Barrington, E., (pseud.) see Beck, Lily Adams
Barrington, Michael
David Arnot 1278
Knight of the Golden Sword, The 1729
Lady of Tripoli, The 757
Reminiscences of Sir Barrington Beaumont, Bart., The 2257
Barron, E.A., see Barrett, Wilson and E. A. Barron
Barry, Jane
Carolinians, The 4388
Long March, The 4389
Maximilian's Gold 5724
. Shadow of Eagles, A 5725
Time in the Sun, A 5726
Barry, William Francis
Dayspring, The 3383
Barry Leroy 2602

Bartlett, Jenniebelle
Cry above the Winds 4703
Bartlett, Lanier
Adios! 4704
Bartlett, Virginia Stivers
Mistress of Monterey 4705
Barton, Florence
Olympia 1635
Barton, Hester
Baron of Ill-Fame, The 807
Bartos-Höppner, B.
Cossacks, The 1678
Save the Khan 1679
Storm over the Caucasus 3721
Bartram, George
Lads of the Fancy 2978
Longshoremen, The 2979
Basil, (pseud.), see King, Richard Ashe
Basilissa 653
Bass, Eduard
Umberto's Circus 3538
Bass, Milton R.
Jory 5727
Basset [Early Victorian] 3109
Basso, Hamilton
Light Infantry Ball, The 5410
Bastard, The 2118
Bataille, Michel
Fire from Heaven 1032
Batchellor, D. O.
Unstrung Bow, The 6192
Bates, Arthur
Cromwell 1730
Bates, Morgan
Martin Brook 4706
Bates House 5416
Bath Comedy, The 2308
Bath Tangle 3121
Baton Sinister (Spinatelli) 1669
Baton Sinister, The (Arthur) 1713
Battalion of Saints 5387
Battle Ground, The 5515
Battle Lanterns 4380
Battle of the Strong, The 2745
Battle of the Weak, The 3055
Battlement and Tower 1997
Bauer, Florence Anne
Abram, Son of Terah 55
Behold Your King 260
Lady Besieged 910
Bauer, Wolfgang and Herbert Frank, (ed.)
Golden Casket, The 1226
Baum, Vicki
Headless Angel 3539
Baumann, Hans
Barque of the Brothers, The 1205

485

Bikelas, Demetrios
  Loukis Laras 3725
Bill, Alfred H.
  Clutch of the Corsican, The
    3387
  Highroads of Peril 3388
Billings, Edith S.
  Cleomenes 266
Billings, Maris Warrington, (pseud.)
  see Billings, Edith S.
Billy the Kid 5794
Binding of the Strong, The 1910
Bindloss, Harold
  Cattle-baron's Daughter, The
    5732
Binns, Archie
  Land Is Bright, The 4721
  Mighty Mountain 4722
  You Rolling River 5733
Binns, Ottwell
  Sword of Fortune, The 1742
Bird, Horace V., see Karig,
  Walter and Horace V. Bird
Bird, Robert Montgomery
  Nick o' the Woods 4723
Bird of Dawning 3831
Bird of Fire 832
Birmingham, George A., (pseud.),
  see Hannay, James Owen
Birney, Hoffman
  Dice of God, The 5734
  Eagle in the Sun 4724
  Grim Journey 4725
Birth of Mischief 2829
Birth of the Gods, The 156
Birthright, The 2385
Bischoff, Ilse
  Proud Heritage 4726
Bishop, Farnham, and Arthur
  Gilchrist Brodeur
  Altar of the Legion, The 516
Bishop of Cottontown, The 5998
Bisno, Beatrice
  Tomorrow's Bread 5735
Bison of Clay 475
Black, Ladbroke and Robert Lynd
  Mantle of the Emperor, The
    3389
Black Angels, The 5105
Black Arrow, The 998
Black Bartlemy's Treasure 2208
Black Cliffs, The 3625
Black Colonel, The 2440
Black Cuirassier, The 2168
Black Daniel 5150
Black Dawn 5948
Black Disc, The 1127
Black Douglas, The (Crockett) 1009

Black Douglas, The (Douglas) 679
Black Dwarf, The 2485
Black Falcon 3840
Black Familiars, The 1454
Black Feather 5323
Black Forest, The 4546
Black Friday 5934
Black Glove, The 1954
Black Gold at Titusville 4861
Black Hunter, The 6308
Black Ivory 4693
Black Jack Davy 6012
Black Jade 6449
Black Majesty 6451
Black Mary 3266
Black Moth, The 2381
Black Pilgrim, The 3731
Black Prophet, The 3323
Black River Captive 4253
Black Rose, The 673
Black Saga [Drums of Destiny] 6429
Black Sheep 3122
Black Spice 3843
Black Symbol, The 5938
Black Thunder 4732
Black Tulip, The 2131
Black William 2453
Black Wolf's Breed, The 4170
Blackbird, The 2245
Blackburn, Thomas Wakefield
  Good Day to Die, A 5736
Blackcock's Feather 1483
Blacker, Irwin R.
  Days of Gold 6384
  Old West in Fiction, The 5737
  Taos 4127
Blackmore, R. D.
  Alice Lorraine 2990
  Lorna Doone 1743
  Maid of Sker, The 2273
  Mary Anerley 2274
  Perlycross 2991
  Springhaven 2992
Blackstock, Charity, (pseud.), see
  Torday, Ursula
Bladys of the Stewponey 2248
Blake, Bass
  Lady's Honour, A 2275
Blake, Forrester
  Franciscan, The 4128
  Johnny Christmas 4727
  Wilderness Passage 5738
Blake, Gladys
  Doña Isabella's Adventures 1612
Blake, M. M.
  Grantley Fenton 3390
Blake, William, (pseud.), see Blech,
  William James

490

Brebner, Percy J. (cont.)
Royal Ward, A 3002
Turbulent Duchess, The 2127
Breck, Vivian, (pseud.), see Breck-
enfeld, Vivian Gurney
Breckenfeld, Vivian Gurney
Maggie 6243
Breem, Wallace
Eagle in the Snow 573
Brenda's Experiment 3892
Breneman, Mary Worthy, (pseud.),
Land They Possessed, The 5744
Breneman, Muriel, see Breneman,
Mary Worthy, (pseud.)
Brenner, Jacques
Nephew to the Emperor 3545
Brentano, Lowell, see Lancaster,
Bruce and Lowell Brentano
Breslin, Howard
Bright Battalions 4136
Concert Grand 4738
Gallowglass, The 521
Hundred Hills, A 5433
Shad Run 4402
Silver Oar, The 4137
Tamarack Tree, The 4739
Bretherton, Vivien
Rock and the Wind 5745
Brethren, The 867
Breton, Frederic
God Save England 913
True Heart 1568
Brick, John
Ben Bryan, Morgan Rifleman
6291
Captives of the Senecas 4403
Eagle of Niagara 4404
Jubilee 5434
King's Rangers, The 4405
Raid, The 4406
Richmond Raid, The 5435
Rifleman, The 4407
Rogues' Kingdom 4740
Strong Men, The 4408
Troubled Spring 5436
Bricks without Straw 6099
Bridal Canopy, The 3533
Bridal Journey 4626
Bridal Wreath, The 1111
Bride, The 1851
Bride for New Orleans 5284
Bride of a Thousand Cedars 6432
Bride of Fortune 5541
Bride of Glory [Miledi] 2346
Bride of Lammermoor, The 1958
Bride of Liberty 4646
Bride of Pilate 336
Bride of the Conqueror 6229

Bride of the MacHugh 1973
Bride of the Nile, The 644
Bride of the River 4995
Brides of the Tiger, The [The Tower
of Wye] 4113
Bridge Between, The 4511
Bridge of San Luis Rey, The 6235
Bridge on the Drina, The 3535
Bridge to Brooklyn 5929
Bridle the Wind 5476
Brief Gaudy Hour 1275
Brier, Royce
Boy in Blue 5437
Brigand, The 1518
Brigham, Johnson
Sinclairs of Old Fort Des Moines,
The 4741
Bright Battalions 4136
Bright Face of Danger, The 4353
Bright Feather (Wilder) 5375
Bright Feathers, The (Culp) 5803
Bright Journey 4850
Bright Land 5502
Bright Pavilions, The 1455
Bright Promise 5165
Bright Shawl, The 6426
Bright Sword, The 5618
Bright to the Wanderer 6339
Brighter Sun 5447
Brimming Cup, The 2562
Bring Larks and Heroes 4067
Bring Me His Ears 5154
Brink, Carol
Buffalo Coat 5746
Snow in the River 5747
Brinton, Selwyn J.
Jacobin, The 2624
Brinton Eliot 4451
Bristow, Gwen
Calico Palace 4742
Celia Garth 4409
Deep Summer 4743
Handsome Road, The 5438
Jubilee Trail, The 4744
Briton, E. Vincent
Some Account of Amyot Brough
2292
Brittle Glass, The 3191
Broad Highway, The 3079
Broad Stripes and Bright Stars 4751
Broadsides 3803
Brod, Max
Master, The 273
Redemption of Tycho Brahe 2128
Brodeur, Arthur Gilchrist, see Bishop,
Farnham and Arthur Gilchrist
Brodeur
Brogger, Mae

495

Collins, Wilkie (cont.)
Antonina 622
Frozen Deep, The 3800
Collis, Maurice
She Was a Queen 1255
Colonel Blood [The King's
Rogue] 2014
Colonel Greatheart [Colonel Stow]
1715
Colonel Kate 2441
Colonel Stow [Colonel Greatheart]
1715
Colonel's Story 5205
Colonial Reformer, A 4043
Colonials, The 4471
Color from a Light Within
1616
Color of Blood 6275
Colors of Vaud, The 2804
Colossus, The 4012
Colum, Padraic
Castle Conquer 3327
Colum of Derry 544
Columbus, A Romance 1132
Colver, Alice
Measure of the Years, The
4152
There Is a Season 4153
Colver, Anne
Listen for the Voices 4813
Theodosia 4814
Colyton, Henry John, (pseud.),
see Zimmermann, Samuel
Comanche 5710
Comancheros, The 5354
Come Home at Even 4143
Come Rack, Come Rope! 1284
Come Spring 4643
Come to the Bower 4754
Comedians, The 286
Comfort, Will
Apache 4815
Coming of Rain, The 5984
Coming of the King, The 1843
Coming of the Preachers, The
2499
Commander of the Mists 2452
Commodore Hornblower 3808
Common Story, A 3742
Compact, The 3974
Companions of Jehu, The
2656
Company of Cowards 5635
Company of Death, The 2187
Company Q 5607
Compton, Herbert
Free Lance in a Far Land, A
3859

Inimitable Mrs. Massingham,
The 2317
Palace of Spies, The 3022
Queen Can Do No Wrong, The
3023
Comrade Jacob 1768
Comstock, Harriet T.
Queen's Hostage, The 1306
Comstock, Seth Cook
Marcelle the Mad 1039
Monsieur le Capitaine Douay
1570
Rebel Prince, The 1571
Comtesse de Charny, La 2651
Conceived in Liberty 4455
Concert Grand 4738
Concord Bridge 4500
Condottiere 1194
Confederate Chieftains, The
2045
Confederate Fiddle, The 5681
Confession of Richard Plantagenet,
The 968
Confessions of a Thug 3916
Confessions of Nat Turner, The
5307
Confessors of the Name 461
Coningsby 2980
Coniston 4798
Conjurer's House 6382
Connie Bell, M.D. 5713
Connor, Ralph, (pseud.)
see Gordon, Charles William
Conquer 654
Conquered, The 238
Conquering Kitty 4831
Conqueror (Marshall) 198
Conqueror (Smith) 6228
Conqueror (Tebbel) 4359
Conqueror, The (Atherton)
4672
Conqueror, The (Heyer) 702
Conqueror's Lady, The 6218
Conqueror's Wife, The 688
Conquest 4873
Conquest of Don Pedro, The
5852
Conrad, Joseph
Almayer's Folly 4081
Arrow of Gold, The 3644
Nigger of the Narcissus, The
3024
Nostromo 6244
Suspense 3676
____, and Ford Madox Hueffer
Romance 3801
Conrader, Constance Stone
Blue Wampum 4816

De Gobineau, Joseph Arthur,
(comte), see Gobineau, Joseph
Arthur (comte de)
Dehan, Richard, (pseud.), see
Graves, Clotilde Inez Mary
De Haven, Aubrey
Scarlet Cloak, The 4437
Dehon, Theodora
Heroic Dust 2642
Deiss, Joseph Jay
Great Infidel, The 809
De Kalb, Eugenie
Far Enough 3975
Dekker, Maurits
Beggars' Revolt 1575
De La Fayette, (Madame)
Princess of Cleves, The 1495
Deland, Margaret
Kays, The 5479
De La Roche, Mazo
Building of Jalna 6310
Mary Wakefield 6390
Morning at Jalna 6311
Delderfield, Ronald Frederick
Farewell the Tranquil 2643
God Is an Englishman 3042
Seven Men of Gascony 3414
Theirs Was the Kingdom 3043
Too Few for Drums 3415
Delectable Country, The 4688
De Leeuw, Cateau
Give Me Your Hand 4847
Deleuze, Bernard, (pseud.), see
Sabran, Jean
Delight Makers, The 5721
Delilah's Mountain 4506
Deliverance, The 5882
Dell, Floyd
Diana Stair 4848
Delmar, Viña
Beloved 4849
Big Family, The 6167
Deluge, The 2163
Delusson Family, The 5826
Delves-Broughton, Josephine
Heart of a Queen, The [Crown
Imperial] 1312
Officer and Gentleman 3733
Dem Good Ole Times 4864
Demarest, Phyllis Gordon
Wilderness Brigade 5480
Demi-Royal 3293
Democracy 5691
Demoiselle of France, A 2073
Demoniacs, The 2307
De Morgan, William
Affair of Dishonour, An 1789
Joseph Vance 3044

Dempster, Charlotte L. H.
Iseulte 3416
Denis Dent 4065
Denounced, The (Banim) 2018
Denounced (Bloundelle-Burton) 2277
Denti di Pirajno, Alberto
Ippolita 3683
Departure of Dermot, The 629
de Queiroz, José María de Eça, see
Eça de Queiroz, José María de
DeQuincy, Thomas
Klosterheim 2130
Derleth, August
Bright Journey 4850
Hills Stand Watch 4851
House on the Mound, The 4852
Restless Is the River 4853
Shadow in the Glass, The 5812
Still Is the Summer Night 5813
Wind Leans West, The 4854
Wind over Wisconsin 4855
De Roberto, Federico, see Roberto,
Federico de
De Ropp, Robert S.
If I Forget Thee 293
Descent of the Idol 2133
Desert 431
Desert Gold 4975
Desiderio 1643
Désirée 2763
Desmond, Alice Curtis
Bewitching Betsy Bonaparte 4856
Marie Antoinette's Daughter 3417
Desmond O'Connor 2703
Desmond's Daughter 3885
Destiny 3084
Destiny in Dallas 6068
Destiny of Fire 769
De Stourton, John, see Lethbridge,
Olive and John de Stourton
Destroyers, The 4442
De Treviño, Elizabeth Borton, see
Treviño, Elizabeth Borton de
Deutsch, Babette
Rogue's Legacy 1042
Devereux, Mary
From Kingdom to Colony 4438
Lafitte of Louisiana 6418
Devereux 2422
Devil, The 1075
Devil Dare 3224
Devil in Velvet, The 1766
Devil Inside, The 3730
Devil Kinsmere 1805
Devil to Pay in the Backlands, The
6274
Devil Water 2492
Devil's Brew 3169

Divine, Arthur Durham (cont.)
Thunder on the Chesapeake 5482
Divine, David, (pseud.), see
Divine, Arthur Durham
Divine Average 5061
Divine Lady, The 2261
Divine Minstrels, The 806
Divine Mistress 1631
Dix, Beulah M.
Fair Maid of Graystones, The
1792
Fighting Blade, The 1793
Life, Treason, and Death of
James Blount of Breckenhow,
The 1794
Making of Christopher Ferring-
ham, The 4173
Mistress Content Cradock 4174
, and Carrie A. Harper
Beau's Comedy, The 4175
Dixelius, Hildur
Minister's Daughter, The 3620
Dixon, Pierson
Farewell, Catullus 216
Dixon, Thomas
Clansman, The 5815
Leopard's Spots, The 5816
Man in Gray, The 5483
Southerner, The 5484
Sun Virgin, The 6199
Traitor, The 5817
Victim, The 5485
Dixon, W. Wilmott
Rogue of Rye, The 3051
Djilas, Milovan, see Dilas Milovan
'Dobe Walls 4773
Dobler, Lavinia
Black Gold at Titusville 4861
Dobraczynski, Jan
Letters of Nicodemus, The 296
Doctor in Buckskin 4658
Doctor, Lawyer, Merchant, Chief
6287
Dr. Sevier 4766
Doctor Thorne 3284
Doctorow, E. L.
Welcome to Hard Times 5818
Dodd, Anna Bowman
On the Knees of the Gods 130
Dodd, Catherine
Clad in Purple Mist 3052
Doderer, Heimito von
Waterfalls of Slunj, The 3552
Dodge, Constance
Dark Stranger, The 4439
Graham of Claverhouse 1795
In Adam's Fall 4176
Pointless Knife, The 1796

Weathercock 4440
Dodge, Louis
American, The 4862
Dodge, Mary Mapes
Hans Brinker 3553
Doherty, Edward J., see Davidson,
Louis B. and Edward J. Doherty
Dohrman, Richard
Last of the Maidens, The 5819
Dolan, Mary
Hannibal of Carthage 217
Dolbier, Maurice
Benjy Boone 4863
Mortal Gods, The 3053
Dole, Nathan Haskell
Omar the Tentmaker 835
Dollar Gold Piece, The 6086
Dom Casmurro 6264
Dombrowski, Katharina von
Land of Women 6247
Domine's Garden, The 4147
Dominion 4024
Domitia 259
Don Gaucho 6271
Don Orsino 3679
Don Pedro and the Devil 6214
Don Quixote de la Mancha 1617
Don Tarquinio 1181
Doña Isabella's Adventures 1612
Doña Lona 4968
Donaldson, Mary E. M.
Isles of Flame, The 530
Donauer, Friedrich
Swords against Carthage 218
Donchev, Anton
Time of Parting 2193
Doneghy, Dagmar
Border, The 5486
Doniphan's Ride 5245
Donovan, Frank R.
Unlucky Hero, The 6419
Don't Tread on Me 4513
Don't You Cry for Me 5352
Dooley, (Mrs.) James H., see
Dooley, Sallie May
Dooley, Sallie May
Dem Good Ole Times 4864
Doom Castle 2449
Doom Trail, The 6372
Doomed City, The 277
Doomsland 3350
Doomswoman, The 4673
Door in the Grimming, The 3563
Door to the North 1209
Dored, Elisabeth
I Loved Tiberius 219
Doris Kingsley, Child and Colonist
4309

518

Field, Bradda
 Bride of Glory [Miledi] 2346
Field, (Mrs.) E. M., see Field,
 Louise
Field, Louise
 Ethne 2025
Field, Rachel L.
 All This, and Heaven Too 4909
Field of Glory, The [On the Field
 of Glory] 2164
Field of Honor, The 3322
Fielding, Henry
 History of Tom Jones, A Found-
 ling, The 2347
Fields, Jonathan, (pseud.)
 Memoirs of Dunstan Barr, The
 6170
Fields, The 5220
Fields Breathe Sweet, The 4214
Fiercest Heart, The 3963
Fierro Blanco, Antonio de
 Journey of the Flame, The 4910
Fiery Dawn, The 3409
Fife and Fandango 3666
Fifield, William
 Devil's Marchioness, The 2076
Fifth Queen, The 1325
Fifth Queen and How She Came
 to Court, The 1326
Fifth Queen Crowned, The 1327
Fifth Trumpet, The 1091
54-40 or Fight 5019
Fig in Winter, A 316
Fighting Blade, The 1793
Fighting Caravans 4976
Fighting Danites, The 5784
Fighting-slogan 6387
Figure in the Sand 497
Filon, Augustin
 Renégat 1320
Findlater, Jane Helen
 Daughter of Strife, A 2348
 Green Graves of Balgowrie, The
 2349
 Story of a Mother, The 3085
Findlay, J. T.
 Deal with the King, A 2350
Fineman, Irving
 Jacob 69
 Ruth 70
Finger, Charles Joseph
 When Guns Thundered at Tripoli
 4911
Finger in Every Pie, A 4787
Finger to Her Lips, A 3540
Finished 3983
Finkel, George
 Long Pilgrimage, The 587

Loyal Virginian, The 1809
Watch Fires to the North [Twilight
 Province] 536
Finlay, Lucile
 Coat I Wore, The 4458
Finlay, T. A.
 Chances of War, The 2026
Finnemore, John
 Red Men of the Dusk, The 1810
Finney, Gertrude E.
 Plums Hang High, The 5853
 Stormy Winter 4912
Fiona 6422
Fire and Ice 483
Fire and Morning 958
Fire and the Hammer 4385
Fire Bell in the Night 5234
Fire from Heaven 1032
Fire in Stubble 1926
Fire in the Heart 5005
Fire in the Ice 613
Fire on the Wind 5877
Fire over England 1402
Firebrand, The (Crockett) 3646
Firebrand, The (Faust) 1156
Firedrake, The 789
First Fleet Family, A 4036
First Rebel, The 4604
First Sir Percy, The 2158
First The Blade (Miller) 5591
First the Blade (Simons) 394
First Thunder, The 3258
Fish, Rachel Ann
 Running Iron 5854
Fish Can Sing, The 3630
Fisher, Aileen Lucia
 Fisherman of Galilee 309
 My Cousin Abe 4913
Fisher, Anne
 Oh Glittering Promise! 4914
Fisher, Clay, (pseud.), see Allen,
 Henry
Fisher, Edward
 Best House in Stratford, The 1321
 Love's Labour's Won 1322
 Shakespeare & Son 1323
Fisher, F. Hope
 Written in the Stars 1094
Fisher, Richard
 Judgment in July 5855
Fisher, Vardis
 Children of God 4915
 City of Illusion 4916
 Darkness and the Deep 480
 Island of the Innocent 190
 Mothers, The 4917
 Mountain Man 4918
 Tale of Valor 4919

France, Anatole, (pseud.) (cont.)
At the Sign of the Queen
Pédauque 2674
Balthazar 503
Gods Are Athirst, The 2675
Procurator of Judaea, The 311
Thais 312
Francezka 2761
Franchere, Ruth
Hannah Herself 4930
Stampede North 6391
Francillon, Robert E.
Ropes of Sand 2358
Francis, M. E., (pseud.), see
Blundell, Mary E.
Francis, Marian
Where Honour Leads 2359
Franciscan, The 4128
Frank, Bruno
Man Called Cervantes, A 1621
Franke, Herbert, (ed.), see Bauer,
Wolfgang and Herbert Franke,
(ed.)
Franzos, Karl Emil
For the Right 3554
Fraser, Hermia H.
Tall Brigade 6320
Fraser, (Mrs.) Hugh, see Fraser,
Mary Crawford
Fraser, Mary Crawford
In the Shadow of the Lord 4196
Stolen Emperor, The 3940
Fray Mario 6200
Frazee, Steve
Year of the Big Snow 4931
Frazier, Neta Lohnes
Sacajawea 4932
Frederic, Harold
In the Valley 4470
Lawton Girl, The 5867
Seth's Brother's Wife 5868
Frederic Uvedale 3694
Frederica 3130
Frederick, John
Bronze Collar, The 4933
Frederick the Great and His Court 2822
Frederick the Great and His
Family 2824
Free Fishers, The 3008
Free Lance in a Far Land, A 3859
Free Land 5954
Free Man 4563
Free Soil 5109
Free to Serve 4310
Free Traders, The 2456
Freebooters of the Wilderness 5958
Freedgood, Morton, see Morton,

Stanley, (pseud.)
Freedgood, Stanley, see Morton,
Stanley, (pseud.)
Freedom, Farewell! 209
Freedom Is the Prize 3838
Freedom or Death 3695
Freedom Road 5846
Freedom Run 5712
Freedom's Way 4178
Freeholder, The 4748
Freelance in Kashmir, A 3904
Fremantle, Anne
James and Joan 1013
French, Alice
Expiation 5869
French, Allen
Colonials, The 4471
French, Maida P.
Boughs Bend Over 6321
French Adventurer, The 4154
French Bride, The 2775
French Dragoon 3513
French Lieutenant's Woman, The
3090
French Nan 2311
French Prisoner, The 3234
Frenchman's Creek 1799
Frenssen, Gustav
Jörn Uhl 3555
Three Comrades, The 3556
Fresh and the Salt, The [Mary
Bravender] 4075
Freuchen, Peter
Law of Larion 6322
Legend of Daniel Williams 6323
White Man 2842
Frey, Ruby
Red Morning 4197
Frey and His Wife 797
Freytag, Gustav
Debit and Credit 3557
Friar Observant, A 1292
Friar of Wittenberg, The 1574
Friday's Child 3131
Frieberger, Kurt
Fisher of Men 313
Friedenthal, Richard
White Gods, The 6206
Friend of Caesar, A 214
Friend of Nelson, A 3160
Friend of the People, The 2751
Friend Olivia 1725
Friend with the Countersign, A 5419
Friendly Cove 2919
Friendly Persuasion, The 5676
Friends of the People, The 3484
Friermood, Elisabeth
Focus the Bright Land 5870

Galt, John (cont.)
  Ringan Gilhaize 1812
  Spaewife 1014
Galván, Manuel de Jesus
  Cross and the Sword, The 6421
Gamble for a Throne 1813
Gamble's Hundred 4177
Game for Empires, A 2360
Game of Kings, The 1313
Gamester, The (Sabatini) 2753
Gamesters, The (Bailey) 2799
Gamo, Jean
  Golden Chain, The 1055
Gamon, Richard B.
  Warren of Oudh 3861
Gann, Ernest K.
  Antagonists, The 315
Gant, Matthew, (pseud.)
  Raven and the Sword, The 4946
Gap of Barnesmore, The 2021
Garden of Paradise, The 845
Garden of Swords, The 3593
Gardiner, Dorothy
  Great Betrayal, The 5511
Gardiner, G. S.
  Rustem, Son of Zal 41
Gardner, Edmund G.
  Desiderio 1643
Gardner, Mona
  Hong Kong 3927
Garfield, Leon
  Smith 2362
Garfield Honor 6152
Garland, Hamlin
  Moccasin Ranch, The 5875
  Spoil of Office, A 5876
  Trail-Makers of the Middle
    Border 4947
Garland of Bays 1374
Garnett, David
  Pocahontas 4200
Garnett, Henry
  Gamble for a Throne 1813
  Red Bonnet, The 2676
Garnett, Martha
  Infamous John Friend, The 3093
Garnett, (Mrs.) R. S. , see
  Garnett, Martha
Garnier, Russell M.
  His Counterpart 1814
  White Queen, The 1333
Garrett, George
  Death of the Fox 1815
Garstin, Crosbie
  High Noon 2926
  Owl's House, The 2925
  West Wind, The 2927
Garth, David

Fire on the Wind 5877
Gray Canaan 5512
Gartner, Chloe
  Drums of Khartoum 3980
  Infidels, The 865
Gasiorowski, Waclaw
  Napoleon's Love-Story 3559
Gaskell, (Mrs.), see Gaskell, Eliza-
  beth C.
Gaskell, Elizabeth C.
  Mary Barton 3094
  North and South 3095
  Sylvia's Lovers 2363
Gaskin, Catherine
  Blake's Reach 2364
  Fiona 6422
  I Know My Love 4060
  Sara Dane 4061
Gaspé, Philippe Aubert de
  Canadians of Old, The [Cameron
    of Lochiel] 6324
Gass, William H.
  Omensetter's Luck 5878
Gaston de Latour 1542
Gate of Ivory, The 6006
Gate-Openers, The 3217
Gate to the Sea 212
Gates of Doom, The 2480
Gates of the Mountains, The 4655
Gathering Clouds 478
Gathering of Brother Hilarius, The
    905
Gathering of the West, The 3092
Gaudy Empire, The [Man of Decem-
    ber] 3485
Gaulot, Paul
  Red Shirts, The 2677
Gaunt, Richard
  Blood for a Borgia 1159
Gautier, Théophile
  Captain Fracasse 2080
  Romance of a Mummy, The 5
Gavin, Catherine Irvine
  Cactus and the Crown, The 6250
  Fortress, The 3741
  Madeleine 3430
  Moon into Blood, The 3687
Gay, Geraldine M.
  Astrologer's Daughter, The 135
Gay, Laverne
  Unspeakables 628
  Wine of Satan 866
Gay, Margaret Cooper
  Hatchet in the Sky 4201
Gay, (Madame) Sophie
  Marie de Mancini 2081
Gay Galliard, The 1366
Gay Lord Robert 1355

Harben, Will N.
  Triumph, The 5521
Harcourt, A. F. P.
  Jenetha's Venture 3897
  Peril of the Sword, The 3898
Hard Cash 3245
Hard Money 5054
Hard Times 3047
Harding, Bertita
  Farewell 'Toinette 2691
  Phantom Crown 6254
Harding, Newman
  Eternal Struggle, The 4227
Harding, T. Walter
  Abbot of Kirkstall, The 937
Hardy, Arthur S.
  Passe Rose 588
Hardy, Blanche
  Dynasty 938
  Sanctuary 939
Hardy, Thomas
  Mayor of Casterbridge, The 3112
  Tess of the d'Urbervilles 3113
  Trumpet-Major, The 3114
Hardy, William George
  All the Trumpets Sounded 13
  City of Libertines 228
  Turn Back the River 229
Hare, Christopher, (pseud.), see
  Andrews, Marian
Hargreaves, Sheba
  Cabin at the Trail's End, The
    4990
  Heroine of the Prairies 4991
Harington, Joy
  Jesus of Nazareth 323
Harland, Marion, (pseud.), see
  Terhune, Mary Virginia
Harlot Queen 962
Harm Wulf 2151
Harnett, Cynthia
  Caxton's Challenge [The Load of
    Unicorn] 940
Harold, the Last of the Saxon Kings
  714
Harold Was My King 710
Harp and the Blade, The 610
Harp into Battle 719
Harp of a Thousand Strings 2640
Harper, Carrie A., see Dix,
  Beulah M. and Carrie A.
  Harper
Harper, Robert S.
  Trumpet in the Wilderness 4992
Harpoon in Eden 3832
Harré, T. Everett
  Behold the Woman! 451
Harris, Bernice

Janey Jeems 5901
Harris, Clare Winger
  Persephone of Eleusis 145
Harris, Corra May
  Circuit Rider's Wife 5902
Harris, Cyril
  One Braver Thing 6331
  Richard Pryne 4492
  Street of Knives 4993
  Trouble at Hungerfords, The 4994
  Trumpets at Dawn 4493
Harris, Edwin
  William d'Albini 697
Harris, Frank
  Bomb, The 5903
Harris, Joel Chandler
  Little Union Scout, A 5522
Harris, John
  Vardy 3444
  see also Harris, Margaret and
    John
Harris, Laura B.
  Bride of the River 4995
Harris, Leon F. and Frank Lee
  Beals
  Look Away, Dixieland 5904
Harris, Margaret and John
  Arrow in the Moon 5905
  Chant of the Hawk 4996
  Medicine Whip 5906
Harrison, Constance
  Carlyles, The 5523
Harrison, Edith
  Princess Sayrane 837
Harrison, Frederic
  Theophano 649
Harrison, Herbert
  Dick Munday 2375
Harrison, Samuel Bertram
  White King 4087
Harrod, Frances, (pseud.), see Ro-
  bertson, Frances F.
Harrowing of Hubertus, The [Huber-
  tus] 6221
Harry Idaho 5188
Harry of Monmouth 973
Harsányi, Zsolt
  Lover of Life 2141
  Star-Gazer, The 2189
Hart, Scott
  Eight April Days 5524
Hartland Forest 2291
Hartley, J. M.
  Way, The 324
Hartley, J. Wesley
  In the Iron Time 1828
Hartley, M.
  Beyond Man's Strength 3691

Hayes, Frederick W.
    Captain Kirke Webbe 3445
    Gwynett of Thornhaugh 2378
    Kent Squire, A 2377
    Shadow of a Throne, The 2379
Hayes, John F.
    Dangerous Cove, The 6333
Hays, Hoffman Reynolds
    Takers of the City 6210
Hazard 2460
Hazardous Wooing, A 2997
Hazelton, George C., Jr.
    Raven, The 5003
He Brings Great News 2950
He Served Two Masters 6209
He Went with Champlain 6337
He Went with Christopher Columbus
    1215
He Went with Hannibal 231
He Went with John Paul Jones 2933
He Went with Magellan 1694
He Went with Marco Polo 1243
He Went with Vasco da Gama 1216
Head of a Hundred in the Colony of
    Virginia, The 4216
Head of Iron, The 4294
Headless Angel 3539
Health unto His Majesty, A
    (Hibbert) 1835
Health unto His Majesty, A (Mc-
    Carthy) 2152
Hear Me, Pilate! 270
Hear the Word 118
Heard, Adrian
    Rose in the Mouth 2692
Hearken unto the Voice 112
Hearn, Lafcadio
    Youma 6423
Heart in Pilgrimage 4874
Heart Is a Stranger 3703
Heart of a Queen, The [Crown Im-
    perial] 1312
Heart of a Slave-Girl, The 427
Heart of Her Highness 1100
Heart of Hope, The 5622
Heart of Jade, The 6215
Heart of Kentucky, The 5194
Heart of Midlothian, The 2487
Heart of the Ancient Firs, The
    5708
Heart of Washington, The 4252
Hearth and Eagle, The 6179
Hearth of Hutton, The 2339
Hearts Courageous 4566
Heart's Delight [The Great Mogul]
    3877
Heart's Highway, The 4375
Hearts in Exile 3773

Heart's Key, The 763
Hearts of Hickory 5148
Hearts of Wales 987
Hearts Triumphant 5330
Hearts Undaunted 4676
Heathen Valley 5098
Heaven Is Too High 5124
Heaven Tree, The (Pargeter) 733
Heaven Trees (Young) 5394
Heckert, Eleanor
    Golden Rock, The 6424
    Muscavado 6425
Hecla Sandwith 5335
Hector, Annie French
    Heritage of Langdale, The 2380
    Maid, Wife, or Widow? 3567
Hedge of Thorns 3318
Heidelberg 2144
Heidenstam, Verner von
    Charles Men, The 2843
Heikē Story 1251
Heinzman, George
    Only the Earth and the Mountains
        5916
Heir of Starvelings, The 2985
Heir to Kings 2336
Heir to Pendarrow 1319
Heirs of the Kingdom, The 881
Helen Adair 4035
Helen Treveryan 3889
Helena 469
Hellfire Jackson 5227
Helmet of Navarre, The 1545
Helon's Pilgrimage to Jerusalem 206
Helps, Arthur
    Ivan de Biron 2898
Hemberger, Andreas, see Bekessy,
    Emery with Andreas Hemberger
Henderson, Daniel M.
    Crown for Carlotta, A 6255
Heney, Helen
    Dark Moon 4064
Hengest's Tale 569
Henham, Ernest George
    Custom of the Manor, The 1352
Henkle, Henrietta
    All the Living 1832
    And Walk in Love 328
    Deep River 5004
    Fire in the Heart 5005
Henri, Florette
    Kings Mountain 4496
Henry, Will, (pseud.), see Allen,
    Henry
Henry Bourland 5900
Henry VIII and His Court 1412
Henry Elizabeth 1391
Henry, King of France 1537

His Majesty's Highwayman 2315
His Majesty's Sloop, "Diamond Rock"
  6445
His Majesty's Well-beloved 1927
His Majesty's Yankees [Son of the
  Hawk] 6365
His Queen 1121
His Serene Highness 2800
His Sovereign Lady 1338
His Was the Fire 3268
Hispaniola Plate, The 6412
History of Aythan Waring, The 3162
History of Clarissa Harlowe, The
  2474
History of Henry Esmond, Esquire,
  The 2522
History of Margaret Catchpole, The
  2316
History of Pendennis, The 3275
History of Rome Hanks and Kindred
  Matters 5616
History of Sir Charles Grandison,
  The 2475
History of Tom Jones, A Foundling,
  The 2347
Hittite Warrior 115
Ho, the Fair Wind 6151
Hobbes, John Oliver, (pseud.), see
  Craigie, (Mrs.) Pearl Mary
Hobbs, Roe R.
  Court of Pilate, The 329
Hocking, Joseph
  Birthright, The 2385
  Chariots of the Lord, The 1842
  Coming of the King, The 1843
  Flame of Fire, A 1624
  Mistress Nancy Molesworth 2386
  Sword of the Lord, The 1585
Hocking, Silas K.
  Strange Adventures of Israel
    Pendray, The 2387
Hockley, William Browne
  Pandurang Hàri 3899
Hodge, Jane Aiken
  Adventurers, The 3448
  Here Comes a Candle 5010
  Marry in Haste 3151
  Maulever Hall 3152
  Savannah Purchase 5011
  Watch the Wall, My Darling
    3153
  Winding Stair, The 3657
Hodges, C. Walter
  Marsh King, The 539
  Namesake, The 540
  Overland Launch, The 3154
Hodgson, W. H.
  Boats of the Glen-Carrig, The
    1691

Hoffenberg, Jack
  Sow Not in Anger 6171
Hoffmann, Margaret Jones
  My Dear Cousin 5012
Hoffmann, Peggy, see Hoffmann,
  Margaret Jones
Hoffman's Row 4783
Hogan, Pendleton
  Dark Comes Early, The 5013
Hohensteins, The 3607
Holborn Hill 3274
Hold Back the Hunter 6030
Holdfast Gaines 5266
Holland, Cecelia
  Antichrist 788
  Earl, The 703
  Firedrake, The 789
  Kings in Winter, The 704
  Rakóssy 1586
  Until the Sun Falls 838
Holland, Clive
  Lovers of Mademoiselle, The
    2695
Holland, Josiah Gilbert
  Bay Path, The 4231
  Miss Gilbert's Career 5014
Holmby House 2011
Holt, Felix
  Dan'l Boone Kissed Me 5015
  Gabriel Horn, The 5016
Holt, Victoria, (pseud.), see Hibbert,
  Eleanor
Holy Lover, The 4287
Holy Sinner, The 630
Holy Week 3380
Home to Kentucky 4826
Home to Tennessee 5468
Home to the Hermitage 4827
Homer
  Iliad, The [The Iliad of Homer]
    146
  Odyssey, The 147
Homespun 4719
Homo Sum 445
Homoselle 5321
Honest Lawyer, The 3203
Hong Kong 3927
Honig, Donald
  Walk Like a Man 5531
Honor Thy Father 6051
Honorable Peter Sterling, The 5861
Honour of Bayard, The 1649
Honour of Henri de Valois, The 3722
Honour of Savelli, The 1652
Honour the King 1873
Honourable Jim, The 1928
Honourable Roger, The 2290
Honour's Fetters 2408

543

Keddie, Henrietta (cont.)
  Sir David's Visitors   3174
  Witch-Wife, The   1870
Keeling, Elsa d'Esterre
  Queen's Serf, The   2403
Keep the Wagons Moving!   5083
Keepers of the House, The   5556
Keith, Chester
  Queen's Knight   541
Keith, Marian
  Silver Maple, The   6395
Kelland, Clarence Budington
  Arizona   5546
  Gold   5942
  Hard Money   5054
  Lady and the Giant, The   5943
  Merchant of Valor   1650
  Valley of the Sun   5944
Kelley, Welbourn
  Alabama Empire   5055
Kellner, Esther
  Bride of Pilate   336
  Mary of Nazareth   337
  Promise, The   82
Kelly, Eleanor
  Richard Walden's Wife   5547
Kelly, Eric P.
  From Star to Star   1098
Kelly, Peter Burrowes
  Manor of Glenmore, The   3345
Kelly, Regina Zimmerman
  Chicago: Big-shouldered City   6173
  Young Geoffrey Chaucer   955
Kelly, William P.
  Assyrian Bride, The   83
  Senator Licinius, The   338
  Stonecutter of Memphis, The   15
  Stranger from Ionia, The   150
Kelston of Kells   1712
Kendrick, Baynard Hardwick
  Flames of Time, The   5056
Keneally, Thomas
  Bring Larks and Heroes   4067
Kenelm Chillingly   3200
Kenilworth   1434
Kennedy, C. Rann
  Winterfeast, The   801
Kennedy, John P.
  Horseshoe Robinson   4514
  Rob of the Bowl   4245
  Swallow Barn   5057
Kennedy, Lucy
  Mr. Audubon's Lucy   5058
Kennedy, Margaret
  Night in Cold Harbor, A   3175
  Troy Chimneys   3176
Kennedy, Sara Beaumont

Cicely   5548
Joscelyn Cheshire   4515
Wooing of Judith, The   4246
Kennedy Square   5276
Kennelly, Ardyth
  Good Morning, Young Lady   5945
  Peaceable Kingdom, The   5946
  Spur, The   5549
  Up Home   5947
Kenny, Louise M. Stacpoole
  At the Court of Il Moro   1170
  Love Is Life   2095
Kent, Alexander
  Enemy in Sight!   2929
  Flag Captain, The   2930
  Form Line of Battle!   2931
  To Glory We Steer   2932
Kent, Louise Andrews
  He Went with Champlain   6337
  He Went with Christopher Columbus   1215
  He Went with Hannibal   231
  He Went with John Paul Jones   2933
  He Went with Magellen   1694
  He Went with Marco Polo   1243
  He Went with Vasco da Gama   1216
Kent, Simon, (pseud.), for Catto, Max
Kent Fort Manor   5407
Kent Squire, A   2377
Kentuckians, The (Fox)   5864
Kentuckians, The (Giles)   4483
Kentucky Chronicle, A   4969
Kentucky Pride   5985
Kentucky Stand   4634
Kenyon, Frank Wilson
  Absorbing Fire, The   3177
  Duke's Mistress, The   2404
  Emma   3178
  Emperor's Lady, The   3453
  Glory and the Dream, The   1871
  Golden Years   3179
  Imperial Courtesan   3454
  Marie Antoinette   2710
  Mary of Scotland   1376
  Mistress Nell [Mrs. Nelly]   1872
  My Brother Napoleon   3455
  Naked Sword, The   1651
  Royal Merry-go-round   2711
  Shadow in the Sun   1377
  That Spanish Woman [I, Eugénia]   3456
Kenyon, Orr, (pseud.), see Carter,
    Russell Kelso
Kenyon, Theda
  Black Dawn   5948
  Golden Feather   4247
Kerr, Archibald W. M.
  By the Pool of Garmoyle   2572

554

Lancaster, Bruce and Lowell
  Brentano (cont.)
  Bride of a Thousand Cedars
    6432
Lancaster, G. B., (pseud.), see
  Lyttleton, Edith J.
Lance, Rupert
  Crowning Hour, The 1174
  Golden Pippin, The 1877
Lancet 2479
Land Beyond, The 4980
Land Beyond the Mountains, The
  4961
Land beyond the Tempest, The 6442
Land Breakers, The 4180
Land for My Sons 4429
Land Is Bright, The (Binns) 4721
Land Is Bright, The (Gerson) 4208
Land is Bright, The (Kjelgaard)
  5555
Land of Bondage, The 4129
Land of Foam, The 500
Land of Last Chance, The 6007
Land of Promises 6014
Land of the Beautiful River 4258
Land of the Golden Mountain, The
  5088
Land of Women 6247
Land They Possessed, The 5744
Land to Tame 5240
Landau, Mark Aleksandrovich
  Before the Deluge 3763
  Ninth Thermidor, The 2719
  Saint Helena, Little Island 3460
Landon, Margaret
  Anna and the King of Siam 3952
Landor, W. Savage
  Pericles and Aspasia 151
Lane, Carl D.
  Fleet in the Forest, The 5081
Lane, Elinor Macartney
  All for the Love of a Lady 1878
  Mills of God, The 5082
  Nancy Stair 2412
Lane, Jane, (pseud.), for Dakers,
  Elaine
Lane, Kenneth Westmacott
  Winter Cherry 1245
Lane, Rose Wilder
  Free Land 5954
  Let the Hurricane Roar 5955
Lang, Andrew
  Monk of Fife, A 1067
  see also Haggard, H. Rider and
    Andrew Lang; and Mason, A.
    E. W. and Andrew Lang
Lang, John
  Wetherbys, The 3903

Langford of the Three Bars 4735
Langworthy Family, The 5790
Lanham, Edwin
  Wind Blew West, The 5956
Lansworth, Lew X.
  Over the River Charlie 3461
Lantern Bearers, The 562
Lantern in Her Hand, A 5697
Lantern Lane 1785
Lanterns of Horn 1923
Lark 2008
Lark and the Laurel, The 1006
Larreta, Enrique
  Glory of Don Ramiro, The 1626
La Scola, Ray
  Creole, The 5957
Last Athenian, The 459
Last Boat out of Cincinnati, The 5327
Last Chronicle of Barset 3287
Last Crusader 1620
Last Days of Pompeii, The 351
Last Duchess of Belgarde, The 2762
Last Englishman, The 752
Last Foray, The 1330
Last Fort 6302
Last Frontier, The (Cooper) 5787
Last Frontier, The (Fast) 5847
Last Full Measure, The 5601
Last Gentleman, The 4115
Last Hope, The 3517
Last Hunt, The 5970
Last Letter Home, The 5146
Last Love, The 3410
Last Monarch of Tara, The 555
Last Night the Nightingale 5820
Last of Britain, The 567
Last of Her Race, The 2855
Last of the Barons, The 967
Last of the Catholic O'Malleys, The
  1482
Last of the Houghtons, The 5442
Last of the Maidens, The 5819
Last of the Mohicans, The 4160
Last of the Vikings, The [The Last
  Viking] 803
Last of the Wine, The 166
Last Plantagenet, The [Richard III:
  The Last Plantagenet] 1001
Last Princess 6213
Last Queen of Hawaii: Liliuokalani
  4104
Last Romans, The 452
Last Valley [Fat Valley] 2160
Last Viking, The [The Last of the
  Vikings] 803
Last Warpath, The 6163
Late George Apley, The 5986
Late Harvest 1465

559

McLaws, Lafayette
  Jezebel 87
  Maid of Athens, The 3767
  Welding, The 5576
  When the Land Was Young 4263
Maclay, A. C.
  Mito Yashiki 3946
McLean, Allan Campbell
  Sound of Trumpets, A 3211
Maclean, Norman
  Hills of Home 2430
McLean, Sydney
  Moment of Time, A 4531
McLennan, William
  Spanish John 2431
  ____, and Jean McIlwraith
  Span o' Life, The 6349
Macleod, Alison
  City of Light 1592
  Heretic, The [The Heretics]
  1396
  Hireling, The 1397
MacLeod, Le Roy
  Years of Peace, The 5977
McMahon, Norbert
  St. John of God 1398
MacMahon, The 1744
MacManus, Francis
  Stand and Give Challenge 2035
McManus, (Miss) L.
  Lally of the Brigade 2871
  Nessa 2036
  Wager, The 2037
MacManus, Seumas
  Lad of the O'Friels, A 3357
McMeekin, Clark, (pseud.)
  City of the Flags 5577
  Fairbrothers, The 5978
  October Fox, The 5979
  Reckon with the River 5121
  Red Raskall 5122
  Show Me a Land 6176
  Tyrone of Kentucky 5980
McMeekin, Isabel, see McMeekin,
  Clark, (pseud.)
Macmillan, Malcolm
  Dagonet the Jester 1900
MacMunn, George Fletcher
  Freelance in Kashmir, A 3904
McNamee, James
  My Uncle Joe 6401
McNeilly, Mildred Masterson
  Each Bright River 5123
  Heaven Is Too High 5124
  Praise at Morning 5578
Macnicol, Eona K.
  Colum of Derry 544
MacOrlan, Pierre

Anchor of Mercy, The 2935
MacPhail, Andrew
  Vine of Sibmah, The 4264
Macpherson, Annie Winifred, see
  Bryher, Winifred
Macquoid, Katharine S.
  Captain Dallington 2432
  His Heart's Desire 2102
  Ward of the King, A 1536
Macrae, J. A.
  For Kirk and King 1901
McVeys, The 5063
Mad Barbara 1786
Mad Grandeur 2566
Mad Sir Peter 1791
Madam Constantia 4412
Madam Flirt 2461
Madame Castel's Lodger 5550
Madame Dorthea 2854
Madame Geneva 2325
Madame Serpent 1512
Madame Thérèse 2664
Madariaga, Salvador de
  Heart of Jade, The 6215
Madeleine (Gavin) 3430
Madeleine (Kavanagh) 3452
Mademoiselle Mathilde 2712
Madonna of the Barricades, The 3523
Madselin 713
Maelcho 1473
Magada, The 1113
Magdalen 386
Magdalen Hepburn 1414
Maggie 6243
Magic Bow 3697
Magic Casements 919
Magic of Dawn 4056
Magician of Lublin, The 3604
Magnay, William
  Amazing Duke, The 1902
Magnificent Adventure, The 5020
Magnificent Destiny 5356
Magnificent Enemies 1102
Magnificent Failure, The 6398
Magnificent Idler, The 5237
Magnificent Traitor, The 161
Magnus Sinclair 1933
Magnus the Magnificent 1463
Mahner-Mons, Hans
  Sword of Satan 2725
Maias, The 3650
Maid and the Miscreant, The 4369
Maid-at-Arms, The 4415
Maid Margaret of Galloway 1010
Maid Marian 734
Maid Marian and Robin Hood 724
Maid Molly 1825
Maid of Athens, The 3767

Maid of Brittany, A 1064
Maid of Florence, The 1674
Maid of Israel 78
Maid of Maiden Lane, The 4697
Maid of Montauks 4275
Maid of Old New York, A 4122
Maid of Sker, The 2273
Maid of the Malverns, A 1938
Maid, Wife, or Widow? 3567
Maiden, Cecil
  Harp into Battle 719
Maids of Paradise, The 3405
Maids of Salem 4276
Maier, Paul L.
  Pontius Pilate 354
Main, Mary Foster
  Girl Who Was Never Queen, The 3212
Mainwaring 3117
Maitland, Alfred L.
  I Lived as I Listed 1903
Major, Charles
  Dorothy Vernon of Haddon Hall 1399
  Gentle Knight of Old Brandenburg, A 2819
  Touchstone of Fortune, The 1904
  When Knighthood Was in Flower 1400
  Yolanda, Maid of Burgundy 1103
Major Grant 3464
Major Weir 1912
Make-Believe, The 4578
Maker of Lenses, The 2173
Maker of Saints 1153
Making and Breaking of Almansur 623
Making of Christopher Ferringham, The 4173
Malcolm Canmore's Pearl 698
Malinche and Cortes 6226
Malkus, Alida Sims
  Caravans to Santa Fe 5125
  There Really Was a Hiawatha 4265
Mallet-Joris, Françoise
  Witches, The 2103
Malling, Matilda
  Immaculate Young Minister, The 2433
  Romance of the First Consul, A 3473
Mally, Emma Louise
  Abigail 5126
  Mockingbird Is Singing, The 5579
  Tides of Dawn, The 1593
Malm, Dorothea
  On a Fated Night 3474

Woman Question, The 5127
Malo, Henri
  Romantic Passion of Don Luis, The 1594
Malory, (Sir) Thomas
  Morte D'Arthur, Le 545
Maltby, A.
  Queen--but No Queen 6216
Malvern, Gladys
  Foreigner, The 88
  Mamzelle 5128
  Patriot's Daughter 2726
  Rhoda of Cyprus 355
  Secret Sign 356
  Tamar 357
Mamzelle 5128
Mamzelle Fifine 2598
Man Apart, A 4010
Man-at-Arms, The (James) 1520
Man-at-Arms, A (Scollard) 1186
Man at Odds, The 2473
Man Born Again, A 1279
Man Called Cervantes, A 1621
Man Cannot Tell 4326
Man for the Ages, A 4685
Man from Cyrene 415
Man from Mt. Vernon 4397
Man from Texas, The 5609
Man in Black, The 2122
Man in Gray, The 5483
Man in the Ancient World 109
Man of December [The Gaudy Empire] 3485
Man of Destiny, The 4936
Man of Good Zeal, A 1564
Man of His Age, A 1498
Man of Montmartre 3469
Man of the Storm, The 5029
Man of the World, The [The Sinner] 3685
Man of Yesterday, The 5950
Man on a Donkey, The 1426
Man on Fire 271
Man They Hanged, The 2920
Man Who Killed Lincoln, The 5653
Man Who Killed the King, The 2786
Man Who Shot Quantrill 5404
Man Who Went Back, The 438
Man with a Sword 747
Man with the Iron Hand, The 6354
Man without a Country, The 4984
Manassas [Theirs Be the Guilt] 5646
Manasseh 3574
Manceron, Claude
  So Brief a Spring 3475
Manchester Man, The 2961
Manchu Empress, The 3928
Manfred, Frederick

566

Manfred, Frederick (cont.)
   Lord Grizzly 5129
   Scarlet Plume 5580
Manhattan Acres 6183
Manhold 2265
Manila Galleon 2937
Mann, E. B.
   Gunsmoke Trail 5981
   Troubled Range 5982
   With Spurs 5983
Mann, F. O.
   Golden Quill, The 970
Mann, Heinrich
   Henry, King of France 1537
   Young Henry of Navarre [King
     Wren] 1538
Mann, Helen R.
   Gallant Warrior 4266
Mann, Millicent E.
   Margot, the Court Shoemaker's
     Child 2104
Mann, Thomas
   Beloved Returns, The 3580
   Buddenbrooks 3581
   Holy Sinner, The 630
   Joseph and His Brothers 89
   Joseph in Egypt 19
   Joseph the Provider 20
   Young Joseph 90
Manning, Anne
   Household of Sir Thomas More,
     The 1401
   Jacques Bonneval 2105
Manor, The 3605
Manor of Glenmore, The 3345
Man's Calling, A 4957
Man's Fear, A 796
Mansfield Park 2952
Mantle of the Emperor, The 3389
Manuela, la Caballeresa del Sol
   6237
Ms. in a Red Box, The 1827
Many a Voyage 5501
Many Are the Hearts 5611
Many Heavens 6079
Many Ways of Love [At the Court
   of Catherine the Great] 2911
Manzoni, Alessandro
   Betrothed, The 2190
Mapmaker, The 1135
Mara, Daughter of the Nile 17
Marassa and Midnight 6448
Marcel Armand 4712
Marcelle the Mad 1039
March of the Innocents, The 895
Marchal, Lucien
   Sage of Canudos 6266
Marching On (Boyd) 5424

Marching On (Strachey) 5304
Marchioness of Brinvilliers, The
   2115
Marco Visconti 1163
Marcus 280
Marcus and Faustina 278
Margaret Brent, Adventurer 4220
Margot, the Court Shoemaker's Child
   2104
Marguerite de Roberval 6350
Marguerite de Valois 1504
Margueritte, Paul and Victor
   Disaster, The 3476
   Strasbourg 3477
Margueritte, Victor
   Frontiers of the Heart, The 3478
   see also Margueritte, Paul and
     Victor
Maria Paluna 6224
Mariamne [Herod and Mariamne]
   344
Marie 3984
Marie Antoinette 2710
Marie Antoinette and Her Son 2730
Marie Antoinette's Daughter 3417
Marie de Mancini 2081
Marie Grubbe 2175
Marie of Lichtenstein [Lichtenstein]
   1582
Marietta 1150
Marius, Richard
   Coming of Rain, The 5984
Marius the Epicurean 371
Marjorie of Scotland 1017
Mark Alston 3272
Mark Eminence 1723
Mark of the Cross, The 2908
Mark of the Horse Lord, The 410
Mark of the Turtle, The 4288
Mark of Vraye, The 1072
Mark Toyman's Inheritance 5351
Markey, Gene
   Kentucky Pride 5985
   That Far Paradise 5130
Markey, Morris
   Band Plays Dixie, The 5581
Markham, Virgil
   Scamp, The 2434
Marlowe, Derek
   Single Summer with Lord B., A
     [A Single Summer with L. B.]
     3582
Marotz 3673
Marquand, John P.
   Late George Apley, The 5986
Marquis, Thomas G.
   Marguerite de Roberval 6350
Marquis, The 2759

Mason, Van Wyck (cont.)
Manila Galleon 2937
Our Valiant Few 5584
Proud New Flags 5585
Rascals' Heaven 4269
Rivers of Glory 4533
"Sea 'Venture," The 6437
Silver Leopard 877
Stars on the Sea 4534
Three Harbours 4535
Valley Forge: 24 December,
1777 4536
Wild Horizon 4537
Young Titan, The 4270
Masqueraders, The 2383
Massingham Affair, The 3105
Master, The 273
Master and Commander 3222
Master-at-arms 2754
Master Beggars, The 1573
Master Entrick, an Adventure 4280
Master Girl, The 494
Master Mosaic-Workers, The 1667
Master of Ballantrae, The 2508
Master of Castile 1119
Master of Chaos, The 4384
Master of Gray, The 1271
Master of Hestviken 804
Master of His Fate [In Spite of
Himself] 2974
Master of the World (O'Neal) 1202
Master of Warlock 5496
Master Secretary 1363
Master Wit, The 1171
Masters, Edgar Lee
Children of the Market Place
5132
Masters, John
Coromandel! 3865
Deceivers, The 3905
Nightrunners of Bengal 3906
Rock, The 488
Masters of the World (Hoppus) 330
Masts to Spear the Stars 3829
Mather, Berkely, (pseud.), see
Davies, John Evan Weston
Mathew, Frank
Defender of the Faith 1404
Love of Comrades 2038
One Queen Triumphant 1405
Royal Sisters, The 1406
Wood of the Brambles, The 2581
Matrix, The 4840
Matschat, Cecile Hulse
Preacher on Horseback 5987
Tavern in the Town 4271
Matthew, Anne Irwin
Warm Wind, West Wind 971

Matthew Early 5076
Matthew Hargraves 3110
Maturin, Charles Robert
Albigenses, The 767
Maude, Sophie
Hermit and the King, The 972
Maugham, H. Neville
Richard Hawkwood 1178
Maughan, A. Margery
Harry of Monmouth 973
Maule, Mary Katherine
Prairie-Schooner Princess 5133
Maulever Hall 3152
Maumbery Rings 3204
Maurice, C. Edmund
Telemachus 455
Maurice Tiernay 2575
Mauthner, Fritz
Mrs. Socrates 155
Mawkin of the Flow, The 1015
Maximilian's Gold 5724
Maxwell, Anna
Pietro the Garibaldian 3701
Maxwell, William H.
O'Hara, 1798 2582
May, Stella Burke
Conqueror's Lady, The 6218
Maya (Oliphant) 3908
Maya: A Story of Yucatan (Foulke)
6205
Mayer, Albert I.
Follow the River 5988
Mayo, (Mrs.) J. R.
Daughter of the Klephts, A 3768
Mayor of Casterbridge, The 3112
Mayor of Troy, The 3237
Mayrant, Drayton, (pseud.), see
Simons, Katherine D. M.
Maze Maker, The 121
Mazeppa 2200
Meacham, Ellis K.
East Indiaman, The 3955
Meade, L. T., (pseud.)
Witch Maid, The 3215
Meader, Stephen W.
Muddy Road to Glory, The 5586
Voyage of the "Javelin," The 3833
Meadows, Denis
Tudor Underground 1407
Meakin, Nevill Myers
Assassins, The 878
Measure of a Man 5717
Measure of the Years, The 4152
Mediation of Ralph Hardelot, The
975
Medicine Man, The 5252
Medicine Whip 5906
Meding, Oskar

Murray, Paul (cont.)
Heart Is a Stranger 3703
Muscavado 6425
Musters, (Mrs.) Chaworth
Cavalier Stronghold, A 1918
Mutineer, The (Becke & Jeffery)
4078
Mutineers, The (Hawes) 3826
Mutiny 3280
Mutiny on the "Bounty" 4098
My Antonia 4789
My Blood and My Treasure 5248
My Brother Napoleon 3455
My Cousin Abe 4913
My Crown, My Love 2192
My Dear Cousin 5012
My Glorious Brothers 189
My Grand Enemy 2513
My Ladie Dundie 1929
My Lady Clancarty 1985
My Lady Greensleeves 1287
My Lady Laughter 4616
My Lady Lucia 1662
My Lady Nan 2333
My Lady of Aros 2289
My Lady of Cleeve (Hartley) 1829
My Lady of Cleves (Barnes) 1277
My Lady of Doubt 4555
My Lady of Intrigue 2093
My Lady of Orange 1562
My Lady of the Bass 2020
My Lady of the North 5613
My Lady of the South 5614
My Lady Pokahontas 4156
My Lady Rotha 2172
My Lady Wentworth 1807
My Lady's Bargain 1845
My Lady's Kiss 2143
My Lord Brother the Lion Heart
868
My Lord Cardinal 1378
My Lord Essex (Eckerson) 1314
My Lord Monleigh 1974
My Lord of Canterbury 1450
My Lord of Essex (Brookfield)
1293
My Lord Winchenden 1847
My Master, Columbus 1207
My Pride, My Folly 6292
My Story 4600
My Sword for Lafayette 2746
My Sword for Patrick Sarsfield
2032
My Theodosia 5260
My Two Kings 1925
My Uncle Joe 6401
My Uncle the Curate 3371
My Vineyard 382

Mydans, Shelley Smith
Thomas 726
Myers, Henry
Our Lives Have Just Begun 879
Utmost Island, The 609
Myers, John
Harp and the Blade, The 610
I, Jack Swilling, Founder of
Phoenix, Arizona 5158
Wild Yazoo, The 5159
Mygatt, Tracy D. and Frances With-
erspoon
Armor of Light 366
Mylechreest, Winifred Brookes
Fairest of the Stuarts, The 1919
Myrick, Herbert
Cache la Poudre 6000
Mysteries 3626
Mysteries of Udolpho, The 1544
Mysterious Monsieur Dumont, The
2718
Mystery at Mycenae 140
Mystery of the Lost Dauphin, The
3496

Nabob, The 3412
Nadir Shah 2896
Nagayo, Yoshiro
Bronze Christ 3948
Naked Came I 3529
Naked Days of the Lost Moon 4139
Naked Sword, The 1651
Nameless Breed 4734
Nameless Castle, The 3575
Namesake, The 540
Nancy Flyer, The 5196
Nancy Kelsey 4903
Nancy Stair 2412
Nantucket Rebel 4595
Napier, Charles
William the Conqueror 727
Napoleon and Blücher 3588
Napoleon and the Queen of Prussia
3587
Napoleon Decrees 2998
Napoleon's Love-Story 3559
Narcissus and Goldmund [Death and
the Lovers; Goldmund] 944
Natalia 6407
Nathalia 2201
Nathan, Leonard
Wind like a Bugle 5160
Nathan, Robert
Fair, The 547
Natives of Hemsö, The 3635
Natsume, Soseki
Grass on the Wayside 3949

O Genesee   4801
O Genteel Lady!   4923
"O King, Live for Ever!"   42
O Western Wind   4169
Oakeshott, Ronald
   Merchant at Arms, The   979
Oakfield   3879
Obliging Husband, The   1727
O'Brian, Patrick
   Master and Commander   3222
O'Brien, Brian, (pseud.), see
   Young-O'Brien, Albert Hayward
O'Brien, Kate
   For One Sweet Grape [That Lady]
     1628
   Without My Cloak   3364
O'Brien, R. B.
   D'Altons of Crag, The   3365
O'Brien, Saliee, (pseud.), see
   Zelley, Frankie Lee
O'Brien, William
   Queen of Men, A   1477
   When We Were Boys   3366
O'Briens and the O'Flahertys, The
   3361
O'Byrne, (Miss) M. L.
   Art MacMurrough Kavanagh,
     Prince of Leinster   1021
   Court of Rath Croghan, The   728
   Leixlip Castle   2041
   Lord Roche's Daughters of
     Fermoy   2042
   Pale and the Septs, The   1478
Ocean Free-Lance, An   3251
Oceans Free   3622
O'Connor, Richard
   Company Q   5607
   Guns of Chickamauga   5608
   Officers and Ladies   4100
   Vandal, The   655
Octavia   414
October Fox, The   5979
Oddsfish!   1738
O'Dell, Scott
   Hill of the Hawk   5168
   Island of the Blue Dolphins, The
     5169
   King's Fifth, The   6225
   Woman of Spain   5170
O'Donnel   3362
O'Donoghue, The   2576
Odyssey, The   147
Oedipus [The Eagle King]   176
Oemler, Marie
   Holy Lover, The   4287
Of Mistress Eve   1934
Off to Philadelphia in the Morning
   5941

Officer and Gentleman   3733
Officers and Ladies   4100
O'Flaherty, Liam
   Famine   3367
O'Flynn, The   1890
Ogden, George W.
   Land of Last Chance, The   6007
   Sooner Land   6008
Ogley, Dorothy and Mabel Cleland
   Iron Land   6009
O'Grady, P. W. and Dorothy Dunn
   Dark Was the Wilderness   6353
O'Grady, Rohan, (pseud.), see
   Skinner, June O'Grady
O'Grady, Standish
   Departure of Dermot, The   729
   Flight of the Eagle, The   1479
   In the Wake of King James   2043
   Ulrick the Ready   2044
Oh Glittering Promise!   4914
Oh, Promised Land   5305
Oh, Susanna!   6141
Oh, Valley Green!   4833
O'Hagan, Howard
   Tay John   6402
O'Hanlon, Richard
   What If This Friend   369
O'Hannrachain, Michael
   Swordsman of the Brigade, A   2586
   When the Norman Came   730
O'Hara, 1798   2582
Ohnet, Georges
   Eagle's Talon, The   3486
O'Houlihan's Jest   2594
Oil of Spikenard   2327
O'Kelly's Eclipse   2534
Oklahoma   5788
Oklahoma Run   5782
Old-Fashioned Girl, An   5696
Old For-Ever   3909
Old Fox, The   3028
Old Fritz and the New Era   2821
Old Hickory   4951
Old Margaret   1099
Old Misery   5190
Old Miss   5452
Old Missionary, The   3900
Old Mortality   1961
Old Motley   3197
Old St. Paul's   1709
Old Score, An   3921
Old Squire   5420
Old West in Fiction, The   5737
Old Wives' Tale, The   2983
Oldenbourg, Zoe
   Cities of the Flesh   768
   Cornerstone, The   880
   Destiny of Fire   769

Oxenham, John, (pseud.) (cont.)
Splendor of the Dawn, The   370
White Fire   4101

Pabo, the Priest   663
Pagan King, The   546
Page, Elizabeth
Tree of Liberty   4553
Wagons West   5177
Wilderness Adventure   4290
Page, Thomas Nelson
Red Riders   6016
Red Rock   6017
Page of the Duke of Savoy, The
1502
Pageant   4092
Painted Minx, The   4418
Painted Queen, The   75
Paiute   5361
Palace of Danger, The   2781
Palace of Spies, The   3022
Pale and the Septs, The   1478
Pale Survivor, The   1886
Palgrave, W. Gifford
Hermann Agha   3958
Palmer, Bruce
Many Are the Hearts   5611
_____, and John C. Giles
Horseshoe Bend   5178
Palmer, Frederick
Vagabond, The   5612
Palmer, John Leslie, see Pilgrim,
David, (pseud.)
Palmer, Marian
White Boar, The   980
Wrong Plantagenet, The   981
Pam the Fiddler   1446
Pamela Pounce   2312
Pan Michael   2165
Pandurang Hàri   3899
Pangborn, Edgar
Wilderness of Spring   4291
Panther Skin, The   33
Papa La-Bas   5766
Paper Cap, The   2975
Paquita   6272
Paradise, Jean
Savage City, The   4292
Paradise, Mary, (pseud.), see
Dorothy Eden
Paradise, Viola I.
Tomorrow the Harvest   4554
Paradise   4194
Paradise Falls   6046
Pardise People, The   3996
Paradise Prairie   5378
Paradise Reclaimed   3631

Parcel of Rogues   1310
Pardo Bazán, Emilia
Mystery of the Lost Dauphin, The
3496
Paretti, Sandra
Rose and the Sword, The   3497
Pargeter, Edith
Heaven Tree, The   733
Paris of Troy [Fidus Achates]   122
Parish, John C.
Man with the Iron Hand, The   6354
Parisians, The   3471
Park, (Mrs.) Kendall
Riquilda   631
Park, Ruth
Frost and the Fire, The   4072
Parker, Cornelia Stratton
Fabulous Valley   5179
Parker, Gilbert
Battle of the Strong, The   2745
Judgment House, The   3228
No Defence   2589
Pomp of the Lavilettes, The   6355
Power and the Glory, The   6356
Promised Land, The   97
Seats of the Mighty, The   6357
Trail of the Sword, The   6358
When Valmond Came to Pontiac
6359
Parker, Katherine
My Ladie Dundie   1929
Parkhill, Forbes
Troopers West   6018
Parmenter, Christine
Golden Age, A   6019
Parrish, Anne
Clouded Star, A   5180
Parrish, Randall
Beyond the Frontier   6360
Bob Hampton of Placer   6020
Devil's Own, The   5181
Molly McDonald   6021
My Lady of Doubt   4555
My Lady of the North   5613
My Lady of the South   5614
Prisoners of Chance   4556
Red Mist, The   5615
Sword of the Old Frontier, A   4293
When Wilderness Was King   5182
Wolves of the Sea   2221
Parry, Edward Abbott
England's Elizabeth   1419
Parson Croft   2388
Parson Kelly   2438
Parson's Wood, The   1966
Partisan, The   4583
Partridge, Bellamy
Big Freeze, The   5183

581

Passe Rose 588
Passengers to Mexico 6268
Passion and the Sword 2845
Passionate Brood, The 664
Passionate Elopement, The 2428
Passionate Pilgrim, The 3785
Passions of the Mind, The 3608
Pater, Walter
  Gaston de Latour 1542
  Marius the Epicurean 371
Pater Maternus [Father Maternus]
  1647
Paterson, Arthur
  Cromwell's Own 1930
  King's Agent, The 1931
  Son of the Plains 6022
Paterson, Isabel
  Fourth Queen, The 1420
  Singing Season, The 1130
Path of Glory, The 6332
Pathfinder, The 4161
Paths Perilous 2747
Pathway to the Stars 5052
Patience of John Morland, The
  4859
Patricia at the Inn 1972
Patrician Street 318
Patrick, Joseph, (pseud.), see
  Walsh, Joseph Patrick
Patriot, The (Fogazzaro) 3684
Patriot of France, A 2707
Patriots, The (Brady) 5429
Patriot's Daughter 2726
Patriot's Progress 4497
Patterns of Wolfpen, The 5907
Patterson, Burd Shippen
  Head of Iron, The 4294
Patterson, Emma L.
  Sun Queen: Nefertiti 24
Patterson, Frances Taylor
  Long Shadow, The 6361
  White Wampum 6362
Paul, Charlotte
  Gold Mountain 6023
Paul, Louis
  Dara, the Cypriot 489
Paul and Christina 2976
Pauli, Hertha
  Two Trumpeters of Vienna, The
  2159
Paulina 2875
Pausanias, the Spartan 153
Pawle, Kathleen
  Mural for a Later Day 4295
Pawn in Frankincense 1507
Pawn in the Game, A 2672
Paxton, S. H., (pseud.), see Smith,
  Ralph

Payne, Robert
  Alexander the God 202
  Blood Royal 3866
  Caravaggio 1658
  Chieftain, The 6024
  House in Peking 3933
  Roaring Boys 1932
  Young Emperor [The Great Mogul]
  3867
Payne, Will
  Mr. Salt 6025
Payson, William Farquhar
  John Vytal 4296
Peace at Bowling Green 5471
Peace, My Daughters 4116
Peaceable Kingdom, The 5946
Peacock, Max, (pseud.), see Wood-
  ruffe-Peacock, Dennis Max
  Cornelius
Peacock, Thomas Love
  Maid Marian 734
Pearce, Charles E.
  Corinthian Jack 3229
  Love Besieged 3910
  Madam Flirt 2461
  Red Revenge 3911
  Star of the East, A 3912
Pearce, Richard Elmo
  Impudent Rifle, The 5184
  Restless Border, The 5185
Peard, Frances M.
  Catherine 3230
Pearl Maiden 321
Pearsall, Robert Brainard
  Young Vargas Lewis 6269
Peart, Hendry
  Red Falcons of Tremoine 735
Pease, Howard
  Burning Cresset, The 2462
  Magnus Sinclair 1933
  Of Mistress Eve 1934
Peattie, Donald Culross
  Forward the Nation 5186
Peck, Theodora
  Sword of Dundee, The 2463
Peder Victorious 6050
Peep into the Twentieth Century, A
  5808
Peeples, Samuel A.
  Dream Ends in Fury, The 5187
  Missourian, The 6026
Peg Woffington 2471
Peggy Gainsborough, the Great
  Painter's Daughter 2243
Pei, Mario Andrew
  Swords of Anjou 632
Pelican Coast 5089
Pemberley Shades 3158

Rayner, Emma (cont.)
Free to Serve 4310
In Castle and Colony 4311
Visiting the Sin 6038
Rayner, William
World Turned Upside Down, The 4561
Raynolds, Robert
Brothers in the West 5213
Paquita 6272
Quality of Quiros, The 1699
Sinner of St. Ambrose, The 633
Reach, Angus B.
Leonard Lindsay 2223
Read, Opie
By the Eternal 5214
Reade, Amos
Norah Moriarty 3368
Reade, Charles
Cloister and the Hearth, The 1106
Foul Play 3244
Hard Cash 3245
It Is Never Too Late to Mend 3246
Peg Woffington 2471
Put Yourself in His Place 3247
Wandering Heir, The 2472
Reback, Janet Taylor Caldwell, see Caldwell, Taylor, (pseud.)
Reback, Marcus. see Caldwell, Taylor, (pseud.)
Rebel, The (Bailey) 3671
Rebel, The (Watson) 2006
Rebel and the Turncoat, The 4435
Rebel Heiress 1921
Rebel in Blue 5665
Rebel in the Night 4512.
Rebel Loyalist, The 4484
Rebel Prince, The 1571
Rebel Princess 2906
Rebel Run 5688
Rebel Sea Raider 3822
Rebel Spurs 6005
Rebellion of the Princess, The 2198
Rebellion Road 5996
Rebels, The (Bodkin) 2554
Reckon with the River 5121
Reckoning, The 4419
Recollections of Geoffrey Hamlyn, The 4068
Red and the Black, The 3385
Red Axe, The 2129
Red Badge of Courage, The 5472
Red Belts 4557
Red Bonnet, The 2676
Red Bridal, A 3615

Red Castle Women 5374
Red City, The 5144
Red Cloak Flying 4374
Red Cock Crows, The 4945
Red Cockade, The 2785
Red Confessor, The 1642
Red Cravat, The 2833
Red Curve, The 2482
Red Doe, The 4589
Red Eve 935
Red Falcons of Tremoine 735
Red Fleur-de-Lys, The 2715
Red Fountain, The 4009
Red Fox, The 1393
Red-hot Crown, The 3766
Red Lances, The 6280
Red Lanterns on St. Michael's 5536
Red Marshal, The 2805
Red Marten, The 2850
Red Mass, The 2794
Red Men and White 6146
Red Men of the Dusk, The 1810
Red Mist, The 5615
Red Morning 4197
Red Mountain 5959
Red Neighbour, The 2075
Red Orm 595
Red Pavilion, The 1241
Red Peony, The 3931
Red Plush 3202
Red Queen, White Queen 412
Red Raskall 5122
Red Reaper, The 1976
Red Republic, The 3404
Red Revenge 3911
Red Riders 6016
Red Road, The 4297
Red Rock 6017
Red Rose of Lancaster, The 956
Red Rover 4427
Red Rust 4777
Red Saint, The 678
Red Shirts, The 2677
Red Spider 2966
Red Sultan, The 3970
Red Towers of Granada, The 830
Red Year, The 3919
Redemption of Tycho Brahe 2128
Redgate, John
Barlow's Kingdom 6039
Redgauntlet 2489
Redhouse on the Hill 5572
Redmond, Count O'Hanlon, the Irish Rapparee 2023
Reds of the Midi, The 2683
Reed, Myrtle
Shadow of Victory, The 5215
Reed, Warren

Robertson, William (cont.)
  Dule Tree of Cassillis, The
    1428
  Kings of Carrick, The 1946
  Lords of Cuninghame, The 1429
  Stone of Dunalter, The 2478
Robin Hood of France, A 2708
Robinson, Emma
  Caesar Borgia 1663
  Westminster Abbey 1430
  Whitefriars 1947
  Whitehall 1948
Robinson, Gertrude
  Sign of the Golden Fish 4318
Robinson, Henry Morton
  Water of Life 6047
Robison, Mabel Otis
  Pioneer Panorama 5235
Robsart Affair 1385
Rochemer Hag, The 3180
Rock, The 488
Rock and the River, The 6329
Rock and the Wind 5745
Rock Cried Out, The 5284
Rock of Chickamauga, The 5554
Rock of Freedom 2136
Rodenberg, Julius
  King by the Grace of God 1949
Roderick Taliaferro 6245
Rodney Stone 3054
Rodocanachi, Emmanuel
  Tolla the Courtesan 2880
Rodomont 2608
Rody the Rover 3324
Roe, Vingie E.
  Great Trace, The 6048
Roe, Virginia
  Splendid Road, The 5236
Rølvaag, Ole E.
  Giants in the Earth 6049
  Peder Victorious 6050
Roger Sudden 6366
Rogers, Cameron
  Magnificent Idler, The 5237
Rogers, Garet, (pseud.)
  Lancet 2479
Rogers, Robert C.
  Will o' the "Wasp" 5238
Rogue and the Witch, The 4286
Rogue Errant 2030
Rogue from Padua, The 1606
Rogue Herries 2528
Rogue of Rye, The 3051
Rogue's Companion 5071
Rogue's Harbor 4189
Rogues' Kingdom 4740
Rogue's Legacy 1042
Rogue's March (Chapman) 4421

Rogue's March, The (Hornung) 4066
Rogue's Tragedy, A 2864
Rogue's Yarn 6430
Roland Blake 5595
Rolfe, Frederick W.
  Don Tarquinio 1181
Roll, Shenandoah 5561
Rolling Years 6104
Roman, The 418
Roman Go Home! 449
Roman Wall 436
Roman Way, The 3206
Romance 3801
Romance of a Mummy, The 5
Romance of a Plain Man, The 5883
Romance of a State Secret, The 1984
Romance of Alexander and Roxana,
  The 197
Romance of Alexander the King, The
  196
Romance of Alexander the Prince,
  The 195
Romance of Dijon, A 2660
Romance of Dollard, The 6299
Romance of Fra Filippo Lippi, The
  1138
Romance of Gilbert Holmes, The
  5065
Romance of Leonardo da Vinci, The
  [The Forerunner; The Resurrec-
  tion of the Gods; Leonardo da
  Vinci] 1655
Romance of Mlle. Aissé, The 2749
Romance of Old Folkestone, A 2435
Romance of Sandro Botticelli, The
  1139
Romance of the Cape Frontier, A
  4005
Romance of the Charter Oak 4331
Romance of the First Consul, A 3473
Romance of the Fountain, The 4255
Romance of the Lady Arbell 1905
Romance of the Three Kingdoms 507
Romance of the Tuileries, A 3441
Romantic Passion of Don Luis, The
  1594
Romantic Prince, The 1546
Rome for Sale 234
Rome Haul 4877
Romola 1155
Ronalds, Mary Teresa
  Nero 378
Ronin, The 1249
Rooke, Daphne
  Diamond Jo 4013
  Mittee 4014
  Wizards' Country 4015
Rookwood 2233

Running Iron 5854
Running of the Tide, The 4925
Running the Gauntlet 5509
Running Thread, The 5643
Rupert, by the Grace of God 1893
Rushing, Jane Gilmore
 Walnut Grove 6057
Russell, George Hansby
 Under the Sjambok 4017
Russell, T. O'Neill
 Dick Massey 3370
Russell, W. Clark
 Ocean Free-Lance, An 3251
 Yarn of Old Harbour Town, The 3252
Rustem, Son of Zal 41
Ruth 70
Rutherford, Mark, (pseud.), see White, William Hale
Ryan, Don
 Devil's Brigadier 5241
Ryan, Marah Ellis
 For the Soul of Rafael 5242
Rydberg, Viktor
 Last Athenian, The 459
 Singoalla 1110
Rye House Plot, The 1943

S. M. C., (pseud.), see Catherine (Sister) Mary
S. P. Q. R. 325
Sabatini, Rafael
 Bellarion 1182
 Birth of Mischief 2829
 Captain Blood 2224
 Carolinian, The 4570
 Chivalry 1183
 Columbus, a Romance 1132
 Fortune's Fool 1950
 Gamester, The 2753
 Gates of Doom, The 2480
 Hounds of God, The 1629
 King's Minion, The 1951
 Lion's Skin, The 2481
 Lost King, The 3514
 Love at Arms 1664
 Master-at-arms 2754
 Nuptials of Corbal, The 2755
 Romantic Prince, The 1546
 St. Martin's Summer 2113
 Scaramouche 2756
 Sea-Hawk, The 1700
 Shame of Motley, The 1665
 Snare, The 3663
 Stalking Horse, The 1952
 Sword of Islam, The 1666
 Tavern Knight, The 1953

Trampling of the Lilies, The 2757
Sabin, Edwin Legrand
 White Indian 5243
Sable Lion, The 2211
Sabran, Jean
 Vengeance of Don Manuel 6276
Sabre General [Proud Canaries] 3450
Sacajawea 4932
Sacajawea of the Shoshones 4900
Sackler, Harry
 Festival at Meron 380
Sacred and Profane 2836
Sacred Jewel, The 479
Saddle and the Plow, The 6094
Sadlier, (Mrs.) James, see Sadlier, Mary Anne
Sadlier, Mary Anne
 Confederate Chieftains, The 2045
 Daughter of Tyrconnell, The 2046
 Fate of Father Sheehy, The 2591
 MacCarthy More! 1481
Safety of the Honours, The 1977
Safford, Henry B.
 Tory Tavern 4571
 Tristram Bent 4319
Sage, William
 Claybornes, The 5633
 Robert Tournay 2758
Sage of Canudos 6266
Saghalien Convict, The 3759
Sagon, Amyot, (pseud.)
 When George III Was King 3253
Said the Fisherman 3776
Sailor Named Jones, A 4489
Saint, The (Fogazzaro) 3686
Saint, The (Unruh) 1192
St. George, Judith
 Turncoat Winter, Rebel Spring 4572
St. George and St. Michael 1895
Saint Helena, Little Island 3460
Saint in Ivory 581
St. Ives 3264
Saint Joan of Arc 1033
St. John of God 1398
Saint Johnson 5755
St. Katherine's by the Tower 2271
St. Leon 1645
St. Lo 1084
St. Martin's Summer 2113
Saint Michael's Gold 2609
Saint of Dragon's Dale, The 785
Saint Patrick's Battalion 5072
St. Patrick's Eve 3353
St. Ronan's Well 3254
St. Thomas's Eve 1359
Saints and Tomahawks 4329

601

Still Is the Summer Night   5813
Stilson, Charles B.
  Ace of Blades, The   2116
  Cavalier of Navarre, A   1554
Stimson, Frederic Jesup
  King Noanett   4348
  My Story   4600
Stirrup Cup, The   4621
Stolen Emperor, The   3940
Stolen Train, The   5405
Stone, Grace
  Cold Journey, The   6375
Stone, Irving
  Agony and the Ecstasy, The
    1672
  Immortal Wife   5295
  Love Is Eternal   5296
  Lust for Life   3522
  Passions of the Mind, The   3608
  President's Lady, The   5297
  Those Who Love   6181
Stone Angel, The   6396
Stone of Dunalter, The   2478
Stonecutter of Memphis, The   15
Stones of the Abbey, The   770
Stonewall's Scout   5533
Stong, Philip
  Buckskin Breeches   5298
  Forty Pounds of Gold   5299
Stooping Lady, The   3118
Store, The   6085
Storm against the Wind   4505
Storm and Treasure   2604
Storm Bird, The   3579
Storm Canvas   3841
Storm Centre, The   5603
Storm Haven   5649
Storm of Time   4054
Storm Out of Cornwall   1299
Storm over the Caucasus   3721
Storm-Rent Sky, A   2661
Storm Signals   5565
Storm the Last Rampart   4609
Storm Tide   5743
Storm to the South   6277
Storme, Peter, (pseud.), see
    Stern, Philip Van Doren
Stormy Life, A   933
Stormy Passage, A   1449
Stormy Winter   4912
Stormy Year   5975
Story at Canons   2341
Story for Icarus   170
Story of a Campaign Estate, The
    3375
Story of a Country Town, The
    5025
Story of a Mother, The   3085

Story of a Peasant, The   2665
Story of Francis Cludde, The   1605
Story of Old Fort Loudon, The   4283
Story of Susan, The   3056
Story of the Plebiscite, The [The
    Plebiscite]   3426
Story of the Trapper, The   6342
Stouman, Knud
  L. Baxter, Medicus   4349
  With Cradle and Clock   4350
Stover, Herbert Elisha
  Copperhead Moon   5656
  Eagle and the Wind   4601
  Men in Buckskin   4602
  Powder Mission   4603
  Song of the Susquehanna   4351
Stowaway to America   4835
Stowe, Harriet Beecher
  Agnes of Sorrento   1190
  Dred   5300
  Minister's Wooing, The   5301
  Uncle Tom's Cabin   5302
  Uncle Tom's Cabin (adapted)   5303
Stowman, Knud, see Stouman, Knud
Strabel, Thelma
  Storm to the South   6277
Strachey, John St. Loe
  Madonna of the Barricades, The
    3523
Strachey, Marjorie
  Nightingale, The   3609
Strachey, Rachel
  Marching On   5305
Strachey, Ray, (pseud.), see
    Strachey, Rachel
Stradella   2188
Strahl, Paul, (pseud.), see Reising,
    Otto
Straight, Michael W.
  Carrington   6083
  Very Small Remnant, A   5657
Strain, Euphans H.
  Prophet's Reward, A   2511
Strained Allegiance   2355
Stranded   5752
Strange Adventures of Israel Pendray,
    The   2387
Strange Adventures of Jonathan Drew
    5345
Strange Brigade   6336
Strange Story of Falconer Thring,
    The   4011
Strange Story of Rab Raby, The   2813
Strange Wives   4118
Strange Woman   5376
Strangeling, The   3115
Stranger, The (Caldwell)   5758
Stranger, The (Ross)   6052

607

608

Synon, Mary (cont.)
  Good Red Bricks, The 6088
Syrett, Netta
  Lady Jem 1982

TR 5879
Tai-Pan 3951
Tailor of Vitre, The 1065
Take Heed of Loving Me 1999
Taken from the Enemy 3221
Takers of the City 6210
Talbot, Hugh, (pseud.), see
  Alington, Argentine
Talbot, L. A.
  Jehanne of the Forest 746
Tale for Midnight, A 1659
Tale of Magali, The 775
Tale of Three Cities 3481
Tale of Two Cities, A 2644
Tale of Valor 4919
Talisman, The 887
Talisman Ring, The 3141
Tall Brigade 6320
Tall Captains, The 6374
Tall Men 5596
Tall Ships, The 5038
Tall Woman, The 5828
Tallentyre, S. G., (pseud.), see
  Hall, Evelyn Beatrice
Tamar 357
Tamarack Tree, The 4739
Tamburas 141
Taming of the Brute, The 2477
Tandrup, Harald
  Reluctant Prophet 108
Tanqueray, (Mrs.) Bertram
  Royal Quaker, The 1983
Tansy Taniard 1443
Taos 4127
Tap Roots 5660
Tapparelli-D'Azeglio, Massimo
  Challenge of Barletta, The 1673
  Maid of Florence, The 1674
Tapsell, R. F.
  Unholy Pilgrim, The 893
  Year of the Horsetails, The 491
Tara 3875
Taras Bulba 1680
Tarbet, W. G.
  Loyal Maid, A 2518
Tarkington, Booth
  Gentleman from Indiana, The 6089
  Monsieur Beaucaire 2519
Tarry Thou Till I Come [Salathiel, the Immortal] 498
Tasma, (pseud.) see Couvreur,

  Jessie C.
Tassles on Her Boots 6103
Taste of Glory 6239
Taste of Infamy, The 6262
Tate, Allen
  Fathers, The 5314
Tate, Ellalice, (pseud.), see Hibbert, Eleanor
Taunton, M.
  Last of the Catholic O'Malleys, The 1482
Taunton, Winefrede Trafford-
  Romance of a State Secrete, The 1984
Tautphoebus, (Baroness) Jemima von
  At Odds 3611
Tavern in the Town 4271
Tavern Knight, The 1953
Tavern Rogue, The 1268
Tavo, Gus, (pseud.)
  Track the Grizzly Down 6090
Tay John 6402
Taylor, Allan
  Morgan's Long Rifles 6378
Taylor, Angeline
  Black Jade 6449
Taylor, Anna
  Gods Are Not Mocked, The 243
Taylor, C. Bryson
  Nikanor, Teller of Tales 564
Taylor, David
  Farewell to Valley Forge 4606
  Lights across the Delaware 4607
  Mistress of the Forge 4608
  Storm the Last Rampart 4609
  Sycamore Men 4610
Taylor, G. W., see Broster, Dorothy
  K. and G. W. Taylor
Taylor, George, (pseud.), see
  Hausrath, Adolf
Taylor, H. C. Chatfield-, see
  Chatfield-Taylor, H. C.
Taylor, James G., Jr.
  Dark Dawn 6450
Taylor, Mary Imlay
  Anne Scarlet 4358
  Cardinal's Musqueteer, The 2117
  House of the Wizard, The 1448
  Imperial Lover, An 2909
  My Lady Clancarty 1985
  On the Red Staircase 2197
  Rebellion of the Princess, The 2198
  Yankee Volunteer, A 4611
Taylor, Meadows, see Taylor,
  Philip Meadows
Taylor, Philip Meadows
  Confessions of a Thug 3916

610

Treece, Henry (cont.)
  Red Queen, White Queen 412
  Ride into Danger 1000
  Road to Miklagard, The 590
  Splintered Sword 618
  Swords from the North 844
  Viking's Dawn 591
  Viking's Sunset 592
  Windswept City, The 177
Treegate's Raiders 4640
Trees, The 5222
Trembling Earth, The 5339
Trembling Land, The 5775
Tremlett, C. H.
  Civil Dudgeon 1992
Trench, W. Stewart
  Ieme 3376
Trevena, John, (pseud.), see
  Henham, Ernest George
Treviño, Elizabeth Borton de
  Casilda of the Rising Moon 635
  I, Juan de Pareja 2185
Trevor, Meriol
  Last of Britain, The 567
Trewern 3279
Trial & Triumph 1199
Trial of Soren Quist 2176
Trinity Bells 4700
Triple Crown, The 992
Tristram Bent 4319
Triton Brig, The 2941
Triumph, The 5521
Triumph of Count Ostermann, The
  2899
Triumph of the Scarlet Pimpernel,
  The 2737
Triumph of Youth, The 2170
Troika Belle, The [The Rake and
  the Rebel] 3752
Trojan, The 136
Trollope, Anthony
  Barchester Towers 3283
  Castle Richmond 3377
  Doctor Thorne 3284
  Framley Parsonage 3285
  Last Chronicle of Barset 3287
  Phineas Finn 3288
  Phineas Redux 3289
  Small House at Alington 3286
  Vendée, La 2779
  Warden, The 3282
  Way We Live Now, The 3290
Trollope, Frances
  Life and Adventures of Michael
    Armstrong 3291
Troopers West 6018
Tros of Samothrace 239
Trouble at Hungerfords, The 4994

Trouble Shooter 5915
Troubled Border 4659
Troubled Range 5982
Troubled Spring 5436
Trouncer, Margaret Lahey
  Nun, The 2120
Troy Chimneys 3176
Troyat, Henri
  Brotherhood of the Red Poppy, The
    3524
Troyer, Howard W.
  Salt and the Savor, The 5328
True Cross, The 884
True Grit 6031
True Heart 1568
True Man and Traitor 3321
Trumpet at the Gates 1005
Trumpet in the City 4544
Trumpet in the Wilderness 4992
Trumpet-Major, The 3114
Trumpet of God (Duncan) 862
Trumpet to Arms 4521
Trumpeter, Sound! 3771
Trumpets at Dawn 4493
Trumpets Calling 5719
Trumpets of God, The [Dawn]
  (Bacheller) 257
Tu Tze-Chun 1225
Tudor Rose 908
Tudor Sunset 1456
Tudor Underground 1407
Tudor Wench, The 1282
Tufts, Anne
  Rails along the Chesapeake 5329
Tumbleweeds 5842
Tunstall, Beatrice
  Long Day Closes, The 2525
Tupper, Edith S.
  Hearts Triumphant 5330
Tur, Eugenia, (pseud.)
  Shalonski Family, The 3788
Turbulent Duchess, The 2127
Turgenev, Ivan
  Fathers and Sons [Fathers and
    Children] 3789
  On the Eve 3790
  Rudin 3791
  Smoke 3792
  Torrents of Spring, The 3793
  Virgin Soil 3794
Turn Back the River 229
Turnbull, Agnes
  Day Must Dawn, The 4620
  King's Orchard, The 6182
  Rolling Years 6104
Turnbull, Clara
  Damsel Dark, The 748
Turnbull, Francese Hubbard

615

616

618

619

Wellman, Paul I. (cont.)
Bowl of Brass, The 6119
Broncho Apache 6120
Buckstones, The 5353
Comancheros, The 5354
Female, The 660
Iron Mistress, The 5355
Magnificent Destiny 5356
Ride the Red Earth 4368
Wells, Evelyn
City for Saint Francis, A 4632
Welty, Eudora
Robber Bridegroom, The 5357
Wentworth, Patricia
Devil's Wind, The 3922
Marriage under the Terror, A 2784
Queen Anne Is Dead 2535
Werewolf, The 2052
Werfel, Franz
Hearken unto the Voice 112
Song of Bernadette 3530
Verdi 3715
West, Jessamyn
Except for Me and Thee 5358
Friendly Persuasion, The 5676
Leafy Rivers 5359
West, Keith, (pseud.), see Lane, Kenneth Westmacott
West, Tom, (pseud.), see East, Fred
West Goes the Road 5203
West of the River 5078
West Wind, The 2927
Westall, William
Red Bridal, A 3615
With the Red Eagle 3616
Westbury, Hugh
Acté 421
Westcotes, The 3239
Westcott, Arthur
Sun God, The 470
Westcott, Edward Noyes
David Harum 6121
Westcott, Jan
Border Lord, The 1457
Captain Barney 4633
Condottiere 1194
Hepburn, The 1458
Queen's Grace, The 1459
Walsingham Woman 1460
White Rose, The 1195
Westerman, Percy F.
Quest of "The Golden Hope," The 2227
Western Union 5891
Westerners, The 6128
Westley, George Hembert

Maid and the Miscreant, The 4369
see also Stephens, Robert Neilson and George Hembert Westley
Westminster Abbey 1430
Westward Ho! 1695
Westward the Monitor's Roar 5720
Westward the River 5340
Westward the Sun 4023
Westward the Tide 4590
Westward to Laughter 6433
Westways 5145
Wetherbys, The 3903
Wetherell, June
Glorious Three, The 5360
Weyman, Stanley J.
Abbess of Vlaye, The 1556
Castle Inn, The 2536
Count Hannibal 1557
Gentleman of France, A 1558
Great House, The 3305
House of the Wolf, The 1559
Long Night, The 2171
Man in Black, The 2122
My Lady Rotha 2172
Ovington's Bank 3306
Red Cockade, The 2785
Shrewsbury 2009
Starvecrow Farm 3307
Story of Francis Cludde, The 1605
Traveller in the Fur Cloak, The 3617
Under the Red Robe 2123
"Whale Off!" 4880
Whaleboat Warriors 4523
Whalen, Will Wilfrid
Golden Squaw 4370
Wharton, Anne Hollingsworth
Rose of Old Quebec, A 6380
Wharton, Anthony, (pseud.), see McAllister, Alister
Wharton, Edith
Age of Innocence 6122
Buccaneers, The 6123
Valley of Decision, The 2886
What If This Friend 369
Wheatley, Dennis
Man Who Killed the King, The 2786
Wheeler, Sessions S.
Paiute 5361
Wheeler, Thomas Gerald
All Men Tall 1004
Wheelwright, Jere Hungerford
Draw Near to Battle 2787
Gray Captain 5677
Kentucky Stand 4634

623

624